CONTEMPORARY RELIGIONS
A WORLD GUIDE

CONTEMPORARY RELIGIONS
A WORLD GUIDE

Ian Harris
Stuart Mews
Paul Morris
John Shepherd

LONGMAN
CURRENT
AFFAIRS

CONTEMPORARY RELIGIONS: A WORLD GUIDE

Published by Longman Group UK Limited, Westgate House,
The High, Harlow, Essex CM20 1YR, United Kingdom.
Telephone (0279) 442601
Telex 81491 Padlog
Facsimile (0279) 444501

DPA
DIRECTORY PUBLISHERS
ASSOCIATION

Distributed exclusively in the United States and Canada
by Gale Research Inc, 835 Penobscot Building, Detroit,
Michigan 48226, USA.

ISBN 0-582-086957 (Longman)

A catalogue record for this publication is available from the British Library.

Phototypeset by The Midlands Book Typesetting Company.
Printed and bound in Great Britain by
William Clowes Limited, Beccles and London

Contents

Preface

There are already in existence a number of one volume encyclopaedias, dictionaries, or reference works on world religions. *Contemporary Religions: A World Guide* differs from these in that it seeks to offer a distinctive and unique three-fold approach to the student or scholar of religion. First, it is important to note, as indicated by the title, that the emphasis is on contemporary religious groups and movements rather than the usual attempt to cover everything from Abraham to the State of Israel; Jesus to present charismatic Christian sects; Muhammad to the 1979 Iranian revolution, etc. We have thus excluded movements of purely historical interest, even those such as Jim Jones' People's Temple, defunct since the mass suicide of members at Jonestown in Guyana in November 1978. Section I contains a series of orienting essays by leading scholars in the field. These essays are designed to allow the reader to contextualize particular group entries within the framework of their religious tradition.

Section II supplies an A–Z gazetteer of currently active religious groups and movements. In addition there are cross-references (written in bold lettering) alerting the reader to other articles in this section. These are in the main larger groups although there are entries for smaller groups if they have, or have had, particular influence or represent the survival of a certain tradition.

The final section presents a country-by-country guide to religions and religious groups. The volume also contains a glossary of religious terms and an index of personal names.

Thus, a reader should be able to track down a specific group, discern its position within the context of the particular religious tradition and discover the geographical locations of the movement in question. Any one of these three entry points could be used.

The inclusion of movements that appear primarily "political" reflects the broader understanding of the category of religion as evidenced particularly in relation to Islam but to a lesser extent in a number of traditions. Despite the use of criteria such as these, the omission of certain groups and movements remains unfortunately inevitable. This is in part due to difficulties inherent in covering certain fields, notably contemporary Chinese religion, and in part because of the limitations of space. Nevertheless, the range of groups and movements covered is considerable and represents an unprecedented attempt at producing a contemporary world guide.

The idea and three-fold model originated with Paul Morris as a development of the successful format utilized in Stuart Mews' *Religion in Politics* (Longman, 1989). Editorial responsibilities were allocated, in broad terms, as follows: Ian Harris — Buddhism, Sikhism, Hinduism (in part), and Chinese and Japanese religion; Stuart Mews — Christianity; Paul Morris — Judaism, Hinduism (in part); John Shepherd — Islam, New Religious Movements, Traditional Religions and Section III. The original version of Section III was prepared by Phil Goodchild, to whom particular thanks are due.

Dr. Ian Harris
Dr. John Shepherd
Religious Studies & Social Ethics
S. Martin's College Lancaster

Dr. Stuart Mews
Dr. Paul Morris
Religious Studies
Lancaster University

Contributors

Ahmed Andrews
University of Glasgow.
Khoja Ithna 'Asharis.

Elisabeth Arweck
Centre for New Religious Movements, King's College, University of London.
Church of Armageddon, Church of Christ (& Crossroads Movement), Family of Love (& Mission South, & Children of God), Jesus Army (Jesus Fellowship), Jesus Movement, Positive Thinking/New Thought, Unification Church/Moonies, Way International, Worldwide Church of God.

Anne Atkinson
Religious Studies Department, Lancaster University.
Christian Fellowship of Zambia, Old Apostolic.

Professor Hugh Baker
School of Oriental and African Studies, University of London.
Chinese Folk Religion, De Jiao.

Dr Fiona Bowie
University College of North Wales.
African New Religious Movements, African Traditional Religions, Aladura, Bangwa religion, Bwiti Cult, Harris Movement, Khoisan religion, Kikuyu religion, Kimbanguist Church, Kitawala, Maria Legio, Nuer and Dinka religion, 'Pygmy' religion.

Dr Bert F. Breiner
Centre for the Study of Islam and Christian–Muslim Relations, Selly Oak Colleges, Birmingham.
Amal, Hizbollah, Islamic Amal, Islamic Jihad.

Dr John Brockington
University of Edinburgh.
Prajapita Brahma, Part I: Hinduism.

Dr Catherine Cantwell
University of Kent.
Entries written jointly with Robert Mayer.

Paul Charman
Religious Studies Department, Lancaster University.
Restorationism/New Churches.

Dr Peter Clarke
Centre for New Religious Movements, King's College, University of London.
Part I: New Religious Movements.

Dr Owen Cole
West Sussex Institute of Higher Education, Chichester. Balmikis, Kabir Panth, Namdharis, Nanaksar Movement, Nirankaris, Ravidas Panth, Sanatan Sikhs, Sarbat Khalsa, Shiromani Gurdwara Prabandhak Committee, Sikh Dharma of the Western Hemisphere, Sikhism, Singh Sabha Movement, Udasis.

Dr Simon Coleman
St John's College, Cambridge.
Word of Life (Livets Ord).

Dr Peter Connolly
West Sussex Institute of Higher Education.
Amaravati Buddhist Centre, British Wheel of Yoga, Buddhist Churches of America, Buddhist Society of Great Britain and Ireland, Buddhist Youth Organisation, Chogye Chong, Chondo Gyo, Friends of the Western Buddhist Order, German Dharmadhuta Society, Iyengar Yoga, Sino–American Buddhist Association, Son, T'aego Chong, Viniyoga, Won.

Dr Guy H. Cooper
Matlock, Derbyshire.
Inuit Religion, Native American Religions, Pan–Indianism, Peyotism, Shamanism.

Thomas Daffern
Institute of Education, University of London.
Australian Aboriginal Religion, Mesoamerican Traditional Religions, South American Traditional Religions; (and jointly with James Veitch): Maori Religion, Melanesian Religion, Polynesian Religion.

Wendy Dossett
St David's University College, Lampeter.
Jinja Shinto, Jodoshinshu, Jodoshu, Komeito, Kyoha Shinto, Minzoku Shinto, Nara Sects, Nichirenshoshu, Nichirenshu, Nipponzan Myohoji, Omotokyo, PL Kyodan, Reiyukai Kyodan, Rinzai Zen, Rissho Koseikai, Seicho no Ie, Sekai Kyuseikyo, Sekai Mahikari Bunmei Kyodan, Shingonshu, Shinto, Shotokushu, Soka Gakkai, Soto Zen, Tendaishu.

Dr Gavin Flood
St David's University College, Lampeter.
Aghoris, Kalikulas, Kashmir Shaivism, Kaulas, Krama, Lingayats, Nagas, Naths, Shaiva Siddhantins, Shaivas, Shaktas, Smartas, Shri Vidya, Spanda, Tantrics, Trika.

Dr Theodore Gabriel
Cheltenham and Gloucester College of Higher Education.
All-India Muslim League, Colanaikans (jointly with Prof Murkot Ramunny), Nagas, Tribal Religions of India.

Philip Goodchild
University of Lancaster.
Part III.

Dr David Gosling
Clare College, University of Cambridge.
All Indonesian Federation of Buddhist Organisations, Buddhayana, Burmese Theravada, Cambodian Buddhism, Cao Dai, Hoa Hao, Kasogatan, Laotian Theravada, Majelis Upasaka Pandita Agama Buddha Indonesia, Samnak Paw Sawan, Singapore Buddhism, Thai Theravada, Theravada Buddhism, Tridharma, Unified Vietnamese Buddhist Church, Vietnamese Buddhism.

Richard Gray
S. Martin's College, Lancaster.
All Ceylon Buddhist Congress, Buddhist Publication Society, Maha Bodhi Society, Ramanna Nikaya, Sarvodaya Sramadana.

Dr Ian Harris
S. Martin's College, Lancaster.
Akhand Kirtani Jatha, All India Sikh Student Federation, Amarapura Nikaya, Amritdhari Sikhs, Anuvrat Movement, Bal Krishnavas, Brahmasampradaya, Buddhist Association of Thailand, Buddhist Sunday Schools Movement, Charan Dasis, Chinese Buddhism, Chinese Buddhist Association, Chinese Daoist Association, Compassion Society, Damdani Taksal, Dasanamis, Dhammadana Association, Dwara Nikaya, English Sangha Trust, Foundation for the Preservation of the Mahayana, Ganapatyas, Gelugpas, Getambe Group, Hingettwin Nikaya, Hooppha Sawan, Hossoshu, International Sikh Federation, Kanji Panth, Kavi Panth, Kegonshu, Keshdhari Sikhs, Lanka Vipassana Bhavana Samitiya, Lao United Buddhists Association, Mahanikay, Manjusri Institute, Mira Bais, Nanak Panth, Neo-Buddhism, Network of Engaged Buddhists, Nishkan Sevak Jatha, Obaku Zen, Patit Sikhs, Ramanandis, Ramdasis, Saddhamma Friends Society, Sahajdhari Sikhs, Sanakasampradaya, Sant Nirankari Mandal, Santi Asok, Satya Samaj, Sauras, Self-Realisation Fellowship, Shinshu Honganjiha, Shinshu Otani, Shugendo, Shwegyin Nikaya, Siddha Yoga, Sikh Missionary Society, Siyam Nikaya, Siyana Vipassana Bhavana Samitiya, Unity Sect, Vinaya Vardhana Society, World Fellowship of Buddhists, Young Men's Buddhist Association, Zen.

Prof. Adrian Hastings
University of Leeds.
Part I: Christianity.

Bradley Hawkins
University of California, Santa Barbara.
Akali Dal, Aurobindo, Bharatiya Janata Party (BPJ), Gandhf, Guru, Melier Baba, Modern Hindu Reform Movements, Radha Seami, Ramakrishna Missien, Ramana Maharsi, Rashtriya Swayamsevak Sangh (RSS), Siv Sena,

Sri Anandamayi Ma, Sri Gedavari Mataji, Sri Narayana Guru, Swami Chinmayananda, Swami Muktananda, Swami Prabhupada, Upasani Babe Maharaj, Vedasta, Yoga.

Dr Paul Heelas
University of Lancaster.
New Age.

Richard Hoch
University of California, Santa Barbara.
Alliance Israelite Universelle, American Council for Judaism, American Jewish Committee, American Jewish Congress, American Jewish Joint Distribution Committee, Ashkenazi, Bene Israel, B'nai B'rith International, Conservative Judaism, Havurat Judaism, Jewish Feminist Groups, Kibbutz, Orthodox Judaism, Reconstructionist Judaism, Reform Judaism, Samaritans, Sephardi. Beta Israel, Jewish New Agers, Karaites jointly with Dr Paul Morris.

Prof Louis Jacobs
University of Lancaster.
Part I: Judaism.

Dr Will Johnson
University of Wales, College of Cardiff.
Bisapanthis, Buddhist Society of India, Buddhists in India, Chittagong Buddhist Association, Digambara Jainas, Irani Zoroastrians, Jainas, Murtipujakas, Parsees, Shrimad Rajchandra, Sthankavasis, Svetambara Jainas, Taranapanthis, Terapanthis, Zoroastrians.

Claudia Liebeskind
Royal Holloway and Bedford New College, University of London.
Bektashiya, Chishtiya, Khatmiya/ Mirghaniya, Madariya, Malang, Rahmaniya, Shattariya, Suhrawardiya.

Dr Denis MacEoin
Newcastle-upon-Tyne.
'Alawis, Ahl-i Haqq, Babis, Bahais, Bahais Under the Provisions of the

Covenant, Batiniya, Dhahabiya, Dhu'l-Riyasatayn, Druzes (Druses), Fiver Shi'ites, Freie Bahai ('Free Bahais'), Gunabadi, Hojjatiya Society, Imamis, Isma'ilis, Ithna 'Asharis, Ja'faris, Kashfiya, Mandaeans, Musta'lis, Ni'matullahiya, Nizaris, Nusayris, Orthodox Bahai Faith, Sabaeans (Sabians), Safi 'Ali Shahi, Sevener Shi'ites (Seveners), Shaykhis, Shi'ism, Twelver Shi'ites, Yazidis, Zaydis.

Dr Freda Matchett
University of Lancaster.
Bauls, Dadu Panthis, Gaudiyasampradaya, International Society for Krishna Consciousness, Mahanubhavs, Shri Shankaradeva Sangha, Shri Vaishnavas, Swaminarayans, Vaikhanasas, Vaishnava Sahajiyas, Vallabhasampradaya, Warkaris.

Robert Mayer
School of Oriental and African Studies, University of London.
Entries written jointly with Catherine Cantwell. Bonpos, Drigung Kagyudpa, Drukpa Kagyudpa, Kagyudpa, Karma Kagyudpa, Mongolian Buddhism, Ngorpa, Nyingmapa, Rimay, Sakyapa, Taklung Kagyudpa, Terma, Tibetan Buddhism, Tsharpa.

Dr Stuart Mews
University of Lancaster.
Anglicans, Anglo-Catholic, Baptist World Alliance, British-Israelites, Charismatic Movement, Council of Churches for Britain and Ireland, Episcopalians, Ethiopian Evangelical Church Mekane Yesus, Faith Movement, Full Gospel Businessmen's Fellowship International, Fundamentalism, House Churches, Malankara Orthodox Syrian, Mission Covenant Church of Sweden, Moral Re-armament, Nippon Kirisuto Kyodan, Nippon Sei Ko Kai, Old Catholic Mariavite Church in Poland, Scientology, Seventh Day Adventists, Uniate Churches, United Church of Christ, Wesleyan, World Council of Churches, World Methodist Council, World Congress of Christian Fundamentalists.

Dr Peter Moore
University of Kent at Canterbury.
Armenian Church, Autocephalous
Church, Coptic Church, Ethiopian
Church, Greek Orthodox Christianity,
Nestorian Church, Old Calendarists, Old
Believers, Orthodox Church (Byzantine
Tradition), Oriental Orthodox Churches,
Russian Orthodox, Syro-Indian,
Syro-Jacobite Church, Zoe.

Dr Paul Morris
University of Lancaster.
Agudat Israel, Belz Hasidism, The Board
of Deputies of British Jews, Bratslav
Hasidism, Cochin Jews, Donmeh,
Ger Hasidism, Gush Emunim (Block
of the Faithful), Haredi (Haredim),
Karlin-Stolin Hasidism, Lubavich
Hasidism, Hasidism, Mafdal (Mizrahi,
National Religious Party), Musar
Movement, Neo-Hasidism, Neturei
Karta, Satmar Hasidism, Sephardi Torah
Guardians Party (SHAS), Synagogue
Council of America, United Jewish
Appeal, United Torah Judaism (United
Torah Party), Vizhitz Hasidism, World
Jewish Congress, World Union of
Progressive Judaism.
Beta Israel, Jewish New Agers,
Karaites, jointly with Richard Hoch.

Keith Munnings
Bristol.
Cargo Cults, John Frum (jointly with
Dr James Veitch); Anthroposophy,
Freemasonry, Occultism, Paganism
(Neo-Paganism), Rosicrucianism (&
AMORC), Satanism, Witchcraft (Wicca,
Old Religion).

Dr Francesca Murphy
S. Martin's College, Lancaster.
Benedictines, Carmelites, Carthusians,
Chaldean Uniate Church, Cistercians,
Pax Christi, Communio e Liberazione,
Dominicans, Eastern Rite Romanian
Church, Eastern Rite Ruthenian
Church, Eastern Rite Ukrainian Church,
Franciscans, Redemptorists, Jesuits,
Maronite Church, Melkite Church, Opus
Dei, Roman Catholic Church.

Dr Petya Nitzova
University of Sofia, Bulgaria.
Qizilbash; Bulgaria (joint author).

Dr Michael S. Northcott
New College, University of Edinburgh.
ABIM, Darul Arqam, PAS; Malaysia
(joint author).

Dr Sarah Potter
*West Sussex Institute of Higher
Education.*
Black Muslims, Moorish (–American)
Science Temple of America, Nation
of Islam.

Elizabeth Puttick
*Centre for New Religious Movements,
King's College, University of London.*
Ananda Marga, Brahma Kumaris,
Buddhist Women's Movement, Elan
Vital/Divine Light Mission, Gurdjieffian
Groups, ISKCON, Krishnamurti
Foundation, Order of Buddhist
Contemplatives, Sahaja Yoga, Satya Sai
Baba, Subud, Theosophy, Transcendental
Meditation.

Professor Murkot Ramunny
University of Calcut, India.
Colanaikans, All-India Muslim League
(jointly with Theodore Gabriel).

Prof. Francis C. R. Robinson
*Royal Holloway and Bedford New
College, University of London.*
Ahl-i Hadith, Ahl-i Quran, Ahmadiya
(Qadianis), Ahmadiya (Lahoris),
Barelvis (Barelwis), Deobandis, Islamic
Modernists (South Asia), Jama'at-i
Islami, Jam'iat ul-Ulama-i Hind, Tablighi
Jama'at.

The Revd. Canon Alan D. Rogers
Weymouth.
Malagasy Religion.

Klaus D. Schold
Heidelberg University.
Apostolic Church (Pentecostal
Congregation of Penygroes), Electronic
Church, Evangelical/Evangelikal,
Lutheran World Federation, New
Apostolic, Waldensians.

CONTRIBUTORS

Dr John J. Shepherd
S. Martin's College, Lancaster.
Afkodré, Afro-American Spiritism, Aga Khanis, Agama (Islam) Jawa, Agama Islam Santri, 'Aidarusiya, Alevis, 'Alia Bohoras ('Aliyas), All-India Muslim Majlis-i Mushawarat, Ansar, Aydinlar Ocagi, Azalis, Badawiya, Bassij-i Mostazafin (Mobilization of the Oppressed), Bohoras, Caritas, Catholic Action, Chisumphi Cult, Church of the Cherubim and Seraphim, Church of God Mission, Church of the Lord (Aladura), Church Universal and Triumphant, Daudis, Da'wa Party (Hizb al-Da'wa), Divana, ECKANKAR, Est, Ethiopian Churches, Etoism, Fada'iyan-i Islam, Fethullahcilar, Fidayin-i Khalq, Free Russian Orthodox Church, Front Islamique du Salut (FIS), Gerakan Pembaharuan, Haddawiya, Hairy Ishans, Halleluja Religion, Halveti-Cerrahis, Hamas (Algeria), Hamadsha, Heavenly Virtue Church, Hibtias (Hibatis, Hiptiyas), Hizb al-Nahda (Renaissance Party; MTI; Ennahda), Human Potential Movement, Ibadiya, Iglesia ni Cristo (jointly with James Veitch), Ikhwan, Insight MSIA, Isikcis, Islami Hareket, Islamic Assembly, Islamic Call Society, Islamic Council of Europe, Islamic Foundation, Islamic Front for the Liberation of Bahrain, Islamic Jihad al-Bait al-Muqaddas, Islamic Progressive Movement, Islamic Renaissance Movement, Islamic Renaissance Party, Islamic Republican Party, Islamic Revolutionary Guards, Islamic Unity Movement, Jama'at-i Islami of Bangladesh, Jama'at-i Islami of India, al-Jama'at al-Islamiya, Jam'iat ul-Ulama-i Ahl-i Hadith, Jihad Organization/al-Jihad, Jihad-i Sazandigi (Reconstruction Crusade), Jocists, Kardecismo, Kebatinan (Aliran Kebatinan), Kepercayaan, Khojas, Kolping Society, Kubrawiya, Kumina, Lassyism, Liborismo, Lord's Army, Mahdavis, Mahdibaghwalas, Mahdiya, Maitatsine, Maldevidan Cult, Maria Lionza, M'Bona Cult, Milli Görüs, Moorish (-American) Science Temple of America, Moro Islamic Liberation Front, Moro National Liberation Front, Mouvement Croix-Koma, Movement for the Enforcement of Ja'fari Law, Muhammadiyah, Mujahidin-i Khalq, Mujahids, Muslim Institute, Muslim Parliament of Great Britain, Muslim World League, Nagoshias, Nahda Movement/Party, Nahdatul Ulama, Nañiguismo, Nurçus, Organization of Islamic Action, Organization of the Islamic Conference, Pangestu, Pocomania, Primal Therapy, Psychosynthesis, Qalandars, Qimbanda, Rajneeshism, Rebirthing, Republican Brothers, Revival Zion, Russian (Orthodox) Church Abroad, Sapta Darma, Satpanthis, Shakers, Shango, Shouters, Silva Mind Control, Society of Militant Clergy, Society for Social Reform, Spiritual Baptists, Sufism, Sulaymanis, Süleymancis, Sumarah, Sunnism, Supreme Assembly for the Islamic Revolution in Iraq (SAIRI), Swedenborgianism, Talaeh al-Fidaa, Taro Cult, Tikhonite Church, True Orthodox Church of Greece, Tayibis, UK Islamic Mission, Union of Muslim Organisations of UK and Eire, Winti, World Conference on Religion and Peace, World Congress of Faiths, World Muslim Congress, 'Yan Tatsine ('Yan Izala), Yasawiya, Zar cult, Zionist Churches.

Part III:
Afghanistan, Algeria, Bahrain, Bangladesh, Egypt, Haiti, Indonesia, Iran, Iraq, Jordan, Kuwait, Lebanon, Libya, Malawi, Malaysia (with Michael Northcott), Mali, Morocco, Oman, Pakistan, Qatar, Saudi Arabia, Sudan, Syria, Tunis, Turkey, United Arab Emirates.

Dr Elizabeth Sirriyeh
University of Leeds.
'Alawiya (Darqawi), 'Alawiya (Hadrami), Darqawiya, Hamalliya, Hamas, Hanafis, Hanbalis, Islamic Liberation Group, Islamic Liberation Organization, Islamic Liberation Party, Khalwatiya, Malikis, Maraboutism, Mawlawiya, Muridiya, Muslim Brotherhood, Naqshbandiya, Qadiriya, Rifa'iya, Salafiya, Sanusiya, Shadhiliya, Shafi'is, al-Takfir wa'l-Hijra, Tijaniya, Wahhabism.

Dr Callum Slipper
London.
Focolare.

Prof. Ninian Smart
University of California, Santa Barbara.
Part I: Religions in the Contemporary
World

Prof. Donald Swearer
Swasrthmoor College, Pennsylvania.
Part I: Buddhism.

Dr Nasir Tamimi
School of Islamic Studies, Jakarta.
Muhammadiyah, Nahdatul Ulama

Dr James Veitch
*Victoria University of Wellington, New
Zealand.*
Aglipayan, Iharaira, Maori Religion,
Maori Religious Movements, Melanesian
Religion, Polynesian Religion (jointly
with Thomas Daffern); Ratana, Ringatu;
Cargo cults, John Frum, (jointly with
Keith Munnings); Iglesia ni Cristo,
(jointly with John Shepherd); New
Zealand, Philippines.

Prof. W. Montgomery Watt
University of Edinburgh.
Part I: Islam.

Rosemary J. Watts
Westminster College, Oxford.
Adventists, Amish, Assemblies of God,
Baptists, Bretheren (German Baptists),
Catholic Apostolic, Christadelphians,
Christian Science, Congregationalists,
Conservative Catholic Churches,
Disciples of Christ (Restorationist),
Dutch Reformed Church, Exclusive
Bretheren, Holiness (Perfectionist),
House Churches, Hutterites, Independent
Evangelical Churches, Interdenominational
Evangelical Churches, Isolated Radio
Churches, Jehovah's Witnesses, Lutherans,
Mennonites (Anabaptists), Methodists,
Moravians, Mormons, Nazarenes, Old
Catholic Churches, Open Bretheren,
Pentecostal (Charismatic), Protestant,
Presbyterian (Reformed), Reformed
Catholic Churches, Salvation Army,
Society of Friends (Quakers), Southern
Baptists, Spiritualists, Taize, Unitarians,
United Churches.

Dr Richard Wilson
University of Essex.
Mesoamerican Traditional Religion
(Mayan).

PART I: MAJOR RELIGIOUS TRADITIONS

RELIGIONS IN THE CONTEMPORARY WORLD

During the 20th century religions have undergone remarkable changes and vicissitudes. The rise of totalitarian ideologies, notably Fascism, Nazism and Communism, have caused considerable suffering to religious traditionalists, notably to **Jews** and **Tibetan Buddhists**, but to many other groups as well. The collapse of Nazism and Fascism at the end of World War II has been followed by the demise of Marxist régimes in Eastern Europe and in the former Soviet Union. All this has brought significant change to traditional religions. But other factors too have brought about transformation. The emergence of a global civilization characterized by instant communication, extensive travel, migrations and an increasingly unified global capitalist system, has encouraged various developments: the emergence of new emphases on ecumenism in many religions, the increased prominence of diaspora groups (such as **Sikhs** outside India supporting movements within India), solidarity between religions and nationalisms (in Iran, Sri Lanka, Ireland and elsewhere), a new self-consciousness of the global significance of each major religion, tendencies towards syncretisms, wider backlashes against religious modernism or liberalism, the growth of new religious movements, a wider spread of individualism and with it a new voluntarism in religion, and the adoption of modern technology in the preaching and spread of religion.

Also, the balance of power has shifted both within religions and between them. The end of the 19th century and the beginning of the 20th was the heyday of the colonial system, and Christian missionaries rode on the backs of empires in a remarkable effort at proselytization, being successful particularly in sub-Saharan Africa and the Pacific region, though not inconsiderable impacts were made in Asia. But particularly since World War II the dignity and power of other traditions have been reasserted. Included here are the relatively small-scale societies of Africa and Native America, which have evolved a wider alliance to express **African religion** as a whole and **Native American religion** (not thus confined to a particular tribe or nation). Meanwhile the post-colonial era has shifted balances. Thus, the majority of Christians now live in the Southern Hemisphere, in sub-Saharan Africa, in Central and South America and in the Pacific region. The majority of Muslims live in South Asia and South-East Asia (notably in Indonesia), and so demographically the Arab region, the traditional heartland of Islam, is less significant. **Buddhism,** still (1992) largely suppressed in Marxist countries, from Vietnam to China and North Korea, has assumed a more Western incarnation. Likewise **Confucianism** and **Taoism** are more vigorous outside than inside China. Judaism since World War II has two major epicentres, Israel and the United States, while its older vitality in Central and Eastern Europe has been largely snuffed out by the Holocaust: its presence in Muslim lands has decisively diminished.

Another phenomenon in the modern period especially has been the growth of new religious movements, both in the West and in most other regions of the world, especially in Africa, where numerous independent churches are making spectacular progress. Some of these new movements are blends of elements from diverse traditions—for instance, African themes intertwined with Christianity, Hindu doctrines and **Gurus** adapted to Western conditions, transformations of indigenous religion as in the **Cargo Cults** of the South Pacific, modernized forms of Japanese **Shinto,** etc. Indeed to some degree all religions have been altered by the impact of capitalism, colonialism and the new globalism. Mainline **Protestantism** for instance is heavily influenced by liberal attitudes and modern scholarship, while Catholicism since Vatican II has felt the impact of the same forces. So in a sense all religions are "new religions". Nevertheless we should not neglect the force of the smaller new religions, which taken together have a lot of power.

It is useful at this point to survey the distribution of the major religions and ideologies in the world, as they have emerged from the colonial period into the new global order—a period which has seen the universalization of the conception (though not always the reality) of the nation-state. The earth's land surface is virtually covered by independent nations, even if there are nations still struggling for such political self-expression.

First, there is a great region, from Europe to North America and from the Arctic to portions of the South, such as Australia and New Zealand, which is predominantly Christian and White. This has been the powerhouse of colonialism, capitalism and a more or less liberal ethos, especially under the influence of Protestantism. Into this Western civilization are mixed in other forces, notably Judaism, especially in the United States of America. But other minorities are important too—Muslims in America, Britain, Germany and France particularly, Chinese and Japanese Buddhists in California, indigenous peoples in North America, Scandinavia, and so on. Attached as a Southern wing of this great bloc of Western culture are Australia and New Zealand, and in an ambiguous way South Africa. Although formally much of the West is Christian, and perhaps more intensely in the USA than elsewhere, it is deeply affected by scientific humanism and a pragmatically agnostic attitude to religion. During the period since World War II the main trends have been democratic, with dictatorships in Southern Europe being overthrown in Greece (1977), Spain (1975) and Portugal (1974). While the whole region of White civilization, both North and South, has been deeply influenced by Christian values, it has entered a phase in which many choose to leave those values behind. At the same time this area has vital minority influences. To signify this transcendence of traditional Christian ideas I shall refer to it as the TransChristian West.

This region abuts upon the countries of Eastern Europe and the former Soviet Union. These are currently in a state of turmoil. There was a period, after World War II, after the Chinese Communist victory in 1949, and subsequent developments in South-East Asia, when the whole region from the River Elbe to Vladivostok, and from Murmansk to Ho Chi Minh City, was Marxist and totalitarian, with little room for traditional religions. In effect Marxism functioned as the state religion. But this Marxist bloc has recently (namely from 1989) been progressively torn apart, with the collapse of Communist régimes in Eastern Europe in 1989, and the demise of the Soviet system in 1991. Actually, though Marxism was like a religion it turned out to be an ineffective one. The emerging countries of the ex-Soviet Union and Eastern Europe have a variety of dominant religions. Poland, Hungary, Slovenia and Croatia are predominantly **Catholic,** with Czechoslovakia mixed. Serbia and other parts of ex-Yugoslavia are mainly **Orthodox** (with Muslims an important presence). Bulgaria and Romania are mainly Orthodox. So too are Ukraine and Belorus, Russia (with its many embedded minorities), Moldava, Armenia and Georgia. But the Central Asian republics are chiefly Muslim. In the Baltics, Protestantism dominates. It looks as if the Muslim republics will join what I below dub "the Islamic Crescent". Meanwhile we may call the area from the Elbe to Vladivostok the TransChristian East.

The third major bloc in the world is constituted by the countries of the Islamic Crescent. Islam dominates from beyond the Australian littoral through Indonesia, Malaysia, Bangladesh, Pakistan (and the Republic of India, which has more than 80,000,000 Muslims within its borders), Afghanistan, Central Asia, Iran, the Arab Middle East and North Africa, to Mauritania and parts of West Africa. There are vital outposts in East Africa. This Crescent is divided primarily between **Shi'a** and **Sunni** Islam, with the latter being most preponderant. Today it is undergoing revival and a new ecumenical self-consciousness, fostered by jet-borne pilgrimage to Mecca.

Within the Arab and related lands there are anomalies. Thus, Turkey, through the reforms and initiative of Kemal Ataturk (1881–1938), became a secular state, attempting, in effect, to join Europe. Its support for Islamic causes has been therefore ambiguous. While some other states in the area, such as Egypt and Iraq, have followed modernist paths, espousing Arab nationalism rather than Islamic solidarity, Turkey has progressed further along the path of modernism than others. The other anomaly in the Islamic Crescent has been the state of Israel, which has (from a Muslim point of view) stuck like a thorn in the flank of Islam: an outpost, in the eyes of many Muslims, of Western imperialism and Jewish–Christian influence.

Another cultural region of the world is Latin America, from just north of the Rio Grande (where its influence on US culture is growing) to Patagonia in the South, comprising largely Spanish-speaking nations, though also the huge Portuguese-speaking Brazil and the multilingual Caribbean. Here the main influence is **Roman Catholicism,** springing from the colonial conquest of the Americas, in this case primarily by Spain and Portugal. In recent times there has been throughout this region a strong surge of Protestantism, especially in its conservative and **Pentecostal** forms. Newish religions, created out of a synthesis of African and other elements are also present, since, especially in Brazil, there is a large African population. The Latin South (as I shall call it) has its own character, and liberal modernism in the Western mode is less dominant.

Below the northern part of the African continent, stretching from Morocco and Mauritania in the West to Egypt, Sudan and Somalia in the East the continent is largely Christian, mostly through modern activities by missionaries, though Ethiopia has its ancient form of Christianity, allied to the **Coptic Church** in Egypt. Sub-Saharan Africa also has many adherents of classical African religions. New, largely Christian, movements are also well represented, even if mainstream Churches often try to deny their legitimacy. Moreover, some parts of sub-Saharan Africa, notably Nigeria and Tanzania, are deeply affected by Islam. Still, Black Africa (as I shall call this zone) is largely Christian, despite its classical African and Islamic minorities.

We have already glanced at the Marxist dominance of East Asia, though it is true that aspects of capitalism are beginning to invade China, especially in the south and around Hong Kong (due to join the People's Republic in 1997, with Macao joining two years later). China has not wished to follow the line of *glasnost* taken by the former Soviet Union. As such political rigidity, with stern suppression of separatism in Tibet, and other non-Han outposts of the Chinese Empire, with special apprehension towards Central Asia goes hand in hand with economic liberalization. What will emerge is obscure at the time of writing (1992). Anyway, China, together with North Korea and much of former Indochina, retains a Marxist autocracy, which is already crumbling, since totalitarian rule is not being efficiently maintained in the face of market liberalization and increasing problems of centralizing the bureaucracy. There is therefore some revival of traditional religions in China. This area can be called the Marxist Bloc.

The final major cultural area in today's world is the region where traditional Asian, mainly Buddhist and Hindu values, have been maintained. In South Asia, there is the predominantly Hindu state of India, though—as we have seen—with a strong minority of Muslims, not to mention smaller minorities of **Sikhs, Parsis,** Christians, **Jainas** and Buddhists. To the South is largely Sinhalese Buddhist Sri Lanka, with, however, powerful minorities of Tamils and Muslims (the former engaged for more than a decade in insurrection). South-East Asia, namely in particular Thailand, Myanmar (Burma), Laos and Cambodia, is **Theravada** Buddhist, and Vietnam is partly Buddhist. Thailand has a substantial minority of Muslims. Vietnam is partly Buddhist, with a Catholic minority.

As well as these areas indebted greatly to Indian civilization there are areas in Asia outside the Marxist Bloc which are chiefly Chinese in culture, such as Taiwan, Hong

Kong and Singapore, together with South Korea (having its distinctive Korean tradition). All these countries are to some degree influenced by Buddhism, and so have an affinity to South Asia. All this underbelly (so to speak) of Asia we can here nominate as the area of Traditional Asia. Actually, it is not that traditional, since some parts of it are hurrying along a modern capitalist path. In the region we need of course to include Japan, with its own distinctive and largely Buddhist civilization, but with ingredients of Shinto, Confucianism, Taoism and Western liberalism, especially in the settlement after World War II.

One might add as a final area the islands of the South and Central Pacific. Though it is now substantially Christian in religion, there are differences of culture from the Northern scene, for here we find Polynesian, Melanesian and other cultural motifs woven into Christian values. And so we can call this the Pacific Region. In short, we have established a number of large cultural areas or blocs in the world, namely: the TransChristian West and the TransChristian East, the Islamic Crescent, the Latin South, Black Africa, Traditional Asia, and the Pacific Region.

These different regions are in differing relations to one another, and to themselves. Generally speaking, the TransChristian West has a majority religious representation side by side with an active minority. Most of the major Christian Churches are either traditionalist or liberal; a more radical fundamentalist wing is dynamic in its opposition to the majority as well as being very energetic in mission. This evangelical minority is also active in the TransChristian East. Similarly, in the Jewish tradition there is an active conservative radicalism, which fastens particularly on developing an outreach in Israel, through such parties as the **Gush Emunim** (Bloc of the Faithful). In the case of Islam, the reaction against modernism and compromise with the West is reinforced by the feeling of opposition to colonialism and possible capitalist oppression. Though so-called fundamentalist movements, such as the **Muslim Brotherhood,** active particularly in Egypt, and analogous movements in Algeria, Pakistan and elsewhere, have a modernizing aspect, at least in practical affairs, they also see themselves as restoring original Islamic values. Similarly the Shi'ite revolution in Iran advocates and implements the notion of an Islamic Republic (an innovative idea), yet also sees itself as restoring a long-betrayed past. In South Asia there are reformist but conservative national movements, among both Hindus in India and Buddhists in Sri Lanka.

Partly because of these more radical movements, there are tensions between the blocs. Already of course there were conflicts between the Islamic Crescent and the West over Israel, regarded as an intrusion on rightful Islamic territory (the *Dar al-Islam*). But especially since the Islamic revolution in Iran there have been difficulties in Western–Islamic relations. These became obscured during the Gulf War of 1991, with differing Islamic nations taking opposing sides.

Conversely, the tensions between the (Asian) Marxist Bloc and the West, on the one hand, and the Islamic Crescent, on the other, have diminished, despite the Beijing massacre of 1989. The TransChristian East and West have largely reconciled their previously bitter differences. While the Southern regions of the world are worried, to put no finer point on it, by economic disparities and a perceived plunder of the South, the fact that these regions are dominated by Christianity modifies the resentment. On the whole, the lands of Traditional Asia have successfully entered the general capitalist system and religions such as Buddhism, Hinduism, **Confucianism, Taoism** and Shinto are happy enough in their, on the whole, fruitful interface with Western and Christian values.

As we have noted, the new global civilization has also tended to foster new religions and borrowings between religions. Forms of both Hindu and Buddhist yoga have made their way into Christian practice here and there, and more generally into Western culture. Conversely, Eastern religions have often adopted Western styles of self-presentation and organization. Many works written in English have incorporated Western philosophical ideas into Eastern doctrine. For instance, **Swami Vivekananda's** articulation of a modernized form of **Vedanta** as presenting the true meaning of the Hindu tradition, which remains popular among the Hindu élite, draws in some degree on motifs derived from 19th century idealism; while both Wittgensteinian and empiricist themes have entered into Sri Lankan Buddhist modernism. As we have noted, there are also conservative movements which represent a reaction against too much accommodation with both modernism and the new global order. They also reflect ways in which tensions between particular religions reinforce or are reinforced by ethnic tensions. Thus religious factors are important in various ongoing trouble zones, as well as some new ones opened up by the demise of the Soviet Union and the devolution of the old system into diverse republics.

The most obvious of the older, partly religion-based conflicts, are those in Northern Ireland and Israel. The division between the two Irish communities is in fact defined by religion, as between the Protestants and Catholics. We have noted how the Jewish state is resented by the Arab countries, partly because it is seen as an alien non-Arab intrusion, but also because of the principle that the territory of Islam (*Dar-al-Islam*) should not be violated by non-Islamic political entities. Conversely, the concern for the land of Israel is more and more being seen as a sacred one, not just as a secular quest for a homeland for the Jews after the tragedy of the Holocaust. But there are plenty of other partially religious conflicts elsewhere. Thus, the Sinhalese nationalist conflict with Tamils (mainly Hindus and Christians) is partly grounded in the belief that Sri Lanka is the true guardian of the Buddha's Law or *Dhamma*. This is reinforced by appeal to the chronicles which piously detail Sinhalese history from a Buddhist perspective. Again, the conflict between India and Pakistan over Kashmir turns on the fact that Kashmir, a largely Muslim state, joined the Republic of India after partition in 1947, because of the action of its then ruler, a Hindu. The rise of revivalist Hindu sentiment in India is seen in the formation of the **Bharatiya Janata Party,** which threatens to disturb the pluralist constitution and policy of the Republic of India. In Afghanistan, much of the energy which motivated the guerrillas (and now the government) fighting against the Soviet Union, and then against the Marxist régime was energized by Islam. The civil war in the South of the Sudan is partly fuelled by the dislike of Christians and adherents of classical African religion for the imposition by the government in Khartoum of Islamic law (*shari'a*). The fighting from 1989 on in Armenia and Azerbaijan is dependent on the perception of national identities which are grounded both in language and religion. Similarly, in Yugoslavia conflict between Croatians and Serbians is heightened by religious differences. There are other struggles in Myanma (Burma), the Philippines, Thailand, Cambodia (Kampuchea), and elsewhere which have a partly religious character.

It is now time to look a little more closely at developments in the various blocs whose disposition in the modern global civilization we have sketched above. First, in the TransChristian West there have been some notable developments. The most significant probably was Vatican II (1962–1965): by bringing *aggiornamento* (updating) to the Church Pope John XXIII (1881–1963) effectively opened the way to liberal modernism within Catholicism. This in turn greatly accelerated Catholic impulses to participate in the ecumenical movement. The latter has brought a high degree of *rapprochement* between most mainline Christian denominations. While Protestant mainline churches in North America and elsewhere have experienced decline, the total impact of liberal Christianity has gained because of the Catholic Church. But this has in turn sparked conservative reactions, particularly over abortion, as a symbol of the division between liberals and others. But also in the late '70s and '80s evangelical and fundamentalist Christianity has shown renewed vigour. This in turn has helped to fuel Protestant missionary activities, significant particularly for Latin America. While in the TransChristian West as a whole

7

new religions have a diminished role, after their flourishing period between the late '60s and the end of the '70s, there has been a growth more generally in themes loosely collected together as the **New Age.** In the United States in particular there has been a significant growth in people who have constructed private religions, drawing on sources in both Christianity and in Eastern religions. Significant too has been the increasing confidence of exponents of Native American religion, beginning too to form alliances with analogous ill-treated minorities such as the **Maoris** and **Australian Aborigines.** More significant is the rooting of originally migrant groups in the West professing traditions not hitherto regarded as Western: notably Muslims from Pakistan and India, North Africa and Turkey in Britain, France and Germany. Other groups such as traditional Sikhs, Hindus and Buddhists, as well as migrants of all kinds, have given most Western countries a pluralist feel. Most major cities contain sizeable groups from all the world's major cultures. This trend will doubtless continue, as frontier controls become more and more ineffective in restraining immigration into the richer countries from the poorer, including the former Soviet Union.

Meanwhile the revival of religion after the Soviet period is evident in the TransChristian East. While Marxism as an ideology is not as dead as might have seemed from the sudden collapse of the system in Eastern Europe and the former Soviet Union, the new freedoms allow churches to recruit and build, while a massive migration of Jews to Israel is beginning to alter the demographics of that country. Also the traditional religions of relatively small-scale groups among Siberian **shamanists** and so on are liable for revival. Russia also has within its border sizeable pockets of Muslims, as in Tatarstan. Islamic minorities in South-Eastern Europe, notably in Bulgaria and in Bosnia-Herzegovina, are significant, while Albania is resuming its role as the only predominantly Muslim state in Europe. Some Western influences are also beginning to penetrate the East, such as Christian evangelicalism and New Age concepts.

The Islamic Crescent possesses a variety of problematical developments. There remains a continuing crisis of Islamic identity. This is due to several factors. First of all, the period after World War II has been characterized by anti-colonial struggle, in the Middle East and North Africa, in South Asia and South-East Asia, and most recently in former Soviet Central Asia. Only in China does there remain a sizeable Islamic minority which has not achieved significant autonomy. During the first phase of anti-colonial nationalism the struggle was often conceived in socialist terms. Thus in the Arab lands, from Algeria to Iraq the primary model was modernizing and not Islamic. Hence the dominance of secular, non-religious régimes in the principal countries, under the aegis of the *Front de Libération Nationale*—FLN in Alberia, the Ba'ath parties of Syria and Iraq, and post-Nasserite régimes in Egypt. Second, the relative failure of these movements in delivering economic strength has led to the growth of neo-Islamic parties and governments, such as the Muslim Brotherhood in Syria and Egypt, suppressed sometimes with brutality, and régimes in the Sudan which have imposed Islamic law. Saudi Arabia has continued a conservative social stance, based on the **Wahhabi** movement dating from the late 18th century but revived as a state ideology from the 1920s. The most spectacular backlash both against monarchism in the Islamic world and against secular modernism was the Islamic revolution of Ayatollah Khomeini in Iran. A less strongly revivalist Islamic régime prevails in Pakistan (a country which was founded on Muslim values in 1947, though a break between the Western region and Bangladesh occurred in 1971—Islam alone being an insufficient bond between the two halves).

The relative ease with which Muslims, even from as far away as Indonesia, can get to Mecca reinforces the sense of unity among the pious. In consequence, a greater unification of practice and belief is becoming evident. There are tendencies opposed to traditional practices not perceived as truly Islamic, such as many of the rituals surrounding the cult of holy men, e.g. in North Africa, and there has been a great erosion of **Sufism,** because fundamentalist revivalism pins some of the blame of the poor state of Islam under the impact of colonialism on the fact that Muslims have not always practised a pure Islamic faith. Though Sufism has had a modest appeal in the West it was suppressed in westernizing Turkey. It maintained influence during the Soviet period in Central Asia, partly because it was adapted to transmitting Islam in a private and secret way. Disillusion both with traditionalism and with secular modernism is a major factor in the new influence of radical revivalism, sometimes called "fundamentalism".

Meanwhile in Israel the struggle between Palestinians and the Jewish state has been largely conceived in secular nationalist and pan-Arab terms. But religious factors are changing, through the growth of influence of the religious right in Israel, notably through the Gush Emunim. The spectrum of Jewish opinion remains highly diverse, from the secular and often socialist **Zionism** of kibbutz pioneers, through the religious agnosticism of many Israelis, to anti-Zionist Jewish conservatism and radical politically-oriented religiosity.

The Latin South has long been dominated by the Roman Catholic Church, which proselytized fairly successfully under the Spanish and Portuguese empires. But since Vatican II in particular there has been some polarization. Liberation theology has been a largely Latin American phenomenon, blending Catholic and Marxist motifs and stressing the Church's need to maintain solidarity with the poor and under-privileged. The establishment of new forms of spiritual and social welfare through the setting up of base communities has helped to foster a new self-consciousness, especially among Indians. Such a polarization of the Church between the more radical priests and the old establishment attitude has expressed itself in a strong tension in areas particularly of civil war (during the late '70s and '80s in Nicaragua and El Salvador). In Peru the Sendero Luminoso or Shining Path movement has exhibited a ruthless and anti-Catholic ideology. But the main tendency in the '80s in Latin America was towards democratic systems, going beyond both older authoritarianism and new revolution. During the '70s and '80s the renewed vigour of conservative Christianity among North American Protestants has helped to fuel a remarkable growth throughout Latin America of Pentecostalism and evangelical faith. Such recruitment is in part among tribal groups but is also evident among Catholics. Also important in Latin America and the Caribbean are a number of African-based new religions, combining often traditional African with Catholic and other elements. Notable among these are the **Santeria, Umbanda** and **Candomblé** in Brazil (though the first originated in Cuba and has been spread in the US, Venezuela and elsewhere by exiles from the Castro revolution of 1959). In Surinam and throughout the whole Caribbean region we find varying groups and movements, perhaps the most important being the **Rastafarians,** who look to Ethiopia and the late emperor Haile Selassie (Ras Tafari) in hope, and Haitian **Voodoo.** All these movements have penetrated into America through migrations.

Black African religion has had to contend with the need to come to terms with the modern world: the impact of colonialism, modern science, capitalism, a new nationalism somewhat arbitrarily expressed in terms of colonial boundaries, struggles for independence, most recently in Zimbabwe and South Africa, and missionary work. The traditional, largely smaller-scale, societies have on the whole accepted Christianity (in some areas Islam). Naturally, classical African religions have maintained themselves to some degree. The second and related problem is the need to synthesize some of the traditional values and those flooding in from the global civilization and from the West. The most important vehicle for such a synthesis are the new religious movements (over 10,000 in sub-Saharan Africa and over 3,000 in South Africa) which are mainly Christian and express through their black leadership a replacement of the previously European-dominated character of the mainline churches. Of these the most prominent perhaps is the **Kimbanguist Church,** originating in Zaire, and now admitted to the **World Council of Churches.** Its founder,

Simon Kimbangu (died 1951), was both healer and prophet, and indeed martyr. The themes of prophetism and healing are prominent in indigenous revivals. The independent churches amount to more than 15 per cent of total Christian membership in Black Africa. In South Africa, taken together, they constitute the single largest religious movement (around 8,000,000).

The missionary churches have been prominent in the struggle for African freedoms. It is true that the **Dutch Reformed churches** of South Africa have generally speaking expressed an ideology of racial separateness. But otherwise the missionary movements, being close to Africans and inspired by ecumenical ideals, have fostered both the education and empowerment of African leaders.

The Marxist bloc, centered on China, has witnessed various vicissitudes. The clampdown associated with the massacre of Tiananmen Square in 1989 cannot conceal the degree of popular disillusion with the Marxist system. While in the '60s and '70s Maoist philosophy itself effectively constituted an evangelical kind of religion, being replete with rituals of solidarity, devotion to the leader, a revolutionary doctrine, a new ethics, and a new mythology, the period since Mao's death in 1976 has seen little new inspiration and much regret at the destruction caused to the fabric of Chinese society by Mao's vision. Further, though restrictions on religion in most of China have been eased, the colonialist oppression of Tibet remains, and to a lesser degree that of other minorities such as the Muslim Uighirs. The influence of Tibetan religion has paradoxically greatly increased through the dispersal of learned Tibetan monks throughout the world and through the example and teaching of the Dalai Lama.

In Marxist South-East Asia much of traditional religion, especially in Cambodia during the Khmer Rouge period (1975–1979), was suppressed. The Khmer Rouge preached a kind of nationalist hermitism, in which Cambodia was to be purified of modern elements, and cut off, from the global capitalist system.

The region which I have called Traditional Asia contains varying tendencies. Some Buddhist countries have experimented with socialism, such as Burma and for a time Sri Lanka. There has been since World War II a revival of the Order or *Sangha,* partly through the greater emphasis on meditation methods, and partly through a new revival of Buddhist learning, fostered also by Western scholarship. New directions have occurred in lay participation and social revival. Meanwhile in India not only have new religious movements sprung up within Hinduism (such as that associated with **Sai Baba,** not to mention older trends such as that expressed through the **Aurobindo Ashram** and the continuing work of the **Ramakrishna Vedanta Mission**). Most importantly there has been a new assertion of Hindu chauvinism, sparked in part by recognition that upper-class Hindus can be disadvantaged by affirmative action to uplift the scheduled castes (viz untouchables and others). The older pluralist philosophy is fading, and a new Hindu self-consciousness is being developed throughout the Hindu diaspora (in the West Indies, South Africa, Fiji and Canada, etc.).

There has been some revival of Confucianism, especially in Singapore. New scholarship is restoring a sense of the Taoist heritage. Meanwhile in Japan and Korea there have occurred vigorous reinterpretations of **Zen,** and in Japan **Pure Land Buddhism.** The new religions of Japan continue to play a role in adapting to new urban social configurations. There has been some revival of Shinto values, going back to the Meiji period (1867–1912) when they were given national prominence. The resurrection of Japanese patriotism in recent years is significant.

Finally, the South Pacific has seen some revival of traditional interests. The notion of a Pacific Way animates the small nations of the South Pacific, while Maori activists in New Zealand have begun to establish a more important place for traditional Polynesian religion in the fabric of New Zealand self-understanding.

One of the late questions on the agenda of non-Western cultures is how to synthesize the varying demands for religious recognition. Within Christianity there are diverse notions deriving basically from the 1970s, such as Black theology, African theology, Asian theologies, Red (Native American) theology and so forth. All the religions are moving into a period when they will need to express both their particular cultural embodiments and their universal or global significance, especially in relation to one another and to the various global ideologies.

Finally, a significant though minor change has been the development of cross-cultural religious studies, which helps to promote mutual understanding between the traditions but also a more objective and analytical knowledge of religion worldwide, without sacrificing the importance of empathy.

Ninian Smart

CHRISTIANITY

Christianity is the largest of world religions and the most extended. Europe, North and South America, Africa south of the Equator, and Australasia may all be described as predominantly Christian continents. Only in Asia is it the religion of a small minority, yet even here it is the majority religion of the Philippines and is also strongly represented in many other areas, notably southern India, Sri Lanka, Vietnam and South Korea. As the dominant religion of the United States of America and western Europe, Christianity is clearly that of the most wealthy, powerful and economically developed parts of the world. Yet Christianity has grown most in the last hundred years in the poorest of societies, principally within the southern hemisphere. Where, even 50 years ago, there were hardly 10 African bishops putting together all the principal Christian traditions, now the figure is nearer 1,000. Moreover, if Christianity's principal global antagonist throughout the 20th century has been communism, that antagonist has now simply collapsed through most of the world, leaving Christians as apparent victors in the conflict, free even to rebuild a long-demolished cathedral in Red Square, Moscow. Finally, Christianity has also continued to provide outstanding leaders of humanity in many fields—not only bishops and popes like the martyred Archbishop Oscar Romero of El Salvador and Pope John Paul II but charismatic and intellectual figures such as Mother Teresa, Teilhard de Chardin and Dietrich Bonhoeffer.

Despite such wide-ranging signs of vitality Christianity may, nevertheless, be undergoing a greater crisis than any other major religion. In western Europe, its traditional heartland, a large majority of people are no longer churchgoers or formal believers, and the society of countries like England and France can better be described as post-Christian than Christian. Secularism and the scientific frame of mind—social and historical science at least as much as the physical sciences—provide the fundamental characteristics of the Western form of modernity and, while they have come to maturity within Christian (particularly **Protestant**) contexts, they appear to many to have undermined the claims of religion in general and of Christianity in particular. The very attempt to respond to such challenges by incorporating modern insights within a theological reinterpretation of Christian belief has often seemed to wreak additional havoc with the tradition, while quite inadequately responding to the external challenge. The use of reason and the formulation of an articulated theology in terms of contemporary intellectual culture have always been characteristics of the mainline Christian tradition but never has the enterprise seemed more in doubt. No other world religion is so close to, so integrally entangled with, the culture of modernity, but that very closeness which, historically, may be seen as creative may, in contemporary terms, be seen as a major cause of disintegration.

It began, and has ever remained identified, with a Jewish prophet of two millennia ago, Jesus of Nazareth. Whatever else Christianity may be, it was in its origins, and in its character has always to a great extent continued to be, a Jewish movement. Christians have never seriously questioned the rightness of continuing to regard the Hebrew scriptures as their own, constitutive of more than three-quarters of the Christian Bible. In regarding the Hebrew scriptures as unquestionably God's word, the followers of Jesus of Nazareth carried over the Jewish sense of identity as God's chosen people on earth, with whom he has established a covenant of grace. Hebraic monotheism, the prayers and prophetic utterances in which it was best expressed, the moral perceptions both personal and social which the law and the prophets saw as consequent upon the nature of God, a theology of history—of the divine concern with humanity being both localized and temporalized—all this was simply taken over by Christianity from Judaic religion: Genesis for a theology of creation, the Psalms for prayer, the prophets for social criticism. At the same time the ritual and dietary rules which had become so central to the practice of devout Jews in the time of Jesus were emphatically rejected, together with the nationalism of religious or political selection. Hence, Christians at one and the same time continued to canonize the Hebrew scriptures and to sit quite lightly to a large part of their contents, regarding much as abrogated. Where Judaism remained a religion of law, Christianity became, more ambiguously, a religion of "grace". It has, however, never been quite clear how the two should be related: as a religion of creation and of political society it tends to be inspired by the Hebrew scriptures, but as a religion of personal salvation it looks more to its own, especially the writings of Paul. The ambiguity of its origins in relation to the religion which it continued, fulfilled, replaced or whatever has always continued to surface in a variety of theologies diversely relating "the New Testament" to "the Old".

What has dominated the Christian movement within this Jewish context has been the figure of Jesus. Whatever theology you settle for, if it is a Christian theology, it has been characterized by its Christology—the interpretation of a teacher, radical moralist, eschatological prophet, miracle worker, the crucified and risen one. The historical Jesus is decisive, but he can only be so by being also the Christ of faith, and that requires a more-than-historical interpretation. The figure of Jesus the Christ relativizes the written scriptures because he, not they, is proclaimed *par excellence* the Word of God. God spoke more absolutely through this person than through any writing.

While the dominance of the church by the figure of Jesus, the Saviour and Son of God, is never in question, what is most decisive about that figure certainly has been. Here again there is ambiguity. Is it the radical moral teaching of the Sermon on the Mount which matters most, the eschatological anticipation of judgement and a divine kingdom, the ultimate acceptance of suffering in the crucifixion, or the triumph of the Resurrection? And what sort of a triumph was that? The sign of the cross, an instrument of inhuman execution, became the primary Christian symbol, yet the faith of the early church is presented again and again as, above all, an Easter faith, a faith in the risen one. The triumph could come so much to dominate the whole that the earthly history, the very untriumphalistic teaching of the Galilean and Jerusalem ministry, could almost be overlooked. And did it signify triumph in the next world or in this? The message could be read as above all sanctifying the experience of suffering embraced, but it could also point to an end to suffering and the overthrow of all powers other than God's. Jesus taught about the "kingdom of God", but ever since there has been argument as to how, when and where that kingdom was to be realized. The earliest disciples seem to have expected its this-worldly imminence. When that did not happen, it was replaced by a very strong preoccupation with life after death. Christianity became for a time a very other-worldly religion of personal salvation and, with the resurrection of Jesus its most characteristic faith affirmation, it is hard to see how it could have been otherwise. "If for this life only we have hoped in Christ, we are of all men most to be pitied" (I Corinthians 15.19). But the complexity and evolution of the figure of Jesus as portrayed in the Gospels (and what was probably the earliest written "gospel", Mark's, appears to have had originally no resurrection narrative at all) have ensured that there can be an almost infinitely varied range of Christianities, each focused upon a different way of interpreting the founder.

What is certain is that he himself is recorded as writing nothing—except once, in the sand! The ambiguity of his role as God's supreme messenger—the *Logos*, divine word, of the preface of John's gospel—is highlighted by that simple fact. The Hebrew scriptures are seen as pointing to him, the New Testament scriptures endeavour to describe and proclaim him, but he as the divine word is somehow beyond and above both. In establishing a "new" covenant in his death, sacramentally communicated to his followers, as Christians believed to be the case in the very first decades of their existence (I Corinthians 11.23–6), Jesus had inexorably relativized the "old" covenant, its rituals, moral obligations and—inevitably—even the scriptures in which they were passed on. But he himself gave them no other scriptures. It is essential for the understanding of Christianity to remind oneself that, for several generations, Christians had no literary "New Testament" to turn to and found it possible to flourish without one. Individual writings, of Paul or another, soon began to circulate but a body of authoritative Christian scriptures, an additional "word of God", was not officially recognized to exist for a couple of centuries. When it came to be established and canonically separated by the church from other writings, orthodox and unorthodox, it was for pragmatic rather than for theoretical reasons. Christianity always needed Jesus. Only secondarily and later did it also need the New Testament and yet, in due course, its only reliable knowledge of Jesus, its only way to avoid deviations, would be through fidelity to this additional collection of sacred scripture—additional to the Hebrew and pre-Christian collection.

The fact that the authority of Jesus in regard to anything specific had to be mediated for future generations across the gap dividing him from the occasional writings of a generation or more later, using a language other than his own, created the second profound ambiguity and source of undefined freedom, even uncertainty, built into the Christian tradition from its start. So much he was not quoted as saying. Thus, central as the Church had become for Christians (and for the theology of Paul) Jesus had, according to the gospels, almost nothing to say about it: the word appears only twice in Matthew's gospel and in none of the other three. Again, he offered no "law" of a precise and practical kind. If the Sermon on the Mount (Matthew 5–7) is the nearest we get, it is pitifully clear that we are just not there. It is ever so much more and ever so much less than a Christian code of law. Unlike Judaism and Islam, Christianity in its essence is in consequence very unlegalistic, however legalistic some Christian groups have become.

It was also in its origins very unritualistic. The highly complex rituals of Judaism, both communal and personal, were swept aside and replaced by an extraordinary freedom in specifically religious terms. There was, beyond baptism, almost nothing else but an at first none-too-formal meal, symbolically repeating the last supper of the Master and his disciples. Jesus had not been of the priestly tribe. He behaved as a prophet, a lay prophet. The sense of laity was continued by the church and only much later did its ministers come to be given sacerdotal titles. Here again there is ambiguity. The priestly character of Jesus is quickly affirmed, his life and death seen in supremely sacerdotal terms, but his sacrifice was a real, not a ritual one, and his clear impatience with ritual, even with preoccupation over sabbath observance, is what was remembered. Ritual, no more than law, can easily take the centre ground in Christianity.

We have seen that even scripture can hardly do so. The final and decisive revelation of God believed to have been received in Jesus had not taken a scriptural form. The first Christians incessantly used the Hebrew scriptures and, little by little, would come to use the new, but both were finally subsidiary to the experience of faith in a person carried onward in a Spirit-guided community by a "tradition" of teaching: "what I received from the Lord I also passed on to you" (I Corinthians 11.23).

The community as such and its identity mattered enormously and its members quickly received the name of "Christians". It was a community of communities, a network of little groups scattered across the towns of the Mediterranean world, consisting first of Jews but then, increasingly, of Gentiles. It accepted the authority of the apostles but soon had to do without their presence and created its own local ministry, which was felt in some way to have an apostolic commissioning. It was, very consciously, a universal community as well as a local one, but it had next to no clear structures of authority to demonstrate this. The universalism, however, was profoundly important, being, in a way, what distinguished it most clearly from the Jews. It was a community intended for everyone "neither Jew nor Greek, neither slave nor free, neither male nor female: you are all one in Christ Jesus" (Galatians 3.28). Here was the intuitive vision of an absolute human unity, possible only because of some strange quality of absolute universality *vis à vis* both God and humanity of Jesus himself. It is tragic that, despite this universalism, the traumatic schism between Christian Jews and the Jewish community as a whole (already so central to the theme of the Epistle to the Romans or the Acts of the Apostles) hardened, as the church became predominantly a Gentile one, into a deep and enduring antagonism towards contemporary Jewry.

What is most significant about the New Testament writings, despite their relatively small extent and profound unity of commitment, is their diversity of authorship, terminology and theology. What this already indicated was that there was no single way of expressing Christianity. Most striking is the contrast between the two absolutely major theologians of the New Testament period, John and Paul, but hardly less influential has been the very fact of a multiplicity of lives of Jesus. Both the harmonies and the disharmonies between the gospels have always been evident and while there have been forceful tendencies within Christianity to achieve a single conflated life of Christ, a single Christology and a single wider theological synthesis, the basic materials of the New Testament writings have always made this impossible. It may be that Paul should be seen as the more decisive influence upon western, Latin, theology, John upon eastern, Greek-speaking, Byzantine, theology, the one more confrontational, the other more monist. That must, nevertheless, be an over-simple way of defining the divergencies which developed within the Christian mind evolving in two different cultures. And there were, of course, others: **Coptic, Syrian, Armenian, Ethiopian.** The point is that the diversities of later centuries were rendered inevitable not just by diversities of culture and language but radically by diversities inherent from the start within the Christian tradition and even constitutive both of its power and of its weakness. That is not at all to say that they needed to be institutionalized.

One further element of the original package requires notice, so influential has it been for the subsequent development of the tradition: the position of Peter. The gospels give him a very clear leadership role among the apostles, recording not only the "Thou art Peter and upon this rock I will build my church" (Matthew 16.16) but several other special sayings of Jesus in his regard. In the *Acts of the Apostles,* while most of the others quickly disappear from sight, Peter retains a central place balancing that of Paul. Between the two a relationship of tension with co-operation is suggested not only by the structure of *Acts* but also by Galatians 2 and 2 Peter 3. The role of Peter in scripture might, however, remain an academic issue of the interpretation of largely unformalized leadership within a very fluid community, if it was not that he (like Paul) ended his days in Rome as a martyr and that—while he was certainly not the founder of the church in Rome any more than was Paul—his tomb in the Vatican cemetery became that church's most treasured possession. The Church of Rome and its bishops saw themselves and were seen more widely by the Christian community as Peter's heir and successor, the most emphatically apostolic episcopal line of succession. It might seem natural that the church in the imperial capital should be allowed some special authority—though in a time of recurrent persecution it might, equally, be judged unnatural to give any preference to Rome, the Babylon of iniquity, on any secular ground. It is, perhaps, surprising that the Church of Jerusalem, originally presided over by "James the Lord's brother", was not preferred as Christianity's central see of authority but, despite the increasing Christianization of Jerusalem in the post 130 era, there is no sign of that. What we have instead is a slowly emerging Roman primacy, undefined in scope, deriving primarily from a sense of Peter's authority but also, if less certainly, from the imperial precedence of the city. In terms of the first centuries this phenomenon might merit only a slight mention but in terms of its impact upon subsequent Christian history, it requires far more.

Until the fourth century the shape of Christianity remained predictable enough but in the fourth and fifth centuries three vast developments occurred, highly decisive for the future, which—if perhaps not to be anticipated in themselves—are clearly explicable in terms of further ambiguity within the original tradition. The first to be mentioned is a transformation of relations with the State, following the "conversion" of Constantine, emperor of the West, in 312. Toleration was quickly followed by privilege and—under his successors, especially Theodosius in the 380s—by the proscription of "pagan" religion. In fact the king of Armenia, Tiridates, had been already converted a little before Constantine. Christianity which in its first centuries had maintained the apolitical and almost pacifist character of its founder turned very suddenly to become a state religion and a mass religion, whose theologians would swiftly come round to justifying the use of force by Christians, and not only for secular purposes but also for religious ones. The "render to Caesar the things that are Caesar's" (Matthew 22.21) of Jesus and the rather heavy state theology of Romans 13 which might seem marginal enough to the life of the earliest Christians, inhibiting them only from total rejection of the political, became instead central textual pillars of a new establishmentarian approach to public life which would dominate Christianity for 1,500 years.

The second development began in Egypt a little before the conversion of Constantine. It was that of monasticism and the institutionalization of the ideal of celibacy, practised first alone but later in an organized community subject to the "Rule" of one of the great founders. Here again the roots go back to the very beginning. By all accounts Jesus was celibate (as was Paul) but his celibacy was not suggested as something to be imitated by others. Nevertheless he did leave one enigmatic saying on the subject: "There are eunuchs who have made themselves such for the sake of the kingdom of heaven. He who is able to receive this, let him receive it" (Matthew 19.12). Certainly there were virgins and widows committed to a life of prayer in the early Christian community, following the belief of Paul that the unmarried state is preferable in that someone is free in it to be concerned "about the affairs of the Lord, how to be holy in body and spirit" (I Corinthians 7.34), but they did not live as a group apart nor did they in any way constitute the leadership of the community. While Christian sexual morality was highly ascetic, it was deeply grounded in a theology of the goodness of the body and it explicitly affirmed the holiness of marriage. It was taken for granted that bishops were normally men who had been married and had children.

The sudden explosion of the monastic movement following the example of Anthony of the Desert led in the course of the fourth century to the establishment of monasteries in most parts of the Christian world. This was in part perhaps a reaction to the increased worldliness of ordinary church life affected by political privilege, power and wealth. It replaced the likelihood of martyrdom in a time of persecution as the cutting edge of Christian moral radicalism. But, while the immediate point of the monastic vocation was to withdraw from all this, even from regular church life, into a separate, wholly prayer-orientated régime of poverty, it was quickly drawn back into affecting the church's ordinary running. More and more monks were chosen to be bishops. The ideal of celibacy became the ideal of the church's regular ministry, required for bishops, at least encouraged for all in major orders. Ideals are one thing, practice is another. It is impossible to know quite how widely the new ideal was really embraced or enforced, but church synods at least endeavoured to do so.

Fourth century propagandists of celibacy like Jerome could seem to undermine any theology of marriage. Henceforth Christianity would struggle with the counter claims of marriage and celibacy as ideal forms of religious living. In this it would come nearer to

Buddhism but contrast with both of its monotheist relatives, Judaism and Islam. Here again there is ambiguity but one which does not allow the complete abandonment of either side: sex, the flesh, marriage have always been affirmed as good by orthodox theology, part of the created order carried up into redemption, but they are not indispensable. The question at issue is whether the normal pursuit of Christian holiness should pass them by.

The third development was the long doctrinal struggle centred upon the formulation of the nature of Christ and the triune character of God in terms of Greek language and philosophy. In general Christians accepted that while Jesus was clearly human he also had a unique relationship with God. Father, Son and Spirit were coming to be seen as being three persons, modes or expressions of the one God. Christians remained emphatically monotheists, but their monotheism would inevitably be questioned by others unable to accept the subtleties of trinitarian theology. But how to define the relationship between the man Jesus and God? Different places—notably Alexandria and Antioch—had developed different stresses, Alexandria upon the divinity, Antioch on the humanity. The implication both of many New Testament affirmations, made in a variety of ways, and of the developing doctrine of the Trinity was that Jesus was fully God, equal to the Father: "I and the Father are one" (John 10.30). Yet there was always another side, strongest too in some of the earliest of New Testament texts. Jesus's cry of dying agony, recorded in Mark's gospel, "My God, My God, why hast thou forsaken me?" (Mark 15.34) does not sound like a dying God.

The ambiguities of the New Testament could be preserved in a variety of devotional and theological traditions but not so easily in ecumenical definitions decreed by councils and enforced by emperors. The church of the imperial age had become a very argumentative and bullying communion. Arguments in the reign of Constantine at Alexandria between Arius and his bishop led to the affirmation of the Council of Nicaea (325) that Father and Son were of one nature; many further arguments led in due course in the fifth century to the Councils of Ephesus (431) and Chalcedon (451). At Ephesus the Alexandrian tradition prevailed over Nestorius, a representative of the Antiochene. Jesus was affirmed to be a single divine person and Mary truly "Mother of God". The unity of the Incarnation, Christianity's most characteristic dogma, was thus defended. Twenty years later, at Chalcedon, a Roman compromise between Alexandrian and **Nestorian** poles affirmed that the one person continued to possess two natures, the fully human as well as the divine. These definitions satisfied most Greeks and most Latins and constituted the "orthodoxy" of both East and West henceforth, but many people to the east of Antioch, including the large Christian church of the Persian empire, remained Nestorian, while Egypt and its daughter church of Ethiopia rejected the two natures of Chalcedon and remained "Monophysite". Both schisms have continued to this day. It seems fairly clear to the modern historian of thought that, under varying terminologies, the faith of these different traditions was far from incompatible. What was incompatible was one precise dogmatic formula with another, each using a metaphysical terminology unknown to scripture. It was the belief of the post-Constantinian church that such things could be settled, generally under imperial pressure, by the vote of a group of bishops and then imposed by the state, which brought the church to irreparable division. Egypt was, anyway, disillusioned with Greek rule from Constantinople while, for the Christians of Persia, it was a relief to be clearly out of communion with the church of its great enemy, the Roman Empire. The political reconstruction of the church had then much to do with its dogmatic reconstruction and division.

For more than 500 years after Chalcedon Greeks and Latins shared a common Christianity within a single communion. The tradition, we can say, had reached a stable form, one which Monophysites and Nestorians also in practice largely shared. For

Greeks and Latins it meant a dogmatic creed, a sacramental, ritualist and monastic shape to religious practice, a strongly developed ecclesiastical hierarchy, and the acceptance that both pope and emperor exercised authority. The West stressed the former, the East the latter, but there was coexistence between them, if also increasing strains. Nominally the breach came with mutual excommunications in 1054, precipitated by the growing ascendancy of the medieval papacy, its increasingly strident claims and the bureaucratic control it was beginning to exercise over the Latin church. Each side had converted or was about to convert much of Northern Europe: as far north as Scandinavia, as far east as Poland and Hungary went Latin, but the Bulgars, the Serbs, the Ukrainians and the Russians owed conversion to Constantinople rather than to Rome.

Under Muslim pressure, Arab and Turkish, the empire of Constantinople and Greek Christianity declined but the conversion of Russia ensured that the **Eastern Orthodox** tradition would continue in strength. At the same time western Europe by the 13th century was developing fast as a unified religious society held together by the ideal of "papal monarchy". A much enlarged canon law and the vast structure of scholasticism, synthesizing every aspect of doctrine and morality, often in a quite rationalistic way with the aid of contemporary philosophy, represent a sustained attempt of great intellectual forcefulness to order the whole world in the light of faith. The theology of Aquinas, the poetry of Dante, the gothic cathedrals, express this ideal at its highest, and western **(Roman) Catholicism** has frequently looked back upon the myth of a golden age in the 13th century.

At the same time the worldliness and intolerance of the medieval church, the power of the papacy, the inevitable politicization the system had brought with it, coupled with a multiplication of devotional practices centred upon relics, pilgrimages and indulgences, a great preoccupation with the devil and hell, the sheer gap between the image of New Testament religion and that of the high Middle Ages, all brought increasing dissatisfaction, especially within the growing literate urban population. The protests of John Wycliffe in the 14th century and John Huss in the 15th were more or less suppressed but prepared the way for the overwhelming 16th century movement of Reformation led by Martin Luther which produced a great variety of Protestantisms to become the dominant religion of northern Europe. The papacy, monasticism, and the ritualism of the medieval church were rejected. Justification by faith was reasserted against a preoccupation with works of piety, while an appeal to "Scripture alone" replaced the idea of the final authority of the voice of the living church. Despite such a common core to Protestantism, large differences emerged to separate Calvin and Zwingli from Luther, **Anglicans** in due course from both, and then others from **Anabaptists** to **Quakers** and (in the 18th century) **Methodists.** The appeal to scripture inevitably brought disagreement rather than concord and there was no common mind on how to cope with all the practices (such as infant baptism) which had developed across the centuries neither supported nor denied by scripture. Furthermore, once the papacy was rejected, the local church in most countries fell victim, willingly or unwillingly, to royal or national control, despite the protests of a more radical wing which resulted in a variety of **"free" churches.**

Early Reformation theology was more fideist, less rationalist, than that of the middle ages. Indeed it was in part a protest precisely against the use of philosophy in relation to matters of faith. It rejected pilgrimages and relics, but not the late medieval obsession with the devil. Yet out of the "conservative" Protestantism of the 16th century developed from the 18th century on a "liberal" Protestantism seeking in ever more innovative ways to restate Christian faith in terms of the contemporary philosophy and culture of Western, post-Enlightenment, society, and to rediscover the Jesus of history from behind the divine Christ of Chalcedonian orthodoxy. In reaction other Protestants, so-called Conservative **Evangelicals,** have turned to a more narrowly and selectively scripturalist interpretation of Christianity. The extreme ritualism central to medieval religion may be contrasted with the extreme scripturalism central to main-line Protestantism, but a pursuit of the rational actually links liberal Protestantism and medieval scholasticism in contrast to evangelical fideism. Each reflects in a rather over-certain form one segment within the ambiguity of Christian origins.

Catholicism, reformed in moral discipline but hardened in its centralized papalism and maintenance of most of the medieval mix of doctrine and piety, revived immensely in the later 16th century and made up in the American and Asian empires of Spain and Portugal for much of what it had lost in northern Europe. Until the close of the 18th century Protestants remained strangely uninterested in missionary endeavour. Then suddenly they rushed into it as western Europe, particularly Britain, expanded to rule the rest of the world in the age of imperialism. In some places the impact of the Victorian missionary was slight in comparison with the effort expended. In Africa, however, it became clear in the course of the 20th century that a vast new Christian world was taking shape, filled not only with all the churches already in existence from the past, especially Protestantism's highly fissiparous past both in Europe and in North America, but also with hundreds of new churches incorporating different varieties of traditional religion and culture and derived from the work of "prophets" like William Wade Harris and Simon **Kimbangu.** Link Africa with Latin America and the principal areas of Christian vitality might now be located in the southern hemisphere.

About half the Christian world today remains within the Roman Catholic communion, while the other half is shared between everything from **Armenian** orthodoxy to the Church of Kimbangu. The highly divided state of the non-Catholic world and the outdated reasons for many of its divisions, deriving from the 16th or even the 19th century, led to the largest general development of 20th century Christianity, the Ecumenical Movement, and the foundation of the **World Council of Churches** (1948). Despite many achievements the Ecumenical Movement appears, nevertheless, to have failed in its principal aim, the reunion of Christians, partly because denominational loyalties and the forces of Conservative Evangelicalism have remained too strong and partly because such a goal can be achieved neither with nor without Rome, the traditional "see of unity". Without Rome the unity of the rest has little appeal for Anglicans and some others, but Rome's own terms for reunion remain too high to be acceptable to many either in Orthodoxy or Protestantism. Yet Catholicism too now shares in many of the diversities and strains of the rest of Christendom, particularly since the second Vatican Council (1962–5) approved characteristically Protestant insistences such as the stress upon a more scripturalist theology, a vernacular liturgy and an active laity. The second Vatican Council may be seen as the moment at which Christianity's largest communion at last moved beyond a medieval form to resume a position (strengthened by enormous growth both in the Americas and Africa) of leadership within the Christian world. However the current Roman reaction against the tendencies at work in Vatican II, a reaction encouraged by the Polish Pope John Paul II, has, at least temporarily, largely closed the vistas opened by the Council but also by the wider ecumenical movement. Nevertheless, developments flowing from the "theology of liberation" of the 1960s in many areas, especially that of feminism and the ordination of women, continue to alter the shape of Christian thinking and behaviour very considerably.

The ambiguity of Christian origins and the vast diversities of Christian history are in consequence mirrored only too faithfully in the ambiguities and immediately uncertain future of Christianity in the 1990s torn between modernizing and conservative pressures. It may be, nevertheless, that no other major religious tradition has proved so translatable and so changeable. This may be explained in terms of the guidance of the Spirit of God, the necessity of "development", the pilgrimage experience of a people through history, or the enigmatically unstructured character of Christian origins. What has remained almost throughout is the ethical monotheism, the filial dependence upon "Our Father" in heaven, the sense of a universal human calling and the memory of a crucified teacher celebrated sacramentally in the eucharistic meal and proclaiming that life is stronger than death, Easter than the tomb.

Adrian Hastings

ISLAM

The Beginnings of Islam

Islam is basically the Arabic word *islam* meaning "surrender" with the implication of surrender to God. The corresponding participle is *muslim*, "one surrendering" (to God). The religion of Islam grew out of certain experiences of a man called Muhammad who was born in Mecca, Arabia, about 570 A.D. Mecca at that period was a prosperous commercial town, because its merchants had obtained something like monopolistic control over the trade between the Indian Ocean and the Mediterranean. This may have come about because frequent warfare between the Byzantine and Persian (Sassanid) empires had made the route through Iraq dangerous, so that the route through western Arabia became more attractive. Mecca thus became prosperous and wealthy, but wealth led to a moral and religious crisis. Though Mecca was now above all a commercial centre, it had retained the religious and moral ideas of the nomadic tribes of the Arabian steppe, but these ideas had little relevance to the new state of affairs in Mecca. Many of the merchants acted unscrupulously and oppressively. Though the new wealth was shared out to some extent, many, especially the younger men, were dissatisfied.

Muhammad was a thoughtful man, deeply concerned with this crisis through which Mecca was passing. This may have been due to the fact that as a posthumous child he had not been able to share in the more lucrative aspects of Meccan trade. When he was about 25 he had looked after the goods of a wealthy widow, Khadija, on a journey to Damascus, and she had subsequently married him. As her husband he was able to do a certain amount of trading, but he remained aware of the crisis in Meccan affairs and meditated on it.

In 610, when he was about 40, in the course of what would now be called a retreat, he had an experience in which a message somehow became present in his mind; and he eventually came to believe that this was a message from God for himself and other Meccans. After this he continued to receive such messages at intervals until the end of his life. The messages were remembered by Muhammed and the followers he began to attract, and were recited in their formal prayer or worship. Only gradually were they written down. Muhammad himself seems to have begun the process of bringing together several separate messages to form *suras* or chapters. After his death all the messages were collected to form the *Quran* as we now have it.

The messages are not dated, though Muslim sources preserve accounts of the circumstances in which some where received; these are technically known as "occasions of revelation" (*asbab an-nuzul*), but they cover only a few of the passages. On this basis Muslim scholars assigned each *sura* either to the Meccan or to the Medinan period of Muhammad's activity, while recognizing that some verses in the *sura* might come from the other period. Modern Western scholars have used stylistic and other criteria to try to date the various passages more accurately, and, while there is a measure of agreement among them, there are also many uncertainties. The traditional view of the *Quran* among Muslims is that it consists of actual speech of God himself conveyed to Muhammad (at least in some cases) by the angel Gabriel, and that it owes nothing to Muhammad's own mind. It is in this sense that Muhammad is a prophet or, as he is more usually called by Muslims, the Messenger of God (*rasul Allah*).

In the early passages God is spoken of as the creator of all things, including each human individual, and there is special emphasis on his goodness towards humanity; but he also punishes evil, sometimes through a temporal calamity, but also at the end of the world on the Last Day, when each person will come before him for judgement, to be assigned either to Heaven (Paradise, the Garden) or to Hell (the Fire) according to his deeds. All are called to be grateful to God for his goodness and to acknowledge him in worship. People are also told not to hoard wealth for themselves but to be generous towards those in need of any kind. Muhammad himself is spoken of as a *nadhir* (warner), who has to warn people of the divine punishment.

Insistence that there is only one God came later, perhaps as a result of the incident of the "satanic verses" or rather "satanic intrusions". Muslim scholars dislike this story and tend to avoid mentioning it, but it occurs in an impeccable source, the commentary of at-Tabari in Sura 22.52:

> Before you we sent neither messenger nor prophet but that, when he desired (or recited), Satan intruded (something) into his desire (recitation). Then God cancels what Satan intrudes.

The story is that once, while Muhammad was sitting with some Meccan merchants and hoping to receive a revelation to win them over to his religion, he began to receive the revelation now in Sura 53.19, 20: "Have you considered Allat and al-'Uzza and Manat the third, the other?". Immediately after these verses, however, Satan inserted words which implied that these goddesses might be asked to intercede with the "high god", Allah. When Muhammad, supposing the words to be a genuine revelation from God, proclaimed them to the merchants, they were overjoyed and joined Muhammad in Muslim worship. Only later, perhaps much later, did Muhammad realize that the words had been intruded and were not from God. From this time onwards the *Quran* insisted that before there is no deity (god) but God—the first half of the Islamic profession of faith (*shahada*).

About 613 Muhammad began to share the divine revelations more widely with friends and acquaintances, and soon had collected a band of followers, mostly youngish men, who worshipped along with him. After a time, however, his opponents began to act oppressively towards those members of their families who had joined him, and life was also made difficult for others. Muhammad encouraged some of his followers to go to Abyssinia, where they were well received by the Christian emperor, the Negus. In Mecca opposition grew into persecution and it became impossible for Muhammad to continue spreading his religion there. He looked for a hospitable milieu elsewhere, and eventually reached an agreement with the main Arab clans in Medina, an oasis over 200 miles north of Mecca. In 622 some 70 Muslims and their families, and then finally Muhammad himself, made the Hijra or Emigration to Medina. This was a turning-point in Muhammad's career, and the Islamic calendar begins with the first day of the Arabian year in which the Hijra took place. Islamic dates are indicated by the letters A.H. (Anno Hegirae).

The polity now formed in Medina was a federation on traditional Arab lines between eight Arab clans in Medina and the "clan" of Emigrants from Mecca. It was not primarily a religious community, but all the main contracting parties were Muslims, and Muhammad had some special privileges as Messenger of God. The Muslims of Medina, who were generous in their hospitality to the Emigrants, came to be known as Muhammad's Ansar or Helpers (a label used again today by the Ansar movement in the Sudan). Some Emigrants engaged in trade, and most took part in raids or *razzias* against Meccan caravans or against the flocks of hostile tribes. On these raids, many Helpers began to accompany them. In 624 one such raiding party of about 320 Muslims encountered a Meccan force of two or three times that number and defeated them decisively in the battle of Badr. Intermittent hostilities followed between Muslims and Meccans. At the battle of Uhud in 625 many Muslims were killed, but the Meccans also came off badly and could not follow up their advantage. An attempted Meccan siege of Medina in 627 failed. Finally in 630 Muhammad, who had steadily become stronger, was able to march on Mecca with 10,000 men and to enter the town virtually unopposed. Most Meccans were now prepared to come to terms with him, and many became Muslims. As a result of his generous treatment of the Meccans the administrative talent of the Meccan merchants later made an important contribution to the establishment of the Islamic empire.

In the remaining two years of Muhammad's life most of the tribes not yet allied to him sought alliance, so that by his death in May 632 nearly all the tribes of Arabia were allies, though in some cases it was not the whole tribe but only a section. Those who became allies were also required to become Muslims. This system developed out of the Arab practice of the *razzia*, a raid to drive off a hostile tribe's camels, where there was seldom any loss of life. Muhammad could not allow his allies to raid one another, and began to direct their energies outwards, northwards to Syria and north-eastwards to Iraq. His policy of sending out raiding expeditions in quest of booty was continued by the caliphs, his successors as political heads of the Islamic state. The expeditions gradually went further and further afield, and met little effective opposition. Many provinces of the Byzantine empire were occupied and the whole of the Persian empire. Forward bases were established to render unnecessary the long journey back to Medina. The final result was that by a century after Muhammad's death the Islamic empire, as it may now be called, extended from Spain through North Africa and the Fertile Crescent to Central Asia and north-west India.

It should be emphasized that this phenomenal expansion of Muhammad's small state was primarily political and not religious. Conquered Jews, Christians, **Zoroastrians** and even Hindus were regarded as "people of the Book", that is, as having a religious scripture from God, and were allowed to become "protected minorities" (*ahl adh-dhimma*), as if they were weak tribes under the protection of the strong "tribe" of Muslims. Only those who did not belong to one of the "peoples of the Book" were forced to become Muslims. The protected minorities paid taxes to the Muslim govenor, but had a measure of autonomy under their religious heads. They were second-class citizens, but on the whole were well treated. There was a trickle of conversions to Islam, the proportion from the Zoroastrians being much greater than that from the Jews and Christians.

Belief and Practice

Islam, unlike Christianity, is less concerned with true belief than with correct practice, that is, it is more interested in orthopraxy than in orthodoxy. Correspondingly the chief Islamic intellectual discipline is not theology but jurisprudence, and of the "five pillars" of Islam only one related to belief. This first pillar is the *shahada* or profession of faith, which is the duty of bearing witness that there is no deity but God and that Muhammad is the Messenger of God. Some Muslims nowadays insist on using the word Allah in English; but *Allah* is simply the Arabic word for God, used by Christians as well as Muslims, while pre-Islamic Arabs believed in Allah as a "high god" but only one among many—a belief countered by the *shahada*.

The second pillar is *salat*, the worship or formal prayer. Every adult Muslim is required to perform the worship five times a day at specified hours. The heart of the worship is essentially a cycle of acts—mainly standing upright, bowing slightly, and prostrating oneself (kneeling to touch the ground with one's forehead)—and these acts are accompanied by prescribed exclamations of praise and adoration. This cycle is repeated two or four times according to the hour of day. There is an introduction in which verses from the *Quran* are recited, and at the close the worshipper wishes peace for his neighbours. When a number of Muslims come together for the worship, they form themselves into rows, and there is one in front as *imam* or leader to give the timing of the acts so that they are performed in unison.

A third pillar is *zakat* or almsgiving, that is the requirement that one should give a specified proportion of one's wealth to the poor and needy. Amounts are fixed according to the different kinds of income and capital. The fourth pillar is the *sawm* or fast. During the month of Ramadan from sunrise to sunset each day a Muslim must not eat or drink anything nor engage in sex. Fifthly there is the *hajj* or pilgrimage. Every Muslim, if his circumstances permit, should make the pilgrimage at least once in his lifetime. This comprises going to Mecca and over several days carrying out certain ceremonies in the town itself and in the neighbourhood. Among the ceremonies is the circumambulation of the Ka'ba, a cube-like building at the centre of the sacred area constituted by the great mosque of Mecca.

Sometimes Muslims include among the pillars the duty of *Jihad* or engaging in the "holy war" against infidels or persons attacking the community of Muslims. The word "jihad" means "striving" and the connotation of fighting comes from the Quranic phrase "striving in the way (cause) of God".

The totality of God's prescriptions for the conduct of human life form the *Shari'a* or divine law. This covers not only matters of individual, social and political morality, but also other aspects of human life such as hygiene (e.g. due care for the teeth). The *Shari'a* is known firstly from the rules stated in the *Quran* and secondly from the *Hadith* (anecdotes about what Muhammad said or did). There have been preserved many thousands of these *Hadith*, which were formerly somewhat confusingly called "traditions". Each has the "support" (*isnad*) of a chain of transmitters, and Muslims distinguish "sound" from unreliable *Hadith* by considering the reputation of the persons named as transmitters. Six early collections of *Hadith* adjudged sound have a kind of canonical status as a basis for determining the *Shari'a*. The two earliest are those of al-Bukhari (d. 870) and Muslim ibn al-Hajjaj (d. 875). Properly qualified jurists may apply the general principles implicit in what is found in the *Quran* and *Hadith* to any fresh matters occurring. In this way the *Shari'a* potentially covers the whole of human life, including whatever new conditions and problems may arise in the future. The call for its implementation today has become a typical feature of modern Muslim "fundamentalist" groups such as the **Muslim Brotherhood** and the **Jama'at-i Islami.** The Muslim countries that have gone furthest in this direction are Saudi Arabia, Pakistan, Iran and the Sudan.

The class of *ulama*, religious scholars who are primarily jurists, developed in the course of the first Islamic century and worked out a system of law for the caliphate. By about 900 A.D. the main body of Muslims had recognized four *madhahib* as equally valid: the **Hanbali, Hanafi, Maliki** and **Shafi'i** (named after their founders Ahmad ibn Hanbal, Abu Hanifa, Malik ibn Anas and ash-Shafi'i). The word *madhahib* is to be translated as "rites" rather than "schools" since each Muslim belongs to a rite and has to follow its prescriptions where they differ from those of the other rites. This can affect various matters from the distribution of a deceased person's estate to minor details of the worship. The sect of **Twelver Shi'ites** had a comparable rite, often called **Ja'fari.** The rites are, however, often referred to as schools of religious (or Islamic) law.

This class of *ulama* had an important place in the united caliphate and in separate Islamic states. No Muslim ruler, however autocratic, was entitled to enact laws for those under him; at most he could make regulations about the detailed implementation of the laws. The formulation of laws was reserved for qualified *ulama*, and for this purpose they had a degree of organization in each Islamic state. They were most highly organized in the Ottoman empire where they had a hierarchical structure and controlled not only the formulation of laws but all the administration of law in the courts and all higher education. After 1850 the Ottoman *ulama* gradually lost much of this power because they were unwilling to say how the *Shari'a* could be adapted to the fresh contemporary needs of the empire.

In Islam there is no official body entitled to say what is the true view on any legal or doctrinal point. Certain jurists known as *Muftis* are qualified to give a "legal opinion" (*fatwa*) on a particular point if appealed to. Even when a jurist is designated as *Mufti* of his country, however, it is open to other Muftis to disagree with him; but in practice Muslims have nearly always reached a large measure of informal consensus, so that to the outside observer there may seem to be something like an official view.

This absence of an official version applies also in doctrinal matters. There is no Islamic creed with the authority of the Christian ecumenical creeds. Men like Abu Hanifa and Ahmad ibn Hanbal composed creeds and also had creeds attributed to them by their followers, and within each legal rite there was a measure of agreement. The basic creed was sometimes said to be belief in God, his angels, his books (revealed scriptures), his messengers (or prophets, among whom Muslims include Moses and Jesus), his determination of all events, resurrection after death, and heaven and hell. Theologians, however, discussed many other matters, sometimes with great subtlety, such as whether God had attributes such as knowledge and speech distinct from his essence.

Some of the earliest doctrinal discussions in Islam were about what non-Muslims might call political matters. Thus when Muhammad died the leading Muslims in Medina met and appointed Abu Bakr to succeed to Muhammad's political position with the title of caliph (*khalifa*, deputy or successor). In time, however, a number of people came to hold that Muhammad should have been succeeded by his cousin and son-in-law 'Ali ibn Abi Talib. This body came to be known as Shi'at 'Ali (the party of 'Ali) or simply the Shi'a. From it has developed the group of sects within Islam known as **Shi'ites,** who constitute about a tenth of the whole Muslim community. 'Ali did in fact become the fourth caliph, but at the heart of the Shi'ite position was the belief that within Muhammad's clan of Hashim there were divinely inspired individuals, first 'Ali, then his sons al-Hasan and al-Husayn. They spoke of these not as caliphs but as *Imams* or leaders, who, as divinely inspired, were infallible. From al-Husayn onwards each *Imam* appointed a son as successor and he then received divine inspiration. Although the believers in these *Imams* regarded each in turn as the rightful ruler of the whole community of Muslims, the Shi'ites were not a revolutionary party but tended to be politically quiescent. This was particularly so after 874 when leading men among them declared that the 12th imam had gone into "occultation" (*ghayba*). This *Imam* is the Mahdi (guided one), who is still alive in occultation and will come forward at an appropriate time to set all things right in the world. Most Shi'ites accept this belief and are known as Twelvers or Ithna 'Asharis, and also as *Imamis*. In 1501, when Shah Isma'il conquered Iran, he made this form of Shi'ism the official religion there and it continues to be so. Under the influence of Ayatollah Khomeini in particular, Iranian Shi'ism has largely shed its political quiescence, although this has proved controversial—by no means all Shi'ite religious authorities concur in this development, and in neighbouring Iraq the supreme authority, Grand Ayatollah Khoi, has continued to endorse political passivity.

Another group maintained that the seventh *Imam* was not Musa, as the Twelvers hold, but his brother Isma'il. At first these **Isma'ilis** were an underground movement, but in 909 they conquered Tunisia and in 969 Egypt, remaining in power there as the Fatimid dynasty until expelled in 1171. Meanwhile a group of Isma'ilis in the lands of the 'Abbasid caliphate gained the name and reputation of Assassins. For most of their subsequent history the many subdivisions of the Isma'ilis are chiefly found in the Indian sub-continent. The best known group are those who acknowledge the Agha Khan as Imam in direct descent from 'Ali. These belong to the sub-division called **Nizāris** or **Khojas** (though now also known as **Aga Khanis**), while the subdivision of **Musta'lis** or **Bohras** became further split into **Daudis, Sulaymanis, Amiris** and **Tayibis.**

The heresiographers reckon as a third group of Shi'ites the **Zaydis.** These held that any descendant of al-Hasan or al-Husayn could become *Imam* by claiming the Imamate and making good his claim by force of arms. They are named after Zayd, a grandson of al-Husayn.

Also involved in the early religio–political discussions were groups collectively known as Khawarij or Kharijites. They insisted that anyone who committed a serious sin was thereby excluded from the community of Muslims. They mostly died out centuries ago, but the subdivision of **Ibadis** still exists as the main population of the sultanate of Oman, with some small groups in Algeria and elsewhere.

The main body of Muslims eventually came to be called **Sunnis.** An early name was Ahl as-Sunna wa-l-Jama‘a (the People of the Sunna and the Community). The Sunna is the example of Muhammad as known from the Hadith, and by emphasizing this as a basis for the *Shari‘a* Sunnis exclude the pronouncements of an inspired *Imam*.

By about 800 some Muslims were beginning to be familiar with Greek philosophy, and found Greek concepts and methods of argument useful against opponents, Muslim or non-Muslim. This led to the development within Islam of *kalam* or philosophical theology. The main early exponents of this, the Mu‘tazila or Mu‘tazilites, were regarded as heretics by the main body of Sunnis because of their belief in the complete freedom of the human will and their denial that God had attributes distinct from his essence (although interestingly their rationalism in theology has recently been invoked as a valuable part of its heritage by the Tunisian "fundamentalist" **Nahda Movement/Party**). In time the methods of *kalam* were used to defend central Sunni positions, notably by al-Ash‘ari (d. 935) in Baghdad and al-Maturidi (d. 944) in Samarqand. The Ash‘aris and Maturidis dominated theology for many centuries. They were opposed by Hanbali theologians, who rejected *kalam* and kept close to Quranic terminology.

In due course much Greek philosophy was translated into Arabic, and some Muslims thought they could combine a form of this philosophy with true Islamic belief. These men are known as *Falasifa* and were regarded as heretics by Sunni theologians. They produced several philosophers of the first rank, above all Avicenna or Ibn Sina (d. 1037), who was roughly a Neoplatonist, and Averroes or Ibn Rushd (d. 1198), who was more Aristotelian. These two men had an important influence on medieval Latin Christian thinkers.

While Islam firmly rejected monasticism, it had a strong ascetic and mystical movement known as **Sufism,** from the word "sufi" meaning one wearing *suf* or wool as a sign of his asceticism. The earliest Sufis were individual ascetics, but some moved on to cultivate mystical and ecstatic experiences. One of the latter was al-Hallaj, executed in 922 for blasphemy in apparently claiming that in ecstasy he had attained union with God. Some early Sufis attracted followers and disciples, but from about 1100 more permanent Sufi brotherhoods were formed such as the **Naqshabandiya, Rifa‘iya, Qadiriya,** and so on: several of these are discussed individually in Part II, as they continue to be of considerable significance in Islam today.

Al-Ghazali (d. 1111) was an Ash‘ari theologian who abandoned his theological professorship to lead a Sufi life; in his long book "The Revival of the Religious Sciences" (*Ihya’ ‘ulum ad-din*) he shows how Sufism can be combined with the practice of standard Sunni Islam. Other Sufis engaged in theological or theosophical speculations which took them far beyond orthodox Sunnism. One such was Muhyi-d-din ibn-al-‘Arabi (d. 1240), whose elaborate system came close to pantheism and who had a great influence on Sufis in many parts of the Islamic world, including for example the **Chishtiya-Sabiriya** in India (where there was a receptive environment for ‘Arabi’s near-pantheism because of its affinities with certain mystical trends in Hinduism).

The spread of Islam

The first four caliphs, the "rightly guided ones" (*Rashidun*), were: Abu Bakr (632–4), 'Umar (634–44), 'Uthman (644–56) and 'Ali (656–61). From 661 the Umayyad dynasty of caliphs masterminded the expansion of Islamic power. In 750 they were replaced by the 'Abbasid dynasty, descendants of Muhammad's uncle al-'Abbas, and these continued as caliphs until their extermination at the sack of Baghdad in 1258 by Mongols. In 945, however, they lost the last of their political power, and thereafter were only figureheads. The actual rule of provinces was in the hands of dynasties of army-leaders, often called sultans. Most of these, however, found it expedient to be nominated by the caliph as governor of the provinces they actually ruled. Despite many political upheavals the Islamic lands possessed a remarkable degree of stability through the social system based on the *Shari'a*.

Recent centuries have seen much of the Islamic world controlled by three empires. The Mogul (*Mughal*) empire, which flourished from 1556 to 1707, controlled much of India but was gradually replaced by the British colonial administration. The Iranian empire, founded in 1501, continued under various dynasties until in 1979 the last shah was expelled by a popular rising headed by religious scholars under Ayatollah Khomeini. The Ottoman empire was founded in Anatolia in the 14th century by a group of Ottoman Turks. In the next century it occupied part of south-east Europe and put an end to the Christian Byzantine empire. In the early 16th century it gained control of Syria, Iraq, Arabia, Egypt and most of Islamic North Africa, and extended its control of south-east Europe to reach from Budapest to the Crimea. After about 1700 its power declined rapidly compared with that of the western European states, provinces were lost, and after World War I it was replaced by the Turkish Republic. Latterly the Ottoman sultans claimed that the caliphate had continued in Egypt after 1258 and had then been transferred to them. This claim was accepted by Sunnis, but conferred no actual powers. When in 1924 the Turkish Republic declared the caliphate abolished, other Muslims failed to agree on proposals for its restoration.

After the first great wave of expansion the spread of the Islamic religion continued sporadically. It made its way into West and East Africa largely through the presence there of Muslim traders. These would marry a local woman, found a family and bring the children up as Muslims. In time local rulers might find it advantageous to be of the same religion as traders playing an important part in regional life. It was probably in a somewhat similar way that Islam spread from the Punjab into other parts of India and then into south-east Asia. The sub-continent was never more than about a third Muslim, but Islam became dominant in Malaysia and Indonesia. It also spread from Central Asia into China. In various ways Islam has thus spread beyond the countries under Islamic rule, and fresh Islamic states have sometimes been created.

Where Islam has once established itself it has seldom subsequently withdrawn. The chief exception is Spain, where the Christian reconquest began with the capture of Toledo in 1085 and was completed in 1492. Those Muslims who remained in Spain were persecuted by Christians and either abandoned their faith or took refuge in North Africa. There were comparatively few Muslims in the European provinces of the Ottoman empire apart from European Turkey, and these have mostly managed to survive as Muslims. Since World War II many Muslims have migrated to Western Europe and North America, chiefly in search of employment and a higher standard of living. In 1990 there were probably about 800,000,000 Muslims in the world.

The modern period

In the history of the Islamic religion the modern period is that in which it has experienced what may be summed up in the phrase "the impact of the West". Within Islam, however, there always seems to have been a potential for religious renewal and reform; Muhammad is reported to have said that there would be a renewer (*mujaddid*) of his religion at the beginning of each century. Two reformers whose influence is still important today antedate any great impact of the West on their communities. One of these was Muhammad ibn 'Abd-al-Wahhab (1703–92) from Arabia, who felt that the Muslim community in which he lived had become decadent through such innovations as the veneration of saints, and recalled it to a stricter observation of the original Islam in its pure form. With the support of what became the Sa'ud dynasty this **Wahhabi** movement, as it is called, brought about changes in Arabia and inspired Muslims elsewhere. The other reformer is Shah Wali Allah of Delhi (1702–62), whose concerns centred in the corruption of popular Islamic practice by Hindu influences and the declining power of the Muslim emperors. He also worked for the restoration of a purer Islam. His continuing influence today can be detected in the **Deobandis.** (On the other hand, the practice of the veneration of saints that he so abhorred also continues to flourish, in India as elsewhere in the Muslim world—apart from Saudi Arabia where all saints' shrines have been destroyed—and is upheld for example by the **Barelvis.**)

It is chiefly since about 1800 that the Muslim community has been experiencing the effect on its life of the impact of the West. This impact has political, economic and intellectual aspects, and has been increasing. The political impact took the form of colonialism, and this in turn led to Muslim movements for political independence which achieved their aim in the course of this century. Although Muslims sometimes blame the colonialist régimes for most of their troubles, it is arguable that the economic impact of the West has had an even more disturbing effect on Muslim life. Western Europeans were chiefly interested in trade, but wealthy Muslims responded by purchasing things offered to them, firstly the products of the industrial revolution, then all the later inventions of scientific technology from cars and television sets to sophisticated weaponry (for governments). Sections of Muslim society have thus come to be dominated by a consumerism and an emphasis on material possessions which are alien to all spiritual life; and the flaunting of luxury has had an adverse effect on other sections of society. Many obvious changes, too, are due to greatly improved communications, both the movement of people and goods and the transmission of news and commands. The vast conurbations of millions of people which are now possible lead to new forms of social structure (or lack of it). The world of the urban Muslim of today is vastly different from that of his grandparents, and this has brought about a widespread crisis of identity. Most of the contemporary movements in Islam may be seen as attempts to deal with this identity crisis.

The Western intellectual impact on Islam has been somewhat different. In the main it followed on from the European Enlightenment of the 18th century. A new scientific outlook developed, and new disciplines of historical and literary criticism. Despite Muslim allegations that the colonialists encouraged scholars to attack and try to destroy Islam, the motive of the early scholars was probably intellectual curiosity, but it should be admitted that most had little positive appreciation of the values of Islam. Muslim difficulties arose from the fact that from the fourth Islamic century or so Muslims had been living on the basis of a self-image which the new historical criticism showed to be inaccurate on some minor points, and which also included the assumptions that Islam was the final and fullest revelation of God to humanity, containing all the human race needed to know of religious and moral truth to the end of time, and that Islam had nothing to learn from any other religious, philosophical or ethical system. This latter assumption of self-sufficiency meant that Ottoman scholars made no attempt to understand the contemporary intellectual movements in Europe following Descartes and Locke, so that when in the 19th century Muslims by travel became exposed to European thought, the scholars could do nothing to help them with the problems raised. This Western intellectual impact has probably had little effect on ordinary Muslims, only on the more educated.

The response of Muslims to the Western impact varies from complete rejection to complete acceptance (in some form of Marxism), but the latter is not relevant here. The so-called resurgence which has become obvious since about 1970 tends towards complete rejection of everything Western (except the material products of Western technology), and calls for a return to the true Islam of Muhammad's time. This is what the Western media call "fundamentalism", though "radical traditionalism" might be a better term (as distinct from the "conservative traditionalism" of the *ulama* who are very often—outside Iran, where the Shi'ite *ulama* have been radicalized in a way that their Sunni counterparts elsewhere have not—among the bitterest opponents of the so-called fundamentalists). Because of its assumption of self-sufficiency it is in danger of shutting Muslims into a kind of ghetto. The resurgence, of course, is many-faceted, especially in respect of the political stance favoured. Some stances lead pragmatically to something less than complete rejection of the West, e.g. those of al-Hasan al-Banna (1906–49) and the **Muslim Brotherhood** in Egypt, and of Mawlana al-Mawdudi (1903–79) and the **Jama'at-i Islami** in Pakistan.

An early exponent of a wide acceptance of Western thought was Sir Sayyid Ahmad Khan (1817–98) who brought Indian Muslims to see that a measure of Western education was essential if they were to share fully in the life of their country, and that it was not incompatible with Islam. He inspired a movement of **Islamic Modernists** in the subcontinent that continue to this day. In Egypt Muhammad 'Abduh (1849–1905), as head of al-Azhar, the traditional university, began to modernize the teaching there. He believed that religion and reason are complementary, but he was selective in his acceptance of Western thought and, though hailed as an early Modernist too (and an inspirer of the **Salafiya**), was actually fairly conservative. Unlike Muhammad 'Abduh, Muhammad Iqbal (1875–1938) readily made use of the ideas of Nietzsche, Bergson and other Western thinkers in his lectures on "The Reconstruction of Religious Thought in Islam" (1930). He became the great inspiration of revivalism in the Indian sub-continent, but there was no close following of his more specific ideas in the lectures mentioned.

Undoubtedly the various movements have helped many Muslims to overcome their feeling of loss of identity, but none has yet shown Muslims how to participate fully as Muslims in the life of the one world of the 21st century. This remains an issue not only for Muslims in the traditional heartlands of Islam, but possibly even more so for the new communities of Muslims in the countries of Western Europe and elsewhere. It remains to be seen what form a "European Islam" may take as Muslim communities make the transition from being immigrant groups to indigenous minorities.

It is important to be aware, in conclusion, that contemporary Islam retains very considerable internal diversity. Certainly there are the headline-catching fundamentalists such as **Hizbollah** in Lebanon, or the **Jihad Organization** in Egypt (members of which assassinated President Sadat); and there are the controversial Quranic punishments applied in Iran, Pakistan, Saudi Arabia and the Sudan; but there are also very different movements concerned, say, with deepening personal piety, like the **Tablighi Jama'at** which originated in India but which today operates world-wide; there are the conservative traditionalists represented by large numbers of the Sunni ulama; there are the Islamic Modernists, less well organized, and currently less influential, yet not necessarily a spent force; and there is the whole gamut of beliefs, attitudes and practices represented in contemporary Sufism, ranging from cults of saints, to community and charity associations, to collective chanting, individual spiritual exercises, and mysticism. Nor is this list exhaustive. Thus Islam remains a varied and fascinating phenomenon which, although often evoking criticism or indeed outright hostility, also merits attention and, in many ways, respect.

This variety is reflected both in the entries on Islamic groups and movements to be found in Part II and also in the entries on individual countries in Part III.

W. Montgomery Watt

CONTEMPORARY JUDAISM

The traditional view of Judaism as a revealed religion governing every aspect of life had to face severe challenges from the end of the 18th century when the Jews began to participate in the life of Western society and share in its values, often in contradiction to traditional Jewish life and values. This period saw the rise of the *Haskalah* (Enlightenment) movement lead by Moses Mendelssohn, a child of the ghetto who became renowned as a foremost German philosopher to become the inspiration for the Maskilim, as Mendelssohn's followers were called, who sought to influence Jewish intellectuals towards a greater appreciation of the need to adapt to the new order. The Maskilim saw themselves, not as rejectionists of the tradition, but rather as the promoters of a new approach in which the tradition could live side by side with the new learning and social forms. The *Haskalah* was, in a sense, a Jewish Renaissance in which, as the historian Zunz said, the Jewish Middle Ages came to an end. The *Haskalah* spread to Eastern Europe where it met with considerable hostility on the part of the traditionalist rabbis but its impact was such that no Jew could be impervious to its claims.

Even more severe challenges to the whole tradition were presented in the 20th century by the Holocaust, in which 6,000,000 Jews, a third of the world population of Jewry, perished, and by the establishment of the State of Israel. These two events, the one catastrophic beyond belief, the other providing a new measure of hope for Jewish survival, both demanded a complete re-thinking of the whole philosophy of Judaism. Questions have been raised for contemporary Jews hitherto unparalleled in the long history of Judaism. Are the Jews an ethnic group or are they the adherents of a religion? Is the main thrust of Judaism universalistic or particularistic? Can the doctrine of God's providential care of His people still be maintained in the light of modern historical investigation into the origins of Judaism and after the Holocaust? Is it still intellectually respectable to continue to affirm the doctrine that the Torah (the Jewish religion) is "from heaven" or does this doctrine now require drastic revision? These kinds of questions have haunted contemporary Judaism, every version of which has now to be seen as a re-interpretation so that even Jews who opt unreservedly for the tradition do so, unlike their mediaeval counterparts, by a conscious act of the will. This article surveys the various responses, their reasoning and their practical implications, as well as the new institutions to which these have given rise.

The divide between **Orthodox Judaism** and **Reform Judaism** is ostensibly on the question of whether the tradition can be changed in the face of new situations, that is, whether the Torah is totally immutable in theory. Yet, since the emphasis in Judaism has been on practice rather than theory, the term Orthodoxy, denoting correct opinions, is somewhat misleading. The differences between Orthodoxy and Reform are especially marked with regard to the rules and regulations of Judaism, Sabbath observance and the dietary laws, for example. The Orthodox, in theory at least and with differing degrees in practice, are committed to keeping all the observances, this being for them the direct will of God. The Reformers, on the other hand, see many of the traditional observances as time-conditioned and not necessarily binding in all their details on contemporary Jews; the degree of observance being decided by individual choice. As the famous 19th century Reform leader, Samuel Holdheim, put it, "The *Talmud* (the source of the detailed rules) was right in its day and I am right in mine". The vast majority of Reform Jews still observe male circumcision, "the covenant of Abraham"; many Reform Jews do not eat pork and some observe the other dietary laws and keep the Sabbath in its strict, traditional form, refraining, for example, from writing or riding on the day, but all as a matter of free personal choice. Yet the reformers tend to see Judaism best expressed in the call of the Hebrew prophets for the pursuit of justice and the life of compassion and holiness rather than its strict observance of the ritual side of Judaism. The Orthodox view such attitudes as heretical. For the Orthodox the ritual observances are of the same order as the ethical, both commanded by God in the Torah, so that there can be as little picking or choosing in the one as in the other. For the Orthodox, the *Halakhah* (the legal side of Judaism), as the very word of God, has never suffered and can never suffer change. **Conservative Judaism** adopts a middle way, in which the *Halakhah* is seen as binding but in dynamic terms, in which the *Halakhah* has been and can be developed in the future in response to changing conditions. To give only one example, Reform Jews would argue that the Pentateuchal prohibition of kindling fire on the Sabbath (Exodus 35:3) is the product of the particular age in which it was first promulgated and has no eternal binding force. The Orthodox see the prohibition as eternally binding and extend it to the switching on of electric lights and the use of electrical appliances. Conservative Jews, while agreeing with the Orthodox that the prohibition is still binding, tend to interpret the *Halakhah* in such a way that a simple operation as switching on an electric light, one which adds to the enjoyment of the Sabbath, is not covered by the prohibition but they would not cook food or bake bread on the Sabbath.

On the doctrinal level, Orthodoxy understands the belief that the Torah is from heaven to preclude all biblical criticism with regard to the Pentateuch and is uneasy with the application of the new discipline to the rest of the Hebrew Bible and even with historical investigation into the other classical source of Judaism, the *Talmud*. Reform accepts modern historical, critical methodology as applied to all the Jewish sources and tends to see the sacred texts as the product of a purely human response to God rather than as divine revelation. Conservative Judaism, like Reform, accepts the findings of modern historical, critical investigation, but, unlike Reform, sees the process itself as a form of divine revelation, God giving the Torah not only *to* the people of Israel but *through* the people in its quest for the divine will.

Both Reform and Conservative Judaism is particularly strong in the USA, where Reform synagogues, or temples, as these are usually called, are organized under the **Union of American Hebrew Congregations** and Conservative synagogues under the **United Synagogue of America.** The major institution for the training of Reform Rabbis is the **Hebrew Union College–Jewish Institute of Religion** (in Cincinnati, Los Angeles and Jerusalem) and for Conservative Rabbis the **Jewish Theological Seminary** in New York and Los Angeles. In England there is a movement known as **Liberal Judaism,** very close in attitude to American Reform, and a Reform movement, closer to, though not identical with, Conservative Judaism in the USA. The institution for the training of English progressive (that is, both Liberal and Reform) rabbis is the Leo Baeck College in London. In England there is also a comparatively small **Masorti** ("traditional") movement, very close in attitude to the version of Conservative Judaism in Israel with the same name. In recent years there has emerged in the USA a more right-wing version of Conservative Judaism known as **Traditional Conservative Judaism** in reaction to the decision by the Jewish Theological Seminary to ordain women as rabbis and other moves to the left in American Conservative Judaism.

Formerly it was unheard of for a rabbi to officiate at the marriage of a Jew to a Gentile but a fairly large minority of Reform rabbis, nowadays, do officiate at such marriage ceremonies in the belief that it is better in this way to retain the loyalty of the Jewish partner than to reject him or her completely. A furore has erupted over the decision by American Reform rabbis to accept as Jewish the child born to a Jewish father and non-Jewish mother, a decision running counter to the traditional rule that the Jewish status of a child is determined by matrilineal descent. Reform Judaism generally does not require the traditional *get* (bill of divorce) for the dissolution of a marriage relying solely on the civil divorce. While all three groups accept proselytes, the Orthodox procedures are stricter and far more demanding of the prospective convert to Judaism than the other two groups.

With regard to eschatological beliefs, Orthodoxy holds fast to the traditional scheme according to which the soul, after the death of the body, awaits the time when it will be reunited with the body at the resurrection. Preceding the resurrection, the *Messiah* will come to redeem the Jewish people from its exile among the nations and, through Israel, usher in for all mankind a state of peace, justice and the establishment of God's kingdom on earth. The Messiah will cause the Temple to be rebuilt in Jerusalem and the ancient sacrificial system restored. This state will endure until the resurrection of the dead when a completely new state of existence will be brought about for all the righteous, Gentiles as well as Jews. Reform Judaism has abandoned belief in a bodily resurrection, substituting for it the belief in the immortality of the soul. And instead of the belief in the coming of a personal Messiah, Reform stresses the advent of the Messianic age in which the ancient hope of redemption will be realized. There is no official Conservative view on these topics but the majority of Conservative Jews no longer pray for the restoration of sacrifices. Naturally, there is considerable vagueness in all three camps about these tremendous mysteries and it might be said that generally the stress is on Judaism as a this-worldly religion in which the will of God is to realized in the here-and-now with the eschatological scheme left in the hands of the Almighty. Even among the Orthodox, while belief in *Gehenna* (the place of afterlife punishment) is still maintained, there is very little hell-fire preaching and few attempts at exploring the geography of heaven and hell.

All contemporary versions of Judaism reject totally, of course, the Christian dogma but there has emerged in modern times a belief in the value of a dialogue with Christianity (and, to a lesser extent, with Islam), though many of the Orthodox grant this low priority.

The comparison in the last century of the division between Orthodoxy and Reform to that between Roman Catholicism and Protestantism, implying the strongest element of schism, is no longer in vogue. Nowadays, all three groups co-operate willingly in welfare work, in supporting the State of Israel and in other spheres of activity. Bodies such as the New York Board of Rabbis have as members rabbis from all three groups, although the more right-wing Orthodox have expressed strong disapproval of this kind of fraternization as weakening Orthodoxy by blurring the distinction between what it considers to be authentic Judaism and spurious substitutes. It is still rare, however, for Orthodox and Reform rabbis to exchange pulpits or to participate together in religious services. Some of the Orthodox deny the right of Reform and Conservative Rabbis to assume the title.

On the contemporary scene, there are few differences among the various groupings with regard to the State of Israel and its centrality in Jewish life. **Zionism** was at first opposed by the Reformers on the grounds that it tended to favour Jewish particularism against universalism; many of the Reform rabbis viewing the *Diaspora* not as exile but as the fulfilment of the prophetic ideal of the people of Israel as a "light to the nations". The Orthodox rabbis opposed Zionism on the different grounds that it tended to replace the Messianic hope of direct divine intervention with, to them, an impious anticipation of the redemption through human, political activity. But some of the Orthodox founded in the **Mizrahi** (in the State of Israel this is now the **Mafdal,** the **National Religious Party)** a movement of religious Zionism in which human efforts to secure a home for Jews in the land of their fathers are praiseworthy as "the beginning of the redemption", that is, as human preparation for the ultimate realization of Messianism. After the Holocaust and the establishment of the State of Israel, most Jews, whether Orthodox or Reform, gave up the old opposition, which seemed now to be anachronistic granted the fulfilment of the Zionist promise and the burning need to repair the devastation caused by the Holocaust. The **Agudat Israel** party, formerly among the fiercest religious opponents of political Zionism, have now accepted, more out of necessity than conviction, the State of Israel and there are members of this party in the Israeli government. The older attitude of opposition only persists among the Hasidim of **Satmar** and the **Neturei Karta.** Sephardi and Oriental Jews were originally largely unaffected by the European movement of Zionism but are now fully active in Israeli political life with their own party of **Shas.**

With a brave insistence that Hitler should not have the last word, there has been an astonishing revival of Orthodoxy in the post-Holocaust world, including an extreme right-wing trend towards the preservation intact of the life of traditional Judaism as it was lived in the great centres of Orthodoxy in Eastern Europe. This trend is often described as that of **Ultra Orthodox Judaism** and its followers as the **haredim** (God-fearing), embracing many Ashkenazi Jews and a lesser number of Sephardi and Oriental Jews who seek to perpetuate, so far as possible, the way of life adopted by their ancestors, different in many respects from that of Eastern European Jewry. The Ashkenazi *haredim* are followers of **Hasidism** or the heirs to the tradition of Lithuanian Jewish piety and learning, hence known as the Litvaks. There are also *haredim* who follow the uncompromising way of Hungarian Orthodoxy, that of Rabbi Moses Sofer in the early 19th century whose slogan was, "anything new is forbidden by the Torah". The main Hasidic groups on the contemporary scene are: **Belz Satmar, Lubavitch, Bratslav, Bobova, Gur, Klausenberg-Zanz, Vizhnitz** and **Karlin-Stolin.** Each of these has its own *rebbe* (the name given to the Hasidic master, to distinguish him from the traditional rabbi) and its own rules and regulations. The Hasidim favour enthusiastic prayer in which the soul soars to its source in the divine. The ultimate aim of the Hasid is to attain to the state of *devekut* (attachment, of the mind to God), a mystical state in which the limitations of the material universe are transcended. This state is only held to be fully possible for the *rebbe* himself, his followers approximating to it through their attachment to him. The *rebbe*'s word is law for his followers, who turn to him for guidance not only in the spiritual path but are advised by him on how to conduct themselves in every aspect of life.

The central institution for the Litvaks is the *Yeshivah*, the college of higher learning, based on the pattern of the great Lithuanian Yeshivot in the pre-Holocaust period. Today many thousands of young men spend years in a Yeshivah, where the main subject studied is the *Talmud.* The major "Lithuanian" Yeshivot today are those of Lakewood in New Jersey; Telz in Cleveland, Ohio, and in Telstone near Jerusalem; Mir, Hevron and Kamenitz in Jerusalem; and, the largest of all, Ponievezh in Bene Berak. The Yeshivah caters to young men, from the age of 18, already fairly advanced in their studies. The main pattern in the Yeshivot is for the students to study by themselves in groups of two; reading through the particular Talmudic tractate designated for the term, and there are twice-weekly lectures by the Rosh Yeshivah, the principal or his assistants. In the majority of the Yeshivot, the language of instruction is Yiddish, as in Eastern Europe of former times, though in some modern Hebrew and English are also used. The usual method adopted is that of keen logical analysis of the difficult legal concepts, with the emphasis on in-depth learning. In these Yeshivot, too, a period is set aside each day for a period of reflection in which the classical works of **Musar** are rehearsed in a melancholy tune, with the aim of perfecting the moral and religious character. In the older Yeshivot of Lithuania there was, at first, strong opposition to the Musar movement, in the belief that the Torah (that is, the study of the Talmud) is sufficient for the improvement of the character. But, eventually, the opposition was silenced and, nowadays, Musar sessions are the norm, with a special moral tutor, known as the Mashgiah, to supervise this aspect of Yeshivah life. In addition to the large Lithuanian-type Yeshivot, there are a number of "Hungarian" Yeshivot in which greater emphasis is placed on the practical rules of Judaism and there are some few Sephardi Yeshivot with their own traditions. In the Hasidic Yeshivot, the study of Hasidic texts is substituted for Musar. Many of the Yeshivot have attached to them a Kolel, in which married students are supported financially so that they can continue their studies without financial care. The aim of the Yeshivot is not to produce rabbis but to encourage the study of the Torah for its own sake (*Torah lishmah*), though, naturally, some students do eventually become practising rabbis. There has emerged as a result a Yeshivah "world" of élitist scholars with a language and vocabulary of its own.

The Yeshivah world is not only opposed to secular studies, unless these are pursued for the furtherance of a career, never for their own sake, but has little use for the modern historical, critical approach to the sacred texts of Judaism. The whole notion of historical development is viewed with strong suspicion as introducing a human element into the revelatory scheme.

Reference should here be made to the recent Baal Teshuvah (penitent) movement. Many hitherto estranged young people have become attracted to the full Ultra-Orthodox life. Their progress towards this aim is assisted by special Yeshivot catering for their special needs, the heads of which are conversant with the inevitable traumas associated with the transition and favour a gradual approach foreign to the either/or of the general Yeshivah world.

The majority of the Orthodox, however, follow, in various degrees, the trend known as Neo-Orthodoxy, in which modernity and secular studies are embraced not only as means to an end but as good and valuable in themselves. As one of the leading figures in the Neo-Orthodox camp put it, "You can have Shakespeare and the Talmud". The two main colleges for the training of modern Orthodox rabbis are Yeshivah University in New York and Jews' College in London. The main organizations of modern Orthodox synagogues are: the **Union of Orthodox Hebrew Congregations** in the USA and the **United Synagogue** in Greater London. A phenomenon not to be overlooked or underestimated is the powerful swing to the right on the part of modern or centrist Orthodoxy in which the attitudes of the Ultra-Orthodox are becoming increasingly popular.

Judaism has not been unaffected by the tendency towards greater equality between the sexes and there are a number of **Jewish Feminist Groups.** In Orthodox synagogues women and men sit separately, women do not officiate in the services and are not called to the Reading of the Torah. The view of Maimonides is generally followed among the Orthodox that women may not occupy any communal office and they cannot serve as rabbis or cantors. But the on-going debate about rabbinic ordination is concerned more with traditional norms rather than, as in the Church debate, with questions of dogma or doctrine. In Reform synagogues and in a majority of Conservative synagogues men and women sit together and women are ordained as rabbis and as cantors. The older view which excluded women from participation in the study of the Torah is no longer held even by the Orthodox, with few exceptions, though women are not admitted as students in the Ultra-Orthodox Yeshivot. In the circle of these Yeshivot, the graduates, whether in the Kolel or studying independently, are not the breadwinners, their wives earning the family living outside the home, usually by teaching children or by secretarial work.

Among all the various groups there has emerged a renewed interest in the Jewish theosophical, mystical system known as the **Kabbalah,** once attacked by the rationalists as sheer superstition but now popular not only in the circle of **Jewish New Agers** but for many other Jews seeking the mystical dimension to the religious life. Hasidism is in any event based on the Kabbalah but, under the influence of Martin Buber and others, **Neo-Hasidism** has emerged in which an attempt is made to translate Hasidic and Kabbalistic ideas and values into the language of the modern world. Followers of this trend will admire the Hasidic masters but, unlike in Hasidism proper, will not owe allegiance to any one particular master. The study of the Kabbalah is also engaged in by Sephardi Jews and there are even one or two Kabbalistic Yeshivot in which this science is an important part of the curriculum together with the *Talmud* and the *Codes*. Some few Jews adhere to what may be termed "pop-Kabbalah" bordering on the occult, far removed from the study of the Kabbalah as a scholarly discipline introduced by Gershom Scholem and his school. But the Scholem approach is purely objective and scientific without any necessary attachment to the Kabbalah as relevant to contemporary religious life. Not all religious Jews see value in the contemporary interest in Kabbalah. Professor Saul Lieberman, once introduced Scholem by declaring, "The Kabbalah is nonsense but the scientific study of Jewish nonsense constitutes Jewish scholarship".

Reconstructionist Judaism, founded by Mordecai Kaplan, was originally not a separate movement but had as a general aim one that cut across the different groups: the reinterpretation of Judaism in naturalistic terms; God as the power that makes for righteousness, not the personal, transcendent God of Jewish tradition. This philosophy of Judaism was popular among scientifically influenced religious Jews who found difficulties with the idea of a God who sets aside the laws of nature to perform miracles and can be dissuaded from His decrees by the act of petitionary prayer. These Jews found attractive Kaplan's description of Judaism as a "religious civilization", embracing art, music and literature, rather than a pure but limited religion. Judaism was seen more as "a way of life", the means of best realizing the Jewish potential and individual Jewish self-expression than as the fulfilment of the commands of a divine being outside the universe. But the renewed interest in the mystical dimension of Judaism and the stark reality of the human situation after the Holocaust seemed to demand, for many Jews, a belief in the God of tradition with whom human beings co-operate in overcoming evil. Consequently, Reconstructionism in the contemporary Jewish world is a philosophy of Judaism adopted by only by a comparatively small group as a separate Jewish religious movement, with its own college for the training of Reconstructionist rabbis in Philadelphia.

External evidence of the particular group to which religious Jews belong is often provided by the mode of dress they adopt. Men belonging to the Ultra-Orthodox are usually bearded and dress in sombre garb, a long black coat or a shorter black jacket. Ultra-Orthodox women dress modestly in long dresses with sleeves reaching to the wrist and have their heads completely covered with a kerchief or, more usually, with a *sheitel,* a wig made of hair other than their own. The modern Orthodox usually adopt Western style fashions and the men are clean-shaven but many of the modern Orthodox women still have their heads completely covered. Hasidic men usually wear on the Sabbath the sable hat known as the *streimel,* originally the type of head covering worn by the Polish nobility but into which various mystical ideas have been read. To the informed observer, subtle distinctions can be observed between the different Hasidic groups. The Lubavitchers, for instance, do not cultivate the curled side-locks (*peot*) worn by other Hasidim and they do not don the *streimel.* The Hasidim of Gur have larger fur hats than the others and the followers of some *rebbes* wear white socks on the Sabbath. All Hasidim attach great significance to regular immersion in the specially constructed ritual bath (*mikveh*) as an aid to purity. All the Orthodox observe the rules of "family purity", according to which a married woman must immerse herself in the ritual bath after her periods before she can be reunited with her husband. The Ultra-Orthodox cover their heads with the prayer-shawl (*tallit*) during the morning prayers and the Hasidim don for all the prayers a girdle made of silk or other materials to divide the upper part of the body from the lower. A number of Hasidim do not wear ties since this belongs to a Gentile form of dress. Reform, Conservative and some of the modern Orthodox Jews adopt unreservedly Western forms of dress although some Conservative Jews and many of the modern Orthodox still observe the ancient law against wearing a garment made of both wool and flax (*shaatnez*).

As if to compensate for the destruction of millions of Jewish books in the Holocaust and as a powerful instrument for the renewal of Jewish life, there has taken place an astonishing amount of publications on every aspect of Judaism. The Yeshivot and other Ultra-Orthodox institutions publish journals of scholarship and monthlies such as The *Jewish Observer* in the USA. Modern Orthodoxy publishes the journal *Tradition* in the USA and *Le'Elah* in England, both of high standard. Among Reform publications are *Reform Judaism* in the USA and *European Judaism* in England. Conservative Judaism publishes in the USA a monthly with this name. It might be remarked that, while the non-Orthodox journals open their pages to all, hardly any of the Orthodox contribute to them and non-Orthodox writers are not normally welcome to contribute to the Orthodox journals. However, the journal *Judaism,* published in the USA by the **World Jewish Congress,** opens its pages to contributors from all the Jewish groups and has published important cross-group symposia; on the question of the role and importance of Jewish law for example. *Commentary,* a monthly published by the **American Jewish Committee,** is not, strictly speaking, a religious journal but often publishes articles of religious significance such as the symposium in the 1960s in which rabbis and scholars belonging to all the groups replied to a number of questions regarding their stance on Jewish theology, later published in book form. On the level of pure scholarship, the learned journals *Zion, Tarbitz,* and the excellent biographical journal *Kirvat Sefer* are published in Israel; the *Hebrew Union College Annual* and the *Jewish Quarterly Review* in the USA; and the *Journal of Jewish Studies* in Oxford. Most of the larger Jewish communities publish a newspaper though none remotely approach the London *Jewish Chronicle,* a paper that has been in regular publication for 150 years and which, in addition to general Jewish themes, covers religious topics in articles, letters and editorial comment, succeeding on the whole in fairly representing all the different viewpoints.

Mossad Ha-Rav Kook in Jerusalem has published hundreds of critical editions of the ancient and mediaeval Jewish religious classics as well as the commentary *Daat Mikra* to the whole of the Bible, carrying through successfully its avowed aim of presenting the modern reader with a digest of the best scholarship, though it does tend to fight shy of biblical criticism, lower or high, in connection with the Pentateuch. The gigantic undertaking, *Enzyklopedia Talmudit,* now half-way through with 22 volumes, covers the whole range of Talmudic and post-Talmudic learning. The *Encyclopedia Judaica* gives a full account of every aspect of Jewish life with much information on the different religious groupings and their history. The Ultra-Orthodox, attractively produced, *ArtScroll* series, in English, covers large parts of the *Bible,* the *Mishnah,* the *Talmud* and other classics, and has produced prayer books for weekdays, the Sabbath and the Festivals; the attitude is that of fundamentalism throughout. The very capable Jewish scholar, Adin Steinsaltz, has produced single-handed fine editions of many Talmudic tractates with his commentary in modern Hebrew. Some of these have also been translated into English, complementing but not supplanting the older translation of the complete *Talmud* into English published by the Soncino Press in London. Numerous works in Hebrew, English and other languages have streamed forth on Hasidism. The Musar movement, too, once somewhat shy of publishing its teachings in print, has now a large number of works to its credit. In the area of traditional Jewish law, hundreds of *Responsa* volumes have seen the light, either as original publications or as photocopies of works long out of print. The work *Otzar ha-Posekim* is a digest of all the *Responsa* on marriage law, now very widely used by Orthodox rabbis.

A particularly strong cult of personality has emerged among the Ultra-Orthodox, not only in Hasidism where it has always been prominent. Photographs of famous rabbinic personalities are on sale in bookshops, despite the earlier reluctance of rabbinic leaders to be photographed. A spate of rabbinic biographies describe the rabbinic and Hasidic heroes in hagiographical terms. Especially among Sephardi/Oriental Jews, the saints are depicted as miracle workers for whom healing the sick, levitation and the ability to turn water in wine are everyday occurrences. There are regular pilgrimages to the graves of the saints, though this stops short of actual intercession.

The departure from tradition is perhaps nowhere to be observed more strikingly than in the rabbinate. The main function of the traditional rabbi, still maintained among the Ultra-Orthodox and some of the modern Orthodox, is to render decisions in Jewish law in all its ramifications and, otherwise closeted in his study, to set the example of total dedication to the study of the Torah. Modern Orthodox, Conservative and Reform rabbis, on the other hand, model their role on that of the Christian clergyman in that they preach regularly, engage in pastoral work, officiate at marriages and funerals, and act as representatives to the non-Jewish world. When a spokesman for Ultra-Orthodoxy was asked what he thought about women rabbis, he replied that, in his book, men rabbis of the new type are also not acknowledged as true rabbis.

It must finally be noted that for all the views from extreme to extreme, Jewish religious life has not yielded to sectarianism and it is incorrect to speak of the various groupings as "denominations". With the exception of those who have embraced a different religion—the "Jews for Jesus", for example—the members of the various groups may dub the others reactionaries or obscurantists or heretics or sinners or even as *goyim* (Gentiles), yet the others still remain in their eyes part of the Jewish community of faith; misguided Jews but Jews nevertheless.

Louis Jacobs

BUDDHISM

The term, Buddhism, refers to the religious tradition derived from a north Indian religious teacher (c.536–476 BCE) who bore the title, the *Buddha,* "Enlightened One". Like other religions which trace their origins to a historic progenitor, the founder's life story and the teachings directly attributed to him constitute an abiding inspiration for subsequent developments.

As with Christianity, Islam and other historic religions, however, Buddhism has developed substantially different shapes and contours during its 2,500 year history. Many of its major systems of thought and practice evolved during its first half millenium of growth on Indian soil, but doctrine, ritual, and forms of institutional life became increasingly varied as Buddhism spread through South East, Central, and East Asia over the next 500 years. For example, the **Nyingmapa** tradition of Tibetan Buddhism begun by Guru Padmasambhava in the eighth century and the **Pure Land School (Jodoshinshu)** founded by Shinran Shonen in Japan in the 13th century represent far-reaching transformations of the early mendicant life style of the followers of the Buddha. From a relatively simple model of religious mendicancy centered around an extraordinary human teacher Buddhism eventually developed ornate and elaborate meditational and devotional rituals and complex theological constructions extrapolated from the historical founder.

By the 20th century Buddhism had become even more variegated as it spread throughout Europe and America. Tibetan monasteries in the Swiss alps, Vietnamese meditation centres outside of Paris, and Cambodian temples ministering to refugee populations in American cities have become the order of the day. From its ascetical, mendicant origins in the area of Lumpini in Nepal and Benaras in Northern India, Buddhism came to play a powerful political, social, and cultural role throughout the subcontinent and in Tibet, China, Korea, Japan, Sri Lanka, Myanmar (Burma), Thailand, Laos, and Cambodia.

Buddhism helped to define 20th century liberation movements against Western colonial imperialism in Sri Lanka, Burma, and Vietnam, and today Buddhists in Asia and the West are speaking out on urgent issues of civil and human rights ranging from the environment to Aids. The tradition which began with an exemplary religious quest in search of individual enlightenment (*nirvana*), became a major educator of ruling élites in India, a theocratic state in Tibet, a dominant philosophical school in China, the primary bearer of high culture in Thailand and Japan, and in its current world-ecumenical form has emerged as a thoughtful critic of the exploitation of the world's human and natural resources by the rapacious appetite of industrial capitalism.

The Buddha and his teachings

Buddhism begins with a story of a young prince, Siddhartha, who, according to legend, enjoyed all the wealth, prestige, and power of royalty. It is a story of worldly success; or, rather, it is a tale of the ultimate limitations of worldly success; the inability of fame, wealth, and honour to provide lasting peace, happiness, and satisfaction. The Siddhartha legend follows the pattern of many heroic myths: a going forth, the achievement of an extraordinary aim, a testing of the hero's mettle, and the hero's return. This structure underlies part, but not all, of the legendary life of Prince Siddhartha whose spiritual journey led to his enlightenment as the Buddha. Several sacred biographies composed in the early centuries of our era also tell of his miraculous birth, childhood and marriage, the Buddha's teachings, and finally his death.

Prince Siddhartha's spiritual journey provides a good starting point to begin the story of Buddhism. It fashions a perspective from which to understand the nature of (i) the Buddha and his teachings; (ii) Buddhist institutions and practice; and (iii) the relationship of the Buddhist tradition to its social and political environment.

Siddhartha was born into an aristocratic family. He was a prince, the son of the ruler of the Sakya clan soon to be incorporated into the larger kingdom of Magadha. Buddhism, thus, emerged out of an atmosphere of political, economic, and social change. Siddhartha's spiritual quest needs to be understood against such a historical backdrop. The quest is contextual, but also timeless; a quest for meaning in uncertain times; a particular setting but persistently relevant.

"Rejoice, O queen! A mighty son has been born to you." "Great Being! There is none your equal." The myths exaggerate Siddhartha's royal status to emphasize the magnitude of his decision to give up the luxury of his station to embark on an uncharted spiritual journey. At the Prince's name-giving ceremony eight astrologers predicted that Siddhartha would become either a universal monarch or a Buddha. The boy's father, distressed that his son might choose not to become a great world ruler thought "It will never do for my son to become a Buddha. What I would wish to see is my son exercising sovereign rule and authority over the four great continents . . .", and so the king sought to satisfy his son's every wish and whim. For 30 years or so Siddhartha enjoyed his luxurious surroundings—seasonal palaces, a beautiful wife, and a soon to be born son, Rahula.

But, as often happens in heroic tales, an abrupt reversal in Prince Siddhartha's life takes place. One day while riding in his chariot through his pleasure gardens the young prince encounters four unfamiliar, startling sights: an old man, a diseased man, a dead man, and a mendicant monk. These encounters cause him to ponder the nature and meaning of his existence so that when he returned to his palace ". . . that magnificent apartment, as splendid as the palace of the chief of the gods, began to seem like a cemetery filled with dead bodies . . .; and the three modes of existence [past, present, future] appeared like houses on fire". Is there no meaning to life beyond old age, suffering, and death? The fourth vision, the mendicant monk, points to an answer: such deep and fundamental questions can only be resolved by a personal journey, a direct encounter with a truth beyond sensual satisfaction and mere sense perception.

Prince Siddhartha embarks on a quest for the truth "gone beyond", studying with teachers of yoga and other philosophies. At one point he nearly dies from the severity of his ascetic practices. Realizing that such austerities can not lead to enlightenment he adopts a more moderate path between the extremes of worldly life and asceticism. For this reason the Buddhist tradition is known as the religion of the Middle Way. After six years of experimentation with different teachings and disciplines, Siddhartha's effort finally ends in victory. Buddhist texts describe his enlightenment in vivid detail, especially the efforts of Mara, the Buddhist equivalent of Satan, to prevent Siddhartha from attaining Buddhahood.

With his goal realized, the Buddha spent the next forty-five years teaching the truths he had discovered about the nature of existence. These teachings are summarized in an oft-repeated formula which appears as part of Sakyamuni's (the sage of the Sakya clan) first public teaching. The formula is called the Four Noble Truths: (i) there is a basic lack of fulfilment or unease in our lives; (ii) this dissatisfaction is rooted in the human tendency towards grasping and selfish attachments; (iii) this dissatisfaction can be eliminated if this grasping nature can be corrected; and (iv) the way to correct selfish craving is charted out in the Eightfold Path which includes moral virtue (right action, right speech, right vocation), mental discipline (right effort, right mindfulness, right concentration), and the attainment of wisdom (right view, right thought).

The Buddhist analysis of suffering or unease focuses on the concepts of *karma* and rebirth (*samsara*). Attachment, craving, and thirst lead not only to suffering and unhappiness, but to re-existence, re-birth or re-becoming. The nature of one's re-existence, furthermore, results inescapably from the nature of one's actions or *karma*. Action motivated by attachment accrues karmic consequences which inevitably bind one to the wheel of becoming. Suffering follows particularly from unjust and immoral acts. *Karma* theory constructs a kind of spiritual justice linking past, present, and future. In Buddhism the dilemma of Job, or why the righteous suffer and the unrighteous prosper, is answered in terms of *karma* and re-birth. While it may not be possible to explain precisely why a righteous person suffers in this life, Buddhists believe that such suffering necessarily follows from karmic acts. The Buddha's Eightfold Noble Path leads beyond attachment and, hence, beyond *karma* and re-birth.

The core story of the Buddha's enlightenment and his first public teaching provides a paradigm for understanding the essential nature of Buddhist teachings and practice. Siddhartha's vision quest begins with an assumption, namely, that we lack knowledge of the true conditions of reality. Our unease, our sense of the time "being out of joint", or our suffering as the texts often put it, derives from our misperception of how things are. The teachings of early Buddhism assert that most of us tend to see things as being independently and substantively perduring. Consequently, we have a sense of self that endures through time, and we live our lives in the expectation of achieving and acquiring equally enduring goals and benefits. In the Buddhist analysis, such expectations inevitably lead to frustration, anxiety and despair, i.e. suffering. In its simplest terms the Buddha's insight affirms that nothing in the world perdures; everything including the "self" is characterized by an impermanence more radical and pervasive than our conventional sense of entities gradually changing over time. Indeed, there is no self-existent "thing" or "self" which gradually changes; reality is nothing more nor less than an interconnected, everchanging web. What we take to be the self is nothing more nor less than an aggregate of material and non-material factors, i.e. body, sensations, perceptions, intentions, consciousness. The knowledge of the truths of impermanence, interdependence, and the non-substantial or "not-self" nature of reality cannot be learned from a book or taught by a teacher. As the story of Siddhartha's vision quest demonstrates, it must be experienced personally, deeply, existentially.

This core teaching pervades much of the Buddhist tradition regardless of sect, school, and culture. By the fourth century of our era the major schools of Buddhist thought had already taken shape, for example *Vaibhashika, Sautantrika, Sarvastivada, Madhyamika, Yogacara,* which informed the basic strands of the tradition—the **Theravada**, *Mahayana, Vajrayana*—as Buddhism spread throughout South East, Central, and East Asia. The Buddha's fundamental insight regarding the radically impermanent nature of things was reaffirmed by the *Perfection of Wisdom* tradition and systematized by the noted Buddhist philosopher, Nagarjuna, in the second century CE under the rubric, "emptiness". Convinced that concepts tend to construct static entities out of ever-changing components of experience (*dharmas*), Nagarjuna asserted that the basic philosophical categories of Buddhist scholastic thought were "empty" (*sunya*). By means of a dialectical logic he sought to prove that all doctrinal assertions were self-contradictory and, hence, insubstantial, that is to say, empty. As we shall see, this view correlates with the Buddhist emphasis on the practice of meditation.

Other doctrinal developments were less deconstructive than the *Madhyamika* school of thought which looks to Nagarjuna as its founder. The continuous emphasis in the Buddhist tradition on the mind had evolved by the fourth century into a school of thought (the *Vijnanavada*) that constructed the mind as the ground which gave continuity to the flux of momentary experiences. Another strand of Buddhist speculation coupled the person of the Buddha with the truth he discovered about the nature of reality (the *dharma*) giving rise to notions of Buddha Nature (*tathata*) and the Body of Dharma (*dharmakaya*). Although Buddhist thinkers fashioned such speculative views in relationship to competing intellectual and spiritual schools of thought, these seemingly divergent ideas continued to reflect the Buddha's insight into the impermanent and interconnected nature of things. Even today, modern Buddhist apologists find this primal Buddhist insight a useful perspective from which to address problems ranging from racism to the ecological crisis.

Buddhist institutions and practice

The basic Buddhist religious institution has been the monastery, a place where, at least in an ideal sense, men and women can pursue Sakyamuni's vision quest. The monastery evolved into a variety of forms, to be sure. Some Buddhist monasteries were located away from towns, an environment where monks and nuns could meditate freed from the distractions of town life. Other monasteries were located in towns where monk scholars wrote doctrinal treatises and taught both fellow monastics and laity. Buddhist monastic centers such as Nalanda and Vikramsila had become India's major universities as early as the fifth century. The fame of their teachers, curricula, and libraries attracted students not only from all over India but also from China and Tibet. The tradition of monastic universities, furthermore, was perpetuated throughout Buddhist Asia. Scholarship and education have been among the enduring legacies of Buddhism throughout Asia, superceded only in the modern period by the advent of secular state-sponsored educational systems. Given the central place of study and education to the Buddhist tradition, the displacement of the monk as the principal educator in countries like Thailand has helped to undermine the status of the Buddhist monk in Thai society.

Buddhist monasteries have also provided the context for contemplative pursuits, in particular meditation. Meditation is, of course, not a spiritual practice unique to Buddhism or for that matter Asian religious traditions with which it has been so closely associated. Buddhist traditions evolved, furthermore, in which meditation disciplines were of peripheral significance. Nevertheless, comparatively speaking meditation can be said to be more central to Buddhism than virtually any of the great world religions: meditation was instrumental to the Buddha's enlightenment; meditation was an essential component of the Noble Eightfold Path put into the Buddha's first public teaching; one of the major schools of East Asian Buddhism is called the meditation school; meditation has been one of the principal reasons for the popularity of Buddhism in the West.

Even though there are continuities in various schools of Buddhist meditation, meditation theory and practice has been no more monolithic than Buddhist doctrine. An early division arose over the merits of tranquillity (*samatha*) or trance (*jhana*) versus insight (*vipassana*) meditation. The former cultivated states of mind associated with the powers of clairvoyance and telekenesis; the latter aimed at comprehending the impermanent, interconnected, and non-substantial nature of reality. Even though various schools evolved particular methods aimed at the attainment of tranquillity or of insight, the two actually complement one another. As Figure 1 suggests, Buddhist wisdom or enlightenment requires both a tranquil psycho-moral state of being as well as an understanding of the deeper truths of human existence.

Throughout Buddhist Asia sectarian traditions were as often based on disagreement regarding the goals and methods of meditation as disputes over doctrine and monastic disciplinary practices. One such disagreement was the sixth century debate between the Ch'an schools of gradual and sudden enlightenment in China. The sudden enlightenment version of the dispute is recounted in the *Platform Sutra* of the Sixth Patriarch, Hui-neng (638–714 CE). According to this tradition Hui-neng, an illiterate peasant from south

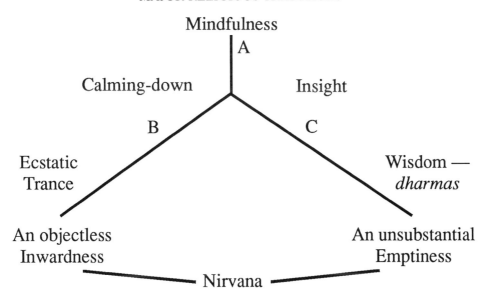

Figure 1 The Buddhist path to enlightenment.

Source. E. Conze (1956) Buddhist Meditation (New York: Harper and Row).

China, heard the *Diamond Sutra* being chanted by a customer in the local market where he sold firewood. Upon being asked to expound the text, the customer urged Hui-neng to seek the wisdom of the monk, Huang-jen, at Wang-mei on East Mountain in north China. Making the journey to Huang-jen's monastery, Hui-neng was allowed to work in the kitchen. The abbot intuitively sensed Hui-neng's spiritual profundity but knew that designating a young illiterate peasant as his Dharma heir would create dissension among the monks. Therefore, he announced that his successor would be chosen by means of a public poetry contest. The abbot's chief disciple and anticipated successor, Shen-hsiu, posted the following poem:

> The body is the tree of enlightenment,
> And the mind is like a bright mirror stand,
> Take care to wipe it all the time,
> Allow no grain of dust to cling.

Then a few days later a second, unsigned poem appeared:

> Enlightenment is not like a tree,
> Nor is the mind a mirror stand.
> Since fundamentally not one thing exists,
> Where, then, is a grain of dust to cling?

This poem, of course, had been dictated by Hui-neng.

The story of Hui-neng exemplifies the teachings of the School of Sudden Enlightenment. Hui-neng's illiteracy illustrates the Ch'an tradition's insistence that enlightenment cannot be achieved through reading Buddhist texts. Hui-neng's poem combines the Buddhist

43

teaching of non-substantiality or emptiness with sudden enlightenment. Continuous polishing of the mirror (gradual enlightenment) suggests that in enlightenment one comprehends a substantive difference between mind (mirror) and body (mirror stand). The Sudden Enlightenment School rejects both the method and the dualistic worldview implicit in Shen-hsiu's poem.

Beyond the content of the story, however, the tale points to a fundamental characteristic of the Buddhist tradition: the centrality to the tradition of the teacher/saint and the importance of sacred biography as a teaching device. Beginning with the story of Buddha's enlightenment sacred biography has held the place of honour in Buddhism. For example, the history as well as the teachings of the Ch'an/Zen tradition are embodied in stories of the patriarchs from Bodhidharma, the reputed founder of Ch'an in China, to Hui-neng to modern teachers in Japan and the West. Such lineages exist in other Buddhist traditions as well, however. What would the Nyingmapa or **Gelugpa** traditions in Tibet be without the stories of Padmasambhava, Milarepa or Naropa, and the Pure Land tradition in Japan without the tales of Honen, Shinran, and Rennyo? Canonical texts and their commentaries should not be ignored in accounting for the doctrinal development of Buddhism, but the emphasis on the existential nature of enlightenment elevates the place of the spiritual exemplar.

Ideally the spiritual exemplar embodies specific, characteristic Buddhist virtues. The Bodhisattva, for example, is not only wise (*prajna*) and compassionate (*karuna*) but patient, upright and so on. Although Buddhist ethics have a prescriptive side such as the five *silas*—not to kill, lie, steal, indulge in sexual misconduct, or consume intoxicants—Buddhism has consistently emphasized the development of virtue or character. Hence, the importance of training and the connection between meditation and morality in the Buddhist tradition. The moral lessons of virtue are most often taught through stories as, for example, the following tale about intellectual pride:

> Nan-in, a Japanese master, received a university professor who came to inquire about Zen. Nan-in served tea. He poured his visitor's cup full, but then kept on pouring. The professor watched the overflow until he could no longer restrain himself. "It is too full. No more will go in!" "Like this cup," Nan-in said, "you are full of your opinions and speculations. How can I show you Zen unless you first empty your cup."

The Buddhist saint, indeed, the Buddha himself, functions on several levels within the tradition. As a moral and spiritual exemplar the saint embodies virtuous ideals valued in the tradition: wisdom, compassion, generosity, patience, equanimity. As we can see, these ideals have a universal, not exclusively a specific Buddhist character. The Buddha and the saint, however, embody not only moral virtue and spiritual wisdom, but power. Cults of the saints are as pervasive in Buddhism as in other religious traditions, perhaps even more so. The stories of Padmasambhava, Milarepa, and Naropa include a host of miraculous and magical elements. In contemporary Thailand and Burma monks famed as meditation teachers are also reputed to have various supernatural powers. Lay devotees revere such monks more for their miraculous abilities than for their wisdom and insight. To be in the presence of such saints can lead to a sense of well-being, and their physical representations or artefacts, for example amulets, are thought to have healing and protective powers.

The cult of saints resonates with the cult of Buddha relics and Buddha images. From the time of King Asoka in India (third century BCE) Buddha relic veneration figured prominently in pilgrimage and popular forms of Buddhist cultic life. Buddha images developed later, shortly after the beginning of the common era. The earliest images appeared at Mathura (near modern Delhi) and in Gandhara in north-west India. Buddha images pre-suppose the development of a Buddha cult. Like Buddha relics and relics of

Buddhist saints, Buddha images were believed to have extraordinary powers. For this reason Buddha relics and images were associated with the rise of classical Buddhist kingdoms and princely states. For example, the Buddhist chronicles of Sri Lanka record that Buddha relics were enshrined at Anuradhapura, the first Buddhist capital city on the island; Chinese rulers sponsored the construction of monumental Buddha images outside of the capital city of Loyang; in modern Thailand the so-called Emerald Buddha image functions as the palladium of the reigning Cakri Dynasty.

As the above observations suggest, Buddhist monasteries are not only places where monks and nuns carry out contemplative pursuits or study and teach, they function as centres of lay religious practice. Furthermore, they have both a symbolic and practical political significance, an issue to be addressed in the final section of this essay. The relationship between Buddhist monastic centres and popular devotional piety first developed in India and then spread to other parts of Asia. Early archaeological evidence in India indicates that relic cults at reliquary mounds or *stupas* existed in close proximity to monastic centres. This co-existence led to a distinction in monastic architectural plans between that part of the monastery devoted to the monastic vocation (*sangha-vasa*) and popular devotional practices such as relic and image veneration (*Buddha-vasa*). Although the distinction between the monastic vocations of meditation and study, on the one hand, and between monastic pursuits and popular forms of devotional piety, on the other, were and continue to be maintained in various ways, the distinctions are also blurred. Thus, for example, in contemporary Thailand monks will meditate, teach, and spend time chanting at various rituals ranging from funerals to house dedications. In short, the monastery and the monastic vocation is, and has been, a complex institution embedded in the cultural, social, political, and economic environments of which they are a part.

It appears that sacred biographies of the Buddha developed simultaneously with Buddha images and Buddha cults. Thus, while the core story of Siddhartha's renunciation appears in many tales, the addition of hagiographic, supernatural detail reflects the development of the cult of Buddha relics and images. In Tibetan traditions the Buddha conceptually takes on a mytho-cosmic character manifested in Tibetan Buddhist art, ritual, and forms of meditation practice. In Japan the Buddha Amida (Amitabha) becomes a dispenser of saving grace for those who utter his name in absolute faith (*Namo Amida Butsu*). In some contemporary reformist movements in South East Asia the Buddha as an object of veneration or devotion has been virtually eliminated. Thailand's **Santi Asok** movement, for example, eschews the use of Buddha images and rejects the tradition of "taking refuge" in the Buddha which initiates many Buddhist rituals.

Buddhism, society, and the state

Buddhism, like other world religions, sanctifies the lives of individuals and communities within the cosmic rhythms of birth, death, and renewal. In Buddhist Asia sacred rituals and celebrations mark major events in the religious calendar, the lunar new year, passages in the individual life cycle, and major events in the life of a given community—village, town, or nation. In short, in traditional Buddhist societies, religion sanctified and, thereby, made meaningful all aspects of life whether cosmic, communal, or individual. We shall examine three examples of the way Buddhism sanctifies and thereby enhances the meaning of the lives of individuals and communities: the celebration of Buddha's Day, New Year's Day, and a funeral or death/rebirth rite of passage.

Buddha's Day, or *Visakha Puja* in the Theravada tradition of South East Asia, is considered the most holy day in the religious calendar, on a par with Christmas and Easter in Christian countries. In South East Asia it commemorates the birth, enlightenment, and death of the Buddha believed by Buddhists to have occurred miraculously on the same day of the week, and is celebrated on the full moon day of the lunar month of Visakha (April–May). The seminal events of the Buddha's career coalesced by the Theravadins are celebrated independently in other Buddhist cultures. In Tibet the traditional religious year included celebration of the Buddha's conception or incarnation on the 15th day of the first lunar month, the attainment of Buddhahood on the eighth day of the fourth month, the Buddha's death on the 15th day of the fourth month, and the Buddha's birth on the fourth day of the sixth month of the Tibetan year. The Buddha's incarnation occupied a pre-eminent place in the Tibetan religious year, partially because it was assimilated into the New Year celebration. Special respects were paid to the Dalai Lama and the Buddha's mother, Mahadevi, was solicited for special boons. In China, Korea, and Japan, Buddha's Day was marked by processions of Buddha images and the bathing of these images.

Buddhism sanctifies seasonal changes of time, the agricultural calendar, and the seasons of human life and death, as well as commemorating events in the life of the founder and history of the tradition. In Japan, for example, seasonal celebrations include New Year's Day; the heralding of Spring on Feb. 3; the Spring and Fall equinox on March 21 and Sept. 23; Buddhist Memorial Day for the spirits of deceased ancestors (o-bon) on July 15; and a Buddhist Thanksgiving Day sometime in the summer. In Thailand the New Year celebration (songkran) falls in the middle of April at the end of the dry season just prior to the coming of the monsoon rains. Although Buddhist temples and monasteries are the site of many New Year ceremonies, the New Year festival, as in Tibet and Japan, seems to have more to do with good luck and a healthy life in the year to come than a specifically Buddhist significance. Various elements of the New Year celebration are obviously intended as acts of sympathetic magic to abet the onset of the monsoon rains necessary for the planting of the rice crop.

Buddhism also sanctifies passage times in the lives of individuals as well as communities, especially death or the end of life. Buddhism throughout Asia has been most consistently connected with death rituals. In China and Japan where **Confucianism** and **Taoism** have competed with Buddhism, funerals and death anniversary celebrations are particularly associated with Buddhist temples. In Theravada countries of South East Asia, funerals are more closely associated with Buddhism than are birth ceremonies or weddings.

Death rituals ease the loss of the deceased for survivors, serve to reinforce the teachings of a particular religion regarding death and the afterlife, and bring together family members and friends who may live apart. Buddhist funerals contain all these elements. In China and Japan they serve to propitiate the spirits of the deceased so they will be happy and not punish those relatives still living. In South East Asian Buddhist countries the funeral is an opportunity to honor the deceased as well as to gain spiritual merit for the living and the dead.

In addition to sanctifying passages times of life for individuals and communities, Buddhism has also defined meaningful patterns of social action. It has upheld the virtues of equanimity and generosity, loving kindness towards humans and animals, and has valued honesty and uprightness. In China, Korea, and Japan the ideas of Buddhist social ethics have competed with Confucianism, and in South and South East Asia Buddhist moral ideals have complemented Brahmanical traditions. In the contemporary period Buddhist leaders such as the Dalai Lama have spoken out on issues of international moment including the destruction of the environment, the exploitation of women and children, the inhumane treatment of labourers, and the world's Aids epidemic. Others such as the Vietnamese Zen monk, Thich Nhat Hahn, have sought to build communities of people who fashion an integrated lifestyle of spiritual discipline and effective social action.

Like other great world religions—Judaism, Christianity, Islam, Hinduism—Buddhism's fortunes as a religion have been closely connected with the state. Buddhism formulated classical conceptions of kingship in the Indianized states of Sri Lanka, Myanmar (Burma), Thailand, Laos, and Cambodia. The Buddhist world view legitimated the king as maintainer of the political, economic, social, and moral orders. The historical model for the mythic Buddhist world ruler was the great Indian monarch, Ashoka (third century BCE) who established hegemony over virtually the entire Indian sub-continent. The quality of later Buddhist rulers—Sinhalese, Burmese, Thai, Lao—was measured by the idealized rule of this strong, righteous, benevolent monarch who, according to the *Mahavamsa* and other Buddhist chronicles, created a welfare state dedicated to the pursuit of religious and humanitarian goals. This ideal has also been operative in the development of the modern nation-state, and still functions as a moral norm for political leadership.

In China, Korea, and Japan, Buddhism competed with **Confucianism** for influence in defining policy as well as influencing court politics. By the end of the ninth century in China the political and economic power of Buddhist monasteries led to an attempt to disestablish the tradition; in eighth century Japan the disruptive political and military power of the Buddhist monasteries in the hills surrounding the ancient city of Nara prompted the emperor to moved the capital to Kyoto; and by the 13th century Tibet had become a Buddhist theocratic state. In short, Buddhism was a major factor in the historical development of the classical states in virtually all mainland South, South East, Central and East Asian countries.

In the modern period the fortunes of Buddhism in various Asian countries have been determined by three major factors: the policies of political régimes, economic and social change, and educational and cultural transformation. Buddhism played a major role in the nationalist resistance to Western colonialism in Sri Lanka and Burma in the late 19th and early 20th centuries. In Vietnam Buddhist protests against the Diem régime as a Catholic police state contributed to Diem's downfall in 1963. The efforts of the **Unified Buddhist Church** to forge a middle way between the policies of China, the Soviet Union, and the United States proved to be ineffective against the unsuccessful US policy to forge a military solution to the conflict. In Thailand support of Buddhism has been a major element in the government's efforts to fashion various nation-building programmes. In Japan, the **Komeito Party,** Japan's third largest political force, is affiliated with the **Soka Gakkai,** a lay organization connected with the **Nichirenshoshu** sect of Japanese Buddhism.

Politically repressive states have undermined Buddhist institutions as in the case of Mao's China and Pol Pot's Cambodia. Mao and Pol Pot saw Buddhism in traditional Marxist terms as a justification of class exploitation and, therefore, as something to be attacked, or, in the extreme case of Cambodia, to be destroyed. Tibetan Buddhist leaders have been in exile in India since the Chinese occupation of that country in 1959. The Dalai Lama has appealed to Western democracies to exert pressure on China to stop what he, and many independent observers, consider to be the cultural genocide of his country.

Classical Asian Buddhism emerged institutionally in relationship to the monarchical state, on the one hand, and a subsistence, village economy on the other. Buddhism has had some difficulty redefining itself in a modern nation-state, urban, increasingly industrialized, world-market economic environment. In this environment Buddhist leaders have sought to create a viable social ethic which speaks with relevance to an increasingly threatened and threatening world. One of the most interesting aspects of this "engaged Buddhism" is its international character.

Today, a new world Buddhism is emerging. Westerners have been interested in Buddhism since the 19th century. Western Buddhist organizations such as the **Buddhist Society of Great Britain and Ireland** were established by men and women who had first-hand acquaintance with Buddhism in Sri Lanka and other countries. Asian Buddhists have also sponsored organizations in the West for decades primarily for their own constituencies, for example the **Buddhist Churches of America.** In the past 30 years however, the picture has changed dramatically partially as a result of sizeable expatriate Buddhist populations who have settled in the West, among whom Tibetans, Lao, Cambodians, but largely as a consequence of a more extensive interaction between Asian and Western Buddhists. Westerners are joining Buddhist communities in Asia in increasing numbers and hundreds of Buddhist monasteries and temples are being built in America and Europe. The Asian-based **World Fellowship of Buddhists** has recently been complemented by the founding of the **International Network of Engaged Buddhists,** a group of Western and Asian Buddhists with a decidedly social activist stance.

A new international Buddhist leadership is emerging—both lay and monastic—which is fashioning a relevant Buddhist spirituality rooted in personal disciplines like meditation coupled with a Buddhist social ethic focused on particular economic, social, and political issues. Generally speaking, this international engaged Buddhism has been critical of the exploitation of the Third World by Western nations. They have joined with concerned religious activists from other religious traditions to work for balanced, humane, and less exploitative forms of development which are more respectful of the cultural, religious, and natural environments of all nations. This broad ecumenical activism represents a crucial voice in a world society increasing determined by economic values and characterized by racial and ethnic violence.

Donald K. Swearer

HINDUISM

By common consent, the four *Vedas* are regarded as attesting the earliest extant form of Hinduism, that were brought into India by the Aryans some time between 1500 and 1000 BCE. The *Vedas* actually comprise hymns of praise and invocation to a wide range of deities but are arranged according to the requirements of an elaborate sacrificial ritual. This is typified by the opening words of the *Rigveda* invoking Agni, the god of fire, whose importance in the ritual as the priestly deity leads to his gaining priority in the ordering of the hymns over Indra, the most frequently invoked of Vedic deities in the *Rigveda,* which provides the earliest and probably the clearest view of the Vedic pantheon. There is from the beginning a blending of more abstract, intellectual elements in the sacrificial ritual with the more personal worship of various gods; I would argue that this is the origin of the tension between the more impersonal and the more theistic trends within Hinduism, the resolution of which tension is repeatedly attempted by the successive new movements arising within the whole.

As the ritual became more elaborate (a trend already visible in later parts of the *Rigveda*), the functions of the various priests were increasingly differentiated, as shown by the *Samaveda* and *Yajurveda* (compiled for the use of the chanting and sacrificing priests respectively) with greater emphasis on the mechanics of the sacrifice itself rather than on the deities to whom it was offered. This shift to a more impersonal pattern takes a slightly different form in the tenth book of the *Rigveda,* with some hymns pondering the nature of the universe and man's place in it. But overall its emphasis is still on the creative function of sacrifice, revealing the continuing links between the ritualistic and speculative approaches. In the *Atharvaveda* also there is a definite speculative element, and it is interesting to note its use of the term *brahman* to denote both its own incantations and the universal principle.

The next stage of the Vedic literature consists of the *Brahmanas,* whose prime task is to expound *brahman,* here the sacred power especially manifested in the sacrificial ritual. As the Vedic term *rta* for the fundamental laws of the universe inherent in the nature of things is replaced by the term *dharma,* so too these fundamental laws came more and more to be equated with the laws of sacrifice. Thus *dharma* in the *Brahmanas* means especially the sacrificial act which in effect conditions and maintains the cosmic order, for the idea found in some later Vedic hymns that sacrifice created the world has developed into the view that the correct performance of sacrifice regulates the maintenance of the world. Consequently, the gods to whom the sacrifices were made became increasingly irrelevant, although certain deities more intimately connected with the ritual and its symbolism became more prominent.

The trend to abstract thought is still more apparent in the older *Upanishads,* which can also be seen as natural continuations of the speculative hymns of the tenth book of the *Rigveda* and of the *Atharvaveda,* while their propensity to link one line of speculation with another is inherited from the elaborate classifications of the *Brahmanas.* Speculation centres on *brahman,* by now seen not just as the power underlying the sacrifice but also as that underlying the universe, and on *atman,* the permanent self or soul lying within the individual; the identification of *atman* with *brahman* may be regarded as the outcome of the same outlook as the systems of correspondences so prominent in the *Brahmanas.* Thus the tendency to abstraction and speculation leads to the emergence of the characteristic impersonal strand in Hinduism which is based on such Upanishadic insights.

Nevertheless, in subsequent *Upanishads,* beginning with the *Isa Upanishad,* there emerges a more theistic trend. Even in the *Katha Upanishad,* with the god of death, Yama, as its teacher, there is a more personal element, which in the *Svetasvatara Upanishad* is subsumed in its theistic emphasis, for it seeks to establish the existence and supremacy of a personal deity on the basis of older Vedic texts, an example already of the way in which developing Hinduism appeals to older authority and at the same time reinterprets it.

This trend towards a theistic outlook, already in these *Upanishads* focusing on Vishnu and Shiva, is seen more fully elsewhere, for the two Sanskrit epics, the *Mahabharata* and the *Ramayana,* are a major source for our understanding of the substantial transformation now occurring. This is particularly interesting since they belong in their origins to the culture of the rulers and no doubt reflect their different outlook on religion. In their earliest layers Indra is still the most prominent and frequently mentioned deity, as the natural standard of comparison for kings and heroes. Slightly later, Brahma becomes more significant, being essentially a fusion of a creator deity with the impersonal absolute, the *brahman* of the *Upanisads,* in a more popular and so personalized form. In their later stages, however, both epics testify to the supremacy of Vishnu and Shiva, although, since ultimately they became Vaishnava works with the identification of one of their main figures (Krishna and Rama respectively) as *avataras* or incarnations of Vishnu, the **Vaishnava** emphasis tends to outweigh the **Shaiva.** In particular, Krishna expounds to Arjuna, one of the *Mahabharata* heroes, a doctrine of action without attachment and of devotion to the deity in the *Bhagavadgita,* which has become one of the favourite texts among Hindus.

The period of the rise of Vaishnavism and Shaivism was, broadly speaking, the most divergent time in Indian religious history, being also the heyday of **Buddhism, Jainism** and other heterodox movements. Already in the *Upanishads,* among the individuals of varied backgrounds who contributed to the debates, were some who had renounced society for life in the forest. Such wandering ascetics, whether singly or in loose groupings, were obviously highly significant for the emergence of the heterodox movements. The existence of considerable numbers of those who had thus rejected society suggests a considerable *malaise* at the period, as does the note of pessimism seen for example in the *Maitri Upanishad* as well as in some aspects of Buddhism; this was the period of the rise of the great states in North India, especially Magadha, with an attendant breakdown of the older way of life. Yet, despite the rejection not only of society but also of much of tradition, underlying the various forms of asceticism now popular we still find the same concern for power and control over the universe which is so basic to the Brahmanas. Equally, it is striking that Buddhism and Jainism accept as axiomatic the belief in *samsara,* the cycle of transmigration and rebirth, which appears in the oldest Upanisads as a novel and esoteric doctrine, along with its corollary in the view of the goal as release from this cycle, *moksa.* Whereas Buddhism later virtually disappeared from India (though becoming dominant in Sri Lanka and spreading through much of Asia), Jainism has survived within India as a significant minority religion. Jain doctrines of the nature of the self's bondage to the world are distinctive, since they say that the cause of bondage is *karma,* is the product of all activity and is a real but subtle substance holding down the self and preventing it resuming its rightful state of free and inactive existence in the state of isolation, which is the usual Jain way of regarding *moksa.* Release can only be achieved by burning off this *karma* by extremes of asceticism, while avoiding its accumulation by various measures including the absolute observance of *ahimsa,* non-violence. The oldest division within Jainism, which may possibly reflect to some extent differences in the teachings of Parsva and Mahavira (the last two and probably the only historical figures among their 24 *Jinas* or Conquerors), is that between the **Svetambara** and **Digambara** sects, but subsequently reform movements such as the **Sthanakvasis** and **Therapanthis** have emerged.

The critical attitude towards all authority so apparent in early Buddhism and Jainism led to the rejection of claims to absolute authority for the *Vedas* or a special status for all brahmans as the class of religious specialists regardless of their qualifications. To this extent these two religions may be seen as a popular reaction to the exaggerated claims made for the status of *brahmans* in some passages of the *Brahmanas*; rather than acting as mediators they had tended to become barriers to the religious aspirations of others, and hence the reaction. The effect of these and similar strictures must have been considerable in forcing a critical reappraisal of more orthodox forms of religion. The response included particularly the formulation of an orthodox synthesis in the *Dharmashastras,* with their emphasis on the duties of station and stage of life (*varnashramadharma*), and the development of the six systems of Hindu thought, with their logical and investigative approaches harnessed to a defence of orthodox values. The *Dharmashastras,* unlike earlier texts on *dharma,* were not tied to a particular group but instead aimed at laying down rules which were valid for the whole of society. They developed from the older social model of the *varnas* (the four classes, which had in the course of time in any case become self-contained hereditary groupings) an elaborate and artificial scheme of mixed marriages and assigned the various offspring to different rungs on the social ladder, in order to account for the actual social realities of their time, which comprised a multitude of separate, hierarchically ranked groups—often occupationally based—which are recognisably the predecessors of modern castes (*jatis*).

The other aspect of the emphasis on the duties of station and stage of life is the formulation of the stages (*ashramas*) into a definite system. Earlier texts had either regarded these *ashramas* as simply alternative life-styles or had rejected them altogether. With the growing importance of renunciation (seen in the rise of Buddhism and Jainism, as well as in the *Upanishads*), both these attitudes were impractical and so the concept of the successive stages was evolved: one could become a renouncer, a *samnyasin,* only after passing through the other three stages of life. At the same time, the main emphasis was placed on the householder stage as the main stage of life, when one's religious and social obligations were fulfilled, with the studentship stage being when the young boy learned his obligation to society, *dharma,* and its practical expression.

The development of the six systems of Hindu philosophy out of various earlier speculations similarly consolidated and formalized trends of thought from the *Upanishads* and elsewhere to provide definite schools of thought with which to counter the doctrines of the heterodox movements. The logical enquiry of the *Nyaya* system can be traced back to the rationalism of, for example, some late Vedic hymns; although its early texts show a relative aloofness from religious questions, the lengthy conflict with Buddhist epistemology prompted an increasingly theistic outlook. So too the *Vaisesika* system was increasingly drawn into a defence of orthodox views against the criticisms of Buddhist logicians, while its basic outlook may be seen as an outcome of the investigation of creation in other late Vedic hymns. The *Samkhya* system can on the one hand be linked with the concern for enumeration and classification seen in the *Brahmanas* and on the other hand has a general resemblance to Jainism in its rigid dualism and fundamental atheism. The *Yoga* system may perhaps be traced back into the Vedic literature but also has similarities to the meditative techniques of Buddhism. Although both *Samkhya* and *Yoga* are found in the *Upanishads*, it is significant that much of the evidence for their early history comes from the *Mahabharata* with its *kshatriya* (ruler, warrior) origins and it is likely that to some extent they originated from the same background as the heterodox faiths but grew towards rather than away from orthodoxy to form in the long run two of the most significant strands in developed theistic Hinduism. The remaining two schools were always directly part of the brahmanical tradition and based on Vedic literature. Whereas *Mimamsa* is based on the *Brahmanas* and is concerned with activity to the exclusion of the deities towards whom the ritual was nominally directed, the *Vedanta* derives from the *Upanishads* and is concerned with knowledge or insight; within it, over the centuries, we see exemplified the continuing creative tension between the impersonal and the theistic in the emergence of the **Advaita, Vishishtadvaita, Dvaita** and other schools.

Over broadly the same period the worship of Vishnu or Shiva as supreme deity developed into fully organized sects. Much of the evidence for this period of the development of Hinduism comes from the *Puranas,* the voluminous compendia of popular Hinduism which in many respects continue where the two epics, the *Mahabharata* and the *Ramayana,* left off. Though composed and edited by *brahmans,* the *Puranas* are very much an expression of popular religion, demonstrating how the *brahmans* have in fact maintained their position as guardians and transmitters of the religious tradition by being receptive, however reluctantly, to innovations which gained a significant following. Indeed, the more popular form of Hinduism from the Gupta period (4th–6th century) onwards has often been called Puranic Hinduism, while they also reflect the growing strength of the sects, since most *Puranas* now have a definite *Vaishnava* or *Shaiva* orientation. However, less sectarian forms of the religion persisted alongside the sects, though increasingly influenced by them; for example, the **Smartas** (who by that name claim to follow *smrti,* the collective term for the traditional literature following the *Vedas*), while worshipping a group of five gods (Vishnu, Shiva, Devi, Surya and Ganesha), also accept Shankara's *Advaita Vedanta.*

Within Vaishnavism the earlier Bhagavata movement gave way to the developed Pancaratra sect, but the more traditionalist **Vaikhanasa** sect continued with less apparent change, although the process by which this sub-school of the Black Yajurveda evolved into an orthodox *Vaishnava* sect is still not entirely clear. Within Shaivism, the originally unorthodox *Pasupata* sect established by Lakulisa developed links with the *Nyaya* system in due course and eventually, it seems, evolved into the *Kalamukhas,* while the more extreme practices of the skull-bearing *Kapalikas* appear to have enjoyed something of a vogue around the seventh century CE. More generally in Shaivism the *Shaiva* scriptures, the *Agamas,* tended effectively to supersede the *Vedas* on the grounds that they contain the essential truths of the *Vedas* in a form more accessible to all; this is therefore in theory a supersession by "completion" rather than rejection. The more intellectual side of Shaivism at this period is represented by **Kashmir Shaivism** or the **Trika** system, originating by the ninth century, which puts forward a monistic viewpoint in some ways similar to Advaita Vedanta: Shiva is the *atman* of the entire universe, the supreme experiencer, whose essence is pure consciousness, and creation is the self-projection of consciousness. The bondage of individual selves is caused by ignorance of reality, and recognition of man's identity with Shiva brings release. Side by side with the development of Vaishnavism and Shaivism there grew the worship of the goddess, Devi, in various forms, of which the most characteristic but least orthodox was **Tantrism,** the combination of ritualistic worship (including several practices abhorrent to orthodoxy) and magical practices to achieve both spiritual advance and worldly powers, of which the nomenclature is, perhaps deliberately, unclear; the main division is usually between **Samaya** and **Kaula.**

The *bhakti* movement which began to flourish in South India from about the seventh century incorporates an unmistakable element of opposition to the *brahmans* as custodians of the Vedic tradition. Yet its characteristic emphasis on a personal relationship between the deity and the devotee revitalized Hinduism and, though finally undermining the older ritualistic pattern, made worship a fervent emotional experience in response to divine grace. The involvement of individuals from various backgrounds and both sexes in the poetry of the movement is interestingly reminiscent of the social composition of the Vedic poets (who included not only some who followed other occupations than those characteristic of the *brahman* class but also a few women), but in reality it is partly a popular protest against the exclusiveness of the *brahmans* of the day. Though largely popular in origin, the *bhakti* movement felt increasing brahmanical influence from the time of the codification of the poems of the *Vaishnava Alvars* and the *Shaiva Nayanmars.* Such collection of their spontaneous and unsystematic responses to the love of their god was just the preliminary to the inevitable emergence of doctrinal systems based on them—the **Shaiva Siddhanta** and the **Sri Vaishnavas** associated especially with the name of Ramanuja. Ramanuja's use of Sanskrit for all his works also marks a move away from the Alvars' use of Tamil in the interests of a wider and more traditional audience.

With the spread of the *bhakti* movement from Tamilnad into the adjacent linguistic areas of South India, other movements sprang up. In Karnataka Basava emerged in the middle of the 12th century as a major social reformer and the founder of the **Lingayat** or **Virashaiva** sect. Though born into a Shaiva *brahman* family, Basava became increasingly alienated from traditional religious and social practices, beginning with the initiation ceremony forced on him at the age of eight. At sixteen he discarded his sacred thread and was thrown out of his home in consequence. Subsequently, when he founded his new movement, Basava institutionalized his rejection of the authority of the *Vedas* and of *brahmans*, replacing the sacred thread worn by *brahmans* alone with the *linga,* worn by all Virashaivas of any caste and either sex. All wearers of the *linga* are equal and there is a pronounced egalitarian emphasis in all Basava's teachings. Yet, despite his rejection of the Vedas and the caste system, along with so many other characteristic features of traditional Hinduism, the Virashaivas have remained a part, though admittedly an unorthodox part, of Hinduism.

As the *bhakti* movement spread northwards, the next major manifestation was the **Warkaris** or **Varkari Panth** of Maharashtra, which also had definite egalitarian tendencies, but without Basava's rejection of brahmanical claims. It has several noteworthy features, in addition to the pilgrimage from which it takes its name, among them the revaluation of the householder status and attendant depreciation of renunciation for its own sake; within its annual (or more frequent) pilgrimages to Pandharpur, caste distinctions are minimised in a way not uncommon in the *bhakti* tradition.

Ramananda, the first major figure of Vaishnava *bhakti* in North India, established a popular movement teaching in Hindi instead of Sanskrit and disregarding caste by admitting all devotees as equals; his followers, the **Ramanandis,** worship Rama as the supreme deity, along with his wife Sita, and have developed a temple-dwelling order of *sadhus,* "holy men". Kabir, traditionally a disciple of Ramananda, shows a still more emphatic rejection of all traditional practices, for he sees the only true religion as lying in the inner experience to which a barrier is formed by all that is external and mechanical, symbolized for him very much in the *brahman* dominance of Hinduism and the *ulama*'s hold on Islam. There is little doubt that at this period of pressure from Islam there was not a little to criticize in traditional *brahman* practices, as the similar strictures of the **Sikh** founder Guru Nanak testify, but equally in time the *brahmans* adapted to the changed situation and maintained their religious leadership. Guru Nanak (1469–1539) preached a message broadly similar to Kabir's, one which is commonly claimed as a synthesis of Hinduism and Islam but which is closest to the *bhakti* tradition. Indeed, in its early years the Sikh religion was not markedly different from other *bhakti* groups, such as the **Kabirpanthis** based on the teachings of Kabir or the **Dadupanthis,** who followed Dadu Dayal (1545–1604). It was given its distinctive identity by the tenth Guru Gobind Singh (1675–1708), who introduced the reforms which distinguished the **Khalsa Sikhs** (also called **kesadhari** from their long hair) from those who continued in the earlier pattern, the **Sahajdharis;** indeed, Sikhism has been more subject to internal dispute than its public image suggests.

Most of the innovators within Hinduism in North India at this period were Vaishnavas, but one should not overlook the popularity of the **Nath cult,** through which tantric ideas and vocabulary became widely current. In its development the Nath cult was undoubtedly indebted to Shaiva and tantric beliefs; in its emphasis on the inward discipline of **Hathayoga** it rejects external rituals, caste distinctions and sacred texts in a manner similar to Kabir and Nanak. But then the Nath cult and the **Sufi** orders of Islam were two of the formative influences which modified Vaishnava *bhakti* into the **Sant** tradition, of which Kabir is one of the major figures and Ravidas is another of contemporary significance, since the modern **Ravidasis** use him as their champion against discrimination. Even less orthodox than the Nath Yogis are the **Aghoris,** notorious for demonstrating their indifference to all worldly conventions by eating anything that comes their way, even—according to popular belief—human corpses.

A more traditional *bhakti* approach is seen in the movements founded by Vallabha (1479–1531) and Chaitanya (1486–1533), which however share a strong erotic flavour in their devotion to Krishna, unlike the poetry of the Rajput princess Mirabai. According to Vaishnava theologians, Vallabha's followers belong to the **Rudrasampradaya,** whereas Chaitanya's followers do not strictly form a *sampradaya* but are commonly known as the **Gaudiyasampradaya.** Both groups were much concerned with the recognition and development of Vrndavana as a temple and pilgrimage centre. Chaitanya became personally acquainted with songs of praise to Krishna among a group of devotees meeting nightly in Nadiya and he developed out of them the methods of chanting and singing (*kirtana*) which became such a feature of his sect and such a factor in its spread; his emotional approach to religion is particularly marked. Another influence on Chaitanya was the **Sahajiya** movement, which allies a tantric approach with an erotic Vaishnavism and an emphasis on spontaneity in religion; in more recent times the **Bauls,** a group of wandering religious singers, though claiming Chaitanya as their founder, are closer to this approach. The **Pushtimarga** of Vallabha developed a strong aesthetic tendency exemplified in the group of poets known as the Eight Seals, among whom traditionally is counted Surdas. Surdas is in fact the outstanding poet of Krishna-*bhakti* in Hindi, just as Tulsidas is the most notable poet of Rama-*bhakti*.

The response to Muslim rule seems largely to have consisted of such popular devotional aspects as those just surveyed. The impact of British rule, with its attendant Westernization, brought a different set of responses, in which the aspects of social reform and political awareness mingled with the purely religious aspects. The first such movement, the **Brahmo Samaj,** was founded in Bengal by Ram Mohan Roy, who was primarily a social reformer, campaigning against the practice of *sati* (widow-burning) and child marriage. Nevertheless, he regularly appealed to tradition and proclaimed his intention as being to restore the ancient tradition of *dharma* by removing the senseless accretions of later times, quoting from the *Dharmashastras* in support of his social campaigns. In religious matters he advocated a return to the rational approach which he saw as the keynote of the *Upanishads*. In Maharashtra the equivalent body was the **Prarthana Samaj,** which favoured the hymns of the Varkari Panth poets for worship and, under M. G. Ranade (1842–1901), devoted itself mainly to social reform.

Return to the basic scriptures is still more clearly a feature of the **Arya Samaj** established by Swami Dayananda Sarasvati, who rejected what he termed the falsehoods of Puranic Hinduism and indeed everything subsequent to the *Vedas,* which he regarded as the sole source of Hinduism and proceeded to interpret in his own "yogic" manner. In his efforts to check the stream of conversions to Islam and Christianity, especially among low-caste Hindus, he evolved a ritual for the readmission of such converts to Hinduism on the basis of procedures laid down in the *Dharmashastras*; this became a major feature of Arya Samaj activity. It also developed quite close links with the **Hindu Mahasabha,** an ultra-orthodox political group, which later became notorious because Mahatma Gandhi's assassin belonged to it. Gandhi is perhaps usually thought of as a political and social reformer, but the religious basis of all his activities is undeniable and in a way links with the reassertion of self-esteem and the call for social service seen in Vivekananda's utterances. The call to social awareness and political self-respect is firmly based nonetheless on traditional values, a point which goes far to explain the many apparent paradoxes of Mahatma Gandhi's life. Even his championing of the Harijans, as he termed the untouchables, has its antecedents in the *bhakti* tradition.

The **Ramakrishna Mission,** under the leadership of Swami Vivekananda, also emphasized the antiquity of Hinduism and claimed as its basis the *Upanishads,* though in practice reformulating Shankara's *Advaita Vedanta* in a more inclusivistic and syncretistic fashion. Similarly, **Aurobindo**'s writings represent a new humanistic interpretation of the *Yoga* system with considerable tantric elements, although he claims that his Integral Yoga stems from the *Rigveda,* the *Upanishads* and the *Bhagavadgita*; certainly he admired Dayananda Sarasvati for his attempt "to re-establish the *Veda* as a living scripture". Originally, Aurobindo had been heavily involved with the Indian nationalist movement but after 1910 shifted from politics to religion—the reverse of what was happening with the Arya Samaj—and established his ashram at Pondicherry, assisted by "the Mother", who continued to run it after his death.

With the achievement of Indian independence, the emphasis changed again, with the stress on social service being subordinated to a reassertion of the spiritual values and intellectual respectability of Hinduism, although the element of political awareness persisted in the new form of the emergence over the years of various Hindu revivalist parties. In addition, a number of movements deriving more or less directly from Hinduism have established themselves in the Western world: the **International Society for Krishna Consciousness (ISKCON,** more popularly known as the **Hare Krishna movement**), the **Divine Life Mission,** the **Divine Light Mission, Ananda Marg, Transcendental Meditation,** the followers of **Satya Sai Baba** or of **Rajneesh** and so on. Most of these movements belong to the monistic or non-theistic strands of Hindu thought, but the Hare Krishna movement has a firmly theistic background.

With its singing and dancing on the streets the Hare Krishna movement has clearly been the most conspicuous of these groups. It is basically a branch of the Gaudiyasampradaya established by Chaitanya and in most respects is impeccably orthodox by the standards of that *bhakti* tradition, as is shown by the extent to which ISKCON has been accepted as a spokesman for Hinduism by Hindus living abroad. The movement was taken overseas by A. C. Bhaktivedanta Swami in 1965, a disciple of the leader of the **Gaudiya Vaishnava Mission** (established in 1886 as a means to propagate belief in Caitanya), who first prompted him to consider spreading the message of Krishna beyond India. The nature of its recruitment in the West has meant that many new members were from Christian or semi-Christian backgrounds and this may well be one factor in its more missionary stance, if such devotees' experience of Vaishnavism has been influenced by attitudes continued subconsciously from that background. One feature of ISKCON has been its conservative and even reactionary nature, which seems to have appealed to a number who were disenchanted with various aspects of the modern West, since the anti-scientific and anti-intellectual aspects of its message suggest a return to the past.

The Divine Life Mission established by Shivananda, though claiming to be a synthesis of the fundamentals of all religions, is based mainly on *Advaita Vedanta* and Shivananda's way of life was broadly that of a traditional renouncer; it has, however, become a world-wide organization. Similarly **Ramana Maharshi**'s ideas came largely from *Advaita Vedanta* but he did not seek to found a movement, although attracting interest from a number of Westerners. Satya Sai Baba represents more the pattern of the traditional, wonder-working guru (claiming also to re-incarnate an earlier figure, Sai Baba of Shirdi) and attracts devotees from well beyond India.

Other movements of Hindu origin exported to the West belong less to the mainstream of Hindu belief and practice. The Divine Light Mission, which gained prominence in the early 1970s with its then teenaged guru, Maharaj Ji, and showed some traditional features (the authority figure of the guru, ecstatic and erotic devotion towards Krishna, and the linking of the two), has since become the less obviously Hindu **Elan Vital.** The Ananda Marg, founded in 1955 by Anandamurti (1923–90), fuses tantric Yoga with Marxist ideas and its reputation for authoritarianism is shown by allegations that the movement murdered followers who wished to leave. Transcendental Meditation (introduced to the West in 1958), though projecting a purely secular and even scientific image as basically a relaxation technique, is based on a rather literalist interpretation of Yoga concepts; its founder, Maharishi Mahesh Yogi, creator of the **Science of Creative Intelligence**, enjoyed a considerable vogue for a time. Bhagwan Shree Rajneesh too attracted numbers of Western hippies to his ashram in Poona during the 1970s with his message of yogic spirituality and the therapeutic value of free sexual expression; after he transferred his activities to Oregon in 1981 he never had quite the same success and in due course he was deported from the United States and died in 1990.

Another aspect of the changing face of Hinduism has been the migration of Hindus abroad in sizeable numbers and the consequences of this for their religious practice. In particular, there has been a shift from the home to the temple as the main focus of religion. While the majority of Hindu temples in Britain are based on mainstream Hindu practice (*sanatan mandirs* or temples), others represent different organizations (such as the **Swaminarayan Hindu Mission,** the **Satya Sai Baba Fellowship** or ISKCON). Several temples are affiliated to the **National Council of Hindu Temples,** a co-ordinating body within Britain, and to the **Vishwa Hindu Parishad,** an international Hindu organization which has links with the right-wing Hindu party, the **Bharatiya Janata Party.**

Other political parties which have been founded on a more or less explicitly religious platform, thereby challenging the secularism espoused by Nehru and so by the Congress Party, include the **Ram Rajya Parishad,** founded in 1948 by Swami Karapatri, the **Jana Sangh Party** with its associated **Rashtriya Svayamsevak Sangh,** and the **Shiva Sena,** formed in 1966 as a Maratha nationalist party. The most directly religious is the Ram Rajya Parishad which harks back to the glorious rule of Rama, the hero of the *Ramayana* and *avatara* of Vishnu, and adopts a distinctly chauvinistic attitude to anything foreign. It has been rather eclipsed by the rise of the Bharatiya Janata Party, which achieved considerable publicity over its campaign for the erection of the Ramjanmabhumi temple at Ayodhya to mark the presumed birthplace of Rama in place of the Baburi Masjid (the mosque which replaced an earlier Hindu temple in 1528–9) and whose attitudes to Muslims over the issue led to great communal unrest in 1990–91. It may not be altogether accurate to term this type of development "Hindu fundamentalism" but it has certainly led to an increase in overt intolerance of a kind which till now has been largely absent within Hinduism.

John Brockington

NEW RELIGIOUS MOVEMENTS

Religious groups and organizations such as the **Hare Krishna** movement, the **Moonies, Rajneeshism, Scientology, Transcendental Meditation, Subud,** and a variety of **New Age** groups have become widely known in the West in the last two or three decades. What is not always realized, however, is that they are part of a very much more general trend manifest in virtually all parts of the world, and in relation to which observers have begun to use the designation "new religious movements"—NRMs—as almost a jargon term. The alternative label, "new religions", is simpler but possibly misleading in relation to the size of some of the groups, which can be very small.

That apart, though, not everyone would accept that contemporary movements of this kind are in fact either new, or to be counted as religion. We shall examine these points in a moment. However, let us ask first why it is that the trend in question has emerged.

Why new religions?

While the United States is regarded as the most fertile breeding ground of new religious movements, this should not be allowed to obscure the fact that new religion, although unevenly distributed across the world, is a global phenomenon.

As far as the West is concerned, the emergence of new religions here has been attributed to the self-limiting nature of the secularization process. Religion had been marginalized to such an extent that a reaction set in, leading to its re-emergence, and one of the clearest signs of this are the new religious movements.

Other explanations include the theory that the new movements, especially those of the 1960s, provided answers for alienated youth. In modern society, where economic calculation and materialism predominate, the individual is primarily a role player rather than a total person. As a person, however, the individual has additional facets which require fulfilment, and here lies the appeal of many of the NRMs in the West. They have recognized this requirement, created by modern life, and have marketed their message accordingly.

In addition, several other factors—the links (linguistic, cultural etc.) established with the countries of Asia during the colonial period, the communications revolution, better welfare, educational and travel opportunities (there are today an estimated 1,000,000 young people from western European countries in the Indian sub-continent), and the relative affluence of the post World War II generation—have all contributed to the interest shown in new religious movements by Westerners, who form the bulk of the membership.

However, the appearance of new religions on a global scale cannot all be explained in these ways, for the features identified in relation to the West are not universal. They account in some measure for the rise of numerous Japanese new movements, especially those that have emerged since World War II; but the new religions of Melanesia (e.g. the **cargo cults**), Latin America (e.g. **Umbanda**), the Caribbean (e.g. **Rastafarianism**) and sub-Saharan Africa (e.g. the **Aladura** movements) need to be accounted for differently. The classification suggested by H. W. Turner (Turner, 1979), and outlined below, contains some useful insights in this regard.

Arguably there has never been a time or place without new religion; yet not everyone would accept that contemporary NRMs are in fact either new, or religion. Let us now consider each of these two points in turn.

New Religious Movements: are they new?

The application of the term "new" to present day religions may be contested by both observers and practitioners alike. For example, members of the **International Society for Krishna Consciousness (ISCKON)** have protested that they are the followers of a tradition of spirituality and philosophy that date back to the spiritual guide or guru Chaitanya Mahaprabhu (1486–1534), who is said to have derived his ideas from the *Bhagavad Gita*, written before the beginning of the Christian era. This emphasis on age, continuity and tradition has to be taken seriously for, among other things, it can have important constitutional and legal implications, and even more importantly such attributes constitute for many movements part of the proof that their message is authentic and true, echoing the poet John Donne who in his *Satyre: On Religion* suggested that "though truth and falsehood bee neare twins, yet truth a little elder is".

However, although the claim made by certain movements that they belong to a long and well-established tradition of spirituality, and are not therefore new, should be taken seriously, it does not in itself exclude the possibility of such movements being perceived as new even by those belonging to the tradition in question. Hare Krishna in India was seen, at first, as new, and the **Unification Church** or Moonies has never successfully established its claim to belong to the mainstream of Christianity. The converse, however is also true; movements claiming to be new and giving the appearance of newness but which derive their beliefs, philosophy and spiritual techniques from an old source, may have difficulty in persuading others that they constitute a new form of religiosity.

One way of resolving some of the problems associated with the use of the term "new" might be to use if in a chronological sense. A date of significance in modern history marking a major turning point might be chosen—for example 1945—and all religious movements that arose in a country from that date would be considered new there irrespective of any links with an established religious tradition elsewhere. Thus, if we take 1945 as the starting point for western Europe and the United States, while both the Hare Krishna movement and the Japanese movement **Soka Gakkai**, can each claim to belong to a well established spiritual and philosophical tradition, they are new in these societies.

However, many of the new religions discussed in this volume are "new" in much more than the date of their emergence or of their arrival in a particular society. As P. Heelas has shown, those movements which he classifies as **"Self-Religions"**—among them the Life Training, the Church of the Movement for Inner Spiritual Awareness/**Insight**, Scientology and **est**—although they derive much of their spirituality from old sources, including various forms of Buddhism, are nevertheless new "in that they fuse two domains which we have become accustomed to see as antagonistic" (Heelas, 1991). Moreover, they have moved beyond religion as established in the West in that participants, instead of acknowledging and surrendering to a God who is wholly other, "live 'as' gods". Furthermore, these "Self-Religions" have gone beyond the traditional purposes of psychology by making psychological techniques serve to uncover the "god" within. In these and other ways the "Self-Religions" are at one and the same time vehicles of religious change and continuity.

Although the actual use of the term "new" to refer to Japan's new religions—one of the major areas of proliferation of NRMs globally—raises no problems of a technical nature, in Japan itself in several senses the religions labelled new are likewise not very new in terms of their content. Soka Gakkai is grounded in the Buddhist teachings of the 13th century monk Nichiren Daishonin, and others, among them **Sekai Mahikari Bumei Kyodan** (World True Light Civilization), and **Seicho no Ie** (House of Growth), have deep roots in **Shinto.** As one observer notes, the new religions of Japan are but new combinations of existing teachings, beliefs and spiritual techniques that are deeply embedded in Japanese society. There are also, we may add, outside influences, Seicho no Ie's content having been strongly influenced by 19th and 20th century **New Thought** movements.

The newness of Japanese movements consists essentially in the way they have been able to make old beliefs and practices relevant to the present day. But the Japanese new religions are in several respects modern, at least from a sociological perspective; the fact that they are all lay movements makes them different, as does the unusual amount of emphasis they place on making religion relevant to today's world.

In the United States one can link contemporary interest in Hinduism and oriental religion generally to the past. The American Transcendentalists of the last century were deeply interested in oriental religions, an interest seen in Emerson's poem "Brahma". The appeal, however, was to an upper class, middle-aged, intellectual sector of society in contrast to the appeal of the contemporary new movements that derive their beliefs and practices largely from oriental beliefs and practices. These, at the outset, attracted in the main the young who, though middle class and often well-educated, were also anti-intellectual. The modern movements, moreover, are also more guru-centred and more concerned with the relevance of their spirituality to the world in which they live.

What has been said concerning the *newness* of contemporary new religions can also be applied to the New Age movement. This movement owes a great deal to New Thought, **Christian Science, Swedenborgianism, Theosophy** and Mesmerism. But once again it has done something new with these sources. For example, once the preserve of the few, by the use of modern means of communication the New Age has made esoteric gnosis available to a much wider public. Present day New Age is much more of a popular religion than its 19th and early 20th century predecessors; it has virtually become a kaleidoscope for almost everything in the domain of New Thought that can be construed as post-modern. Further, its attempt to spiritualize the whole of the contemporary social milieu so that it becomes a new religion, its use of the electronic communications network as a means of association among "members," and its endorsement of both the rational and the irrational in the pursuit of self and world transformation, give it a degree of distinctiveness and newness.

Its informal, networking arrangements create immense difficulties for anyone attempting to classify the New Age movement or, perhaps more accurately, movements, for it is not unreasonable to speak of a Christian New Age movement, of a **neo-Pagan** New Age movement and so on.

New Religious Movements: are they religious?

Not only is the label "new" controversial from both an observer's and a participant's perspective, but so also is the application of the term "*religion*" to many of the movements covered in this volume. The problem of finding a suitable definition to apply to all forms of religion is something I have discussed at great length elsewhere, and concluded that such a definition is neither possible or necessarily desirable (Byrne and Clarke, 1992). Here space permits no more than a brief glance at what a limited number of observers and participants think about the ascription of the term "religion" to the movements under discussion.

Some observers have argued that Scientology is more a form of modern magic than a religion, and the same might be said of other movements, among them Mahikari. But there is little agreement among scholars on this matter.

Clearly, many new movements possess many of the features, in terms of beliefs, practices and structures, traditionally associated with religion, and fulfil a number of religious purposes and can, therefore, be regarded as such providing the definition used is sufficiently comprehensive without being too vague as to be of no use. Of course, not all new religious movements seek to be classified as religions, and some even strongly object to the label, among them the Rajneesh movement, at least in its early days, and Transcendental Meditation.

For other movements, being a religion is not a permanent condition, at least not in each and every situation. Some have become religions over a period of time, some are religions in one context but not in another, while others have claimed to be one kind of religion in one context and another kind in another. Thus the situation is extremely fluid.

Their diversity and their spread across so many cultures make new religions as difficult to classify as religion is to define, although there have been some impressive endeavours in this area, among them Wallis' classification of new religious movements on the basis of their response to the world.

Classifying new religions

The diversity of new religions makes classification well nigh impossible. Wallis abandoned any attempt to classify new religions according to their origins—indigenous traditions, imported traditions, and psychological roots—on the grounds that this offered little by way of an understanding of the structure, functioning and sources of support of these movements. He went on to suggest that a better way could be found by examining their orientation to the world around them.

From an examination of their orientation to the world, three types of new religion were identified: world-denying, world-affirming and world-accommodating. The first type of movement, in rejecting the world, awaits or helps to bring about its overall transformation, and this is what Hare Krishna, the Moonies, the **Children of God** and in a special sense the New Age is all about. ("In a special sense" because New Age does not have the communal structure and other characteristics associated by Wallis with the world-rejecting kind of movement, nor does it actively engage in recruitment or manifest that contempt or disrespect for social norms sometimes found in these movements.)

The second type, world-affirming movements, are typically committed to active participation in society and, moreover, are engaged in providing the techniques and spirituality that they claim will enable people to unlock their full potential, something the majority apparently fails to do, and thereby participate with even greater success in the world. Transcendental Meditation, Scientology and many Japanese new movements, including **Perfect Liberty Kyodan** and Soka Gakkai, are of this kind. However, they are not necessarily as materialistic and this-worldly oriented as this terminology may suggest. World-affirming movements can also be concerned with questions of spiritual development *per se* and with such ultimate questions as life after what they would describe as mere physical death, the true self being immortal.

The third of Wallis' types, world-accommodating new religions, include charismatic renewal movements, the **House Churches** and Subud, the latter being a movement of Indonesian Islamic and traditional religious content and very similar in several respects to charismatic renewal movements. Although members of these movements, as in the case of world-affirming movements, remain engaged in the wider society, unlike participants in the latter they turn to religion not for increased worldly success but more out of a desire for that spiritual growth just mentioned. As Wallis states, participants in world-accommodating movements seek "a clear experience of the divine", something they find absent in conventional religious institutions.

Clearly, new religions emerge in very different contexts and tend not only to be highly syncretistic, but to be syncretistic in many different ways, and all of this makes it difficult to classify them in terms of their orientation towards the world. But most of them are millennarian and seek the transformation of society, and this also creates serious difficulties for anyone attempting to classify them in terms of a three-fold typology based on their orientation toward the world. Nevertheless, Wallis' classification sheds light on certain features of new movements despite various criticisms that can with some justification be levelled at it.

Other attempts at classifications of new religious movements such as Turner's are related more to the so called Third World. Covering the last 100 years and more, Turner provides a four-fold classification of new religions in primal societies with special reference to sub-Saharan Africa, this time based largely on content and response to other so-called world religions (Turner, 1979). He begins with what he refers to as neo-primal movements, that is movements attempting to renew traditional religions under Christian influence, for example Godianism in Nigeria.

The next group are Hebraist movements, where faith corresponds to the prophetic religion of Israel and the movements see themselves as descendants of the ancient Israelites. The Rastafarian movement is of this kind, as are, Turner believes, some of the Maori movements in New Zealand such as **Ratana** and **Ringatu**. Turner also speaks of synthetist movements which develop a new religion from traditional and Christian elements, and independent churches which are intentionally Christian but are African-founded and -led and include the Aladura or praying churches of western Africa and the **Zionist** and **Ethiopian** churches of southern Africa.

The category of independent churches may well be applied beyond the context of Africa to churches among North American Indians, or in fact to any new Christocentric religion in a part of the world formerly colonized by European "Christian" powers.

There are numerous examples from the late 19th century of neo-primal, Hebraist, synthetist and independent new movements not only in sub-Saharan Africa but also in Melanesia and elsewhere, although it is worth noting that some regions were more prolific in the creation of these movements than others. Likewise, today there is considerable variation in the number of new religions in western Europe due to history, geography, language, communications and social organization and constitutional arrangements. Finland and Eire, for example, have far fewer new movements than Denmark and the United Kingdom.

In Japan post-World War II new religions have been referred to as "crisis" religions. They arose as responses to the momentous changes in that society to which defeat, occupation, democratization and rebuilding in all areas of life gave rise.

Sources of recruitment

As far as all three of Wallis' types of new religion are concerned the sources of support have changed with time and especially during the past decade. Initially their focus was on the young, those aged between 18 and 35. Now they involve a much wider age range and a much larger social constituency, reaching out beyond the middle classes and the well educated to people of all social backgrounds. Some movements have always been noticeably less class-conscious than others, among them Soka Gakkai, which has drawn its support from a wide range of social and economic groups, albeit mainly from the lower middle and upper working class sectors of society.

Some movements also have an ethnic appeal, for example, the Rastafarian movement, the **Swami Narayan** movement, the **Black Muslim** movement and others. The Rastafarian movement, however, is increasingly attracting members of non-African descent and in this it is not so different from Umbanda in Brazil.

In Brazil and I suspect elsewhere in Latin America a majority of members of new movements come from the ranks of those who have retained strong ties with their non-

Brazilian past. Japanese new movements—among them Soka Gakkai, Seicho no Ie (House of Growth), and **Mahikari**—attract Japanese-Brazilians, often first and second generation descendants of the Japanese who arrived in the country in the early years of this century, principally to work on the coffee plantations in São Paulo. Soka Gakkai also appeals to Brazilian professionals and business people as well as the shop floor manager and skilled worker. Seicho no Ie appeals, it would seem, to a very wide spectrum of Brazilian society but perhaps its main support comes from middle-aged, non-salaried middle-class women, rather than the educated young who, it seems, are increasingly attracted by Kardecian spiritualism (also known as **Kardecism**).

In the West African context the previously mentioned Aladura churches made a strong appeal to women, but in this case it was women in search of specific forms of healing. Like so many of the new movements we are concerned with, the Aladura of western Africa—known as Zionist churches in southern Africa—and many other "new" African churches were founded by prophets and, as Turner points out, might equally appropriately be described as "prophet-healing churches" (Turner, 1989). These churches have not only promoted spiritual healing but also the cause of African leadership in the spheres of religion and culture and at least indirectly in political matters; and this has been a large part of their appeal. Outside Africa, in Europe and the United States, the new black led churches, e.g. the **Church of the Cherubim and Seraphim** or the **New Testament Church of God,** attract in the main the more alienated Africans in exile, or West Indians. However, they are in no sense as exclusivist as the Rastafarian movement once was, or as militant and separatist as the Black Muslim movement.

The wider society's response

The growth of the so called Anti-Cult movement, which comprises numerous voluntary organizations, has contributed to the widespread belief, at least in Europe and the United States, that new religion, if it be religion at all, is bad religion. Likewise in Japan there is a distrust of a number of movements including the Unification Church (Moonies). Among the earlier Japanese anti-cult movements to be founded was the movement calling itself the "Parents of Victims of the Unification Association" which came into existence in 1973. Another, "Parents Opposed", followed in 1975. The Japanese Communist Party is also said to have been a strong opponent of the Unification Church.

Beckford has argued that the mode of insertion into society employed by a movement is a crucial factor in determining the society's response to it. Where the mode of insertion is perceived as oppositional and disruptive of important social institutions such as family and education, then the response of the society in question will usually be hostile, and especially so when the movement is not indigenous. This appears to have happened in the case of the Unification Church in Japan. This church, which is strongly associated through its founder and in other ways with Korea, and therefore automatically suspect in Japan, attempted to establish itself there by recruiting young adults and then withdrawing them from their jobs, colleges and families, thus going against the trend found in indigenous Japanese new religions which was to recruit on a family basis and leave members in their employment. Thus the Unification Church created the impression that its purpose was to usurp the functions of three key socialization agencies—the family, school and workplace. There was, however, opposition to new religions in Japan prior to the arrival of the Unification Church, opposition generated by the aggressive methods of evangelization once used, but later abandoned, by Soka Gakkai.

Anti-cult organizations are not all equally opposed to new religions; they range along a continuum from the strongly opposed groups such as the American Spiritual Counterfeits

Project (SPF) and the British Deo Gloria Outreach (DGO), at least in their early history, to the more tolerant groups such as the British-based Family Action for Information and Rescue (FAIR). Moreover, those who believe that members have been systematically brainwashed and deprived of their freedom, argue for the necessity of, and even justify, kidnapping as a means of rescuing participants from the clutches of new movements, while other groups that disapprove of much that goes on in new religious movements in the name of religion are, nevertheless, opposed in principle to the use of such measures against members.

Centres have also been established for the purpose of researching the new religions, among them the Centre for New Religions at King's College, University of London, the former Centre for New Religions at Selly Oak Colleges, Birmingham—now known as the Interact Research Centre—which focuses on the interaction between local and world religions, the Gurutek in the Faculty of Theology and Missiology at the University of Aarhus in Denmark, the Centre for the Study of New Religions (CESNUR) in Turin, Italy and the Institute for the Study of American Religion at the University of California at Santa Barbara. Scholars, and in particular social scientists, it can be noted in passing, are usually regarded as being more sympathetic to the new religions than the lay person.

Other institutions such as the Dialogue Centre at Aarhus in Denmark, the American Conference on Religious Movements based in Rockville, and INFORM based at the London School of Economics and Political Science, seek to provide the wider public with accurate information and advice.

New religions have received much criticism from many quarters, including the media. Of course, some of them have sought to be noticed without giving much thought to the kind of publicity they might be given, believing that bad publicity is better than no publicity. Litigation has also brought movements to the attention of the wider society, and often in an unfavourable way. An example would be the Unification Church, which was involved in the most costly libel trial to date in the United Kingdom in 1980, and lost. Indeed, after this trial newspapers began to use the term "moon-struck" outside the context of new religions to refer to anyone who was believed to have been unwittingly and unwillingly led astray or deceived. This trial came in the wake of the mass suicide by members of a new movement, the People's Temple, in Jonestown, Guyana in 1979, and not unexpectedly there followed a period of intense hostility among the wider public to new religions.

It would appear that the volume of litigation in the United States over new religions has been greater than anywhere else. In theory, in countries such as the United States there are, constitutionally, no marginal religions; but marginality does in fact exist where new religions are concerned as a result of the popular unacceptability of these movements and the political and social tensions to which they give rise.

Size of membership and impact

There has been much disagreement over the extent and depth of the impact of the contemporary new religions on the wider society. Sometimes they have been dismissed as having done nothing to reverse the process of secularization, while for others they constitute a clear sign of the return of the sacred and provide indisputable evidence that secularization is a self-limiting process.

A number of observers have chosen to assess their impact on the basis of their numerical strength, and discovering that they have attracted a very small percentage of the population, conclude that their impact has been extremely limited. It has even been claimed that the idea that the influence of new religions has been deep and widespread is a media creation and has come about because most of those involved were middle-class, well-educated people with articulate relatives and friends of means who made much of what they perceived as the dangerous effects of these religions.

But if the impact of new religions is going to be decided on the basis of the number of those who have joined, then the difficult question of what actually constitutes membership or belonging to a new religious movement needs to be discussed here, however briefly. Membership of new religions takes many different forms, from full-time to part-time to very loose spiritual, affective and physical links with a community, to nothing more than spiritual and intellectual bonds kept alive through such activities as meditation, the receiving of relevant literature and possibly tithing. Many of Scientology's "members" are simply people who order or are sent its literature. There are even cases where membership is "involuntary"; **Sahaja Yoga** recruits "members" by spiritual contact—sometimes mediated through a glance or a stare—which can result in people becoming members without any knowledge whatsoever that they now belong to a new religion. More often, however, membership is similar to membership of one or the other voluntary organization where levels of commitment and involvement can vary greatly.

The difficulty of determining membership is compounded when we come to the New Age movement which functions on the basis of networking and has no formal membership as such, although various individual movements/organizations within it do. There is also the associated and prickly problem of "syncretism", many new religions accepting the idea of membership of more than one religion at the same time, and this has led to continuing membership of an "old" religion while at the same time participating in a new religion. This writer has frequently encountered this situation among members of, for example, Subud, some of whom are, at one and the same time, Muslims, **Roman Catholics, Anglicans** and so on. One also meets devout Anglican and Catholic Scientologists. Moreover, all Hare Krishna members claim to be orthodox Hindus. By way of contrast, one also finds groups who would appear to be part of an older religious tradition but who draw a clear line between themselves and that tradition; for example there exists a **Sufi** or mystical order in Britain, Beshara, which claims not to be Muslim in any formal sense of the term.

It is probably the case that in the United States and western Europe less than one per cent of the population has at some time in their life been involved in full-time, direct, active commitment to a new religion on a relatively long-term basis, that is two years or more. However, it is also the case that if we include **Tibetan Buddhist** centres in western Europe among new religious movements, these centres are attracting more novices of European birth and education than religious orders such as the **Jesuits,** with a long history, a well developed infrastructure and with access through the media, churches and schools to the wider society. This is the case in the United Kingdom and Germany and perhaps also in France and elsewhere.

Granted the necessity of qualifying the meaning of the term "membership", there are, of course, parts of the world where full-time participation in new religions is by any standards on a large scale. For example, in Japan Soka Gakkai alone has an estimated 18,000,000 members and in Nigeria the Aladura churches have millions of members.

The impact of new religions cannot, however, be adequately assessed solely by reference to statistics of full-time, part-time or any other form of membership, whether these be large or small. It is certainly the case, if we take the question of their impact in the West, that many more people today, as a result of participation in new religious movements, are much more knowledgeable about, and have experience of, a variety of non-Christian spiritualities and techniques than was ever previously the case. Moreover, as a result of media coverage and litigation, among other things, the circle of non-participants in new religions with some knowledge of non-Christian spiritualities and insights is probably far wider than ever before. A wide range of publications on New Age spirituality is available in general bookstores.

Furthermore, members of mainstream religions have taken over and incorporated into their spiritual programmes ideas and techniques pioneered by influential figures in the development of new religions. The enneagram of **Gurdjieff** is but one example of this; it is now used in Catholic circles, particularly in retreats, although the users are not always aware of its origins.

The new religions have had a considerable indirect influence on mainstream Christian churches who, realizing the appeal to the young of meditation and mysticism, have begun to pay greater attention to the mystical and experiential, and less to the social gospel, with a view to attracting support in a world in which faith appears increasingly to be turning inwards.

There is hardly an area of modern life which has not to some extent been affected by new religions, from mainstream church life to management training and business life, and from the law to politics to medicine—especially, but not exclusively, psychology and psychotherapy—to diet and matters of the environment and peace. Not all new religions are madly health-conscious, "green" and "pacifist", but some, among them Soka Gakkai and the **Brahma Kumaris** movements, have made a cleaner environment and non-violence essential prerequisites of serious commitment, and campaign widely for these causes.

Conclusions

New religions either die or become "old" new religions in time. A number of those established in the 1960s and 1970s are already dead or dying, among them Ishvara or Lifewaves in Britain and **Convince** in Jamaica.

The survival of a religion is a question of many things, including the strength or fragility of its content or belief system, and the skill, efficiency and enthusiasm with which it is marketed. Finance, leadership, the methods of recruitment employed and the cultural and political climate are also important factors in the success or failure of a movement.

Among the movements that have survived some have become much more accommodating to the wider society, even defending its main agencies of socialization, including the nuclear family, which they once ridiculed. These movements have taken on the form and structure of established religions or churches. There are also movements which have made the transition over the past 30 years or so from **Human Potential Movement** to religion and/or church and back.

Many new movements have universalistic ambitions. This is certainly true of the Moonies, the **Satya Sai Baba** movement and Soka Gakkai, albeit in different ways. This leads to evangelization on a global scale and the increasing presence, consequently, of many of the new movements discussed in this volume in Eastern Europe, the Soviet Union and the so called Third World. Of course, and, somewhat paradoxically, these same movements now engaged in missionary activity in the Third World once gave the evangelization of the West—said to be advanced technologically and materially but spiritually immature—as the main reason for their presence throughout Europe and the United States.

The future is unclear. In parts of the Third World such as Latin America, evangelical **Protestantism/Pentecostalism** is clearly making most headway. And in several European countries there has been a steady rise in the number of converts to older new movements such as the **Jehovah's Witnesses** and **Mormons**. Although there are indications that it has now peaked, the Witnesses have in the last quarter of a century made spectacular progress in Italy, mainly among the economic migrants from the south of the country who have travelled in search of work to the large industrial cities of the North.

As for the future development of those newer forms of religion which are our principal concern here, New Age—perhaps the nearest thing to post-modernist religion—will perhaps retain its appeal throughout the 1990s, and there may also be a steady growth in Buddhist movements—not, however, in **Zen** as in the 1960s—but in those movements where the approach is both intellectually more rigorous and the spirituality relevant to everyday life in a world that increasingly seeks security legitimation from technology.

References

Byrne, P. and Clarke, P. (1992) *Religion Defined and Explained* (Basingstoke: Macmillan).
Heelas, P. (1991) "Western Europe: Self Religions," in S. Sutherland and P. Clarke (eds) *The Study of Religion: Traditional and New Religion* (London: Routledge).
Turner, H. (1979) *Religious Innovation in Africa* (Boston).
Turner, H. (1989) *Religious Movements in Primal Societies* (Elkhart).
Wallis, R. (1984) *The Elementary Forms of the New Religious Life* (London: Routledge).
Wallis, R. (1991) "North America's New Religions" in S. Sutherland and P. Clarke (eds), op. cit.

Peter B. Clarke

PART II: RELIGIOUS GROUPS AND MOVEMENTS

A

Adat Israel. See **Orthodox Judaism.**

Adventists. There are three main Adventist groups, of which by far the largest is the **Seventh Day Adventists**, so called because they celebrate the "seventh day" i.e. Friday sunset to Saturday sunset, as the day of rest (the other Adventist sects follow the rest of the Christian Church and set aside Sunday for worship).

Adventists trace their origin to William Miller, a Baptist preacher in Massachusetts USA, who in 1836 published a book setting out the results of his Bible studies which had led him to believe that Jesus Christ would come again to earth in 1844 (the "Second Advent"). Many people followed his teaching but when 1844 came and went most fell away. However a few adherents remained and announced that Miller's interpretation of the Bible had been correct, but the event foretold was not Christ's return but the beginning of an investigation in heaven of those who have died, to determine who is worthy of resurrection.

At this time Ellen G. White became influential in the movement as a result of her revelations and prophecies. In 1863 the Adventists organized themselves into a denomination with its headquarters at Battle Creek, Ellen White's home town. The first missionary was sent out in 1874, and the movement began in England in Southampton in 1878 with the work of W. Ing.

Adventists base their beliefs on their interpretation of the Bible. They receive communion four times a year in a service preceded by foot-washing, and practise believers' baptism. Tithing (giving one-tenth of one's income to the church) is expected of all Seventh Day Adventists. Believing that "your body is the temple of the Holy Spirit" (I Corinthians 6.19) they favour vegetarianism and avoid tobacco, alcohol and other drugs.

It was the dietary requirements of the patients in the Adventists own sanatorium at Battle Creek that led a local baker, J. H. Kellogg to provide baked cereal dough as a readily digestible food. The popularity of this was such that his brother, W. K. Kellogg founded a company to manufacture the product and distribute it to a wider market—hence the corn flakes and other breakfast cereals we know today.

Seventh Day Adventists are enthusiastic missionaries and have churches throughout the world. Adventist membership is currently estimated at over 5,000,000. Since 1903 the headquarters has been in Washington DC, USA.

Afkodré. The name Afkodré is taken from the Dutch word for idolatry (*afgoderij*), and is used as an alternative designation for **Winti,** the folk religion of Surinamese Creoles.

African New Religious Movements. There has been a steady increase in the number of New Religious Movements (NRMs) and their adherents since the turn of the century, although NRMs in Africa date back to the 17th century with the Antonian sect in the Kingdom of Congo. The vast majority are in sub-Saharan Africa, where by 1978 there were an estimated 10,000 movements with 10,000,000–12,000,000 active members. They are often messianic or millenarian in character, with prophetic leaders and an emphasis on healing, visions and dreams. The extent to which NRMs engage in political or welfare activities varies, both with regard to one another and within one movement over time. Some are highly fissiparous (such as the **Harris** churches in West Africa), and may decline or dissolve on the death of a charismatic founder (e.g. Alice Lenshina's Lumpa Church in Zambia). Others continue to expand and to adopt structures closer to the pattern of mission churches (e.g. the **Kimbanguist Church** in Zaire).

Attempts have been made to classify African NRMs along a continuum between traditional religion and mission Christianity (their degree of religious syncretism), according to origin, or by reference to organizational and leadership structures. At best such descriptions can only provide a rough guide with few NRMs falling neatly into any one category. Three broad types are commonly recognized: (i) The most numerous and fastest growing are the African Instituted, Independent or Indigenous churches, also known as **Zionist,** prophet-healing or spiritual churches. They are broadly **Pentecostal** in character with an emphasis on charismatic leadership and healing (e.g. the prophetic **Aladura**, Harrist and Kimbanguist churches; the messianic Mai Chaza Church and Johane Masowe's Apostolic Church in Zimbabwe, and the millenarian **Kitawala** (Watch Tower movement); (ii) Separatist, African, Orthodox or **Ethiopian** churches, so called because of their separation from a parent body (usually a mission church) in response to a desire for greater independence and indigenization of leadership, sometimes with accommodation of customs such as polygyny. The Jamaa Movement (Zaire), **Maria Legio** (Kenya) and Catholic Church of the Sacred Heart (Zambia) originated in **Roman Catholic** missions while the Church of Christ in Africa (Kenya), Providence Industrial Mission (Malawi) and the Cameroon **Baptist** Convention separated from **Protestant** bodies. The ancient **Coptic** Church in Ethiopia and Old Testament prophets often provide inspiration for a more African form of Christianity than that offered by the mission churches; (iii) Neo-traditional or syncretist movements which attempt to reform or revive traditional customs while incorporating some Christian (or occasionally Muslim) elements (e.g. the **Bwiti** cult in

Gabon, the Poro and Sande cults among Mande-speakers in West Africa and the National Church of Nigeria).

African Traditional Religions. Traditional religions, Christianity and Islam have coexisted for many centuries in Africa and have frequently interacted, influencing one another's practices and beliefs. The term "African Traditional Religions" (ATRs) is used to refer to the oral religious traditions of peoples who have not subscribed to either of these two "religions of the book", and are found mainly south of the Sahara. The pervasive, implicit nature of African Traditional Religions led some early Western observers to deny the existence of "religion" among peoples without a written tradition. More recently, however, scholars have appreciated that the term "religion" is itself a Western cultural construct. Examples of African "religiosity" abound, but based upon a cosmology in which the entire world can be viewed as a source of power to be held in balance, controlled, checked, and channelled, rather than on Western notions which distinguish between the sacred and secular, natural and supernatural.

There has been some discussion as to whether it is correct to speak of African Traditional Religion, or only of a multitude of different religions. While anthropologists have tended to examine the specificity of particular religious traditions, African theologians have sought to map out the common ground between traditional religions. Geographical, historical, linguistic and social forces have certainly produced a bewildering variety of religious expressions and customs, yet some common characteristics do emerge, particularly regarding underlying attitudes and assumptions about the nature and role of human beings and their place within the world. The comments that follow indicate some features which are common to many ATRs, none of which, however, are ubiquitous, or take precisely the same form in different societies.

African Traditional Religions have been described as forms of "diffused monotheism" or "refracted theism". There is a common belief in a supreme creator, who is generally beneficent and can be petitioned directly in times of crisis, (known as *kwoth* among the Nuer of the Southern Sudan), and may even be associated with a particular sacred place (Mount Meru in Kenya for the **Kikuyu**) but who acts more commonly through intermediaries in the form of lesser divinities, spirits or ancestors. These intermediaries may be regarded as symbols or conceptualizations of the power inherent in the world and in people (as for the Shona of Zimbabwe). For the Uduk, of the Sudan/Ethiopian border, deities emanating from outside, be it from Muslim neighbours, Christian missionaries or Nilotic peoples to the south, can be contrasted to an implicit form of "moral knowledge" based on their experience of the hunt, human existence and mortality and conceptualized as an animating life force (*Arum*), which has become differentiated within the world.

Creation myths commonly relate a time when a creator god lived close to human beings, who were immortal. Through accident, chance, or as a result of human misbehaviour, the creator withdrew from intimate contact with human society and the connection between heaven and earth was severed, introducing mortality. Cosmogonies are usually explanatory— they describe the situation in which human beings find themselves—rather than apportioning blame, suggesting a means of salvation, or the restoration of a primordial state. The world as it is experienced, the reality of life, mortality and regeneration, is the starting point for ritual activity and worship.

The degree of centralization and elaboration of religious authority mirrors the political and economic situation of a particular people. In the medieval centralized kingdoms of West Africa, Zimbabwe and the Sudan, traditions of divine kingship sought accommodation with older more diffuse sources of authority. Among the Yoruba peoples of Nigeria, Benin and Togo, for instance, modern rituals re-enact struggles between local cults and a centralized imperial religion. In agricultural societies the king of chief is often associated with the fertility of the land and will usually sacrifice at a sacred shrine on behalf of his people. For the Zulu of southern Africa fertility is conceptualized as a female deity, who plays an important role in girls' initiation ceremonies in this patrilineal society in which women, through marriage, form a link between clans. Zulu women are also frequently healers and ritual specialists, suited by their social role to mediate also between the spirits and human society, or to repair rifts in the social fabric. Nomadic peoples, such as the **Mbuti** of Zaire, the **Khoisan** peoples of southern and south-west Africa, or the **Nuer and Dinka** of the southern Sudan, with a decentralized or segmentary social structure, are unlikely to recognize centralized spiritual authorities or shrines with permanent religious specialists to serve them.

Continuity between the living and the dead is expressed through contact with ancestors, particularly the recent or "living dead" (also referred to in the literature as "shades"), who have the power to intervene in individual or communal affairs. When they have no one left alive who remembers and pays respect to them, seeking their good will and mediation through libations by offering sacrifices to their skulls or to carved wooden ancestor statues (as among the **Bangwa** of south-west Cameroon), they may become disembodied spirits, lacking in individual personality. Access to ancestral skulls is, for the Bangwa, itself a source of political and spiritual authority. The male successor of the patrigroup sacrifices skulls on behalf of those related to the deceased. For women, who can inherit the skulls of female, but not male kin, and whose skulls do not form patrigroup lineages, prayer is more personal and the relationship between a deceased woman and her children less threatening. For the Mbuti the spirits of the dead merge with the other spirits of the forest and can become a potential menace to those who dwell there.

Belief in multiple selves or disparate psychic powers within an individual are common. Thus that part of a person which represents continuity with a family or clan can be reincarnated, while the dead individual retains his or her position as an ancestor. Other "selves" may manifest their presence through dreams or witchcraft activity, either volitionally or without the knowledge of the conscious self. Witchcraft may be used for the benefit of the individual or community, or for anti-social ends (sorcery—associated with night time activity, shape-changing, cannibalism, incestuous behaviour and the beasts of the bush or forest). Witch-curing cults, which ward off or counteract the activities of sorcerers and witches, have gained in popularity in recent years, as have healing cults in general. All sickness has a potentially "supernatural" source, as it is the diminution of personal power either through possession by a deity, spirit or ancestor, or the maleficent effects of sorcery or witchcraft. Divination, often by a specialist using some form of oracle, determines the source of the illness and allows for appropriate remedies. (Western understandings of curing can sometimes co-exist with traditional beliefs, as the former are more concerned with mechanical processes than with the underlying rationale of sickness and health.) Where sickness results from spirit possession the afflicted individual may become a mouthpiece for that particular deity or spirit, and can build up a reputation as a **shamanic** healer (cf. **Khoisan religion**).

The powers and forces which are possessed by and emanate from people, as well as from other animate and inanimate sources, continually interact, and must be kept in balance. Music can play an important part in restoring harmony, as in the Mbuti *elima* female initiation ceremony, in which the slumbering forest is reawakened. Securing the blessings of life, and maintaining fertility, economic prosperity and harmony within the community, while countering the threats of war, disease, drought and death, require continual vigilance and appropriate ritual activity. Christianity and Islam may be harnessed as sources of power and directed towards these ends (cf. Shona Spirit Churches and other **African New Religious Movements**). Traditional religions are far from static, with new cults (such as the **Bwiti** in Gabon), rituals and religious responses developing and interacting with one another in reply to 20th century demands. ATRs show little inclination, as some 19th century missionaries had assumed, to wither away with the advance of Christianity and "Western civilization".

Afro-American Spiritists. This is a general designation sometimes used to cover a cluster of cults and movements found in the Caribbean and surrounding countries (including Brazil—hence, sometimes, the more particular designation, where appropriate, of Afro–Brazilian cults). They incorporate, in various ways and to different extents, belief in spirits and rites of spirit-possession. Examples include **Candomblé, Convince, Macumba, Obeah, Pocomania, Qimbanda, Revival Zion, Santería, Shango, Umbanda, Voodoo (Vodun)**, and **Winti**.

Aga Khanis. In 1817 the Shah of Iran conferred the honorific title Aga Khan (or Aqa Khan) on the spiritual leader (Imam) of the **Nizaris,** the larger of the two main surviving branches of **Isma'ili Shi'ism** within Islam. Following an unsuccessful rebellion against the Shah in 1841, the Aga Khan fled to India, eventually making Bombay his headquarters in 1848. The hereditary title has passed to his successors as Imams, and as a result "Aga Khanis" has come to be used as a common designation for the Nizari sect within Isma'ili Shi'ism. Thus the Agha Khanis and the Nizaris are one and the same group, with the different names indicating different aspects of their history and tradition.

The Aga Khanis are sometimes also referred to as **Khojas,** but strictly speaking this is inaccurate: it is not the case either that all Khojas are Aga Khanis, or that all Aga Khanis are Khojas.

Not all Khojas are Aga Khanis: a few are not Nizaris at all, but **Twelvers** (and indeed a few are even Hindus). Conversely, not all Aga Khanis are Khojas: some Nizaris within India, and those elsewhere (e.g. in Syria and Iran), are drawn from quite different groups.

The confusion has presumably arisen because, under the Agha Khan's leadership, the Nizari Khojas have become a wealthy and widely distributed community, with a major presence in East Africa.

The religious centres of the Nizaris are known as *jama'at khanas*, being assembly and prayer halls which also function as mosques. Aga Khan III (d. 1957) established the practice of using these for the dissemination of modern adaptations of the faith, both in religious matters and also on social issues: he regularly sent *farmans* (religious guidance) to be read out in all jama'at khanas. He encouraged not only younger people, but also women, to lead public prayers.

Aga Khan III was also—playing a non-sectarian role—one of the main forces behind the foundation of the **All-India Muslim League** in 1906, and was elected President of the League of Nations in 1937. The tradition he established of a variety of charity work—building schools, hospitals, clinics, welfare organizations—has been continued by Aga Khan IV, now resident in France, who in 1967 established the Aga Khan Foundation to promote humanitarian and cultural causes. The Aga Khanis remain a well organized and influential community both within India and beyond.

Agama (Islam) Jawa. Islam is officially recognized by the state as the religion of the overwhelming majority of Indonesians (approximately 87 per cent), but beyond the confines of government bureaucratic thinking a major cleavage is recognized within the Muslim community. On the one hand are those who adhere to the Five Pillars of the faith and acknowledge the authority of the shari'a (*syaria*), the Islamic law; on the other hand are those, sometimes referred to as nominal Muslims, who adhere to a local blend of certain Islamic tenets (such as belief in Allah and acknowledgement of the Prophet Muhammad) with older Hindu, Buddhist and indigenous Indonesian animist elements, and who are more likely to recognize the authority of local customary law (*adat*) than the shari'a.

This kind of division is to be found throughout Indonesia, but only in the central island of Java have members of the two segments of the community been identified by different labels—the stricter Muslims as *santri*, the more nominal Muslims as *abangan*. Correlatively, the religion of the former is known as **Agama Islam Santri,** and that of the latter, Agama Jawa or Agama Islam Jawa. These are not labels for two distinct religions, however; they are labels for two variants of the Islamic religion in Indonesia.

Believers who designate their religion as Agama Islam Jawa (Javanese Islam) instinctively balance recognition of their links with mainstream international Islam against the purely local roots of much of their inheritance. Those who use the label Agama Jawa (Javanese Religion) emphasize the primacy of the local character of their faith. However, this is a difference of emphasis whose significance should not be exaggerated, and need not be pursued here. The prime distinction is the santri/abangan one (with the religion of the latter at times receiving even more localized labels, e.g. *Agama Sunda*—Sundanese religion—in Sundanese West Java).

Agama Jawa (or Agami Jawi) has clear affinities with aspects of **Sufism,** which historically played a major role in the diffusion of Islam throughout the Indonesian archipelago. Healers and spiritual leaders become revered as saints and after their death cults involving the veneration of their graves develop. Of particular significance are the shrines of nine saints, *wali sanga*, credited with first preaching Islam in Java. For adherents of Agama Jawa, pilgrimage to these shrines in northern Java can be an adequate substitute for the otherwise normative pilgrimage to Mecca.

Again, Sufi-style chanting, *dhikr*, commonly occurs as part of the ceremonies known as *slametan*. These are sacred communal meals in which customary dishes blessed by a mosque official are shared by a family, friends and neighbours. A *slametan* may be connected with a variety of occasions—for example, circumcision, marriage, illness, death, business promotion, academic success, changes of season.

Meanwhile, from the Hindu–Buddhist complex comes belief in numerous subsidiary deities, now associated for example with fertility and rice cultivation, or accidents or death. Such is the affinity between Agama Jawa and the Balinese brand of Hinduism in various ways, indeed, that many *abangan* have preferred to be classed officially as Hindu rather than Muslim, and Hinduism is now spreading somewhat in Java.

In addition, a belief in ghosts, ancestral spirits, guardian spirits, and various kinds of magic have been incorporated from earlier indigenous primal religious (the remnants of which are today officially classified by the state as "animism"). Veneration of ancestors is important in a manner somewhat reminiscent of **Chinese folk religion**.

Many adherents of Agama Jawa have been drawn to the numerous new religious movements, or **kebatinan** sects, that continue to flourish, usually with a mystical aspect of some kind.

Agama Islam Santri. The overwhelming majority of Indonesians are recognized officially by the state as being Muslim, but in fact there is a major difference between the unambiguously Muslim believer who practises a mainstream form of Islam based on the Five Pillars, and the less purely Muslim believer whose religion incorporates elements of a Hindu–Buddhist–animist synthesis. The former is known as *santri*, the latter as *abangan*, terms originating in Java but now applied more generally. Agama Islam Santri refers, as will readily be inferred, to the kind of orthodox Islam practised by the *santri*, as opposed to that of the *abangan*, known in Java as **Agama Jawa**, but identifiable throughout the archipelago.

The focal points of Agama Islam Santri are the mosque (*mesjid, masigit*—or, in the case of small mosques in small villages, *langgar*), mosque organiser (*penghulu*), the religious judge (*hakim* or *pengadilan agama*), and the village religious teacher (*kiyayi*), who may own as well as run a school or boarding school (*pesantren*) where young *santri* can learn the teachings of Muhammad and learn to read the Quran. The *penghulu* authorizes marriages and divorces as well as organizing times of prayer and various mosque ceremonies, but is probably less well informed about Islam than the *kiyayi*: rivalry between them is common.

The current Muslim revival has taken root among the *santri*, but largely outside the bounds of their two main surviving traditional organizations, the **Muhammadiyah** and the **Nahdatul Ulama.**

Aghoris. Aghoris are Indian ascetics living in and around cremation grounds, renowned for their unorthodox and antinomian practices. They are the successors to the, now defunct, ascetic tradition of the **Kapalikas.** The Aghoris worship Shiva in his terrifying form as Aghora; imitating their god by wearing long, matted hair, going naked or draped in a stolen shroud, covered with ashes from the cremation ground, garlanded with bones, carrying a skull begging bowl taken from a corpse found in a river and behaving as if mad. The ascetics aim at liberation from *karma* and the cycle of reincarnation by embracing the impure and abandoning social norms. In some rituals the Aghori worships Shiva seated upon the chest of a corpse and might consume the corpses's flesh, as well as excrement and urine. Aghori ritual involves the use of the five "m"s of **Tantrism,** namely alcohol, meat, fish, parched grain (perceived as an aphrodisiac) and performing sexual intercourse with a menstruating, low-caste woman or prostitute. Through these rites the Aghori is breaking brahmanical taboos and acting out his monistic theology. At death an Aghori is buried in a meditation posture in a tomb called a *samadh*. This becomes as place of reverence for devotees. Few Aghoris remain in India, though there is a centre or *ashram* at Varanasi established in the 18th century by the sect's founder Kina Ram, who is said to have been an incarnation of Shiva.

Aglipayan. This independent church was founded in the chaos which marked the end of Spanish rule in the Philippines. A revolutionary, nationalistic movement led by Isabelo de los Reyes headed the rebellion. A Filipino priest, Gregorio Aglipay, identified with the struggle and became chaplain to the movement. When he refused instructions to return to the **Roman Catholic** Church, he was excommunicated in 1899 by Archbishop Nozaleda. Forced into independence, Aglipay suddenly found himself at the centre of a new church. Catholics, in a major exodus, left the church to join him. By 1906 one in every four Filipinos identified with the new movement, attracted by its opposition to Spain, to the Catholic Church and to the power of priests and friars.

At one point it looked as if some kind of alliance might be forged between the new Catholics and Protestants, but this floundered in 1909 when the Philippine Supreme Court decided that, in spite of defections by priests and people, the vacated church property and premises belonged to the hierarchy of the Roman Catholic Church.

Aglipay also found unitarian ideas conducive doctrinally (the influence upon him of the American Governor-General of the Philippines), and this offended many Protestants. The high point, as far as numbers were concerned, was reached around 1918 with 15 per cent of the population identifying with the Aglipayan. However, by the late 1960s this had declined to 5% of the population. Aglipay was consecrated "Supreme Bishop" by a council of priests (no Catholic bishops having defected with him), but the problem of "apostolic succession" continued to worry him and the new church.

After his death in 1940 there was a split: part sought to return to the Catholic Church of the Philippines, and the other to maintain, in some way, its independence. After years of struggle and litigation, the Philippine Supreme Court, in 1955, recognised Isabelo de los Reyes Junior as the Supreme Bishop of the Independent Church. He then led negotiations for recognition from the Philippine **Episcopal** Church. Success led to an impressive service on April 7, 1948, when three Filippino Independent Church bishops were ordained, including de los Reyes, by the Rt Rev. N. S. Binsted of the Philippine Episcopal Church. Soon after, the latter entered into a fruitful relationship with the Philippine Independent Church.

In 1961 the American Episcopal Church approved a concordat of intercommunion with the Independent Church, thus giving the Aglipayan increased stature and authenticity. Priests continue to be trained at the Episcopal Seminary of St Andrew's in Manila as they have been since 1947, and the church is slowly gaining ground as an indigenous episcopal church in the Philippines.

Agudat Israel. (See also **Orthodox Judaism, Hasidism,** and **Zionism.**) Agudat Israel (Hebrew, Association or Union of Israel) is the single most important, international

Jewish **Orthodox** organization, and later also an Israeli political party. It was founded in Kattowitz (Upper Silesia) in 1912 as an attempt to preserve and protect the strictly Orthodox way of life against a plethora of modern challenges. Like **Zionism** it sought to develop a mass movement among the Jews of Europe. The actual context of the formation of Agudat Israel was to counter the growing Zionist Organization but other threats included **Reform Judaism,** the assimilation of Jews into European culture and socialism. The founders, who included some of the greatest rabbinic authorities of the day (e.g. Rabbis Israel Meir Hacohen, Haim Soloveitchik of Brisk, Haim Oser Grodenski of Vilna and Abraham Mordecai Alter of **Ger (Hasidism)**), sought to re-establish the historical position of the great rabbis of the Jewish community as its leaders. They formed a Council of Torah Sages (Moetzet Gedolei Hatorah) as Agudat's ruling advisory body and a Great Assembly (Kenesiyyah Hagedolah) which included representatives of German **Neo-Orthodoxy;** Polish and Lithuanian Orthodoxy (Hasidic and non-Hasidic) and Hungarian Orthodoxy. Thus under the umbrella of Agudat Israel were a wide variety of opinions and styles of Orthodox Judaism. Agudat centres, youth movements and women's groups were established throughout the **Ashkenazi** world.

Jewish education was a priority concern. The movement was particularly influential in Poland and took an active part in Polish politics with a number of Agudat candidates being elected to the Polish parliament.

Agudat's attitude to the Zionists' aim of Jewish resettlement in Israel was ambiguous—while supporting Orthodox Jewish communities in Israel, the idea of a non-religious state was rejected. The rise of Nazism in the 1930s gave rise to a change in Agudat policy and settlement in Israel was supported and Agudat members were encouraged to emigrate

there. Also Israel came to be recognized and accepted as the centre of Jewish Orthodox life. The *Holocaust* wiped out the European heartland of Agudat Israel and the movement, while still represented in most centres of Jewish population, is now based in Israel and the USA.

In America since 1939, Agudat Israel supports Jewish educational and other facilities and publishes the monthly *Jewish Observer.* It opposes the inclusion of non-Orthodox elements in communal organizations.

In Israel since 1919, Agudat Israel set about the task of building a separate **Ultra-Orthodox** community in the land, totally independent of the Zionist Organization and Jewish Agency. Immigrants after 1935, particularly from Poland, led to a change in their separatist policy and the development of a more accommodating stand on working with the Zionists. This development led to **Neturei Karta** and other extreme anti-Zionist groups leaving Agudat Israel. From Agudat Israel's ranks the Agudat Workers' Party had also emerged in Poland. In time this party became independent and pursued separate policies and later took part in a number of Israeli coalition governments.

Agudat Israel joined the provisional government of the State in 1948 and was part of the ruling coalition until leaving following a dispute over religious education in 1952. In 1953 Agudat established an independent religious school system that was government funded. Agudat has, and is, represented at the national and municipal levels. From 1952 until 1977, when Agudat joined Menahem Begin's ruling Likud coalition, Agudat did not participate in the government. In 1973 it re-combined with its Workers' Party. Its position is still somewhat ambiguous in that it does not fully recognise the legitimacy of the non-religious state yet it takes part in the political process and even accepts senior committee posts.

Agudat Israel has consistently fought for the support of its institutions and over issues of *Halakhah* and the state. It insists on fighting what it understands as "secular" coercion, such as the conscription of religious women, abortion, etc., and holds that values cannot be generated by society alone and thus there is need for the authoritative interpretation of religious texts as the guide for contemporary values. Traditionally it sought to develop the *Torah*-state in Israel and limited its energies to direct religious issues, however, in recent years Agudat has developed concerns relating to foreign policy and national security. For example in the 1988 elections, largely under the influence of the **Lubavich** Rebbe, Menahem Schneersohn, it took a hard line on the return of the occupied territories ("not an inch").

Agudat Israel was for a generation the only major **Haredi** party and the second religious party in Israel after the religious Zionist, **Mafdal** party. In 1984 **Shas (Sephardi Torah Guardians' Party)** was formed to counter the **Ashkenazi** domination of Agudat, thus splitting the Haredi vote. Just before the 1988 general election, a further split took place when a new **Haredi** party was founded, **Degel Hatorah (Torah Flag)** to counter the Hasidic domination of Agudat Israel (largely by **Ger** and **Lubavich**) and give a voice to the Lithuanian Haredi (and **Belz** Hasidic) communities. Degel Hatorah took 2 seats in the Knesset (Israeli parliament), Agudat gained 5 seats and Shas an unexpected 6 seats, giving the Haredi community as a whole an unprecedented 13 seats. After the 1988 elections it appeared as if there had been an increase in the power of Agudat and the Haredi community as a whole. However for the 1992 Israeli general election in an unsuccessful attempt to consolidate the Ashkenazi Haredi vote, Agudat Israel and Degel Hatorah joined forces as the **United Judaism Party.** This new alliance took only 4 seats, while Shas retained its 6 seats. While Agudat is no longer the sole political voice of the **Ultra-Orthodox,** it still represents the voice of the Ashkenazi, especially Hasidic communities.

Ahl al-Da'wa. This is the name—meaning "People of the Call"—under which the Algerian branch of the **Muslim Brother hood** is known.

Ahl-i Hadith. The Indian Muslim movement known as *Ahl-i Hadith*, which means "People of the Traditions", came from a similar intellectual background and shared similar concerns to those of the **Deobandis**. They were, however, more extreme in their ideas, more intense in their commitment, more élitist in social background, more consciously sectarian in their behaviour, and less influential. Many came from once great Muslim families which had fallen on hard times. By the 20th century the movement had developed madrasahs, mosques, journals, and from 1912 its annual All-India Ahl-i Hadith Conference.

Like the Deobandis, the Ahl-i Hadith are committed to purifying Muslim behaviour of all practices not sanctioned by Islamic law. In doing so, however, they reject the decisions of the medieval law schools, and use only the *Quran* and the Traditions as guidance, and only those jurisprudential techniques sanctioned by the Traditions as method. Their approach means very great individual responsibility for the believer; they condemn almost all expressions of Islamic mysticism.

The ways of the Ahl-i Hadith are puritanical. They insist, for instance, on simple marriage celebrations and scrupulous fulfilment of the requirements of the faith. Their style is sectarian and embattled; they sport their own cut of beard and insist on their form of prayer which involves, amongst other things, saying *Amen* aloud and a different positioning of the hands. In British India they were often the focus of disturbances. Furthermore, as is not unusual in the case of such intense ideological sects, a group split off in the late nineteenth century to form the **Ahl-i Quran.** There is much similarity between the Islamic stance of the Ahl-i Hadith and that of the **Wahhabis** of Saudi Arabia.

They have spread with the South Asian diaspora of the 20th century and currently have branches in all the major cities of Britain as well as in Europe.

Ahl-i Haqq. The *Ahl-i Haqq* ("People of the Truth") are adherents of a small but scattered religion found in western Iran and parts of north-eastern Iraq and Soviet Central Asia. There are also members in most major Iranian cities. Followers are often misleadingly termed 'Ali-Ilahis ("believers in the divinity of 'Ali"), but in fact the **Shi'ite** Imam 'Ali plays only a minor part in their system. The sect combines extremist Shi'ite beliefs with elements from **Sufism** and local legend. Doctrine centres around the notion of successive manifestations of the divinity and repeated metempsychosis, while religious practices have clear links with those of some Sufi brotherhoods, including entry into trance states, during which burning coals are handled. The Ahl-i Haqq are split into numerous ethnic, tribal, and religious groups. There is no central organization, nor do they have a canonical scripture.

Ahl-i Quran. The Ahl-i Quran stem from a splinter group of the **Ahl-i Hadith**, led by Maulana Abdullah Chakralavi in Lahore, which asserted from the late 19th century that only the *Quran* could be used as a source of authority. They are exclusive and have a history of strife with the Ahl-i Hadith. A notable developer of the position of the Ahl-i Quran was the Pakistani thinker Ghulam Ahmad Parvez (1903–1985). His followers, the Parvezis, are based in London and hold annual functions.

Ahl-i Sunnat wa Jama'at. This is the self-designation, as "true Sunnis", of the Indian Muslim movement known as the **Barelvis**.

Ahmadiya (Lahoris). A group of highly educated men who split from the **Ahmadiya (Qadianis)** in 1914 over the succession to the leadership of the community. They felt that the leader should be selected; the bulk of the community wanted to confine the choice to the family of the founder, Ghulam Ahmad. The Lahoris have gradually edged their way back to the mainstream of Islam.

Ahmadiya (Qadianis). The Ahmadiya were the last major Islamic movement to develop in 19th century India. The founder was Mirza Ghulam Ahmad (1839–1908), who came from an old Mughal service family of the Punjab, a province wracked by competition between Christian and Hindu missionaries. Ghulam Ahmad began as a champion of Islamic orthodoxy, but in the process claimed to be an incarnation of the Hindu God, Krishna, the true Christian Messiah (Jesus, he argued, had not died on the Cross but had lived to carry his mission to northern India and was buried in Kashmir), and a Muslim prophet — Muhammad, he declared, had been the last of the law-giving prophets, but he, Ghulam Ahmad, was a prophet as a reviver of religion (*mujaddid*). These claims were bitterly contested by nearly all Muslims. Ghulam Ahmad and his followers were forced to separate from the **Sunnis** and pray in their own mosques, being known as Qadianis.

The Ahmadiya are one of the most highly organized Muslim communities. Leadership has passed down through the descendants of Ghulam Ahmad, who are regarded as having the gift of prophecy—a claim opposed by the rival **Ahmadiya (Lahoris)**. They are most efficiently organized as a great multinational concern, with their headquarters first at Qadian and then, after the partition of India, at the purpose-built town of Rabwa in Pakistan. All members of the community pay a tithe of 6.5 per cent of their income each year.

The Ahmadiya are also amongst the most vigorous proselytizers of Islam. Currently they have a presence in 120 countries, and missionaries at work in 48. Around 10,000,000 followers are claimed worldwide; the most successful area of proselytization outside Pakistan has been West Africa. Ahmadis are present in all Western European countries. In Britain they have 45 branch associations and two notable centres, the London Mosque at Wandsworth, and Islamabad, near Tilford in Surrey, where they have printing facilities in 30 different languages.

The Ahmadiya are hated by all Muslims, being deemed to have betrayed Islam by the nature of their heteredox beliefs. They have suffered appalling persecution in Pakistan and in other Muslim countries; the current head of the community lives in exile in London. They have many similarities with another (erstwhile) Islamic messianic movement, the **Bahais**, who emerged in 19th century Iran. There is, however, one difference; the Bahais have left Islam, the Ahmadiya have not—although they have in effect been expelled.

'Aidarusiya. The 'Aidarusiya is an important sub-branch of a **Sufi** order, the **'Alawiya (Hadrami)**, and contributed very significantly to its spread from its base in the Yemen to South Asia and Indonesia.

Aisiah. The women's section of the major Indonesian Muslim organization, the **Muhammadiyah.**

Akali Dal. The Sikh party known as the Akali Dal (the Immortal Party) has its roots in the Shiromani Akali Dal formed in 1920. Always militant in orientation, its aim was to secure the religious and political rights of the Sikh minority, particularly in the Punjab. Originally its interest was to wrest control of the *gurdwaras* (Sikh shrines) from the control of the British, but its leadership soon made common cause with Gandhi and entered into the struggle for independence. The Akali Dal was led in the crucial years 1935 to 1961

by Master Tara Singh, a converted Hindu who welded the Sikhs into a formidable political force which began to demand increased autonomy from New Delhi. In recent years, however, the Akali Dal has become increasingly the voice of moderation in Punjabi politics, opposing more militant Sikh groups such as the **Damdani Taksal** led by Jarnail Singh Bhindranwale, who call for all-out civil war against the central government.

Despite the power of the party in Punjab politics, it is currently split by factionalism.

Akhand Kirtani Jatha. An important *khalsa*-based movement for the reconversion of lapsed (i.e. **Patit**) **Sikhs.** Based on the activities of Bhai Randir Singh (1878–1961) who was imprisoned by the British in the pre-Independence period in India, the Jatha combines a concern for political libertarianism with strongly devotional strains. A characteristic of the movement are its overnight hymn-singing sessions undertaken by its initiated and vegetarian devotees. The Jatha is active in the UK.

Akshar Purushottam Sanstha. A sub-group within the **Swaminarayan** movement. Devotees revere both Swami Narayan and Gunatitananda, an early follower of the former.

al-Takfir wa'l-Hijra. Al-Takfir wa'l-Hijra emerged in the 1970s in Egypt as a radical offshoot from the **Muslim Brotherhood.** Shukri Mustafa (1942–78), a young agricultural student, was imprisoned in 1965 for distributing Brotherhood leaflets at Asyut University. It was the time of a wave of arrests following the discovery of a plot against Nasser centred on the leading ideologue of the Brothers, Sayyid Qutb. In prison Shukri Mustafa became disillusioned with the Brothers, and laid plans for a new movement before his release in

1971. He completed his studies and formed a group around him called the Society of Muslims. They believed, following Sayyid Qutb, that Egyptian society had strayed so far from Islam that it was no longer Muslim, but unbelieving. Therefore, they thought it necessary to practise *takfir*, the act of declaring someone an unbeliever, and *hijrah*, emigration away from an unbelieving community to live as an exclusive group of true believers. Hence their name: al-Takfir wa'l-Hijra.

The group's expenses were met largely by the remittances of members sent for short periods to work in Saudi Arabia and the Gulf. Members lived communally in furnished flats, married among themselves, and refused to send their children to state schools or to do military service. This was preparatory to the time when they would be strong enough to launch a *jihad* against corrupt un-Islamic society.

In January 1977 they began this phase, attacking nightclubs and bars in Cairo as their contribution to a more widespread pattern of rioting against the Sadat régime. In July they kidnapped and later murdered a former minister of religious endowments who had written against them. Security forces then hunted down and arrested hundreds of members of the group out of an estimated 3,000–5,000. Shukri Mustafa and four others were executed in March 1978.

Al-Takfir wa'l-Hijra appeared to have been crushed in 1978, but organizations of the same name were still active in 1991 among the Islamic opposition in Libya and Algeria, as well as among Palestinians under Israeli occupation. In Egypt, surviving members have apparently continued their activities in comparable groups such as al-Jihad (the **Jihad Organisation**).

Aladura. Aladura (Yoruba, "owners of prayer") is a term used to describe various prophet-healing churches, going under names such as the Celestial Church of Christ, the Brotherhood of the Cross and Star and the numerous **Cherubim and Seraphim** societies, primarily in Nigeria and neighbouring West African countries, although there are offshoots in Europe and the USA. Aladura churches originated around 1918, with considerable expansion in the 1930s under Jospeh Babalola's mass healing movement, and gaining in respectability and size since Nigeria's independence (1960). Although now also making converts in Nigeria's Muslim north, the majority of members are still drawn from former mission churches, appearing less élitist and offering greater scope for participation and leadership, particularly for women. Relations between Aladura churches are generally cordial but attempts at union have met with little success. Links with Western **Pentecostal** churches are common, and Oshitelu's **Church of the Lord, Aladura,** with over 1,000,000 members, is affiliated to the **World Council of Churches.**

'Alawis. This is a general term applied to various political and religious groupings with particular connections to the **Shi'ite** Imam 'Ali. Nowadays it is mainly used to refer to the **Nusayri** sect found in Syria and to a lesser extent in Turkey, especially around Antakya.

The Nusayris, under the label 'Alawis, should not be confused with members of either of the two **'Alawiya Sufi** orders; nor should they be confused with the **Alevis** of Turkey.)

'Alawiya (Darqawi). Two quite separate *Sufi* orders are known by the name 'Alawiya, and they need to be distinguished from each other. (Their adherents, 'Alawis, need further to be distinguished from the **'Alawis** who form a **Shi'ite** group also known as the **Nusayris,** as well as from the **Alevis** of Turkey.)

The 'Alawiya (Darqawi), as one of the two 'Alawiya orders is sometimes known, is an offshoot of the **Darqawiya,** and was founded in 1918 at Mostaganem in Algeria by Ahmad ibn al-'Alawi. Despite its 20th century origin, it is thoroughly traditional. It differs from the Darqawiya in the adoption of Indian-inspired rituals introduced by al-'Alawi following a journey to India. The 'Alawiya has attracted European converts and Martin Lings, an English Muslim, has produced a moving biography of the ascetic and saintly founder, entitled *A Moslêm Saint of the Twentieth Century*.

Found in Algeria and scattered elsewhere in North Africa and the Middle East, including Gaza, Jerusalem and Jordan, its founder's writings have been edited and disseminated by followers in Damascus particularly. Its meetings in Jerusalem and in a few other places in Israel since 1967 have been viewed with suspicion by the **Muslim Brotherhood** as representing a very different style of Islam.

'Alawiya (Hadrami). The older of the two 'Alawiya **Sufi** orders was founded by Muhammad ibn 'Ali (1178–1255), and has been established in Hadramawt in southern Yemen ever since. From there it spread, mainly through a sub-branch, the 'Aidarusiya, to South Asia and later, in the 19th century, to Indonesia (then the Dutch East Indies), where its members achieved notable commercial success. More recently, restrictions on repatriation of money by 'Alawis from Indonesia to the Yemen have led to some weakening of the 'Alawiya in its traditional Yemeni base. 'Alawis are found too in East Africa, e.g. in Kenya, and have been especially influential in Zanzibar (now part of Tanzania).

In all these regions the 'Alawiya has retained a somewhat exclusive character, members being drawn almost without exception from various branches of the Ba 'Alawi, a sayyid family, i.e. one tracing its descent from the Prophet Muhammad.

Alevis. The Alevis are a heterodox Islamic group in Turkey, where they are claimed by some observers to constitute as many as a quarter of the total population—a claim which, however, it is impossible to verify. They are sometimes confused with the **'Alawis,** some of whom are also found in Turkey, but the distinction remains clear if the latter are referred to by their other name, **Nusayris**.

One thing that Alevis and 'Alawis do have in common is, as these names imply, a veneration for 'Ali, the nephew and son-in-law of the Prophet Muhammad, and for this reason they are often classified as **Shi'ites.** The **Twelver Shi'ites** of Iran, however, although they have begun to establish links with the 'Alawis of Syria, reject the Alevis as heretics. Nor do the Alevis regard themselves as being Shi'ites. They are close to, if not indeed identical with the **Qizilbash**.

They distinguish themselves from their **Sunni** neighbours, however, in several ways additional to their veneration of 'Ali, to whom they attribute divinity. They reject the Sunni practice of prayer five times a day as mere external ritual; they reject the month of fasting at Ramadan—replacing it with 12 days (in memory of the 12 *Imams* of the Twelvers, and generally observed during the month of Muharram when Twelvers commemorate the martyrdom of Imam Hussain at Karbala); they reject the pilgrimage to Mecca; and they observe less strict rules of ritual purity. Distinctive of them too is their veneration of the rabbit, against the eating of which there is a taboo.

They have their own independent religious organization in eastern Turkey (many Alevis are Kurds), which is hierarchical in structure: in a given region a *mursid* (professor) is in charge, with elders or *pirs* under him, and guides or *rehbers* under them in turn. *Mursids* and *pirs* both come from sacred lineages, and intermarriage with ordinary villagers is forbidden, being widely regarded as equivalent to incest.

The pir—known too as the *dede*—visits villages in his jurisdiction, and the villagers collect funds to give him. He also presides over the central annual ritual known as the ayn-i cem, (service of union). This involves prayer, the sacrifice of a ram (symbolic of submission—islam—to God as in the story of Abraham's readiness to sacrifice his son) followed by a communal meal in which food and wine are shared by all equally, preaching, singing, slow-turning dances similar to those of the Whirling Dervishes (**Mawlawiya**), and communal recitations of the oft-repeated name of God (*zikr*), in a session which lasts the whole night until the following morning.

There are clear similarities here to practices of certain **Sufi** orders, especially the **Bektashiya**, whose founder, Hajji Bektash, they particularly venerate (along with Jalal al-Din Rumi, the famous mystic-poet founder of the Mawlawiya). Indeed, the Alevis may have originated as an offshoot of the Bektashis, and the two groups—along with the Nusayris—are regarded as in some sense kinsfolk.

Another practice which reinforces the Alevi sense of community is the tradition of each young person being "paired" with another (known as a *musahip*) from a very early age; and of married couples being paired too (known as *eş tutma*).

Within Turkey Alevis have been regarded with suspicion by the Sunni majority, both because of their allegedly grave heresy, and because of their alleged links with Kurdish nationalism and/or extreme leftism/Communism. They in turn have sought to claim the equality that is their due according to the principles of the Kemalist secular state. In 1966 they began publishing a bi-monthly political and cultural journal, *Cem*. This has often contained attacks on two modern Sunni movements, the **Nurcus** and the **Süleymancis**.

From the '60s on, there has been a trend towards politicizing the faith, and particularly among Alevi migrant groups in Germany, for example, songs in praise of egalitarian social justice have been introduced into the Ayn-i Cem alongside the traditional devotional ones. Cassettes and videos celebrating, say, the life of Pir Sultan Abdal, the great Alevi poet, as a battle on behalf of the poor and powerless against a strong and tyrannical centralized power, are also in wide circulation: they have clear contemporary implications, and the Turkish state remains suspicious.

'Alia Bohoras ('Aliyas). The 'Alia Bohoras are a tiny sub-sect of the **Daudis** within Indian Islam. The Daudis, in turn, form a branch of the **Musta'li** sect of **Isma'ili Shi'ism**. They are commonly (though slightly inaccurately) identified as **Bohoras**. The 'Aliyas have retained a separate group identity under their own line of religious leaders (Da'is), resident in Baroda, since 1621, when they split from the main community of Daudis over the leadership issue.

'Ali-Ilahis. A term erroneously applied to the **Ahl-i Haqq**.

Aliran kebatinan. The aliran kebatinan—**kebatinan** sects or movements—are a feature of the religious life of Indonesia. Generally initiated by a guru-like figure who makes claims to having been the recipient of revelation, they usually incorporate some kind of mystical emphasis: the word kebatinan is derived from the Arabic *batin* used by **Sufis** in particular to refer to the inner aspect of reality. The most famous example internationally is **Subud**, and these kebatinan movements fall into the category of New Religious Movements (see the essay in Part I).

All Ceylon Buddhist Congress (ACBC). The name applied to the leadership of the **Young Men's Buddhist Association (YMBA)**. It was founded in 1918 by several Buddhist leaders (G. P. Malalasekera; C. A. Hewawitarane; F. R. Senanayake; D. B. Jayatillake) and initially called The All Ceylon Congress (ACC) of the YMBA. After an alternative title of The ACC of Buddhist Associations in the early 1920s it was finally designated The All Ceylon Buddhist Congress (ACBC). It has been a powerful influence upon the state as a voice for maintaining Buddhism and Buddhist institutions, especially under the leadership of G. P. Malalasekera, when, in 1953, following two years of campaigning to instigate a Buddhist Sasana Commission to investigate the state of Buddhism in Ceylon (D. S. Senanayake announcing and retracting such a promise), the ACBC went ahead in appointing such a commission. It has been active outside Sri Lanka, in the Buddhist crisis of Vietnam, and in the cause of **Tibetan Buddhism**, as well as in internal activities such as promoting Sinhalese as the official language of Ceylon. At a famous meeting in April 1946 it decided that under no circumstances whatsoever should a monk be engaged in politics. Although concentrated in Colombo, it is active throughout the whole island.

Alliance Israelite Universelle. Based in Paris, the Alliance Israelite Universelle, modern Jewry's first international organization, was founded in 1860 to both fight for universal Jewish emancipation and to provide aid for persecuted Jews. Until World War I, it focused on the Ottoman Empire and North Africa; afterwards, mainly North Africa, primarily through educational institutions. Before 1945, it was anti-Zionist, favouring universal Jewish rights over a separate state but in 1945 reversed its stand, becoming **Zionist,** today maintaining programmes in Israel. During the 1960s it began increasing its educational projects in France, home of many North African Jewish refugees. Although always a philanthropic body it was viewed by some antisemites as the model of the "international Jewish conspiracy", largely because of its international focus. In recent years the Alliance has been criticized by Israeli religious authorities for its anti-religious stance and as being an agent of secularism in its education programmes.

All-India Muslim League. The All-India Muslim League is to some extent the product of the crystallization of the apprehensions and aspirations of the Muslim community of the Indian subcontinent into what is sometimes termed the Two-Nation Theory, namely the concept that the Muslim inhabitants of the regions, in spite of centuries of co-existence, constitute a distinct and totally incompatible group of people from the Hindus of India. It is believed by many Indians to owe its genesis to the British colonial policy of *Divide et impera*, voiced by Lord Elphinstone, Governor of Bombay and others, leading Lord Dufferin to encourage the formation of the Indian National Congress, a political organization which by its composition was essentially Hindu dominated, though avowedly secular in ideology. Sir Sayyid Ahmad Khan, the leading Muslim *savant* of the time, warned Muslims to keep away from the Indian National Congress and its nationalistic aspirations, which would, according to him, lead to Hindu majority rule in India and the inevitable oppression of Muslims. The presence of Hindu extremist figures in the Congress, such as Balagangadhara Tilak, the initiator of the anti-cow slaughter movement, added strength to Sir Sayyid's caveats and his voicing of the two-nation theory. The Mahatma's vision of Rama Rajya, though entirely devoid of communalistic implications, added to the apprehension of the Muslims. On Oct. 1, 1906 a Muslim delegation to Lord Minto, viceroy, was able to secure separate electoral representation for Muslims—hailed at the time as a great triumph for the Muslims. To further safeguard the interests of the Muslims, on Dec. 30 of that year the All-India Muslim League was formed under the leadership of Nawab al Mulk and the Nawab of Dacca.

The avowed objectives of the new organization were: (i) To promote among the Muslims of India loyalty to the British administration, and to remove their misconceptions regarding the intentions of the Government; (ii) To protect and advance the political rights and interests of the Muslims of India and respectfully represent their needs and aspirations to the Government; and (iii) to prevent the rise among them of any feelings of hostility to other communities without prejudice to the aforementioned objectives.

The advent of the fiery Ali brothers and Abul Kalam Azad to the scene, however, changed the loyalist stance of the Muslim League. Its objectives became nationalistic like that of the Indian National Congress, and the League entered into an uneasy pact with the Congress and supported their aspirations for self rule. Thus in 1916 the League, in what is known as the Lucknow pact, adopted, albeit reluctantly, non-violence as the central principle of the movement for independence.

In 1934 another charismatic figure entered the Indian political scene. This was Mohammedali Jinnah, returning from England after higher studies. His initial aspiration was to unite Hindus and Muslims and thus he joined both the League and the Congress. In 1935, however, he became disillusioned about hopes for Hindu–Muslim unity and declared that the Muslims of India were a separate nation. The two-nation theory re-emerged in Indian politics. In 1940 he first mooted the idea of Pakistan, a homeland for the Muslims of India. Jinnah now emerged as the foremost figure in the Muslim League and the voice of the Muslims of India. He was called Qaid e Azam (Great Leader).

Aug. 16, 1946 was declared as direct action day by the League, with demonstrations, *hartal* (closing of shops) and other acts of an agitational nature. In the communal conflict that ensued 500 lives were lost. Sept. 2, 1946 was declared a day of mourning by the League. Members went about wearing black badges and carrying black flags. "Pakistan or Kabaristan" (land of corpses) was the slogan shouted by the demonstrators.

At midnight on Aug. 15, 1947 India became free, but as two nations—the Republic of India, and Pakistan. The two-nation theory of the Muslim League had at last triumphed.

The majority of the All-India Muslim League migrated to Pakistan after independence. However, a substantial number of Muslims still remained in India, so that the Muslim League still remained a viable political party in India. However, its significance was much reduced, and its impact is today mainly confined to one region of India, Kerala state. There it has been a member of coalition governments which have ruled this Indian state ever since its inception in 1957. Indeed the Muslim League holds the balance in the rather unstable political climate of the region. It has thus gained advantages from successive "United Front" governments of the State, such as a separate Muslim district, Malappuram, the teaching of Arabic in schools, a university in the Muslim majority district greatly enhancing the opportunities of Muslim youth for higher education, a Muslim judge in the Kerala High Court, and Muslim members in the State Public Service Commission.

The Muslim League has been extremely pragmatic, compromising its essentially religious ideology to the extent of allying with the Communist parties of the state, especially the left wing Marxist party of Kerala, entering into electoral understanding with the Marxists, and participating in coalition governments led by the Communist Party of India, and the CPI (Marxist). Under the aegis of the Marxists the image of the League in Kerala has perhaps undergone a significant change. It is no longer viewed as a communalistic organization.

However, in 1975 a split occurred within the party. The schism was engendered mainly by personality clashes between leaders, regional loyalties, and the question of support for the Congress Party (Indira) in elections. Thus a dissident group led by Ummer Bafaki Thangal formed a rival party known as the Indian Union Muslim League. They fielded rival candidates in the Parliamentary Elections of 1977. The rift has now healed and the All-India Muslim League has the united support of all Muslim League members in the state. It remains a potent force in the political arena of Kerala State, though its impact on the rest of India is but a shadow of its pre-independence status.

All-India Muslim Majlis-i Mushawarat.
Formed in 1963 as a coalition of a variety
of Muslim political parties and educational
organizations, the Majlis seeks to unite
and channel the efforts of India's Muslims
to secure and strengthen their position in
a predominantly Hindu environment. The
very variety of views accommodated has
meant that the organization is somewhat
politically passive in character. A breakaway group, the U.P. Muslim Majlis, was
politically successful in elections in the late
1960s, but the success was short-lived.

Amal. AMAL is an acronym for the
Arabic *afwāj al-muqāwamah al-lubnānīyah*
(Lebanese Resistance Detachments) and
forms the Arabic word for "hope". AMAL
—or commonly "Amal"—was founded by
Imam Musa al-Sadr in July 1975 as the
military and political wing of an organization
known as *Harakat al-mahrūmīn* (The Movement of the Deprived). Imam Al-Sadr was
a charismatic **Shi'ite** leader who became
president of the Supreme Islamic Shi'a
Council of Lebanon in 1969, two years after
its foundation as the first recognized political
institution to represent the interests of the
Lebanese Shi'ites. In 1974, he founded the
Movement of the Deprived which grew
out of his deep concern for the plight
of the Lebanese poor, many of whom
were Shi'ites. He worked closely with the
Melkite Bishop George Haddad in their
common fight for the rights of the poor.
The formation of a militia by a religious and
political movement is typical of Lebanese
communalism, where most political groups
represent a religious constituency and have
their own militias (for example the **Maronite**
Christian Phalangists and the **Sunni** Muslim
Murābitūn).

Imam al-Sadr's disappearance while visit-
ing Libya in 1978 remains a mystery.
Following his disappearance his leadership
role was divided. Shaikh Shamsuddin con-
tinued as deputy head of the Supreme
Shi'ite Council, and by mid-1980 Nabih
Birri, a lawyer, was President of the Amal
Leadership Council. In spite of personal

rivalry between the two leaders, the
leadership of both organizations remained
generally faithful to Imam Al-Sadr's vision
as expressed in the 1975 Charter of the
Movement of the Deprived and later
accepted as Amal's Charter. The Charter
comes out strongly against traditional
Lebanese confessionalism and in favour of
complete equality of all Lebanese citizens.
It argues that the political confessionalism
of the Lebanese system hinders constructive political development and divides
the citizenry into mutually exclusive categories which destroy national unity.

In contrast to its more radical rival,
Hizbollah, Amal's aim is for a reformed
Lebanese system rather than the establishment of an Islamic state modelled on Iran.
In this it differs too from **Islamic Amal**. It
has opposed Hizbollah's policy of hostage-
taking, and fierce fighting broke out
between the two groups in 1988 and 1989
over a number of issues. This fighting was
followed by a ceasefire and an agreement
which may, however, prove to be purely
temporary.

All India Sikh Student Federation (AISSF).
A militant **Sikh** youth group which has its
origins within the less hardline **Akali Dal.**
Banned by government decree in March
1984, the federation claims, along with two
other groups, responsibility for planting
a bomb on an Air India flight which
crashed off the west coast of Ireland on
June 23, 1985, with 329 fatalities. Under
its secretary, H. S. Kahlon, the federation
emerged as an influential grouping within
the radical Sikh movement which took
control of the Golden Temple in January
1986. Subsequently Kahlon led a splinter
group out of the AISSF towards greater
alignment with the militant **Damdani
Taksal** Sikh religious school. Since 1988,
and against a perceived background of
greater government intransigency, splits
within the AISSF have been healed and
in March of that year Jasbir Singh Rode,
an AISSF nominee, was appointed chief
priest (*jathedar*) of the Akali Takht in

Amritsar. The AISSF has, perhaps, 20,000 active members.

All Indonesia Federation of Buddhist Organizations. A federation of all the major Buddhist sects in Indonesia popularly known by the acronym **WALUBI** (which is derived from the Indonesian Per-*WAL*-ian *U*mat *B*uddha *I*ndonesia). The total Buddhist population is difficult to estimate but is probably in the region of 3,000,000, or between 1 and 2 per cent of Indonesia's predominantly Muslim population of 180,000,000.

The federation was founded in Jogyakarta in May 1978 with the main aim of promoting union among Buddhists. Its genesis owed much to its first chairman, a journalist called Suparto (now deceased), and it is currently led by Bhikkhu Girirakkhito, a prominent monk. WALUBI includes both **Theravada** and **Mahayana** Buddhist groups and **Buddhayana,** a syncretistic combination of both these two plus **Kasogatan,** a local variety of Javanese Buddhism. **Nichiren Shoshu** of Indonesia was originally part of WALUBI, but has more recently been excommunicated on account of its allegedly heretical teaching.

Ordained and lay Buddhists are strongly represented in most branches of the Federation, the current aims of which are the promotion of union among all Buddhists and mutual understanding between Indonesian Buddhists and the government.

Amarapura Nikaya. One of the three main divisions of the **Theravada** Buddhist *Sangha* in Sri Lanka. Founded in the 19th century as a protest against the royal sponsorship and casteism of the **Siyam Nikaya**, its ordination lineage derives from the **Shwegyin** order based at Amarapura, Burma, hence its name. Once established on Sri Lankan soil entry to the order was not dependent on caste, though as time has progressed caste specific sub-groups have emerged. Of the current 18 fraternities, the most

prominent are the **Mulavamsa, Saddhamma-vamsa, Kalyanavamsa** and **Dhammarak-khitavamsa**. Organization is rather loose and the united order is presently presided over by Ven. Balangoda Ananda Maitreya, a scholar, visionary and astrologer. Amarapura's approximately 3,000 monks reside in about 1,000 monasteries throughout the island and are thought to be more puritanical than members of other orders. Distinctively, they cover both shoulders with their robe and leave their eyebrows unshaven.

Amaravati Buddhist Centre and Associated Monasteries. Amaravati Buddhist Centre and its three related monasteries in Devon, Northumberland and Sussex were founded in 1984, 1983, 1981 and 1979 respectively, the first and last under the auspices of the soon-to-be-renamed **English Sangha Trust,** a Buddhist charity. Residents and supporters of these centres follow the **Theravada** Buddhist tradition as practised and taught by the Venerable Ajahn Chah of Wat Nang Pah Pong in north-east Thailand. The spiritual director of all four English centres is the Venerable Sumedho Mahathera. Branch monasteries have been established in Australia, Italy, Switzerland and New Zealand.

The parent monasteries in Thailand are part of the forest tradition of Theravada Buddhism where meditation is given priority over other kinds of activities carried out by monks such as study or education. The same emphasis is found in the western centres. Other activities engaged in by the monks (*bhikkhu*) and nuns (*siladhara*) are teaching the laity, running meditation retreats, prison visiting, hospice work and inter-faith dialogue. At the Sussex monastery the monks and nuns are restoring a 120 acre commercial forest to the condition of variegated English woodland and the 25 acres of grounds around the monastery to traditional English meadowland.

The constitution of the monastic *sangha* is quite international. In the community of 80 monks and nuns (in the four centres) 15 nationalities are represented.

American Council for Judaism. American anti-**Zionist** organization founded in 1942 by group of Reform rabbis who disagreed with the decision of the **Central Conference of American Rabbis** (the Reform Rabbinate) to support the creation of a Jewish army in Palestine. At one time, it claimed a membership of 20,000. Isolated since its inception, it lost further support among American Jews following the *Six-Day War* (1967). Many of the Reform *temples* previously associated with it no longer support it. The Council continues to represent the anti-Zionist position characteristic of the "classical" **Reform Judaism** of the late 19th century.

American Jewish Committee. Founded in 1906 in response to Russian *pogroms,* the American Jewish Committee, has continued to fight for the rights of Jews worldwide. Originally supporting the *Balfour Declaration,* it also insisted that Jewish rights throughout the world be protected. After a split with the **Zionist** leadership in 1942, it decided in 1946 to support an independent Jewish state as opposed to its previous hope that the United Nations could guarantee Jewish rights without the creation of a state. Since 1947, it has also fought on behalf of non-Jews, becoming involved in the Civil Rights movement. Originally limiting itself to a membership of 60, the Committee was reorganized in 1944 with a broader membership base numbering today in the tens of thousands with offices in New York, Jerusalem, Paris, Mexico, and South America. It sponsors *Commentary* and along with The Jewish Publication Society of America, publishes the *The American Jewish Yearbook.*

American Jewish Congress. A community relations organization, The American Jewish Congress began as a short-term coalition of Jewish groups following World War I but due to participants' demands became an established institution, led by Stephen S. Wise, in 1928. It later organized anti-Nazi protests, creating along with the Jewish Labor Council a boycott of German products. The Congress has fought American anti-Semitism and since 1945 has been involved in activities to strengthen American pluralism such as the Civil Rights Movement and efforts to maintain church–state separation. Consistently pro-**Zionist,** the Congress today attempts to create understanding between American and Israeli Jews. There are currently over 300 chapters across America.

American Jewish Joint Distribution Committee. Founded in 1914, "the Joint", as it is popularly known is a worldwide Jewish charitable organization. Created during World War I to aid European and Palestinian Jews, its activities continued throughout World War II after which it took responsibility for providing services to 250,000 European Jews and another 50,000 in the displaced persons' camp of Cyprus. It currently aids Jews in 40 countries and has recently assisted in relief efforts for Iraqi Kurds and non-Jewish Ethiopians. Since 1939, it has been part of **United Jewish Appeal.**

American Muslim Mission. This is the name currently used by the US organization formerly known as the Nation of Islam, but which became famous under the more popular label of the **Black Muslims**.

Amish. The Amish are a branch of the **Mennonite** Church. They were originally followers of Jakob Ammann, a Swiss 17th century Mennonite elder who set high, rigid standards of behaviour and dress and withdrew his followers from the mainstream Mennonites. Amish families migrated to America in the 18th century and settled in Pennsylvania, later spreading out to other states. The movement eventually died out in Europe.

Old Order Mennonite Amish live in settlements made up of districts each of up to 200 people. There are no church buildings, members meet in each other's homes. The leader of the settlement is the bishop, aided in worship by preachers and deacons. Services are conducted in a distinctive language known as Pennsylvanian Dutch (a mixture of Old German and English).

Amish men have beards (but not moustaches) and their clothes fasten with hooks and eyes not buttons. They wear distinctive broadbrimmed black hats. Women wear long full dresses without jewellery, black stockings and shoes, plus bonnets and shawls. They do not have electric light, telephones or motor cars, but despite refusing to use modern machinery have a high reputation as farmers. Each community is independent, and a community may divide into two if it is too large.

Amish beliefs are very similar to Mennonites; they practise adult baptism and celebrate Holy Communion and footwashing. It is believed there are over 50,000 Amish.

Amorc. Amorc—or strictly AMORC: the Ancient and Mystical Order Rosae Crucis—is an international organization founded in 1915 by the prolific writer H. Spencer-Lewis and, as its name implies, claiming a **Rosicrucian** origin.

Amritdhari Sikhs. A Sikh who has undergone initiation into the *khalsa*, or Sikh community established by the tenth *guru*, Gobind Singh in 1699. A **Khalsa Sikh** who has therefore "taken *amrit*", the sweetened water central to the initiation ceremony. All Amritdharis are also **Keshdhari.**

Ananda Marga. Ananda Marga is a new religious movement founded in 1955 in Bihar, India, by Sri Anandmurti (b. 1921). He taught a form of **Tantric Yoga** based on chanting, meditation and Yoga. It is highly structured and ascetic, with strict regulations on cleanliness, conduct, diet

(vegetarian), and sex. Fully committed members (*acharyas*)—estimated at several hundred thousand worldwide—wear Indian dress, take an Indian name, and are celibate, though part-time members blend in with society.

The movement has been accused of violent terrorism, and believes the use of force is justified against tyranny and exploitation. It was banned in India during the 1970s emergency, when its leader was imprisoned, though finally acquitted, on murder charges.

The movement used to have a large following in Europe, especially Germany, but numbers are now diminishing. It runs schools, orphanages and projects for the poor in several Third World countries.

Angkatan Belia Islam Malaysiam (ABIM). ABIM, the Malaysian Islamic Youth Movement, is one of the most important *dakwah* (Muslim renewal) organizations in Malaysia. Founded by students of the University of Malaya in 1971, this campus-based movement was in the 1970s responsible for the radicalizing of Malay students at home and overseas. ABIM's founders saw Islam as a force for change throughout society, including political change, and as a comprehensive way of life relevant to all areas of society. ABIM lays much emphasis on international Muslim brotherhood, and on justice in all spheres, campaigning for example against government corruption. Close ideological similarities are claimed with two well-established Islamic movements abroad, the **Jama'at-i Islami** and the **Muslim Brotherhood.**

Like most dakwah organizations, ABIM operates through a network of cell groups, on campuses and in university halls. It also publishes magazines and pamphlets, and promotes training and education in true Islamic principles. Its influence has changed the whole nature of student life in Malaysia, symbolized perhaps by increasingly strict Islamic dress becoming standard on campus. For a while, especially between 1979 and

1981, it also commanded increasing respect in rural areas through its championing of social as well as religious issues.

ABIM is now a relatively declining force. UMNO (United Malay National Organization), the main, Malay–Muslim, party in the government coalition, moved to counter its influence, for example by setting up rival schools, and rival programmes of talks and seminars. In 1982 UMNO actually recruited the charismatic ABIM president, Anwar Ibrahim, to its ranks—which he quickly ascended to ministerial level. This "defection" induced many ABIM members to transfer their allegiance to the fundamentalist opposition group PAS (**Parti Islam Se-Malaysia**), leaving ABIM appreciably weakened. Its progressive emphases have been displaced by more radical fundamentalist groups and influences, including **Darul Arqam.**

Anglicans. Adherents of the Church of England are called Anglicans in Britain. All the churches which belong to the Anglican Communion trace their origins to the Church of England and send bishops to the Lambeth Conference. They are independent, autonomous churches, except in England where the mother-church has restrictions placed on it by Parliament. Anglicanism outside Britain is largely the result of missionary and imperialist outreach. The beliefs and practices of the Church of England were carried to the American colonies (where they were originally under the episcopal oversight of the bishop of London), to Canada, India, Australia and New Zealand, and to those parts of Africa, Asia, and the Caribbean where British colonies were established.

The Church of England claims to be a reformed Catholic Church. The Reformation in England was partly an act of state, decided by King Henry VIII, but made possible also by the influence of **Protestant** ideas from the continent, and by an upsurge of popular piety. In England, the authority of the Pope was renounced by the *Act of Supremacy* in 1534. The *Book of Common Prayer* was authorized in 1559, and for centuries provided the only permissible forms of service which could be used in Anglican churches. Doctrine and ritual were defined in the *Thirty-nine Articles* of 1571, and the Bible was translated into English in the Authorized Version of 1611. The Church of England attempts to be inclusive, and contain those with widely differing theological emphases. These include **Evangelicals,** who include the present Archbishop of Canterbury, Dr. George Carey, who stress individual commitment to Christ. Then there are those like the Archbishop of York, Dr. John Habgood, who values its historical role as the church of the kingdom of England, by law established, with the monarch as Supreme Governor, and bishops in the House of Lords. Dr. Habgood sees it also as the national church of the English people, though many choose to dissent. There are high churchmen, sometimes called **Anglo-Catholics,** who see themselves as heirs to a fusion of the Celtic Church pioneered in the north by Aidan of Lindisfarne in 634, and also of the mission from Rome sent by Pope Gregory and led by Augustine who reached Canterbury in 597. As an episcopal church, value is placed on the historic succession of bishops.

The creation of bishops outside England inevitably presented problems for united action. In 1867 Archbishop Longley invited all the diocesan bishops to a conference at Lambeth, and his successors have normally repeated the invitation every 10 years. Lambeth Conferences provide an indication of the Anglican instinct on a wide range of doctrinal, moral and social questions, but their decisions are not legally binding. At the 1988 Conference, the most explosive issue was the ordination of women to the priesthood and their consecration to the episcopate.

Anglo–Catholics. The name given to those priests and people in the Church of England who hold high church views. They value the apostolic succession conveyed in the laying-on of hands by a bishop at ordination. Anglo–Catholicism is a product of the Oxford Movement which was a reaction to government interference in the affairs of the church in 1833. It came to value ritual, the wearing of vestments, and the use of incense. Supporters often long for the recognition of Anglican orders by the Pope. Some of them work in the downtown parts of cities and feel a particular commitment to Christian Socialism. Through the *Alternative Service Book 1980,* Anglo–Catholics have largely succeeded in one of their aims which was to make Holy Communion the principal service of the Church of England. In recent years some of those who accept the Catholic vision have become concerned that it has become associated with opposition to women priests and a tolerance of homosexuality. The bishop of Edinburgh, Richard Holloway and the theologian, Rowan Williams, have launched Affirming Catholicism to emphasize the positive aspects of this tradition.

Ansar. The Ansar (Helpers) are a Sudanese religious movement loyal to the memory of Muhammad Ahmad (1848–1885), the Mahdi. Originally a revolutionary messianic movement, or **Mahdiya,** which established an Islamic state in the Sudan from 1885 to 1899, they have survived as a religious grouping with a powerful influence in the Sudan through support of their political extension, the Umma Party. Their militancy can still be reactivated, despite their military defeat by President Nimeiri's forces in the attack on their Aba Island base in 1970. At the height of Nimeiri's Islamization programme in 1984, they marched in force to the Mahdi's tomb to pledge an oath of allegiance to a great grandson of the Mahdi, Sadiq al-Mahdi, as their leader and the Mahdi's successor. Sadiq, leader of the Umma Party, and one of the leading politicians of independent Sudan, was a vocal critic of Nimeiri's shari'a policy. With Ansar support, he played a key role in

the brief democratic interlude between the elections of 1986 (Nimeiri was deposed in 1985) and the military *coup* of 1989.

Anthroposophy. Anthroposophy (wisdom of humanity) shares the same tenets as **Theosophy** (wisdom of God), but emphasizes the central place of humanity in the spiritual science. It was founded by Rudolf Steiner in 1913 when he broke away from the Theosophical Society in Germany. Knowledge of higher worlds is attained through mental, physical and spiritual exercises and the celebration of the sacrament is central to the Anthrosophical Society's Christian Fellowships. Steiner's ideas have been used as the basis for experimental work in agriculture and education. Steiner schools are most numerous in Germany, but are held in high regard in all countries where they occur.

Anti-Bahai Society. This is the name by which the **Hojjatiya Society** of Iran used to be known.

Anuvrat Movement. A modern **Jain** lay movement founded in 1949 by the **Terapanthin** monk Acarya Tulsi. Conceived as an attempt to uproot corruption from India, and open to all regardless of religious affiliation, the movement stresses the centrality of the five Jain lay vows of non-injury (*ahimsa*), truthfulness (*satya*), non-steadling, avoidance of illicit sex, and non-attachment.

Apostolic Church (Pentecostal Congregation of Penygroes). The Apostolic Church (AC) was founded by the brothers Daniel Power Williams (1882–1947) and William Jones Williams (1891–1945) in 1916. The brothers were converted during the Welsh revival 1904–5 and became associated with the Apostolic Faith Church of W. O. Hutchinson (1864–1924) in Bournemouth where Daniel was called into office as an apostle in 1913.

In 1915 there were disagreements between the AFC and the Welsh assemblies which resulted in the founding of the AC and William, a miner, was called into the new office of prophet. Soon a number of other churches joined the AC, the Burning Bush Assembly of Andrew Turnbull (1872–1937) of Glasgow in 1918, the assembly of Frank Hodges of Hereford in 1922, and in 1924 a group of churches under the leadership of H. V. Chander of Bradford. Administrative headquarters were established at Penygroes, Carmarthen Wales, with the Apostolic Convention Hall (3,000 seats) where an annual convention is held and a Bible School whilst the centre for missionary activities is in Bradford and the financial control in Glasgow (members give tithes and other donations).

In the AC organization and doctrine is closely linked. On the one hand there is a strict hierarchy of apostles (who lay on hands to impart the holy spirit, ordain the elders and govern the church), prophets, shepherds, teachers, evangelists, elders, deacons and deaconesses, whilst on the other hand the gifts of the Spirit are given full scope. After a period of growth in the 1930s, the AC is today one of the smallest Pentecostal groups in the UK and actually in decline. The AC is a member of the British Apostolic Fellowship but its relationship with other Pentecostal churches must be described as not without problems and tensions. The AC is of some importance through its extensive missionary work in Nigeria, where it is the largest Protestant church, and in France, Italy, Denmark and New Zealand.

Armenian Church. The Armenian Church, officially the "Armenian Apostolic Church", represents one of three main traditions among the **Oriental Orthodox** Churches. The ancient kingdom of Armenia was the first nation officially to adopt Christianity,

converted by St Gregory the Illuminator around 300, whence its alternative title of "Armenian Gregorian Church". It became separated from the mainstream Church in 506, after repudiating, partly for ecclesio-political reasons, the decrees of the Council of Chalcedon (451), which made the Church at least nominally monophysite in its theology. Armenian worship, celebrated in an archaic form of Armenian but based substantially on the Byzantine (Greek) Liturgy, preserves some of the oldest forms of Christian chant. The supreme head is theoretically the Catholicos-Patriarch of all the Armenians, whose seat is at Etshmiadzin monastery in the ex-Soviet but now independent republic of Armenia. The hierarchy's alleged complicity with the Soviet régime led many Armenians to acknowledge the Catholicos of Sis (resident near Beirut) as supreme head.

The Armenians have suffered centuries of invasion and persecution, becoming widely scattered outside their original homeland (now divided between the Armenian Republic and north-east Turkey). During World War I, c.500,000 Armenians were massacred by the Turks, while in Soviet Armenia the Church was all but completely suppressed. Throughout, the Church has remained a potent symbol of Armenian national identity. Today Armenian communities preserve their religious traditions in many countries of the Middle East, Europe and the Americas, numbering around 4,000,000 individuals worldwide. There is a small but well-known community in Jerusalem. Since 1742 there has also been a Uniate Armenian Church, governed by a Patriarch residing in Beirut and numbering around 1,000,000 faithful. These have shared the suffering and exile of the Oriental Orthodox Armenians, and communities exist in many parts of the Middle East and North America.

Armstrongism. This name, based on that of the founder, Herbert W. Armstrong, is an alternative designation for the **Worldwide Church of God.**

Asali Nirankaris. Literally, the true **Nirankaris.** A designation employed to distinguish the **Sikh**-derived Nirankari movement from the move recent splinter group, the **Sant Nirankari Mandal.**

Ashkenazi. (See also **Sephardi.**) Refers to Jews from Central and Eastern Europe and their descendants. The community began in the Middle Ages along the Rhine valley in Northern Germany and France being referred to by the name of the Biblically-mentioned Ashkenaz (Genesis 10:3, 1 Chronicles 1:6 and Jeremiah 51:27) for reasons that are disputed among scholars. The originally geographic designation became the label for a specific Jewish cultural tradition. The Ashkenazim gradually spread throughout Central and Eastern Europe as well as to England and later to America. Following the outbreak of the Russian *pogroms* (1881), Ashkenazim fled in large numbers to America and in lesser numbers to the land of Israel. Ashkenazim outnumbered Sephardim (Jews from Spain and Portugal) from the 17th century onwards, comprising 90 per cent of world Jewry before the *Holocaust.*

Ashkenazi and **Sephardi** cultures developed their own cultural, liturgical and linguistic differences (differing pronunciation of *Hebrew* along with Ashkenazim speaking German-influenced languages such as *Yiddish*). Though upholding both the *Written and Oral Torahs,* Ashkenazi and Sephardi interpretations of Jewish law differ to some degree, being most pronounced during Passover when Sephardim permit and Ashkenazim prohibit certain foods.

Today, Ashkenazim comprise the majority of Jews in Europe, North America, South Africa, Australia, and New Zealand, and just less than half of the population of Israel. The Ashkenazim in Israel have their own Chief *Rabbi* and systems of education and law courts.

Assemblies of God. The Assemblies of God is the largest **Pentecostal** denomination in the United States. It was founded from a number of pentecostal groups at Hot Springs, Arkansas in April 1914 at the initiative of Howard Goss.

The church has an ordained ministry and a democratic system of church government. It administers a number of Bible Colleges and a publishing house, and sends missionaries throughout the world.

As in all pentecostal churches the gifts of the Holy Spirit (1 Corinthians 12) are expected and practised, in particular speaking in tongues, healing and prophecy.

Assemblies of God. *See* **Pentecostal**.

Association of Combatant Clergy. This Iranian **Shi'ite** organization is described under the alternative name of **Society of Militant Clergy.**

Association of Reform Zionists of America (ARZA). *See* **Reform Judaism.**

Association of Sect Shinto. A Japanese religious organization formed to oversee the administration and development of **Kyoha Shinto.**

Association of Shinto Shrines. Also known as **Jinja Honcho,** this organization was founded in 1946 to co-ordinate the affairs of Shrine or **Jinja Shinto.**

Assyrian Church. This is an alternative name for the **Nestorian Church.**

Australian Aboriginal Religion. The Australian Aborigines retain one of the oldest of all living religious traditions on the planet, having lived for millennia untouched in Australia before the coming of the Europeans.

The understanding of human nature in Aboriginal religion is profound in that each person is seen as a partial incarnation of a totemic ancestor, with all people having two souls, one being from its human parents, and the other being immortal and deriving from its totemic ancestor. This latter soul returns at death to the sacred realm of the dream time. The totemic ancestors are seen as archetypes pre-existing in nature out of which the shapes and forms of the natural world, including the animal and human realms, are created. It is thanks to their continued activity that life as we know it is possible. The greatest of all totemic ancestors is the Great Rainbow Snake who is conceived as the primary totemic deity of the dream time, the giver of life, dweller in deep pools, with a body shining like quartz, brilliant with light, shimmering like mother of pearl. In its moistness and effervescence the Rainbow Snake is the giver of all fertility, liquid, blood, water and hence life itself. The Rainbow Snake is also seen as underlying the energy of sexuality and is hence accompanied by sexual companions, the "Green Parrot Girls". For Aboriginal culture the sacred and the secular co-exist; sacred time, "Altajiranga", or the "dream time" comprises the depth and resonance within which our own world is sustained.

Central to Aboriginal spirituality is the idea that certain particular regions of the landscape or certain sacred objects are more deeply charged with the numinous than others, and act as channels or interconnection points between the different levels of being in the cosmos as a whole. "Tjurunga" are particular sacred objects or activities which act as agents of intersection in this manner, such as the bullroarer, or tshals, or yams, or special boards with elongated ends. Aboriginal religion is concerned with the control and channelling of the sacred into forms which can sustain and uphold the community, through individual or collective initiation rites. This process of initiation is important to Aboriginal culture and involves elaborate and painful mutilations, periods of fasting and solitude, and the ceremonial decoration of one's body through sacred cosmetics. Collective times of transformation included "corroborees", namely festive ceremonies which involved the re-enactment of myths seen as co-existing in the dream time performed on sacred ground, which has been decorated and prepared in advance. The Aboriginal sense of art, including colour and design, is closely interlinked with their spirituality, and integrated into their religious practices, unlike more sophisticated cultures where "art" is seen as something other than spirituality.

Aboriginal spirituality remains a living tradition for the minority indigenous population of Australia, comprising some 2 per cent of the population, namely 250,000 people. It remains a rallying force in the face of the growing contemporary problems of the country, such as racism, unemployment, and landlessness.

Aydinlar Ocagi. "The Intellectuals' Hearth" was founded in the late 1960s in Turkey as a club or discussion group for the elaboration of a right-wing ideology suited to counter the appeal of the 1968 student movement (university professors being prominent among the founders). The result was a "Turkish-Islamic Synthesis" which has become increasingly influential in government circles since the 1980s as the Hearth's members have gained senior positions in the state.

The ideology may be described as a blend of elements of putatively distinctive Turkish national culture reinforced by a common religious faith and heritage. The family, the mosque and the military are regarded as key institutions which should be mutually reinforcing—and indeed were so before Turkish intellectuals' capitulation to ideologies of Communism and humanism, combined with unreflective imitation of the West. Modernization should be combined with national culture—in which Islam is a central component—in the manner successfully pioneered by the Japanese integration of traditional religious values with technological advance.

Education has a fundamental role to play in re-establishing or strengthening Turkish–Islamic culture, and since 1982 religious education has become compulsory for all secondary school pupils. An Islamic upbringing is seen as essential for inculcating the requisite spiritual and moral values. With these in place, youthful rebellion and social conflict will be averted, and a harmonious process of industrialization can occur.

From the perspective of groups like the **Nurcus** and **Süleymancis,** all this remains tantamount to a variation on the policy of attempted state control of Islam for nationalist purposes to which they have always been opposed.

Azalis. Azalis (or Azali Babis) are a tiny minority in Iran who continue to adhere to the beliefs and laws of the **Babis.** Their name is derived from Mirza Yahya Nuri Subh-i Azal (c.1830–1912), the Bab's appointed successor. The Azalis remained loyal to him when, in the mid-nineteenth century, other Babis followed his half-brother Mirza Husayn 'Ali Baha Allah, and created the independent religion of **Bahaism.**

Aztecan Religion. Elements of the spiritual legacy of the Aztecs have been retained in **Mesoamerican Traditional Religions** in Mexico.

B

Baalei Teshuvah. *See* **Orthodox Judaism; Zionism.**

Babis. Babism began in Iran and Iraq as a radical millenarian movement within **Twelver Shi'ism.** The founder, Sayyid 'Ali Muhammad Shirazi, the Bab (1819–50), was a merchant who had been deeply influenced by **Shi'ite** esotericism. In 1844, following the death of the head of the semi-heterodox **Shaykhi** school, Shirazi proclaimed himself the Gate (*bab*) to the twelfth Imam, the Shi'ite messiah.

Subsequently, he claimed to be the hidden Imam in person and a prophet bringing a new faith to abrogate Islam. Large numbers converted throughout Iran, leading to widespread controversy. The Babis themselves adopted a militant policy, anticipating a holy war and the inauguration of a theocratic state.

Defeat in fierce clashes with state troops led to the collapse of the movement's appeal as an instrument for social and political change. The Bab himself was executed in 1850, and the remaining leadership forced into exile in Baghdad in 1852, after an abortive attempt on the Shah's life.

By the 1860s, a split had occurred between the Bab's appointed successor, Mirza Yahya Nuri Subh-i Azal (c. 1830–1912) and his half-brother, Mirza Husayn 'Ali Baha Allah, whose followers created an independent religion, **Baha'ism.** Only the small minority remaining faithful to Azal retained the beliefs and laws of the original movement.

Many **Azali** Babis became prominent in radical Iranian politics around the turn of the century, but Babism has remained an insignificant minority movement increasingly marginalized from wider society and lacking a clear leadership or organization. There are now only a few hundred Azali families in Iran.

Badawiya. The Badawiya is one of the most important **Sufi** orders in Egypt. It was founded by Ahmad al-Badawi, a Moroccan educated in Mecca who began to have mystical experiences when he was about 30, followed by a vision impelling him to go to Tanta in Egypt. Here he remained until his death in 1276, attracting disciples and establishing a reputation for miracles, mysticism and saintly conduct.

Today a large city in the Egyptian delta, Tanta remains the centre of the cult of "Sidi Ahmad". Its highlight is a week-long autumn festival which attracts well over 1,000,000 pilgrims. Other Sufi orders are prominently represented too, setting up their tents, displaying their flags, and taking part in the colourful procession which culminates in the present leader of the Badawiya entering the great mosque-tomb for a special Sufi service.

The government is also well represented at this gathering, although among sophisticated Egyptians there is a tendency to dismiss the whole thing as popular superstition. At the popular level, certainly, the Sidi Ahmad cult remains spiritually potent throughout Egypt today. (Moreover, Tanta is also a prominent centre of Islamic learning: it is where, for example, Muhammad 'Abduh, so important in the **Salafiya** movement, was educated.)

Bahais. With a world membership claimed to lie between 3,000,000–4,000,000, over 100,000 centres in almost every part of the globe, and an active international missionary campaign, Bahaism (the Bahai Faith) may yet prove the most successful of the numerous new religions that have come to prominence since World War II. The question of how to "place" Bahaism is a little problematic. Although it originated as a sectarian movement within **Shi'ite** Islam, there is now no sense in which Bahais would regard themselves as Muslims, nor would they be recognized as such by any branch of Islam.

Bahais themselves have for some time now proclaimed their faith to be a "world religion" on a par with Islam, Christianity, and other established creeds. This however, presents obvious problems in the case of a movement at most 150 years old, without a distinct culture, and lacking a major presence in any one country. Actual status varies from place to place. In Iran, the movement's birthplace, Bahais represent the largest religious minority (about 300,000), but are the object of severe official and popular disapproval and periodic persecution. Elsewhere in the Muslim world, they are a negligible minority subject to legal and social restrictions or, in many cases, an absolute ban.

Since the 1960s, there has been considerable growth of the movement in developing countries, to the extent that Bahaism, it has been said, has started to become a predominantly Third World religion. "Mass conversion" of largely rural peoples in Latin America, Africa, and Asia has been the chief cause of expansion in the modern period. The largest Bahai community in the world is now that of India, where there are almost 1,000,000 adherents.

The faith's founder, Mirza Husayn 'Ali Nuri Baha Allah (Baha'u'llah) (1817–1892) was the son of an Iranian government official. One of the first individuals in Tehran to convert to the radical **Babi** sect in 1844, Husayn 'Ali came to prominence following the death of the Bab and most of his leading disciples (drawn from the ranks of the Shi'ite clergy) by 1852, and went on to become the most prominent of a new generation of non-clerical claimants to divine inspiration in the 1850s.

In the course of successive exiles (Baghdad 1853–1863, Istanbul, Edirne 1864–1868, and Palestine 1868–1892), Husayn 'Ali, now terming himself Baha Allah (the Beauty of God), transformed the militant sect of the Bab into a semi-pacifist, universalist religion that owed much to Islam but proclaimed the advent of a new dispensa-tion in which all earlier religions would be fulfilled.

Both Baha Allah and his son and successor, 'Abbas Effendi 'Abd al-Baha (1844–1921) did more than just modify the eccentricities of Babism. Influenced by Western ideas on matters such as the equal status of men and women, the harmony of science and religion, universal peace, world government, or the adoption of an international language, they created an eclectic movement designed to be attractive far beyond the Islamic confines within which it had had its origins. 'Abd al-Baha in particular preached a universalist creed equally divorced from Islamic legalism and Far Eastern mysticism, and from the 1890s the faith attracted a following in Europe and America, principally among middle-class religious dilettantes.

'Abbas's successor, Shoghi Effendi Rabbani (1897–1957) carried the Westernization of Bahaism much further. He was one of the first spiritual leaders in his century to introduce Western managerial techniques into the realm of religious organization, creating bye-laws and administrative methods for the numerous local and national "Spiritual Assemblies" which formed the basic units of an increasingly complex organizational hierarchy. By his death in 1957, he had successfully laid the basis for the continued international expansion and bureaucratization of the movement and, like his predecessors, bequeathed to its followers a substantial body of writing (including numerous original works and translations in English).

It had originally been intended that Shoghi be the first of a line of Baha'i Guardians (modelled on the Shi'ite *imams*), but he left neither children nor will, and in 1963 an internationally elected body known as the Universal House of Justice took control of the faith. The vast majority of Bahais gave their allegiance to this nine-man council, although a number of small splinter groups have challenged their authority and advanced their own leaders.

Bahai belief is a complex development of Islamic doctrine modified by general

Shi'ite and Babi concepts and manifestly influenced by modern Western social and political theory (although Bahais ascribe their beliefs solely to divine inspiration). Within the Bahai system, a transcendent divinity periodically reveals Himself to mankind through the medium of "Manifestations" (*mazahir ilahiyya*), among whom the most notable have been Moses, Jesus, Muhammad, the Bab, and Baha Allah. Bahais include among the prophets of the past several figures not recognized in conventional Islamic doctrine, such as Zoroaster, Krishna, and Buddha.

Apart from spiritual teachings modelled on Jewish, Christian, and Islamic norms, Baha Alla "revealed" a body of laws and social teachings deemed to constitute a *shari'a* or legislative canon binding on believers and covering such areas as prayer, fasting, pilgrimage, marriage, divorce, burial, inheritance, punishments for criminal offences, and taxation. This rudimentary system may in future be supplemented (but not abrogated) by the Universal House of Justice, which is regarded as a divinely inspired legislative body.

Modern Bahaism since 'Abd al-Baha has laid much emphasis on religio–social teachings such as those mentioned above, and there tends to be a greater emphasis on administrative than devotional activities. A small number of Bahai temples (*Mashriq al-Adhkar*) have been built on a continental basis, but in most places meetings take place in rented premises or believers' homes. The Bahai world centre at Haifa, Israel, has been elaborately developed and landscaped, and is the focus for pilgrimage in the absence of access to holy sites in Shiraz (Iran) and Baghdad.

Bahais are formally prohibited from engaging in politics, but the writings of Shoghi Effendi in particular make it clear that the long-term aim of the movement is to enter the political process through the creation of theocratic states, leading to the eventual emergence of a universal Bahai commonwealth ruled by the Universal House of Justice and subsidiary national Houses of Justice. (*See also* **Orthodox Bahai Faith,**

Freie Bahai, Bahais Under the Provisions of the Covenant.)

Bahais Under the Provisions of the Covenant. A small **Bahai** sectarian group established by Leland Jensen and based in Missoula, Montana, USA.

Bal Krishnavas. Hindu devotees of Krishna conceived as the divine child, Balaji. Bal Krishnavas are mainly found in south India and numerous sub-cults, in which Balaji is honoured in a variety of forms, exist within the overall, highly fluid, movement.

Balmikis. This is the Punjabi form of the name of the author of the Hindu *Ramayana*. He is said to have been a member of the *chuhra* (i.e. sweeper) caste. Many *chuhra* attempted to improve their status by converting *en masse* to **Sikhism** in the late 19th and early 20th centuries. They discovered, however, that religious acceptance did not necessarily improve their depressed social position so they adopted Balmiki as their *guru* and have established a *sabha* (society) which is neither Hindu nor Sikh though in their places of worship, also known as *sabhas*, copies of the *Guru Granth Sahib* and *Ramayana* will be seen installed side by side. Balmikis also tend to adopt the insignia of **Keshdari Sikhs.**

Bangwa Religion. Bangwa religion is an example of **African traditional religions**. The Bangwa, who probably number under 100,000, live on the forested southwestern edge of the much larger (numbering approximately 1,000,000) Bamileke peoples, speaking semi-Bantu languages, who inhabit the grassfield plateau between the equatorial forest and savannah zones of Cameroon. Commerce, in particular the trans-Atlantic slave trade, allowed Bangwa chiefs to accumulate wealth, measured in women and ceremonial objects. The nine paramount chiefs, who in the past might have had 50 or more wives, together with their children and palace retainers, form the focus of territorial groups, and control the main markets. Sub-chiefs and quarter-heads reproduce the same pattern on a smaller scale. In the religious sphere the supreme god, Ndem, parallels the paramount chief, who sacrifices to Ndem on behalf of his people at a territorial shrine (natural rather than man-made). Sub-chiefs, quarter-heads and compound heads sacrifice to lesser gods on behalf of their respective territorial units.

Shallow ancestral groups are also the focus of offerings and prayers, centred on the ancestors' skulls. Patrilineal skulls are inherited by a male patrigroup head whereas female skulls are dispersed in the care of female kin.

Spirits and witches inhabit water, the forest and natural phenomena, and are generally capricious and need to be placated. A diviner will diagnose the source of sickness (ancestors, spirits, witchcraft) and suggest appropriate remedies.

Witchcraft is inherited from a parent of the same sex and can be activated without an individual's knowledge. Chiefs and their retinue may form witch covens with the power to transform into were-animals and attack their enemies. If used for the good of the community witchcraft is an accepted weapon, but if it is motivated by spite and results in disharmony within the community it is condemned. Anti-witchcraft cults and medicines are used as protection from the attack of witches, usually patrilineal kin or co-wives. Post-mortems (now illegal) determined whether the deceased was a witch killed by anti-witchcraft devices. Witchcraft is associated with heat and anti-witchcraft medicines cool its power.

Twin births are particularly auspicious and twin parents become ritual specialists. In the world of unborn children people move around in pairs or groups. Single births result in the break up of these groups and sickly children, who are tempted by their unborn friends to return, need to have their "spirit eyes" ritually closed.

For the many Bangwa who have moved to the towns, witchcraft remains the most enduring aspect of traditional belief. Christianity has also had an impact, and the ancestral skull cult has declined in importance, although Christianity can in no way replace a whole cosmology and system of beliefs embedded in the life of the people.

Baptists. In 1611 Thomas Helwys returned to England from Amsterdam, Holland, inspired by the teaching he had received from John Smyth. He founded a church in Newgate Street, Spitalfields, London. Its distinctive belief was in believers' baptism, rather than the infant baptism practised by the established church. In addition, members supported Armenian theology which maintained that Christ died for all, but that it was possible even for Christians to fall from grace and resist the work of the Holy Spirit.

The movement flourished, but 20 years later there was a schism by Baptists influenced by the Calvinist doctrine that God chooses who will be saved and those who are "elected" to salvation can never be lost because God's grace is irresistible. This group became known as **"Particular Baptists"**.

Both groups grew during the 17th century, despite persecution. A lasting legacy from this time is *The Pilgrim's Progress* written by a Baptist pastor, John Bunyan, whilst in prison. During the 18th century the General Baptists (Armenian) were influenced by unitarian doctrine (denying the three persons of the Trinity) but returned to trinitarian orthodoxy under the teaching of Dan Taylor.

In 1792, following the work of William Carey, the Baptist Missionary Society was formed at Kettering, Northamptonshire, "for propagating the Gospel among the Heathen". This was the first Protestant missionary society and inspired other denominations to set up their own similar societies during the next 10 years. Once established in India as a missionary, William Carey translated the whole Bible into six different Asian languages with the aim of making God's word available to all.

The Baptist Church spread to America in 1639 with the founding of the community at Providence, Rhode Island by Roger Williams. (The English Baptists were separate from the **Mennonites** from Europe who also believed in adult baptism.) It has grown to be one of the largest denominations in the USA and was the origin of the black Baptist Church movement which has its own denominations. As in England there were doctrinal schisms: the **Southern Baptist** Convention (with over 14,000,000 members and extensive worldwide missionary work) is more fundamental and conservative than its northern equivalent the **American Baptist Churches** in the USA (2,000,000 members). The civil rights leader Martin Luther King came from the black Baptist church, Billy Graham, whose evangelistic campaigns take place all over the world is also from the American Baptist tradition.

In Europe Baptist doctrine "returned" in 1834 through work in Hamburg, Germany, and spread throughout the continent. In recent years Russian Baptists have been subjected to particular oppression by communist régimes because of their refusal to compromise with state suppression of religion and their insistence on evangelizing. The work of Baptist missionaries has spread the Baptist church into all continents.

Most Baptist churches in Britain now belong to the Baptist Union of Great Britain and Ireland, though some more conservative Baptist churches have formed their own groupings (in Wales, Scotland and Ireland). Very few Baptist churches are independent; from the earliest times there has been a tendency for Baptists to work together. However Baptists are divided about church unity, some support ecumenical bodies such as the World Council of Churches, others refuse to work with other denominations, particularly Roman Catholics.

Church leadership is from ministers with the assistance of elected deacons (lay). Worship usually consists of hymns, prayers and a sermon, with regular celebration of the Lord's Supper which Christians of other denominations are mostly welcome to share. Worldwide membership is estimated at 40,000,000 (not including the black denominations).

Baptist World Alliance. Originally the Baptist World Congress which first met in 1905, the Alliance is a voluntary association which is largely financed by **Southern Baptists.** Its headquarters are near Washington DC. Although many millions of **Baptists** throughout the world have no link with the Alliance, it does have the support of unions and conventions with 37,000,000 members.

Barelvis (Barelwis). The Barelvi movement is derived from one of several attempts by the Muslims of South Asia to find ways of being Muslim under colonial rule. However, whereas most of these attempts had their origins in a process of Islamic revival and reform, those of the Barelvis were in large part in resistance to this process. If the **Deobandis** wanted to conserve Islam as they found it in the law books of the Middle Ages, the Barelvis wished to conserve it as they found it in 19th century India, laden with local customs and imbued with the belief that saints could intercede for men with God. The movement crystallized in the late-19th century around the scholar and polymath, Ahmad Riza Khan of Bareilly (1856–1911), whose followers call themselves the true **Sunnis**, *Ahl-i Sunnat wa Jama'at.*

All Muslims honour the Prophet Muhammad. In the teaching of Ahmad Riza Khan, however, the Prophet is pre-eminent. He stresses the **Sufi** concept of the Light of Muhammad (Nur-i Muhammadi), which was derived from God's own light and which existed like the Word in Christian theology from the beginning of creation. It had played a part in the very process of creation; it was omnipresent; it meant that the Prophet, though human, was also more than human. He could intercede for man with God. In consequence, Ahmad Riza Khan's followers display enormous respect for the Prophet in their religious practice, paying great attention to *maulud* (celebrations of the Prophet's birth), to a particular moment in *maulud* when it is believed the Prophet is present, as well as to the annual death celebrations of many saints who, it is believed, also have intercessory powers.

Under the British the Barelvis tended to avoid politics, although eventually, like other non-reforming groups, they supported the demand for Pakistan. Since Independence in 1947, the movement has burgeoned both inside and outside South Asia. In Pakistan its organization is the Jam'iat ul-Ulama-i Pakistan, which boasts at least one notable political figure in Maulana Noorani. In Britain they form the largest group of Muslims and one which has been notable for its continuing quarrels with the Deobandis and the **Ahl-i Hadith,** and for the leading role its members played in the agitation against Salman Rushdie's *Satanic Verses*.

Bassij-i Mostazafin. Bassij-i Mostazafin, or Mobilization of the Oppressed, is an Iranian paramilitary organization which has become a vehicle of mass participation in the defence of the Islamic Republic by tens of thousands of volunteers, mostly young people under 18 years of age. In the 1980–1988 Iran–Iraq war they featured prominently in human wave attacks, being labelled by some observers the "boy warriors". Dedicated to the cause of Islam, the bassijis saw it as their duty to court martyrdom.

The Bassij has functioned under the Pasdaran organization, the **Islamic Revolutionary Guards,** since its inception in 1980.

Batiniya. Batiniya is an alternative name for the **Isma'ilis.** It is derived from their emphasis on the importance of esoteric in-

terpretations of religious belief, or inward (batini) truths.

Batuque. One of the names used in the central regions of Brazil for the **Afro-American spiritist** movement **Candomblé**.

Bauddha Dharmankur Sabha. Inaugurated in Calcutta in 1892, this association, along with the **Maha Bodhi** Society, has been instrumental in the revival of Buddhism in West Bengal.

Bauls. A Bengali Hindu movement noted for the poetic quality of its songs and the strangeness of its members' appearance. The name *baul* means "mad", and the tattered garments of these low-caste wandering mendicants give an impression of wildness which is in keeping with their refusal to accept social or religious conventions. They have neither ritual nor ceremonies, regarding their songs as their only worship and their spiritual path as the reverse of what is usually accepted. They have affinities with both the **Vaishnava Sahajiyas** and the **Sufis,** and come from both Hindu and Muslim families. The content and style of Baul songs was an influence upon the poetry of Rabindranath Tagore (1861–1941). He and his associates preserved many *Baul* songs, which had formerly been part of a completely oral tradition.

Bektashiya. The Bektashiya is a **Sufi** order founded by Hajji Bektash Wali (d. about 1337) in the 14th century; its organization and practices were reformed in the 16th century by Balim Sultan. It was one of the most important orders in the Ottoman Empire and flourished particularly in areas with a Christian population, in Albania and South Anatolia. Today it is found still mainly in Turkey, although there are a few centres in Yugoslavia (in Macedonia and Kosovo), and it may be expected to resurface in Albania, where it continued until its suppression, along with all organized religion, in 1967. (An Albanian Bektashi community is also to be found in Detroit.)

Registered officially as a **Sunni** organization under Ottoman rule, it might more aptly have been designated **Shi'ite.** Bektashi worship centres around 'Ali, adherents having evolved the concept of a trinity uniting 'Ali with Allah and Muhammad. The order has placed no great emphasis on the formal requirements of Islam, preserving some pre-Islamic Turkic **shamanic** traditions (e.g. a taboo on contact with the hare, or the necessity of revering the threshold of a door). It also includes Christian elements in its practices, such as the participation of women with unveiled faces in rituals, the confession of sins with absolution, and the distribution of wine, bread and cheese to new members. After the impressive initiation ceremony, men and women dance together.

The Bektashi order has a strict authoritarian structure with a *celebi* (chief) at its apex. It is famous for guarding a great secret, about whose content—whether theological, political, or social—there has been a variety of speculation.

The fortunes of the order have varied considerably. It was closely connected with the Janissaries (the slave military corps of the Ottoman army raised from the Christian population), and the destruction of these in 1826 was followed by a persecution of the Bektashiya. The order revived by the mid-19th century and played its part in politics through an alliance with the Young Turks. During World War I the order supported Kemal Ataturk. Together with all other Sufi orders, however, the Bektashiya was prohibited in Turkey in the autumn of 1925. It went underground and only re-emerged with the introduction of party politics after World War II. The Bektashis' main lodge, in Hacibektaş in central Anatolia, was restored and opened as a museum in 1964. The annual celebrations have been promoted as a tourist attraction, although they have at times become rather politicised: they have also

become a rallying point for **Alevis.** The fate of the Bektashiya has continued to depend from year to year on which government is in power.

The survival of the Bektashiya has depended on its flexibility in re-interpreting its role in Turkish society. The order began to re-interpret its history according to political necessities. Great emphasis has been placed on Turkishness, and the order's contribution to the Turkish language and literature. The Bektashis have also described their founder as an opponent of foreign influences, such as capitalism and fascism. The Bektashiya became very politicized; its structure and emphasis on secrecy have been a useful political resource for opposition to Turkish central government. Through re-interpretation of its tradition the Baktashi order has coped with the repression of various authorities over the centuries. It is cautiously finding a new mode of co-existence with the contemporary secular state.

Belz Hasidism. (See also **Orthodox Judaism, Zionism.**) One of the Eastern European Hasidic dynasties re-established after the *Holocaust* in the land of Israel (Jerusalem, Bene Berak, Haifa, Ashdod) with centres in Europe (London, Manchester, Antwerp) and North America (New York, Montreal, Toronto). Part of the **Haredi (Ultra-Orthodox)** sector of contemporary Jewry. Named after the town, in Galacia, where the founder, Rabbi Shalom Rokeah (1779–1856), established his "court". Under his leadership and that of his family dynasty, Belz became the major Hasidic centre in Galacia, with other centres at Lvov and Cracow, and through their involvement in communal affairs, Belz Hasidim came to exercise great influence on the development and character of Galacian Hasidism. Shalom Rokeah was a renown Talmudic scholar and began the traditional Belz stress on Rabbinic learning in addition to the practice of the commandments and Hasidic practices. He was also an opponent of the **Haskalah** and the Belz were, and still are, noted for their opposition to innovation and modernization. In Galacia the Belz were anti-**Zionist** and initially opposed to **Agudat Israel,** a tension that has re-surfaced in recent times.

Rabbi Aaron Rokeah (1880–1957), the fourth Rebbe, who helped establish the influence of Belz Hasidism among Hungarian Jewry (1914–18), moved to Israel in 1944. Establishing *Yeshivot* in Israel and a Belz centre in Tel Aviv, Aaron sanctioned the Belz affiliation with Agudat Israel. His grave in Tel Aviv is a place of pilgrimage for the Belz Hasidim. The current Rebbe is Rabbi Issachar Dov (1948) who moved his court to Jerusalem, now the centre of Belz life.

In recent years the Belz have resisted the growing dominance of Agudat Israel by **Ger** and **Lubavich Hasidim** and were the only Hasidic group to join the Lithuanian-dominated *Mitnaggdim* to form the **Degel Hatorah** party for the 1988 Israeli general election. The Belz supported the **United Torah Party** (created for the 1992 elections and made up of Agudat Israel and Degel Hatorah).

The Belz are characterized by their attention to their distinctive version of traditional Hasidic modes of dress, the absolute centrality of the Rebbe, *Torah* study and their attempt to preserve in its entirety the structure of their Hasidic lifestyle. Although their numbers are comparatively small, the Belz Rebbe and his Hasidim play a major role in the Haredi world, both in Israel and the *diaspora.*

Benedictines. Members of **Roman Catholic** monastic communities which observe the Rule of St Benedict. The basis of Benedictine monasticism is not the personality, nor the monastery—Monte Cassino—but the *Rule* of St Benedict of Nursia (c480–542). St Benedict created in his *Rule* the laws by which ". . . to establish a school of God's service, in which we hope to ordain nothing which is harsh or burdensome". The way of life in which the *Rule* issued was enduringly unique. It departs from the severe asceticism and the hermetic individualism of Egyptian monasticism. Benedictine monasticism is cenobitical, or communal. The monks' "work" is to praise God in the liturgy. The *Rule* enjoins seven daily offices: these are Lauds, Prime, Terce, Sext, None, Vespers and Compline. Obedience to the *Rule* is intended to impress upon the monk the successive stages of the ladder of "humility": this is to train him to suppress his self. Benedictine monasticism differs from the post-medieval religious orders in that its primary aim is not, as with the **Carmelites**, for example, to perfect the "interior castle", but rather, objectively to perform the liturgy. Moreover, the Benedictines have never been an order, answering to a central authority. Within the framework of adherence to *Rule* each abbey has relative autonomy; the *Rule* has been variously interpreted.

The *Rule* was practical: it could be applied to diverse circumstances with ease. Thus did its ethic, once espoused by Pope Gregory the Great (c540–604), become by the eighth century the basis of all European monasticism, and of much of her civilization. After the Oxford Movement, Victorians such as J. H. Newman depicted the Benedictines as the heroes of the Dark Ages, quietly rebuilding Europe after the depredations of the Vandals and Goths. In this case, romanticism ran close to the grain of history. The writings of the Early Church Fathers, and the Latin poetry of Ovid, Catullus and Virgil, survived the Dark Ages because they were endlessly copied by the monks. This was soon to be the only thing which the monks did by hand. By the year 1000 a new development had taken root: all choir monks were also ordained as priests. The abbeys' rural acres were now tilled by serfs. The leisure thus created was spent in the celebration of divine offices: highly scented psalmodies proliferated. The abbey of Cluny, founded in 910, lay behind this. A century later, the **Cistercians** broke away to recreate the simplicity of Egyptian monasticism: they founded Citeaux in 1098. St Bernard left there in 1115 in order to found Clairvaux. From Clairvaux, he preached a theology of experience: Peter the Venerable, last great Benedictine Abbot of Cluny, and the first high Tory, protected the dying Abelard from the consequences of both Bernard's puritanical zeal and Abelard's own eccentricities.

Cluny became a mother-house, presiding over smaller monasteries. Such administrative systematization received ecclesiastical approval at the Fourth Lateran Council of 1215. According to Cardinal Gasquet, "no country but England appeared to have taken the Council seriously". English Benedictine abbots and priors were thus the first triennially to meet in the new chapters; English monasteries were the first, perhaps, to enjoy visitations by Bishops. In 1408, the first Benedictine Congregation was born: this was the "Cassinese", a federation of Italian abbeys, created by Luigi Barbo. After the Council of Trent (1545–63), each abbey had by law to be affiliated to a Congregation. Henry VIII's suppression of the monasteries dispersed the English Benedictines. In 1619, Pope Paul V reunited them in the English Congregation. Many gathered at St Gregory's of Douai for the "English Mission". English Benedictines still call pastoral work "going on the Mission".

The near death of Benedictine monasticism in the 18th century, and its recovery, by the late 19th may be a source of optimism today, when numbers have once more fallen. The French Revolution, Napoleon and Joseph II of Austria each laid waste to the Benedictines. In 1800, only 30 Benedictine abbeys remained. By 1914, numbers had doubled. In the 1850s, the Benedictines returned to England, there to found the abbeys of Downside and Ampleforth: there are now 10 English abbeys. One major debate among modern English Benedictines has been whether monks should be first and foremost "missioners" or monks within the abbey: the latter have won the day. The present finds 21 Benedictine Congregations: the

largest, the Subiaco, is a group of 34 abbeys; an average Congregation contains 10 abbeys. The Benedictines now muster 9,453 monks, 8,425 nuns, and 11,564 sisters. An Abbot Primate presides over the united congregations. Since 1977, he has been the Reverend Dom Victor Dammertz. His powers are limited. Benedictines still vigorously subscribe to the principle of the subsidiarity of individual abbeys. Benedictine practice is thus diverse. Some French abbeys are contemplative, whilst the largest abbey, St John's, in Minnesota USA, is home to a university campus. Benedictines are, perhaps rightly, cheerful about their future: they are not prey to the cult of personality which has spoiled many modern Catholic religious movements. Alasdair MacIntyre claims that Europe now awaits its new St Benedict: it remains an open question whether he or she will be a Benedictine.

Bene Israel. The Bene Israel ("Sons of Israel") comprise the largest Jewish community in India, centred around Bombay (there are smaller communities in **Cochin,** Calcutta and Surat). Unknown to other Jews until the 18th century, the Bene Israel maintained a separate Jewish identity while having a unique niche in the caste system as well as adopting Hindu practices such as the prohibition of the eating of beef and the banning of widows from remarrying. According to their own traditions they are descendants of the lost 10 tribes of Israel and came to India as early as the 2nd century BCE. The Bene Israel underwent something of a "renaissance" in the 19th century and have since adopted **Sephardi** rites and traditions.

From a base of some 6,000 in the 1830s, their numbers peaked at more than 20,000 in 1948 but since then the majority have emigrated to England and Israel (some 7,000), where after some controversy over their Jewishness they were fully accepted by both the **Ashkenazi** and Sephardi Chief Rabbis in 1982.

Beta Israel. Literally the "House of Israel" (in the Ge'ez language), the self-designation of Ethiopian Jews. Their oral traditions recall "coming from the west" and following Jewish traditions from ancient times. Often referred as "**Falashas**" (Ge'ez for "strangers") although this name is not used by the Beta Israel themselves. In the past century their population declined from 250,000 (according to one report) to approximately 40,000. Identified by some traditionalists as the lost Israelite tribe of Dan, dating from the 8th century BCE and by other scholars as 4th century CE converts to Judaism, their origins are still a matter of debate. Their "Judaism" is very different in that unlike most Jewish communities, shaped by the mainline rabbinic developments in theology and practice as reflected in the *Oral Torah,* the Beta Israel had no access to these sources and have a number of their own specific traditions. They studied the Bible in Ge'ez translations.

In the mid-1970s American Jews took up their cause and after some questioning of their Jewish status, Israel began bringing them out covertly. The first major rescue attempt, Operation Moses in 1984 brought out more than 8,000 and was only halted due to publicity. Operation Solomon was launched in May 1991 to rescue Ethiopian Jews caught up in the civil war. More than 14,000 were brought to Israel in 24 hours. By April 1992, a further 2,560 had emigrated with the last 1,500 expected in Israel before the end of the year. The Beta Israel leadership patterns (the *kes* or "priest") have been somewhat assimilated to Jewish norms with a number of their leaders being ordained as **Orthodox** rabbis who encourage the community to follow contemporary Jewish rabbinic norms. Although recognized as Jews by the **Sephardi** Chief rabbi in 1973 and the **Ashkenazi** Chief Rabbi in 1975 there have been some difficulties over issues of marriage and legitimacy. There is also evidence of tensions between the traditional religious leaders and a new generation of non-religious spokesmen.

More than 30,000 Beta Israel now live in Israel.

Bharatiya Janata Party. The Bharatiya Janata Party (BJP), formed in April of 1980, represents a coalition of Hindu sectarian groups which has attempted to wrest power from the ruling Congress Party. Its major component is formed of former members of the Bharatiya Jana Sangh (BJS). This party was formed soon after Independence in 1951. Originally strongest in Uttar Pradesh, Madhya Pradesh, Rajastan, the Punjab, and around Delhi, the BJS managed in 1967 to wield enough power to exert considerable influence on the coalition governments of the period, but its influence declined in the early 1970s. After the lifting of the Emergency in January, 1977, it joined with other parties to form the Janata Party which held power until 1980. All of these parties espoused a platform founded on Hindu sectarian principles. Such principles include an activist version of Hindu nationalism closely allied to Brahminism and the regional interests of the northern, Hindi-speaking areas. It drew heavily on the RSS for manpower. Its influence declined in the early 1980s but, with the resurgence of Hindu sectarian feelings, it has returned to prominence.

Bisapanthis. A sub-sect of the **Digambara Jainas**, led by a non-mendicant guru and characterized by a liberal attitude to temple worship.

BKS Iyengar Yoga Teachers' Association. Founded in 1977 as a professional body for the training of teachers in **Iyengar Yoga.**

Black Muslims. The scholar C. Eric Lincoln first used this term to describe the Nation of Islam, a 20th century movement of black Americans to restore a black nation. It began as a "proto-Islamic" religion with

Christian and black nationalist elements, but through its influence most new converts to Islam in North America are now African-Americans, totalling about 1,000,000 in a number of organizations, in an American Muslim population of some 4,000,000.

In 1913, Noble Drew Ali founded the **Moorish-American Science Temple** in Newark, teaching that blacks must recognize their true Islamic identity and reject the name "negro" by which whites stripped them of their heritage. In 1929 in Detroit, Wallace D. Fard (also known as Wallace Fard Muhammad), an immigrant possibly of Turco-Persian parentage, claimed to be Noble Drew Ali reincarnate. He became leader of part of this movement which grew into a separate organization under the new name of (in full) the Lost-Found Nation of Islam in the Wilderness of North America (generally abbreviated to Nation of Islam), but proclaimed a similar message to the effect that blacks must be restored to Allah and their original high status as the Asiatic tribe of Shabazz.

After Fard disappeared mysteriously in 1933, Elijah Muhammad (born Elijah Poole, son of a Baptist preacher in Georgia, who moved to Detroit in 1923) headed the movement from 1933 to his death in 1975. He believed that Fard was Allah, and that he himself was Allah's messenger to African-Americans. Black Muslims expected the imminent destruction of white rule, when blacks would inherit the earth, and taught that Original Man was black and that whites had been selectively bred by a wicked scientist, Yakub, and are wholly inferior and evil.

This racial mythology, and Elijah Muhammad's claim to prophethood, were in fact beliefs contrary to authentic Islam, as was impressed upon him during extensive journeying in the Muslim world in 1959, but he found it impossible to repudiate them. His message of black pride and separatism was significant in the black nationalism which opposed integration and the focus on civil rights in the 1960s and '70s.

Malcolm X, the leading Black Muslim minister from 1953 to 1964, and a hero for blacks today, was a prominent black nationalist. His autobiography is the chief primary source on the Black Muslims, as well as an outstanding account of religious conversion, but by the time of his assassination in 1965 he had moved to embrace orthodox Islam and an advocacy of human rights, leaving the Nation of Islam to found his own Muslim Mosque Incorporated and Organization of Afro-American Unity. Although the Nation of Islam grew rapidly during his ministry to perhaps 100,000, membership was limited by its "black Puritanism", which included abstention from smoking, alcohol, drugs and gambling; refusal of military service (Elijah Muhammad was imprisoned during World War II as a conscientious objector, and Muhammad Ali's boxing career was notoriously interrupted in consequence of his refusal to fight in Vietnam); and an emphasis on an ordered family life, clothing and dietary restrictions, hard work, economic and educational self-help, as well as daily prayers and regular mosque attendance.

Elijah Muhammad's son and successor, Warith Deen Muhammad (also known as Wallace D. Muhammad), changed the profile of the movement, rejecting the earlier racial mythology of black superiority and the claims, unacceptable to orthodox Muslims, to the divinity of Fard Muhammad and the prophethood of Elijah Muhammad. Thus he has led his followers to mainstream **Sunni** Islam, and has relaxed some of the lifestyle restrictions. All blacks are now known as Bilalians, after Bilal, the black ex-slave who was Muhammad's first *muezzin,* and the enemy is now racist states of mind rather than "white devils"—indeed some whites have been admitted into membership.

In 1976 the name was changed to World Community of al-Islam in the West, and again in 1980 to American Muslim Mission, its current title. The organization moved to establish good relations with the previously excoriated US government, as also with a number of foreign Muslim governments and associations. In 1985, however, the organization's national structure was disbanded (Warith Deen Muhammad resigning as leader), and the movement became completely decentralized.

Meanwhile in 1978 the controversial Black Muslim Minister, Louis Farrakhan (formerly Louis X), whom many had thought would succeed Elijah Muhammad as leader, claimed to have been excommunicated from the World Community of Islam, and revived the Nation of Islam with its original black nationalist apocalyptic and lifestyle, and with its disciplined order of men—some would say its security force—the Fruit of Islam.

One authority suggests, without statistical evidence, that the American Muslim Mission is now more middle-class, as well as closer to the American mainstream, while Farrakhan retains the increasingly dispossessed urban working-class male membership which was the original strength of the Black Muslims. The black separatist position is now, however, a minority stance among African-American Muslims, who have mainly joined the Islamic mainstream.

B'nai B'rith International. B'nai B'rith International was founded in New York City in 1843 as an American Jewish fraternal organization. Since then it has become the largest international Jewish service organization with lodges in over 45 countries, the first of which was opened in 1882 in Germany. B'nai B'rith is the sponsor of a number of other organizations including: the Anti-Defamation League (founded in 1913) which combats all forms of prejudice, the B'nai B'rith Youth Organization (founded in 1924), and the Hillel Foundations and Counselorships (founded in 1923), which provide services to Jewish students at over 400 campuses worldwide.

Board of Deputies of British Jews. This national committee was founded in 1760 by the **Sephardi** and **Ashkenasi** communities

of England and after being reorganized in 1835 was officially recognized by the government as the representative body of British Jewry. In 1886 the **Reform** community joined the existing **Orthodox** representatives. Originally membership was limited to delegates from synagogues but more recently other Jewish organizations are represented. Organized into a number of committees, ranging from education and youth to law, the Board has worked for a series of Jewish interests, including: Jewish emancipation (before 1858); the settlement of Jewish immigrants to Britain; countering anti-semitism and Israel (before 1918 the Board was anti-**Zionist**). Currently there are more than 400 members.

Bodhi Society. A Singapore based Buddhist organization founded to encourage and to finance the missionary visits of Thai **Theravada** monks to Singapore.

Bohoras. The Bohoras (Bohras) are an Indian community who mostly adhere to the **Daudi** branch of the **Musta'li** sect of **Isma'ili Shi'ism** within Islam. Their name derives from the Gujarati word Vohoras, meaning "traders". They are often regarded as identical with the Daudis, although strictly speaking this is inaccurate: some Daudis in the Yemen are not Bohoras, while conversely a few Bohoras belong to the rival branch of the Musta'li sect, the **Sulaymanis,** and a few are **Sunnis** or even Hindus.

The reasons for this confusing configuration lie in their history. This goes back to successful Musta'li missionary activity in Gujarat as early as the 11th century, which resulted in a thriving Musta'li community, perhaps based on the conversion of a whole caste or caste grouping. These converts became known as Bohoras. By the late 16th century, these Indian Musta'lis emerged as more important than the Musta'lis in the Yemen, which had been the centre of the movement since the twelfth century, and the centre was transferred to Gujarat.

At this point, however, there occurred the split between the Daudis and the Sulaymanis. Most Bohoras identified themselves with the Daudis, a situation that has continued until today. A few, however, became Sulaymanis.

Meanwhile in the mid-15th century a schism had occurred amongst the Bohoras, one group becoming Sunni. These Sunni Bohoras have developed independently as a largely agricultural community.

In general, however, as their name implies, the Bohoras have a well-founded reputation as prosperous traders. While Gujarat remains their centre, Bohoras are to be found in most towns in the subcontinent, and there are numbers in the commercial centres of East Africa, and in Mauritius, Myanmar (Burma) and elsewhere. Some estimates put their number at around 1,000,000, while others suggest fewer than half that figure. In any event, their significance is disproportionate to their numbers.

Bonpos. "Followers of the Bon Faith", an ostensibly non-Buddhist religious minority of about one per cent of Tibetans. A monastic tradition, the Bonpo curriculum is identical to that of **Tibetan Buddhism** in all but name; yet the Bonpos claim greater antiquity, accusing Buddhism of plagiarisation. This has earned the Bonpos occasional persecution from irritated Buddhists.

Bonpos believe their religion was founded in the distant past by Lord Shenrab Mibo, in the Olmo Lungrig district of Tajik (modern Iran?), from where it spread throughout the world, reaching Tibet centuries before Buddhism via the old western Tibetan kingdom of Zhang Zhung. Although there were priests called Bonpos in pre-Buddhist Tibet, Bon since the 10th century effectively became a multiform of Buddhism, and Bonpos extensively participate in Buddhist institutions and doctrines. Hence Bonpo logicians freely study and debate with their **Gelugpa** or

Sakyapa counterparts, while others partake of the **Nyingmapa** (Great Perfection) or **Terma** traditions.

The basic Bonpo scriptures (*Kanjur*) fill 113 volumes, and their commentaries (*Katen*) a further 293, mostly copied from Buddhist prototypes. Their pantheon is huge and their main symbol is the *svastika*. Before the Chinese invasion of 1959, Bonpos had some 330 monasteries in Tibet. They have successfully established a refugee monastery in Dolanji, India, and, as an endangered cultural minority, have attracted vigorous support from western academics. They retain their reputation for exemplary piety and discipline.

Boston Church of Christ. This is the parent organization of the **Church of Christ** movement.

Bougists. Members of the Congolese new religious movement popularly known as **Lassyism** but whose official designation is the Mission de Dieu du Bougie—the Church of God of the Candle.

Brahma Kumaris. The Brahma Kumaris World Spiritual University was founded in India in 1937 by a diamond merchant and devout Hindu now known as Brahma Baba (1877–1969), who believed he was sent to save chosen souls from a forthcoming cataclysm. The millennialist dimension is played down in the West, where the movement presents itself as primarily educational and philanthropic.

The teachings, called Raj **Yoga**, are based on Hindu meditation. The aim is to realize one's essential nature as a soul, purifying the body through an ascetic régime, including vegetarianism and celibacy.

The movement is unusual in being run almost entirely by women, as teachers and administrators. Its headquarters are in Mount Abu, India, with centres throughout the world. Estimated numbers are 250,000 worldwide (about 800 in Britain), though the movement's influence is much larger, with many sympathizers and patrons in high places. Its latest peace project, Global Vision, is backed by the United Nations, to which it is affiliated as a non-governmental organization.

Brahmasampradaya. One of the four contemporary Indian **Vaishnava** teaching and monastic traditions which has its origins in the writings of the orthodox Hindu thinker Madhva (1238–1317). Madhva taught a dualistic (*dvaita*) version of the **Vedanta** philosophy which holds that Visnu is the supreme, transcendent being and that humans are a true reflection of his divine nature. Liberation consists of servitude to god for all eternity. Madhva lived in Karnataka and today the *sampradaya* is still a mainly south Indian phenomenon. The thriving main temple, at Udipi, is consecrated to Balakrishna and is still administered by direct descendants of Madhva. The Brahmasampradaya possesses a monastic order of committed renunciants (*samnyasins*) called the **Madhva Gaudiya Vairagins.** Founded by the Bengali saint Chaitanya (1485–1533), they are distinguished in appearance by their white *dhoti,* three-stranded necklace of beads and V-shaped white forehead marking, and are particularly prominent in Orissa state.

Bratslav Hasidism (Bratslaver). Rabbi Nahman of Bratslav (1772–1811), a great-grandson of the Baal Shem Tov, was one of the most original Hasidic teachers and the founder of a new movement within Hasidism. Nahman made a pilgrimage to the land of Israel in 1798 and taught small groups of disciples in the Ukraine and in the Podolian town of Bratslav (1802–10). During his short life he was involved in a series of acrimonious controversies with other Hasidic leaders. Nahman died at 39

in Uman (Ukraine) and his grave was, and is, a place of pilgrimage for his followers. His devotees, in accordance with their master's instructions, dance around his grave on the annual anniversary of his death.

In a number of ways his teachings differ from those of other Hasidic Rebbes *(Tzaddikim),* most significantly in relation to his "doctrine" of the *Tzaddik* (Rebbe) itself. Whereas other Hasidic movements developed dynastic and hereditary, charismatic patterns of leadership, Nahman taught that there can only ever be one "true Tzaddik" (referring to himself), with whom it was essential to be in contact. Further, the Messiah would be an incarnation of this "true Tzaddik". This messianic doctrine marks off the Bratslav from other Hasidic groups adding an historical element to their concerns largely absent in the others. Bratslav Hasidim have maintained this tradition and even after Nahman's death they have continued to "be led" by their dead Rebbe—they are often referred to as the *Toiter* (Yiddish, "dead") Hasidim.

Nahman's teachings were collected and disseminated by his disciple, Nathan Sternhartz (1780–1845), including the famous collection of 13 folk tales, *The Tales of Rabbi Nahman* (1815). These stories have secret, allegorical and mystical interpretations taught only to initiates.

Bratslav Hasidism developed a following in Poland in the late 19th century and there was a centre in Uman until recent years. Nahman was influenced by Lurianic Kabbalah and taught that doubt in God's existence was part of the structure of creation itself. He was strongly opposed to the study of Jewish philosophy, undermining reason while greatly emphasizing the vital importance of faith ("Better a superstitious believer than a rationalistic unbeliever"). Only faith, and he limited this, in the main, to faith in himself as the true Tzaddik, was of true spiritual value and this should be developed along with practice of the commandments.

Nahman insisted that his followers spend a period of each day in total solitude for prayer, which he understood as a dialogue between man and God. This stress on intense, isolated meditative dialogue *(hitbodedut)* with God is one of the distinctive features of Bratslav Hasidic practice. Others include moving with a shuffling gait during communal prayers in order to lose the "ego" ("Man must lose himself in prayer and entirely forget his own existence"); attendance at three annual sessions at the Jerusalem centre (originally the tradition was a thrice-yearly meeting with Rabbi Nahman himself) and a concern with the spiritual importance of music ("Melody and song lead the heart of man to God"), in particular the Hasidic melody *(niggun)*.

There are Bratslav centres in Brooklyn (New York) and in Israel. Rabbi Nahman's influence can be discerned in a number of different quarters. Rabbis Shlomo Carlebach and Zalman Schachter-Shalomi and others draw heavily on his teachings in their presentations of New Age Judaism (see **Jewish New Agers**). The continued popularity of Martin Buber's interpretations of Hasidism which include his retelling of Nahman's *Tales* (see **Neo-Kabbalah; Hasidism**) also attest to this influence. The works of major figures such as, the Jerusalem based, Talmudic authority Rabbi Adin Steinsalz evidence the impact of Nahman's writings.

There are also two distinct bands of direct "devotees"—a number of "inner circles" of disciples and groups of more general followers. The former includes the circle of Rabbis Rosenfeld and Fleer in Brooklyn, where membership is limited to initiates who have already made at least one pilgrimage to Nahman's tomb in Uman, and Rabbi Gedaliah Koenig's circle attached to the main Bratslav synagogue in Jerusalem. There is also a Bratslav community in Bene Berak in Israel. Although the numbers of devotees is comparatively small, Rabbi Nahman continues to be a spiritual force in contemporary Judaism.

Brethren (German Baptists). This movement originated in 1708 in Schwarzenau, Germany, under the leadership of Alexander Mack. However, persecution drove members out of Europe, and in 1719 they settled in Pennsylvania USA. Throughout the 18th and 19th centuries they moved west and reached the Pacific in 1850. The church, which consists of three groups, the largest being the **Church of the Brethren**, is now almost entirely in North America.

The church founders believed in Pietism, a 17th century doctrine which encouraged Christians in holy living, a knowledge of the Bible and in sharing their faith with unbelievers. Members today refuse to fight in wars and will not take oaths.

Distinctive features of their worship are footwashing, a practice based on Jesus' washing of his disciples' feet as an act of humility (John 13.4–15) and believer's baptism by immersion *three* times (for the Father, Son and Holy Spirit). This triune immersion has led to the epithets **Tunkers** (from the German *tunken*—"to dip"), "Dunkers" and "Dippers".

Total membership today is about 600,000.

British Israelites. Those who believe that the British, and perhaps, more widely, the Anglo–Saxon peoples are the literal descendants of the 10 lost tribes of Israel which were deported by the Assyrians in 722–721 BC. Acceptance of the theory, partly on a literal interpretation of the Bible, carries the assumption that the British are a chosen people. Believers in this theory have not found it necessary to form a sect, but have been found, particularly in the 19th century, when Britain ruled the waves, in all churches and sects. Their teaching aroused particular opposition from **Christadelphians.**

British Wheel of Yoga (BWY). The British Wheel of Yoga is a registered charity which aims to promote the study and practice of yoga through the provision of education and teacher training and by co-operation with other organizations having similar aims. Founded in 1963 by Wilfred Clark under the title of the West Midlands Yoga Association, the organization has been growing steadily, taking up the present title in 1973.

The three principal levels of activity and responsibility within the Wheel are county, regional and national. Representatives in the 57 counties distribute their region's newsletter and the quarterly national magazine *Spectrum*. They also organize local seminars and collect subscriptions. Regional affairs are dealt with by an annually elected regional committee. Its job is to further the aims of the Wheel through the organization of seminars, the production of newsletters and representing regional interests at national level.

Nationally, the Wheel produces *Spectrum*, organizes the Annual Congress and AGM (a residential conference, workshop and discussion forum) and provides professional diploma courses to qualify people as yoga teachers. National policy, funding and activities are overseen by the National Committee, made up of 11 regional officers, four executive officers and four trustees. The training of teachers is the responsibility of the Education Committee, which devises the syllabus and arranges for the assessment of diploma candidates. The Wheel also sponsors visits to Britain by yoga practitioners from overseas and an international network is gradually being developed.

At the present time there are approximately 4,000 members of the BWY, 1,000 certified teachers and over 100 Teacher Education Tutors. The honorary president of the Wheel is Swami Satcidananda of Virginia, USA.

Brotherhood of the Cross and Star. The Brotherhood of the Cross and Star is one of the West African (especially Nigerian) prophet-healing churches of the type referred to generically as **Aladura.**

Buddhayana. The **Indonesian Buddhayana Council** or **Majelis Buddhayana Indonesia** (MBI) was first established at Watu Gong, Semarang, in Central Java, in 1954, as a result of the initiative of Sthavira A. Jinarakkhita, an Indonesian Buddhist monk who had been ordained in Burma. MBI is based on three scriptures, the Pali and Sanskrit *Pitakas* and the Indonesian *dan Kawi Pitaka*. Members worship Sang Hyang Adi Buddha and always begin sessions with the invocation *"Namo sang Hyang Adi Buddhayana"*, from which the name derives, expressing homage to the Buddha. Tjoetjoe Ali Hartono is currently the sect's leader.

Buddhist Association of Thailand. The largest lay Buddhist organization in Thailand was established in 1934 to encourage the study and practice of Buddhism. It presently works in the social welfare and public services field, though many of its activities are directed towards the accumulation of religious merit. By the early '80s there were 75 provincial associations linked to the Bangkok headquarters, 14 of which were controlled by Chinese Buddhists. It places great stress on radio and television broadcasting for the propagation of the *dhamma* and publishes a monthly magazine (*Buddha Dhamma*) and an English-language annual, *Visakha Puja*.

Buddhist Churches of America. The Buddhist Churches of America constitute the American wing of the True Pure Land School (**Jodoshinshu**) and are formally affiliated to the western branch of its Japanese headquarters in Kyoto. Originally, the Churches were called The Buddhist Mission of North America, founded in 1899 by two Jodo Shinshu missionaries from Japan: Rev. Shuei Sonoda and Rev. Kakuryo Nishijima. The aim of the Mission was to serve the religious needs of the Japanese immigrant community on the West Coast. During World War II many

American Japanese were relocated to the interior of the country and after the war many of them remained in their new places of residence. In this way the movement broadened its geographical base. It was also during the war years (in 1942) that the Mission changed its name to the Buddhist Churches of America.

Doctrinally, the Churches subscribe to the tenets of Jodoshinshu (or **Shin**) Buddhism with their emphasis on the saving power of Amida Buddha. Services are simple and are usually conducted in Japanese, though special English-language ceremonies are becoming more frequent. The head of the Churches is the bishop, who is assisted by a Board of Directors and a Ministerial Association made up of Jodoshinshu clergy. The Board of Directors includes a ministerial representative from each of the eight districts into which the Churches are organized. Seven of them are located in the western half of the USA, the eighth, the Eastern District, covers the eastern half. This arrangement gives some idea of the current geographical distribution of Church members.

At the present time the Buddhist Churches of America claim over 100,000 adherents, almost all of whom are of Japanese extraction. One of the major issues facing the Churches as they approach the 21st century is, therefore, that of whether to seek expansion into the wider American community or to simply maintain a stable Japanese-rooted membership.

Buddhist Publication Society (BPS). Founded in 1958 by Nyanaponika Thera, a **Theravada** monk of German extraction, along with two lay devotees, the Society has been an influential vehicle for the transmission of Buddhism to the West. Its main English language publications are a journal, *The Wheel,* and occasional pamphlets entitled *Bodhi Leaves.* Based in Kandy, Sri Lanka some of the "honorary workers" within the organization are Chinese Buddhists. The BPS has close links with the **Maha Bodhi Society.**

Buddhist Society of Great Britain and Ireland. The Buddhist Society was founded in 1907 " . . . to welcome and serve as the vehicle for the teachings of . . . Ananda Metteya", the first Briton to ordain as a Buddhist monk and return to teach. Two years later the Society published a journal, *The Buddhist Review*, which appeared fairly continuously until 1922. The 1920s were a period of upheaval for the Buddhist Society. Scholars and practitioners often failed to agree on its aims and emphases and so, in 1926, it was formally dissolved.

During this same period Buddhists within the Theosopical Society began to organize themselves and founded a Buddhist Lodge in 1924. The following year they began publishing a journal, first under the title of *The Buddhist Lodge Monthly Bulletin* and then as *Buddhism in England*. In 1926 the Lodge detached itself from the Theosophical Society and, under the presidency of Christmas Humphreys, became The Buddhist Society, London; the journal was renamed *The Middle Way*. Both titles are in use at the present time.

The aims of the Society are set out in a statement of intent on the back of each issue of *The Middle Way*. They are " . . . to publish and make known the principles of Buddhism and to encourage the study and application of these principles". The same statement also makes clear that the Society adheres to no one school of Buddhism and is concerned to offer the newcomer an impartial introduction to the variety of Buddhist teachings and practices. Hence members can attend classes on one or more of **Theravada, Zen** and **Tibetan Buddhism.**

In 1979 the Society published *The Buddhist Directory*, a guide to Buddhist groups in the UK and, in a more limited fashion, abroad. This has been revised every few years since then and is probably the most up-to-date publication on the British Buddhist scene. At the present time the Society has around 3,000 paid-up members.

Buddhist Society of India. Founded in 1951 as the focal organization for the "**neo-Buddhism**" established in India by Dr B. R. Ambedkar (1891–1956). Although interested in Buddhism for most of his life, it was not until two months before his death that Ambedkar and his followers officially converted at a dramatic public ceremony in Nagpur. That occasion was merely the prelude to the rapid conversion of almost 4,000,000 people, most of them from the untouchable or "scheduled" caste to which Ambedkar himself belonged (the *mahars* of Maharashtra).

A major impetus in Ambedkar's espousal of Buddhism was his conviction that untouchables could only find freedom outside Hinduism. His interpretation of **Theravada** Buddhist texts, as propagating his own ideals of egalitarianism, justice and rationality, made Buddhism seem the perfect vehicle for this liberation.

Many of his untouchable followers came to regard him as a *bodhisattva* or "saviour", and since his death they have built Buddhist temples throughout Maharashtra state, as well as publishing much literature, mainly in Marathi, on various aspects of Buddhism. Ambedkar's grandson, Prakash Ambedkar, is now the head of the Society. The early growth of neo-Buddhism in India has now peaked at about 6,000,000 persons, and some reconversion to Hinduism has taken place in recent times.

Buddhist Sunday Schools Movement.
Founded in 1958 by students and teachers at Mahachulalongkorn University, Bangkok to revive Buddhist education among young people and to help them deal with the increasing impact of modernity by providing a traditional framework of ideas. By 1987 297 schools, normally attached to monasteries, existed in Bangkok and surrounding provinces. A similar Sunday school movement, originally set up by the **Young Men's Buddhist Association** (YMBA), also exists in Sri Lanka.

Buddhist Women's Movement. In America, women now comprise half the Buddhist

practitioners and a small but growing number of teachers. Ordination for women was lost for 1,000 years in the **Theravada** and **Vajrayana** traditions. However, Pema Chodron discovered a Vajrayana ceremony in Hong Kong and was the first nun to be ordained in the West. In some **Zen** monasteries, such as the **Order of Buddhist Contemplatives** run by a woman, Kennett Roshi, women are ordained on equal terms with men. Other well known Buddhist teachers include Tsultrim Allione, Maurine Stuart, Ruth Dennison, Joanna Macy, and Ayya Khema in Australia.

Women are beginning to challenge the patriarchal power structure of Buddhism, discussing problems of male leadership, especially the abuse of power, including sexual exploitation. They are also exploring alternative solutions to basic issues such as monasticism; how far meditation can be integrated with daily life; the appropriateness of Asian ceremonial procedures. Women-only retreats first started in Britain, within the **Friends of the Western Buddhist Order** (FWBO), and are now happening in America too.

Women are generally seen as making a positive contribution to Buddhism, being warmer with their students, and pragmatic and flexible in adapting the traditions to Western conditions. Some women are conservative, but most are "strong voices for change". Structures are becoming more democratic and fluid, and there is more emphasis on relationship, family, and caring values. Conservatives feel that Buddhism transcends gender, so concern with women's issues is inappropriate. But most women feel that this ideal is all the more reason to challenge and overcome sexism, and create a new, less hierarchical and more holistic style of Buddhism which will encompass both male and female needs.

Buddhist Youth Organization (BYO). The Buddhist Youth Organization of Korea is effectively the youth wing of the **Chogye**

Chong. Much of their work is concerned with helping society through charitable work. The rationale for this comes from a practical interpretation of *Mahayana* teaching about seeking the enlightenment of all living beings. Many **BYO** members belong to the educated classes of Korean society and have managed to establish centres at many universities across the country. From there they seek to propagate Buddhist teachings through lectures, discussion groups and other related activities.

Another major dimension of BYO work is the organization of retreats for young people. These usually take place in rural **Son** monasteries for periods ranging from a couple of days to a fortnight. The idea behind the retreats is to provide young people with an opportunity for personal development in a Buddhist context. A typical programme will include lectures, discussions, Son meditation, work and chanting of the scriptures. By Western standards the regime is austere. Participants rise between three and four a.m. to chant, meditate and do chores until breakfast at six. Despite (or perhaps because of) this, such retreats are growing in popularity. They provide young Koreans with an opportunity to take a break from the increasingly Westernized, competitive and materialistic society of modern Korea whilst at the same time tapping into their country's traditional roots.

Buddhists in India (Assam, Arunachal Pradesh, Tripura and Mizoram). The Buddhism practised in the valley and hill regions of these areas, when not derived from the **Tibetan** tradition, has been re-introduced into India from neighbouring Myanmar. The vehicle for this influx has been either immigration or simply the flow of a common culture across political boundaries. Nevertheless, the religion of these hill people of Tripura, Mizoram, and the extreme east of Arunachal Pradesh, although Burmese, and thus **Theravada,** in origin, is strongly flavoured by local practices.

Buo Son Ky Hong. A modern Vietnamese millenial movement, also known as **Hoa Hao.**

Burmese Theravada. Burmese Buddhism is essentially **Theravada.** It was preceded, however, by the animistic beliefs of the hill tribes and by the Hinduism of early traders from India, and these have profoundly changed its cosmology.

According to Burmese cosmology the European–Asian continent, called Jambudipa, is the southern of four islands situated at the cardinal points surrounding Mount Meru, the centre of the universe. The Buddhist inhabitants of Jambudipa live lives of suffering in comparison with their counterparts on the northern island, where everybody lives for 1,000 years without ageing, but in consequence cannot gain merit through improvement. Thus future Buddhas, with their potential for good deeds, can only be born in Jambudipa.

Above and below Mount Meru are 31 places of existence. Four of the 31 realms are beneath the human plane of existence; these are the worlds of animals, demons, ghosts, purgatories and hells. Humans who accrue insufficient merit during their lifetimes may be reborn in one of these.

It is important to distinguish the demons and ghosts of the sub-human realms from the inhabitants of the higher planes of existence on and above Mount Meru. These are the *nats, devas, nagas, garudas* and gods of many kinds, which are an integral part of everyday Burmese life, and feature prominently in Burmese architecture.

It has been said that for the Burmese, *nats* serve much the same purpose as do saints in relation to popular **Roman Catholicism.** Theravada Buddhists cannot turn to the Buddha in times of need, but if the *nats* are suitably appeased with offerings of flowers, food and money, or approached through soothsayers, they may be of assistance.

Originally each tree and field in a village was inhabited by a *nat*, and there were additional *nats* of the wind, rain and harvest. The unification of Burma as a great centre of Buddhist culture in the 11th century led to the suppression of many *nats*, though 36 managed to survive under the aegis of Thagyamin (or Sakka; similar to the Hindu god Indra), who was elevated by King Anawrahta for the purpose of keeping the others in line with Buddhist principles.

During the next centuries Burmese Buddhism contributed much to the stability and progress of Asian Buddhism, and became famous for its *Abhidhamma* tests. The Fifth Great Council was held in Mandalay in 1871. British rule from 1886–1948 provoked a strong feeling of nationalism which combined the desire for political independence with the need to protect and promote national religion. The Sixth Great Council, celebrating the 2,500th anniversary of the Buddha's demise, was held in Rangoon in 1954 and lasted two years.

Monks (*pongyis*, literally "great glory") played a prominent part in the early independence movement, and actively supported U Nu's election campaign in 1960. U Nu's distinctive Buddhist socialism, with its goal of *loka-nibban*, the perfect society on earth, was influenced by U Ba Swe, a prominent Burmese Marxist, who used Buddhist terminology to denote social liberation through revolutionary struggle. Thus, for example, the Burmese strike slogan "turn down, turn down" is based on the traditional phrase for a refusal by *pongyis* to accept alms by inverting their bowls against the givers.

In 1965 many young *pongyis* denounced the revolutionary government of Ne Win as anti-religious; many were arrested, and the Sangha has subsequently become much less influential in political and national affairs. Eighty-five per cent of Burma's population of 42,000,000 is Buddhist. There are now estimated to be between 100,000 and 300,000 *pongyis* in Burma, of which 30,000 to 50,000 are novices. Among the various groups of Burmese Theravada, the **Thuddama** is most numerous, while the **Shwegyin** is important and influential. There are also a number of Theravada subgroups which accommodate, to a greater or lesser extent, animism and *nat* veneration and reflect the importance of various sacred sites and temples. The Shwedagon Pagoda in Rangoon, which dates back to the eleventh century, is a focal point of Burmese religious and national aspirations.

Bwiti Cult. The Bwiti Cult, also known as the *Église des Banzie* ("Church of the Initiates"), is one of the **African New Religious Movements**. It originated among the Fang of Gabon as a neo-traditional movement which attempted to revitalize an ancestral cult, incorporating beliefs and rituals from neighbouring peoples. The Cult has since adopted a messianic/prophetic type of leadership similar to some African Instituted Churches, with increased synthesis of Christian and indigenous elements. Converts are now drawn from mainstream Protestant and **Roman Catholic** churches, as well as from **African traditional religions.**

C

Cambodian Buddhism. From ruins and objects of art it is clear Buddhism had been introduced into Cambodia by the 5th century CE. The name of the country at that time—Founan—is derived from a Khmer word meaning "mountain". According to Hindu mythology carried to South East Asia by Indian traders, the mountain was Mount Meru, centre of the universe and throne of the god, where divinity on earth (i.e. the king) guaranteed order and agricultural prosperity through his just and perfect rule.

Thus the king links the past to the future and integrates spiritual and worldly life, a fusion which modern South East Asian governments have found convenient with regard to the parallel roles of *Sangha* and State. This also explains, in the case of Cambodia, why Prince Norodom Sihanouk, as last representative of the god-kings, has been and remains such a powerful political influence, and why the Khmer Rouge, in overthrowing the government which succeeded him, destroyed the *Sangha* as well.

Hindu, **Theravada** and **Mahayana** influences all played a part in Cambodia's religious life to varying degrees until approximately the 12th century, when Buddhist reforms in Sri Lanka and developments in Thailand brought the Theravada to prominence. In 1887 Cambodia became part of the French Union Indochinoise, with the result that Cambodians became exposed to a wide range of external influences, some of which were readily assimilated, while others provoked hostility and rejection. The *Sangha* was stimulated to modernize its schools and raise their standards to college level. The Université Bouddhique Preah Sihanouk began functioning in 1961, and monks became increasingly involved in educational and community welfare projects. As in Thailand, there were two "orders" known as **Mahanikay** and **Thomayat**, the latter being smaller, royalist and more conservative, with close links with Thailand. Unlike Thailand, though, the Cambodian orders each had their own patriarchs, the last of whom was publicly disembowelled by the Khmer Rouge.

In 1970 it was estimated that there were 3,369 monasteries in Cambodia, of which 3,230 were Mahanikay and 139 Thomayat. The total number of monks was 65,000, of which 62,700 and 2,300 respectively were members of the two orders.

In 1975 Cambodia's capital, Phnom Penh, fell to Pol Pot's Khmer Rouge, and four years later the Vietnam-backed People's Revolutionary Council of Cambodia replaced them. Between 3,000,000 and 4,000,000 Cambodians died, including possibly as many as 50,000 monks. Tens of thousands of refugees, fleeing from both Pol Pot and the Vietnamese, took refuge in holding centres inside the Thai border. At two of these, Sa-kaeo and Khao-I-Dang, a remarkable Cambodian monk, Phra Maha Ghosananda, set up temples and organized days of prayer and meditation for peace between April and June 1980. These were attended by more than 150,000 refugees of all religions, and messages of support were received from the Pope, the Dalai Lama and other major religious leaders. Under the Heng Samrin regime the two monastic fraternities were merged as "our monks are neither Mahanikay nor Thomayat but are Nationalist monks" (1985).

As far as one can tell religious observance, though greatly curtailed, is much as it was in the past, though strongly coloured by Mahanikay custom and practice. Government restrictions, determined by considerations of a vastly reduced population, allow ordination of monks only over the age of 50. Similar restrictions are placed on potential nuns though the government Office of Religious

Affairs has difficulty in enforcing the law in rural areas. Monastic education is in a particularly poor state and Buddhist literature sent from neighbouring states tends to be held up by an unsympathetic bureaucracy. It is hoped that, with the return of Prince Sihanouk to the country in 1991, the *Sangha* will rapidly regenerate.

For a brief period visitors from outside Cambodia were allowed to visit Angkor Wat, Cambodian Buddhism's largest and most sacred shrine, which dates back to the 9th century.

Candomblé. Candomblé, more than likely an onomatopoeic term referring to an African musical instrument, was brought by African slaves to Brazil during the trans-Atlantic slave trade and began to establish itself as a religion in its own right in the first quarter of the 19th century in the states of Bahía, Maranhão and Pernambuco in north-eastern Brazil. It is known by different names in different regions: as **Shango** (Portuguese: Xangô)—the name of the Yoruba god of thunder—in Pernambuco, **Macumba** in Rio in the south-east, Tambor de Mina and Nagô in Maranhão, and Pajelança, Catimbó and Batuque in the central regions. The congregations of believers remain independent of each other, with no moves comparable to those in **Umbanda** to seek to develop a national organization, and this, together with the variety of names, is a reflection of Candomblé's origins as the continuation in Brazil of local or tribal **African traditional** cults which are centred on worship and rites of spirit possession.

Based today very largely on Brazilian versions of Yoruba myths and rituals, Candomblé mixes, or as some would say juxtaposes, African and **Roman Catholic** beliefs (notably the conflation of Catholic saints with African deities), and to a lesser extent Amerindian ones, but, in contrast to Umbanda, not the spiritism of Allan Kardec (**Kardecismo**). Members are in the main Afro–Brazilians, largely from underprivileged groups in society.

In Bahía especially, the mediums of the Yoruba gods are women.

Although persecuted in the late 19th century, and again during the Vargas dictatorship (1937–1945), Candomblé, like Umbanda (and perhaps because of it) is now legal, and participation in the various cults is open.

Cao Dai. Cao Dai, more formally known as **Dai Dao Tam Ky Pho Do,** is a syncretistic Vietnamese sect, founded in 1926. It tries to draw together **Confucianism, Buddhism, Taoism** and **Christianity** into a single religion of the Way (**Tao**). Its full title means "The Great Way of the Three Epochs of Salvation". During the first two epochs God had used different religions to save humanity from materialism; now, during the third, all these religions are coming together. Thus Confucianism traces the road to a just society, Buddhism serves as a guide to devotion and charity, and Taoism teaches the value of truth and discipline of character.

Cao Dai teaching is derived from texts based on revelation by mediums, often teenagers, who claim to be in touch with either the Supreme Being (**Cao Dai**) or the spirits of famous historical figures. These include the Buddha, Confucius, Jesus Christ, Muhammad, Sun Yat-sen, Victor Hugo and Joan of Arc. The Cao Dai hierarchy was modelled on that of the **Roman Catholic Church,** having a pope, cardinals, archbishops, etc. The movement rejects family worship and the role of apostle healers, both characteristics of the related **Hoa Hao.**

By 1935 Cao Dai had grown extensively and had split into about 10 different branches, each with its own leader. It was much too highly organized to be an umbrella for other groups, and until 1955 even fielded its own army. Resolutely anti-Communist, its hope was for an independent Vietnam which would lead a "middle way" between the superpowers. In the mid-1960s such an approach harmonized with the moderate elements of the **Unified Vietnamese Buddhist Church,** and contributed to the collapse of the Diem government.

Cao Dai and Hoa Hao have been described as millenarian movements, in that they represent the fusion of the secular and the sacred to form a socio–religious grass-roots movement. Both await the imminent return of Maitreya, the future Budha. The current membership of Cao Dai is still large in traditional areas.

Cargo Cults. Cargo cults are new religious movements that have sprung up in great numbers this century, primarily where traditional religions in New Guinea, Melanesia and the Pacific Islands have encountered European colonization. They are based on a belief that the greater wealth and happiness associated with Western materialism can become available to indigenous groups through certain religious rituals.

Western material prosperity became apparent with the arrival of bulk supplies of European, later American, goods (cargo), by air or sea. In cargo cults, further supplies are sought which are to be delivered supernaturally by God or the gods, perhaps aided by the spirits of the dead or to be brought by returning ancestors. Wharves, airstrips and warehouses were built, facilities prepared and new rituals created to replace traditional customs in order to hasten the arrival of this new order of equality with whites (so that observers have often characterized the cults as millennarian movements).

Cargo cults sprang up most notably in Irian Jaya, Papua New Guinea, the Solomon Islands, Fiji and Vanuatu. In the last of these, the **John Frum movement** made its appearance in 1939–40, and maintains a following still today.

Caritas. Founded in Freiburg in 1887, Caritas (or in full, Deutscher Caritasverband) is a notable **Roman Catholic** organization providing a system of medical care and social service in Germany. It sponsors hospitals, homes for the elderly, and a variety of day institutions. With responsibility for some 36,000 centres of this kind, served by over 200,000 lay and religious personnel, it is a major organization.

Carmelites. The Carmelites have been from the outset one of the strictest penitential Orders in the **Roman Catholic** Church. There are two wholly separate branches of the Order. Both rivers originate in the 12th century, among certain Christian settlers in Palestine. In imitation of Elijah, these pilgrims and ex-crusaders lived as hermits on Mount Carmel, the Biblical site of the prophet's meeting with God. They were dedicated to the Mother of God. St. Berthold persuaded the hermits to live cenobitically, in communities; St. Brocard told St. Albert, the Latin Patriarch of Jerusalem, that the communities required a *Rule* to regulate their practical and spiritual conduct. The *Rule* was devised by St. Albert between 1206 and 1214 and authorized by Pope Innocent IV in 1247. It required that "All . . . remain in their own cells . . . meditating on the Law of the Lord day and night and watching in prayer."

Driven back to Europe upon the dissolution of the Latin Kingdom, the Carmelites dispersed and became preaching friars. Arriving in England in 1242, they built friaries in Aylesford in Kent and in Hulne, Northumberland. Expelled thence by Henry VIII, they returned to England in 1926 and to Aylesford in 1949. There are now 2,000 friars, 900 nuns and 3,000 sisters. Numbers are in some places beginning to climb. The original Order of Carmelites ("O. Carm.") retain their devotion to Elijah, and to the Mother of God; they are still inspired by St. Albert's Rule. They are divided into 23 provinces world-wide. Fr. John Malley oversees the Order as a whole, as Prior-General.

On the question of the division of

the Carmelites, history gives way to interpretation. The Reformed Order have considered that, after the return to Europe and the mitigation of St. Albert's *Rule* by Pope Eugene IV, the salt lost some of its savour. St. Teresa of Jesus (1515–1582), a sturdy Spanish woman of Jewish stock, set out on the religious life within the mitigated Order, entering the Monastery of the Incarnation in Avila in 1535. In 1562 St. Teresa left her monastery to found the first reformed house, the convent of St. Joseph. Her friend and spiritual director, St. John of the Cross, set up a house for reformed Carmelite brothers in Duruelo in 1568. Their efforts to "return to the sources" annoyed ecclesiastical and secular authorities, and affronted some, as it were, un-reformed Carmelites. St. John was questioned by the Inquisition and imprisoned in Toledo, in a monastery of the mitigated Rule. Mobs set out to dismantle St. Joseph's: through the grille, the enclosed nuns blew a raspberry at their tormentors. The new houses were forbidden to take in novices, a move which if successful would have speedily curtailed the Reform. The wrangle was discussed in Rome. Having been told by a sympathetic Cardinal that ". . . those with the mitigated Rule fear that the reform will finally reform them also", Pope Gregory XIII decided in 1580 that the reformed Order must become an autonomous Province, with its own Provincial. By the time of her death, St. Teresa had helped to found 36 houses; the Order spread from Spain to Europe and the New World. The two names for the reformed order are the Order of Discalced Carmelites ("O.D.C."), because they wear peasants' sandals ("Discalced", shoeless), and the Teresian Carmelites, after their foundress.

St. John of the Cross was one of the great mystics of Christian history. In the poetry of *The Spiritual Canticle,* he described the "blessed adventure" of the soul's journey to God. St. John travelled the "dark night" of the way of the negation of all images. He taught his disciples to "Desire . . . the knowledge of

nothing . . . . Desire to be nothing,. . . . To come to be what you are not, you must go by a way in which you are not." The forthright Teresa told him that "It would be a bad business for us if we could not seek God until we were dead to the world. Neither the Magdalene, nor the woman of Samaria . . . was dead to the world when she found him." St. Teresa was also a mystic, the author of an *Autobiography,* and of *The Interior Castle.* She wrote that: "The Saviour almost always appeared to me *visibly* in risen form. When I saw him in the holy Host, he was in this transfigured form,. . . his body was always glorified." St. Teresa was the first woman to be pronounced a "Doctor" of the Catholic Church.

St. John and St. Teresa have remained at the heart of Teresian Carmelite contemplation. According to Fr. Noel O'Donoghue O.D.C., in his *Mystics for Our Time* (1991), a study of St. Teresa of Jesus, St. John, and St. Thérèse of Lisieux, Carmelite spirituality is specifically "feminine". St. Thérèse of Lisieux (1872–1897), taught the "Little Way" to God in her autobiography, *The Story of a Soul,* and in her "hidden" life. She was the woman who in the first half of this century most fired the devotional imagination of Catholics. The saint concealed beneath their sentimental glossings still inspires Carmelite nuns and priests. The German Jewess, Edith Stein, who has lately been beatified as Sister Teresa Benedicta of the Cross, is another Carmelite woman of distinction. Born on the Day of Atonement, 1891, Edith Stein took her doctorate in Göttingen under Edmund Husserl, and became the great phenomenologist's assistant. She was converted by reading St. Teresa of Avila's *Autobiography.* Directed by the Jesuit Erich Przywara, she translated Newman's *Diaries* and Thomas Aquinas' *Questiones Disputatae* into German. Having been an important figure in the German Catholic renaissance of the 1920s, Edith began in the Germany of the 1930s deliberately to prepare for "my own holocaustum". When Jews lost the right to lecture in German universities in 1933, Edith gave up her teaching vocation for membership of the Discalced Carmelites. She now composed a great treatise on *Finite and Eternal Being,* which combines Thomism and realistic phenomenology. Sent for safety after Kristallnacht to Holland, she was arrested there by the Nazis and died in Auschwitz in 1942. The convent which the Carmelites built at Auschwitz in the late 1980s in her memory has been a cause of conflict between Jews and Polish Roman Catholics. Edith Stein's unflinching intellectual and moral clarity and her personal reappraisal of the Carmelite vocation of penance, or atonement, will continue to vivify her Order in the decades to come. The Order of Discalced Carmelites is growing in numbers throughout the world. The most fruitful areas are Latin America, Asia and Africa. There are now 3,681 Teresian Carmelite Brothers and Friars and 11,402 nuns. 60 congregations are affiliated to the order. "Secular" or lay orders of Teresian Carmelites also thrive. Teresian Carmelite women live in enclosed houses. The men combine contemplation with preaching. All of their houses attempt to observe a rule of silence. Daily prayer includes the saying of the Liturgy of Hours and two hours of personal prayer. Carmelites are divided by country into Provinces. Vincent O'Hara is Father-Provincial of the Teresian Carmelites of Ireland and England. The Father General of the Order is Fr. Camilo Maccise.

CARP. The Collegiate Association for Research of Principles (CARP) is the youth organization of the **Unification Church** and recruits on university and college campuses.

Carthusians. In the late 11th century, many monks and nuns were driven to return to the austere and hermetic way of life which characterized primitive Egyptian monasticism. St. Bruno, the founder of the Carthusian order, was one of these. He left his post as rector of Reims University to live as a hermit in the wilds outside Grenoble. Having been joined by several like-minded fellows, he founded in 1084 the monastery of the Grande Chartreuse; the monastery and the **Roman Catholic** Order to which it gave rise take their name from the near-by village of Cartusia. The Carthusian rule, the **Consuetudines,** was composed by St. Guigo and published in 1136. The basic principle of the Order was, and remains, commitment to solitude: each brother was to live in his own cell, within which he said his Office; each was to cultivate his own garden, and to prepare his own meals from its produce. Members of the Order are still committed to a life of complete solitude and unbroken silence. They are occasionally permitted short walks, for a chat with a fellow Carthusian. There are currently 394 Carthusian monks, 86 nuns, 14 postulants and 36 novices. There are now four Carthusian monasteries in Spain, two in Italy, and one each in Germany, Slovenia, Switzerland, Brazil, Portugal and the USA. Two Carthusian convents survive in Italy, two in France and one in Spain. The Carthusians' way of life has been too demanding to draw more than a handful of particularly self-sacrificing souls in any century.

Catacomb Church. An alternative designation for the underground **True Orthodox Church** in the former Soviet Union.

Catholic Action. A **Roman Catholic** lay movement promoted by Pope Pius XI, and strongly influenced by the thought of French philosopher Jacques Maritain. Beginning in the 1920s, it became active in Latin America where it encouraged the development of a social conscience among the upper class initially, although in recent decades it has become heavily involved with the poor.

In France it has been completely reorganized in the wake of Vatican 2, and exercises considerable influence. It is accorded a certain priority, compared with other groups, by the hierarchy, and in turn it influences the appointment of priests and bishops. It has developed special programmes, e.g. for workers, or in the field of education, and through these it draws in an estimated 8 per cent of practising Catholics.

Catholic Apostolic Church. The Catholic Apostolic Church began in Britain in 1832. Based initially at the Newman Street church in London (off Oxford Street) partly inspired by former Scottish Presbyterian minister Edward Irving, the sect is sometimes referred to as "Irvingites".

The church was charismatic and catholic, members spoke in tongues but developed elaborate rituals out of a belief in the "Real Presence" and "Perpetual Reservation". Membership was achieved by the "Sacrament of Sealing" which included the person among the 144,000 mentioned in Revelation 7.

Believing that the Second Coming of Christ was imminent, the church chose 12 "apostles" who together with the original 12 would occupy the 24 thrones of Revelation 4. In 1836 these new apostles delivered a statement to King William IV and the Anglican Church. In 1842 a service book was issued created from Roman Catholic, Greek and Anglican sources. By 1853 a new church had been built in Gordon Square.

The 12 new apostles were each given an area of Europe or America to evangelize. However, no provision was made for a replacement when an apostle died. Furthermore, once the 144,000 members had been "sealed" no additional sealing of members was possible, so the movement has now almost died out.

In 1863 in Germany a new apostle was recognized after the original Apostle to Germany had died. This caused a split with the Catholic Apostolic Church and a New Apostolic Church was formed, with a Patriarch, regarded as the Apostle's successor, rather as the Pope is regarded as the successor of St Peter. When Hitler came to power the then Patriarch called him "God's special emissary".

A number of other splits have occurred in the New Apostolic Church and the movement is now strongest in Germany and the Netherlands with offshoots in areas with German and Dutch immigrant communities such as the USA and South Africa. Global membership is approximately 25,000.

Catimbó. One of the names used in the central regions of Brazil for the **Afro-American spiritist** movement **Candomblé**.

CAUSA. The Confederation of the Association for the Unification of the Societies of America (CAUSA) is an offshoot or branch of the **Unification Church**.

Central Conference of American Rabbis (CCAR). *See* **Reform Judaism**.

Centre for Yoga Studies. A British based centre for the dissemination of the **Viniyoga** tradition of T.V.K. Desikachar.

Chaldean Uniate Church. Nearly all of Iraq's Christians are Catholics; nearly all of these are Chaldean. The Church as a whole numbers 335,000; a small group of 93,000 reside in Eastern Syria. Iraq's Christians were originally Nestorian. The efforts which were made after 1200 to recover them for the Catholic Church ripened in a reunion pact in 1553. This issued in the Chaldean Uniate Church. The Chaldeans used to swell the villages of northern Iraq. From the mid-1970s, violent repression of the Kurds by the Iraqi government, and discomfort between Christian minority and Muslim majority, have encouraged those Chaldeans who

have not abandoned Iraq for less unfortunate climes to move to the cities.
Baghdad is especially favoured. It is seat to
their Patriarch, and home to the Church's
central administration. Raphael I. Bidawid
has been the incumbent of the See since
1989. Some Western journalists view his
failure to criticize Saddam Hussein, President of Iraq's military–socialist government, in a poor light. The Chaldeans have
abstained from ordaining married men
since 1948. They have 17 bishops. Iraq's
major seminary, shared between Chaldean
and Syrian Catholics, is in Mosul.

Charan Dasis. A Hindu devotional movement in which the god Krishna is regarded
as the sole source of all things. Founded
by Charan Das, an 18th century merchant
from Delhi, the sect is opposed to the
worship of images and, in theory, is open
to all. In fact, members are mainly of the
mercantile castes and the sect flourishes in
the north of the country. Members wear
distinctive yellow garments and a small
pointed cap ornamented with a yellow scarf
tied around the rim.

Charismatic Movement. This name has
been given to the developments which
began to occur in the mainstream churches
in the late 1950s and the early 1960s.
Emphasizing the personal experience of
God's gift of the Holy Spirit to believers,
and also the variety of spiritual gifts,
the name is taken from the Greek
word *charismata* which means "spiritual
gifts" and is used in 1 Corinthians 12,
Romans 12, and Ephesians 4. It is
a Jesus-centred movement. Charismatics
believe it is Jesus who baptizes believers
in the Spirit (Acts 1:5). The key event for
Charismatics is held to be "baptism in the
Spirit", a non-Biblical expression, derived
from Matt. 3:1, Mark 1:8, Luke 3:16. This
is held to be a second blessing subsequent
to conversion which often seems to find
expression in "speaking in tongues". It is
argued that this replicates the experience

recorded in *Acts* of the disciples on the
day of Pentecost. Whether true or not,
it is undisputed that the gift of tongues
disappeared from the Church for centuries,
though this may only mean that as church
leaders moved up the social and cultural
ladder, they ceased to recognize and value
the phenomenon.

An important moment in the restoration
of "tongues" came with Edward Irving
(1792–1834) and the **Catholic Apostolic**
Church. Thereafter the phenomenon was
manifested by followers of the **holiness
and perfectionist** movements. In interpretations of what is now seen as
classical **Pentecostalism,** note has often
been taken of the low social status
of those who parade élitist spiritual
gifts. These were the people swept into
Pentecostal experience as a consequence
of the Welsh revival of 1904–5, and which
spilled over to Azusa Street, Los Angeles
in 1906. However, few were prepared
when charismatic phenomena appeared in
the historic churches and denominations.

In 1962 Michael Harper, an English
Anglican clergyman, founded the Fountain
Trust in England to encourage charismatic
understanding and experience. At Duquesne
University in Pittsburgh, USA in 1967 it
spread rapidly among **Roman Catholic**
students and faculty. From there it seems to
have spread to both Catholic and **Protestant**
colleges and universities. The difference
between classical and neo-Pentecostalism
is that the latter appeared within existing
churches and did not require withdrawal
to form a new sect. However although
the charismatic movement has powerfully
affected Roman Catholics, especially in
Holland, Anglicans, particularly in South
Africa, and the Baptists in Britain, existing
institutions have failed to contain the
phenomena which has often moved out
into **house churches, Restorationist and New
Churches.**

Cherubim and Seraphim. A common name
for **Aladura** Churches of African origin,
as in the **Church of the Cherubim and
Seraphim.**

Children of God. This was, during the first decade or so of its existence, the name of the new religious movement currently known as **Family of Love.**

Chinese Buddhism. It is exceptionally difficult to determine the condition of Buddhism in China at the present time. Neither the numbers of monks, nuns and laity nor the denominational allegiance of believers are known with any certainty. What is certain is that Buddhism is only slowly recovering from the horrors of the Cultural Revolution (1966–1979). In that 13-year period public worship was suppressed, many clergy were imprisoned or forced into labour camps and temples, monasteries and Buddhist libraries were destroyed. The temple complex at Zhaojue, for example, was turned into a municipal zoo in this period, though some temples, for reasons not fully understood, were protected by order of Zhou Enlai. Since the early '80s the situation has improved a little and the government sponsored **Chinese Buddhist Association** has encouraged clergy training on a limited scale. A monastic training school, the Buddhist Institute, is established in Beijing and a similar institute for nuns exists in Sichuan. Courses last from two to four years depending on previous schooling and it is estimated that the countrywide figure for enrolment in all institutes and temples is about 1,500 persons per year. A 15-day ordination ceremony of 800 monks and nuns was reported at a temple in Guangdong Province in 1988 but the numbers of fully trained members of the *Sangha* are still woefully low. Temples are expected to be self-supporting. Those on the tourist routes prosper, but most must rely on profit-making enterprises such as weaving, bookbinding or agriculture. Donations from visiting ex-patriots can be a significant element of income. The government decrees that "all monks shall take part in productive labour" though this is interpreted in a more liberal manner as time passes. Nevertheless many restrictions remain. Monks are prohibited from holding religious services in homes of the faithful, a traditional duty, and no new monasteries may be built.

Conditions for Buddhists in the Tibetan Autonomous Region remain poor and any statistics to the contrary may be regarded with the utmost suspicion. The vigour of **Tibetan Buddhism** before the 1959 Chinese invasion will take many centuries to recover. Of the 6,254 monasteries standing in 1951, virtually none remain. The vast majority of the monastic population are either dead, imprisoned, forcibly returned to secular life or in exile in India and beyond. Nevertheless many party officials recognize that 30 years of atheist propaganda have been a failure in Tibet and outside observers have noted that, despite the absence of a thriving monastic sector, lay pilgrimages and other devotions continue to attract large numbers. There are now some signs of a softer official approach. The Dalai Lama's family have visited the Lhasa area within the last few years and some temples and monasteries have been reopened. The number of monks officially allowed in residence is strictly limited though. Buddhist higher education is almost non-existent. On a more positive note, the establishment of a **Gelugpa** training institute in 1985 marks the reintroduction of a 10-year course leading to the degree of *geshe*.

Chinese Buddhists Association (CBA). Founded in 1954 this central-government-sponsored organization oversees the development of Buddhism throughout the People's Republic. It is not clear how provincial delegates are chosen for the "national representatives meetings" but the primary task of the CBA is to "help the government in implementing the policy of freedom of religious belief". To this end the Association attends to the training of monks and nuns, produces and circulates Buddhist scriptures and related literature, fosters Buddhist research and promotes exchanges with Buddhists from other lands. The national CBA has little direct control over individual temples and monasteries though it does determine the monasteries which may be reopened. The organization disburses government funds but also has the authority to solicit donations from ex-patriot benefactors in Hong Kong and overseas. The current president is Zhao Puchu; the Panchen Lama was honorary president until his death in 1989. The CBA produces a quarterly journal, *Fa Yin*.

Chinese Taoist Association (CTA). A government-sponsored organization designed to regulate **Taoism** in much the same way that the **Chinese Buddhist Association** oversees the development of Buddhism. Taoism is the most difficult Chinese religion to accurately evaluate and the number of priests and nuns is unknown. Perhaps 200 Taoist monasteries and temples are now functioning and a small proportion of these are officially permitted to train priests. The CTA runs a, one-year, clergy-training course in Beijing and this appears particularly popular with young women students. Popular Taoism, essentially unregulated by the state, retains some vigour with temples packed during major festivals.

Chinese Folk Religion. In the 19th century when the population was thought to be about 400,000,000, it was common to call China "the land of 400,000,000 Buddhists". It would have been equally true to call it "the land of 400,000,000 ancestor-worshippers" or "of 400,000,000 Taoists" or "400,000,000 nature worshippers". The vast mass of the Chinese people were all of these. The population now is over 1,100 million, but no figures or even estimates are available for the number practising any or all of these beliefs—probably it is a long way short of the old figure of 400,000,000.

The most deeply held of all Chinese beliefs is ancestor worship, and many of the very earliest writings describe ancestor worshipping ceremonies. When a mature person dies, his or her soul survives as a kind of minor god which can be worshipped by the children and by other later descendants. The worship confers benefits both ways: on the ancestor, because without the care of the living the dead soul is thought to fade away to extinction, and on the descendants, because the ancestors are considered able to bring spiritual influence to bear on their worldly well-being. It is assumed that the ancestors inhabit an after-world much like this one, and worship consists largely of providing the goods necessary for comfortable existence in that world—food, money, housing, clothing and transport. The food is real (eaten by the worshippers after the ancestors have taken their spiritual fill), but the other goods are made of paper and are burned to transmit them to the after-world.

Buddhism came to China from India in about the 1st century AD, and was soon embraced by the common people to whom it promised salvation. They did not cease to worship the ancestors, however, and for those (few) who worried about such things it became necessary to think of a split soul, part of which went on as an ancestor god and part of which went through the cycle of rebirths. One of the Boddhisatvas, Avalokitesvara, under the name Kuan Yin ("Hearer of cries") has been probably the most revered deity in all China, worshipped by all in need of help.

Taoism began as a philosophy which stressed man's unity with nature, but Taoists began to seek eternal life as a means of emulating nature's constant renewal, and they turned to alchemy and to dietary, breathing and sexual techniques designed to prolong life. By about the same time as Buddhism arrived they had separated soul from body and begun to worship ancient nature gods and the deified souls of great men. Magical practices such as rain-making and plague exorcism remain associated with Taoism.

Chinese folk religion developed as an amalgam of different religious elements. In addition to worshipping ancestors, Buddhist gods, Taoist gods, and nature gods, people worshipped "heaven", an impersonal force much like "destiny". They also took care to make offerings to the hordes of evil spirits which swarmed around them and might otherwise do them mischief. The mix of religious practice varied (and varies) from area to area, from village to village, and from home to home, so that it would really be more true to speak of Chinese folk religion*s* rather than of one folk religion.

Chishtiya. The Chishtiya is the most widespread and most popular **Sufi** order in South Asia today. Its original seat was in Chisht near Herat in present-day Afghanistan. Khwaja Abu Ishak of Syria has been credited with founding the order, and through him it is traced back to the Prophet Muhammad. Its effective founder, however, was Khwaja Mu'in al-din Chishti (d. 1233) who introduced the order to India in the late 12th century. His shrine at Ajmer today attracts the largest number of pilgrims in South Asia, especially at the annual 'urs, or festival celebrating the anniversary of his death. The early development of the order was shaped by a number of charismatic "great Shaikhs", venerated still as saints, who were active in the northern part of the sub-continent—the tomb of Baba Farid (d. 1265) at Pak Pattan in the Punjab also attracts huge crowds each year on the occasion of the 'urs. The disciples of the "great Shaikhs" then disseminated the order in most areas of South Asia. This early branching out in the 14th century explains the mass following of the Chishtiya today, and its supra-regional appeal.

The two most important branches of the order developed in the 14th century, the Nizamiya and the Sabiriya.

The Nizamiya derives its name from Nizam al-din Auliya (d.1325), whose tomb is situated in Delhi where it functions as a centre of pilgrimage and is visited by many Hindus and Sikhs as well as Muslims. Visits by diplomatic representative from various Muslim countries serve further to underline its importance. Silsilas (lines of discipleship), spread all over the sub-continent, are traced back to him, jointly constituting this branch of the Chishtiya.

The Nizamiya experienced a revival and reorganization from the 18th century onwards as a response to the declining central power of the Mughals. Emphasis was placed on the active propagation of Islam and the internal spiritual regeneration of Muslims. Successors of the Sufi revivalist saints became active in politics in the 20th century, joining the cause of the reformist *ulama* (**Jam'iat ul-Ulama-i Hind**), and using their mass appeal in electoral processes.

The silsilas of the Sabiriya are traced back to Ala uddin 'Ali ibn Ahmad Sabir (d. 1291). This second branch, however, did not come into prominence until the 15th century when Ahmad 'Abd al-Haqq set up a great mystic centre at Rudauli in Awadh, Uttar Pradesh. The Sabiris spread especially in North India, their main centres developing in Uttar Pradesh. Leading representatives of the branch in the 16th and 17th centuries were Shaikh 'Abd al-Quddus Gangohi (d. 1537) and Shaikh Muhibullah Allahabadi (d. 1648). The latter, especially, promulgated liberal and syncretic trends in Indian Islam, reinvigorating the theory of *wahdat al-wujud*, or ontological monism, promulgated by Ibn al-'Arabi. Amongst the most notable Chishti-Sabiris of recent times have been Haji Imdadullah (d. 1899), the spiritual master of many **Deobandis,** Ashraf 'Ali Thanvi (d. 1943), the leading North Indian mystic of the early 20th century, and Muhammad Ilyas (d. 1944), the founder of the **Tablighi Jama'at.**

The early ideological concepts of the Chishti saints were firmly based on the concept of *wahdat al-wujud*, the negation of private property, and the undesirability of working for one's living. Their desire was to live for God alone. They avoided contact with, and dependence on, the state.

An important feature was that they did not demand formal conversion to Islam before they initiated a new disciple: ideally they expected such conversion to come out of that person's religious experiences. Up to the present day many Chishti saints are venerated not only by Muslims but also by Hindus.

A characteristic of the Chishtiya is the practice of *sama*, the listening to hymns and mystical songs sung with or without the accompaniment of instruments. Khwaja Muin al-din Chishti gave this institution a new dimension, a local colour and character. Listening to music was a contentious issue among Sufis, and if it was allowed, then only in front of a spiritually immaculate audience. Other practices of the Chishtiya involve the silent and loud repetition of phrases, contemplation and confinement of a person for a prescribed period. A more indigenous feature used by the order is the practice of regulating their breath.

Migration from South Asia does not mean that followers relinquish their ties with the order. Devotees will return to the shrine of their saint on the annual feast day ('*urs*). Those who cannot do this will organize their own festival in their new local community. This then centres around a descendant of the shrine who can act as a regional representative.

Chisumphi cult. No longer the important cult it once was, it is still to be found among the northern Chewa of Malawi. A sacred drum is regarded as a symbol of God, Chisumphi, who, in former times at least, was believed to enter into certain mediums, or cultic spirit wives (the Makewana), at a central shrine. *See too* **African traditional religions.**

Chittagong Buddhist Association. Formed in 1887 to co-ordinate the conduct of the 30,000 **Theravada** Buddhists (monks and lay people) in Chittagong and the Chittagong Hill Tracts in the south-eastern parts of East Bengal (now Bangladesh). The movement that led to its formation was begun by a Theravada monk, Saramedha, who, in the middle of the 19th century, reformed the *Sangha* by removing Hindu practices and restoring proper ordination. The Association constitutes the oldest modern Buddhist society in the sub-continent.

Chogye Chong. The first distinctively Korean school of **Son (Zen)** Buddhism; also the name given to the single, unified school of Korean Buddhism which was established in 1935. After the Japanese occupation of Korea (1910–1945) the Chogye Chong was the school which represented the traditional Korean approach to monastic life, emphasizing celibacy and discipline. They are opposed by the **T'aego Chong,** a school representing the more liberal Japanese tradition of married monks.

Chondo Gyo. Chondo Gyo (The Religion of the Heavenly Way) was founded in 1860 by one Ch'oe Suun. Ostensibly based on Ch'oe's personal revelation, the teaching is, in fact, a synthesis of **Confucian, Taoist** and native Korean thought. Initially it was propagated under the name **Tonghak** (Eastern Learning) as a counterweight to Christianity, referred to by the Koreans as **Sohak** (Western Learning). In 1905 Tonghak was renamed Chondo Gyo and its numbers grew rapidly. Today it claims over 1,000,000 members in South Korea.

Doctrinally the Chondo Gyo could be described as a form of pantheism. There is one **God (Hanullim)** who embraces the whole of existence. Human beings are thus part of God and carry the divine within them. The aim of the religion is to help people realize their innate divinity and to bring about a heaven on earth. This is achieved through a combination of religious practice, ethical conduct and charitable works. Christian influences are discernible in some of the movement's practices such as prayer, reading from scripture, singing hymns and also, perhaps, in the earthy focus of its utopian aspirations.

In the years following its establishment and also during the period of Japanese occupation (1910–1945) the movement was heavily involved in the political struggle of the common people for democratic government and for Korean independence. At the present time, however, it is not an active participant in South Korean politics.

Christadelphians. The Christadelphians ("Christ's Brethren") were founded in America in 1848 by John Thomas (b. 1805) who had emigrated there in 1832 after studying medicine in London. He initially joined the **Disciples of Christ** but broke away to form his own movement. The doctrines spread to England through the work of Robert Roberts.

Christadelphians base their faith on the Bible, particularly the Hebrew prophets and the book of Revelation which they use to predict future events. They believe Jesus will return and reign for 1,000 years in Jerusalem, but reject the doctrine of the Trinity. Salvation is received on the basis of good works and an acceptance of Christadelphian doctrines; members are baptized by immersion.

They have no ministers or clergy and publish no statistics on membership. There are believed to be 30,000 members in the United Kingdom. Churches meet in rented halls or private homes, the Christadelphian message is spread through literature and public lectures.

Christian Fellowship Church. The official title of the indigenous church in the Solomon Islands more popularly known as **Etoism.**

Christian Fellowship of Zambia (CFZ). This church was founded by a former

Brethren missionary on the global wave of the **charismatic** movement. More specifically in the context of Zambia, it represents a breakaway from the austere Brethren orientation. An unemotional dedication to New Testament exposition has been replaced by a concentration on the power and gifts of the Holy Spirit.

CFZ services are characterized by the tidal ebb and flow of emotion. Members of the congregation fall down, dance, raise their arms in the air, speak in tongues, and the women ululate. The singing is accompanied by drumming and swaying. There is frequent prophesying, interpretation of dreams, and casting out of demons. Interestingly the latter often have a local flavour, including demons of snakes, lions, crocodiles or even beer-drinking (a cultural practice condemned by the Brethren missionaries).

The CFZ congregation is predominantly poor: the attraction of the church being the cathartic nature of the worship in a culture where emotion is generally repressed, and its full schedule of activities which helps alleviate the tedium of the common lifestyle. For the leaders there is an incentive of potential travel and material benefits through the international connections of the church's founder.

Christian Science. Christian Science was founded by Mary Baker Eddy (1821–1910) and is based on the teaching in her book *Science and Healing with a key to the Scriptures* published in 1875. Mary Baker Eddy came from New Hampshire USA and had been healed from various illnesses by a spiritual healer P. P. Quimby.

Christian Scientists are sometimes described as neither Christian nor Scientist. They believe that God is spirit, and that matter, sin, suffering, and illness are unreal. Death is an illusion: in consequence Jesus did not die on the cross. Accepting these beliefs leads to salvation.

The first church was opened in Boston USA in 1879 and the movement spread to England and Germany. Churches are run according to Mary Baker Eddy's directives in *The Manual of the Mother Church* (1895). There are no sermons, comment or interpretation: instead there are readings from the Bible and Mary Baker Eddy's writings. Church buildings are referred to as Reading Rooms. There are no ordained clergy, the movement is run by a board of directors.

The *Christian Science Monitor* is a newspaper published by the movement which has an international reputation for the quality of its reporting. It does not accept advertisements for alcohol or tobacco.

The entertainer Joyce Grenfell was a Christian Scientist. Present worldwide membership is over 1,500,000, of whom 1,000,000 are in the United States.

Chundo-Kyo. *See* **Chondo-Gyo.**

Church of Armageddon. Also known as Love Family (not to be confused with Family of Love) or Love Israel Family, and founded in Seattle, Washington, by Paul Erdman, known as Love Israel. The group derives its name from Revelation 16:16 which states that the nations of the world will be gathered in Armageddon. Love Israel claims to be Jesus Christ's representative on earth and his instrument to gather God's true family. The group's beliefs are centred on the Bible and its charter. On joining the Family, a member is baptized and given a new name, either biblical or one representing a virtue, such as Prudence, Strength etc. Members believe that they "die to their past" and that death is an illusion. New members are given a new age, 66 years older than their actual age, but they profess to be timeless. A new calendar replaces the conventional one. Members are encouraged to break with their past completely, including severing ties with their natural parents and with the world outside; there are no TV, radio, or newspapers. Members live communally

in houses owned or rented by the Family under the guidance of an elder. All assets are managed by the leader and members are encouraged to give all their possessions "to God".

In 1983 accusations and lawsuits by dissenting members against Love Israel led to a breakup of the Family. Israel was accused of "sexual opportunism" and of using Family money to pay for a luxurious lifestyle and drugs while children had neither shoes or books. The leader went to Los Angeles and worked in a friend's investment bank. The Seattle members (several dozens) joined the handful of members living on a farm in Arlington. Total membership was reported to be 300 then. In 1985 Love Israel moved to the farm bringing with him some 45 members including six of his children. In 1989 the Arlington group counted 90 members.

The outlook of the community of 1989 differed somewhat from its former image. While monogamy and strict regulations are not an integral part of the community, members live a fairly traditional lifestyle with an emphasis on close-knit family units. The leader said in an interview that he had changed as he matured and that drugs had no place in the Family.

Church of Christ. Its parent church is the Boston Church of Christ, with satellite congregations having formed in major cities in the UK, notably London, Birmingham and Manchester. Its roots go back to The Crossroads Church of Christ in Florida, USA, begun by Kip McKean who while a student at the University in Florida, converted to Christianity and started discipling ministries in other churches. McKean founded the Boston Church of Christ in 1979 with his wife Elena, from where teams were sent out to Britain in the early 1980s. By the late 1980s the movement had about 70 centres worldwide, their leaders often being young, highly motivated young couples.

The structure of the movement is based on "shepherding", with a "discipler" in charge of converts to monitor their "spiritual growth". This means continuous contact, passing on instructions and involvement in personal matters. Theologically, the Church appears to follow the Protestant tradition, accepting its teachings of Jesus, the nature of the trinity and the authority of the Bible. However, there seems to be a claim to absolute truth which explains efforts to recruit members of other churches. Further, the Church teaches that salvation cannot be obtained by faith alone and that baptism by full immersion is the moment of conversion.

Usually young people attracted to the Church are said to be pressured into joining and kept busy once they are involved. Members may use different names for their organization when recruiting.

Church of Christ is also the English designation of the Philippine **Iglesia ni Cristo.**

Church of God International. This is a splinter group of the **Worldwide Church of God** (WCG). It was established in 1978 by Garner Ted Armstrong, son of the founder of the WCG.

Church of God Mission. A Nigerian new religious movement founded and led by Benson Idahosa, a charismatic preacher and talented organizer. With links to the PTL Ministry of Jim Bakker in the United States, Idahosa set up a religious broadcasting station in Benin City, although a government ban on religious broadcasting has prevented its use hitherto. The movement has a further international dimension through mass crusades conducted in a number of countries outside Africa, including Australia.

Church of God of Prophecy. This is a West Indian **Pentecostal** church which is one of the black churches which has become well established in the UK with a national headquarters and regional organizations.

Church of Manalo. The **Iglesia ni Cristo,** a new religious movement in the Philippines, is sometimes referred to as the Church of Manalo after its founder, Felix Manalo (1886–1963).

Church of Perfect Liberty. A Japanese new religious movement, more commonly known as **PL Kyodan.**

Church of South India. *See* United Churches.

Church of the Cherubim and Seraphim. This church is established in the UK, mainly in London and the West Midlands, but is in origin a Nigerian sect in the **Aladura** tradition. It is not **Pentecostal,** although services bear certain similarities to those of black churches of West Indian origin such as the **New Testament Church of God.** During their services, members are barefoot and wear long white prayer gowns. Powerful congregational singing creates a mood of excitement, and individuals may engage in acts of prophesying. Preaching, on the other hand, is little emphasized, being in effect displaced by the interpretation of dreams and visions, which, however, must be in accordance with the Bible treated in a fundamentalist manner. Strongly authoritarian, the church insists on separate offices for men and women, but there is no emphasis on a distinctive ethical lifestyle.

Church of the Lord (Aladura). An important independent indigenous prophet-healing church based in Nigeria, and a product of the wider **Aladura** movement. It was founded in Nigeria in 1930 by a former Anglican teacher and catechist, Josiah Oshitelu, and then after World War II it branched out into Liberia, Sierra Leone and Ghana in particular. In 1964 the first branch outside Africa was established, in Britain.

Membership entails baptism by immersion. The ministry has a dual hierarchical structure, with apostles and bishops at the head of the two strands respectively. The Apostles are pre-eminent in a line of prophets, with gifts of visions, revelations and prophecy; the bishops are pre-eminent in a line of evangelists, with gifts of preaching, pastoral care and administration. An apostle ranks above a bishop, and above everyone stands the primate. Women have found gradual acceptance in these roles. The church has over 1,000,000 members, and is now affiliated to the **World Councils of Churches,** as well as being linked to the **Pentecostal** movement.

Church of the Movement of Spiritual Inner Awareness. This new religious movement is generally known by its acronym **MSIA**.

Church of the Twelve Apostles. This Ghanaian church is a product of the influential **Harris movement**.

Church of the Watchtower. This African organization of **Jehovah's Witnesses** is described elsewhere under the heading **Kitawala**.

Church Universal and Triumphant. Since 1974, a year after the death of its founder, this has been the official designation of a new religious movement originally called Summit Lighthouse. It began in Washinton, DC in 1958, founded by Mark L. Prophet (1918–1973), and spiritual leadership now rests with his widow Elizabeth née Wulf, also known as Guru Ma. God is believed to use Ascended Masters (of whom Mark Prophet is now one) to train his dedicated servants on earth to proclaim his word in the "last days". Members are baptized, renounce alcohol, tobacco and drugs, and pledge themselves to give 10 per cent of their income to the movement—which, re-

latedly, is accused by critics of becoming wealthy at its members' expense. It owns the extensive Royal Teton Ranch near Yellowstone Park in Montana, where it holds a large annual conference of members. Membership figures are not released, but there are adherents in a number of countries worldwide, including the UK.

Cistercians. A Roman Catholic religious order, the Cistercians spring from the reformist groups which, in the late 11th century, broke away from the Benedictine Order. They found its monastic practice overly leisured, its cuisine unduly filling, for a monastic order, its liturgy cluttered, and its architecture, as typified by the great Abbey at Cluny, unsuitably elaborate. The Cistercians would return to the simplicity of St. Benedict's *Rule*. Where the Benedictines interpreted the *Rule's* prohibition of the consumption of "four-footed animals" as leaving ample space for the ingestion of chicken, pheasant, grouse, and so forth, the Cistercians became vegetarians; large repasts had been necessary at Cluny to provide the energy for the Black Monk's chief pastime of singing profuse offices and psalmodic litanies: the Cistercians overthrew the "dictatorship of the choir", a common phenomenon, by excavating, at the instigation of St. Stephen Harding, the Order's original liturgy; the Cistercians stand against the excesses of Romanesque architecture resulted in the invention of the Gothic cathedral. The first Cistercian house was founded in 1098 at Cîteaux in Burgundy, by Robert of Molesme. Their *Institutes* were composed shortly afterwards by St. Alberic. In the 12th century, St. Bernard of Clairvaux explained that the aim of the Cistercians' hard penitential life is the soul's mystical union with God.

There are now two separate Cisterician orders, a consequence of a revolt against the laxity of the monks of what later came to be named the "Cistercians of the Common Observance". The newer group are the "Order of Cistercians of the Strict Observance" OCSO, or in the vernacular, "Trappists". Their founder was Armand-Jean le Bouthillier de Rancé. In 1664, de Rancé imposed reform upon the French Cistercian house at La Trappe. His legacy survived, and as a result of the French revolution, which drove those monks who survived it to emigrate, spread to Switzerland, and thence to Belgium, Germany, Spain, and Italy.

After Napoleon's demise, the French Cistercians of the Strict Observance flourished once more. Their house at Port du Salut has become renowned for its eponymous cheese. In 1848, they detached a successful expedition to Kentucky, where the first American Cistercian abbey was founded, at Gethsemani. The reformed Order was fissiparous until 1892, when Pope Leo XIII directed all Cistercian abbots of the Strict Observance to volunteer to become a single Order. Pope Leo also provided the means for Cistercians to study theology. Thomas Merton (1915–1968) was a monk of Gethsemani: his autobiography, the *Seven Storey Mountain* was a bestseller in the 1950s. Merton's flirtation in the 1960s with, amongst other things, Zen Buddhism, may indicate the openness of the Order to new religious styles; or it may reflect the mood of the time. More recently, Henri Nouwen's sane account of the year's stay at another American Abbey, *The Genesee Diary*, indicates the continuing popularity of the contemplative life. Cistercians of the Strict Observance are still vegetarians, fast for half the year, live by manual labour within the monastery confines, keep a rule of silence which has entailed the elaboration of a Cistercian sign language, and wake in the middle of the night for prayer. There are currently 2,000 Cistercian nuns in the Strict Observance, and 3,000 Fathers. Numbers are slightly lower in the Common Observance. Members of the Common Observance work in parishes and in schools. Clothed in white cassocks, they are known as the "White Fathers".

Clean Government Party. *See* **Komeito.**

Cochin Jews. Jewish communities developed in the city of Cochin (now in the Indian State of Kerala) and in a number of the surrounding areas. Although scholars have traced the history of Jewish settlement back to the 10th century CE, and its origins are obscure, one of the communities (the Pardesi, see below) celebrated its 1,900th anniversary in 1968. Jews organized themselves into three discrete and endogomous communities somewhat along Indian caste lines. The "Black Jews" were physically similar to the local population, had their own synagogues and were engaged in trade and crafts. The lighter skinned, "White Jews" (or Pardesi, "foreigners") were a combination of Jews from the area together with **Sephardim** (from Spain, Holland and the Middle East) and **Ashkenasim** (from Germany). Professionals and merchants, they had their own synagogues following a largely Sephardi rite with Ashkenazi elements. A third group (*meshuhrarim*–"emancipated") was made up of freed slaves who joined either community but did not have communal rights until the 20th century.

The communities, centred around an area still known as Jew Town, were protected by the Rajah of Cochin during the period of Portuguese control (1502–1663) and thrived under Dutch rule (1663–1795) with the increased opportunities for trade and commerce. Links were established between the Cochin and Amsterdam Jewish communities and subsequently with the wider Jewish world. Cochin Jews produced religious works in Hebrew and local languages. The emergence of the **Zionist** movement in Europe was supported by Cochin Jews and after the establishment of the State of Israel (1948), and in a process initiated by the "Black Jews", many emigrated there in the 1950s. Approximately 5,000 Cochin Jews currently live in Israel. Small communities remain in the Cochin area represented at the national and state levels by the South Indian Jews' Association.

Colanaikans. The Colanaikans of Kerala are the only remaining cave dwelling tribe in India. All efforts to "develop" them have failed. In common with other Indian tribal groups they have interesting religious beliefs and practices, which form part of the composite picture of the **tribal religions of India**.

The Colanaikans believe in three types of deities. The foremost is a god called Banasu, who sometimes appears to them as a man or as an animal. The second group of deities are the gods of the plains, who they believe can be kept off by propitiating their own deities. They also believe in a river god known as Ola Devva. The Colanaikans therefore do not bathe in rivers at night or early in the morning, and caution their children not to throw stones in the river for fear of offending this god. The Colanaikans have idols which are kept in the caves and transported along with them when they shift their residence to other caves. Some idols which are especially sacred are kept in the interior forests far away from human habitation so that they are not contaminated by human presence. If these idols are touched by people, the Colanaikans believe that they become powerless and unable to protect them from the deities of the plains.

The chieftain of the tribe is also the chief religious functionary. He propitiates the spirits, and cures people of sickness, which they believe is due to spirit possession. The "treatment" involves blowing on the patient's face and body, invoking other gods to help in exorcising the spirit, and ringing a bell round the victim's head. If these measures fail, the chief dances to the music of a religious instrument called the Bida.

The territorial chiefs are highly respected

as they control many spirits, and can not only cure sickness, but also inflict sickness through sorcery.

Communio è Liberazione. At the turn of this century, a Bishop of Rome predicted that the religious orders would decline and the secular orders flourish and multiply. In sheer force of numbers, secular orders such as Communio è Liberazione outweigh all of the combined **Roman Catholic** religious Orders enumerated elsewhere in this book.

Communio è Liberazione members sometimes come across as exuberant to the point of obstreperousness (readers will not go far amiss if they picture Italian **Protestant Evangelicals**), with a great delight in community pastimes, a strong and informed sense of the importance of conversion, and a Catholic faith modern in its lack of interest in the liturgical accoutrements of earlier times, and conservative in its commitment to Roman Catholic doctrine. Communio è Liberazione was founded in the late 1960s by the Italian Luigi Giussani. Don Giussani realized that Italian students and schoolchildren had a weak knowledge of the basic tenets of Catholic faith, and even less understanding of the purpose of what little they had been taught. He set out to remedy this. Drawing on the thought of the French theologian Henri de Lubac, he spoke of God as the "object of human desire". Communio è Liberazione currently has upwards of 100,000 members. Although the "Italian connection" is still important, the movement has spread across Europe and has strongholds in South America and elsewhere. It is unhesitating in its loyalty to the Pope in Rome.

Compassion Society. Also known as **Tz'u Hui T'ang** this modern Taiwanese group was founded in the eastern part of the island. Its prime deity is the Venerable Mother or Golden Mother of the Jasper Pool who rules over a paradise of immortals in the mountains of the west. Society members believe that she revealed herself to the spirit medium Su Lieh-tung near Hualien in 1949. The movement places great emphasis on spirit writing and has a large body of sacred texts, many of which come from this source. There are thought to be about 200 "Branch Halls" and 400 smaller groups throughout the island with the main temple situated in Hualien. Members total between 10,000 and 15,000 and the society possesses a quite complex administrative structure. A small splinter group exists called the **Palace of Sacred Peace** though relations with the Society remain cordial.

Congregationalists. Congregational churches are united not by a tenet of theology but by a system of church government. Taking seriously the words of St Paul, "Christ is the head of his body, the church" (Col. 1. 18) and the description of Christians by Peter "You are the chosen race, the King's priests, the holy nation, God's own people" (1 Peter 2. 9) Congregationalists reject external authority and give every local church the right to make its own decisions.

This has led to both liberal and evangelical strands in the church. Congregational churches, because of their autonomy have had the freedom to listen to all the new ideas of modern theological scholarship and Bible criticism and accept or reject as they feel God opens their minds. Most Congregational churches believe in the need for a personal faith in Christ, and express this through the sacraments of Baptism and the Lord's Supper.

Since the 19th century Congregational churches have worked together through national and later international councils. Since 1970 they have been part of the **World Alliance of Reformed Churches** which also includes the **Presbyterians** with which they often have a theological affinity.

As well as Congregational churches all over the world arising from missionary activity initiated in the USA and the UK, two other main areas have a strong Congregational tradition. These are the **Mission Covenant** churches of Scandinavia, and the **Eastern European Congregational** churches, particularly in Bulgaria, Czechoslovakia and scattered communities of Armenians.

In England most Congregationalists have united with the Presbyterian Church to form the **United Reformed Church**. However the Congregational Union in Scotland and the Union of Welsh Independents (Welsh-speaking) have remained separate. Worldwide specifically Congregational membership is estimated at over 2,000,000.

Conservative Catholic Churches. These are a group of about 60, mostly small, denominations, which opposed recent reforms in the **Roman Catholic** Church, particularly those of the Second Vatican Council (1962). In Britain they are represented by the Catholic Tridentine Church which supports the beliefs of Archbishop Lefebvre. Following his insistence on the Latin Mass and other traditional practices, Archbishop Lefebvre defied the pope by training and ordaining priests, leading to his excommunication from the Roman Catholic Church.

Although fragmented the movement is worldwide and numbers over 250,000.

Conservative Judaism. Conservative Judaism simultaneously teaches that the Jewish people must be committed to *halakhah* (Jewish law) but they are also empowered to modify it, as long as such changes are consistent with what are seen to be the dynamic processes of change in the *halakhah* and Judaism. The movement has its origins in the thought of Zecharius Frankel (1801–1875) who called for a "positive—historical" approach to Judaism, arguing that while post-Biblical Judaism had developed historically, and thus, change was permitted, any alterations of *halakhah* must come slowly, reflecting the will of the Jewish people. At first he found common cause with some moderate Reform leaders but in 1845, he left a Reform-organized rabbinic conference in Frankfort after a majority approved a measure stating that use of Hebrew prayers was "advisable" but not mandatory. In 1854, Frankel was chosen over Abraham Geiger, the noted radical Reform scholar, to head the newly-formed *Jüdisch-Theologisches Seminar* ("Jewish Theological Seminary") in Wroclaw (Breslau) which became the centre for what was then known as "Historical Judaism".

In America, the Conservative movement also began as a reaction to **Reform Judaism,** which by 1880, had become the dominant strand of Judaism. Some traditionalists and moderate Reform rabbis united in 1886 to found the **Jewish Theological Seminary** in response to the 1885 "Pittsburgh Platform" which although not formally approved by the conference was clearly favoured by many of its members, becoming the guiding principle of American Reform for the next 50 years. (The platform was adopted by the founding meeting of **The Central Conference of American Rabbis,** the Reform rabbinate, in 1889). The traditionalists and moderate Reform leaders were shocked by the Platform's rejection of rituals such as *kashrut* (the dietary code), the beliefs in Heaven, Hell, and the coming of the Messiah and the re-establishment of Jewish sovereignty in their ancestral home. The Seminary was the centre for both those who favoured moderate change, while accepting the Bible and *Talmud* and those who opposed change, although there were traditionalists who did not support the Seminary. By the end of the century, the Seminary was floundering, as Reform Jews maintained their ties and the new immigrants from Russia tended towards **Orthodoxy** (or secularism).

Under the urging of men like Cyrus Adler, Louis Marshall, and Simon Guggenheim, the Jewish Theological Seminary was reorganized in 1902 with Solomon Schechter (1850–1915) at its head. Now, the Seminary aimed to help "Americanize" the new immigrants by training rabbis who could both appeal to the tradition and integrate their congregants into America. Under Schechter's leadership, the Seminary and the movement, began to grow in influence and call itself "Conservative Judaism". In 1913, Schechter organized a union of congregations to support the seminary, **The United Synagogue of America,** but at its start, it was not clear if this was to be a specifically Conservative organization (as was desired by some *alumni* of the seminary) or if it were to be an "Orthodox–Conservative" union, as other leaders (including Schechter) wanted. Eventually, it became an organization of exclusively Conservative congregations.

Under the leadership (1915–1940) of Cyrus Adler, the movement grew, with the seminary, the United Synagogue, and the Rabbinical Assembly of America (reorganized in 1929 after its original founding in 1901; renamed in 1962 as **The Rabbinical Assembly,** the international association of Conservative rabbis) all being strengthened. The movement grew rapidly under the 1940–1972 tenure of Adler's successor, Louis Finkelstein. During those three decades, Conservative Judaism became the largest American denomination, meeting the needs of a large number of congregants who wished to feel part of both modern America and tradition. This blend can be seen in the 1960 decisions of the Rabbinical Assembly of America to permit the use of electricity on the Sabbath, which Orthodoxy considers unethical, as well as driving automobiles to synagogue on this day.

In recent years, this modernizing trend has continued with the Jewish Theological Seminary's 1981 decision to admit women into its rabbinic and cantoral programmes. This change of policy led to some dissent, with a group of Conservative rabbis, led by David Novack, splintered from Conservative Judaism, founding

The Union of Traditional Conservative Judaism, later renamed **The Institute for Traditional Judaism** (Rabbi Novack remained a member of the Rabbinic Assembly and was otherwise involved in Conservative Judaism until 1988). In 1985, the Rabbinical Assembly voted to accept women rabbis, with Amy Eilberg becoming the first Conservative woman rabbi. After some controversy, women were also admitted into the Cantors Assembly, although a group of cantors opposed this decision, The International Federation of Traditional Cantors, was formed in 1991, with Cantor Eliezer Kirshblum as Acting President.

That there are limits on the movement's liberalism were shown in the 1985 decision to reaffirm the traditional position that only those whose mothers are Jewish or have been converted according to *halakhah* are Jews (a rejection of Reform's decision that people with Jewish fathers and non-Jewish mothers or whose conversion was not conducted accorded to *halakhah* are considered Jews) as well as the 1992 decision not to maintain the "status quo" and not admit gay and lesbians to the Jewish Theological Seminary or Rabbinic Assembly (The decision prohibits any expulsion of gays or lesbians in the groups and established a commission to further study the issue).

Conservative Judaism is represented in Israel by the **Masorati** ("Traditional") movement, with more than 40 congregations and its own rabbinic seminary in Jerusalem, *Beit Midrash le-Limodai Yahadut* ("Institute for Jewish Studies" founded in 1984), where American rabbinic students also study for a year. The movement also established **Kibbutz** *Honaton* in the Galilee region. Currently, the Rabbinical Assembly has more than 1,200 members and the United Synagogue of America represents more than 830 congregations (approximately 1,250,000 persons).

Worldwide, the movement is represented by the World Council of Synagogues (1959). In addition to its seminaries in America (JTS and the Los Angeles University of Judaism where students may do part of their studying after their year in Israel) and Israel, there is the Seminario Latinamericano in Buenos Aires (1959). Currently, there are an estimated 2,000,000 Conservative Jews worldwide.

Convince. A small ancestral cult in eastern Jamaica where the ritual centres on Bongo ghosts, that is, the spirits of people who belonged to it during their lifetime. Unlike **Candomblé, Vodun, Shango** and **Santería,** which comprise a syncretic mix of **African traditional religions** and **Roman Catholicism,** Convince combines elements of African religion with others typical of **Protestant** Christian worship, such as prayers, hymns and Bible readings. An annual ceremony of animal sacrifice is held, and spirits of the ancestors may possess a devotee during Convince rituals. However, the movement has declined rapidly in the last two or three decades, providing little more at present than occasions for festivities.

Coptic Church. From the arabized Greek word for Egyptian, the term "Copt" has come to mean an Egyptian Christian of the monophysite tradition. The Coptic Church is one of the main **Oriental Orthodox** Churches and the largest of three rival representatives of the ancient Patriarchate of Alexandria, the others being the Greek-speaking Patriarchal Church of Alexandria (Byzantine Orthodox tradition) and the Uniate Coptic Church (Roman Catholic) established in the 18th century. The now independent **Ethiopian Church** was under the jurisdiction of the Coptic Church until 1959.

Mediterranean Egypt was part of greater Greece and the patriarchal Church founded by St Mark at Alexandria in the 2nd century was a Greek Church. The vast majority of Christians in Egypt rejected the authority of the Council of Chalcedon, thereby associating themselves with the monophysite view of Christ's nature. Up until the Muslim conquest in the 7th century most Egyptians were Coptic Christians. Their descendants today probably number somewhere between 6–8,000,000, roughly 15 per cent of the total population.

The primate, who bears the title "Pope of Alexandria and Patriarch of the See of St Mark of Egypt, the Near East and All Africa", has in modern times resided in Cairo. The best known of the dioceses outside Egypt is that of Jerusalem. The Coptic liturgy, based on the originally Greek Liturgy of St Mark, is celebrated in an ancient form of Coptic to which much Arabic has been added. Monasticism, which in the early Christian Church largely developed in Egypt, remains an important part of the Coptic tradition.

Throughout most of their history the Copts have suffered discrimination and occasional bouts of persecution, and have enjoyed complete freedom of religion in the modern sense only since the end of the 19th century. The current primate, Pope Shenouda III, was from 1981 to 1985 banished to a desert monastery following unrest between "revivalist" Copts and "fundamentalist" Muslims, and just prior to the assassination of President Sadat. The government has tried to act even-handedly, but as a minority the Copts are bound to find themselves increasingly under pressure if militant Islam gains significant ground in Egypt.

Coptic Evangelical Church. A Presbyterian church in Egypt and the largest single **Protestant** grouping in the Middle East.

Council of Churches for Britain and Ireland. The British Council of Churches which **Roman Catholics** felt unable to join has now been replaced by a new body, the Council of Churches for Britain and Ireland, which includes Catholics and **Protestants.** National bodies have been set up: Churches Together in England, Action of Churches Together in Scotland (ACTS), Churches Together in Wales (CYTUN).

Carried over into the new CCBI is Christian Aid, set up in 1944 to help refugees, and now a major provider and enabler of relief and development projects in disaster areas. Since 1957 a special week has been set aside to collect money from every house in Britain.

Craft. "The Craft" is a common designation for **Witchcraft.**

Crossroads Movement. This movement is also known as the **Church of Christ** movement. The Crossroads Church of Christ was begun in Florida by Kip McKean, who went on to found the Boston Church of Christ, the current base of the movement, in 1979.

Cumina. *See* **Kumina.**

Custom. The term by which traditional **Melanesian religion** is known in Vanuatu (formerly New Hebrides).

D

Dadu Panthis. An Indian devotional movement founded by the poet–saint Dadu Dayal (1545–1604). The chief influences upon Dadu's thinking appear to have been Ramananda and Kabir, so that although born a Muslim he worked out a spiritual path which attracted Hindus and Muslims alike and proclaimed the true religion as being higher than either. His hymns speak both of longing for personal union with God and of absorption into an impersonal divine reality. These hymns were brought together by his followers to form the *Bani,* the inspired speech of Dadu. This book is the chief focus of worship in the Dadu Panthi temples or *dadudwaras.* Most Dadu Panthis today live in or near Naraina, Rajasthan, the place of Dadu's death, which is a pilgrimage centre for his followers.

Dai Dao Tam Ky Pho Do. A synchretic Vietnamese sect, more widely known as **Cao Dai.**

Damdani Taksal. A militant **Sikh** religious school closely associated with the name of Sant Bhindranwale, a charismatic Sikh leader killed in the army assault on the Golden Temple in June 1984. From time to time aligned with the **All India Sikh Student Federation (AISSF),** the Damdani Taksal has been bitterly opposed to more moderate Sikh religious organizations, particularly the **Shiromani Gurdwara Prabandhak Committee (SGPC).** In 1986 a committee of senior Damdani members appointed Manjit Singh and Harminder Singh Sandhu, general secretary of the AISSF, to look after the "religious and political affairs of the Sikhs". Harminder Singh was assassinated, presumably in an internecine power struggle, in Amritsar, on Jan. 29, 1990.

Dancing Dervishes. A colloquial designation for members of the **Mawlawiya Sufi** order.

Dar al-Quran. A modern branch of the notable **Sufi** order, the **Shadhiliya,** which is active in Jordan. Some members are also politically active, including the prominent deputies Laith Shbailat and Yaqub Kush, who form part of the Islamic bloc in the Jordanian Parliament.

Darqawiya. A popular, traditional-style **Sufi** order, the Darqawiya was established in 19th century Morocco and named after Abu Hamid al-'Arabi al-Darqawi (1760–1823). Al-Darqawi was himself a **Shadhili** and laid no claims to establishing a new order. He preached against what he perceived as the excesses of local saint cults and against involvement in worldly affairs, although later in his life he supported revolts against the Moroccan sultan.

In imitation of their master, a number of Darqawis live the life of wandering mendicant dervishes, dressed in a patched frock and carrying a staff and large wooden rosary, while others are attached to Sufi centres. The order is widespread in Morocco and Algeria, and was introduced to the UK by a convert, Shaykh 'Abd al-Qadir al-Sufi, who established a Darqawi centre in a Norfolk village in 1976. Since then he has moved on to establish another community in Granada in Spain, but the Norfolk members remain a well-organized group.

Darul Arqam. The Darul Arqam is an important and controversial dakwah (Muslim renewal) organization in Malaysia. Established in 1968, it attracted numerous followers in the 1970s from among the young and educated, being in this respect a rival to ABIM (**Angkatan Belia Islam Malaysiam,** the Malaysian Islamic Youth Movement) in its quest for student support. More recently its activities have been centred in three rural villages in particular, where its followers practise an austere communal lifestyle. Its members dress in green or black—the men with turbans and a long green shirt, the women in black or green purdah dress. Instead of waiting for the creation of an Islamic state in Malaysia, Darul Arqam seeks to establish an alternative Islamic community on its own land. It aims to convert society by converting individuals to a truly Islamic lifestyle (and criticizes the Islamic fundamentalist political opposition group PAS—**Parti Islam Se-Malaysia**—for having failed to inculcate true spiritual strength in its members). It imposes strict segregation of the sexes, among both adults and young school-age children. Great emphasis is placed on correct practice, not just on religious ritual (as tends to be the case with one of the other dakwah groups, the **Jama'at Tabligh**) in all areas of life, familial, social, economic and political.

Its emphasis on separateness from the wider plural society of Malaysia, and its radical social vision, which includes a commitment to economic self-sufficiency, set it apart from other dakwah organizations in Malaysia.

Besides its three communes, Darul Arqam runs various schools, kindergartens, student groups, agricultural projects and halal food factories. In its social form as well as its practice and teachings, Darul Arqam is effectively a New Religious Movement in an Islamic context, similar to commune based NRMs in the West such as **Hari Krishna**.

Its radical critique of the partnership of UMNO (United Malay National Organization) with non-Muslims in the ruling coalition governments since independence in 1957, as of wider social and political arrangements, has earned it the disapprobation of government leaders and of the state *ulama*.

Both ABIM and PAS have also been targets of sharp criticism by Darul Arqam, as have Islamic movements abroad, including the **Jama'at-i Islami** and the **Muslim Brotherhood**.

In recent years the leadership has been involved in a series of theological controversies, and has attracted much unfavourable publicity in the government-controlled media. Its appeal has consequently been considerably weakened. In 1991 the federal government declared Darul Arqam a proscribed organization.

Dashanamis. Literally, "the 10 names". The Dashanamis are constituted by 10 orders of Hindu renunciants (*samnyasins*) founded, according to legend, by the great Indian philosopher Shankara (c. 788–820). These orders are, more-or-less, caste specific with four of the 10 being assigned exclusively to brahmins. The philosophical outlook of the movement is non-dualist absolutism (*advaita vedanta*) and the majority of sub-groups demonstrate a strongly **Shaivite** orientation. Dashanami ascetics, on full initiation by a guru, sever links with their family and reside within a monastery (*math*) usually situated in an urban environment and often associated with the temple dedicated to an important deity. Bhubaneswar, in the east Indian state of Orissa, possesses many such *maths,* the earliest of which date back to, perhaps, the 10th century, though many are quite modern.

Maths are fully autonomous institutions usually presided over by a head ascetic or pontiff who is regarded as the ultimate arbitrator in theological disputes. He may be aided in the day-to-day running of the community by a management committee and on his death headship tends to pass in a hereditary line running through the nephew. Some *maths* contain schools and/or dispensaries for traditional medicaments. Dashanamis are physically distinguished by an ochre loincloth, a necklace of 54 *rudraksa* beads, a single-pronged staff and three horizontal white forehead markings.

Daudis. The Daudis are a branch of the **Musta'li** sect of **Isma'ili Shi'ism** within Islam. Their main centre is in Gujarat, and most Daudis are Indian, although a few are to be found in the Yemen. In India the Daudis are also known as **Bohoras** (Bohras), although strictly speaking the identification is inaccurate (since a minority of Bohoras are not Daudis, and a minority of Daudis are not Bohoras).

The Daudis emerged as a branch of the Musta'lis in contradistinction to the other branch, the **Sulaymanis,** when a split occurred over the leadership. The religious leader of the Musta'lis was known as the Da'i Mutlaq, and in 1591 two rivals for this position emerged: Daud ibn Qutb Shah, and Sulayman ibn Hasan. Most Indian Musta'lis supported the former, hence coming to be known as Daudis. (Most Yemeni Musta'lis, by contrast, supported the latter, hence coming to be known as Sulaymanis.)

The Daudis have traditionally shown great reverence for their leaders, and tombs of the Da'is are often visited in the manner of **Sufi** shrine cults. The Da'i is also known in India as the Mulla-ji, and is resident in Bombay. In the 20th century his authority has to some extent weakened, being strongly supported by conservatives, but challenged on certain issues of policy (e.g. education, and control of communal funds) by more modernist followers.

Outside Gujarat, the Daudis are to be found in most of the large towns and cities of the sub-continent, and in Burma (Myanmar) and East Africa, where, as Bohoras, they have established a strong reputation as successful businessmen and traders.

A few small sub-sects of the Daudis exist, having emerged typically over leadership issues rather than issues of Isma'ili doctrine. Thus the 'Alia Bohoras (or 'Aliyas) date from 1621 and have a separate line of Da'is resident in Baroda; and a vegetarian group, the Nagoshias (or Nagushis—"not meat eaters"), split from the 'Alia Bohoras in 1789. Meanwhile the Hibtias (Hibatis, Hiptiyas) had seceded in 1761 — they

were in fact persecuted by the Daudis, and very few remain (in Ujjain). The Mahdibaghwalas (Mahdibagh-wallas) seceded in 1897, and for a while flourished as a somewhat isolated community in Nagpur. However, none of these groups is numerically significant.

Da'wa Party. The Da'wa Party (Hizb al-Da'wa al-Islamiya, or Islamic Call Party—not to be confused with Libya's **Islamic Call Society**), is one of the most important of the **Shi'ite** Islamist groups in Iraq. It apparently began in Najaf in the late 1950s as a renewal movement inspired by the important Shi'ite writer and religious authority, Ayatollah Muhammad Baqir al-Sadr (1933–1980), and in response to the growing threat of atheistic Communism in the period 1958–1963 under the republican rule of 'Abd al-Karim Qasim. By the late 1970s, however, it had become much more political, and a target of repression by Saddam Hussein's Ba'th government, in power from 1968 onwards.

Baqir al-Sadr, who had developed a theory of an ideal Islamic state under "the rule of the jurist" rather similar to that of Ayatollah Khomeini (himself in exile in Najaf between 1964 and 1968), was executed by the Ba'thist régime in 1980. So too was his sister, Bint Huda. By this time the Da'wa had begun to attack police posts and Ba'th party offices. Since then it has also been engaged in sabotage actions elsewhere in the Gulf, for example in Kuwait and Bahrain. In the 1980s it had some involvement with international terrorism, but this has ceased.

Al-Da'wa is a strong supporter of Khomeini's Iran, where it has a large number of members, mostly Iraqi refugees, and where it has established a multitude of cultural and social organizations. It also has an organized unit in the Iranian army.

There are some branches in Britain, and they publish several magazines supportive of their cause. Further branches exist in Syria, Lebanon and Afghanistan.

Since the severe repression at the time of al-Sadr's execution, the leadership has become less clerical and more lay. The Da'wa now opposes the theory of the rule of the jurist (*wilayat al-faqih*), differing importantly on this from SAIRI (the **Supreme Assembly for the Islamic Revolution in Iraq**).

Al-Da'wa was fiercely critical of Iraq's invasion of Kuwait, and dismayed by the considerable popularity enjoyed by Saddam Hussein in the **Sunni** world in his subsequent confrontation with the West. As longstanding critics of American imperialism, they could hardly condone the presence of American soldiers on Muslim soil; yet they were apparently not opposed to limited military intervention by Muslim troops (although fearful of the possible military destruction of Iraq). They were actively involved in the post-war Shi'ite uprising in the south, but with what degree of influence is not clear.

De Jiao. De Jiao (Tak Kaau in Cantonese) means "Religion of Virtue" and originated in the Chaozhou (Teochiu) area of South China in about 1939. It is most firmly established in Singapore and Malaysia, where there are more than 60 "churches", but is also found in Hong Kong and among other Chinese communities. Adherents believe that there is truth in all the major world religions, and they worship before an altar on which are figures of Laotse (**Taoism**), Kuan Yin (Buddhism), Confucius, the Virgin Mary or Jesus Christ, and Muhammad. They recite from scriptures which are made up of extracts from the Taoist *Tao Te Ching*, Buddhist sutras, the **Confucian** *Analects*, the Bible and the Quran, and their leaders act as spirit mediums to give advice and healing, usually employing the technique of writing in sand with a stick to convey the spiritual message. Many of the groups look after the social welfare of their members through burial clubs, youth clubs, and medical clinics.

Deliverance Church. One of the largest independent African **Pentecostal** churches in Kenya (and, to a lesser extent, Uganda). It has links with the Morris Cerrullo Ministries based in California, and is working to establish a wider international base.

Deobandis. The Deoband movement emerged from one of several attempts by the Muslims of South Asia in the 19th century to find a way of being Muslim under colonial rule. Education was the Deobandi answer to being good (**Sunni**) Muslims without political power. The focus of the movement was a *madrasah* (Islamic secondary school) founded at Deoband, a small country town some 90 miles north-east of Delhi. The *madrasah* has subsequently grown to the extent that it is now regarded by many as the most important traditional university in the Islamic world after al-Azhar in Cairo. The movement itself has been spread in large part by the foundation of *madrasahs* associated with Deoband. By 1900 it acknowledged 40 attached schools; by its centenary in 1967, 8,934.

Deoband offered a way of being Muslim with as limited a relationship as possible with the state. In terms of beliefs this meant following the Islamic holy law as it had been handed down from the Middle Ages, tolerating only those expressions of **Sufism** that admitted no hint of intercession, and avoiding forms of behaviour which might suggest **Shi'ite,** Hindu or Western influences. It was a scriptual religion. Knowledge of God's word was central to knowing how to behave as a Muslim. As the state was controlled by a non-Muslim power, Muslims had to get their knowledge for themselves and ensure that they followed its meaning, the promptings of individual human conscience being the main sanction. Appropriately this has come to be termed a "protestant" form of Islam, which in its association, for instance, with literacy, the printing press and personal responsibility, bears comparison with Protestantism in

Christian Europe. In the Islamic world it is to be compared with the **Muhammadiyah** of Indonesia and the **Salafiya** of North Africa.

In terms of organization Deoband's concern to sustain Islamic society outside the framework of the colonial state meant total dependence on public subscription, bureaucratic provision of guidance in Islamic law, a programme for the translation of Arabic and Persian Islamic texts into the vernaculars, and most vigorous use of the printing press. A typical Deobandi book is Maulana Ashraf 'Ali Thanvi's still popular *Bihishti Zevar*, which was first published in the 1890s and offers complete guidance to women on how to behave as Muslims. (For a translation and commentary see B. D. Metcalf, (1990) *Perfecting Women* (Berkeley: University of California Press.)

Deoband's Islamic stance has, by and large, been reflected in its politics to the present. Having created systems to operate outside the state, their idea of a properly ordered society was ultimately one ruled by scholars like themselves. Consistently with this they did not as a group support the movement for Pakistan, since they envisaged that it would be an Islamic state in name only, ruled by secular Muslims. They preferred a future in a secular independent India where, somewhat optimistically, they hoped some form of jurisprudential apartheid would be achieved between secular Hindu India and themselves.

Since 1919 their main voice in Indian affairs has been the **Jami'at ul-Ulama-i Hind,** which after Partition developed a Pakistani wing, the Jam'iat ul-Ulama-i Islam. Deobandis have spread with the South Asian diaspora of the 20th century. They remain notable for their concern to maintain a traditional Islamic education, and for their bitter disputes with the **Barelvis** over a range of issues but, most particularly, belief in intercession at saints' shrines. They are sometimes referred to by their Barelvi critics as **Wahhabis**: it is not intended as a compliment.

Dhahabiya. One of the few Iranian **Shi'ite Sufi** orders, Dhahabiya began life as a branch of the Kubrawiya in the 15th century. Revived in the mid-19th century by Hadrat-i Raz, it now exists in two divisions, both of which have their headquarters in the southern Iranian city of Shiraz.

Dhammadana Association. A modern Thai **Theravada** Buddhist grouping founded to foster the dharmic socialism associated with the radical thinker Buddhadasa Bhikkhu. Based at Wat Suanmokkhabalaram, in the south of the country, the association has published Buddhadasa's writings, which attack popular superstitions and rites, since 1951. The group mainly appeals to an urban *intelligentsia*.

Dhammarakkhitavamsa. A prominent **Theravada** Buddhist monastic grouping within the Sri Lankan **Amarapura Nikaya**.

Dhammayut. An alternative rendering of the Thai **Theravada** monastic fraternity, the **Thammayutika Nikaya**.

Dharmadasis. One of only two extant groups which make up the original 12 branches of the Indian **Kabir Panth**.

Dhu'l-Riyasatayn. A branch of the Iranian **Ni'matullahi Sufi** order.

Dhundiyas. An alternative name of the **Sthanakavasis**, a reformed sub-group within **Svetambara Jainism**.

Dianetics. This is the "science of mental health" taught by the **Church of Scientology**.

Digambara Jainas. "Sky-clad" **Jainas**—one of the two major sects of the Jainas, so-called because their monks go naked. They hold that the possession of clothing is tantamount to remaining a householder and therefore acts as a disqualification from the mendicant path to liberation. For this reason, they deny that **Svetambara** mendicants are monks at all. They also differ from the Svetambaras in their contention that souls cannot be liberated from female bodies. Digambaras reject the Svetambara canon as inauthentic, referring instead to other works, especially those ascribed to Kundakunda (2nd century BCE, or later).

Digambara mendicants are restricted to a single begged meal daily, which they receive in their upturned palms. Their *Sangha* presently contains perhaps as few as 65 full (naked) monks, 60 "junior" (clothed monks) and 50 nuns, although mendicant numbers have always been relatively small.

Traditionally, Digambara strength has been in south-west India—Maharashtra and Karnataka. The pilgrimage site of Sravana Belgola (in Karnataka) contains what has become probably the best known Jaina image, the monolithic figure of Bahubali. Its ritual "heat-anointing" every 15 years attracts tens of thousands of Jainas from all over India. Such sites are usually under the direction of a non-mendicant official, who may at various times combine the functions of caste guru, teacher and librarian. The status of this official is peculiar to the Digambaras, and especially to those of the **Bisapanthi** sub-sect. However, the **Terapanthis** (not to be confused with a Svetambara sub-sect of the same name) reject his authority. A further sub-sect, the **Taranapanthis,** are opposed to image worship. In this century the **Kanji Panth**, has attracted a large Digambara following through Kanji Swami's reinterpretation of Kundakunda's teachings.

Dini Dawat. Dini Dawat (Religious Mission) is an alternative name for the Indian—and now international—Muslim reform movement, the **Tablighi Jama'at.**

Dinka Religion. Dinka religion is discussed here in conjunction with Nuer religion as an example of **African traditional religions**: *see* **Nuer and Dinka Religion.**

Disciples of Christ (Restorationist). In 1809 Alexander Campbell arrived in America to join his father, a minister of the presbyterian Church of Scotland. Following the influence of his father he came to believe that existing churches had wandered away from the ideals laid down in the New Testament. In 20 years they had founded a denomination which became known as the "Disciples of Christ" based on the principles of Christian life and church government which they believed were found in the Bible. They campaigned for other churches to unite by "restoring" what they claimed was God's original intention for the church.

In 1905 a major split occurred in the movement, partly caused by questions on the interpretation of the Bible in the light of modern Bible criticism. The more conservative members called themselves the **"Church of Christ"** and are now the larger of the two bodies. Most of the membership is still in the USA (7,000,000) but there are strong churches in Britain, Australia and New Zealand. Both groups have a weekly Communion service, practise believer's baptism and regard the New Testament as the sole authority for church life, rejecting other ecclesiastical traditions.

Worldwide membership is over 8,000,000. The Disciples of Christ are members of the **World Council of Churches**, continuing the founders' aim of a united church.

Divana. These "possessed ones" have been described as a cross between a **Sufi** adept and a witch-doctor. They are at best "irregular" (*bi-shar'*) Sufis who lead a mendicant life in the Central Asian states of the former USSR, and comparable in many ways to the **Malang** of South Asia.

Divine Light Mission. The Divine Light Mission is a new religious movement of Indian origin and known in the West since the visit to England in 1971 of the "boy-guru" Maharaji. Since the early 1980s it has been known by a different name, **Elan Vital**.

Dolma. A sub-group within the **Sakyapa** school of **Tibetan Buddhism**.

Dominicans. The Dominican Order, conceived by St Dominic as theologically knowledgeable missionaries, received Papal recognition in 1216. The Dominicans or "Order of Preachers" were, alongside the **Franciscans**, the first Order of friars. Friars were expected to be more flexible than their landed, monkish forebears. The Dominicans' first task was to catechize the untutored populace of Europe's new cities and to recover those of the French *intelligentsia* who had succumbed to heresies of dualistic stripe.

The Dominican contribution to the Church has been broadly in the realm of ideas. Most still have university degrees. A few explain their faith in modern idiom. The Dutch Fr. Schillebeeckx draws on the experientialism originated by the Protestant theologian, F. D. Schleiermacher (1768–1834), taking it to have contemporary resonance. Matthew Fox propagates a peculiarly Californian fusion of the spirit of Christianity with that of nature. Most, such as the 500 Dominicans deployed in television and in publishing, win no notoriety for their blameless teaching and preaching works. Numbers have dropped steadily since 1958: there are now 7,000 Dominican friars, 4,500 Dominican nuns, and 40,000 sisters. Half live in Europe, a quarter in the Third World.

Dominicans prefer to live and to pray in community. Their priories contain at least six friars; smaller groups are called houses. The priory elects its own prior; the houses' superiors are chosen by the Provincial. The Provincial is selected by a Chapter of priors and house delegates. He has four years in office. The Master is elected by the provincials and other Dominican officials. He has nine years' tenure and cannot be re-elected. The last was Fr. Damian Byrne. The new Master elected in 1992, is Father Timothy Radcliffe, the first Englishman to hold the office in the Order's 777 years.

Donmeh. The Donmeh (Turkish, "apostates"), also known as **Sabbateans,** are the followers of the 17th century Jewish "messiah" Shabetai Tzevi. Born into an **Ashkenazi** family in Izmir (Smyrna) in 1626, Tzevi, after studying *Talmud* and **Kabbalah** and always something of an eccentric, was banished from the community for religious deviations. He travelled extensively and lived in Jerusalem and Cairo before being proclaimed the long-awaited messiah by one Nathan of Gaza. He renounced many of the commandments and advocated a series of antinomian practices (his doctrine of the "holy sinner"). Thus began a wave of messianic fervour that swept across Europe and the Middle East as large numbers of Jews prepared for the imminent "end-times". Tzevi's campaign came to an abrupt end in 1666 when he was captured, taken to Istanbul and given the option of death or conversion to Islam. The Jewish world was stunned by Tzevi's decision to accept the latter! A few hundred families followed him into Islam and became known as the Donmeh. Tzevi died in exile in Albania in 1676.

The Donmeh formally and outwardly followed Muslim traditions but maintained secret Jewish and Shabbatean practices, including an orgiastic spring equinox festival which included wife-swapping. Salonika, proclaimed a holy city by Tzevi, became the centre of Donmeh life. In the late 17th century the Donmeh split into two groups—the Izmirilis (following Tzevi) and the Yakubis (followers of Tzevi's brother-in-law, Jacob, heralded as a reincarnation of Tzevi). In the early

18th century a second schism occurred and a new "incarnation" of Tzevi, in the person of Baruhiah Russo, led a third faction known as the Karakash. None of the "sects" permitted intermarriage with Donmeh of other groups and the groups themselves were distinguished by status and occupation—the Izmirilis were merchants and intellectuals; the Yakubis, clerks and officials; and the Karakash, artisans and workers.

In 1913 there were some 16,000 Donmeh in Salonika (out of more than 60,000 Jews) and in 1924 the Donmeh, rejected by Salonika Jewry, were moved into Turkey. Donmeh were influential in the Young Turk movement and the 1909 government included three Donmeh ministers. By the end of World War II the Yakubis and Izmirilis had largely assimilated into Turkish society, leaving only the Karakash as an active Donmeh group. Presently there are approximately 3,000 Karakash, mainly in Istanbul where they have their own synagogue containing a statute of Baruhiah Russo brought with them from Salonika. Continuing outwardly as part of the broader Muslim community, the Karakash do not let outsiders into their homes and only reveal their secrets on wedding days to brides and grooms. They await the imminent return of their messiah.

Drigung Kagyudpa. Third largest of the surviving **Kagyudpa** schools of **Tibetan Buddhism,** founded by Jigten Sumgon of the Kyura clan (1143–1217), who was a disciple of Gampopa's illustrious student Phagmodrupa (1110–1170). Named after their mother monastery of Drigung Til in Central Tibet, the Drigungpas soon achieved vast wealth and spread throughout Tibet and Ladakh. Jigten Sumgon's special doctrine is called *Gong Chik*, "One Thought", and the Drigungpas are famous for their emphasis on prolonged solitary retreats and the practice of esoteric yoga, especially *Phowa*, the "Transference of Consciousness". Drigungpas are very closely interconnected with the **Nyingmapas,** and have a substantial **Terma** tradition. The many Drigung monasteries in Ladakh remained untouched by the Chinese destruction of Tibetan Buddhism, and the Drigungpas have also begun activities in the West.

Drigungpas. *See* **Drigung Kagyudpa.**

Drukpa Kagyudpa. "Dragon Kagyudpa". Second largest of the four surviving **Kagyudpa** schools of **Tibetan Buddhism,** the Drukpas are divided into three sub-groupings of "Middle", "Lower" and "Upper". Founded by a student of Gampopa's disciple Phagmodrupa called Ling Repa (1128–1189), and his disciple Tsangpa Gyare (1161–1211), the school received its name from a vision of nine roaring dragons which filled the sky during the consecration of one of their early monasteries. The Drukpas are renowned for their renunciation, simplicity and deep commitment to practice, and are one of the few Tibetan schools to still maintain the tradition of *Repas*, "cotton-clad yogins" who practice *Tummo* or "inner heat", thereby living in freezing caves above the Himalayan snow line with virtually no food or clothing. Despite their tendency to decentralization, the Drukpas became the state religion of Bhutan, where they survive in great strength. Noted for their skill in the arts, especially mystic songs, the Drukpas also produced a very great scholar in Pema Karpo (1527–1592), whose current reincarnation, the 12th Drukchen Rinpoche, is the Drukpa's major incarnate lama. With bases in Ladakh and Darjeeling, and fluent in English, H. H. Drukchen Rinpoche is now a popular teacher all over the world.

Druzes (Druses). A quasi-Muslim community of between 200,000 and 400,000, mainly found in Lebanon, Syria, Jordan, and Israel. The religion began as a branch of **Isma'ili Shi'ism,** originating in a belief in the divinity of the sixth Fatimid caliph, the despotic al-Hakim (d. 1021), a doctrine first preached in Syria by an Isma'ili missionary called al-Darazi (who gave his name to the sect). The Druze era begins in the year 1017, when an Iranian disciple, Hamza ibn 'Ali, proclaimed the faith of al-Hakim to be independent of both **Sunnism** and Isma'ilism.

The Druze still believe that al-Hakim (whom they regard as still alive) will return at the end of time as their Messiah. They do not observe either Sunni or Shi'ite beliefs or practices, but their particular doctrines have generally been kept secret, even from the majority of Druzes themselves. The essential belief is a strict monotheism centred in the divinity of al-Hakim. As in several forms of Shi'ism, there is a cyclic theory of seven prophets, and a belief in reincarnation common to several extremist sects. The central scriptural text is a collection of letters by different individuals, known as the *Rasail al-hikma*. The community is sharply divided between a religious élite known as *'uqqal* and the remainder (*juhhal*—the ignorant).

Dunkers. Based on the German word meaning to dip or duck (e.g. in water), this is a label for members of the **Brethren** (German Baptists).

Dutch Reformed Church. The Dutch Reformed Church is a branch of the **Presbyterian (Reformed)** tradition, and is highly influential in South African politics. Dutch immigrants to South Africa organized the church into a main white denomination (NGK) and three "mission" churches for African, Coloured and Indian members.

The NGK, to which the former president P. W. Botha belonged, held to a theological defence of apartheid until 1986. However in 1990 the newly-elected Moderator of the NGK, Pieter Potgieter publicly confessed his church's guilt in supporting the policy which he now believed to be wrong. However other minority white denominations, notably the NHK and the newly formed APK (1987) have not withdrawn support for apartheid. The present president of South Africa, F. W. de Klerk belongs to the Gereformeerde Kerk, a branch of NGK.

The Coloured church (NGS) has been the most liberal and prominent of the mission churches, under the leadership of Dr. Allan Boesak. In 1990 he resigned as Moderator of the church after admitting an extra-marital affair, although he is still active politically.

Dwara Nikaya. A small monastic fraternity (*gaing*) within the **Burmese Theravada** Buddhist *Sangha* presently containing some 3,000 ordained monks. Founded in the mid-19th century at Okpo monastery, Lower Burma, the order eschews superstition and ritual and is rationalist in orientation. The Nikaya places great emphasis on the intentionality of acts, hence its name, Dwara—which means source.

E

Eastern Orthodox Church. The popular label "Eastern Orthodox" is sometimes used to distinguish these churches from the **Oriental Orthodox churches**, but at other times the two are conflated. Here the label **Orthodox Church (Byzantine tradition)** is used.

East Syrian Church. This is an alternative name for the **Nestorian Church**.

ECKANKAR. The ECK is the Spirit, the divine essence of God within each person. The "secret science" of ECKANKAR enables people, through the practice of spiritual exercises, to allow their souls to travel to the higher spiritual realms and link with Spirit, thus freeing them from the necessity of future reincarnations on earth. The movement, founded in Las Vegas in 1965 by John Paul Twitchell, is estimated to have perhaps 50,000 members worldwide.

Edah Haredi. *See* **Orthodox Judaism.**

Eglise des Banzie. The Eglise des Banzie (Church of the Initiates), is an **African New Religious Movement** better known to many as the **Bwiti Cult.**

Elan Vital. Formerly known as the Divine Light Mission, this new religious movement was founded in the 1930s by Shri Hans Ji Maharaj (d 1966), but only became known in the West when the founder's youngest, 13-year-old son, the "boy-guru" Maharaji, came to England in 1971. The teaching is called "Knowledge", and this knowledge is achieved by training the senses to focus on inner rather than external experiences. Part-time members lead a normal lifestyle and can marry, but contribute 10 per cent of their income to the group. Ashram members are unmarried and donate their salaries.

The movement grew rapidly, until Maharaji fell out with his mother after marrying his American secretary. She took over in India, where his brother is now recognized as head of the movement, but he is still in control in the West. Elan Vital (as the movement began to be called in the early 1980s) then became less Indian, and adopted a lower profile. Numbers, once claimed as hundreds of thousands, are down to about 7,000 in Britain and 15,000 in the USA, but growing slowly.

Electronic Church. The term "Electronic Church" (EC) is a modernization of the term "Electric Church", invented by the early prophet of the EC, Ben Armstrong in the 1970s. Two criteria can be used for a definition: (a) The use of modern technology for the communication of programmes with a religious content; and (b) the funding of these programmes by money generated by the programmes themselves, which means they generate enough income to cover their own production costs, directly or indirectly. (eg. by fund-raising appeals, incentives by interested parties, advertising etc.) Whilst (a) describes religious broadcasting in its widest sense, (b) draws a line between religious broadcasting *per se* and the EC. The history of the EC is very closely connected with the history of religious broadcasting in the USA. It began in 1921 with the broadcasting of evening prayer from Calvary Episcopal Church, Pittsburg and the first Christian-owned radio station KFUO (Keep Forward, Upward, Onward) in 1924 was only a logical step forward. The 1920s and 30s were marked by stringent new licensing standards introduced in

1927 by the Federal Communications Commission (F.C.C.). Of the approximately 60 stations which were licensed and operated by religious groups in 1927, nearly 50 per cent went out of business. Those years also brought the ecumenical age conflict between the so-called "liberals" and **fundamentalist** groups which organized themselves in 1944 into the National Religious Broadcasters (NRB). Both national networks, CBN and NBC, sold airtime to every religious broadcaster who was able to pay the fees. Scandals about controversial religious and political statements persuaded the national networks in the 1930s to stop the sale of airtime and offer free network time to three mainstream partners only. The 1940s and 50s saw a parallel development of religious network broadcasting on a national level and the increase of bought time by the EC on a local level until 1960 when the FCC released a new deregulation statement with the result that a few stations and networks could now afford the luxury of giving free airtime. Mainstream religious programmes were pushed aside. Aggressive and now legal methods of fundraising made the financing of EC programmes possible.

In the 1960s, 70s and 80s full use was made of the deregulations and the new technological possibilities. Whereas in 1959, 53 per cent of religious broadcasting was on "bought time", by 1977 this had risen to 92 per cent. The EC became an ambitious and powerful religious and political force. At the end of the 1980s the EC fell into crisis. The pillars of the EC began to crumble as financial, political and theological difficulties occurred. The EC always claimed to be a popular mass movement, but research showed that the audience of the EC was relatively small (with a maximum 5,000,000–20,000,000 viewers per week).

The same was the case in regard to EC affiliated political pressure groups like the "Moral Majority", which proved to be neither moral nor a majority, and polls showed that the activities of the EC had little, none or even a negative effect for political candidates supported by the EC. By the end of the 1980s the EC had overreached itself, the myth of the large and powerful EC was destroyed. A number of scandals resulted in a "cleaning up", which helped the EC to adapt to a new situation. New markets have to be cultivated, especially in the rich, industrialized areas of the world (for example the European Broadcasting Network (EBN) based in Oslo, Norway). The present changes in Eastern Europe mean that soon the EC can operate here freely. The keyword is mission, the target is to reach the whole world by the year 2000.

Elim Fellowship. An association of classical **Pentecostalist** congregations and ministers, which grew out of revivals in Northern Ireland (1911–20) and subsequently in England and Wales. Their earliest full title was Elim Foursquare Gospel Alliance.

Elim Pentecostalists. *See* Pentecostalists.

English Sangha Trust. A soon-to-be-renamed charity. It supports British-based monks of the **Theravada** tradition and has been influential in the establishment of both the **Amaravati Buddhist Centres** and the **Friends of the Western Buddhist Order** (FWBO).

Ennahda. This is a name sometimes used for the Tunisian Islamist organization described here under the heading **Hizb al-Nahda**.

Episcopalians. Some settlers in the American colonies took their **Anglican** beliefs and traditions with them and accepted the ecclesiastical oversight of the Bishop of London. After the War of Independence, in 1789 the name "Protestant Episcopal

Church in the USA" was adopted. Samuel Seabury was elected bishop by the clergy of Connecticut and consecrated by Scottish Anglican bishops. In 1967 "The Episcopal Church" was accepted as an alternative name. It claims 2,750,000 members, which include President George Bush. It belongs to the Anglican Communion. One of their most controversial leaders is Bishop Spong of Newark.

est. Erhard Seminar Training is one of the movements which have been called **"self religions",** and which may also be seen as part of the **Human Potential Movement.** Thousands of Americans and Europeans have been attracted to it, with many claiming that its notorious method of enhancing personality by encouraging participants to scream and shout abuse at each other has proved surprisingly effective.

Ethiopian Church. Ethiopia became Christian in the 4th century, falling within the jurisdiction of the original Church of Alexandria. Since the monophysite controversy of the 5th century, the Ethiopian Church has followed the theological and ecclesiastical traditions of the Coptic Church. Until the mid-20th century its primate and senior bishops were Copts rather than native Ethiopians. In 1959 it became completely independent of Coptic jurisdiction, and now constitutes a separate body among the Oriental Orthodox Churches. It numbers around 8,000,000, nearly half the country's population.

The Ethiopic liturgy is a version of the Coptic liturgy translated into the originally vernacular but now defunct Ge'ez language. A distinctive feature of Ethiopian worship is the use of percussion instruments and dance. The Ethiopians have over the centuries been variously subject to native African, Islamic and especially Jewish influences. From Judaism they have adopted circumcision,

a Saturday Sabbath, and certain dietary observances. The Patriarch-Catholicos, or *abuna,* reside at Addis Ababa. Since the 19th century there has also been a Roman Catholic Uniate Church in Ethiopia, also using the Ethiopic rite.

Ethiopian Evangelical Church Mekane Yesus. With 500,000 members, this church which was constituted in 1959, was officially recognized by the Government as second to the Ethiopian **Orthodox** Church. Mekane Yesus means "the place of Jesus" and was the name given to the first congregation in Addis Ababa. Native evangelists, Swedish, German and American **Lutheran** missionaries before their expulsion in 1936, gathered congregations. Committed to both spiritual, physical and material human needs, the Church has set up over 1,400 literacy schools, over 30 clinics, as well as agricultural and vocational training centres. It is a member of the **World Council of Churches.**

Ethiopian Jews. *See* **Beta Israel.**

Etoism. Known officially as the Christian Fellowship Church, Etoism is an indigenous church in the Solomon Islands founded by one Silas Eto. It arose in 1959–61 as a product of a schism from the former **Methodist** church on the island of New Georgia. It has established a dozen or so primary schools, and attracts a membership of approximately 3 per cent of the population.

Evangelicals (Evangelikals). The terms "evangelicals" and "evangelicalism" were subject to many changes and reflect the convergence of a number of traditions. By 1700 they had become a synonym for **"Protestant"** or **"Lutheran".** In Britain the Wesleyan **Methodist** religious awakening around 1750 was described as the evangelical revival, slightly later revivalists inside the Anglican and Free Churches used the term. Evangelicals of all classes came together to support William Wilberforce's crusade against the slave trade, to found the modern missionary societies and to collaborate in the work of the British and Foreign Bible Society.

Today many Protestant Churches in Latin America call themselves evangelicals (*evangelicos*). Europeans and North Americans whose theology was founded in the historic Protestantism, early pietism and evangelical revival formed in 1846 in London the Evangelical Alliance to co-ordinate their various activities. Then American Calvinists divided and the revivalist party inherited the name "evangelical". "Conversion" as an internal religious experience took the place of social concern. About 1900 American Methodism had divided into three parties, each seeing itself as "evangelical". By the late 1910s the **Reformed** tradition was in upheaval. On the one side was the liberal tradition, on the other a revivalist confessional coalition under the names "conservatives", "evangelicals" and fundamentalists. The revivalist became more and more Reformed, the conservatives opened up to evangelicalism. Conservative Wesleyanism, especially the Church of the Nazarene (1904), joined the reformed evangelicals in the war against liberal secularization.

In the 1940s, a number of reformed evangelicals (J. Ockenga, H. Henry, J. Carnell) organized a "neo-evangelical movement" as a reaction against the narrowness and separatist tendency of fundamentalism and to open up evangelicalism with the purpose of giving it a wider base. They established the National Association of Evangelicals (1942), Fuller's Theological Seminary (1947) and the magazine *Christianity Today* (1956).

The final split between Evangelicals and fundamentalists came as Billy Graham accepted the help of liberal church leaders for his New York Crusade (1957). Prominent fundamentalists accused Graham and the neo-evangelicals of being "traitors from within". It was also clear that the neo-evangelicals intended to claim sole copyright for the title "evangelical". Some neo-evangelicals try to separate themselves from the traditions which are more directly rooted in 19th century evangelicalism by describing them as "Evangelikals" and themselves as "evangelicals". So another clear split is developing as was the case with the fundamentalists. The evangelicals are today organized worldwide in the World Evangelical Fellowship and the Lausanne Committee for World Evangelization.

Exclusive Brethren. The Exclusive Brethren came into being as a result of a split in the Brethren movement in 1849 (*see* **Open Brethren**). They were originally the followers of J. N. Darby (Darbyites), a former lawyer and Church of Ireland minister who was associated with the start of the Brethren. Darby rejected everything he regarded as evil, and was involved in many conflicts over doctrine and behaviour.

Exclusive Brethren try to avoid the influence of "the World", for example by not watching television, attending only Exclusive Brethren meetings, not drinking alcohol etc. They do not share Communion with other Christians. Leaders are chosen from within the Church and some may be supported in full-time ministry. The movement has continued to fragment over doctrinal differences and at times extreme members have attracted hostile media attention (James Taylor in America). Worldwide membership is over 150,000, mostly in Britain but also in America and Australasia.

F

Fada'iyan-i Islam. The Fada'iyan Islam (Devotees of Islam) is an Iranian organization founded in Tehran in 1945 by a **Shi'ite** cleric (and putative descendant of the Prophet Muhammad), Sayyid Mujtaba Navvab Safavi. Under his leadership, and that of two devoted followers, the Imami brothers, the Fada'iyan swiftly developed into a ruthless terrorist group, prominent victims being an Iranian Minister and a Prime Minister, both assassinated in mosques—a second Prime Minister was injured but escaped with his life.

On the one hand the Fada'iyan opposed deviant interpretations of Islam (their first major act had been to murder the distinguished intellectual, Ahmad Kasravi, a prominent critic of traditional Shi'ism), what they regarded as Jewish terrorism in Palestine, and Western control of Iranian economic assets; on the other hand they advocated Quranic punishments and holy war: all themes which continue to resonate in post-1979 revolutionary Iran.

By 1956 the leaders and assassins had been caught and executed, though former Fada'iyan members were involved in the assassination of yet another Prime Minister in 1965, this time as members of a new organization, the Hizb-i Millal-i Islami (Islamic Nations Party). It is possible, however, that the Fada'iyan may have continued underground after 1956. Certainly Ayatollah Khalkhali, the notorious "hanging judge" of Khomeini's Iran, claimed to have been a member ever since his days as a religious student. He publicized their cause by encouraging members, in 1980, to demolish a marble mausoleum built in honour of the late Shah's father, Reza Shah.

Since then, however, the Fada'iyan appear to have been eclipsed—although they apparently still exist—by other organizations, ranging from the local Revolutionary Committee, or Komiteh, to mass movements like the Pasdaran, the **Islamic Revolutionary Guards.** They should not be confused with the **Fidayin-i Khalq,** active at the time of the 1979 revolution.

Faith Movement. Faith teaching in **Protestant charismatic** Christianity is frequently called the "Gospel of Prosperity". **Pentecostal** healing revivalism is combined with a form of positive thinking. Financial prosperity and physical well-being are seen as inevitable consequences of true spiritual re-birth. Prosperity of all kinds is believed to be the right of Christian believers. Poverty is the result of personal sin and inadequate faith. Biblical support for these views is found by proponents in Deuteronomy 28–30 and Mark 4.

The best-known exponent of the prosperity gospel is Kenneth E. Hagin, of Rhema Bible Church, Tulsa, Oklahoma, USA. Hagin came to these views in 1950, but seems to have drawn upon ideas put forward by E. W. Kenyon in Boston in the 1890s. As expounded by Hagin these ideas have found a wide resonance, not only in America, but in Europe through movements like **The Word of Life,** Asia, especially South Korea, where Paul Yonggi Cho's Full Gospel Church in Seoul with its 500,000 members is said to be the biggest church in the world, and sub-Saharan Africa. Rhema Bible Churches are flourishing in South Africa. The "Fire Congress", convened by Reinhard Bonnke in Harare, Zimbabwe, in 1986, with delegates from 41 African states, gave a prime slot to a seminar on "Evangelism and Prosperity", led by American TV evangelist, Kenneth Copeland.

Faith Movement (of Maulana Ilyas). The Faith Movement (Tahrik-i Iman) is an alternative name for the Indian—and now international—Muslim reform movement, the **Tablighi Jama'at,** founded by Maulana Muhammad Ilyas.

Falashas. *See* **Beta Israel.**

Family of Love. The movement was founded in California in 1968 by David Brandt Berg, later known as Moses David or "Mo". It was first called Children of God, but since the late 1970s it has been known as the Family of Love. It is a millennarian movement which emerged out of the **Jesus People** movement of the late 1970s in America with a more radical style and message. A number of communes were established there before the headquarters moved to London in 1971. By the mid-1970s the movement had spread to 60 different countries.

The Children of God/Family of Love claims to be a truly Christian movement which is based on the Bible and the "Mo Letters", written by the founder as a modern equivalent to St. Paul's epistles. Their often pornographic content provoked outrage and opposition, as does the practice of "flirty fishing": female members are exhorted to prostitute themselves (become "hookers for Jesus") in order to win new members.

Berg teaches that mankind is living its Last Days and that the signs of the Second Coming are close: capitalism and communism are on the verge of being destroyed by God and will be replaced by "godly socialism".

The structure of the movement is pyramidical, with Berg at the top, and counsellors, bishops, shepherds and under-shepherds beneath. The grassroots members "forsake all" their possessions to the movement, to which they devote themselves full-time. Mo's word holds the final authority over the teachings which are revealed to him from God. A distinction is made between "acts done in the spirit" and "acts done in the flesh", the latter

belong to the "deluded" outside world and support "the system". Being a member and acting "in the spirit", i.e. in faith and obedience to Berg, all one's actions become sanctified and free from "worldly" laws, which explains the virtual absence of restrictions on sexual behaviour, both for adults and children alike. In the late 1970s, the movement changed from a large-scale community to widely scattered, mobile family units and small groups. These are encouraged to support themselves through jobs, hold bible study meetings and get involved in existing churches. The number of members worldwide has been estimated as up to 10,000. However, this may be a considerable overestimate.

Federation of Buddhists of Thailand (FBT). Founded in the mid-1970s by monks of the **Mahanikaya,** the FBT has agitated for a less autocratic system of *Sangha* government. It is strongly opposed to the influence of the **Thammayut** in ecclesiastical affairs.

Federation of Students' Islamic Societies. This British student organization draws much inspiration from the **Muslim Brotherhood.**

Federation of Synagogues. *See* **Orthodox Judaism.**

Fethullahcilar. The Fethullahcilar is a new Islamic group in Turkey with certain affinities to already established groups like the **Süleymancis.** Founded by Fethullah Gülen, it appeals to the educated young. However, it remains to be seen whether it takes proper root.

Fidayin-i Khalq. The Fidayin-i Khalq, or People's Fighters, emerged in the Shah's Iran as a Marxist-inspired urban guerrilla organization. At first a supporter of the

Islamic revolution of 1979, which indeed its fighters helped to create, it soon began to clash with the Pasdaran, or **Islamic Revolutionary Guards,** and was forced to resume its previous clandestine existence, much as happened to its Islamic counterpart, the **Mujahidin-i Khalq.** With leaders in exile since the mid-1980s, its present condition remains unclear. It is not to be confused with the **Fada'iyan-i Islam.**

Fiver Shi'ites. The label Fiver Shi'ites (or simply Fivers) is sometimes given to the **Zaydis** as a convenient way of distinguishing them from both the **Isma'ilis** (or Sevener Shi'ites) and the **Twelver Shi'ites.** It derives from the fact that the Zaydi line of leadership deviates from those of the two other groups at the fifth Imam.

Focolare. The Focolare Movement is inspired by Jesus' prayer on the eve of his death: "Father, may they all be one" (John 17:21). It seeks to build this unity by dialogue: with people of no religious faith, with people of different religious traditions and between members of the various Christian Churches and communities.

It has a number of wide-ranging movements within it that are important means of its work for unity. These are: *New Humanity*, which focuses upon the world in all its social, political, cultural and economic dimensions; *Young People for a United World*, which strives to promote the idea of unity among young adults and older teenagers; and *Youth for Unity*, which seeks to do the same among children and younger teenagers; the *New Families*, which concentrate upon family life and all related issues as a means of fostering unity; the *Parish Movement*, which works in parishes for the renewal of the Church by encouraging the spirit of unity.

The members of the Movement are, in the first place, all equally members of the same body, with the same spirituality, though there are many different ways of expressing the same basic calling. At

the Movement's root are the *Focolarini*, who form the focolares, small, single-sex communities of married and celibate people who have the vocation to keep the presence of Jesus permanently among them (Matt. 18:20), though only the celibate members of the communities actually live together. At the very heart of the Movement are people with different kinds of vocation. There are the *Volunteers* who meet together regularly and feel called to renew the structures of society according to the Gospel, with the light of the presence of Jesus among them. There are the *Gen*, young people who meet with those of their own ages: the *Gen 2* (approximately 18–30 year-olds); the *Gen 3* (approximately 9–17 year-olds); and the *Gen 4* (approximately 3–8 year-olds). And there are also priests and religious individuals who belong in their own fashion, as appropriate for them, as well as bishops who are closely associated with the Movement.

Despite the number of structured ways of belonging to it, the Focolare Movement is also a large, loose-knit net of relationships, with many people being part of its general life without needing any formal association. Its membership spans Church boundaries, and includes Christians of all traditions, and there are, indeed, people of faiths older than Christianity who feel called to its life and structures, as well as non-believers. These people all meet together at the various events held by the Movement, in its formation centres and in the number of little towns of Gospel life that the Movement has established throughout the world.

Beginning in Trent, northern Italy in 1943, and based on the profound spiritual experience of Chiara Lubich, its founder, the Movement has been officially sanctioned by the **Roman Catholic** Church, first of all, as *Opera di Maria* (the Work of Mary) in 1962 by Pope John XXIII and then, most recently, in 1990 by Pope John Paul II, when the Movement's General Statutes were approved. It has received official approval by other Churches and, in 1981, the Archbishop of Canterbury appointed an Episcopal Guardian for **Anglican** members. The Focolare Movement exists in most countries of the world and in 1992 had about 2,000,000 members.

Foundation for the Preservation of the Mahayana. An organization founded in the 1980s by Lama Zopa, an exiled **Tibetan Buddhist** monk. In the **Gelugpa** tradition, the foundation is closely associated with the **Manjusri Institutes.**

Franciscans. John Bernardone (1182–1226) was a spiritual "troubadour", dedicated to "Lady Poverty". He was known to his friends as "Francis", the "Frenchman", and to posterity as St. Francis of Assisi. He was called to live in great austerity and to preach the Christian gospel. He gathered a group of friends who lived by begging alms in order to share the lot of the very poor.

The *joculatores domines* ("jugglers of God") sought acceptance at Rome. Their way of life was informally condoned by Pope Innocent III in 1209. By 1217, they had spread from Italy to Europe; the groups were now divided into "provinces", over which St. Francis appointed ministers. The homeless and mendicant origins of the barefooted *fratres minores* led to the creation of one of the two new preaching orders of *Friars* of the 13th century.

In 1221, St. Francis was asked to write a more detailed *Rule* for his Order. When this was taken to be too arduous, he composed a third: this was formally ratified by Pope Honorius III in 1223. St. Francis regretted the social, human, or ecclesiastical compulsion to fix and to modify his rule. In popular **Roman Catholic** belief, St. Francis was the first "stigmatist", bearing on his body the marks of the crucifixion.

The story is told in St. Bonaventure's *Life of St. Francis:* Bonaventure's presence at the University of Paris in the late 13th century is a sign of the Franciscan Friars' response to the contemporary need to teach about Christianity in cities. There are now 25,000 Franciscan friars and priests, living in most countries of the world. They are prominent in Japan. The Franciscans still take the call to evangelization as their most serious duty.

An **Anglican** Society of St. Francis was founded for men in 1922, but was preceded by a Community of St. Francis, created in 1905 for women.

Freemasons. Freemasonry today has a large membership, nearly 2,000 lodges existing in the Greater London area alone. As one of the world's oldest fraternal societies of men concerned with spiritual values, its members learn its mysteries through a series of rituals whose symbolism is based around the tools and customs of the stonemason. The basic principles of Freemasonry are Brotherly Love, Relief (assisting the community) and Truth.

The Brotherhood has come in for considerable media attack in recent years on grounds of corruption and misuse of power. Masonic meetings have a total ban on discussion of politics and organized or official religion, and freemasonry expresses no opinions on such matters. The recent public attention, by arousing a self-scrutiny of its own ranks, has probably strengthened Masonry.

Free Russian Orthodox Church. This is the name of the branch of the emigré **Russian (Orthodox) Church Abroad** which now operates within Russia. Its first parish was established in June 1990, and the number is increasing rapidly although there is fierce opposition from the Moscow Patriarchate and many priests still operate from their flats. It has three bishops who are subject to the Synod of the Russian Church Abroad located in New York. The senior of the three, Archbishop Lazar of Tambov and Moshansk, was for many years a member of the underground

True Orthodox Church, and many other True Orthodox members are now joining FROC. Members of both organizations actively opposed the *coup* of August 1991, but they are in competition for churches and parishes, and FROC, in line with its parent organization, repudiates the validity of most True Orthodox priestly orders and sacraments.

Freie Bahai ("Free Bahais"). A small, anti-organizational group of **Bahais** centred in Germany, which claims the inauthenticity of the document appointing Shoghi Effendi as Guardian of the religion.

Friends. Quakers are known as Friends, and their organization is the **Society of Friends**.

Friends of the Western Buddhist Order. The Friends of the Western Buddhist Order (FWBO) was founded in 1967 by Maha Sthavira Sangharakshita (formerly Dennis Lingwood). Born in 1925, he was stationed in India during World War II. After the cessation of hostilities he remained in India and, in 1949, was ordained as a novice. The following year he took full ordination as a monk in the **Theravada** tradition. Whilst resident in India Sangharakshita (Protector of the Community), as he became known, studied both **Tibetan** and **Zen** traditions and worked extensively with ex-untouchable converts to Dr Ambedkar's **Neo-Buddhism.** On his return to London in 1964 the need for a kind of Buddhism that Westerners could practice in a Western context impressed itself upon him. The result was the founding of the FWBO and, in 1968, the **WBO (Western Buddhist Order).**

The organization of the FWBO allows for three levels of involvement. At the heart are the Order Members. These are male and female, some married, some single; the latter practise celibacy. Order Members are called *Dharmachari* (m.) or *Dharmacharini* (f.), which means, loosely,

"follower of the doctrine". They are the FWBO equivalent of monks and nuns. At ordination they accept the 10 precepts of the novice and apply them as extensively and compassionately as they can to all areas of their life. Such a régime, they argue, is better for committed Buddhists in the Western world than the traditional set of over 200 *Vinaya* rules that regulate the lives of fully ordained Buddhist monks.

The next level of involvement is that of the *mitra* (lit. friend). These are lay Buddhists who have made a formal commitment to the FWBO. Some, but by no means all, *mitras* go on to become Order Members. All have close contact with Order Members, two of whom become the *mitra's* "spiritual friends" and take a special interest in his or her welfare. At the third level are the "friends", sympathetic and supportive lay people who want to be involved without making the degree of commitment expected from a *mitra*.

Each local group is attached to a Centre, which will accommodate at least five order members. The Centre provides a focus for friends, *mitras* and Order Members. Most operate Right Livelihood businesses such as vegetarian restaurants, wholefood shops and building companies. All Centres donate a portion of their income to finance centrally organized activities and the Indian wing of the organization which, because of its predominantly ex-untouchable membership, is dependent on donations for its effective functioning. Each centre is, nevertheless, autonomous and self-financing.

From humble beginnings the FWBO has increased its membership and extended its activities into various parts of Europe and North America. It obviously meets a need for many Westerners who are interested in Buddhism. Although criticized by many of the more traditional Buddhist groups the FWBO has established itself as a prominent feature on the Buddhist scene. A crisis point will obviously come when the founder passes away but if the organization can survive this intact the likelihood of it having a viable future is high.

Front Islamique du Salut—FIS. The FIS (al-Jabha al-Islamiya li-Inqadh, or Islamic Salvation Front) was founded in 1989, the first Islamic political party to appear in Algeria, and by far the largest. Within a year it had achieved 54 per cent of the vote in municipal and provincial elections in June 1990, gaining control of two thirds of Algeria's Popular Assemblies (i.e. in 32 out of 48 of the provinces). Its further astonishing success in the first round of the national election in 1991 led to the suspension, in January 1992, of the second round of the election which was universally expected to pave the way for the formation of a fundamentalist Islamic government.

FIS's roots lie in the broad movement of Islamic renewal, **Ahl al-Da'wa,** that emerged in Algeria in the late 1970s and flourished after the death of President Boumedienne in 1978. This period also coincided with the success of the Islamic revolution in Iran, but in Algeria Islamist tendencies had been apparent already in the 1960s, their inspiration going back indeed to the **Salafiya.**

The FIS aims to re-establish the state and the society on the basis of Islamic law, the shari'a. The stricter lifestyle it advocates would include traditional restrictions on women, some of whom claim to have been ordered to vote for FIS by their husbands. Presenting itself as the necessary solution to Algeria's severe problems, which include large-scale youth unemployment, it has so far produced little in the way of practical policy. Appealing as it does to a wide variety of constituents, this may reflect a deep-seated difficulty, rather than being simply the consequence of its rapid success. Nevertheless, it is clearly extremely well organized, and capable of mobilizing very considerable numbers of people, using its own network of mosques as a popular base.

The Iraqi invasion of Kuwait in 1990 led to a crisis: the leadership, conscious of the need to secure continued financial support from the Saudis (and Kuwaitis), had little option but to support Saudi Arabia, while at the grassroots level there was massive popular support for Saddam Hussein.

Following the army intervention of 1992 to prevent certain FIS victory at the polls, the movement's leaders were detained, leaving the initiative to more militant elements within the movement. Sporadic acts of violence occurred, perpetrated in part, it is thought, by former mujahideen fighters in the war in Afghanistan, for which a number of Algerians volunteered. At the time of going to press, the future of the movement remains uncertain.

Full Gospel Business Men's Fellowship International. Founded in the USA in 1952 by an Armenian dairy farmer with **Pentecostal** beliefs, Demos Shakarian, its chapters of businessmen meet over a meal to hear and tell about God's blessings on their lives and businesses. Now represented in five continents, it claims to reach more than 1,000 million people a year. In sub-Saharan Africa, it is similar in some respects to **Christian Faith Action Ministries,** and has spread rapidly to 29 countries from an initial base in Nigeria. Shakarian's story is told in *The Happiest People on Earth* (1975).

Fundamentalism. The label "Fundamentalist" is often applied now to those who hold strict, traditional religious positions in a vehemently assertive and illiberal way. It is accepted with pride by those like the American, Dr. Bob Jones and the Rev. Ian Paisley of Northern Ireland. They both maintain the verbal inerrancy of the Bible, and support the positions adopted by the **World Congress of Christian Fundamentalists.** In recent years, Fundamentalism has also been applied by outside observers to Shi'ite Islam in Iran and elsewhere, though its appropriateness is contested by Islamic scholars. In India, the Vishwa Hindu Parishad emerged as a form of Hindu revivalism in reaction to Muslim resurgence.

Fusokyo. A Japanese mountain worship group, based on Mt. Fuji, and one of the traditional 13 constituent sects of **Kyoha Shinto.**

G

Ganapatyas. A popular Hindu devotional movement which regards Ganapati, or Ganesha—the elephant-headed god and one of the five traditional deities of **Smarta** worship, as the highest form of Brahman available to the senses. Widespread in western India, most particularly in Maharashtra, devotees are mainly found amongst the higher castes. Though the worship of Ganesh is found throughout the sub-continent, this specific form of devotion is based on eight sacred sites in and around the city of Pune. The origins of the Ganapatyas can be traced back to the 6–9th centuries CE, though the sect itself holds Moraya Gosavi (d. 1651) to be the founder. A noted Maharashtrian saint and devotee of Ganesha, Moravi experienced many visions of the god and is believed to have been buried alive, in a state of *samadhi,* at the Cincvad shrine on the outskirts of Pune. Several of Moravi's descendants have been influential in the movement and much devotional literature, in both Sanskrit and Marathi, has been produced since the 17th century. There are two main annual pilgrimages to the eight shrines and these can attract very large crowds. The most important of the two is the *Ganesha Caturthi* (August–September) which was given a fresh impetus in the early years of this century by the influential Maharashtrian nationalist and Ganapatya, B. G. Tilak (1856–1920). The festival has, from time to time, acted as a platform for militant Hindu nationalist agitation.

Gaudiya-sampradaya. The best-known form of Bengali devotionalism. The inspiration for this *sampradaya* springs from the life and personality of Sri Chaitanya (born Vishvambara Mishra, 1486–1533), though the Vaishnava movement in Bengal originated some centuries earlier. Caitanya grew up in a milieu in which the love of Krishna and

Radha was given poetic form by a number of important Bengal writers. The **Sahajiya** movement may also have influenced him. The *Bhagavata-purana* was adapted into Bengali just before Caitanya's lifetime, and the emotional type of *bhakti* which it describes and recommends in Krishna's devotees is richly exemplified in the stories of Caitanya's behaviour which are given in his biography, the *Caitanya-caritamrita*. Caitanya's followers did not, however, regard him merely as a great devotee of Krishna. For many of them he was Krishna himself—or greater still, Krishna and Radha in one body.

Although not a theologian himself, Caitanya chose six theologians among his followers to settle in Vrndavana, where Krishna had spent his childhood and youth among the cowherds, and to work out there a system of doctrine, based on the *Bhagavata-purana*. In this system the highest reality is identical with Krishna. *Bhakti* is the only way to enjoy this reality, and the devotee is called upon to imitate the *gopis,* the women and girls of the cowherd community who loved Krishna. The nine forms of *bhakti* which are listed in the *Bhagavata-purana* are systematized and combined with aesthetic theories about the value of emotional states.

The Caitanya movement has had a profound effect upon the religious life of Bengal, even though membership of the Gaudiya-sampradaya declined between the 17th and 19th centuries. In the late 19th century there was a revival under the leadership of Bhaktivinoda Thakura (1838–1914), who founded the **Gaudiya Vaisnava Mission.** His son and successor Bhaktisiddhanta Sarasvati (1874–1937) was the *guru* of A. C. Bhaktivedanta, who gave the Caitanya movement a world-wide scope through the organization **ISKCON** which he founded.

RELIGIOUS GROUPS AND MOVEMENTS

Gaudiya Vaishnava Mission. Founded in the late 19th century, this Bengali Hindu missionary society promotes devotion to Krishna. Its teachings derive from the **Gaudiyasampradaya** and it was instrumental in the formation of **ISKCON.**

Gelugpas. "The Virtuous Ones." A monastic order of **Tibetan Buddhists** known as "Yellow Hats" because of their distinctive ceremonial headgear. Its most prominent member is H. H. Dalai Lama though, strictly speaking, he is not the head of the order. The *Gelugpas* originated in 15th century Tibet as a reform movement placing great stress on strict monastic discipline and the elimination of certain magico–sexual practices that had begun to dominate the Buddhism of the region. The founder, Tsong-kha-pa (1357–1419), though not an independent thinker, was a skillful logician and was able to harmonize *Mahayanist* philosophical thought into a coherent system for the benefit of his followers. He also laid the foundations of a graduated intellectual and meditative training scheme, modelled on a curriculum established at the great monastic universities of northern India. Monks are expected to progress through a rigorous study of selected Sanskrit and Tibetan philosophical texts to the degree of *geshe*. Beyond this stage a candidate may opt for further spiritual training in the Buddhist tantras.

The first monastery, Ganden, was established by Tsong-kha-pa in Lhasa and the influence of the school gradually extended throughout the country, though the *Gelugpa* powerbase has always been in Central Tibet. In the 16th century, the third successor to Tsong-kha-pa was influential in converting the Mongols to the Buddhist faith and was awarded the title "Dalai" (Ocean) by Altan Khan. Since this time it has been customary to regard successive Dalai Lamas as serial incarnations of the celestial bodhisattva Avalokitesvara. The present Dalai Lama (1935–), who is 14th in the line, was forced to flee from Tibet following the Chinese invasion of 1959. Now settled in Dharmasala, N. India with a considerable number of fellow Tibetans both monastic and lay, he is the head of the Tibetan government in exile. His changed circumstances are such that he is the focus of the spiritual and nationalist aspirations of all Tibetans irrespective of precise religious affiliation. The second most prominent lama in the order, the Panchen Lama, was forced by the Chinese authorities to spend his adult life in Beijing. He died in 1989. In recent years the *Gelugpas* have begun an extensive printing project, the **Library of Tibetan Works and Archives** based in Dharmasala, aimed at preserving the literary culture of Tibetan Buddhism. The Gelugpas have also had good success in gaining converts, mainly through the tours of prominent teachers such as Lama Thubten Yeshe and Lama Zopa, and there are now a considerable number of Western *Gelugpa* monks, nuns and lay people located in centres throughout the world. In Tibet itself *Gelugpa* monks have been an influential focus of popular discontent with the Chinese occupation and have suffered accordingly.

Gerakan Pembaharuan. The Gerakan Pembaharuan, or Renewal Movement, is an Indonesian Muslim movement originated by Nurcholis Madjid which flourished in the 1970s. Described variously as liberal and modernist, it represents a major departure from mainstream Muslim thinking (as found in Indonesia in the **Nahdatul Ulama** and the **Muhammadiyah**, for example) by urging that the faith find expression through the light of individual consciences rather than through separate Muslim institutions (educational, social, political etc).

The rise of a diametrically opposed militant Islam in the 1980s has ensured that this Renewal Movement remains tiny, and in any case its appeal has tended to be confined to members of the younger educated élite.

157

Ger Hasidism (Gur). (See also **Orthodox Judaism.**) Following the destruction of the major centres of Jewish life in Eastern Europe during the Holocaust a number of Hasidic dynasties, including the Ger, were re-established in the land of Israel, with centres in Europe and North America. Thousands of Ger Hasidim and others pay visits to the Jerusalem court of the current Ger *Rebbe,* Rabbi Israel Alter, each year. He is one of the major figures in the Jewish world and his influence is widespread in both Israel and the *diaspora.*

Ger Hasidism is named after the small town near Warsaw, Poland, of that name (Hebrew, "Ger"; Yiddish, "Gur"; Polish, "Gora Kalwaria"), where their founding Rebbe, Rabbi Isaac Meir Alter (1799–1866), established his family dynasty (1859). A noted scholar, Isaac Meir was influenced by the Przysucha-Kotsk school of Hasidism and promoted *Torah* study among his followers. He, and his successors, were active in public affairs and evidenced a particular concern with the situation of the Polish Jewish masses. His grandson, Rabbi Judah Aryeh Leib (1864–94), introduced a philosophical element into his teachings, drawing on the writings of Rabbi Judah Loewe of Prague.

Ger Hasidism became the most powerful Jewish Orthodox movement in Poland and the Ger Rebbe the pre-eminent spokesman for Orthodoxy until the Holocaust. This was particularly evident under the leadership and organization of Rabbi Abraham Mordecai Alter (1866–1948), the great-grandson of the founder, who was recognized as the leading figure in European **Orthodox Judaism** and was one of the founders of **Agudat Israel.** He was especially active in the creation of youth movements and educational institutions. In 1940 he moved to Israel. The current Rebbe is his son.

The Ger were one of the few Orthodox groups who were supportive of the programme of the return of Jews to the land of Israel and the rebuilding of Jewish life there, they are still, along with the

Lubavich Hasidim the main groups within **Agudat Israel.**

Ger Hasidim are characterized by their traditional garb including the tall fur hat (spodik), their *Torah* study and strict observance of the commandments, and represent the continuity of Polish Hasidism in the contemporary Jewish world.

German Dhammaduta Society. The *German Society for the Proclamation of the Doctrine (Dhammaduta)* is the German wing of an international Buddhist missionary endeavour. Essentially concerned with the propagation of Buddhist teachings according to the **Theravada** school, its origins can be traced back to the Buddhist Mission for Germany which, in turn, was sponsored by the **Sri Lankan Dhammaduta Society** (founded in 1952) through their International Buddhist Service (founded in 1954). In 1957 the German Dhammaduta Society took over the Berlin "Buddhist House" built by Paul Dahlke in 1924. This now serves as a residence for Sri Lankan monks and a base for the Society's missionary activities in Germany.

German Society for the Proclamation of the Doctrine. *See* **German Dhammaduta Society.**

Getambe Group. A lay meditation society founded in 1980 by Ven. P. Sorada at the Getambe Buddhist temple near Peradeniya, Sri Lanka. The group promotes **Theravada** insight (*vipassana*) meditational practice amongst the laity, in part, to help overcome illness, anxiety and the like. It is one of many such groups in Sri Lanka today, though it is far less hostile to the *sangha* than some.

Greek Orthodox (Church). Institutionally there is no such entity as the "Greek Orthodox Church". The term has sometimes been used to describe the entire **Orthodox Church (Byzantine** tradition), but very misleadingly in view of the important role played by the Slavonic (and other) elements in this tradition. A misleading (though understandable) usage of the opposite kind identifies the term with the Orthodox Church of Greece, since a number of institutionally quite distinct Orthodox Churches can be described as "Greek Orthodox". These include the Church of Greece, the Church of Cyprus, the Ecumenical Patriarchate of Constantinople (the original Church of the Byzantine Empire), the Patriarchal Church of Alexandria, and (at least nominally) the Patriarchal Church of Jerusalem, together with the semi-independent Church of Sinai. The Ecumenical Patriarchate (based in Istanbul in Turkey) also has jurisdiction over four semi-independent Churches located within the territory of modern Greece but for historical reasons never incorporated into the Church of Greece: those of Patmos, Crete, the Dodecanese islands, and Mount Athos. What basically defines a Church as Greek are the common language of worship, and the associated culture and customs. To what particular Church a Greek-speaking Orthodox belongs is not always obvious. For example, Greeks and Greek Cypriots living in the United Kingdom come under the jurisdiction of the Ecumenical Patriarchate, not that of the Churches of their respective countries of origin.

Gunabadi. A branch of the Iranian **Ni'matullahi Sufi** order.

Gurdjieffian Groups. George Gurdjieff (c.1872–1949) attracted many leading members of the inter-war *intelligentsia* (for instance Katherine Mansfield) with his radical teachings, developed during his travels throughout Asia, and bearing many resemblances to **Sufism.** His theory was that most human beings are so mechanical and "asleep" that they do not develop souls, unless they receive a "shock" to wake them up. His method, known as the Fourth Way and also as "the Work", involved supreme tests of energy and endurance, but also meditations and sacred dances, which are still preserved in the Gurdjieff schools.

The main centre of his work in Britain is now the Gurdjieff Society, which currently has about 600 members. There are many other small groups, often at odds with each other, some of which have no direct link with Gurdjieff. There are about 1,000 Gurdjieffians in Britain. There are also groups practising the "System" of Ouspensky, Gurdjieff's most famous disciple, who founded his own movement.

Gurdjieff's therapeutic approach was one of the main influences on the **Human Potential Movement.** His unusual cosmology, including the doctrine of "reciprocal maintenance", was influential on the "green" movement. Along with **Krishnamurti** he is the most highly regarded of contemporary Eastern spiritual teachers, even in academic circles, and his books are still widely read.

Guru. "Guru" is the term used in most Indian religions for a spiritual teacher or preceptor and the relationship which is established between the guru and his or her *chela* (disciple) is one of the fundamental features of virtually all the sects of Hinduism. Generally it is held that some deity or other is the founder of any particular lineage of gurus, being, in fact, that lineage's *ādiguru*. Thus the living guru comes to be seen as the living embodiment of that founder-deity. As such, he or she is worthy of utter veneration, since it is only through the intercession of the deity, incarnated in the guru, that salvation is possible. This "divinity" passes from guru to guru in a supposedly unbroken chain. Very often the guru is seen as possessing the ability to enlighten the disciple through initiatory acts (*dīkṣā*). Such actions are often seen as actual transfers of mystical energy (*śakti*) which fundamentally changes the disciple's psycho-physical constitution in a way that is impossible through self-effort alone.

The centrality of the guru is mandated by a number of cultural factors found in Indian society. Serious truths have always been held to be too powerful for inclusion in books, and, therefore, have always been stored in the "divine" vessel of the guru. Thus even the most esoteric of mantras, for example, can only be activated through their being imparted to the *chela* by the guru. All practical initiation is impossible without the guru, as is the learning and application of those meditative techniques which form the heart of Hindu practical religion. Consequently the *chela* is more than willing to accede to the guru's every whim, since it is only through the guru that the *chela* may reach salvation. As a result, many gurus receive more homage than the cult's titular deity and the guru is actually worshipped, with money and flowers being laid at his "lotus feet" in much the same way as is a god.

Guru Panth. Literally, the path of the Guru. A term employed to denote the **Sikh** community as embodiment of Sikh ideals.

Gurzmar. In the Indian sub-continent, members of a particular **Sufi** order, the **Rifa'iya,** are referred to as Gurzmar because of their practice of striking their bodies with a sort of mace (*gurz*).

Gush Emunim (Block of the Faithful). (See also **Zionism**.) The major settlement group in Judea and Samaria (the "administered" or occupied territories) is the Gush Emunim, founded in 1974 (although its origins can be traced back to the Gahelet youth group in 1952). It is held to be "the major extra-parliamentary force within Israel", and its members, after supporting Likud in 1977, have since voted for a variety of parties. They represent a faction developing out of **Mafdal** and number only

about 2,000. No other group has raised the core issues of the meaning of the Jewish state and the relationship between **Zionism** and Judaism so forcefully.

Gush Emunim offers a theological "answer" to the tensions between traditional **Orthodox Judaism** and modern secular Zionism—"there is no Zionism without Judaism and no Judaism without Zionism". This "answer" is based on the teachings of the spiritual leader of the Merkaz Harav *Yeshivah,* Rabbi Abraham Isaac Kook, and his son and successor, Rabbi Tzvi Yehuda Kook. The major figures in the Gahelet youth group were students at the Yeshivah and it represents the link between this group and the Gush Emunim.

Rabbi A. I. Kook, the first **Ashkenazi** Chief Rabbi of Palestine, taught that the apparently secular activities of the Zionist pioneers were, when correctly understood, to be seen as possessing the "hidden spark" of the sacred. In explicating his doctrine of the "sacralization of the secular", he had recourse to a number of analogies, such as the building of the Holy of Holies in the Jerusalem Temple (the Jewish "state") where the holiness was preceded by the activities of "secular" workmen. His "theological" efforts failed to unite the different factions of pre-state Palestinian Jewry. His son, Tz. Y. Kook, understands the state to be of ultimate religious significance, and the in-gathering of the exiles and the re-establishment of Jewish sovereignty in the land to be signs of the impending redemption. The Gush Emunim share their teacher's views of the sanctity of the "whole" land of Israel.

The Gush Emunim are generally tolerant of secularists and understand the present state of Israel to be "the kingdom in the making", although they insist that God's law always takes precedence over the democratic process. They seek to unite the different elements of Jewish Israel by their practical activities, that is, the establishment of religious settlement-communities (legal and illegal) in the occupied territories ("divinely mandated

Israel"), and see themselves as the true heirs to the Labour-Zionist pioneers. Their settlement plans have been both supported and opposed by both major political parties.

In the 1992 general election the Labour alliance gained victory on a platform of advancing the peace process. This will almost certainly entail calling a halt to the building of new settlements in order to free up American loan guarantees needed to help settle Russian immigrants. The Labour manifesto also promised Palestinian autonomy within nine months. These developments will limit the options open to the Gush Emunim and may well see the decline of their broad appeal to the Israeli Jewish populace.

H

Habad (Chabad) Hasidism. *See* **Lubavich Hasidism.**

Haddawiya. The Haddawa are a **Sufi** order of wandering dervishes whose base is in Morocco. Founded by Sidi Haddi (d. 1805), a shadowy figure about whom little is known, they uphold an ideal of celibacy, and this is mostly adhered to although married members are not unknown. There is a tendency to homosexuality. Their lodge lacks dormitory facilities, and in their itinerant lifestyle they sleep wherever they happen to be.

They are noted for a particular devotion to cats, having taken over, it is thought, a pre-Islamic cat cult (the cat having been widely venerated in the ancient Near East). The ritual eating of cats is part of their practice, as is the use of cannabis to induce prophetic utterances. Like wandering fakirs in the Indian sub-continent and elsewhere, they employ a peculiar slang of their own. Increasingly they are to be found in the countryside rather than in the towns.

Hairy Ishans. A radical offshoot of the **Yasawiya Sufi** order located in Kirghizstan and Uzbekistan. As a brotherhood that has operated clandestinely, its strength is impossible to gauge, but it is thought to be found mainly among city-dwellers. Unlike other Yasawiya groups, its members practise a silent chant (*dhikr*). (**Ishanism** is an alternative name for Sufism in the former USSR.)

Halleluja Religion. This is a syncretic mix of Christianity and Amerindian religion found in Guyana among the Akawaio Indians, and among related Indian groups in Venezuela and Brazil. It has a geographical focus in a holy village and its church—this has been the central sanctuary since the death in 1911 of an Indian named Abel who was the alleged recipient of revelation. The movement is respected by the **Anglican** church, which has missionaries who work with it, and which recognizes its baptism.

Halveti-Cerrahis. The Halveti-Cerrahis are a Turkish **Sufi** order whose weekly meetings in Istanbul are often attended by visiting foreigners. There are branches in Germany and the USA, and the movement's leaders are learned and respected.

Hamadsha. The Hamadsha are a socially despised **Sufi** order in northern Morocco, allegedly founded by 'Ali ibn Hamdush (d. c1720). Trances are induced by particular tunes, each thought to be connected with a particular member of the *jinn*, or spirits, and some adherents slash their heads. During dances to musical accompaniment in which both men and women participate and go into trance, an effeminately dressed man features prominently, slashing his head until it bleeds, and the blood then being licked by women as a source of blessing. Scholars suggest that there is strong influence here from pre-Islamic practices.

Hamalliya. The Hamalliya is a **Sufi** order which is an offshoot of the **Tijaniya,** and sometimes described as reformed Tijaniya. It arose in Mauritania early in the 20th century, where it was propagated by a Tijani mystic known as Hamallah (1883–1943). Not highly educated, he stressed the importance of the Sufi life rather than scholarship, and claimed to be reviving the authentic doctrine of al-Tijani. In 1925 he was deported by the French to southern

Mauritania on account of his opposition to their colonialist rule, and was subsequently deported to the Ivory Coast. Hamallis began at this time to deviate from the main Tijaniya and other Muslims, adding to the profession of faith the words "and Hamallah is our *shaykh*", shortening their prayers, and facing the West in prayer.

After the death of the founder, the Hamalliya increased in numbers and adopted further unorthodox practices, such as shouting prayers, and confessing sins in public. A section of the movement stressed a simple lifestyle, giving up all luxuries and handing over their earnings to their group head for distribution among them. Often in conflict with the colonial administration, the Hamalliya spread rapidly among the underprivileged and less educated throughout the French-controlled territories of West Africa, reaching East to Niger by the late 1930s. Since World War II it has also spread successfully in Nigeria, and has some followers in Algeria and Morocco.

Hamas (Algeria). Hamas is the acronym for Al-Haraqa li-Mujtama' Islami, the Movement for an Islamic Society, founded in Algeria in 1990. In contrast to **FIS,** it advocates Islamic renewal within society prior to, and as a necessary condition of success in, exercising government power to reform the state along Islamic lines. Nevertheless, electoral support of FIS is not ruled out.

The choice of name is an allusion to the **Hamas** active in Gaza and the West Bank, but there are no known organizational links. Hamas in Algeria represents the development into a political party of an earlier non-political association known as Guidance and Reform (Al-Irshad wa'l-Islah). The leader in both cases is Shaikh Mahfoud Nahnah.

Hamas (West Bank and Gaza*)*. Hamas is a Palestinian Islamic organization founded in August 1988 by Shaikh Ahmad Yasin, a local leader of the **Muslim Brotherhood** in order to participate in the *intifada* (uprising) to confront the Israeli occupation authorities in the West Bank and Gaza. In May 1989 Yasin was arrested and on Oct. 16, 1991 an Israeli military court in Gaza sentenced him to life imprisonment plus 15 years for ordering the killings of Israeli soldiers and Palestinians collaborating with the Israelis. Hamas is opposed to any peace negotiations with Israel and does not accept any plan to partition historic Palestine into Jewish and Arab states. It has declared its readiness to continue and escalate the *intifada*. In January 1992 its supporters were clashing with Palestinians in favour of the peace process and Israel was seeking to deport some leading activists.

Hamidiya Shadhiliya. An Egyptian branch of a notable **Sufi** order, the **Shadhiliya.**

Hanafis. The Hanafi school or rite (*madhhab*) is the oldest and largest of the four **Sunni** schools of Islamic law (the other three being the **Maliki, Shafi'i** and **Hanbali**). It was founded in 8th century Iraq by Abu Hanifa (d. 767), a silk merchant, whose system was to be granted official recognition by the 'Abbasid caliphs of Baghdad and later to enjoy the same status in the Ottoman and Indian Moghul Empires.

Early Hanafi jurists had considerable powers to make use of their personal opinions in forming judgements. Later on these powers were curtailed, but, where the Quran and Traditions offered no clear guidance, they frequently resorted to analogical reasoning (*qiyas*) in order to deal with new situations. This could be done in two ways. The first was to look for material similarities with a case already decided by the sacred texts, thus burglary could be considered similar to theft because both involve taking another's goods. The second was to establish the motive behind the Quranic or Prophetic ruling, hence since the consumption of wine is to be punished because of its intoxicating effects, similarly the consumption of drinks and substances that intoxicate is to be punished in the same way. Hanafi jurists generally laid stress on the need to consider the public interest in reaching their decisions, and to adapt the law to meet changing circumstances.

At present the Hanafi school is predominant in Turkey, the Indian sub-continent, Afghanistan and Central Asia. There are also large numbers of Hanafis among the Arabs of the Fertile Crescent, and most Chinese Muslims are Hanafis.

Hanbalis. The Hanbali rite or school of Islamic law (*madhhab*) takes its name from Ahmad b. Hanbal (d. 855), a famous collector and teacher of Traditions in Baghdad. Ibn Hanbal is the author of a number of works, including the *Musnad*, containing some 28,000 Traditions arranged according to the transmitters rather than the topics. He admired al-Shafi'i, founder of the **Shafi'i** school and agreed with him on the importance of the Prophetic Traditions as a source of law. However, he differed from him in holding to the view that only the Quran and Traditions constituted the sources of the Holy Law. Hanbalis since his time have normally rejected analogical reasoning (*qiyas*), although they have admitted a consensus confined to the early Islamic community.

The Hanbali school had few followers after the 14th century, but experienced a revival in the 18th century with its adoption by the Arabian **Wahhabis**. In modern times its thought has also influenced the reform movement of the **Salafiya**. It is usually regarded as the strictest of the four **Sunni** schools (the remaining three being **Maliki, Hanafi** and **Shafi'i**), but it can accommodate developments in more liberal directions. An example of this is its doctrine of permissibility, according to which acts are judged to be permissible where there is no specific reference in Quran or Traditions prohibiting them. Following this principle, only the Hanbalis allow a clause to be inserted in the marriage contract stipulating that the husband shall take no additional wives.

Today the Hanbali school is followed in the Kingdom of Saudi Arabia.

Happy, Healthy and Holy Organization (3HO). Another name for the California-based **Sikh Dharma of the Western Hemisphere**.

Harakat al-Tawhid al-Islami. This **Sunni** Muslim organization is a fundamentalist group in the Lebanon. Its name translates as **Islamic Unity Movement** (or Islamic Unification Movement).

Haredi (Haredim). (See also **Orthodox Judaism, Hasidism.**) Haredim (Hebrew, those that "tremble" (before the word of God), taken from Isaiah 66:5) refers to the **Ultra-Orthodox** Jewish communities in Israel and in the *diaspora*. They number approximately 300,000 in Israel, mainly in Jerusalem and Bene Berak. Referred to also by the Hebrew term *dati* ("observant"), they live in Haredi neighbourhoods and distinguish themselves from the modern **Orthodox** and **Neo-Orthodox** in terms of their conscious refusal to compromise with the modern world. Their own perception is of continuing the ways of traditional Judaism, unchanged, living lives fully within the framework of the commandments and customs as Yidn or erlicher Yidn (Yiddish, (true) Jews or virtuous Jews). The Holocaust and the horrendous losses of the centres of Ultra-Orthodox Jewish life loom large and are reflected in their programmes of renewal and development. Their particular form of Judaism arose in the late 18th and early 19th century largely as a reaction to the *haskalah* and the collapse of *shethl* (Jewish town or townlet) and ghetto life in Europe. Their leaders, such as Rabbi Naftali Zvi Yehuda Berlin (1817–93); Rabbi Moses Sofer (1762–1839); and Rabbi Shlomo

Halberstam of Bobova (1848–1906) rejected secular studies and developed *Yeshivot* in order to educate Jews in traditional *Torah*-learning.

The Haredi community is made up of two distinct strands—the groups of Hasidim and the Lithuanian-dominated Mitnaggdim. The former are divided into a number of different movements each led by its charismatic leader or Rebbe (see **Hasidism**). The latter often refer to themselves as Bene Torah (the sons or followers of *Torah*) or Bene Yeshivah (the sons or followers of the *Yeshivah*) and are based on groups affiliated to a particular *Yeshivah* (e.g. Mir and Kamenitz in Jerusalem and Ponievezh in Bene Berak). There is considerable variety in both groups. By the late 19th and early 20th centuries Hasidim and Litvaks (Lithuanians) found themselves no longer arch-enemies but sharing a concern for the defence of traditional Jewish life and learning. Tensions, however, are still evident between the two groups. For example, the Hasidic dominated **Agudat Israel** stands against the Lithuanian **Degel Hatorah,** although they joined forces for the 1992 Israel general election. The Haredi community as a whole is non-**Zionist** but there are different levels of involvement, ranging from total rejection (**Neturei Karta,** Reb Arelah) to more moderate positions.

Yiddish is the vernacular for both groups and Hebrew is pronounced in an Eastern European fashion. In a number of ways the two groups have grown alike, for example, the Hasidim have also developed the *Yeshivah* as a central institution. Also in terms of leadership, although the Hasidic Rebbe derives his authority from piety and spirituality and not from his scholarship as in the case of the Lithuanian *Rosh Yeshivah* (the principal or head of a Talmudic academy), often the *Rosh Yeshivah* is a hereditary position.

Smaller groups of **Sephardim** have also in recent years adopted Haredi lifestyles and are part of this community. Many of these attend Lithuanian (and in some cases Hasidic) *Yeshivot*. In 1984 the **Sephardi Torah Guardian Party (Shas)** was established with the blessing of the leading Litvak authority, Rabbi Eliezer Schach (Rosh Yeshivah of Ponievezh) to gain political representation for Ultra-Orthodox Sephardi communities. Sephardim, however, tend to remain separate and follow their own traditions although in recent years there is evidence of some intermarriage between them and other Haredim.

There are Haredi communities in New York (with Litvak Yeshivot in Lakewood, New Jersey; Telz in Cleveland, Ohio), Antwerp, London (with a Litvak *Yeshivah* in Gateshead near Newcastle) and in other Jewish centres worldwide.

The Haredi community, in Israel and the *diaspora,* continues to grow, mainly due to its large birth-rate and to develop greater involvement with the politics of the wider Jewish community.

Hare Krishnas. This is a popular designation of members of **ISKCON**.

Harris Movement. The Harris (or Harrist) churches originated with a Grebo catechist from Liberia, William Wade Harris (c 1850–1929), who received his calling from the Angel Gabriel in a vision. Between 1913 and 1915, Harris baptized some 120,000 people in the Ivory Coast and Ghana, before being deported back to Liberia. In 1924 British **Methodist** missionaries came across Harris' converts and many became Methodists, but independent Harrist churches have continued to expand under prophetic leaders and healers such as John Ahue and Albert Atcho, and to found new offshoots, such as the Church of the Twelve Apostles in Ghana. Followers of Harrist churches are now numbered in the 100,000s and in the Ivory Coast enjoy official recognition.

Hasidism. See **Orthodox Judaism, Lubavich Hasidism, Satmar Hadism, Belz Hasidism, Bratslav Hasidism, Ger Hasidism.**

Havurat Judaism. See **Jewish New Agers.** *Havurot* (fellowships) are small Jewish worship and study and/or communal groups that create intimate communities and stress active /participation and the creative and spiritual dimensions of Jewish life. Many *havurot* have collectively produced their own prayerbooks and distinctive patterns of worship, including Sabbath observance, communal meals and often Hasidic stories, music and dance. A significant number of *havurot* have been connected with university campuses. Havurot Judaism is closely linked to the development of New Age Judaism. Many of the New Age communal groups were established as *havurot* and leading Jewish New Age figures have been associated with *havurot*. Influences include: Rabbi Zalman Schachter-Shalomi's 1960s Jewish renewal groups; articles in *The Reconstructionist* by Ira Eisenstein, Jacob Neusner and others; *The Jewish Catalogs* (a series of books on "Do-It-Yourself Judaism"); and Rabbi Arthur Green's founding of Havurat Shalom in Boston in 1968. A number of national organizations exist including: Schachter-Shalomi's P'nai Or ("Faces of Light") Religious Fellowship; The Network of Jewish Renewal Communities and The National *Havurot* Co-ordinating Committee (now aligned to the Federation of Reconstructionist congregations, see **Reconstructionist Judaism**). In addition, many "mainstream" congregations (especially **Reform** and **Conservative**) contain smaller *havurot* which serve to increase members' interaction and level of participation.

Heavenly Virtue Church. This is a new religious movement found e.g. in Hong Kong and Malaysia. It stresses ethics, virtue and wisdom, bringing together elements of five major traditions—Confucianism, Taoism, Buddhism, Islam and Christianity—which it claims to complete. Adherents, numbering perhaps over 200,000, are drawn overwhelmingly from the Chinese community, as its original name, Tien Te Sheng Hui, would lead one to expect. (See also **De Jiao**.)

Hebrew Union College/Jewish Institute of Religion (HUC/JIR). See **Reform Judaism.**

Hibtias (Hibatis, Hiptiyas). The Hibtias are a tiny sub-sect of the **Daudis** within Indian Islam. The Daudis, in turn, form a branch of the **Musta'li** sect of **Isma'ili Shi'ism.** They are commonly (though slightly inaccurately) identified with the **Bohoras.** The Hibtias seceded in 1761, and subsequently they were persecuted by their Daudi former co-religionists. Only very few remain today, in Ujjain.

Hito no Michi Kyodan. A Japanese new religious movement, now part of **PL Kyodan.**

Hizb al-Da'wa. The Hizb al-Da'wa al-Islamiya, to give it its full name, is one of the most important Shi'ite fundamentalist groups in Iraq: see **Da'wa Party.**

al-Hizb al-Islami. This is the name—Islamic Party—under which the Tunisian branch of the **Muslim Brotherhood** is known.

al-Hizb al-Jumhari. Al-Hizb al-Jumhari is a reformist Islamic movement in the Sudan. Known until 1969 as the Republican Party, it refers to itself in English today as the **Republican Brothers.**

Hizb al-Nahda. The Hizb al-Nahda, or Renascence Party, was known as the Islamic Tendency Movement (Mouvement de la Tendance Islamique—MTI, Harakat al-Ittijah al-Islami) until November 1988 when it formally declared itself a political party under the new name. Official recognition was, however, denied it, both then and subsequently.

The Nahda is the largest of the Islamist movements in Tunisia. Its origins lie in a movement of Islamic renewal radiating out from Tunisia's traditional centre of learning, the Grand Mosque of Zaytouna, in the 1970s. This movement included the Association for the Preservation of the *Quran* founded in 1970, and a loose number of study groups established to discuss Islamic topics, including matters of doctrine and of individual and social ethics.

In 1981 the MTI was sufficiently well established to seek official recognition as a political party, but action by Islamists to enforce the fast of Ramadan by using threats to induce cafes and shops to close after they had chosen to remain open, and to close the bar in a Club Mediterranée centre, led to arrests and the imprisonment of significant numbers of MTI members, including 61 identified as MTI leaders. Although most were released in 1984, the state cracked down again in 1987: seven members were sentenced to death, and two were indeed hanged. Leader Rashid Ghanouchi was sentenced to life imprisonment. However, following the 1987 *coup* against President Bourguiba, the state's policy changed again, and many MTI members, including Ghanouchi himself, benefitted from an amnesty. The change from MTI to Nahda occurred soon afterwards.

Nahda policies differ from those of many Islamist groups. The Nahda rejects violence (in contrast to the **Islamic Liberation Party**), accepts political and confessional pluralism, and advocates a modern interpretation of the Shari'a (Islamic law) according to general Quranic principles. The establishment of an Islamic state in Tunisia must be preceded by an active process of Islamic renewal so that the state will emerge democratically and not be imposed dictatorially.

Critics have contended that Nahda's commitment to democracy and tolerance is a facade, and point to the existence, admitted by the party, of an extensive underground network alongside the public organization.

Appealing mainly to students, the Nahda nevertheless has a broader constituency. In elections in 1989, candidates sympathetic to its policies (it was not accorded official recognition as a political party and so could not field official candidates of its own) gained 15 per cent of the national vote, and up to 30 per cent in some of the towns. Rashid Ghanouchi retired to Paris and was replaced as president by Ali Laaridh. Along with the six legal opposition parties, however, al-Nahda boycotted the June 1990 parliamentary elections.

The 1990 Iraqi invasion of Kuwait was supported by Ghanouchi, and received wide popular support in Tunisia. Al-Nahda's leaders, on the other hand, remained mindful of the need to support the Saudis in order to secure continued financial support. During the Gulf War of January–February 1991, significant anti-government disturbances led to violent clashes and the arrest of many leaders and hundreds of members of al-Nahda. The party officially suspended all activity in March 1991. In present circumstances its future remains unclear.

Hizb al-Tahrir al-Islami. *See* **Islamic Liberation Party**.

Hizbollah. (In Arabic *Hizb Alláh*, the Party of God.) Hizbollah was founded in 1983 with the direct involvement and support of the Islamic Republic of Iran. The name had been earlier used in Iran and applied to participants in popular demonstrations and paramilitary groups which worked to counter the influence of any dissident movements in the wake of the Iranian Revolution. Hizbollah remains closely linked to the Iranian government. The movement is concerned with morality within the **Shi'ite** community as much as with politics and has adopted a number of measures to try to enforce Islamic dress for women and to prevent the consumption of alcohol. Its goal is the establishment of an Islamic state in Lebanon, but its leaders have often shown a willingness to compromise. Shaikh Fadlallah, who often serves as unofficial spokesman for the organization, has spoken of an Islamic state developing out of the free choice of Lebanese Muslims rather than being imposed upon them. In order for this to happen, however, Lebanese Muslims must be in a political position which makes such self-determination possible. Hizbollah is committed to the cause of creating such a political situation in Lebanon.

Together with **Islamic Amal** it represents a religiously militant strand of the Lebanese Shi'ite community which stands in marked contrast to the (by Western standards) more moderate position of **Amal** and the Supreme Shi'ite Council of Lebanon. Hizbollah and Amal came to armed conflict with each other, not least over the question of the taking of hostages. Hizbollah is believed to be involved in a number of activities which have been undertaken in the name of the **Islamic Jihad**. These range from the taking of hostages to a number of suicide attacks on various foreign (principally American) institutions in Lebanon. Hizbollah co-operates with the **Sunni** group *Harakat al-Tawhid al-Islami* (Islamic Unity Movement) which shares its puritanical moral views and commitment to an Islamic state in Lebanon.

In May 1991 the leadership of Hizbollah fell to Abbas Mousawi. Hizbollah was the only militia to refuse to be disarmed in accordance with the Taif agreement, and it has been permitted by the Lebanese government to continue guerrilla warfare against the Israeli troops occupying southern Lebanon (and their proxy, the South Lebanon Army). In February 1992 the Israelis responded by bombing the car in which Mousawi and his family were travelling, killing all its occupants. The future direction of Hizbollah policy is now likely to become all the more uncompromising (symbolized perhaps by

its recent self-designation as the Islamic Resistance). Following the assassination of Sheikh Mousawi, the leadership has been taken up by the 31-year old Sheikh Hassan Nasrallah, who is a Sayid (ie someone claiming descent from the Prophet Muhammad).

Hngettwin Nikaya. The smallest monastic fraternity (*gaing*) within the **Burmese Theravada** Buddhist *Sangha* presently containing some 1,000 ordained monks. Founded in the mid-19th century by the abbot of Hngettwin ("cave of birds") monastery at Sagaing, the order is now concentrated in the Mandalay region. The order is strongly rationalistic—particularly in its ethical outlook, is opposed to the worship of Buddha images and denies the efficacy of prayer. It places great emphasis on the practice of meditation.

Hoa Hao. A millenarian tradition known, in the Mekong delta of Vietnam, as **Buo Son Ky Huong**. Hoa Hao was founded by Huynh Phu So, who revealed the principles of a new "Buddhism of Great Peace" in 1939. Hoa Hao is similar in some respects to **Cao Dai,** but more orthodox in relation to Buddhism, and less syncretistic. Its adherents believe that Huynh Phu So is the Emergent Buddha.

Hoa Hao, named after the spiritual centre in south Vietnam where it was founded, does not attempt to unite religions and is opposed to elaborate rituals. During the forties it was strongly anti-Communist, and Huynh Phu So was murdered by the Viet Minh in 1946. During the Vietnam War Hoa Hao attracted thousands of anti-communist followers who wore amulets bearing the inscription "Buo Son Ky Huong", the first of these having been distributed in the 19th century by a mystic called Buddha Master of Western Peace. Buddha Master claimed to be a messenger from heaven who came to warn mankind of the imminence of apocalypse. Only those who took refuge in the Seven Mountains (where Maitreya would descend after the world had been purified) and practised true religion would be spared. Healing was the most common skill claimed by the early apostles.

Its current membership is large in certain traditional areas. Hoa Hao and Cao Dai both tried to attract Japanese assistance during World War II.

Hojjatiya Society. The Hojjatiya (Hujjatiya, Hojjatiyeh), or the Charitable Society of Mahdi, the Proof of God (Anjuman-i Khayriya-yi Mahdaviya-yi Hojjatiya) is a **Twelver Shi'ite** organization founded in the 1950s by Shaykh Mahmud Halabi, a close ally of Imam Khomeini, for the express purpose of propagating Islam. In fact, its activities centred in the persecution of members of the **Bahai** religion. Between then and the Islamic Revolution it was generally known as the "Anti-Bahai Society". In the early 1980s, however, the movement took its current name and adopted wider political policies, infiltrating the Islamic Republican Party and the government. Its chief enemy was now Marxism. In the religious field, however, the society opposed Khomeini's attempt to extend the authority of the clergy to political rule (something they believed to be the prerogative of the Hidden Imam or Mahdi). In 1983, government and Tudeh (Communist) party pressure forced the Society to suspend its activities on the grounds both of their refusal to endorse Khomeini's theory of political rule by the clergy (*wilayat-i faqih*), and also of a tendency to socio–economic conservatism. Its current status is unclear.

Holiness (Perfectionist) Movement. Holiness churches originated in America, and grew out of the **Methodist** movement.

One of the distinctive doctrines of Methodism was Christian Perfection (holiness, entire sanctification) which stated that God has the power, through the Holy Spirit, to enable Christians to fulfil the command of Matthew 5, 48 "You must be perfect—just as your Father in heaven is perfect". This inward holiness—being so filled with God's love that there is no desire to sin—was believed to be a "second blessing" coming after the experience of conversion.

The doctrine became less central to Methodism in America during the 19th century. The mainstream Methodist Church supported slavery, opposed Holiness movements within the church (of which the strongest was the "Tuesday Meeting for the Promotion of Holiness" founded in the 1830s by Phoebe Palmer) and refused to lay down strict rules about Christian living. Those supporting the Holiness doctrine felt forced at various times to take a stand and to form their own churches.

Today, consequently, there are many different Holiness denominations committed to the doctrine of Christian Perfection. Many have sent missionaries abroad. The largest is the **Church of the Nazarene** with over 800,000 members. This reached Britain in 1906 through the work of George Sharpe in Scotland. Members of Holiness churches reject worldly pastimes such as drinking alcohol, smoking or going to the cinema and concentrate on holy living based on Bible principles. Membership worldwide is about 5,500,000.

Holy Spirit Association for the Unification of World Christianity. This is the full official designation of the Reverend Sun Myung Moon's **Unification Church** (whose members are popularly known as "the Moonies").

Hooppha Sawan. Hooppha Sawan (the Religious Land), 80 miles south of Bangkok, was founded in the early 1970s by Suchart Kosolkitiwong, a Thai Buddhist novice in search of a place for meditation, who subsequently established the site as headquarters of the **International Federation of Religions** to promote world peace and fraternity in 1975.

169

Hossoshu. One of the six **Nara** sects of Japanese Buddhism. It propounds an idealistic philosophy and has approximately 40 temples and 600,000 adherents at the present time. **Hosso** is a philosophical school which views consciousness as the basis for the appearance of the phenomenal world. Its head temples are the Kofukuji and the Yakushiji. The **Shotokushu** seceded from **Hossoshu** in 1950.

House Churches. A movement amongst **Protestants** which in Britain began in the 1970s, and grew from the feeling that the existing denominations were dormant. Strongly influenced by the **Charismatic** movement, house churches are in part a rejection of traditional church buildings, formal liturgies, and a separated, trained ministry. Meetings often called Christian Fellowships may be held in private homes or hired public buildings. Chains of house churches exist in various groupings like the Harvestime group, in which Bryn Jones, Goos Vedder, Terry Virgo and Arthur Wallis have played key roles and which is particularly strong in West Yorkshire. Harvestime has acquired a permanent home by buying the **Anglican** Diocesan offices in Bradford. A high point in their annual calendar is the Dales Bible Week which attracts 8,000 residents for prayer, praise, Bible study, and ministry. Other groups include the Pioneers led by Gerald Coates in London, G. Wally North, who exercises an itinerant international ministry from near Prestwick airport in Scotland, and the Ichthus movement led by Roger Forster. *See* **Restorationism/New Churches.**

House of Growth. *See* **Seicho no Ie.**

Howling Dervishes. A colloquial label sometimes given to members of the **Rifaʻiya Sufi** order.

Hua Yen. The Chinese name of the Japanese Buddhist **Nara** sect, **Kegonshu.**

Human Potential Movement. Regarded by many as the psychological wing of the **New Age** movement, it typically involves the development of emotional competence, perhaps through a prior restructuring of one's concepts. Methods involved may include **Primal Therapy, Rebirthing,** and **Psychosynthesis.**

Hutterites. A group of **Anabaptists** which has kept separate from the **Mennonites,** although sharing most of their beliefs. They were formed in Moravia and were followers of Jakob Hutter who was martyred by burning in 1536. They developed as groups of agricultural collectives "holding everything in common" as the early disciples had done (Acts 4, v32). These collectives are known as "Bruderhofs". This group also migrated to both North America and Russia.

I

Ibadiya. The Ibadis (hence, sometimes, "Ibadism") are a small group of Muslims, the origins of whose movement antedate the **Sunni-Shi'ite** split. The Ibadis are in a line of descent from the original "secessionists" from (what became) mainstream Islam, the Khawarij or Kharijites. The latter were involved in early religio-political disputes and civil war. They took the view that believers who committed a grave sin should be expelled from the Muslim community; and they resisted the trend towards making the leadership of the *umma* in some sense hereditary in the family of the Prophet. Both features have been retained among the Ibadis, whose traditions have evolved from this source.

Ibadi communities choose as their leader, or *imam,* the person whom they regard as best qualified in terms of the two criteria of religious knowledge and political (including military but also administrative) skills. Should the imam commit a crime, he must repent or abdicate. Members of the group who commit a serious sin may be excommunicated, or suffer imposed isolation until they repent publicly after the Friday prayers. The particular penalty is decided upon by a council (*mutawa'a* or *azzaba*) of perhaps a dozen people, and it is from this circle that a new imam is generally drawn. The council also act as arbiters in tribal disputes.

As these features perhaps indicate, the Ibadi movement has remained confined to relatively isolated tribal groups who have preserved an ancient way of life. Some Ibadi communities are found today in the Mzab area of southern Algeria and in Tunisia, but their main centre is in Oman, where, however, the traditional fusion of religious and political leadership gave way in the 18th century to a separation of powers, the *imam* retaining religious leadership in the traditional Ibadi centres in the mountains, and the political leadership being relocated in the Sultan of Muscat on the coast. As a result of civil strife in the 1960s, the present *imam,* Imam Ghalib, went into exile in Saudi Arabia.

ICUS. The International Conference on the Unity of the Sciences (ICUS) is a branch of the **Unification Church.** It invites academics and scholars from all over the world to attend regularly organized conferences.

Idrisiya. A branch of the notable **Sufi** order, the **Shadhiliya.**

Iglesia ni Cristo. The Church of Christ is by far the largest of over 300 indigenous denominations in the Philippines which jointly constitute some 20 per cent of the population. It is sometimes known as the Church of Manalo, and members may be known as Manalistas—after the name of its founder, Félix Manalo (1886–1963).

Manalo was converted in 1904 to **Protestantism** through the **Methodist** Church, and began to study for the ministry. Part way through this training he shifted to the **Presbyterian** Ellinwood Bible School. The **Disciples of Christ** next received his attention because he was attracted to their view of believers' baptism, and he was appointed one of their first evangelists in the Philippines. In 1912 the Seventh Day **Adventists** received him into membership and he worked for them.

Two years later, disillusioned with all the groups in which he had been involved, Manalo moved out on his own, believing himself specially called by God to this new responsibility. On July 27, 1914 the Iglesia ni Cristo was founded and incorporated as a church. The church grew fast in the first five years, with members drawn mainly from the Disciples. It also attracted attention for its very public debates over baptism, use of icons/statues in worship and its forbidding of the eating of blood-red mcat.

In 1919 Manalo studied for a year at the Pacific School of Religion, USA. Upon his return he had to re-impose and re-establish his leadership in a church badly divided by dissension. Initially, growth was slow, but after the independence of the Philippines, membership rapidly expanded as the church adopted a strong, nationalistic stance. It spread throughout the Philippines and overseas with Philippino emigrants and workers. The wealth and power of the church can be judged from the many churches (known as chapels) which have been built on a grand scale. This church's success is due largely to the way in which it has indigenized Protestant Christianity. It uses Tagalog as its official language, and encourages the use of regional and local languages in services—it is *the* church for the Philippino, and is in touch with ordinary people, seeking to mobilize their support and encouragement.

The church fosters strong bonds with the community, and is highly organized with a centralized authority and power structure. Leaders exert considerable power, especially at election time, often dictating the outcome of local elections by the use of a block vote. The membership is thus highly disciplined—its Sunday and Thursday meetings are obligatory, and members are required to give a specific amount of their income (decided by the leaders) to the Church.

The church has a strong influence on business and social life. Members employ one another and support one another in business. The church also aids members in their businesses. The church is strongly anti-Catholic and anti-American, and trains its members to defend their own beliefs and to attack the beliefs of those with whom it disagrees.

Theologically, the Trinity is vigorously denied. Jesus, though Saviour, is truly human in all respects. Baptism is by immersion upon joining the church. It is a sin against the Holy Spirit to eat blood or meat cooked in blood. The dinuguan, a culinary delicacy of the Philippines, is cooked in blood, but forbidden to the members of this group. Salvation is only to be found by joining the true church. It is held as a cardinal belief that the true church disappeared in history (Romans 16:16), only to re-appear in the Philippines according to the prophecy of Isaiah 43:5–6. Manalo's leadership is affirmed by the prophecy in Revelation 7:2–3.

The church has an influential magazine, *Pasugo*, roughly translated as "God's Message", and operates a network of radio stations.

Iharaira. Te Kooti, founder of the **Ringatu Church**, died in 1893. He designated no successor, but one of the influential people who was to follow in his footsteps was Rua Kenana. Rua was born in 1869 and, in 1904, underwent religious experiences in which the voice of God spoke and Jesus appeared to him. When word spread of these experiences, many people came to consult him and to seek healing. Rua established his "New Jerusalem" in 1906. This became the centre of his activities and a place of pilgrimage for Maori people. He was leader, friend and prophet to the Maori for over 30 years. He identified himself with Moses and drew a parallel between himself and the exiled people.

In his childhood he had experienced alienation and rejection, and had seen his people experiencing similar things at the hands of the colonizing Europeans. He was an astute leader, and established a community of apostles and councillors who enabled him to lead in a constructive and positive way. In 1904 on a nearby mountain, Rua had a mystical experience in which he claimed to have spoken with God and met with Jesus. The mountain came to be compared to the Holy Mountain where Moses had conversed with God, so this gave the area of the "New Jerusalem" a sacredness that it would otherwise not have had.

In 1906 Rua was baptized as the Messiah and selected 12 disciples—more on the Old Testament model than the Christian—and followed the practices of Saturday sabbath. When he died in 1937 this prophet of charisma left behind a major influence amongst the Maori of the East Coast of New Zealand's North Island. Over recent years this influence has been Christianized.

Ikhwan. Ikhwan (or al-Ikhwan) means the Brothers. Some care is needed, though, in that it is a term with three possible referents.

First, it may refer to fiercely dedicated (some would say fanatical) Bedouin **Wahhabi** Muslims instrumental, through their military prowess, in the gradual establishment of the Kingdom of Saudi Arabia (completed in 1934).

Second, it may refer to their modern successors, the followers of the charismatic Juhayman al-Utaybi who seized the famous mosque in Mecca in 1979 in an attempt to launch an insurrection against the ruling royal family whom they saw as a corrupt élite who had betrayed the Wahhabi ideals they claimed to uphold. The rebels were eventually overpowered, and al-Utaybi was killed.

Third, it may refer to the Ikhwan al-Muslimin, the members of the **Muslim Brotherhood**.

Ikhwan al-Muslimin. Meaning Muslim Brethren, this is the Arabic designation for the **Muslim Brotherhood**.

I Kuan Tao. *See* **Unity Sect.**

Imamis. The term Imamis is a more formal designation of the branch of Islam which is known more generally in the West as the **Twelver Shi'ites** (Ithna 'Asharis).

Imam-Shahis. The Imam-Shahis are a small sub-group of the **Nizari Khojas** in India, where they are perhaps better known as the **Satpanthis.**

Independent Evangelical Churches. Evangelical Christians believe that everyone is in need of God's forgiveness, and that God's forgiveness is available to all by His grace, through faith in Jesus Christ. They want to tell this good news (gospel) to everyone who they believe is not yet a Christian.

There are many independent evangelical denominations and they fall roughly into three types. The first type are churches in many different countries which result from the work of a single, non-denominational, missionary society, (often based in the USA or the UK). Examples are the Worldwide Mission churches (for instance the Worldwide Mission Church of Bermuda, the Worldwide Mission Church of India) which were founded by the **Worldwide** Mission organization based in Pasadena, California, USA. The largest of these churches is the Worldwide Mission Church of Ghana (90,000 members) but some are as small as a few hundred.

The second type are groups of evangelical churches which join together for primarily administrative purposes. In the United Kingdom an example is the **Fellowship of Independent Evangelical Churches** which has over 30,000 members and is still growing.

The final group consists of churches which represent evangelical views in a particular area or ethnic group. The **Sudanese Church of Christ** is active primarily in the Nuba mountains of Sudan. In India (Assam) and Burma the **Lakher Independent Evangelical Church** is said to have a membership of 95 per cent of the Lakher tribe who were previously headhunters.

Estimated global membership of these churches is 1,500,000.

173

Indonesian Buddhayana Council. *See* **Buddhayana.**

Insight. Insight Transformational Seminars was founded in 1978 by John-Roger Hinkins (born 1934) and its international headquarters are located in Santa Monica, California. Insight became well known in Britain in 1979 through the enthusiastic support for them evinced by Arianna Stassinopoulos Huffington. The movement belongs to what P. Heelas has designated the **"self religions"**. Participants in the seminars are often middle-class professionals, and a typical introductory seminar would occupy six evenings. Participants often report important gains in self-confidence and ability to communicate successfully with others.

Institute for Traditional Judaism. See **Conservative Judaism.**

International Church of Christ. This is the name used to describe the **Church of Christ** movement based on the Boston Church of Christ but now also including the London Church of Christ, the Birmingham Church of Christ, and the Manchester Church of Christ in the UK.

International Federation of Religions. An organization founded in 1975 by the Thai new religious movement **Hooppha Sawan** to promote world peace and fraternity.

International Network of Engaged Buddhists (INEB). Founded in Thailand in 1989 at a conference of monks and laity from 11 different countries, the Network has Buddhadasa Bhikkhu, Thich Nhat Hanh and Dalai Lama as its patrons. Affiliated groups may be found in 26 countries including France, Japan, USA, and the UK. The INEB aims to promote understanding between differing Buddhist traditions and is concerned with articulating authentic Buddhist responses to a wide range of issues such as alternative education and spiritual training, women's rights, the environment and development. It also serves as a clearing house for information on other engaged Buddhist groups and from time to time operates with spiritual activists from other religious traditions. The greatest concern of the Network is to empower Buddhists in areas under great duress such as Bangladesh, Burma, Cambodia and Sri Lanka. The Network publishes a tri-annual magazine, *Seeds of Peace*, in conjunction with the Thai Interreligious Commission for Development and has sponsored a variety of conflict resolution seminars for monks in the SE Asian region.

International Sikh Federation. A shadowy militant **Sikh** organization allegedly led by Jasbir Singh, a nephew of Sant Bhindranwale. Although never proved, Jasbir Singh has been widely cited as the "co-ordinating mastermind" behind the assassination of Mrs. Gandhi in October 1984. In January 1986 he was elected by radical Sikhs to be head priest (*jathedar*) of the Akali Takht in Amritsar, though this attempt to gain power at the religious centre of Sikhism was ultimately foiled by moderates.

International Society for Krishna Consciousness (ISKCON). ISKCON was founded in 1966 in New York by Bhaktivedanta Prabhupada, but traces its origins back to the 16th-century mystic Chaitanya, being in the tradition of **Gaudiya Vaishnava** Hinduism which recognises Krishna as the "Supreme personality of Godhead". It is essentially a fundamentalist Hindu sect (and as such, a member of the European Council of Hindu Organizations), with a simple practice, consisting mainly of the Hare Krishna chant (*mantra*), hence its alternative name, the Hare Krishnar. It was the first of the new religious movements to attract media attention, partly through the saffron robes and shaved heads of its followers. Its best known sympathizer, George Harrison, turned the chant into a pop song, and also donated Bhaktivedanta Manor, the British headquarters.

The lifestyle is very disciplined and restrictive: vegetarianism, no drugs or other stimulants, minimal sex for pro-creation only. The leadership is entirely male, and the movement's derogatory attitudes towards women have provoked criticism inside and outside the community.

Controversy followed Prabhupada's death, when some of the 11 gurus he had in some sense appointed (although it is somewhat unclear what that sense is) abused their leadership. There was some evidence of drug use and smuggling, deceptive fundraising, and even murder. Indeed, about half the gurus have now left or been expelled from ISKCON, leading to schism. However, the movement claims to be reformed since these scandals.

A Governing Body Commission meets annually to guide the worldwide con-federation of over 100 temples, centres and schools. The official estimate of numbers is 3,000 full-time members worldwide with 200,000 "congregational" members. Of these about 300 full-time and 4,000 part-time members are British, with an additional 300,000 sympathizers in the Hindu community. Unlike most new religious movements, ISKCON has a large following among working-class youth.

Inuit Religion. The Inuit (Eskimo) inhabit an enormous area of the arctic and sub-arctic, from Alaska to Greenland. They traditionally lived by hunting in a severe and dangerous environment and much of Inuit religion centred around animals and hunting rituals. Each animal was believed to have a spirit owner and the availability of animals was profoundly affected by the behaviour of humans. Animals were treated with great respect and many rituals

surrounded their hunting. In Canada and Greenland the Inuit believed that all sea animals were under the control of a female Sea deity, who would hold back the animals when humans transgressed taboos. This then necessitated the trance journey of the Shaman to her home at the bottom of the sea to placate her and release the animals. Shamans played a central role in Inuit life in their capacities as game magicians and healers of the sick. **Shamanism** has declined with the decline in traditional culture, but hunting still forms a major part of many Inuit communities and a respectful attitude towards animals persists.

Irani Zoroastrians. The Zoroastrians who preserved their tradition in Iran after the rise of Islam, as opposed to those who migrated to India (the **Parsis**). Forced by persecution and social pressures to retreat, with their two most sacred fires, into remote villages (notably, near the desert cities of Yazd and Kermān), most Zoroastrians subsisted in Islamic Iran in obscurity and poverty.

Between the 15th and 17th centuries, Irani Zoroastrian priests were in contact by correspondence with the Indian Parsis and, from the late 19th century on-wards, Parsi reform movements influenced Zoroastrian city dwellers in Iran. The rural population has, however, remained "orthodox" in its isolation. During the Pahlavi dynasty (1925–1979) Zoroastrians enjoyed greater freedom because of their historical association with the pre-Islamic past. That association once again became a disadvantage with the Islamic revolution of 1979. At present there are approximately 30,000 Irani Zoroastrians.

Irvingites. An informal label for members of the **Catholic Apostolic Church**.

Ishanism. An alternative name for **Sufism** in the former Soviet Union. 'Ishan' is in origin a Persian term of respect for a Sufi master.

Isikcis. A Turkish Islamic renewal group rather similar to the **Süleymancis** and **Nurcus**. They are opposed to the officially secular nature of the Turkish state, and consequently tend to be regarded as subversives by the state. Their current size and influence remains rather unclear.

ISKCON. Acronym for **International Society for Krishna Consciousness,** commonly known as the **Hare Krishna movement**. Although it is often regarded as a new cult, it is in fact firmly rooted in the **Gaudiyasampradaya** of Bengal. The founder of ISKCON, His Divine Grace A. C. Bhaktivedanta Swami Prabhupada (born Abhay Chai an De in Calcutta, 1896–1977), spent most of his life as a pharmacist, a family man and a devout member of the **Gaudiya Vaisnava Mission,** which had been established in 1886 by Bhaktivinoda Thakura in order to promote the Chaitanya tradition and the way of life based upon it. Bhaktivedanta's guru, Thakura's son, laid upon him the responsibility of spreading the worship of Krishna in the West. In 1959 he became a *samnyasi* in order to devote himself to preaching, and in 1965 he sailed to New York and founded ISKCON there the following year.

The members of ISKCON worship Krishna as "the supreme personality of God-head", not an *avatara* of Visnu, but the Supreme Being himself, who has manifested himself in other figures also, for example Rama, the Buddha and Caitanya. The latter is particularly important for ISKCON members who see him as embodying both Krishna and his beloved Radha. Initiated members of ISKCON, usually known as devotees, may live as *brahmacharis* (celibate students) or as married *grihasthas* (householders). In either case they lead a somewhat austere life, rising early, taking a daily cold shower, keeping to a diet of vegetables, fruit, pulses, grains and dairy products. Alcohol, tea and coffee are prohibited, as is the use of drugs. For the householders sex is regarded as only for procreation within marriage. Both *brahmacharis* and *grihasthas* adopt Hindu dress and names. Much of their time is spent in chanting and in studying the scriptures of the Caitanya tradition, all translated and provided with a commentary by Prabhupada. In public they take part in street processions in which they sing the praises of Krishna, and distribute their scriptures to any who wish to have them.

ISKCON is a world-wide movement, which has a considerable appeal to many Westerners, mostly young people who see their own culture as too materialistic. Both in India and the West, it is regarded by Hindus as an authentic expression of the *bhakti* tradition. Since Prabhupada's death the international management of the movement has been in the hands of the Governing Body Commission which he set up, with gurus chosen by Prabhupada himself to give spiritual leadership and continuity.

Islamic Hareket. See p. 181.

Islamic Amal. The period following the 1982 Israeli invasion of Lebanon was marked by the increasing radicalization of the **Shi'ite** community. A number of Shi'ites became disenchanted with the moderate stance of **Amal**. In 1982, Husain al-Musawi formed the Islamic Amal (al-Amal al-Islami, or the Islamic Hope). Originally intended as a reform movement within Amal, Islamic Amal rejected the secularized leadership of the traditional Amal. Instead, it looked for inspiration to the Islamic Republic of Iran, particularly to the political ideology of Ayatollah Khomeini. It became powerful in the Bekaa valley during the period of Syrian and Iranian co-operation in the early 1980s while Syrian troops were occupying that part of Lebanon. The Islamic Amal is committed to an Islamic state in Lebanon. Having a puritanical moral outlook it works also to influence the personal lives of members of the Shi'ite community in Lebanon. In 1983, another group with similar aims and with direct Iranian support, called **Hizbollah**, was formed. Owing to the obvious overlap in interests and clientele, Islamic Amal has been virtually absorbed by Hizbollah.

Islamic Assembly. The Islamic Assembly (al-Mujtamma' al-Islami) was a local movement in the Gaza Strip inspired by, or an offshoot of, the **Muslim Brotherhood**. Most mosques came to be influenced by it during the 1980s, and it gained control of the Islamic University, winning 65–75 per cent of the student vote. Its leader was the charismatic Shaikh Ahmad Yasin who went on to lead **Hamas**, and the Islamic Assembly was subsumed within the latter organization.

Islamic Call Party. The Hizb al-Da'wa al-Islamiya, one of the most important **Shi'ite** fundamentalist groups in Iraq (and not to be confused with Libya's **Islamic Call Society**): see **Da'wa Party**.

Islamic Call Society. The Islamic Call Society (Jam'iyat al-Da'wa al-Islamiya), established in 1970 and based in Tripoli, seeks in many ways to emulate the Saudi-based **Muslim World League**, whose structure as an international Muslim organization—general conference, world council, and regional meetings—it has increasingly imitated since its restructuring in 1982. The crucial difference, however, lies in the fact that it promotes the atypical interpretation of Islam developed by Libya's Qaddafi.

It established its own Islamic college in Libya in 1974, followed by branches in Damascus (1982) and London (1986), the first two in particular training quite large numbers of preachers and teachers. Other Islamic schools and centres have been sponsored in a dozen African countries, as have "Islamic hospitals" further afield

in Bangladesh and the Philippines: Black Africa and South-East Asia are the focus of a great deal of the Society's activities.

As well as its religious educational and medical care work, the Society organizes a variety of conferences, including, every four years, the major meeting of its International Council. Like its publications, these serve among other things as a channel for presenting Qaddafi's religio–political interpretation of the USA, Britain, France and other Western nations as latter-day Crusaders intent on battle against Islam, and against whom in turn *jihad* is necessary.

In connection with its claim to international significance, the Society has begun to call itself the World Islamic Call Society (Jam'iyat al-Da'wa al-Islami al-'Alamiya), but its shorter original title remains in common use.

Islamic Congress. An alternative label in English for the **Islamic Assembly** movement in the Gaza Strip.

Islamic Council of Europe. This London-based organization was set up in 1973 with encouragement and support from the Saudi government, and with the aim of coordinating the activities and efforts of the numerous Muslim organizations in Europe. It has organized major conferences, and funded a number of research projects. The provision of Islamic literature to meet the needs of European Muslim communities has been an important task. Co-operation between the Islamic world and Europe, and the breaking down of prejudices and misunderstandings, has also been a prominent goal.

Islamic Foundation. Based in Leicester (UK), this organization publishes an attractive range of literature on Islam. Prominent on its lists are works by the late Saiyid Abul A'la Maududi (1903–1979), founder of the **Jama'at-i Islami**. The

Islamic Foundation has personal links to this organization and to the **UK Islamic Mission**.

Islamic Front for the Liberation of Bahrain. The IFLB (al-Jabha al-Islamiya li-Tahrir al-Bahrain) was established in Tehran in 1979 in the wake of the Iranian revolution. Iran's long-standing claims to the island were doubtless a factor leading to its establishment. Its leader was one of an influential group of **Shi'ite** clerics trained in Karbala, the centre of **Twelver** learning in Iraq: Hadi al-Mudarrisi, brother of the erstwhile leader of the Iraqi oppositional **Organization of Islamic Action**.

In collaboration with underground cells of the Iraq-based Hizb al-Da'wa, or **Da'wa Party**, the IFLB engaged in acts of sabotage, and in 1981 mounted a *coup* attempt. In response, the authorities handed out lengthy prison sentences but refrained from the death penalty. Perhaps partly as a result of this relative leniency, combined with a generally more accommodating attitude towards the majority Shi'ite community in Bahrain, the IFLB has failed to engage widespread popular support.

Islamic Groups. This vague title is sometimes used in relation to the situation in Egypt in order to refer to the rather ill-defined, but increasingly prominent, cluster of organizations known as **al-Jama'at al-Islamiya**.

Islamic Jihad. The Islamic Jihad (*al-Jihad al-Islami*) has been described as a loose association of particularly dedicated and daring members from other Islamic militant organizations. It is not known for sure whether the Islamic Jihad exists as a specific organization with its own structures and leadership. It is possible that the name refers to various *ad hoc* groups which come together for a specific purpose. Alternatively, it might be a cover name used to preserve the anonymity of other more visible organizations such

as **Hizbollah, Islamic Amal**, the PLO and others. A number of suicide commandos have acted in the name of the Islamic Jihad and the organization has claimed responsibility for explosions at various foreign embassies, including the American Embassy in Beirut in 1983. Following the assassination of Sheikh Mousawi, the leadership has been taken up by Sheikh Hassan Nasrallah, who is a Sayid (i.e. someone claiming descent from the Prophet Muhammad). Most recently it claimed responsibility for the suicide bombing of the Israeli Embassy in Buenos Aires in March 1992 in retaliation for the assassination, along with his wife and 5-year old son, of the Hizbollah leader Sheikh Abbas Mousawi by the Israelis.

Islamic Jihad al-Bait al-Muqaddas. A radical Palestinian Islamist group based in Amman in Jordan. Its name refers to "the Holy House", i.e. Jerusalem. It is led by Shaikh Asad al-Tamimi, who called on supporters to engage in suicide attacks on Western interests at the time of the Gulf war against Iraq. He called for a holy war in defence of the Muslim believer, Saddam Hussein, against the side supportive of atheism, America. The organization is believed to be relatively small and not, at present, particularly influential.

Islamic Leagues. This is a label sometimes used instead of Islamic Groups to refer to the increasingly important **al-Jama'at al-Islamiya** in Egypt.

Islamic Liberation Group. This once dramatically significant group is more accurately known as the **Islamic Liberation Organization**.

Islamic Liberation Organization. The Islamic Liberation Organization (Munazzamat al-Tahrir al-Islami)—also known as the Islamic Liberation Group—was established in Egypt in 1971 by Salih Sirriya (1933–76), a Palestinian with a Ph.D. in science education. Sirriya had previously been a member of the **Islamic**

Liberation Party. He had lived in Jordan until the suppression of the Palestinian guerrillas in 1970, after which he spent a year in Iraq before moving on to Cairo where he worked for the Arab League and began building up the secret cells of his own organization. Sirriya saw the problems of society as coming from the un-Islamic rulers, who must be removed in order to implement Islam from above. In April 1974 he organized an attempt to assassinate Sadat by first taking over the Technical Military Academy before marching on the Arab Socialist Union where the President was due to make a speech. The plot failed, Sirriya and his top aide were sentenced to death and executed in 1976, and the Islamic Liberation Organization disintegrated.

Islamic Liberation Party. The Islamic Liberation Party (Hizb al Tahrir al-Islami) was founded in the early 1950s by Taqi al-din al-Nabahani (d. 1978), an Islamic judge in the Shari'a court in Haifa (in the days when it was a town in the state of Palestine) who later settled in the West Bank town of Nablus after the creation of the state of Israel in 1948. The party bears similarities to the **Muslim Brotherhood**, but was explicitly formed as a political party concerned with seizing power, and was consequently banned almost from its inception in Jordan and other Arab states. Members seek the establishment of an Islamic state in common with other Islamist groups. Although largely Palestinian and Jordanian, the party has been reported as an active opposition element in several Arab countries, including Lebanon, Libya, Tunisia and Egypt.

Islamic Modernists (South Asia). The Modernists formed an élite stream of Islamic thought, but one of great importance in 19th and 20th century South Asia. It flowed from the movements of revival and reform in early 19th century Delhi; its source was Saiyid Ahmad Khan (1817–98), the

descendant of high-ranking Muslim service families.

After the Mutiny uprising of 1857, Saiyid Ahmad decided that the answer to the problem of how Muslims should survive without power was to reconcile them to British rule. His method was to demonstrate that there was nothing in Western civilization that intrinsically undermined Islam. Like the **Ahl-i Hadith** he circumvented the medieval law schools and went straight to the Quran and Hadith for guidance. The basis of his exegetical principles was that the laws of Creation were the work of God, and the Quran was the word of God, and they just could not be contradictory. If they seemed so, it was because men failed to understand them correctly. As Saiyid Ahmad tested this basis in such areas as *jihad,* slavery and polygamy, he developed the dynamic principle of modernist thought, which is to distinguish between what is central to revelation and what is merely the historical wrapping in which it came. His concern was to translate that central purpose into modern circumstances.

This dynamic principle has been developed in modernist thought down to the present. It is there in Muhammad Iqbal's (1877?–1938) bridging of the gulf between Islamic universalism and the modern national state; it is there too in his bridging of the gulf between the sovereignty of God and that of the people in his transference of the main support of the shari'a from the consensus of the *ulama* to that of the people. It is most clearly worked out by the leading modernist thinker of recent times, and one time head of Pakistan's constitutionally established Institute of Islamic Research, Fazlur Rahman (d. 1988), in his explanation of the reasoning behind the most important piece of modernist legislation, Pakistan's Muslim Family Laws Ordinance of 1961. Key institutions in carrying forward modernist ideas have been the Muhammadan Anglo-Oriental College at Aligarh (1877), the All-India Muslim Educational Conference (1886) and the **All-India Muslim**

League (1906). Once Pakistan was won, Modernists hoped that it would be a laboratory in which their thought could be developed. In fact it came to be an arena in which they had to defend their corner against other heirs of South Asian Islamic responses to the West, most notably the **Deobandis**, the **Barelvis** and supporters of the **Jama'at-i Islami**.

Islamic Progressive Movement. The Islamic Progressive Movement (Harakat al-Taqaddum al-Islami, or MPI—Mouvement du Progrès Islamiste) is a rival Islamist organization in Tunisia to the better-known and more successful Islamic Tendency Movement (Mouvement de Tendance Islamique, now a political party, **Hizb al-Nahda**). Unlike most Islamist groups, which tend to use earliest Islam as a criterion of an ideal Islamic society, the MPI denies the existence of a model society in the past, and emphasizes the task of working towards what will at best be an increasingly better historical approximation of one in the future. Their ideal is a society in which Islamic law continues to be developed in modern circumstances, and in a way which incorporates humanist notions of individual self-fulfilment. In contrast to groups which take their cue from Mawdudi's **Jama'at-i Islami**, they regard political power as being rooted in the will of the people rather than in God.

Islamic Renaissance Movement. The Islamic Renaissance Movement (Mouvement de la Nahda Islamique) was founded legally in Algeria in 1990, although it claims to have existed underground since 1974. An Islamist movement, it differentiates itself from **FIS** and **Hamas** by opposing government moves towards privatization. In this respect it is akin to the left wing of the **Muslim Brotherhood**. Led by Shaikh Abdullah Djaballah, it appears to attract support amongst intellectuals in particular, and has not yet established a popular base.

Islamic Republican Party. This once-powerful organization was a product of the Iranian revolution, and a major channel for the dissemination of Khomeini's ideals, both through its country-wide organization and through its dominance of the Iranian parliament. After a number of years, however, it began to reflect the deep dissensions that had emerged among the *ulama* and the country's leaders, and in 1987 Khomeini ordered its dissolution.

Islamic Resistance. Islamic Resistance is a self-designation which the Lebanese **Shi'ite** organization **Hizbollah** began to use in 1992.

Islamic Resistance Movement. This important Islamic group in the West Bank and Gaza Strip is better known as **Hamas** (the acronym of its Arabic title, Harakat al-Muqawama al-Islamiya).

Islamic Revolutionary Guards. The Sipah-i Pasdaran-i Inquilabi Islami, to give the full title, or Corps of the Guardians of the Islamic Revolution—more simply, the Islamic Revolutionary Guards, are one of the mainstays of the Islamic state in Iran. As an institution, they had their origins in some of the street fighter groups active against the army in the closing days of the rule of the Shah. Following the revolution, on Khomeini's orders, they became organized by the new Islamic Republican Party, which had been founded as the political arm of the *ulama,* and used against the two guerrilla opposition groups, the **Fidayin-i Khalq** and the **Mujahidin-i Khalq**.

Subsequently the guards (*pasdars*) were built up as a military force loyal to the *ulama* and ready to protect the Islamic state against any attempted *coup* by the army. The protracted Iran–Iraq war of 1980–1988 facilitated this process, the guards eventually being accorded a ministry in their own right (although it was dissolved at the end of the war). Following the Israeli invasion of Lebanon in 1982, three thousand Pasdaran were sent to that country, where their presence contributed to the relative decline of **Amal**, and the growing influence of **Hizbollah**. They remain a significant power base for the radicals against the pragmatists in the country's leadership, although the latter are currently dominant under Ayatollah Rafsanjani, the President.

Under the Pasdaran organization, a further movement, of "boy warriors", emerged (the **Bassij**).

Islamic Salvation Front. This Algerian Islamist movement is better known by its name in French, **Front Islamique du Salut—FIS**.

Islamic Tendency Movement. The leading Muslim fundamentalist organization in Tunisia, the MTI (Mouvement de la Tendance Islamique) has been known since November 1988 as the Renaissance Party, **Hizb al-Nahda**.

Islamic Unity Movement. This **Sunni** Muslim organization, also known as the Islamic Unification Movement (Harakat al-Tawhid al-Islami), is a fundamentalist group in the Lebanon which co-operates with the **Shi'ite** organization, **Hizbollah**, whose puritanical moral views and commitment to an Islamic state in Lebanon it shares.

Islami Hareket. The Islami Hareket—Islamic Movement—is an extremist Turkish group about which little is known but which has claimed responsibility for the murder of several prominent secularists in 1990. Links have been alleged between this organization and **Hizbollah**, but there is no clear public evidence of the claim (although it is true that supporters of Hizbollah—Hizbullahiler—have published periodicals in Turkey).

Isma'ilis. With a modern following of several million dispersed through India, Pakistan, East Africa and the Middle East, the Isma'ilis represent the largest branch of **Shi'ite** *Islam after the Imamis or* **Twelvers**. The sect emerged after the death of the sixth of the Shi'ite Imams, Ja'far al-Sadiq, in 765. Ja'far had originally intended his eldest son, Isma'il, to succeed him, but the latter died prematurely and the imamate passed to his brother Musa instead, in the line of Imams which went on to form the basis of Twelver Shi'ism. However, various factions dissented, some claiming that Isma'il was still alive, others that the imamate rightfully belonged to his son Muhammad. They are all commonly referred to as Isma'ilis (collectively Isma'iliya), or sometimes Seveners, since they diverge from the Twelvers in recognizing Isma'il as the seventh Imam.

In various guises, Isma'ili Shi'ism rapidly became the most militant alternative to **Sunni** orthodoxy and the political control of the dominant Abbasid dynasty. An efficient propaganda system developed under the first Isma'ili Imams, and in 909 the North African branch of the sect established the powerful Fatimid dynasty in Egypt, which flourished until 1171. Sub-branches such as the Qaramita (Carmathians) caused political upheaval in Arabia, the Yemen, and elsewhere.

Following a split in 1094, the Fatimid Isma'ilis divided into two main branches: **Musta'lis** and **Nizaris**. It is this latter branch which today represents the majority of the world's Isma'ili population, and which has become well known through the activities of its *imams,* who have used the title Agha Khan since the 19th century (hence the label **Aga Khanis**). The most radical group to break away from the Fatimid Isma'ilis was that of the **Druzes**.

Isma'ili doctrine emphasizes the esoteric interpretation of religious belief, distinguishing outward (*zahir*) from inward (*batin*) truths—hence the widespread use of the alternative name Batiniya for the sect. Outward Isma'ili thought and practice is essentially orthodox in structure, with little divergence from either Sunni or Twelver Shi'ite norms. The esoteric doctrine presents Islamic ideas within a perspective influenced by Greek philosophy, particularly Neoplatonism, to which alchemical, **kabbalistic**, and astrological ideas have been grafted. A cyclical theory of revelation divides history into seven periods, each initiated by a prophet, followed by six *imams*.

Isolated Radio–Church Groups. During the past 50 years radios have become much more widely available throughout the world. This has enabled church organizations to maintain a Christian presence in countries where the Christian religion (or certain forms of it) is banned. The two main organizations broadcasting **Protestant** programmes worldwide are Trans World Radio, based in Monaco (with an additional major radio station in the Netherlands Antilles) and Voice of the Andes (HCJB) in Quito, Ecuador. Both use high-powered transmitters and broadcast in many different languages all over the world. A similar service for **Roman Catholics** is operated by Radio Vatican. An alternative approach is the radio correspondence course, run by such organizations as the International Correspondence Institute based in Belgium.

Christians converted by such radio broadcasts beamed to anti-Christian countries are entirely dependent on the radio for their Christian teaching and nurture. They are not members of any specific denomination. Such small groups may number up to 20 adults, isolated from any other Christian contact. It is very difficult to estimate numbers; calculations have been based on the number of letters to the major Christian broadcasting stations, but these are dependent on the level of adult literacy and the reliability (including the absence of censorship) of the postal system.

In the 1980s it was estimated that there were up to 2,000,000 such isolated radio–church Christians in Europe, of which three-quarters were believed to be in the USSR and the rest in Eastern European countries. Now that Soviet states are declaring independence and Christian worship and even evangelization is more widely accepted, the role of such broadcasting is changing and it is possible that these previously isolated groups may be integrated into the wider church.

Ithna 'Asharis. The "Ithna 'Asharis" are the "Twelvers" within Shi'ism, and thus the **Twelver Shi'ites**.

Iyengar Yoga. Iyengar Yoga is the system of yogic teaching and practice associated with the name of BKS Iyengar. Born in India in 1918, Iyengar suffered from a weak constitution but through the practice of yoga under the guidance of various teachers, including his *guru* Professor T. Krishnamacharya, the founder of **Viniyoga**, he brought himself to an exemplary state of health. As he writes, in the essay "The Body Is My Temple". '. . . in the year 1934–35 a doctor examined me in school. My height then was four feet 10 inches. I weighed 70 pounds. My chest measurement was twenty two inches and chest expansion was only half an inch. Today my height is five feet six inches, weight is 145 pounds and my chest expands by five inches'.

All who came into contact with Iyengar were impressed by his mastery in the performance of yogic postures (*asana*). Among his more well-known students were the religious thinker **J. Krishnamurti** and the violinist Yehudi Menuhin. It was Menuhin who, in 1961, first invited Iyengar to teach yoga in the West. From that time onwards Iyengar made regular visits to London to offer instruction in yoga. In 1969 the Iyengar method was recommended for use in the Inner London Education Authority's adult education classes. The following year a teacher's certificate for Iyengar teachers was introduced and then, in 1977, the **BKS Iyengar Yoga Teachers'**

Association was founded as the professional body for Iyengar trained teachers. Practitioners of this method now teach yoga in many countries across the world.

Despite the emphasis placed on yoga postures, the Iyengar approach seeks to integrate this practice with breath control and spiritual development. This is attested by, among other things, the fact that Iyengar has published a translation of and commentary on Patanjali's classic yoga text *The Yoga Sutras*. In some circles Iyengar's style of teaching is regarded as harsh and potentially harmful. However, those who have worked closely with him liken his approach to that of a rather stern **Zen** master, who might appear frightening to the student but who, through acute perception and skilful intervention, facilitates rapid progress in those under his guidance.

Like many eminent men, BKS Iyengar is a controversial figure. What cannot be doubted is that he has been a leader in the dissemination of yoga to the west and one of the outstanding personalities in the yoga world of the 20th century. His book *Light on Yoga* is a bestseller which, along with his other publications and the **Light on Yoga Association** he founded, will ensure that his approach continues to be a major influence on the development of yoga in the West during the 21st century.

Izumo Oyashirokyo. A Japanese revivalist **Shinto** group and one of the traditional 13 constituent sects of **Kyoha Shinto.**

J

Ja'faris. The term derives from the concept of **Twelver Shi'ism** as a fifth law school within Islam, with its origins in the legal teachings of the sixth Imam, Ja'far al-Sadiq (d. 765). The other four law schools—**Maliki**, **Hanafi**, **Shafi'i**, **Hanbali**— are found in **Sunnism**.

Jainas. Followers of the ancient and unbroken Indian religious tradition of Jainism, named after the *Jinas* or "Victors". According to traditional accounts, reflected in iconography and devotional practice, there are 24 such *Jinas* or *Tirthankaras* (Ford Builders) in each half-cycle of cosmic time. Mahāvīra (The Great Hero—c599–527 BCE is the most recent as well as the last *Tirthankaras* in the current half-cycle. For historical purposes, he is considered the founder of Jainism, and many of the earliest surviving texts claim to record his teaching. After his death, Jainism flourished, especially in north-east India, with many groups of wandering ascetics relying upon a substantial lay following to provide them both with begged food and new recruits. The majority of these ascetics, as appears to have been the case throughout Jaina history, were nuns.

According to traditional accounts, a famine (c300 BCE) caused part of the community to migrate south, a geographical redistribution that apparently led to a religious dispute when the two groups resumed contact. Starting as an argument about accurate memory of the oral tradition (and thus about what constitutes the scriptural canon), this eventually (79CE) engendered a major schism in the ascetic community, dividing it into **Svetambaras** (the white-clad) and **Digambaras** (the sky-clad), a division maintained to the present day. The names used reflect what became the chief point at issue: does the renunciation of all possessions, which is one of the prerequi-

sites for becoming a true monk, require the complete abandonment of clothing?

In doctrinal terms, little divides the two major Jaina sects. Early practice was conditioned by three beliefs: (i) that nearly all matter, including the elements, is alive (in the sense of containing living beings or souls); (ii) that doing harm to these beings is wrong; and (iii) that such wrong action will have a deleterious effect upon the future condition and births of the actor. This effect is produced through the mechanism of *karma,* which, according to Jaina doctrine, consists of subtle matter that invades the soul of the passionate agent and literally weighs it down. Through the operation of diligent care and dispassionate restraint in all circumstances, and the cultivation of rigorous ascetic practice, accumulated *karma* can be shed and fresh accumulations prevented. The object is to attain complete liberation from the bonds of matter, a state of omniscient and blissful isolation at the apex of the inhabited universe.

The key element in Jaina practice is strict adherence to the principle of non-violence (*ahimsa*). Given that souls are ubiquitous, it is particularly important to restrict one's range and consumption of food. All Jainas are therefore strictly vegetarian, and fasting plays a central role in both ascetic and lay practice. The ideal death is one of ritually controlled starvation.

The development of a technical philosophy which stresses the manifold nature of reality and the relative nature of any possible statement about it has helped to check potential threats to ascetic practice from theoretical speculation about such matters as, for example, the reality of karmic bondage. Asceticism, through the living example of the monks and nuns, as well as through extensive and precisely formulated lay practices such as fasting has always been a focal point for the Jaina community's sense of its own identity.

Ascetics have a pedagogical and exemplary rather than a priestly function. For the majority of the laity, however, the practice of religion has been concentrated in temple worship (*puja*). Devotion to the *Tirthankaras*, who have gone beyond human contact, is considered fundamentally reflexive and meditative in nature; there are, however, numerous attendant deities who can be influenced on the Hindu pattern.

Both of the main Jaina sects enjoyed substantial royal patronage at various times. By the 12th century, however, the Muslim invasions in north India, and the increasing strength of Hindu sectarianism in the south, ensured a decline in both numbers and political influence. Further divisions took place within the two main sects, mainly concerning the use of images in temple worship.

Today there are concentrations of Svetambaras in north-east India and Digambaras in the south, and all main cities have Jain communities. Although there are perhaps less than 3,000,000 Jainas in India (including 6,150 ascetics, nearly three-quarters of whom are nuns), their economic and ethical influence is disproportionately great. Much of their prosperity is channelled into temple building and other religious activities. In the second half of the 20th century, Jainas have migrated, largely via East Africa, to establish small communities throughout the world. The first Jain temple in Europe was opened in Leicester in 1988.

The Jains have built many temples and produced outstanding examples of religious art and architecture throughout the subcontinent. As well as preserving Prākrit and Sanskrit classical religious texts in their temple libraries, they have also played a major role in the production of narrative literature of all kinds in various vernaculars. The pervasive influence of their cardinal doctrine of *ahimsā* on Indian thought and culture has been highlighted again in the 20th century by **Mahatma Gandhi**'s espousal of non-violence under the influence of the Jaina layman, **Srimad Rajchandra** (Raychandbai Mehta).

Jalaliya. The Jalaliya is a branch of the South Asian **Sufi** order, the **Suhrawardiya**. Its members have tended to move outside the shari'a, favouring the use of drugs, and to become identified with **Shi'ism**.

Jama'at al-Ikhwan al-Muslimin. The Society of the Muslim Brothers is the full title of the important organization more commonly referred to simply as the **Muslim Brotherhood**.

al-Jama'at al-Islamiya. Although described in some press accounts as a particular organization, the designation al-Jama'at al-Islamiya is better understood as referring to a cluster of militant Islamist groups that have become a feature of Egyptian society in the last two decades. The labels Islamic Groups and Islamic Leagues have both been used to refer to the organizations in question. They recruit among university students and also in deprived suburbs e.g. of Cairo, especially among new arrivals from the countryside. Links are thought to exist between various of these groups and al-Jihad (the **Jihad Organization**)—responsibility has been variously attributed to both for the assassination in Cairo in May 1992 of a prominent critic of Islamist movements, Farag Fouda.

Membership of the Islamic Groups is believed to have swollen into thousands in recent years, and in some villages of Upper Egypt they have virtually replaced the forces of the state in the provision of various services including law and order. The government has responded from time to time with attempted crackdowns, particularly in the wake of incidents such as the shooting of 13 villagers, mostly **Copts**, in the volatile governorate of Asyut in June 1992, and also revenge attacks on the police in the same area.

Meanwhile the banned but tolerated **Muslim Brotherhood** distances itself from violence, but failed to condemn the murder of Dr Fouda, leading to surmises that there may have developed at least a tacit alliance between the Brotherhood and the Jama'at.

Jama'at al-Nur. The Jama'at al-Nur, or Association of Light, is an alternative name for the Turkish Muslim renewal group more generally referred to as the **Nurcus** (or Nurcular Camaati).

Jama'at al-Takfir wa'l-Hijra. The "Atonement and Flight from Sin Society" is (or was) an extremist Islamist group in Egypt. It is commonly referred to more simply as **al-Takfir wa'l-Hijra**.

Jama'at-i Islami. The Jama'at-i Islami is a leading part of what has come to be called the "Islamic movement" in the second half of the 20th century. It is at the same time a prime example of "Muslim fundamentalism", which may be defined as a concern to return to what Muslims feel is the original form and intent of Islamic doctrine, but one which is much influenced by its 20th-century context. As such it shares similarities of concern and of approach with the leaders of the Iranian revolution, and with the **Muslim Brotherhood** and its more recent offshoots in Egypt. Indeed, its ideas played a significant role in the second stage in the ideological development of the Brotherhood from the 1950s onwards. Unlike other movements from South Asia, which were primarily concerned to develop ways of surviving as Muslims under colonial rule, the Jama'at has been concerned to answer the larger question of how to be Muslim in the face of the dominance of Western civilization. Power, it argues, is essential to the preservation of Islamic civilization. The Jama'at is an élite party of the righteous which is concerned to unite Islam with that prime expression of 20th century power, the modern state.

The origins of the Jama'at lie in the ideas of Saiyid Abul A'la Maududi (1903–1979), who was a journalist and a theologian but not a man with the training of a traditional Islamic scholar. By the 1930s, when he became editor of *Tarjuman al-Quran,* which was to be the vehicle of his ideas for the rest of his life, Maududi knew that his life's mission was, as he wrote, to "break the hold which Western culture and ideas had come to acquire over the Muslim intelligentsia, and to instill in them the fact that Islam has a code of life of its own". He opposed the movement for Pakistan on the grounds that what was needed was not a nation-state of Muslims but an Islamic state. In 1941 he founded the Jama'at to put this idea into practice.

Maududi's political vision may be expressed thus. Central is the belief that God alone is sovereign; man has gone astray because he has accepted sovereigns other than God—for instance, kings, nation-states or custom. All the guidance which man needs can be found in the Islamic Holy Law (Shari'a) which offers a complete scheme of life where nothing is superfluous and nothing lacking. Political power is essential to put this divinely ordained pattern into effect; the Islamic state has a missionary purpose. Moreover, because God's guidance extends to all human activity, this state must be universal and all-embracing, and because the state's purpose is to establish Islamic ideology it must be run by those who believe in it and comprehend its spirit—those who do not may just live within the confines of the state as non-Muslim citizens (zimmis). Naturally this state recognizes that God, not man, is the source of all law. The state is merely God's vice-regent (khalifa) on earth.

The Jama'at is highly organized from the head of the organization, or Amir (Maududi held this position until 1970), to its provincial and district branches. The central organization is based in Lahore—despite his original opposition to the creation of Pakistan, Maududi moved there after its founding in 1947. Normal membership is restricted: often an applicant is kept under observation for months to see whether his behaviour meets the Jama'at's standards. Thus in 1971 the organization had only 2,500 members, but several hundred thousand postulants. Finance comes mainly from donations, and from the royalties derived from Maududi's many books.

Despite its small numbers the Jama'at has had a considerable impact on the politics of Pakistan. It campaigned successfully for the introduction of Islamic clauses to the Pakistani constitution of 1956, it consistently opposed the martial law régime of Ayub Khan, played an important role in the overthrow of Mr Bhutto in 1977, and had significant influence in the first few years of Zia ul-Haq's régime when Shariat (Shari'a) courts—operative still today—were established. The December 1991 Lahore High Court decision upholding the supremacy of Islamic law over all other laws in Pakistan demonstrates its influence. Its members constantly seek positions of influence from which they can advance their Islamic purpose, and up to May 1992 the Jama'at constituted the second most powerful part of Pakistan's ruling Islamic Democratic Alliance: it walked out in protest against the Prime Minister's refusal to continue backing its long standing ally among the Afghan mujahadeen leader, Gulbaddin Hekmatyar.

In Bangladesh the Jama'at has considerable organizational strength, deriving support in particular from the younger generation who have been through higher education. In recent elections it has managed to win up to 20 seats in the Bangladesh parliament. In India, on the other hand, the Jama'at is of little political significance. In Britain it is represented by the UK Islamic Mission based in Leicester, its publications being produced by the associated Islamic Foundation, also in Leicester.

Jama'at-i Islami of Bangladesh. The **Jama'at-i Islami**, with its main base in Pakistan, remains a significant and controversial organization in the former East Pakistan too. Its leader, Golam Azam, is believed by many in Bangladesh to have led the collaborators with Pakistan during the brutal civil war of 1971 which gave birth to Bangladesh as a separate country, and to have organized the killing of leading intellectuals at that time. The Jama'at was formally banned until 1975, since when it has grown considerably, and in the 1991 general election it gained 18 seats in the National Assembly. It apparently receives strong funding from Saudi Arabia, and members of its powerful student wing at Chittagong University are known to carry arms. Violent clashes between its supporters and detractors occur with some frequency.

Jama'at-i Islami of India. The Jama'at-i Islami of India is the sister organization of Maududi's **Jama'at-i Islami**, now based in Pakistan. Whereas the latter, however, works to promote an Islamic state, its Indian counterpart continues the policy—developed in pre-Partition days—of distancing itself from this objective. Reflecting the minority, relatively vulnerable, status of Muslims in India, the Indian Jama'at is committed to the defence of a secular Indian state as a guarantee, at least in principle, of a safe future for Islam in the country. It is of little contemporary political significance, in contrast to the Jama'at in Pakistan (and Bangladesh).

Jama'at Tabligh. Jama'at Tabligh is an alternative way of referring to the important Islamic reform movement **Tablighi Jama'at**.

Jam'iat ul-Ulama-i Ahl-i Hadith. This Society of Ulama of the People of the Hadith is a Pakistani **Sunni** Muslim organization whose members are often known as **Wahhabis** because of their strict views. The South Asian **Ahl-i Hadith** movement of which they are an expression is described elsewhere. They are close to the Saudi religious establishment, as their views would lead one to expect, and oppose Iranian influence on Pakistan (prominent in a rival organization, the **Movement for the Enforcement of Ja'fari Law**). Support is drawn mainly from the business community in Karachi and parts of the Punjab.

Jam'iat ul-Ulama-i Hind. The Association of Indian Ulama, founded in 1919, is an organization of India's Muslim clerics which is concerned with the welfare of Muslims throughout the nation. It has its seat in Delhi. Inspired by the **Deobandi** movement, it has sought to avoid involvement in politics while supporting the idea of a democratic secular state. It opposed the two-nation theory of Jinnah which formed the ideological basis for the creation of Pakistan as a Muslim state. Relatedly, it advocates co-operation between Muslims and non-Muslims, and between Muslims and government in India, as means for the creation and maintenance of a prosperous, integrated country. It actively encourages the spread of Islamic education, promotes the study of Urdu, organises religious courts for settling matrimonial disputes (it sees itself as the guardian of Muslim personal law), and provides assistance for widows, orphans, and people hurt or harmed in communal disturbances.

After partition in 1947, a Pakistani wing developed, the Jam'iat ul-Ulama-i Islam.

In 1988 a split occurred, leading to the emergence of a breakaway group, the Milli Jam'iat ul-Ulama-i Hind.

Jam'iat ul-Ulama-i Islam. The Pakistani wing of the **Jam'iat ul-Ulama-i Hind**.

Jam'iat ul-Ulama-i Pakistan. The Pakistani organization of the **Barelvi** movement in South Asian Islam. The notable political figure, Maulana Noorani, is a prominent member.

Jam'iyat al-Islah al-Ijtima'i. A **Sunni** Islamist organization based in Kuwait and known in English as the **Society for Social Reform**.

Jehovah's Witnesses. An **Adventist** sect founded by Charles Taze Russell who in 1872 started the International Bible Students' Association in Pittsburgh, USA. Soon he became the pastor of his own independent church and in 1879 began publishing a magazine *The Watchtower* to publicize his beliefs.

Having rejected his **Presbyterian** background, he was influenced by **Adventists** who believed the Bible could be used to predict the time and manner of the end of the world. Russell's studies led him to believe that Christ's coming took place invisibly in 1874 and that the Second Coming would be in 1914. He also concluded that the correct name for God is Jehovah and that Jesus was not one person of the divine Trinity but was originally the Archangel Michael, one of the sons of Jehovah (the other being Satan). His followers took the name Jehovah's Witnesses and called their meeting places "Kingdom Halls".

The Jehovah's Witnesses have always concentrated on getting converts. This is done by going out to people's homes, trying to get into discussion and to disseminate their literature. Their study of the Bible has led them to reject blood transfusions, participation in politics (on the grounds that since the Second Coming, national governments are in conflict with the rule of Christ) and the celebrating of festivals such as Christmas, Easter and birthdays. Their meetings focus on Bible study and methods of winning converts.

The organization has always been authoritarian and is now controlled by a Governing Body in Brooklyn, USA. All members are assigned an area to evangelize, and are required to report on their activities. Members may be disciplined by being expelled from the fellowship of believers. There is an intense antipathy to the established churches whose beliefs are misrepresented and abused.

There are believed to be about 6,000,000 Jehovah's Witnesses worldwide.

Jesuits. A **Roman Catholic** religious order founded by Ignatius Loyola, who was born in 1491 in the Spanish Basque country. His new Order, the Jesuits, or "Society of Jesus" (S.J.), won Papal recognition in 1540. Hans Urs von Balthasar, an ex-Jesuit theologian, notes Ignatius's "strange affinities" with Cervantes's Don Quixote. The Society was intended to combat Protestantism, to convert unbelievers and to educate the young. It has retained, especially, the latter aim. Its arsenal has been Ignatius's *Spiritual Exercises*— imaginative meditations on the life of Christ—arduous intellectual training, and military discipline. During the religious conflicts of the 16th century, many Jesuits were trained to undergo martyrdom; some achieved it. By the time of Ignatius's death in 1556, Jesuit missionaries had taken the gospel to China and to India. From 1609, in the virgin territory of South America, they created the "Reductions of Paraguay" (spread across Uruguay, part of Brazil and most of Argentina). These were self-supporting settlements, governed by the Indians under Jesuit supervision. The Jesuits' watchful gaze also deterred Portuguese slave traders. The Society undertook to convert the South American Indians, and to construct the Reductions, on the condition that their charges would not be subject to colonial exploitation. By 1767 the Jesuits had been driven from Spain, Portugal and South America. Political pressure compelled Pope Clement XIV to dissolve their Order in 1773. The Society was recalled to life in 1814 by Pius VII. Much as the **Benedictines** had illumined pre-Reformation Christianity, so the Jesuits' heroism and theatricality, with a strong suggestion of political intrigue, crimsoned the Catholicism of the baroque age.

Having been the engineers of the Counter-Reformation Church, the Jesuits were also its creatures. Vatican II brought revision. At the Society's 31st General Congregation in 1965–1966, Pope Paul VI intimated that their new enterprise must be the struggle against "atheism". The new General, Fr. Pedro Arrupe, interpreted the fresh direction in what became a characteristic manner: "The battle against atheism is identical in part with the battle against poverty . . .". The 32nd and 33rd General Congregations stated that the primary aim of the Society is the propagation of justice. Some of the young Jesuits of South America, where the Society is once more concentrated, took this to entail the overthrow of established régimes. Pope John Paul I warned them against "temptations to secularism"; so has John Paul II. Fr. Peter-Hans Kolvenbach, the Dutch man who was elected General at the 33rd Congregation in 1983, forbids members to be government ministers or to indulge in "negative criticism" of the Church. He is committed to the Jesuits' identification with "the poorest of the poor", considering that this must be woven into the curricula of their 2,000 universities, colleges and schools. In addition to the three vows taken in all Orders, of poverty, chastity and obedience, some (currently 63 per cent) Jesuits take a fourth vow: to be loyal to the Pope. Although the fourth vow has not, as many wish, been extended to all, it is now offered on the basis of pastoral work as well as academic achievement. The Jesuits' long academic initiation has also been abbreviated. There were 36,000 Jesuits in 1965; there are now about 24,000, including students and lay brothers. Fr. Kolvenbach attributes the decline to ". . . the absence of spiritual vitality in our ecclesial communities" and to the "diminishing attraction of austere apostolic labours . . .". They must bear in mind that Quixote is "the true patron saint of Catholic Action".

Jesus Army. Formerly known as the "Bugbrooke Community" after the village in Northants (UK) where it began, "Jesus Fellowship", or "Jesus Fellowship (Baptist)", or "Jesus People", this British movement was founded in 1969, after a mystical experience by Noel Stanton, a lay pastor since 1957. He is regarded as "the prophet" who expounds an authoritative interpretation of "God's will". The 1970s saw a significant expansion of the movement with houses opening for former drug addicts, the purchase of New Creation Hall and New Creation Farm, and community businesses. Discipling and shepherding groups began, with an "elder", said to be "in the Spirit", acting as guardian over 25–30 members in his spiritual care. For communal living an austere and spartan lifestyle was adopted with no contraception, celibacy as the "higher way", separation from worldly things, i.e. TV, cinema, non-Christian literature.

From a **Protestant** point of view the Jesus Army appears orthodox. It is the movement's lifestyle and practices, especially shepherding, which have provoked controversy. The death of five members in the late 1970s stirred a widespread campaign, with accusations against the movement as a "cult", similar to those levelled against "the **Moonies**": breaking-up of families, brainwashing and aggressive authoritarianism. This led to an enquiry by the Evangelical Alliance (EA)—an umbrella organization for **evangelical** groups—in 1986 resulting in the exclusion of the Fellowship from the EA and the **Baptist** Union.

By the mid-1980s the organization had a 700-strong following with some continuing to live as ordinary church members and others in communal residence in one of the movement-owned houses. After starting up in the Midlands, the organization now works nationwide and has stepped up its activities in London. Of central importance is evangelism which is organized in great public events such as "Jesus Marches", "tent missions", and "street witnessing"; members are instantly recognizable by their army combat jackets, banners and badges. The Jesus Army (as the former Jesus Fellowship has called itself since 1986) target the "forgotten people"—the working class and the fringes of society.

Jesus Fellowship. This, prior to 1986, was the name of the movement currently called the **Jesus Army.**

Jesus Movement. The Jesus Movement, better known as the Jesus People or Jesus Freaks, and occasionally referred to as "Street Christians", consisted of a wide range of groups, ministries and evangelistic endeavours which emerged late in the 1960s. Although they differed considerably in terms of style, details of theology and practice, as well as social organization, they shared a commitment to a fundamentalist interpretation of the Bible, coupled with expectations of the millennium. They focused on the worship of Jesus, including a belief in the working of the Holy Spirit through Pentecostal gifts. This type of worship—characteristic of traditional American evangelism—was combined with features of a countercultural way of life. While members of the movement abstained from sex and drugs, they retained hippy garb, long hair, rock music and a communal lifestyle. In some cases more fundamentalist and evangelical churches supported Jesus People type groups as a means of winning young people back from the counter culture. The first following was drawn from that (hippies, drop-outs, drug users), typically aged between fourteen and twenty-four, from a middle or upper-middle class white background. Claiming to be "spiritual revolutionaries" or the "revolution for Jesus" they sought to bring about change through spiritual efforts, after the secular ones had obviously failed. The musical "Jesus Christ Superstar" acted as a medium for these ideas. At the same time the movement offered a meaningful community where worldly materialism, competition and achievement had no place.

During the gradual decline of the counter culture, most of the Jesus People groups withered away; some of their followers have found their way back to the more **evangelical** of the conventional denominations, others have become more "respectable" by moving closer to **Pentecostalism.**

Jewish Feminist Groups. Jewish feminist groups are united by their desire for active participation in Jewish ritual, whether they are composed of observant or non-observant women. Group activities vary from religious retreats organized by B'not Ash ("daughters of fire" (annually)) and Nishmat Nashim ("Women's Soul" (bi-annually)) to organized prayer groups, in cities such as Baltimore, Chicago, Houston, and New York City.

Some groups, such as the Washington Heights Women's Service, use the traditional prayerbook; others rewrite traditional ceremonies, as shown by the various "women's *haggadot*" (prayerbook used for the festive evening meal(s) of Passover). Many women's groups gather once a month to celebrate *Rosh Hodesh* (New Moon), a holiday that was generally ignored until discussion of it in *The Jewish Catalog* prompted new interest in it, especially by women, who according to tradition, do not work on that day as a reward for not participating in the worship of the Golden Calf. *Rosh Hodesh* groups exist in a number of cities, including Boston, Montreal, and New York City. Additionally, many groups, including those that use the traditional prayerbook, have written new naming services for their daughters. In the late 1980s, a group of women who wished to read from the Torah on the women's side of the Western Wall, aroused great controversy, despite the group's leaders being Orthodox women. The Israeli Supreme Court (August 1989) ruled that the "women of the wall" must pray "in accordance with the custom of the site". At the end of 1988 the

"First International Conference on the Empowerment of Jewish Women" was held in Jerusalem, co-sponsored by the American Jewish Congress, the World Jewish Congress and the Israeli Women's Network. Jewish lesbians, in addition to being part of larger groups, also have their own separate synagogues and prayer groups.

Jewish New Agers. See also **Havurat Judaism.**) Jewish New Age movements are part of the wider emergence of New Age groups in the contemporary world, especially Europe and the USA. While these Jewish groups share interests in spiritual, experiential, therapeutic and meditative practices, and mystical theologies with other New Agers, they draw on specifically Jewish sources and traditions, particularly **Kabbalah** and **Hasidism.** New Age Judaism is made up of a number of diverse groups. Leaders include Rabbis Shlomo Carlebach (born 1926), Zalman Schachter-Shalomi (born 1924), Joseph H. Gelberman (born 1912) and Dr. Philip S. Berg.

Carlebach ("the singing rabbi"), an **Orthodox** rabbi and well-known composer and singer of Hasidic songs and teller of Hasidic tales, travelled in the late 1960s, teaching of the coming New Age of universal oneness; the life of celebration; methods for the transformation of consciousness, and outlining the crucial part that Jews are to play in this process. Carlebach teaches not only the ways of Jewish life but its "innerness" (Pnimiyyut). Influenced by many of ideas of the counterculture, he was the inspiration behind the establishment of a number of communal houses—for example, The House of Love and Prayer (San Francisco) and Or Chadash ("New Light", in Los Angeles). Approximately 40 families currently live in Moshav Me'or Mod'in, a communal settlement in Israel, involved in the production of organic and other health foods, founded by Carlebach in the 1970s. The Network for Conscious

Judaism, founded by David Zeller, serves to disseminate Carlebach's form of New Age Judaism.

Schachter-Shalomi, a **Lubavitch** Hasidic rabbi and Religious Studies professor, found his life changing after "dropping acid" with Timothy Leary in 1959. This experience both re-affirmed his commitment to his Jewish tradition (although he later cut his ties with the Lubavitch Hasidim) and created an openness to other spiritual teachings. He was involved in Havurat Shalom (see **Havurat Judaism**) and in 1962 began formulating his plans for a centre to promote "Jewish renewal". This centre was to be a forum for experiments in prayer, the study of Jewish sources, the development of spirituality and the exploration of other forms of creativity. In 1975 he founded the B'nai Or ("Sons of Light") spiritual community in Philadelphia (renamed less chauvinistically as the P'nai Or ("Faces of Light") Religious Fellowship in 1985). Practices at the centre include Jungian psychotherapy, Hindu and Buddhist meditative techniques, Kabbalistic and Hasidic study and contemporary music and dance. Schachter-Sholomi became the leading "guru" for Jewish New Agers and groups across the USA and Canada affiliated to B'nai Or. He was influential in the setting up of one of the best known Jewish New Age groups, the Aquarian *Minyan* in Berkeley, California. There were seven P'Nai Or fellowships in the USA and Canada and two in Europe. Schachter-Sholomi is the author of many influential articles and books on New Age Judaism, including the guidebooks, *The First Step: A Guide for the New Jewish Spirituality* (1975; 1983, with D. Gropman) and *Fragments of a Future Scroll: Hassidism for the Aquarian Age* (1975). Recently, the Aquarian Minyan and a number of fellowships that have broken away from Schachter-Sholomi's organization together with other groups have formed The Network Renewal Communities.

Gelberman is an Orthodox rabbi who has developed a New Age Judaism, that brings together *Kabbalah* and Hasidic teachings (particularly as mediated by Martin Buber) with psychotherapy and New Age metaphysics. He has founded a number of institutions, including The Little Synagogue (New York); The Mid-Way Counseling Center; The Foundation for Spiritual Living; The Kabbalah Centre, and two inter-faith organizations, The Metaphysical Centre and The New Seminary.

Yehudah Ashlag (1886–1955) founded a *Yeshivah* in Bene Berak in Israel where particular attention is given to the study of the *Zohar* (a 13th century mystical commentary on the Hebrew Bible and the foundational text of the *Kabbalah*). The translator of sections of the *Zohar* from Aramaic to Hebrew and the author of *Ha-Sullam (The Ladder)*, a commentary on this text, he also established the Research Centre of Kabbalah in Jerusalem. Dr. Berg, the current head of the Centre, is the author of a number of books on *Kabbalah* which stress its use as a source of knowledge about astrology, reincarnation, energy and other New Age concerns. The Centre has branches in New York, Los Angeles, Chicago, Tel Aviv, Paris, Mexico City, London, Antwerp and Hong Kong.

Other figures include, Rabbi Joel DeKoven who teaches yoga and Rabbi Alvin Boboff, the co-founder of Dynamic Judaism, who practises psychic healing. Jewish New Age groups continue to grow and to network with each other as they develop new forms of the Jewish tradition that integrate New Age teachings.

Jewish Theological Seminary (JTS). *See* **Conservative Judaism.**

Jihad-i Sazandigi. Jihad-i Sazandigi, or Reconstruction Crusade, is an organization formed in Iran in 1979, immediately after the revolution that brought Ayatollah Khomeini to power, for the purpose (among others) of taking the Islamic

Revolution to the countryside. It became an important channel through which the new Islamic Republican Party, the political arm of the *ulama,* was able to extend its influence throughout the country.

Originally intended as a mass organization, it has become rather more exclusive—some would say narrow and doctrinaire—through insisting on purging itself of members regarded as being insufficiently committed to the cause of the Islamic Republic. Unlike the Pasdaran (**Islamic Revolutionary Guards**) or **Bassij**, the Jihad has a non-military character, and has been very active, especially in parts of the country ravaged during the war with Iraq, in rural development projects and reconstruction. Its members have built and staffed clinics and schools, as well as labouring on roads and other infrastructural projects such as bringing water and electricity to the villages. Membership falls predominantly in the 20–30 years age range.

Jihad Organization. The Jihad Organization (Tanzim al-Jihad) is the deadliest of the Egyptian Islamist groups committed to the use of violence. It was responsible for the assassination of President Sadat in 1981. Despite widespread arrests, and the imposition of death sentences or varying terms of imprisonment in trials in 1981–82 and again in 1984, further outbreaks of violence and, in 1987, assassination attempts on two former government ministers have been the responsibility of al-Jihad (as it is often known) and its splinter groups.

Violent clashes with the police have continued, and in 1988 there were also clashes with members of the **Muslim Brotherhood**. In contrast to the latter, al-Jihad regards its country's Muslim leaders as guilty of apostasy from Islam, and as ruling the state by heathen laws. These laws should be replaced by the Shari‘a (Islamic law), and the means to this end is to fight to overthrow the heretical and despotic rulers. Muslims have neglected the *jihad,* a duty they must rediscover. Should it cost them their lives—whether in battle or as a

result of state execution—paradise will be their martyr's reward.

Al-Jihad is among the groups believed to have sent members to fight with the Islamic resistance in Afghanistan. It refrained from calling for *jihad* on behalf of Iraq in the Gulf War of 1991, while at the same time warning against America's alleged objective of conditioning Muslims to accept their continued humiliation and the supremacy of the West.

Jikokyo. A Japanese mountain worship group, based on Mt. Fuji, and one of the traditional 13 constituent sects of **Kyoha Shinto.**

Jinja Honcho. Also known as the **Association of Shinto Shrines.**

Jinja Shinto. Until the end of World War II Shinto was intimately related to the state. Emperors were seen as *kami,* as descendants of the Sun goddess Amaterasu O Mikami (venerated at the Grand Ise Shrine, Mie Prefecture). The sacrality of state galvanized Japanese national identity and facilitated all kinds of political expedients at different points in history. Before the Meiji Restoration in 1867 it was quite possible to be Buddhist and still participate in Shinto activities, as Shintoism was perceived more as a cultural expression, than as a religion. To a certain extent this still holds true. In fact Shinto and Buddhism fused to such an extent that theories emerged to rationalize this phenomenon. During the anti-Buddhist purging of the Meiji era (1867–1912), however, Shinto once again stood alone as the unifier of the Japanese consciousness and carried the country through various wars, culminating in World War II. The war dead are enshrined at the controversial Yasukuni Shrine in Tokyo. After the war, in December 1945, under the American Shinto Directive, State Shinto was abolished; constitutional separation of religion and state was promulgated, and the Emperor was called upon to renounce his divinity. The new situation of religious freedom provided the basis for the establishment in February 1946 of the **Association of Shinto Shrines** (*Jinja Honcho*), a voluntary liaison body which now oversees the affairs of Shrine (*Jinja*) Shinto. Jinja Shinto claims around 62,000,000 adherents, but this figure must be qualified by the fact that Shinto membership is in no way binding or exclusivist, and that the public interact with Shinto activities selectively, in accordance with their perceived needs. The priesthood number around 26,000 and are trained at seminaries, or the Universities of Kokugakuin and Kogakkan.

Jocists. Members of the **Roman Catholic** organization, Jeunesse Ouvrière Chrétienne (Young Christian Workers), which was founded in Belgium after World War I by Father Joseph Cardijn. Established with the aim of taking root among factory workers in particular, its members meet in small groups where they discuss passages from the Bible and social problems.

Jodoshinshu. A form of Japanese **Pure Land Buddhism**, founded by Shinran (1173– 1262), a trained **Tendai** priest who sought inspiration from the **Pure Land** scriptures. He followed the Pure Land master Honen until 1202 when he was exiled as a result of the disapproval of the authorities over the rising interest in Pure Land devotion amongst the masses, who had hitherto had little contact with Buddhist teachings. During and after his exile Shinran wrote commentaries on the scriptures, the most famous of which is the *Kyogyoshinsho,* and hundreds of hymns in a vernacular style.

After his death, Jodoshinshu, the **True Pure Land School** (as differentiated from Honen's **Jodoshu** or **Pure Land School**) was disseminated variously by Shinran's descendants and disciples. The largest denominations today are those headed by direct descendants of Shinran, a continuing reminder of the founder's revolutionary marriage, which symbolically brought Buddhism into the realm of the previously secular Japanese family.

The Pure Land scriptures, believed to have been spoken by Sakyamuni Buddha, are *Mahayana* texts charting the career of Amida, the transhistorical Buddha venerated by Pure Land devotees. Shinran believed that during this age of degeneracy the individual has no choice but to rely completely on the grace of Amida to bring him to the Pure Land. Through the power of Amida, even an individual deeply bound by *karma* may, if the grace of Amida is invoked, achieve rebirth in the Pure Land.

Although Shinran claimed only to be continuing the work of his master, certain clear differences arose between Jodoshinshu and Jodoshu, due mainly to Shinran's insistence upon the worthlessness of self-effort for most people. Jodoshu maintains that the constant repetition of the *nembutsu* will secure rebirth, whilst for Shinran the fulcrum of the relationship between Amida and sentient beings is faith in Amida's boundless compassion, which arises from the realization of the individual's *karma*-bound and spiritually destitute nature. For him the *nembutsu* need only be called once.

Institutional Jodoshinshu is organized around a sense of gratitude to Amida, to the exclusion of all other Buddhas and Bodhisattvas. The veneration of Shinran is also important. The most significant festival on the Jodoshinshu calendar is *Ho-on-ko,* the yearly memorial of Shinran's death. As a distinctly Japanese form of Buddhism (one of the few that did not arrive in a package from China) institutional Jodoshinshu also embraces such aspects of Japanese ritual life as funerals and ancestor memorial services, which provide its financial basis.

Historically there are 10 sects of Jodoshinshu, the largest of which are the **Takadaha**, and two headed by Shinran's descendants who were originally caretakers of his mausoleum, **Shinshu Honganjiha** and **Shinshu Otaniha**. In these groups temple mastership frequently passes from father to son. In recent years however Otaniha has been torn by internal disputes and more than 400 disaffected temples have seceded.

As with all Japanese religions statistical status is inconclusive, partly because a whole household registers with a temple, regardless of the religious tendencies of individuals concerned, and because many Japanese tend to belong to more than one sect. Since Jodoshinshu provides the social function of dealing with death, this is often the only time members of the public encounter the institution. However, Jodoshinshu is one of the biggest single Buddhist sects in Japan, with something like 14,000,000 adherents.

Jodoshu. Jodoshu was the first major Buddhist **Pure Land** movement to gain firm foundations in Japanese society in the Kamakura era. The founder was Honen (1133–1212) who had practised **Tendai** *nembutsu* meditation on Mount Hiei, which he ultimately rejected in favour of single practice *nembutsu* repetition based on faith in the saving power of Amida. The *nembutsu* ("*Namu Amida Butsu*"—"I take refuge in Amida Buddha") was regarded by Honen to be the only operable vehicle to Enlightenment in this age of degeneracy and was seen as a means of purification. Jodoshu stresses the believer's own power to influence rebirth, a factor later to be eliminated by Honen's disciple Shinran, the founder of the **Jodoshinshu** movement.

The Chionin in Kyoto is the head temple of this sect, which claims around 3,000,000 adherents.

John Frum Movement. This is an example of the phenomena known as **cargo cults**. It is found in Vanuatu in the Pacific. "Frum" means "broom", and John Frum was thought of as someone in the tradition of John the Baptist who would sweep away the inequalities between New Hebrideans and Europeans, and usher in a new age of justice, happiness and prosperity.

During World War II, 300,000 Americans suddenly arrived to set up, in a matter of months, their biggest base in the Pacific—complete with eight hospitals and 19 cinemas. The islanders were struck by the way in which blacks and whites worked together, and by their generosity and openness. In contrast to the British and French, who expected deference, the Americans treated people equally, restoring a sense of dignity. Yet they had wealth and power—their God was clearly pleased with them.

Missionaries had already introduced the idea of John the Baptist. This was now in effect combined with the idea of the mysterious, invisible generous benefactor "Uncle Sam" who provided the Americans with all their cargo, plus perhaps the equally mysterious Santa Claus who brought presents at Christmas for Europeans, to produce the messianic figure of John Frum.

He allegedly appeared on a beach of the island Tanna at sundown, dressed in white man's clothes but speaking the native language, and with a shining walking stick. He always went and stood in the same place, and people went to the beach to listen. (According to other accounts, it was a villager who stood up claiming to be a manifestation of John Frum, whom he described in the preceding terms.) His face remained invisible, but he urged people to have faith in America. People would come from America again to help them, and provide roads and proper houses. He urged them to leave the missionary churches, and they did. His promises were the same as the Bible's, and he was the road to Jesus. If they were patient, they would get money.

And they did: tourists came! Such is the current belief among adherents of the movement today. Their numbers are not known, and the movement appears to have splintered into several smaller groups, but it has not disappeared. Members perform a Volcano Dance to John, who said that he controlled the volcano, and that a road leads there from America. His army is believed to live inside it. Members also believe that if they are faithful to the memory of John Frum, then one day he will return.

K

Kabir Chaura. One of only two extant groups which make up the original 12 branches of the Indian **Kabir Panth.**

Kabir Panthis. The great Indian guru Kabir lived in north India from about 1440 to 1518 CE though accounts of the duration and period of his life vary considerably. He rejected distinctions of caste and religion to the extent that it is difficult to locate him within the Hindu tradition, (by caste he was a *jullaha* weaver), or Islam to which he had converted. He taught the oneness of God who is without form, the equality of all human beings, thus denying the validity of caste or gender distinctions, and the rejection of the efficacy of rituals and of ritual purity to the extent that he deliberately chose not to die in the holy city of Varanasi. There is no convincing reason for accepting the tradition that he was a disciple of the brahmin *guru* Ramanand. This association seems to be device for legitimizing the Panth of a non-brahmin *guru*. Some of Kabir's hymns are contained in the Sikh Guru Granth Sahib but evidence of a meeting between Guru Nanak and Kabir is weak and similarities in their teachings are not usually regarded as indicating dependence.

The Panth is traditionally held to have broken down into 12 sub-groups within a hundred years of the death of Kabir; one of these may have been the **Udasis.** Nowadays only two recognizable groups remain, the **Dharmadasis** with headquarters in the Chattisgarh district of northern India, and the **Kabir Chaura** based in Benares. In general the Panth has a lower caste membership of Hindus and Muslims, though amongst the Dharmadasis merchants are prominent. The Panth includes both lay and monastic groups and is found throughout the north from Gujerat to Bihar.

Kagyudpas. "Followers of the Oral Teaching Lineages." One of the four main traditions of **Tibetan Buddhism**, comprising a number of closely related but completely independent religious orders with a shared spiritual heritage. Four of these, the **Karmapa**, **Drukpa**, **Drigungpa** and **Taklungpa**, still survive as independent institutions; but the teachings alone now remain of the Phagdru, Tshalpa, Baram, Yamzang, Tropu, Shugseb, Yelpa and Martshang, passed on by lamas of other denominations.

All Kagyudpa schools originate from the master to pupil succession of the following five great exemplary founding saints: Tilopa (988–1069) was an élite Bengali Brahmin whose career progressed from head of state, to monk, to outcaste tantric yogin, inhabiting cemeteries and practising sexual yogas. Although enlightened, he was widely considered insane. Naropa (1016–1100), a Bengali noble turned monk, progressed from famous academic to obscure wandering yogin, obeying Tilopa with unswerving devotion. Marpa the Translator (1012–1097), Tibet's first Kagyudpa, outwardly remained an ordinary married farmer, revealing the spiritual and scholarly treasures he had learned from Naropa to a few chosen disciples. His student Milarepa (1052–1135), Tibet's most popular saint, was a major poet and penitent murderer whose renunciation, devotion, and unparalleled zeal in ascetic yoga brought him full enlightenment. The physician Gampopa (1075–1139) took to monasticism on his wife's death; systematizer of Milarepa's teachings, he created the organizational basis that served all subsequent Kagyudpa monastic and scholastic institutions.

Kagyudpas are Tibet's leading yoga experts, practitioners of the famous "Six Doctrines of Naropa". Renowned for their devotion, *Mahamudra* meditation, and spiritual songs, their emphasis on prolonged meditational retreats has earned them the sobriquet "Practice Lineage". Kagyudpas have from early times been intimately associated with the **Nyingmapas**, whose tantras and **Termas** they continue to practise. For several centuries Tibet's largest tradition, they are now successfully spreading internationally.

Kakai. This is the name in Iraq for the heterodox Muslim sect **Ahl-i Haqq**.

Kalikulas. Hindu **Shaktas** of the Kalikula tradition worship the terrifying, ugly goddess Kali; emaciated, garlanded with severed heads, girdled with arms, with lolling tongue and eyes rolling with intoxication. Kali worship takes an esoteric and exoteric form. In its esoteric form Kali is the centre of secret ritual in which she is visualized as identical with the light of absolute, pure consciousness, transcendi.., her male spouse Shiva, while exoterically she demands blood sacrifice. There is a famous temple to Kali at which blood sacrifice is offered in Calcutta. Indeed the occasional human sacrifice still occurs in remote areas.

Kalyanavamsa. A prominent **Theravada** Buddhist monastic grouping within the Sri Lankan **Amarapura Nikaya**.

Kanji Panth. A 20th century **Jaina** reform movement based on the charismatic personality of Kanji Swami. The Panth is a sub-group within **Digambara Jainism**.

Kanphatas. *See* **Naths**.

Kapalikas. A defunct and highly unorthodox Hindu **Shaivite** ascetic tradition now largely subsumed by the **Aghoris**.

Karaites. The Karaites (literally "scripturalists"), a Jewish sectarian movement, accept only scripture (the Hebrew Bible or written *Torah*) as authoritative and reject the rabbinic traditions of interpretation (oral *Torah*). While the name appears in the 9th century CE, the movement's origins are to be found in the previous century when Anan ben David lost his bid for the leadership of the Babylonian Jewish community due to his heterodox views and began his own movement. The Karaite movement initially grew rapidly and the Karaite–Rabbinite (the Judaism of the rabbis) schism divided the Jewish world. By the end of the 11th century, however, and after a Rabbinic "counterattack", the issue became resolved with the complete separation of the Karaites as a small schismatic group outside of "mainstream" Judaism.

Karaism developed its own traditions and rituals (characterized by a literalism in interpretation), calendar, order of services and did not permit intermarriage with non-Karaites. Currently, there are a number of communities in Russia; 1,500 in the USA (mainly in the Bay Area in California), and some 100 families in Istanbul. The majority of Karaites now live in Israel (20,000) under the leadership of Haim Hallevi of Ashdod, the Karaite Chief Rabbi.

Karakash. *See* **Donmeh**.

Kardecismo. Allan Kardec (1804–1869) was a French codifier of spiritism/**spiritualism,** which he regarded more as a scientific philosophy than as a religion. Spirits of the deceased can communicate with the living through mediums—but in contrast to British spiritism, Kardec's system incorporated belief in reincarnation, also claiming that out of the hierarchy of spirits that inhabit the invisible spirit world, Christ was the highest ever to become incarnate.

It is in Brazil that Kardecismo has taken on the character of a religion, appealing to significant numbers of the urban middle classes. Perhaps more importantly, it has interacted with movements of African spiritism which have developed from **African traditional religions** brought across by slaves, leading to the syncretic and currently more widespread and influential **Umbanda** religious movement.

Karlin–Stolin Hasidism. Karlin and Stolin are the Lithuanian towns associated with the beginnings of the Perlov Hasidic dynasty, whose followers are referred to as Karlin–Stolin Hasidim. The first Rebbe and founder of this Hasidic movement, Rabbi Aaron ben Jacob (1736–1772), a disciple of Dov Ber the Maggid of Mezhirech, exercised great influence on the development of Lithuanian Hasidism. Renowned for their Hasidic melodies; their stress on joy; Talmudic study and strict observance of the commandments; the purificatory value of ritual immersion; fervour and solitary self-surrender in prayer and the education of women, the Karlin–Stolin established centres in the land of Israel (Tiberias and Jerusalem) in the 19th century and in America in the 20th. The Lithuanian dynastic leaders, the great-grandsons of Aaron, together with many of their followers were killed in the Holocaust. Currently, the movement has centres in America and Israel.

Karma Kagyudpa. Also known as the **Karmapas**, this is the largest of the surviving **Kagyudpa** schools of **Tibetan Buddhism**, founded by Karmapa Dusum Khyenpa (1110– 1193), a student of Gampopa. His reincarnation Karma Pakshi (1206–1283) is often believed to be the first incarnate lama (*tulku*) to be recognized in Tibet, and ever since then the Karma Kagyudpa school has been headed by successive serial Karmapa reincarnations, who are always the objects of intense devotion from their followers. Regarded as emanations of the celestial bodhisattva

Avalokitesvara, the Karmapas remained Tibet's foremost incarnations until the coming of the Dalai Lamas some centuries later. The Karmapas are famous for their unique black hat, said to be a material replica of a spiritual crown woven from the hair of 100,000 goddesses, and the Karma Kagyudpas, heirs to Gampopa, specialize in combining monastic discipline and scholarship with advanced *tantric* practice and intensive meditation. The charismatic 16th Karmapa, Rangjung Rigpay Dorje, died in Chicago in 1981, after establishing over 100 centres in the West, and the activities of other Karma Kagyudpa lamas, such as Chogyam Trungpa the founder of Samye Ling in the Scottish borders and the Naropa Institute in Boulder, Colorado, and Kalu Rinpoche, have helped give this school exceptionally sound foundations in exile. The current headquarters of the Karma Kagyudpas is at Rumtek in Sikkim.

Karmapas. *See* **Karma Kagyudpa.**

Kashfiya. The Kashfiya is a quasi-heterodox school within **Twelver Shi'ism**, its members being more widely known as **Shaykhis**.

Kashmir Shaivism. Kashmir Shaivism is a form of Hinduism which developed in the Kashmir valley from the ninth to 11th centuries CE, supplanting Buddhism and **Shaiva Siddhanta.** This tradition was "monistic", maintaining the identity of the self and absolute, and forms the basis of the contemporary, popular religion of Hindus remaining in the valley, as well as an esoteric tradition which has been transplanted to the West.

A number of schools comprise Kashmir Shaivism, but three traditions are especially important, namely the **Trika** ("Threefold"), **Spanda** ("Vibration") and **Pratyabhijna** ("Recognition"). These traditions recognized a group of Sanskrit texts called **Tantras** as their

199

revealed source of authority, as opposed to the Vedas of orthodox Hinduism. The Trika tradition, so called due to its veneration of the three goddesses Para, Parapara and Apara, is mainly concerned with initiation, ritual and cosmology. The Spanda reveres the revelations of Shiva to Vasugupta (c875–925). In a dream Shiva revealed to Vasugupta a group of verses inscribed on a rock at the top of a mountain, which Vasugupta wrote down as the *Shiva Sutras*. Lastly the monistic Shaiva theology of the Pratyabhijna is represented in the works of Abhi-navagupta (c975–1025), particularly in his *Tantraloka*. The Tantric **Krama** tradition should be noted as having a significant influence on Kashmir Shaivism. Apart from this esoteric tradition, the popular cult among Hindus in the valley has been that of the god Svacchanda Bhairava.

The central philosophy of monistic Shaivism is that there is only one reality identified as consciousness (*caitanya, samvit*), but also referred to in more personal terms as the god Shiva or by some other synonym. Shakti is the consort of Shiva, the female force in the universe which is its material cause. The descent of Shakti through the grace of Shiva lifts the veil of illusion which prevents us from seeing the all-pervading reality of absolute consciousness. Through Shakti, Shiva is both concealed and revealed. To realize the identity of the self with the supreme Shiva is to wake up to our pure subjectivity and to be liberated from the cycle of reincarnation (*samsara*).

Although providing the ideological backdrop, the sophistication and complexity of the Trika teachings are not particularly in evidence in the daily lives of the remaining Shaiva brahmins of Kashmir or Kashmiri *pandits*, although Svacchanda Bhairava is worshipped. Their main concerns are the fulfilling of moral law (*dharma*) and social obligations with respect to their caste or *zat* (from the Sanskrit *jati*), a term which denotes an occupational group and connotes that group's innate or essential nature. Social obligation entails paying debts incurred over innumerable past lives to one's fellow humans, ancestors and gods, and to performing the necessary life-cycle and daily rituals. While being preoccupied with the concerns of this world, the brahmins accept that liberation (*moksa*), going beyond the veil of illusion, is a desired, if distant, goal. However, some *pandits* do become *shaktas*, followers of Shakti, or seekers after spiritual power, within the social institution of the householder.

The more esoteric aspects of Kashmir Shaivism have been preserved in an oral tradition, finding expression in the teachings of the guru Swami Lakshman Jee (d. 1992) who retained many of the ideas of Abhinavagupta. The universe is an unfolding of consciousness in a hierarchical sequence, codified in the system of the 36 categories, ranging from Shiva at the top to earth at the bottom. This process is also regarded as the manifestation of sound from subtle to gross levels, expressed in the letters of the Sanskrit alphabet. These letters make up *mantras* or sacred formulas which reflect this subtle sound. Through Kashmir Shaiva *yogas* Swami Lakshman Jee claims that we can free ourselves of these impurities and realize our identity with the absolute. Lakshman Jee teaches the awakening of an energy (*shakti*) within the body called Kundalini. Once awakened by yoga practices such as breath control, Kundalini rises through a central channel of the body, piercing various centres of power (*cakras*) as she rises, until she unites with Shiva at or above the crown of the head. The practitioner then experiences the bliss of union with Shiva.

Contemporary versions of Kashmir Shaivism now exist in the West. The **Universal Shaiva Trust** based in California propagates the teachings of Swami Lakshman Jee; Swami Cetanananda, the American abbot of the **Nityananda Institute** in Massachusetts, teaches a form of the Trika tradition; and the **Siddha Yoga** of the late Swami Muktananda claims to be based on the teachings of Kashmir Shaivism.

Kasogatan. Derived from Sugato (the well-gone), one of the nine epithets of the Buddha. A popular form of Javanese Buddhism of obscure origin but which claims to be related to the Majapahit kingdom—the last pre-Islamic Buddhist kingdom in Java c1500AD. Its adherents currently number several thousand. Leading figures have included Oka Diputera, a Balinese government official who served for a time as Director of Buddhist Affairs in the Ministry of Religious Affairs, and General Suraji.

Kaulas. Kaulism is a Hindu **tantric** tradition going back to the cremation grounds of Kashmir and Swat (400–800 CE), centred on the worship of "families" (*kulas*) of female deities (*yoginis*) and the supreme Goddess Kulesvari as internal to consciousness. There are four lines of transmission of the tradition: the eastern transmission forming the **Trika** of **Kashmir Shaivism;** the northern transmission forming the **Krama;** the western transmission forming the cult of the hunched Goddess Kujika; and the southern transmission of the cult of the Goddess Tripurasundari or Kamesvari. This latter tradition developed away from its more sectarian tantric roots and is now called the **Sri Vidya.** It became and remains popular in south India.

Kavi Panth. A modern **Jain** lay reform movement established in 1924 to reconcile **Svetambara** and **Digambara** beliefs. The movement (*panth*) takes its name from its founders, the poet (*kavi*) Raychandrabai Mehta and his wife Devabhai. Kavipanthis have one sacred text, called **Srimad Rajchandra,** which is a collection of letters from the founder to various correspondents, hence the alternative name of the group. Devotees worship the image of their founder along with images of other Jain *Tirthankaras*. The Panth is particularly influential in the cities of Gujerat and

Kathiawar with perhaps 10,000 members overall.

Kebatinan. New religious movements (NRMs), as indicated in one of the essays in Part I, are a major contemporary religious phenomenon. In Indonesia large numbers of NRMs have proliferated since World War II, drawing in particular on the strong **Sufi** and Hindu traditions of mysticism in the islands, and these are referred to generically as *kebatinan* groups or sects (*aliran kebatinan*)—the term being derived from the Arabic "*batin*", a term used in Sufism to refer to the inner aspect of reality. Most are small, with up to about 200 members, while others such as **Subud**, **Sapta Darma**, **Sumarah** and **Pangestu** number their followers in the thousands, and Subud, of course, has become an internationally significant movement.

Most of the groups are broadly mystical in their orientation ("*kebatinan*" is variously translated as "mysticism", "the science of supernature", "the science of the inner"), using various mixtures of meditation, ascetic discipline and psychological theory to achieve a sense of inner balance or unity with God and the world. Some groups, however, have a different orientation, being concerned perhaps with moral purity or with magic, or being millenarian in character. In most cases adherence to one of the sects involves attaching oneself to a guru figure who is qualified to act as a spiritual guide because of a claimed experience of revelation—*wahy*: the term used in Islam for the final revelation to Muhammad.

The *kebatinan* groups are, however, firmly rejected by the *santri* adherents of strict Islam, **Agama Islam Santri**, although they often attract the nominal Muslims known as *abangan,* whose version of the faith is known—in Java at least—as **Agama (Islam) Jawa**. With the ruling élite drawn largely from the latter group, it is perhaps not surprising that some well-known *kebatinan* leaders advise the government and military.

Some groups, for example Subud, engage in healing, while others, for instance Sumarah, regard this as taboo. Controversy also attends the issue of seeking monetary gain through the exercise of one's special powers, for example by giving lottery predictions.

Critics—inter alia *santri* Muslims—accuse the kebatinan groups of indulging in a jumble of superstition at best, or worse, in black magic and occultism (*klenik*). Since 1973, however, the government has given semi-official status to the *kebatinan* movement by recognizing it as a legitimate form of the Godliness, *keTuhanan,* required of all Indonesians by their Constitution, even though it remains classified as "faith" or "beliefs", (*kepercayaan*) rather than "religion" (*agama*)—a distinction enshrined in the Constitution, but whose meaning has remained controversial. Hence it is administered, not by the Ministry of Religion, which supervises the affairs of the six officially recognized religions (Islam, Roman Catholicism, Protestantism, Hinduism, Buddhism, and Confucianism), but through the Direktorat Pembinaan Penghayat Kepercayaan in the Ministry of Education and Culture.

Nevertheless, in the 1980 census no record of affiliation to *kebatinan* groups was included, and more recently the government has begun insisting that *kebatinan* is to be seen as complementary to *agama* and not a substitute for it. Thus in terms of the recognition of the validity of the *kebatinan* form of spirituality, the pendulum appears to have swung back to something approaching the pre-1973 position. The important difference remains, however, that *kebatinan* sects are now permitted to conduct weddings, administer oaths of office, offer religious instruction in schools, and celebrate *1 Suro,* a Javanese holy day, as a national holiday.

In their quest for respectability and recognition, the groups have increasingly operated through an umbrella organization, whose name, however, has changed several times. Originally (in 1955) known as the Badan Kongres Kebatinan Indonesia, in 1970 it became the Sekretariat Kerjasama Kepercayaan, and then in 1979 the Himpunan Penghayat Kepercayaan.

Kegon emphasises the mutual identity of phenomena and the great Buddha Dainichi. Its central scripture is the *Kegonkyo*. The Todaiji in Nara remains the head temple, and Kegon claims over 700,000 adherents. The great Buddha at Nara is Dainichi, completed in 749 during the reign of Emperor Shomu, a champion of Kegon.

Kegonshu. One of the surviving **Nara** sects of Japanese Buddhism. The teachings of the sect are based on the Mahayanist *Avatamsaka* (Flower Garland) *Sutra* which holds the mutual interpenetration and unity of all things. The sect approximates closely to the Chinese Buddhist **Hua Yen** school and has its headquarters at Todaiji. There are about 60 temples, 900 clergy—over two thirds of whom are women, and 45,000 adherents in Japan today.

Kepercayaan. *Kepercayaan,* "faith" or "beliefs", is the official designation by the Indonesian state of the numerous **kebatinan** groups, mostly mystical sects, that have spring up since the war. Since 1973 the government has accorded them a degree of recognition under the collective title *kepercayaan,* and along with this new status they have acquired certain powers and privileges previously reserved for the officially recognized religions such as Islam. Nevertheless, the attitude of the state towards them remains somewhat ambivalent.

Keshdhari Sikhs. A Sikh who retains uncut hair (*kesh*), one of the five Ks associated with initiation into the *khalsa*, or Sikh community established by the 10th *Guru*, Gobind Singh in 1699. It does not strictly follow that a Keshdhari is also **Amritdhari,** i.e. a properly initiated **Khalsa Sikh,** though this is usually the case.

Khalidiya. An offshoot of the **Mujaddidiya Sufi** order, originally established in 19th century Damascus by a Kurdish shaikh, and subsequently widespread, including in the Indian sub-continent.

Khalsa Sikhs. In 1699 Guru Gobind Singh created a new body within the Sikh Panth, the *Khalsa* or Pure Ones, Membership was by a new form of initiation (*amritsankar*). Besides keeping the outward form of the five Ks there are certain moral regulations which must be observed. These *kurahts*, intended to lead to purity of living are; not to smoke, use drugs, drink alcohol, or commit adultery. They are in addition to the general precepts which require Sikhs to be honest, trustworthy, hard working, and to observe the equality of all people regardless of caste, class, or gender. The **Nihangs** are a sub-group of warriors within the *khalsa*, believed to have been created by Gobind Singh as a fighting force.

It is said that the idea was inspired by the suicide squads of the Mughal army who first used the name. They are formed into four armies (*dals*), each with a *jathedar* (captain). They live in encampments (*deras*), and are easily recognized by their blue clothes, and turbans, and their weapons which often consist of spears and swords but also modern rifles and automatic weapons.

Khalwatiya. The Khalwatiya is a **Sufi** order which dates back to the 14th century but unlike many other orders does not recognize an individual founder. Several

Persian, Kurdish and Turkish Sufis are associated with its early development, two with the name of al-Khalwati, thought to be derived from their practice of going into retreat (*khalwa*). Yahya al-Shirwani (d. 1464 at Baku) is sometimes regarded as the real founder, his litany being recited at Khalwati gatherings.

Khalwatis are noted for their strict training of initiates, and some branches are unwilling to accept illiterates. Preparation for entry to the order varies in different branches, but often involves a period spent in prayers, fasting, night vigils and the characteristic retreat from three to a maximum of 40 days.

In its early stages the Khalwatiya seems to have been involved in the cult of 'Ali, but aspects of this were suppressed or went underground when the order spread among **Sunni** Turks in Anatolia with encouragement from the Ottoman sultan Bayezid II (1481–1511), himself a member. From Turkey the order was introduced into Ottoman Egypt in the 16th century, but remained largely confined to Turks until the 18th century, when it enjoyed a notable revival, due in part to the activities of the Syrian Sufi Mustafa al-Bakri (1688–1749). The Khalwatiya has shown a tendency to split into many sub-orders, including the Bakriya (from al-Bakri), very popular in Egypt, and the Sammaniya, which has penetrated into the Sudan, Ethiopia and across to South East Asia (Indonesia for example). The Sudanese Mahdi, Muhammad Ahmad, whose **Ansar** movement continues to be influential, was a shaikh of the Sammaniya.

At present the Khalwatiya in various branches is reported as active in Lebanon and Syria. In Turkey it was suppressed in 1925 with the banning of Sufi orders and it is not clear whether it has survived. In Albania it continued until the Albanian Cultural Revolution of 1967, after which it could only carry on in secret, but may resurface in the changed circumstances. In Yugoslavia a small number of very active groups is still to be found in Kosovo and Macedonia.

Khatmiya. The Khatmiya, or Mirghaniya as it is also known, is a **Sufi** order which developed out of the Idrisiya of Ahmad ibn Idris (1760–1837), the influential reformist Sufi teacher. Of particular importance among his pupils were Muhammad ibn 'Ali al-Sanusi, founder of the **Sanusiya**, and Muhammad 'Uthman al-Mirghani (1793–1851), founder of the Khatmiya/Mirghaniya. Both orders claimed to be comprehensive, incorporating the essential ideas of the **Naqshabandiya**, **Shadhiliya** and **Qadiriya**.

Muhammad 'Uthman had gained followers in several countries prior to his death in 1851—in India, Arabia, Egypt and the Sudan. It was in the last of these, however, that the order became particularly important, being established there initially by his son al-Hasan, who founded the township of Khatmiya. The subsequent development of the Khatmiya is very much intertwined with the political development of the country.

The Khatmiya established itself in the north of the Sudan and became closely connected with the largest tribe there. It also acquired vested interests in the Turco–Egyptian government. The rise of the **Mahdiya**, with its declared aim of creating an Islamic state, was perceived as a threat to the position of the Khatmiya. During the existence of this Islamic state the leadership of the Khatmiya order went into exile, only to return and re-establish its authority after the reconquest of the Sudan in 1898, although it was to find itself out of government favour in the early 20th century.

With the formation of political parties, the two main opposing ones were supported by the Khatmiya and the Mahdiya respectively (members of the latter now being known as the **Ansar**). With independence in 1953 the two parties, and hence the two movements, both struggled for political power. Neither of the two parties was strong enough to form a government on its own. Coalition governments and the fusion of politics and religion are two features of political life in Sudan. Military *coups* have interfered with the political activities of the

Sufi orders. But the Khatmiya still wields religious and political power in its regional centres.

Khoisan Religion. Khoisan religion is an example of **African traditional religions**. The Khoisan are the aboriginal peoples of southern Africa. They consist of two closely related groups—genetically, culturally and linguistically—the Khoi (Hottentot), who are cattle herders and agriculturalists, and the San (Bushmen), who are hunter-gatherers. The Khoisan languages are characterized by consonantal clicks. Throughout most of their former territories, Khoisan peoples have been replaced by Bantu and European settlers. There are an estimated 50,000 Khoi, the majority in Namibia. About 20 per cent of the population live in South Africa, where they are mainly wage-labourers. The largest populations of San, who may number around 40,000 in total, are in Botswana.

Creation myths provide the key to Khoisan cosmology and ritual activity. Accurate ethnographic information from different groups is scarce, and what follows is a generalized account of some Khoisan beliefs and practices as recorded over the past few decades. A creator ordered the different species of animal and plant life, including human beings, and then withdrew into the sky to play a negligible role in human affairs. An "administrator" controls phenomena such as rainfall, human health and fertility. The creator is envisaged in positive terms, but the administrator negatively. Humans would be immortal but for the administrator's mishandling of the world. The positive and negative attributes of the creator and administrator are sometimes regarded as alternative aspects of human personality.

The *shaman* has the role of restoring order in the face of misfortune or social tension by means of a divinatory dance, during which the influence of the administrator can be counteracted. The participation of all those involved in a dispute, or area of concern, is essential to the **shamanic** ritual, which serves to unite the cosmological and experiential levels of existence.

Khoja Ithna'Asharis. According to many of the Muslims who describe themselves as **Khojas**, the term means businessman, or professional, and should be considered as a caste (the Khojas are an Indian group by origin) or ethnic term rather than a sectarian one. However, the addition of the label **Ithna'Ashari** clearly introduces a "sectarian" factor. For unlike the majority of Khojas, who are **Isma'ili Shi'ites**, the Khoja Ithna'Asharis are **Twelver Shi'ites**. As followers of the twelfth Imam, who they believe to be in occultation, these members of the Khoja community share the religious beliefs and practices of many Iranian and Pakistani Shi'ites, and are known to intermarry with these communities, and also with European Twelvers. One can in fact achieve Khoja status by marrying a Khoja.

Unlike the Isma'ili Khojas, the Twelver Khojas do not seek to incorporate, or adapt, elements of Hinduism into Shi'ism, but the observer cannot help but draw similarities between the five revered persons of Muhammad, 'Ali, Fatima, Hassan and Hussain, with the five major divinities of **Smarta** Hinduism.

Like the Isma'ilis, the Khoja Twelvers are mostly prosperous traders and professionals, and outside India have been prominent in the economy of East Africa. The community now present in countries such as Canada and the United Kingdom have mostly come from Africa, and maintain close networks through their World Centre based in Stanmore, Middlesex (UK).

Khojas. The Khojas are an Indian community who mostly adhere to the **Nizari** sect of **Isma'ili Shi'ism** within Islam. Their name derives from the Persian word *Khwaja* (Lord). A 14th–15th century Nizari missionary converted a caste, the Lohanas, and bestowed upon them the name of

Khojas. Subsequently some Khojas transferred their allegiance to **Sunni** Islam, others to **Twelver Shi'ism** (a group now known as **Khoja Ithna 'Asharis**), and a few even reverted to Hinduism. Thus not all Khojas are Nizaris, although the identification is commonly made. (A similar qualification applies to the common identification of the Khojas with the **Aga Khanis**.)

The Khojas are not themselves an Islamic sect—they belong (mostly) to the Nizari sect. In many ways they retain characteristics of caste: one is born a Khoja, and caste rules of marriage and inheritance have obtained until quite recently (when customs associated with Hinduism have begun to lapse). They have a distinctive body of religious literature known as *Sat Panth* (True Path), and this incorporates and adapts certain elements from Hinduism: for example, 'Ali is regarded as an avatar of Vishnu, the *Quran* as the last of the *Vedas,* and the Prophet Muhammad is identified with Brahma.

Also characteristic of the Khojas are their *jama'at khanas*, or assembly and prayer halls, which form a focus of their community activities and function as mosques. Their communities are well organized under a religious community leader (*mukhi*) and an account keeper (*kamadiya*).

Khojas have a reputation as prosperous traders which they have consolidated under the leadership of the Aga Khans. In India they are located mainly in Sind, Gujarat and Bombay, although communities are to be found scattered throughout the country. Outside India they are particularly important in East Africa, although there are groups elsewhere, including Europe and America. A split which occurred in the 16th century resulted in the formation of a sub-group known as the Imam-Shahis (Imamshahis) or **Satpanthis**. As the latter name implies, they share much of the religious literature of the Nizari Khojas.

Kibbutz. (*See also* **Zionism.**) (Pl. *kibbutzim*) —one of a number of Israeli socialist collective settlements in which all property is communally owned and all members' needs are provided for. The movement has its roots in the attempt of secular Russian immigrants to the Land of Israel in the 1904–1906 immigration wave to "return" the Jews to their original condition by making them into communal farmers in their ancestral home. The first agricultural settlement, then called a *kevutzah* ("group") was founded in Deganyah in 1909. After World War I, the farms added industrial components, calling themselves *kibbutzim*. *Kibbutz* members saw themselves as the elite of the new Jewish society and provided many leaders for the new state of Israel.

Ideological always, the movement branched into four groups, three secular organizations; *Ha-kibbutz ha-Artzi ha-Shomir ha-Tza'ir* ("The National Young Guard *Kibbutz*"), *ha-Kibbutz ha-Me'uhed* ("The United *Kibbutz*"), *Ihud ha-Kevuzot ve-ha-Kibbutzim* ("the Union of *Kevutzot* and *Kibbutzim*"), all of which differ somewhat in their approach to socialism and Zionism, and a smaller religious group, *Kibbutz ha-Dati,* ("The Religious *Kibbutz*"), which rejects the secular *kibbutz* members' claim that traditional Judaism was an inauthentic product of *diaspora* conditions. Approximately 4 per cent of the Jewish population in Israel live in *Kibbutzim*.

Kikuyu Religion. Kikuyu religion is an example of **African traditional religions**. The Kikuyu (Gikuyu) comprise an eastern Bantu branch of the Niger–Congo language family, and occupy a large area of southern Kenya. Like other East African peoples, the Kikuyu believe in a supreme god, *Ngai,* whom they associate with Mount Kenya (*Kere-Nyaga*) and other lesser mountains. Sacrifices to *Ngai,* addressed as "*Mwene-Nyaga*" ("possessor of brightness"), are performed by elders on behalf of the community (a patrilineal lineage group) at sacred trees. *Ngai* is not approached on personal or trivial matters but may be petitioned in the case of crises, such as drought,

epidemics, or serious illness. Some elders belonging to the senior age-set may be regarded as seers and healers, and have special powers which enable them to communicate directly with "*Mwene-Nyaga*". Natural phenomena such as thunder and lightning, the sun, moon, stars, rain and rainbows are considered to be manifestations of *Ngai* and may be regarded as omens.

Ancestral spirits are regarded with the respect due to senior clansmen and women and live in a parallel social world to that of their descendants, in whom they continue to take an interest. If angered by dissension among their living kinsmen and women, or because of a lack of respect shown to them, the ancestors may cause illness, which can be diagnosed through divination and corrected through propitiatary sacrifices. Spirits are thought to lurk in natural phenomena, and may be identified by sudden swirling gusts of wind. They are capable of causing sickness and may be driven into a river or stream with shouting and blunted weapons. Sacrificial units are bounded by rivers, and in common with many other Bantu peoples, the Kikuyu believe that ancestral or other spirits cannot cross water. Witches, unlike practitioners of traditional medicine or dealers in charms, are greatly feared and are believed to poison their victims.

Rites of passage mark important life events and are accompanied by periods of seclusion, symbolizing death and rebirth into a different state. Initiation into adulthood includes circumcision for boys and, in the past, clitoridectomy for girls (a practice which has been defended by the Kikuyu, despite mission opposition and attempts at its suppression by colonial governments). The sacrifice of a sheep or goat marks most important rituals.

The Kikuyu have been influenced by both Islam and Christianity in the course of the 20th century. Many of their number hold to one of these two religions, without necessarily rejecting all traditional practices. Independent churches and traditional revivalist movements (*see* **African New**

Religious Movements) have also claimed large numbers of adherents.

Kimbanguist Church. The church, officially known as L'Eglise de Jésus Christ par le Prophète Simon Kimbangu, was founded in 1921 by a **Baptist** catechist, Simon Kimbangu (1889–1951), in the Lower Congo (Zaire), and it is one of the most important **African New Religious Movements**. Kimbangu, a prophet and healer, was imprisoned on a charge of sedition and his followers persecuted. Despite such pressures the church, now led by Kimbangu's three sons, has transformed itself from a revivalist movement with political overtones into an established church with over 4,000,000 members, official recognition and affiliation to the **World Council of Churches**.

Kitawala. The Church of the Watchtower or Kitawala is a widespread African New Religious Movement in central Africa influenced by the American Watchtower and Bible Tract Society (**Jehovah's Witnesses**). African versions of the parent organization have arisen in Malawi, Zambia and Zaire, dating from around 1907, under leaders such as Elliott Kamwana in northern Nyasaland (Malawi), Nyirenda in the Belgian Congo (Zaire) and Jeremiah Gondwe in Zambia. Refusal to swear allegiance to secular authorities has led to widespread persecution (Kamwana was deported in 1909 and Nyirenda executed in 1926: Jehovah's Witnesses are also currently banned in Malawi), but Kitawala churches continue to attract adherents. Gondwe's Independent Watchtower Church, for example, was estimated to have 4,000 members in 1971, rising to 19,000 by 1976.

Kizilbash. *See* **Qizilbash.**

Kolping Society. This **Roman Catholic** organization was founded in Germany in 1849 by A. Kolping to offer support to young workers both socially and spiritually. Today it is concerned with wider questions of social justice and renewal. Consonant with its full title, the International Kolping Society (Kolpingwerk International), it now operates in 17 countries, although its headquarters remain in Germany. In the mid-1970s it had some 300,000 members.

Komeito. The "Clean Government Party", Komeito, began as the political wing of **Soka Gakkai** and is now a substantial Japanese opposition party in its own right (it was officially separated from Soka Gakkai in 1970). Its official ideology is "humanitarian socialism", and reflecting the spirit of **Nichiren Buddhism**, it promotes peace and social equality from a pragmatic rather than idealistic orientation.

Konkokyo. A Japanese faith-healing movement and one of the traditional 13 constituent sects of **Kyoha Shinto.**

Krama. A **tantric** tradition originating in the cremation-ground cults of the Swat Valley, now in Pakistan, between 400 and 800 CE. The Krama was an ecstatic, visionary tradition concerned with possession by female deities, the *yoginis,* in order to gain supernatural power, and with the worship of Kali in successive stages (*krama*). This tradition is preserved in a less esoteric form among the **Newar** brahmins of Nepal, where the Krama structure of worship is expressed in the iconography and cult of the goddess Guhyesvari. Her cult is centred at Pasupatinatha, a place of pilgrimage, where the vagina of the goddess Sati is said to have fallen after her corpse was dismembered by Vishnu, as Shiva danced frenziedly with it. The image of Guhyesvari can also be found elsewhere in Nepal within temples to the goddess Taleju, a form of Durga.

Krishnamurti Foundation. The young Krishnamurti (1895–1985) was "discovered" on an Indian beach by the Theosophists C. W. Leadbeater and Annie Besant, and brought up to be the new World Teacher. In 1929 he repudiated this role, and denounced organized religion, ritual, dogma and gurus. The **Theosophy** movement then split in two, half of the members following him. For the rest of his life he travelled the world, teaching informally. His spiritual vision is close to Buddhism in its insistence that truth is formless and timeless and cannot be known by the conditioned mind, but only by direct perception.

The main centres of the Krishnamurti Foundation are in England, Switzerland, America and India. These function mainly as study centres, though there are also 11 schools; many pupils go on to university. Although he had no formal disciples, he influenced many people, and along with **Gurdieff** is the most highly regarded Eastern teacher among the Western *intelligentsia,* acknowledged by leading scientists and philosophers.

Kubrawiya. A **Sufi** order whose founder, Najmuddin Kubra, is buried in Kunia-Urgench in Turkmenistan. His tomb is the spiritual centre of a brotherhood which has always been confined to parts of Central Asia, and which has now been absorbed to a great extent, it seems, by the **Naqshabandiya** in that region.

Kukas. An alternative name for the **Sikh**-derived, **Namdhari** movement.

Kumina. A small ancestor cult of African origin which is similar in some respects to **Convince,** and still found in parts of Jamaica. There are three ranks of spirits, known as zombies: sky gods, earthbound gods, and ancestors. They are invoked through drumming and singing. The ritual ends with the sacrifice of a goat. The most

common rationale of ritual dances is the paying of respect to the dead ancestors of the people present.

Kurozumikyo. A Japanese faith-healing movement and one of the traditional 13 constituent sects of **Kyoha Shinto.**

Kyo Chong. A sect of Korean Buddhism amalgamated with **Son** in 1935 to form the **Chogye Chong,** the first distinctively Korean version of **Zen.**

Kyoha Shinto. Traditionally, there are 13 sects of Kyoha or **Shuha** (Sect) Shinto. These originated either with a charismatic founder or out of an amalgam of Traditional and Restoration Shinto and various non-Shinto's influences (**Buddhism, Confucianism, Taoism, Shugendo** folk beliefs and so on.) Common characteristics include founder veneration, worship of tutelary and national *kami,* purification, supplication and appeasement rituals and prayers, and the promotion of a virtuous life. Most of the sects have sacred scriptures written or revealed by their founder.

The sects are loosely classified into five types:

1. Mountain worship sects: **Fusokyo** and **Jikokyo** (Mount Fuji), and **Ontakekyo** (Mount Ontake);
2. Faith healing sects: **Kurozumikyo, Konkokyo** and **Tenrikyo;**
3. Purification sects: **Misogikyo** and **Shinshukyo;**
4. Confucian sects: **Shinto Shuseiha** and **Shinto Taiseikyo;**
5. Revival Shinto sects: **Izumo Oyashirokyo, Shinrikyo** and **Shinto Taikyo.**

Tenrikyo, the largest of the traditional 13 now has independent status, and will be dealt with separately as will **Omotokyo,** a new sect which is sometimes included under the Kyoha Shinto umbrella. Almost all the above have spawned splinter sects which have gained legal recognition since government controls over religion were lifted after World War II. As a whole **Sect Shinto** claims around 6,000,000 adherents, and a further 2,000,000 claim to belong to **New Sect Shinto**. Sect Shinto has no shrines. Its meeting places are commonly called churches. Its affairs are overseen by the **Association of Sect Shinto**, directorship of which rotates annually amongst the member sects.

L

Laachi. A highly politicized branch of the **Yasawiya Sufi** order to be found in Kirghizstan.

Lahoris. *See* **Ahmadiya (Lahoris)**.

Lanka Insight Meditation Society. Also known as the **Lanka Vipassana Bhavana Samitiya.**

Lanka Vipassana Bhavana Samitiya. The Insight (*vipassana*) Meditation Society of Sri Lanka. A lay meditation group founded in the early 1950s by an influential group of **Theravada** Buddhist laymen, led by H. Sri Nissanka, to promote the meditational programme of Mahasi Sayadaw, a prominent Burmese spiritual teacher. The use of Burmese monks to introduce the practice in Sri Lanka led to some nationalist hostility to the movement in its early years of existence. Lay meditation is held to be beneficial in a variety of non-traditional ways, for instance in the alleviation of illness and anxiety. The society has been rather unsympathetic towards the established *sangha* and appeals to a predominantly English-educated urban élite. Its membership is consequently rather small.

Laotian Theravada. Laotian Theravada Buddhism followed much the same history as that of Cambodia and Thailand. Laos became independent of French rule in 1954. Prior to the Communist takeover in 1975 Buddhism was the state religion under royal patronage with no divisions into "orders" (as in Thailand and Cambodia), and a single patriarch. In 1975 virtually all 3,000,000 Laotians were Buddhists.

Prior to Communist rule Laotian Bud-

dhism was at an earlier stage of modernization than its neighbours. The monks enjoyed a high degree of public respect and played a major role in public education. In 1965, the Institute of Buddhist Studies was established under the Ministry of Education, subsequently being transferred to the Ministry of Religious Affairs in 1975. Many monks continued their studies in Thailand and India, returning to important ecclesiastical and lay positions on their return.

Following the protracted civil war between the Laotian government forces and the Laotian People's Revolutionary Party (or Pathet Lao), the 600-year-old monarchy was abolished in 1975. Many monks fled to Thailand, Europe and the USA. Little is known with any degree of accuracy about the current state of the Laotian Sangha though leadership is provided by the **Lao United Buddhists Association (LUBA)**.

Lao United Buddhists' Association. The LUBA was founded in the late 1970s, under the supervision of the Lao People's Revolutionary Party (LPRP), in an attempt to abolish the traditional hierarchical structure of the Laotian **Theravada** *Sangha* and to subordinate Buddhist teachings to the ideology of the party. Monks were urged to propagate socialism, though on a theoretical level the party accepts that socialism and Buddhism are compatible. Since the early '80s the status of monks has improved and many, who had previously fled to Thailand, have now returned. *Sangha* membership is improving, popular festivals are being revived (despite official party disapproval of superstition), *wats* are receiving government money for refurbishment, and Pali studies and meditation courses are becoming widespread. The President of the LUBA,

Maha Thongkhoune Anantasounthone, estimated (August 1985) that 6,897 fully ordained monks and 9,415 novices, in 2,812 *wats,* are spread throughout the country, with 20 per cent of that number in and around Vientiane. The morning alms round is becoming an increasing feature of Lao life once again and the hostility of the authorities has eased a good deal. Since 1985 Party members may temporarily enter the *Sangha* and several monks participate in the Lao Front for National Construction at the highest level.

Lassyism. An indigenous prophet-healing church in the Congo which originated with a former Salvation Army member, and charismatic prophetic figure, Zepherin Lassy, in 1953. Members are sometimes referred to as Bougists, from the church's full official name, Mission de Dieu du Bougie (or Nzambi ya Bougie, God of the Candle). Growth was rapid, and by 1961 members made up nearly 9 per cent of the population of the Congo. Subsequently decline set in, and the organization is currently noticeably less influential than another indigenous movement in the Congo, the **Mouvement Croix-Koma**.

Latin-rite Catholics. See the entry on **Roman Catholics**.

Latter-day Saints. An alternative name for the **Mormons**.

Liberal Judaism. *See* **Reform Judaism.**

Liborismo. An **Afro-American spiritist** cult in the Dominican Republic. It originated at the turn of the century with one Liborio, and has been revived in recent decades. The majority of adherents also continue to practise as **Roman Catholics.**

Library of Tibetan Works and Archives. Established in the 1970s by exiled **Gelugpa** monks in northern India, the library exists to preserve and disseminate the Buddhist, and related, literary traditions of Tibet. It publishes many writings by the Dalai Lama.

Light on Yoga Association. An organization founded by B. K. S. Iyengar to foster the spread of **Iyengar Yoga.**

Lingayats. Lingayats or **Virashaivas** are the dominant religious community in Karnataka in South India, who worship Shiva in the phallic form of the *linga*. This is worn around the neck and is worshipped daily. Rather than performing the usual Hindu rites of passage, the Lingayats initiate their children into the tradition soon after birth. Part of the wider *bhakti* movement, the tradition traces its origin to Basava (d.c1167), who rejected the orthodox values of Hinduism such as caste hierarchy, the mediation of Brahmin priests between devotee and God, and the authority of the Veda, saying that knowledge of God (i.e. Shiva) is available to all regardless of caste or gender. Basava and other poets composed free-verse devotional poems in the Kannada language which criticized ritual as being useless and praised the body as the true temple of Shiva. Lingayat doctrine is not dissimilar to that of **Kashmir Shaivism.**

There is a Lingayat order of ascetics, the *jangama,* though most members are householders. The Lingayats are free of many of the social restrictions of orthodox Hinduism: for example, the women participate in the choice of marriage partner and can re-marry upon the death of a husband.

London Church of Christ. This is a major UK base of the **Church of Christ** movement which is anchored in the Boston

Church of Christ. Similar bases exist in Birmingham and Manchester.

Lord's Army. A movement of lay renewal within the Romanian **Orthodox Church**. It was founded in 1923, but under Communist rule in Romania its members were persecuted: one of the main leaders, Traian Dorz, spent 17 years in prison followed by further years of house arrest and intimidation. As well as organizing meetings for prayer and Bible study, it has also been able to produce a certain amount of Christian literature, including Bibles.

Love Family. This movement, not to be confused with **Family of Love,** is also known as the **Church of Armageddon** (or Love Israel Family).

Lubavich (Lubavitch) Hasidism. (See also **Hasidism, Agudat Israel.**) Habad was founded as a new movement in Hasidism by Rabbi Schneur Zalman of Lyady (1745–1812). The word Habad is an acronym of Hokhmah (Wisdom), Binah (Understanding) and Daat (Knowledge). These are the three highest ("intellectual") emanations of the divine mind (*sefirot*) which according to the Kabbalistic microcosm–macrocosm doctrine are to be found also in man. Schneur Zalman taught that the true basis of religious life was the intellectual meditation on God (the awakening of the higher potentialities ("Habad") and only on this secure foundation could the emotional sphere, so highly stressed in Hasidism, be properly developed. Habad, thus, represents a particular stress on the priority of the intellect compared with other Hasidic groups.

Schneur Zalman's *Collected Writings* (*Likutei Amarim*, 1796), normally referred to as (the) *Tanya*, is the first systematic work of Hasidic "theology" and remains the core Habad text. He taught a two-

fold "perspectivism" concerning the nature of reality. From one perspective there is a process of the "going out" of divinity (the realm of emanation) and this divine creativity serves to invest all "creation" with the divinity (that constitutes "reality"). This notion led to the charge of pantheism, levelled against Habad, by its opponents. From the second (and divine) viewpoint there are no emanations of divinity only the appearance of the (many) emanations, which merely conceals the (One) divinity. The world is thus "nothing", that is, there is no "creation" at all—there is only God. The Hasid participates in this divine process in two ways. Firstly, the physical performance of the commandments reflects, and is reflected in, the outward movement of divinity. Secondly, by intellectual meditation on the *sefirot,* as manifest in the mind, the individual Hasid can re-unify the *sefirot* in their source (En Sof).

He was also opposed to the growing tendency among Hasidim to venerate the *Tzaddik* (Rebbe) as miracle-worker and understood the Rebbe as the intellectual and spiritual leader of his Hasidim.

His son and the second Habad Rebbe, Rabbi Dov Ber (1773–1827), established a centre in Lubavich in Belroussia, and Habad Hasidism is also commonly referred to Lubavich Hasidism. Dov Ber developed his father's teachings and was the author of *Tract on Ecstasy,* in which he sought to distinguish the spurious levels of emotional ecstasy from the "real thing". Lubavich became the largest and most prominent Hasidic movement in northern Russia.

Habad teaches that a portion of divinity (En Sof) is to be found in every Jew but that this "spark" is obscured by the "ego" and only when this is transcended can the spark be awoken. This awakening is the result of intellectual insight but can be fostered by ritual practice.

Rabbi Joseph Isaac Schneerson (1880–1950), the 6th Rebbe in the line of succession, was the leader of **Orthodox Jewry** in the Russia and after 1917 devoted his considerable energies to working for the preservation of traditional Jewish life under Soviet rule. He was exiled by the Soviet government in 1927 for his activities and with many of his followers moved to Brooklyn (New York) where he established his headquarters in 1941. J. I. Schneersohn was a major figure in the general and widespread post-War revival of Orthodoxy in America. Under his leadership, Lubavich developed its "outreach" programme to non-Lubavich Jews and offered many the opportunity to return to a traditional form of Jewish life (see **Baalei Teshuvah**).

The present Lubavich Rebbe, Rabbi Menahem Mendel Schneersohn (1902), the son-in-law of Joseph Isaac Schneersohn (7th in the dynastic line), presides over the largest contemporary Hasidic group and a veritable international empire of educational facilities (high schools and *Yeshivot*), publishing ventures (Kehot publishing company) and media services (radio and television stations and channels).

As the absolute authoritative and venerated Rebbe for his tens of thousands of Hasidim and the even larger number of sympathizers, he is one of the most significant figures in the contemporary Jewish world. His immediate followers live in close proximity to the Lubavich headquarters in Brooklyn and live lives centred around their Rebbe. Many Lubavich are engaged in a life-long programme of the study of Habad and other Jewish sources with specialists teaching the Habad interpretation of *Kabbalah*. They will often carry a copy of *Tanya* and can be seen studying around the city. Many spend an hour a day or more reciting the Shema (a particular prayer) in order to focus their energy on unifying the upper and lower forces in their minds. Usual Hasidic practices, including song and dance, also feature prominently in the Lubavich path. In addition, thousands regularly visit the Rebbe for a personal audience in order to ask for advice and guidance on all aspects of their existence.

The current Rebbe has continued to develop his father's "outreach" programme and many thousands of Jews from a non-Orthodox programme have become Lubavich Hasidim or have adopted to some degree a more traditional, observant, Orthodox lifestyle. At Jewish centres around the world Lubavich Hasidim encourage and sometimes cajole Jews into performing the commandments. They have a fleet of trucks and buses ("(Command-ment) Mitvah-tanks") which offer instruc-tion and the opportunity to fulfil command-ments. On Friday nights, all over Israel and in New York, they encourage Jewish women to light Sabbath candles and they are particularly evident at Jewish festival times attempting to persuade Jews to follow the patterns of traditional observance. The Lubavich strive for a high public profile, for example, they light Hannukah candles in Times Square and in other centres. They have also focussed attention on Jewish students at university campuses around the world. The Rebbe has forged an "army" who work tirelessly for their perception of the good of Jewry.

A theological position underlies these practical efforts at reviving traditional Jewish practice. Habad holds that each Jew possesses, however apparently hidden, a portion of the divine spark. This spark when awoken, will move towards others and they attempt to create a "critical mass" of such sparks in order to hasten the redemption. Often the analogy of the human body is utilized to talk of Jewry, with each limb and cell necessary for the healthy functioning of the whole. Every Jew, thus, is of "supreme" value and, in general, Habad is more open to *gentile* converts than is usual among Orthodox Jewish groups. These efforts have been highly successful.

Habad has an ambiguous relationship to the modern world. They see little, or no, value in secular education and yet have a graduate Rebbe. They rail against the evils of the modern world and yet have a most positive, albeit selective, "instrumental" attitude to modern technology (videos, films, facsimiles, satellite broadcasting, etc.).

Again, and much more importantly, they have an uneasy relationship with the reality of the State of Israel. They supported the establishment of the Jewish state in 1948 but the Rebbe has never visited the country. Since 1967, however, Habad has been heavily involved in Israeli party politics. Lubavich (along with **Ger Hasidism**) have come to dominate **Agudat Israel** and play a dominant role in the political activities of the **Ultra-Orthodox** community. The Rebbe has consistently taken a hard line on the "occupied territories" and has rejected the "land for peace" option. Lubavich involvement in Haredi politics was a significant factor in the fragmentation of Haredi parties. The Rebbe and Rabbi Eliezer Schach have challenged each other for the Haredi vote.

Before the recent collapse of the USSR, Lubavich worked clandestinely in the Soviet Union and since the collapse of state socialism have been active throughout the countries of eastern and central Europe. Radiating out from the Brooklyn centre, there are Lubavich centres in North Africa, Israel (Kfar Habad, Jerusalem and Tel Aviv); France, Britain, Canada, Italy, Australia and other Jewish communities.

Most recently (1992) there have been rumours and newspaper and magazine article claiming that the Rebbe (who is without an heir) is the *messiah* and that the redemption is at hand and will be marked by the Rebbe's triumphant arrival in Israel.

Lui-ists. One of the two major sects within the modern Taiwanese **Unity Society.**

Lusitanian Church. *See* Reformed Catholic.

Lutherans. Martin Luther (1483–1546), often regarded as the founder of the **Protestant** Reformation, was a monk, priest and theological lecturer at the University of Wittenberg, Germany. His studies led him to the belief that, through the grace of God, faith alone is necessary for salvation, churches, priests and even good works are not essential. These beliefs were summarized in the *95 Theses* which he is said to have nailed to the door of Wittenberg Church in 1517. Later he deduced there were only two true sacraments, Baptism and the Eucharist, rather than the seven defined by the **Roman Catholic** Church. In 1521 that church excommunicated him.

He continued to teach and his views spread through Europe. Within 20 years the Lutheran Church had become the state church of Germany, Scandinavia and much of Eastern Europe. Luther translated the Bible into German, wrote a number of hymns (of which the best known is "A safe stronghold our God is still") and married a former nun, Katherine von Bora.

The Lutheran Church is still the state church in most Scandinavian countries. In Sweden membership is automatic, one must choose to opt out. In Germany some Lutheran churches have joined with **Reformed** (Presbyterian) churches to form a united church. Lutherans believe that the Bible is the sole rule of faith, to which creeds and tradition are subservient. For this reason much modern biblical criticism has been led by Lutherans. The *Book of Concord,* first published in 1580 collects together the beliefs of Lutherans in the words of the creeds, of Luther, and in an agreed statement of faith drawn up in 1577. There is a single order of priesthood, although oversight is given by a "General Superintendent" of an area, who in some countries is known as a bishop. However methods of church government vary from country to country. Services are liturgical and will normally include a sermon based on the Bible. Celebration of the Eucharist has, as in other denominations, become more frequent in recent years. Hymns are still an important part of worship, many Lutheran hymns are well known throughout the church, for example "Now thank we all our God" and "Wake O wake", owing much to their settings by J. S. Bach.

In many countries (as in the case of the United Kingdom) there are small Lutheran churches ministering primarily to ethnic groups, particularly former refugees from Eastern Europe such as Latvia or Estonia. Most Lutheran churches belong to the **Lutheran World Foundation** whose headquarters are in Geneva, Switzerland. The Lutheran Church is one of the largest denominations in the world with global membership estimated at over 60,000,000.

Lutheran World Federation. Relief work by Lutheran Churches after World War I, extensive contacts between and unifying movements inside Lutheran Churches created the desire to establish a body where common interests could be discussed. These efforts led to the 1st Lutheran World Conferences in Eisenach 1923 and two further conferences in Copenhagen (1929) and Paris (1935). The fourth meeting, planned for 1940 in Philadelphia was, because of World War II, postponed to Lund, Sweden in 1947. Here Lutheran Churches of 23 different countries adopted a constitution and the name was changed to The Lutheran World Federation (LWF).

The LWF sees itself as a "free association of Lutheran Churches" and eight General Assemblies have been held. At the second assembly in Hanover, Germany, it was decided to create the Lutheran World Service to serve people regardless of race, creed, or political affiliation. (In 1990 there were around 5,000 employees.) The eighth assembly in Curitiba, Brazil, adopted a new constitution which includes the statement "The Lutheran World Federation is a communion of Churches which confess the Triune God, agree in the proclamation of the word of God and are united in pulpit and altar fellowship", and also a new organizational structure with the LWF secretariat in the Ecumenical Centre, Geneva, and the three departments: theology and studies, mission and development and the LWS.

The LWF is governed by the Assemblies which meet every eight years. The governing body is served by a council of 48 members (50 per cent Churches from First World and 50 per cent from Third World countries). In 1990 the LWF had 105 member churches. It is very much involved in the ecumenical process and dialogue with other churches, though its strong confessional emphasis and political conservatism has led to tensions with the WCC.

M

Macumba. An Afro–Brazilian spirit possession cult which is similar in its syncretism and in other respects to **Candomblé, Vodun** and **Shango.** It has gradually passed from religion to magic, and is often associated with immorality and wrong-doing.

Madariya. The Madariya is a **Sufi** order found in India and Nepal. It was founded by Shah Badi al-din Madar, a Syrian who settled in India until his death in 1440. Shah Madar, sometimes called Zinda Pir, or Living Guide, is also venerated by the **Malangs**—and as is the case with the latter, the practices of the Madaris are regarded as being unorthodox. The saint's tomb, and the seat of the order still today, is in Makanpur, Uttar Pradesh. A great fair is held there annually on the occasion of the *'urs,* or anniversary of his death. Large numbers of pilgrims visit the shrine every year. Recent attendance figures show the fair to be visited by 50,000 people.

The practices of the Madaris are very much akin to those of Hindu holy men. No emphasis is placed on fasting and prayer, and devotees of the order are noted for their black flags and turbans, and the iron chains they carry. They do not eat either fish or meat. An important feature of the order is the use of drugs.

Madaris are either settled or move around, being particularly noticeable as mendicants at the time of Eid when they travel around receiving the *zakat* gifts that higher caste Muslims would find it dishonourable to accept. The reverence which they accord to the Imams 'Ali and Husayn indicates a devotion to the family of the Prophet similar to that in **Shi'ism.**

The Madariya was very popular and influential in Bengal from at least the 15th to the 17th century; and in north India at the end of the last century, the Madariya was considered to be a mass order—it

then made up 2.3 per cent of the Muslim population. No recent figures are available, but the order is widespread in South Asia, where it functions in many ways as one of the lower castes—members are born into it rather than joining voluntarily, and are often found in the role of keepers of cemeteries.

Madhva Gaudiya Vairagins. An order of Hindu **Vaishnava** ascetics closely linked to the **Brahmasampradaya** and particularly prevalent in Orissa state.

Mafdal (Mizrahi, National Religious Party). (*See also* **Zionism, Orthodoxy.**) Mizrahi was founded in 1904 as a religious, **Orthodox** party joining the **Zionist** Organization with "The land of Israel for the people of Israel according to the *Torah* of Israel" as its motto. Mizrahi developed into an international organization of religious Jews who support the State of Israel. In the land of Israel, two independent groups were formed—the Mizrahi party and the Mizrahi Workers' Party. These two joined together to form Mafdal (National Religious Party) in 1956. Mafdal (and earlier as its component parts) has been a coalition partner in every Israeli government (Labour and Likud) and have been a major factor in Israel's political stability since 1948.

Traditionally, under pressure from both its non-religious coalition partners (seeking to limit its proposed religious legislation) and from the more separatist Orthodox parties, Mafdal has sought a pragmatic accommodation of the religious sector in Israel's mainly non-religious society, while maintaining its long-term aim of the establishment of a Torah-state. It has defended religious interests against secular pressures and worked for co-operation between the non-religious and religious in the building of the Jewish state, the establishment of which Mafdal considers to be of religious–messianic significance.

Mafdal followers have been ardent supporters of the state and have generally accepted their national service, unlike the non-Zionist Orthodox, and this has often been combined with *Yeshivah* study. Mafdal institutions, where there is an attempted synthesis between religious and "secular" values, include the state–religious schools, Bar Ilan University, and the religious *Kibbutzim* and Moshavim, with their practical synthesis of Zionist labour and Orthodox values.

Mafdal's strategy of co-operation with the ruling non-religious parties has ensured its almost continuous control of the Ministry of Religious Affairs. This has allowed Mafdal to wield great influence over the Chief Rabbinate and religious courts and councils and to operate an extensive system of patronage.

After holding between 10 and 12 Knesset seats from 1949 until 1977, Mafdal's electoral support fell dramatically to only five seats in the 1988 election (the six seats won in 1981 were reduced to four in 1984).

Significant factors in this decline include the radicalism of its younger members—many of the ultra-nationalist groups have their origins in Mafdal—and the ethnic/ **Sephardi** factor. Mafdal's view that the 1967 victory has "messianic" import and that the occupied territories are "God given" run counter to much current thinking and in the 1992 general election Mafdal secured six seats. It appears as if its reduced status might be permanent.

Maha Bodhi Society. The founder, Angarika Dharmapala (1864–1933), born Don David Hewavitarne, came from a middle-class family in Colombo and grew up within the colonial British Christian education system. His dislike for Christianity provoked passionate nationalist feelings for Ceylon as a Buddhist nation. When, in 1880, he encountered the **Theosophists** he formed a special relationship with Madame Blavatsky (it was she who encouraged him to study Pali and Buddhism). In 1891 he visited Bodh Gaya, the place of the Buddha's *maha bodhi* ("great enlightenment"), but was disappointed to find it dilapidated and under Hindu ownership. He formed the Maha Bodhi Society (**MBS**) in Calcutta that same year with the aim of redeeming the site for Buddhism. He also intended to set up a Buddhist high school at Bodh Gaya. The MBS became a forceful manifestation of Sinhalese nationalism and revived the awareness that Buddhism had its roots in India. Dharmapala's nationalist cause came to fruition only after his death when in 1948 Ceylon won independence. Hikkaduve Sumangala was the first President of the society with Dharmapala as organizing secretary. The MBS has developed centres in many Indian cities and due to Dharmapala's role in the World Parliament of Religions (Chicago, 1934) the MBS achieved international publicity and received foreign patronage. The society, now based in Colombo, sponsors all Sinhala Buddhist monasteries and funds missions beyond Sri Lanka. The **Buddhist Publication Society** is closely allied to the MBS. Although a Buddhist high school has not to this day been established at Bodh Gaya, Dharmapala's vision did not fail; on the site there is a Tibetan and a Burmese monastery and a Chinese and a Japanese temple.

Mahanikay. The largest fraternity of **Theravada** Buddhist monks in Thailand. Of the over 28,000 monasteries presently operating in the country, 26,694 belong to the Mahanikay. The order escaped the monastic reforms imposed by the kings of the late 19th century and it remains more closely aligned with the common people. In the 1930s the order became imbued with a democratic spirit and as a result the mid-century saw fairly intense conflict with the other, more aristocratic fraternity, the **Thammayut**. Disagreements are primarily organizational and political but do not affect the doctrinal domain, in which there is virtual accord. In the mid '70s some, mostly well-educated, monks of peasant stock formed the **Federation of Buddhists of Thailand (FBT)** to press for a less autocratic system of *Sangha* government. The fraternity has been prominent in the popular democracy movement which led to the downfall of Prime Minister General Kraprayoon in May 1992. The Mahanikay was also found in Cambodia, though it was merged with its rival fraternity, the **Thomayat**, by the Heng Samrin government in 1975.

Mahanubhavs. An Indian **Vaishnava** devotional movement particularly strong in Maharashtra state. Adherents focus their devotions on a group of five historical figures known as the "five Krishnas" who are believed to be manifestations (*avatara*) of the Supreme Being. The most prominent of the five, Chakradhar (1194–1276), is held to be the founder of the group. Although their devotion to Krishna links them to the mainstream Hindu tradition, the Mahanubhavs reject caste and pollution laws and the authority of the Vedas. The main text of the movement is a collection of Chakradhar's sayings, the *Sutrapatha,* and devotees tend to adopt a fairly ascetic lifestyle. Also known as the **Manbhavs,** or Manbhaus, the group show family resemblances to their larger Marathi rival, the **Warkaris.**

Mahdavis. The Mahdavis originated as followers of an Indian mahdi figure, Sayyid Ahmad of Jaunpur (1443–1504). At one time small communities could be found in all regions of the sub-continent, but opposition by the Mughal state and the religious establishment prevailed, and today only a few Mahdavi groups survive in Hyderabad and Gujarat.

Mahdibaghwalas (Mahdibagh-Wallas). The Mahdibaghwalas are a tiny sub-sect of the **Daudis** within Indian Islam. The Daudis, in turn, form a branch of the **Musta'li** sect of **Isma'ili Shi'ism.** They are commonly (though slightly inaccurately) identified as **Bohoras.** The Mahdibaghwalas seceded in 1897, and for a while flourished as a somewhat isolated community in Nagpur. The few remaining today attract little attention.

Mahdiya. Mahdism is a generic term for Mahdi-led messianic movements in Islam. More particularly it refers to a movement in the Sudan that has continued to be influential down to today.

Muhammad Ahmad (1848–1885), a member of the Sammaniya **Sufi** order, proclaimed himself Mahdi in 1881, and with the capture of Khartoum in 1885 (and the death of General Gordon and his garrison) established an Islamic state in the Sudan. Drawing a parallel between himself and the Prophet Muhammad, he called his movement the **Ansar**—the Helpers—as Muhammad called those who assisted his move from Mecca to Medina. After his death six months later, leadership of the movement fell to a deputy, and the Islamic state lasted 14 years until defeated by an Anglo–Egyptian army under General Kitchener in 1899.

Despite initial British attempts to suppress the movement, the Ansar continued and eventually revived and regained legitimacy under the Mahdi's charismatic posthumous son Abd al-Rahman al-Mahdi (who retained the leadership until his death in 1959). Yet it had now changed character considerably, entering into limited cooperation with its former foes, the British (and also the Sufi orders). Following independence in 1956, it has been influential through its support for its own political organization, the Umma Party.

In elections scheduled for June 1969, two Ansar leaders, Sadiq al-Mahdi, a great grandson of the Mahdi, and al-Hadi al-Mahdi (Sadiq's uncle), were widely expected to come to power as Prime Minister and President respectively. They represented two wings that had emerged in the Ansar movement, the pragmatic modernism of Sadiq and the religious conservatism of al-Hadi. Sadiq exercised political control of the Umma Party, while al-Hadi exercised spiritual leadership of the Ansar with the title *imam*.

In the event, Colonel Nimeiri's military *coup* intervened. In 1970 the Ansar stronghold on Aba Island was bombarded, and thousands of Ansar, including their *imam* al-Hadi al-Mahdi, were killed. This was not, however, the end of their influence. Sadiq al-Mahdi, with traditional Ansar support, remained a leading political figure throughout Nimeiri's rule (running the gamut from leader of an attempted *coup,* exile, prime ministerial office, and imprisonment). After Nimeiri's deposition in 1985 he emerged yet again, following the elections in 1986, as Prime Minister, until the further military *coup* of 1989.

A long-time supporter, with the **Muslim Brotherhood**, of introducing Islamic law in the Sudan (Sadiq al-Mahdi has at times been quite close to Hassan Turabi, the gifted leader of the country's Muslim Brotherhood), al-Mahdi nevertheless, in marked contrast to Turabi, strongly opposed the autocratic imposition of Shari'a by President Nimeiri in 1983. He had led a commission to develop a modern interpretation of Shari'a based on the Quran and Sunna but, unlike Nimeiri's policy, sidestepping the medieval law manuals. Also unlike Nimeiri, he opposed the imposition of Shari'a on the non-Muslim peoples of the southern Sudan. In the post-Nimeiri period the Islamic laws were frozen, but the Shari'a issue remains a live one.

Mahikari. *See* **Sekai Mahikari Bunmei Kyodan.**

Maitatsine. This Hausa word meaning "he who curses" was applied to the leader of a millenarian Muslim sect in Nigeria, Alhaji Muhammadu Marwa, and is sometimes used as a label for the sect itself. The more widely used name for the latter, however, is **'Yan Tatsine**. Marwa was killed in an attempted takeover of the city of Kano in 1980, but the sect has survived.

Majelis Buddhayana Indonesia (MBI). A popular Indonesian Buddhist sect more usually referred to as **Buddhayana.**

Majelis Upasaka Pandita Agama Buddha Indonesia. "Council of Buddhist lay spiritual advisers of Indonesia." A Buddhist lay organization which came into being in the 1970s partly on account of a shortage of monks. The "spiritual advisers" (*panditas*) are not subject to monastic rules and can therefore marry and are also authorized to issue certificates of marriage. The *MUABI* is a member of the **All Indonesia Federation of Buddhist Organizations (WALUBI)**. A leading figure is Soemantri M. S., a retired Army General, who lectures in Trisakti University in Jakarta, and who recently translated some of the works of the Thai scholar-monk Buddhadasa Bhikkhu into Indonesian.

Majlis-i Mushawarat. A widely used abbreviation for the **All-India Muslim Majlis-i Mushawarat**.

Malabar Christians. *See* Syro-Indian Churches.

Malagasy Religion. The Malagasy people, perhaps 10,000,000 in number, originated a millenium ago, crossing the Indian Ocean in canoes from their homeland in South East Asia. They speak a language akin to Bahasa Indonesia. There has been some intermingling with African and Arab elements, and they are divided into a dozen tribal units, some of which have social castes.

The Malagasy have little concern for religious beliefs, and lack an extended mythological system. Their chief concern is with conduct. They stress the interdependence of persons within society, but "society" includes the dead as well as the living. "The living share one home: the dead share one home" is an often quoted proverb, one of the hundreds of proverbial sayings that play the part that holy books do in other religions. The dead are honoured with sacrifices and elaborate rituals, sometimes including the exhumation of the essential eight bones of the skeleton, which are danced round the family property with great festivity.

God is to all Malagasy a remote but basically benevolent being, all-seeing and all-rewarding. He is called Andriamanitra, the fragrant lord, and Zanahary, the creator. As in most peasant communities, people's chief concerns are with health, food and plenty of children to be a support in old age. These blessings flow from not offending God, and, more importantly, from assiduously cultivating the ancestors. "May you be blessed by God and the ancestors" is a customary form of goodbye.

Circumcision is almost universal. Taboos (*fady*) abound, and apply not only to things and actions but even to words. The calendar, based on Arab sources, is full of lucky and unlucky days. Religious specialists include the guardians of shrines and diviners. Witches, the only people who go out at night, strike fear into young and old alike, and with good reason, for they are skilled in the use of poisons. Travellers honour local spirits by making offerings at holy trees, rocks, or rivers, and a bad omen will cause an enterprise to be abandoned.

Many of the basic aspects of ancestral religion are held by the near half of the population that is Christian (chiefly **Roman Catholic** or **Protestant**, but with some **Anglicans** and a few new sects). The same applies to the small number of Malagasy Muslims. To try to break away from ancestral customs and ancestral

ways of viewing the world is almost impossible, even for the highly educated and Europeanized minority.

Malangs. Malangs are male religious mendicants who belong to the bi-shar' (without the Shari'a) group of **Sufi** orders. They are mainly to be found in northern India (especially the Punjab) and the Deccan. Other Muslims consider them to be unorthodox. The difference between the bi-shar' and the ba-shar' (with the shari'a) orders lies in the concept of inner and outer world. Like other Sufis, the Malangs believe in the existence of both worlds. The ba-shar' Sufis, however, live in the outer world and attempt to purify this outer world to bring it on the same level as the inner world. They have to make a transition from one world to the other. The Malangs totally disregard the outer world and concentrate only on the inner one. Henceforth, they have no need for the Shari'a which is used for regulating the outer world. The Malang communicates directly with God without mediation by external prescriptions. This communication takes place in a state of intoxication through hashish or other narcotics. In this state the Malang can also disregard his body, the only connection with the outer world.

A characteristic of the Malang is his particular style of dress. He sees himself to be the bride of God and thus to be subservient to God. Malangs wear female ornaments, bangles and rings to emphasise this position. An iron bangle is often found, indicating that their tie with God cannot be broken. They wander from shrine to shrine but might also, on the command of God or a living saint, attach themselves to a particular shrine. In spite of their emphasis on equality, theirs is a hierarchically structured community.

Maldevidan Cult. This is a syncretic mix of Hinduism and **Roman Catholicism** found in Martinique. The god Vishnu is identified with Christ, the goddess Mari-eman with the Virgin Mary, and various minor gods with Catholic saints (as happens too in Afro-Catholic cults such as **Candomblé, Shango** and **Santería**). In rites of spirit-possession, Vishnu/Christ is believed to possess a priest and speak through him while he stands bare-footed on sharp implements, for instance machetes. A fellow priest interprets this revelation. There follow the sacrifice of a sheep or a cock, and a feast.

Malikis. The Maliki rite or school of Islamic law (*madhhab*) was founded by Malik b. Anas (d. 795), a lawyer of Medina and pupil of Abu Hanifa, founder of the **Hanafi** school. Malik's main views are contained in *al-Muwatta* (*The Beaten Path*), which outlines the practice followed in Medina, supported by numerous Traditions (sayings and deeds of the Prophet and his close companions). It represents one of the earliest collections of such material, and Malik is also highly regarded as a traditionist.

Malikis, one of four **Sunni** schools of law alongside the **Hanafis**, the **Shafi'is**, and the **Hanbalis**, are currently predominant in North and West Africa and Upper Egypt. They are generally thought to be more tradition-conscious and conservative than the Hanafis or Shafi'is, and are opposed to the strategems (*hiyal*) used by Hanafis to circumvent Shari'a rulings that appear to be inconvenient or unsuited to new situations, for example the ban on taking interest. They also oppose the excessive use of analogy (*qiyas*), particularly as practised by the Hanafis. In common with other schools they accept the consensus of religious scholars (*ijma'*) as a source of Law. They base their acceptance of this consensus on consideration of the public interest.

In modern times Maliki interpretation of law has shown signs of greater flexibility than the classical theory seems to allow. In Morocco from the 15th century onwards Maliki jurists developed a practical approach to formulating law to suit actual

conditions, recognizing that this might not meet the requirements of strict Maliki doctrine. In Egypt the famous modernist Muhammad 'Abduh (1845–1905), so influential for the **Salafiya**, was himself a Maliki. Working from the Maliki view that a jurist should assume God's desire for human welfare in choosing between Quranic and Prophetic texts, he held that in framing laws a jurist should always seek to promote the general welfare and should do this by the use of human reason, working from general Islamic moral principles. 'Abduh's views are consistent with the generally moralistic outlook of the Malikis regarding the purpose of Holy Law.

Manalistas. Members of the **Iglesia ni Cristo** in the Philippines may be referred to as Manalistas after the movement's founder, Felix Manalo (1886–1963).

Manbhavs. An alternative name given to the **Mahanubhavs,** a Hindu devotional movement.

Mandaeans. An extremely small, virtually extinct religious community concentrated in south-western Iran and southern Iraq, once erroneously referred to as "Christians of St. John the Baptist", in allusion to their baptismal rituals. They are possibly of Palestinian or Syrian origin and were identified by some Muslims with the Sabaeans (*Sabi'in*), a scriptural group referred to in the *Quran*. A large body of religious literature, written in a form of Aramaic in the Mandaean language, has been studied, and some of it published. Their beliefs, which involve a system of emanations from the Godhead, suggest a Gnostic influence or origin.

Manjusri Institute. Founded in 1976 by the followers of two Tibetan monks, Lama Thubten Yeshe and Lama Zopa, at Conishead Priory, Cumbria, England as an

early attempt to bring **Gelugpa** teachings to
the West. Now run by Geshe Kelsang, it is
part of the **Foundation for the Preservation
of the Mahayana Tradition** established by
Lama Zopa. The Institute offers visitors a
range of Buddhist, and related, meditative
and intellectual training. Already the home
to a growing number of Western monks and
nuns, an educational programme leading to
the monastic degree of *geshe* is underway.
The Manjusri Institute has a number of
associated *dharma* centres throughout the
world, and a flourishing publishing arm,
Wisdom Publications.

Maori Religion. The Maori comprise 10 per
cent of New Zealand's population and
are closely related to other Polynesian
groups in language, culture and religion
(*see* **Polynesian Religion**).

The supreme being, Io, resides in the
highest of 12 heavens, and acts through
a hierarchy of gods, spirits, guardians and
ancestors. Creation occurred when Rangi,
the sky god, mated with Papa-tua-Nuku,
the earth mother, to generate numerous
gods such as Tane, Tangaroa and Rongo
to rule over nature and human activity.
The realm of gods also includes the *wairua*
(spirits), the *tipuna* ("ancestors"), the
kaitiaki ("guardians") as well as the *kehu*
("ghosts") and the *taniwha* ("monsters").

There are no strictly maintained barriers
between the realm of the gods and that
of humans. The *tipuna*, for example, the
remembered ancestors or the living dead,
belong to both realms. Community is what
binds the living and the dead—the latter
live on because they are remembered by
the former, and if appropriately recognized
and regarded, can bring blessing to
the former. The people, the nobility
(*rangatira*) and the high chiefs (*ariki*)
are bound together by loyalties in the
extended family (*whanau*), the sub-tribe
(*hapu*) and the tribe (*iwi*).

The religious practitioners (*tohunga*) are
specialists in maintaining equilibrium in the
community, and assuring its quality. Some
are experts in magic and others in the

sacred. The realm of the dead, which
also inter-penetrates the human sphere, is
presided over by the guardian of the third
realm, the underworld (*hinenuiotepo*).
This is where death, disease and evil
have their origin. All three realms are
infused with *mana* (undifferentiated "holy
power") which can erupt in people or
places or endow certain objects such as
the greenstone tiki with a sense of primary
value and worth. Where and in whom
mana erupts there is danger, and caution
is essential when humans approach such
places or people. Before normality can
return, the *tapu* (the sacredness) must be
lifted. But even in the course of ordinary
life, a person is special. Each has, within
the life principle (*mauri*), a soul, and one's
mana (status, prestige or "face") endowed
at birth must be protected at all costs.

The Maori is conscious of the sacredness
of the whole of creation. Kinship with
nature and the land was essential for
human well-being. In approaching the
sacred there was a set form of words
to use (*karakia*)—the words once uttered
were said to release power, and thus bring
about change in a particular situation or
achieve a certain purpose.

Sickness and disease were thought to
have their origin in an evil force, and
were taken seriously, not only with a
prescription of herbal medicine, but in the
choice of *karakia*: there was a *karakia* for
the lifting of *tapu* and a different *karakia*
for the lifting of *makutu* (curse) laid by
someone with evil intent. The tohunga
were experts not only with words and
herbal remedies, but were also aware of
what we would call the psychology of
sickness.

Death is a time of intense sensitivity.
It is essential for the family and tribe
that the appropriate *karakia* are used to
release the spirit of the person (*wairua*)
which waits until the rituals have been
completed before it begins its journey
to Cape Reinga at the northernmost tip
of New Zealand. From there it descends
to the floor of the ocean to travel on
to the abode of the dead (*hinenuitepo*).

The funeral ceremonies (*tangi*) around an open casket are conducted in the meeting house on the *marae*. Visitors are received with a *karanga* and conduct themselves with solemnity, acknowledging first the ancestors of the *marae* and its family, then addressing the deceased person and the family in mourning, before receiving the visitors into the community with a handshake and "hongi"—the pressing of noses and the sharing of living breath—the most delicate of all personal contacts. The visitors are then asked to eat and drink. At an announced time, the final funeral rites are performed, the casket sealed and burial in the tribal area then takes place.

The *marae*, the grass area in front of the meeting house, is where speeches are delivered and visitors received. The Maori is a skilful orator: all who speak demonstrate an extensive knowledge of tribal traditions and mythologies. The *whare tupuna* (meeting house) is where the community meets, sleeps and conducts its affairs.

The Maori in recent years are open about their beliefs, values and traditions. A bicultural relationship is being forged with difficulty, but with measurable success, between the Maori and the European New Zealander. A visit to a *marea* is an essential part of a young person's education; tertiary institutions have a *marae* on campus. A Maori university has been founded and Maori studies are readily available at all other New Zealand universities.

Thus, the ancient form of Maori religion is experiencing an open renaissance in the latter part of the 20th century, going a long way to restore dignity to the Maori people of New Zealand.

Maori Religious Movements. The Maori response to the missionary movement and the European colonization of early New Zealand was to protect their identity and their traditions. An affinity with the Jews and the Old Testament was the cornerstone of the Maori defence against Christianity. Between 1830 and 1850 there

were 10 major religious movements which arose with this background.

The 1850s was the decade of healers with nine main movements identified. The colonial struggle culminated in the Land Wars of the 1860s which saw the Maori increasingly defranchized of land, and thus of their spiritual identity. Prophetic movements arose during this period of which 16 were of major importance, with many more of minor or local significance. By the turn of the century the struggle over land had concluded with the Maori defeated. Their leaders were to turn their attention to influencing the political process in order to retrieve some pride.

During the Land Wars, Maori were increasingly disillusioned with Christianity, seeing it as the vehicle of colonization. Reform movements were thus often a direct response to oppression and disillusionment. In the 20th century Maori have increasingly sought spiritual roots in Maori churches (**Ringatu** and **Ratana**) and, in many cases, *tohungas* (Maori religious specialists) have kept alive the values and ideals of pre- (Christian) European religion, and have passed on their knowledge and skill to successive generations.

In the 1980s, after a century of quiet struggle, the *Treaty of Waitangi*, signed in 1840 between Queen Victoria and the Maori tribal chiefs, was given an important place in New Zealand law. A tribunal was established to attempt to unravel and resolve problems arising out of the early colonial history of New Zealand and the clash between the European and the Maori.

Maraboutism. The French term "*marabout*" (from Arabic *murabit*) originally meant a warrior for Islam living in a *ribat* (frontier-post) but later came to be applied in North and West Africa to an adept of **Sufism**, or quite generally to a holy man in a loose sense. Thus maraboutism is used to refer to the range of Islamic beliefs and practices associated with the *marabouts*, including aspects of popular Islam frowned upon by stricter believers, such as reliance on talismans and amulets.

The *marabout* is thought by those who venerate him to possess *baraka* (sacred power) which "rubs off" on to believers through physical contact during his life, and through contact with his tomb-shrine after his death. Such shrines are very numerous in North and West Africa. The *baraka* may also be thought to be passed down through the *marabout*'s living descendants. In cases where he is—or is thought to be—descended from Muhammad, the *baraka* is of exceptional importance as that of the Prophet himself.

Maraboutism was a major target of Muslim reformers inspired by the **Salafiya** and also by **Wahhabism**, but it continues to exercise a powerful appeal.

Maria Legio. Founded by two Luo Catholics, Gaudencia Aoko and Simon Ondeto, in western Kenya in 1963 and named after a **Roman Catholic** organization, the Legion of Mary, Aoko was a charismatic figure who sought to combine RC and **Pentecostal** elements in worship. The movement, which in the 1970s claimed over 90,000 members (mainly among the Luo), emphasizes healing, exorcism, community and morality. Numbers declined with the departure of Aoko, but Maria Legio remains the largest African Instituted Church (*see* **African New Religious Movements**) to spring from a Roman Catholic background.

Maria Lionza. Maria Lionza is an Afro–Catholic cult found in Venezuela. Like **Shango** and **Santería,** both of which have now spread to Venezuela, it is a syncretic mix of **African traditional religions** and elements drawn from **Roman Catholicism.**

Mariavites. *See* Old Catholic Mariavite Church in Poland.

Maronites. The various branches of the Maronite Church chose affiliation to the **Roman Catholic** Church between the 14th and 16th centuries, thereby engendering one of the largest Catholic Uniate communities in the Middle East. In 1985, the Church numbered 1,576,462 members. A high proportion live in Syria and in Lebanon, although many have emigrated in recent years. Maronites have been deeply affected by the civil strife which has been endemic to these regions in the last half century. Most of the Maronites of Syria are concentrated in the west. Here they practise conservative forms of Catholicism. Survival takes priority over innovation. They are also relatively open-minded. The situation entails pragmatic co-operation amongst Christians of different traditions, and with moderate Muslims.

Twenty-nine per cent of the Lebanese people are Maronite. In 1926, France made Lebanon an independent State. Article 9 of the 1926 Constitution requires that "The state in rendering homage to the Most High shall respect all religions and creeds". However, France accepted that Maronites should be the majority in that state. In the 1940s Muslims and Maronites allied in the struggle for Lebanon's independence. When it was achieved in 1943, both tacitly agreed to a "National Pact". This ensures that the political system is confessionalist. Each religious community acquired, and retains, that degree of political representation which their proportional numbers then warranted. In 1943, there was a ratio of six Maronites to five Muslims. The Pact provides for a Maronite President, two Muslim Premiers (one **Sunni** and one **Shi'a**), and two **Greek Orthodox** Vice-presidents: the principle is carried over into every political institution, such as the Army and civil service. Lebanon's confessional system worked for 30 years. It has now collapsed, under the pressure of massive Palestinian immigration, in the wake of the 1967 Arab–Israeli War. The former was sanctioned by the 1969 *Cairo Agreement* which altered the delicate Christian–Muslim equilibrium. The Maronites now support Israel's war against the Palestinian Liberation Organization, to which Lebanon gives shelter. Lebanese Muslims, whose numerical strength now exceeds the degree of participation in the political process accorded them, now forcibly reject the National Pact. Both sides are armed. In 1975, civil war broke out between Muslims and Christians, after gunmen fired upon Pierre Gemayel, then leader of the Maronite Phalange Party; Maronite gunmen responded in kind. Gemayel became President from 1982–1988 and was, as a Maronite figurehead, a target for Muslim ill-feeling. The Maronites have proposed, first, in 1977, in a statement entitled "The Lebanon We Want", that each religious community should form a separate federal entity within the state of Lebanon; in 1984, after the Lausanne Conference, that Lebanese politics be secularized (both proposals are equally unacceptable to the Muslims); in 1986, that the National Pact be revised and reformed; in 1988, some, including President Gemayel, leaned toward abandoning the confessional system. The most important Maronite groups today, usually divided among themselves, are the religious leadership in Bkirki, centred on the Patriarch Nasrallah Sfair, those attached to Gemayel, those following the Phalange Party Leader George Saadeh, and those engaged in the Christian Brigades of the Lebanese Army, led by General Michael Aoun. Any long-term solution to the Middle Eastern crisis depends partly upon the Maronites.

Masorti (Masorati). *See* **Conservative Judaism.**

Mawlawiya. The Mawlawiya is a **Sufi** order associated in particular with Turkey, and popularly known as the Whirling Dervishes. Members of the order are known as Mawlawis (from the Arabic) or Mevlevis (from the Turkish).

Taking its name from the great mystical poet Mawlana ("Our Master") Jalal al-din Rumi (1207–73), the Mawlawiya was one of the earliest orders to attract European interest, largely due to the distinctive dance which gave rise to the label Whirling Dervishes. Born in Khurasan, an area of north-east Iran known for its ecstatic Sufis, Rumi moved during the Mongol invasion to settle in the Turkish town of Konya, which was to become the centre of his order. Under the influence of a wandering dervish, Shams al-din of Tabriz, in whom he recognized "the perfect man", he turned increasingly from sober to ecstatic Sufism, composing a vast quantity of Persian mystical verse. Rumi's famous work, the *Mathnawi,* in about 25,000 rhyming couplets, is regarded by the Mawlawis as revealing the inner meaning of the *Quran.* The Mawlawiya developed into a major urban, aristocratic and wealthy organization in the Ottoman Empire (in contrast to the **Bektashiya** which retained a more popular rural base). It spread from Turkey into Eastern Europe, but its centres in the Arab world remained almost entirely Turkish in membership.

Mawlawi initiates face a demanding period of preparation, totalling almost three years (1,001 days), before being admitted to full rank in the order. After performing a prayer of repentance they must devote themselves to a series of menial tasks, such as sweeping floors, cleaning latrines, shopping and working in the kitchens, with the aim of fostering humility. In addition to regular prayers, they have to attend for training in the symbolic ritual dance of the Mawlawiya and, like the **Khalwatiya**, to undergo times of retreat. Only when they have completed the novitiate can they participate in the famous whirling dance to achieve a controlled, highly disciplined ecstasy. The dance is full of symbolic significance, alluded to in the poetry of Rumi, the turning of the dancers being said to represent the circling movement of the spirit, culminating in leaping up to a state of union with the Divine. Mawlawis emphasize the importance of love and the need to respect everything of use to humanity, including the inanimate. In the past they have been noted for their tolerance towards other faiths, despite their poor relations at times with other orders. Their chief rivals have been the Bektashiya, and they have been condemnatory of the more extravagant practices of the **Rifd'iya**.

Today the Mawlawiya is in decline and confined to Turkey, where the ecstatic dance is performed annually in Konya, the site of Rumi's tomb, from Dec 11–17, the anniversary of his death. A once major order has become in danger of being relegated to a tourist attraction. The order appears to have died out in Greece since the 1920s, and in Yugoslavia since World War II. In the Arab lands the Mawlawi centres have been closing down since the 1950s. One of the best known at Tripoli in northern Lebanon survived into the 1970s, and in Beirut the last shaikh of the Mawlawiya was killed in May 1982 during the Israeli bombardment of the city. The decline appears to be due to a number of factors, the most important being official suppression, the close association of the order with Turkish aristocracy, and the difficulty of reconciling the Mawlawi Way with a modern working lifestyle.

Mayan Religion. Mayan Indians in Guatemala and southern Mexico retain elements of their traditional religion, which is an example of **Mesoamerican Traditional Religions** (*see* both entries under this heading).

M'Bona cult. This cult is found among the southern Chewa in Malawi. The god M'Bona is believed once to have been human. Subsequent to the arrival of Christianity, he has also been identified as a Black Jesus, as the cult has become more syncretistic.

Mbuti Religion. *See* **Pygmy Religion.**

Melanesian Religions. Melanesia comprises a number of different island cultures. They are situated north-east and east of Australia and comprise Iriyan Jaya (which is part of Indonesia), Papua New Guinea, the breakaway island of Bouganville, the Solomon Islands, Vanuatu, the Loyalty Islands, Wallis and Futuna, and Fiji. The phosphate island of Nauru in the mid-Pacific is also related to this area. The inhabitants of these island groups are dark skinned (hence the name), and the area is particularly rich in religious practices which have attracted the attention of anthropologists and interpreters of religious traditions.

Since Christianity came to this area, it has largely overshadowed the primal religious traditions. However, in more recent times, as independence has come to these island groups, attention has been given to the primal religions of each island group, as Christians have begun to rethink Christianity, whether **Roman Catholic** or **Protestant**, in the context of a new, emergent Pacific identity. A considerable lead has been given to the task of finding suitable expressions for indigenous theologies by the Pacific Council of Churches, and at the centre of this thrust is the Pacific Theological College situated in Fiji, and its Catholic counterpart. A pivotal role has been played in the gathering of Pacific histories and interpreting cultures by the University of the South Pacific which is also situated in Fiji. The University of Papua New Guinea, situated in Port Moresby, is also playing a major role in gathering together the traditions of the past, and in interpreting the varieties of cultures emergent in these areas.

The tradition of male cults is particularly strong in Melanesia. The initiation cults in particular guarantee entrance into the stages of adulthood and through the difficult passages of life, from birth, adolescence, marriage and death. Often the rituals of the male cults involve elements of mutilation, including circumcision, blood letting, tattooing and strengthening the males in their relations with females. There are different cults that specialize in equipping their members with various qualities which are deemed to be necessary for tribal life. Initiations take place in special "spirit houses" called "haus tambaran". An important part of Melanesian religion are the frequent "Sing Sings": elaborate festivals of song and dance in which the entire community becomes involved, and which follow a seasonal rhythm. These festivals are inter-connected with the economic life of the community since such festivals often lead to complex trading arrangements. "Sing Sings" often involve the use of masks which comprise the most important artefact of Melanesian religion, central to the male cults. They embody various spiritual beings and spirits from the Melanesian pantheon of deities. Bull roarers are used to create sound effects and to generate an atmosphere of the extra-ordinary.

Among the most interesting new religious movements, particularly in Vanuatu, are the **cargo cults.** They also occur in the Solomon Islands and are intimately connected with the coming-of-age of these island communities.

Fiji's spirituality is also very complex. Fire walking ceremonies are a particular feature of island life, demonstrating the mastery of spiritual consciousness over physical pain. The **Methodist** Church has played an important role in Fiji politics and, over more recent years, with the rise in nationalism, there has been a recovery of Fijian primal religious identity. This identity has begun to find its way into expressions of Christianity, particularly at the edges of culture. A striking feature of Fijian life is also the development of Indian religions, Hinduism and Islam in particular, but also some Buddhism. Although the Indian and the Fijian communities have a tense relationship, there is a growing awareness of the religious strands of the peoples of these islands.

The rich heritage of primal religion in this area has drawn attention to the characteristics described by the terms *Mana* and *Taboo*. R. H. Codrington brought the attention of the scholarly world to these concepts, and his study of the way in which *Mana* and *Taboo* operated has been refined in more recent studies. They are explained briefly in relation to **Polynesian religion.** The religious world is rich with gods, spirits (good and bad) and ghosts. The living have strong relationships with the dead as communities seek to balance their lives. In this the use of religious practitioners is essential. This concern with primal religion is often overlaid with the Christian tradition, Roman Catholic or Protestant. As these island communities rediscover their primal religious traditions, a rich heritage is being revealed, and this will be increasingly used in the search for viable and authentic expressions of religious faith.

Melkites. Syria is home to six Catholic rite communions (Melkite, **Armenian**, Syrian, **Maronite, Latin** and **Chaldean**), of whom the Melkites are the most numerous. There are currently 924,202 Melkite believers. Melkites follow the Byzantine rite. They are drawn from the most highly cultured echelons of Syrian society. Their Patriarch lives in Damascus. During the 1960s, they suffered under the Baathist government, which closed Melkite schools and proscribed Melkite youth organizations. Since then, the cultivation of adult catechetics has been essential. Accordingly, Melkite clergy, already in receipt of a sophisticated theological education, are also well versed in pastoral skills. The Congress of Melkite Catholic Clergy was established in 1969. Its annual assemblies provide a forum for ecumenical dialogue. Most Melkites live in Syria, but they are also to be found in Lebanon, Jordan, Egypt, America, Australia, Europe and Africa.

Mennonites (Anabaptists). The Menno-nites get their name from Menno Simons, a former **Roman Catholic** priest who in 1537 became the leader of the **Anabaptist** community in Holland. The Anabaptists' distinctive doctrine was that the Bible taught that Christians are a community of believers and that therefore baptism, the sign of membership of the Christian community, could only be given to believers. At that time all babies were baptized as infants, so a mature person being baptized as a sign of commitment was, said the Anabaptists' opponents, being "re-baptized". The Anabaptists, however, denied that infant baptism had any effect and did not have their infants baptized.

Their views brought them into conflict with the church and the state: they were severely persecuted and attempts were made to suppress their teaching. As a result many Mennonites emigrated to North America from the middle of the 17th century. In Europe the Mennonite flair for agriculture and a capacity for hard work led in 1788 to an invitation from Catherine the Great for them to settle in the Ukraine and teach local farmers their methods. There are Mennonites in the Ukraine and other ex-Socialist Republics to this day.

The Mennonite desire to follow Bible teaching as closely as possible led to their refusal to accept military service, refusal to take oaths and refusal of public office. In 1693 an extreme group formed the first of the **Amish** communities, which survive today as closed, primarily agricultural communities, rejecting all forms of modern technology.

Another group of 16th century Anabaptists were centred on Zurich in Switzerland. They were initially known as the Swiss Brethren, but their beliefs were the same as those in Northern Europe. Menno worked successfully to unite these two groups into a single movement.

One group of Anabaptists which has kept separate from the Mennonites, although sharing most of their beliefs, is the **Hutterites**.

The Mennonites also travelled to South America and set up communities in such places as Mexico and Paraguay. Today they are strongest in America and Canada although there are many internal divisions based on minor differences of doctrine or ethnic origin. The worldwide membership is about 1,250,000.

Mesoamerican Traditional Religions. The primal religions of Central America present a complex and ambiguous face in the contemporary context. The total population of indigenous peoples, i.e. descendants of the original inhabitants of America before the European conquest number some 30,000,000 throughout the region. The religious outlook of a great majority of these remains coloured by their pre-Christian traditions, even if the majority are normally **Roman Catholic** in the regions.

In Mexico some 11 per cent of the population, or 8,000,000 people, descend from the Aztec cultures and include the Zapotec, Huichol, Yaqui, Mixtec, Yucatec cultures, each of which have managed to preserve intact, often in conditions of considerable secrecy, their own spiritual legacy. The Huichol Indians of Northern Mexico have kept the pre-Columbian traditions more than any other groups. The Yaqui tribes and others also retain considerable vestiges of pagan spirituality. There is a strong degree of magic and witchcraft mixed up with this heritage, such that their world view is concerned with ritual actions undertaken by people in order to sustain the cycles of nature. Huichol medicine men (Maracamen) continue to uphold a role among the communities similar to that performed by the ancient pagan priesthood. The **peyote cult** and other hallucinogens are still actively used for achieving transcendental awareness among these peoples, as is true of many indigenous peoples worldwide.

The contemporary writings about the Yaqui Indian, Don Juan, by the anthropologist Carlos Castaneda, whatever their authenticity is eventually revealed to be, have managed to bring alive the traditions of these peoples in a most graphic way to the modern world. The legacy is ambiguous because Mexican paganism was notorious for its brutality and the glorification of human sacrifice at the heart of its cult. The human sacrificial practices of American indigenous cultures were undertaken in the "surrational" belief that the offering of human hearts to the sun deity would contrive to sustain the sun and the world from its imminent 5th cyclical destruction. The Aztec peoples in particular understood themselves to have a sacred calling to undertake this work of preservation. Their mythology elevated the status of the warrior, creating historically a disciplined priestly and warrior caste which dominated central American civilizations. To be seen in the contemporary world as an inheritor of this tradition is to be held somewhat as something of an outcast from the mainstream of Central American societies, which are European and Roman Catholic dominated.

The descendants of the Mayan civilization of southern Central America have an even more difficult situation in the contemporary world. In Guatemala the 5,600,000 Mayan descendants comprise something over 50 per cent of the population of the country, and modern **Mayan religion** maintains profound links with the religion of the Maya of the Classical period. From the date of the 16th century conquest by the Spanish, the Mayan descendants have suffered continuous and sustained oppression and denial of basic human rights. Only in the 1940s and 1950s was there an attempt to improve the plight of the indigenous cultures with the establishment of a National Indian Institute and the undertaking of certain land reforms. After the reform minded President Arbenz was overthrown in a coup in 1954, however, 35 years of uninterrupted dictatorships saw the oppression of the Indian's religious and political rights intensify. Death squads were (and are) used by the ruling military élites to massacre wholesale whole Indian communities and villages. In 1982 Gen. Rios Montt announced "all Indians are subversives" and instructed his troops to destroy all vestiges of traditional Mayan culture, forbidding religious rituals, burning fields of maize, which for the Mayan civilization was an act of supreme desecration due to the sacred importance of maize in Mayan spiritual culture. Ancient Mayan culture was again highly stratified with a ruling priestly warrior élite and a large mass of peasants. The irony of the current situation is therefore that the new ruling élites of the region are essentially non-indigenous. Human sacrifice of captives was an essential component of Mayan military culture.

The modern descendants of the Mayans in Guatemala have managed to retain traditions of spiritual initiation in which initiates undergo a series of "cargos" or burdens on retreat at special religious sanctuaries scattered in the mountainous highlands. Such practices continue to be persecuted so what is known about them is often fragmentary and the Indians' indigenous cultures retain their spiritual traditions underground, as is true of the region of Central America in general. To all indigenous cultures of Central America places of power become associated with the possibility of achieving states of transcendental being, and pilgrimage to such places is an important feature of Central American paganism to this day. So too are the festivals and ceremonies of these cultures, often nominally overlaid with Catholic flavouring. Patron saints are often identified with native gods in a Christo–pagan hierarchy of divine beings and intercessors.

In El Salvador the 1,000,000 indigenous peoples comprise some 20 per cent of the population and have been caught up in the brutal civil wars for decades. In Honduras, Panama and Costa Rica the indigenous cultures comprise a smaller percentage of the population, as a result of sustained persecution by the Spanish élites over centuries. It is not always the case that the Indian cultures automatically side with left-wing peasant guerrillas throughout the region. For example in Nicaragua the Mesuitos, Suyla and Ama peoples resisted the rule of the Sandanista government and managed to achieve a certain autonomy in their area along the Atlantic coast.

The prospects for all the indigenous religious cultures of Central America are in the balance. The region has been beset with conflict and civil war, often at a level of intense ferocity and brutality, together with the immense problems of environmental degradation, urbanization, illiteracy and poverty etc. The strategies needed for the region to prosper demand inter-cultural and inter-religious co-operation as a precondition of mutual survival.

Mesoamerican Traditional Religions (Mayan). The ferocity of the Spanish invasion in northern and central Mexico meant that the **Aztecan religion** was all but obliterated in the wake of advancing Christian armies. The same cannot be said for the Mayan area to the south, where traditional religious beliefs and practices continue in a dynamic form. At present, some 8,000,000 descendants of the Maya live in Southern Mexico and Guatemala, still adhering to many aspects of the world view of their more famous ancestors.

The religion of the modern Maya is not exactly equivalent to that of the Maya of the Classic period since the high priests' theocratic centres such as Tikal and Chichén Itzà have long since been deposed. In addition, the last 500 years have seen much syncretism with **Roman Catholic** orthodoxy. Yet the majority of Mayas still work the land on isolated small-holdings and maintain a profound link with the old gods of agricultural fertility. The Earth Lord provides the creative energy to successfully cultivate the staples of maize, beans and squash. The Earth Lord is often represented as a fat *ladino* (non-Indian) who jealously guards his treasures, but can be tempted into a fruitful relationship of reciprocity by sacrifices of candles and

incense on the mountain tops and in the caves. Other lesser deities play a role in the agricultural enterprise, such as Catholic saints who each protect a particular crop, and the fertile Mother Moon who is often linked with the Virgin Mary. The Father Sun, unlike during the times of the Mayan empire, plays only a supporting role, as does the Morning Star, who was the warrior god of the ancient Maya.

In southern Mexico and western Guatemala, Mayan peasants believe that each person has an animal spirit (or *nagual*). The animal spirit is like an *alter ego*, which lives with the Earth Lord deep inside the mountain. A powerful person may have a strong animal spirit such as a jaguar or hummingbird, and a meek person may have a butterfly or deer as their *nagual*. The animal spirit has an ethical dimension, since if the person breaks moral codes, the Earth Lord will release the animal spirit into the forest, thus exposing the person to grave physical danger. If the animal spirit were killed, the person will die also. Many **shamanic** healing practices are concerned with returning the animal spirit to its corral inside the mountain. This set of beliefs, however, is not shared by the Maya of eastern and central Guatemala. We must be careful, then, not to over-generalize about the Maya, since there is a great deal of variation at the level of both the village and 20-odd linguistic groups.

The community structure which has served as the vessel for traditional Mayan beliefs is the religious brotherhood (or *cofradía*). Catholic priests formed the brotherhoods in the 16th century in order to better evangelize the indigenous groups, but the villagers have made them all their own. The religious brotherhoods still organize fiestas for the village saint, as was originally intended, but they also became the whole social structure of the community, the fora for political decisions, economic strategies and Mayan and Catholic religious practices. During a man's life, he moves up the hierarchy, each time taking on a greater civil or religious duty. One year he may be mayor, the next year in charge of the saint's feast-day and the following year responsible for feeding the Earth Lord. Ultimately, he becomes an elder, responsible for the material and spiritual well-being of the community.

In recent years, the religious brotherhoods have ceased to be the main structure of local religious life. The unity of the community has been undermined by economic differentiation, migration, an intervening state and civil war (in Guatemala). In addition there have been a number of massive changes within orthodox religions. Protestantism has been very successful in converting Mayan peoples, and it is estimated that **evangelicals** now represent 35 per cent of the Guatemalan population and the majority of active churchgoers. There have now been two **Protestant** presidents of Guatemala in the space of the last 10 years. The Catholic church has also gone through profound changes, and from the 1970s on began forming base groups in each community. These Bible-based groups displaced the traditional religious brotherhoods in many areas and are now the main force in local Catholic life. The leaders of the base groups, or catechists, have waged a campaign against what was seen as the idolatry of Mayan beliefs. The Christ-centred religious ethic of the catechists has resulted in the demise of the Earth Lord and the importance of saints.

Yet the old gods have not left the scene completely. There are at present many ethnic revivalist movements throughout the Mayan area, seeking to renovate the ancient agricultural rituals. They seek to construct a new Mayan identity, incorporating many traditional religious practices. This revivalism is a prominent feature of Mayan religion, and played an important role in historical political movements such as the Tzeltal rebellion in 1712 and the War of the Castes in the 1860s. The latter rebellion was centred around a Talking Cross, expressing a Mayan content in a Christian form, and to this day armed Mayan guards protect the Talking Cross in a church in the Yucatán.

Methodists. A **Protestant** denomination which owes its origins to the preaching and organizational skill of John Wesley. On Monday April 2, 1739 Wesley, a high church **Anglican** clergyman "submitted to be more vile" (as he says in his journal) and preached to a crowd of 3,000 people on land outside the city of Bristol. It was the start of a life of preaching all over the country, frequently outdoors, often to people who through poverty or despair would never enter a church, but always calling people to repentance from sin, and a faith in Jesus Christ leading to justification with God and the inner assurance of salvation. Banned from many Anglican pulpits he said "The world is my parish" and travelled the length and breadth of the country on horseback.

John Wesley always encouraged his followers to go to their local church for worship and the sacraments. However he organized them into "classes", groups of believers who met together each week to learn and encourage each other in the Christian faith. The system may have been based on his contacts with the **Moravians**. They became known as "Methodists"—a name originally applied to a similar group which John and his brother Charles had belonged to whilst at university. Charles wrote hymns which were set to inspiring tunes (often the popular songs of the times by such composers as Handel and Mozart which were a means of teaching the Arminian theology of universal grace which the Wesleys espoused. Examples are "O come to my saviour! His grace is for all", and "Ah, Lord, with trembling I confess, A gracious soul may fall from grace". In 1784 John Wesley ordained two men as presbyters (or priests) and another as a Superintendent (or bishop) prior to their travelling to work in America where there was a desperate shortage of Anglican clergy. This act, which denied the doctrine of the Apostolic Succession caused an inevitable split between the Anglicans and Methodists, although it did not take place until after Wesley's death in 1791.

Methodism spread rapidly outside

Britain as a result of emigration and missionary activity. American Methodists early became independent of the British Methodist Conference. In the USA most of them belong to the United Methodist Church. In the 19th century splits occurred in the British Methodist body caused by differences between those who emphasized lay (i.e. non-priestly) ministry, and worship led by the inspiration and style of the preacher (Primitive Methodists) and those who preferred a liturgy very similar to that of the Church of England (Wesleyan Methodists). The Primitive Methodists were active in social reform, particularly trade unionism.

In the 20th century the various Methodist denominations in Britain have mostly come together to form a single Methodist Church. Both ministers and local preachers have been retained, but it has become normal for only ministers to administer communion, though this right may be given to lay people in exceptional circumstances. Each Methodist society belongs to a circuit, in which the senior minister is called a superintendent. Circuits are part of a District (comparable to an Anglican diocese) led by a Chairman of District. Each level has a representative body and at national level there is the annual Methodist Conference. The President of the Methodist Conference is elected annually. In 1992 Kathleen Richardson became the first woman President.

Most Methodist Churches belong to the **World Methodist Council**. Many churches overseas, brought into being through missionary work, are now autonomous bodies. Estimated worldwide membership is 26,000,000.

Mevlevis. Members of the **Mawlawiya Sufi** order are sometimes referred to as Mevlevis (from the Turkish) rather than Mawlawis (from the Arabic). They are also popularly known as the Whirling Dervishes.

Milli Görüs. Milli Görüs—"national view" —is a conservative Turkish religio–political grouping which promotes a particular synthesis of Islam and nationalism. It was closely associated with the religious National Salvation Party in the 1970s, but was banned in the wake of the 1980 military *coup*. Currently it supports the National Salvation Party's successor, the Welfare Party. It is particularly active among the Turkish community in Germany (where, however, it is overshadowed by the **Süleymancis**).

Milli Jam'iat ul-Ulama-i Hind. A breakaway group from the **Jam'iat ul-Ulama-i Hind** which emerged as the result of a split in 1988.

Minzoku Shinto. Folk Shinto. Mainly, although by no means exclusively, Japanese folk religion has been preserved through Shinto. It is basically magico–religious in character, and emphasis is on ritual and taboos, not doctrine or ideas. The calendar year is dotted with festivals, mostly thanksgivings and purifications, which clearly relate to ancient totemistic beliefs. Divination plays a major part in folk belief, and even today palmistry, astrology, fortune-telling the setting of auspicious and inauspicious days and so on are commonplace. The petitioning of *kami* for mundane benefits or protection, ancestor veneration, worship at family altars, and so on have all been embraced by the various religious institutions, but are basically rooted in folk belief.

Many new religious movements take their inspiration from these deep rooted aspects of the Japanese psyche, and shamanism, possession and mediumship proliferate, especially among founder figures.

Mira Bais. Hindu **Vaishnava** followers of the Rajput princess and poet, Mira Bai (1498–1546). Mira Bai's highly popular devotional songs are still sung today. Dedicated to the god Krishna, visualized as the raiser of Mt. Govardhana, and tinged with erotic elements, they did much to revive Hindu devotionalism in her own time. Mira Bai is said to have physically merged with a temple image of Krishna at the end of her life. The movement remains popular in Rajasthan and in parts of Gujerat.

Mirghaniya. The Mirghaniya is an important **Sufi** order in the Sudan. It takes its name from its founder, Muhammad 'Uthman al-Mirghani (1793–1851). However, it is perhaps more generally referred to as the **Khatmiya**.

Misogikyo. A Japanese purification movement and one of the traditional 13 constituent sects of **Kyoha Shinto.**

Mission de Dieu du Bougie. A Congolese new religious movement popularly known as **Lassyism**, from the name of the founder, Zepherin Lassy.

Mission South. This was, during the first decade or so of its existence, the name of the new religious movement currently known as **Family of Love.**

Mizrahi. *See* **Mafdal.**

Modern Hindu Reform Movements. These began in the early 19th century in response to the pressures exerted on Hindu society by British rule. The first of these was the Brāhmo Samāj (Society of God), founded in 1828 by Rāmohan Roy, a Bengali brahmin. The Brāhmo Samāj forbad images, icons or statues in the place of worship, condoning only monotheistic services, hymns and prayers, and espoused a programme of social

reforms to improve the status of women and the lower castes. Often seen as a form of Hindu Protestantism, Society doctrine held that there was truth to be found in all religions, but in practice the Society became a purely Hindu theistic organization. After Roy's death in 1833, the Samāj was eventually presided over by Keshab Chandra Sen, who expanded its activities and gave its religious aspects an increasingly mystical slant which many Hindus saw as Christianity in disguise. Eventually he broke with the parent organization, afterwards known as the Ādi Samāj, and founded the Bhāratvarshīya Brāhmo Samāj (the Brāhmo Samāj of India), which he wanted to be pan-racial, pan-scriptural and pan-national. Unfortunately, Sen's inability to adhere to his own ideals eventually resulted in a schism in his organization and the formation of the Sādhāran Brāhmo Samāj in 1878. All of these organizations have persisted, albeit in a moribund way, up to the present day.

In western India, a society similar to the Brāhmo Samāj, the Prārthanā Samāj (the Prayer Society), was formed by such prominent figures as R. G. Bhandārkar and M. G. Ranade in 1867. A successor to an earlier and unsuccessful group known as the Paramahaṁsa Sabhā, the Prārthanā Samāj espoused a programme of social reform which gained strength in Mahārāṣṭra, claiming spiritual descent from the famous medieval poet-saints of that region. The movement which was to have the most effect on Modern India, however, was the Ārya Samāj (the Noble Society), founded by Dayānanda Sarasvatī in 1875. Dayānanda harked back to the Vedas as the pure source of the Hindu tradition. While promoting many European innovations such as societies for the training of young men and women, Sunday worship, and sundry social reforms, Dayānanda vigorously denounced Christianity and opposed European influences on what he perceived to be the core of the Hindu identity. Many of the Hindu fundamentalist movements in India to-day trace their origins back to the Ārya Samāj.

Mongolian Buddhism. Following their 13th century conquest of Tibet, some of the Mongol elite, notably Khubilai Khan, were converted to **Tibetan Buddhism** by their erstwhile hostage, the **Sakyapa** hierarch Phagpa (1235–1280). But it was the third Dalai Lama, Sonam Gyamtsho (1543–88), who brought the process of converting the Mongols to completion by devoting the last 10 years of his life to missionary work in Mongolia. When his reincarnation, the fourth Dalai Lama, was recognized in Altan Khan's great grandson, the "Golden Descendants" of Genghis Khan became firmly identified with **Gelugpa** Buddhism, and soon all Mongolia adopted the Gelugpa religion.

Yet the deep sincerity and faith so characteristic of Mongolian Buddhism was quickly exploited by China's Manchu emperors, who ingeniously established institutions to control and use Gelugpa Buddhism as a means of eroding Mongolian political and military power. Thus by the early 20th century, even many deeply religious Mongolians perceived a conflict between their religious institutions and their national aspirations for independence from Manchu China.

After 1948, Inner Mongolia remained under Communist China, with the result that Mongolian Buddhism and culture as a whole have been virtually eradicated throughout that region through the permanent resettlement there of a vast preponderance of Chinese immigrants. But Outer Mongolia survived as an independent state under Soviet control, and Mongolian culture and Buddhism have fared much better there, despite Communist persecution. With the decline of Soviet Communism, a Buddhist revival is beginning in Outer Mongolia, although political threats from China remained strong enough to have prevented the Dalai Lama from visiting in 1991. A large quantity of Tibetan-language

Buddhist books have survived in Ulan Bator.

Some Mongolian peoples such as the Buryats live in territories now part of Russia, and practise the Gelugpa tradition of Tibetan Buddhism. At the time of writing their future remains unclear, although hopeful. A Gelugpa monastery founded in Tsarist times in St. Petersburg has recently been re-opened, but the full extent of European Russian participation in Tibeto–Mongolian Buddhism is not yet clear.

Moonies. The followers of the Reverend Sun Myung Moon are popularly known as the Moonies. Their organization is more formally known as the **Unification Church.**

Moorish (–American) Science Temple of America. This organization originated in Newark, New Jersey, in 1913 in the preaching of Noble Drew Ali (born Timothy Drew: 1886–1929). Its name was based on Drew's claim that black people were descended from the Moabites of Biblical fame, with Morocco as their true homeland. Moreover, Islam was their (and the) true religion.

Following its founder's death in 1929, the movement's leadership was assumed by a young member, R. German Ali, who supervised the steady growth of the movement during the 1940s and 1950s. Since then, however, it has been eclipsed by a rival organization founded by one of Drew Ali's followers, Wallace Fard Muhammad: the Nation of Islam, more popularly known as the **Black Muslims**.

Nevertheless, it still exists in much reduced form, with its particular version of the message of black superiority as contained in its small sacred book, compiled by Drew, entitled *The Holy Koran of the Moorish Science Temple of America*.

Moral Re-armament. This international movement was founded by an American

Lutheran minister, Dr. Frank Buchman (1878–1961). It began shortly after World War I when Buchman began a tour of European universities holding house-parties and recommending the idea of a "quiet time" in which divine guidance was to be sought. Stress was placed on the four "absolutes": absolute purity, absolute honesty, absolute love, and absolute unselfishness. In the 1920s, groups were set up in more than 60 countries, and in South Africa the name "The Oxford Group" was mistakenly used but came to be adopted with pride. The group was always anxious to secure the good will of important and famous people, which led to suspicions that it had been too uncritical in its attempts to court Hitler.

In 1938, the name "Moral Re-Armament" was adopted and the emphasis shifted from individuals to nations. The aim now was to strengthen national morale, create a better spirit in industry, and provide whole-hearted opposition to Communism. From 1946, MRA world assemblies began to be held at Caux-sur-Montreux, Switzerland. Efforts to promote reconciliation began with meetings at Caux attended by French premier, Robert Schuman, and German chancellor, Konrad Ardenauer.

Buchman's undenominationalism came in the post-war years to be extended to all religions as he tried to reconcile those of different faith-communities. What had begun as a movement for individual Christian commitment appeared to have become a global ideology. There are signs that the removal of the threat of Communism in 1989 could bring a shift to the movement's original emphases.

Moravians. In 1722 a Moravian lay preacher, Christian David, visited Count Zinzendorf of Saxony and persuaded him to allow a group of Moravian religious exiles to settle on the Count's estate. This group belonged to the Unitas Fratrum (Unity of the Brethren) and believed in Pietism, a 17th century doctrine

which encouraged simple, holy living, closely based on biblical principles, and in sharing faith with unbelievers. They had been exiled from Moravia (now part of Czechoslovakia) following the victory of the Catholics at the Battle of White Mountain in 1620.

These Moravians built a community which they called Herrnhut ("In the Lord's care"). Their communal life was very disciplined: single men lived together in households separate from single women and married couples lived separately from single persons. These separate groups were known as choirs. Soon the Moravians began to travel abroad to share their beliefs. They went to the rest of Europe, North America (where they first settled in Pennsylvania), Greenland, the West Indies and parts of South and East Africa. In England a community was founded in Fetter Lane, London and was attended by John Wesley, the founder of **Methodism**. He first met Moravians on board ship when he was travelling to America in 1735, and was greatly impressed by the depth of their faith. In 1738 he visited and stayed at Herrnhut.

Moravian worship is based on the church year, but with an emphasis on Christ and his suffering. The Church has its own hymnbook (Unitas Fratrum produced the first Protestant hymnbook in 1501) and liturgy. Central is the Easter Litany (1749) used at the Easter Dawn service, which is a statement of the Moravian's faith. Moravians have the three traditional orders of ministry—deacon, priest and bishop; only bishops may ordain.

Membership is about 500,000 world-wide, with the largest communities in USA, South Africa and Tanzania. The headquarters is still at Herrnhut in Germany.

Mormons (Church of Latter Day Saints). In 1830 Joseph Smith from New York, USA published *The Book of Mormon*. This was, he said, the history of a group of Israelites who emigrated from Jerusalem to America in Biblical times. He claimed that the book had been written by the prophet Mormon on gold plates buried in the ground. The prophet's son, Moroni had appeared to Joseph Smith in 1827 (when Joseph was aged 22) telling him where to find the plates. Using special crystal spectacles (called Urim and Thummim) Joseph was able to translate the plates, and said the *Book of Mormon* was a supplement to the Bible. He said that in 1829 he had been given authority by John the Baptist and the apostles to found a new Church.

Joseph Smith attracted many followers—and enemies. He was murdered while in prison in 1844. His successor, Brigham Young led a trek across America to Utah, where Salt Lake City became the headquarters of the movement. From 1843 till 1890 Mormons accepted the practice of polygamy which brought them into conflict with neighbouring states. However Mormons also believe in tithing (giving up one-tenth of your income to the church) and many young Mormons go overseas for two years at the age of 18 as missionaries—at their parents' expense.

Mormons believe that God has a body of flesh and has evolved from man. By his own efforts man may become a god (as Christ did). Membership of the Mormon community is essential for salvation. For this reason they are very active in the study of Family History. Almost every church (or Church of Jesus Christ of Latter-Day Saints which is the official title) has a genealogical library attached, whose extensive resources are available to the public. Dead ancestors who are identified by Mormons are baptized by proxy in a special service.

Mormons have clear standards of behaviour, they avoid tobacco, tea, coffee and alcohol (the communion service is celebrated with water, not wine). There is a strong emphasis on family and on community involvement. Worldwide membership is estimated at about 5,000,000.

Moro Islamic Liberation Front. A Vice-Chairman of the **Moro National Liberation Front**, Hashim Salamat, led a faction against the leader, Nur Misuari, in 1977, accusing him of various defects of character and of being soft on Communism. They expelled each other. Eventually Salamat's faction was named the Moro Islamic Liberation Front and established its headquarters in Pakistan. Like the MNLF, it is more a political than a religious organization. By the mid-1980s it was estimated to have 10,600 fighters in Mindanao, just over half the number mobilized by its rival, and it was the latter that was the main participant in negotiations with the government of President Aquino.

Moro National Liberation Front. The Moros are the Muslims of the Philippines. The name "Moors" was bestowed on them by the Spaniards. The Moro National Liberation Front first came to prominence following President Marcos' imposition of martial law in 1972. Led by Nur Misuari, who was forced to leave the country and subsequently established his base in Libya, it is more a political than a religious organization, unlike many of the Islamist religio–political groups in the Middle East and elsewhere. It has been consistently supported by the **Organization of the Islamic Conference** in its quest for security and justice for the Muslims of Mindanao and Sulu in the southern Philippines. By the mid-1980s, with an estimated 30,600 fighters in Mindanao, it was advocating independence rather than autonomy for 13 provinces, but following the demise of the Marcos régime it has negotiated on the basis of autonomy while pressing for a radical interpretation of that concept.

Mouvement Croix-Koma. An indigenous new African Christian movement (literally, the Nailed to the Cross movement) in the Congo. It originated in 1964 when a Roman

Catholic layman, Ta Malanda, began to attract massive followings in a campaign against witchcraft. Malanda regarded his campaign as a movement within the **Roman Catholic** church rather than as a separate church. He organized week-long courses, or retreats, at his headquarters in Kankata during which participants learnt to renounce their fetishes (which were then placed on public display). By the time of his death in 1971, an estimated 20 per cent of the population of the Congo—and virtually the entire population of some regions or tribes—had visited Kankata, which became something of a centre of pilgrimage. Subsequently the movement gradually severed its links with the Roman Catholic church, becoming an independent organization.

Mouvement de la Nahda Islamique (MNI). An Islamist organization in Algeria: see **Islamic Renaissance Movement**.

Mouvement de la Tendance Islamique (MTI). The MTI, the leading Muslim fundamentalist organization in Tunisia, has been known since November 1988 as the Renaissance Party, **Hizb al-Nahda**.

Mouvement du Progrès Islamiste (MPI). An Islamist organization in Tunisia: see **Islamic Progressive Movement**.

Movement for the Enforcement of Ja'fari Law. This Pakistani Muslim movement (Tahrik-i Nifaz-i Fiqh-i Ja'fariya) was established in the early 1980s as a channel for the expression of the concerns of the **Shi'ite** minority in Pakistan faced with the specifically **Sunni** Islamization measures being introduced by General Zia ul-Haq. It advocates the introduction of (**Twelver Shi'ite**) **Ja'fari** law for Shi'ites, and full freedom for Shi'ites to observe their own distinctive rites publicly. It maintains close links with Iran, of whose government it is generally supportive.

Movement of Islamic Resistance. This is a translation of Harakat al-Muqawama al-Islamiya, better known by its acronym of **Hamas**. It is the main Islamic group in the West Bank and Gaza Strip.

MSIA. Pronounced Messiah, this is an acronym for Church of the Movement of Spiritual Inner Awareness founded in the late 1960s by John-Roger Hinkins (b. 1934). The movement is now usually bracketed with a later product of Hinkins' known as **Insight**.

Muhammadiyah. The Muhammadiyah (Followers of Muhammad) is a major Muslim socio-religious organization in Indonesia, with several million members. Founded in 1912 by H. Achmad Dahlan and some fellow *ulama* at the traditional Javanese court in Jogjakarta, its origins reflect the influence on South-East Asian Islam of the Islamic modernist **Salafiya** movement in the Middle East.

With increased steamship travel consequent upon the opening of the Suez Canal in 1870, the number of Muslims embarking on the pilgrimage to Mecca also increased, with many of them staying on to study for a while before returning to South East Asia. Having themselves absorbed the reforming modernist ideals, they sought to propagate and implement them through their publications and new schools and organizations in Singapore, Malaysia and Indonesia, coming to be known collectively as the Kaum Muda, or "new faction", in contrast to the "old faction", Kaum Tua.

Focusing on the *Quran* and *Hadith* at the expense both of medieval tradition and the syncretistic beliefs and practices of local folk Islam, the Kaum Muda sought to develop a form of faith which combined fidelity to the teaching and example of Muhammad with clear relevance to the circumstances of the modern world. The Muhammadiyah was founded in Java to pursue these twin aims through establishing a new system of Islamic education to rival—and ideally, perhaps, to replace—the traditional Indonesian *pesantren* system.

Pesantren are a centuries old institution consisting of local, often rural, centres of Muslim education run by *kiai* (*kiyayi*), the traditional religious leaders. The content of their teaching lacked, from an Islamic modernist's perspective, both doctrinal purity and contemporary relevance. The new schools and boarding schools (*madrasas*), often urban, set up by the Muhammadiyah sought to remedy these defects, and with considerable success, establishing a strong reputation for a good modern education which has incorporated technologies and new methods imported from the West. Such has been the growth and development of the Muhammadiyah education system that it today virtually rivals that of the state, from infant school level right through to university level.

Moreover, in addition to its impressive record in education, Muhammadiyah has been active in welfare work, and now runs a range of orphanages, clinics and hospitals. Also its women's movement, Aisiah, has been noted for its vigour. As an organization, however, Muhammadiyah no longer stands out for creative reformist religious thinking, and young Indonesians inspired by the Islamic renewal of the 1980s have tended to gravitate to local mosque-based associations and Usroh groups outside the older organizations like Muhammadiyah and its traditional rival, **Nahdatul Ulama**.

Unlike Nahdatul Ulama, Muhammadiyah has by and large eschewed political activity, and does not evoke government hostility today under President Suharto any more than previously under Sukarno, or indeed during wartime Japanese or earlier colonial Dutch rule.

Finding its support originally among merchants and traders, the Muhammadiyah has successfully broadened its appeal and now draws widely on members of the state bureaucracy as well as on the rural population.

Mujaddidiya. Originally an Indian subbranch of a major **Sufi** order, the **Naqshabandiya**, it subsequently spread to other areas.

Mujahidin-i Khalq. The Mujahidin-i Khalq, or People's Holy Warriors, emerged in the 1970s as an Iranian organization which used urban-based guerrilla tactics against the Shah's regime. Their thinking was inspired by an attempted synthesis of Marxism and Islam. Active, indeed prominent, in the Iranian revolution, they subsequently soon found themselves, with their more flexible interpretation of Islam, aligned with the liberal and secular opposition, and persecuted by the Khomeini régime, whose leaders they in turn sought to assassinate. Since 1981 their leader, Massoud Rajavi, has been in exile, and inside Iran the Mujahidin have been arrested and tortured by the thousands, and hundreds have been executed.

Towards the end of the Iran–Iraq war, they organized a National Liberation Army to enter Iran alongside Iraqi forces (or, after the ceasefire of 1988, alone), but met with little success. Their leadership, having moved from Paris to Iraq in 1986, were expelled from Iraq in 1989, after the war, presumably having outlived their usefulness to Saddam Hussain.

How much support they still command within Iran remains unclear, but they no longer appear to be a significant force, ruthless repression by the state having exacted a terrible toll.

Mujahids. The Mujahids are a reform movement within Islam in the Mappila community of Kerala, southern India. A formal organization, Nadvat-ul-Mujahideen, was officially constituted in 1952. Dubbed "Wahhabis" by the traditional **Sunni**

leadership, they have in fact developed their own distinctive approach to reform and education, although the original impetus may have derived partly from personal visits by some Mappilas to Saudi Arabia, but partly too from the **Salafiya**.

They have placed great emphasis on the need for an Islamic education that goes beyond rote learning, and have established their own religious schools, and even in certain areas separate mosques. They oppose invoking saints in prayer, emphasize the important place of reason and freedom of thought and opinion in religion, and the use of the vernacular in the mosque. A Malayalam translation of the Quran was produced by their major thinker, C. N. Ahmed Maulavi (b. 1906), who also translated, with a commentary, the authoritative *hadith* collection of al-Bukhari. His often free interpretations of Quran and *hadith*—with the former given strict precedence over the latter—have invoked the hostility of the traditional Muslim teachers who have proscribed his numerous publications. They in turn, however, have been forced, in response to the challenge of the Mujahids, to a more explicit coherent statement of the authority of tradition over and against individual interpretation.

Mulavamsa. A prominent **Theravada** Buddhist monastic grouping within the Sri Lankan **Amarapura Nikaya.**

Multiplying Ministry Movement. This is an alternative designation for the **Church of Christ** movement based on the Boston Church of Christ but now also including the London Church of Christ and similar bases in Birmingham and Manchester in the UK.

Muridism. An alternative name for **Sufism** in the former Soviet Union. It is taken from the term *murid* meaning a Sufi follower.

Muridiya. This 20th century **Sufi** order was founded by Amadu Bamba Mbacke (c1850–1927). The establishment of the order is sometimes seen as an adjustment to the new circumstances of occupation in Senegal after the final defeat of the Wolof by the French in 1886. Amadu Bamba was a member of the **Qadiriya** for a number of years, noted for his personal piety, his unworldliness, learning and poetic skills. In 1891, or thereabouts, he claimed to have seen the angel Gabriel in a vision, calling on him to spread the faith. The site of this experience was later called Touba ("repentance"). The French, concerned that he might lead a *jihad* against them, exiled him to Gabon (1895–1902) and Mauritania (1903–7), during which time he built up a reputation for miracles, such as spreading his prayer mat on the ocean and surviving a fiery furnace and an island of snakes and devils. He is thought to have left the **Qadiriya** while in Mauritania, teaching the rituals of his own new order. His relations with the French later improved, as he counselled his followers against *jihad,* urging them to "go and work". Before his death in 1927 the Muridiya built a great mosque at Touba, where he was buried, and which was to become the object of annual pilgrimages.

The Murids venerated their founder as a saint in his lifetime and some even regarded him as God on earth and openly addressed him as such. Crowds gathered around him in the hope of receiving blessing (*baraka*) transmitted in his saliva. The Muridiya has built up a strong economic base in Senegal through taking their founder's advice on work seriously and cultivating peanuts as a major cash crop. Murids are also very active in Senegalese politics, building on the foundations laid between 1920 and 1960 when, it has been said, France governed the economically and politically crucial peanut basin in conjunction with the Murid hierarchy in a kind of indirect rule; a tradition largely continued in independent Senegal under Leopold Senghor and Abdou Diouf.

Murtipujakas. Literally, "image-worshippers", also known as **Pujeras** the largest group of the **Svetambara Jainas**, so-called because their temple ritual involves the "worship" of *tirthankara* images.

Musar Movement. (*See also* **Orthodox Judaism.**) Musar (Hebrew, instruction) in its general sense refers to Jewish ethical literature, more narrowly it refers the late 19th century ethical movement founded in Lithuania by Rabbi Israel (Lipkin) Salanter (1810–83). He created a system of vigorous self-examination that he insisted was a vital part of religious and spiritual development alongside *Torah* study and observance of the commandments. Its aim was not merely a formal intellectual study of ethical literature but the development of the emotions and the spiritual virtues, such as humility. It involved directed meditation on ethical literature and practical exercises. The Musar *shmooz* (or *shmues*—ethical discourse and associated practices) as directed by the *Masgiah Ruhani* (Hebrew, spiritual supervisor) are now part of the curriculum in Lithuanian-type *Yeshivot*.

Muslim Brotherhood. The Muslim Brotherhood (Ikhwan al-Muslimin) is the most visibly successful of the 20th century Islamic reformist organizations in the Arab world. It was founded in 1928 or 1929 by Hasan al-Banna (1906–49), a primary schoolteacher in the Suez Canal port of Ismailiyya, Egypt. His father had studied under the great modernist scholar Muhammad 'Abduh at al-Azhar, and he himself came under the influence of 'Abduh's disciple, Rashid Rida, while training in Cairo to be a teacher. He was strongly affected by the reformist ideas of the **Salafiya**, but was also an active member of a minor **Sufi** order, the Hasafiya, into which he was initiated by the son of its founder. The new movement clearly bore the marks of both these tendencies in al-Banna's thought and he described it as "a Salafi message, a **Sunni** way, a Sufi truth, a political organization, an athletic group, a

scientific and cultural union, an economic enterprise and a social idea".

The Brotherhood may be seen as arising out of the frustration of Egyptian Muslims with the unwillingness, or inability, of the official religious scholars and Sufi orders to confront the actualities of occupation by the unbelieving British, and corruption and growing secularism in the upper *échelons* of Egyptian society. It may be seen as no accident that the Brotherhood should have thrived in Ismailiyya, the town housing the headquarters of the Suez Canal Company and the British forces stationed in Egypt. Al-Banna became the first Supreme Guide of the Brothers, providing a leadership not unlike that of a Sufi shaikh to his disciples. Below him the movement was organized in a strict hierarchy under a Guidance Council with several committees. Members belonged to "families", cells of five to 10 Brothers, families then being formed into clans, clans into groups and groups into battalions, the largest units. From 1942 a special section was established, devoted to the *jihad* against both foreign occupiers and the decadent society within.

The early membership of the Brotherhood was drawn largely from the rural working class in the 1930s. By the 1940s it was becoming more firmly based among the urban lower middle class, and subsequently gaining support among university students and staff, civil servants and professionals. The Brotherhood operated as a highly successful propaganda machine through its publishing ventures, schools, athletics clubs, and campaigns to promote literacy and hygiene, in addition to more traditional-style mosque addresses. The message was essentially of the need to break away from the blind imitation of past authorities, to accept only the *Quran* and the most reliable *hadith*s as sources of the Holy Law (Shari'a), to work towards a totally just Islamic society. Brothers were to perform their religious duties strictly and lead good moral lives, abstaining from alcohol, gambling and fornication, avoiding usury and not playing or listening to music, dancing or watching corrupting entertainments. Their womenfolk were to be educated to become good wives and mothers, to wear "legal" dress, not to work alongside men or attend mixed gatherings. Despite al-Banna's personal commitment to Sufism, most Brothers came to oppose it as no true part of Islam. The movement had from its beginnings been anti-imperialist and became also anti-**Zionist**, anti-Communist and frequently hostile to Christians viewed as the new Crusaders threatening the Islamic world.

On the death of al-Banna, murdered by the secret police in 1949, the number of Muslim Brothers in Egypt was estimated at around 500,000. The leadership of the movement was assumed by Hasan al-Hudaybi, a judge, who was anxious to promote the image of the Brotherhood as a respectable, moderate organization that renounced terrorism. Nevertheless, the Brothers continued to be involved in anti-British agitation and took an active part in the riots of January 1952, allying themselves with the Free Officers who took over in the July coup. Yet relations soured between Nasser and the Brothers, since the new régime's brand of socialism and nationalism conflicted with their desire for an Islamic state and allegiance to a wider Islamic community. In November 1954 a Brotherhood plot against Nasser was uncovered, leading to the arrest of many members, including al-Hudaybi, and the official dissolution of the movement.

Among those arrested was Sayyid Qutb (1906–66), the radical ideologue of the Muslim Brothers. During his 10 years in gaol he became ever more convinced of the need for a tougher approach to seeking the reformation of Egyptian society, sunk so far in corruption and decadence as to constitute a society that was no longer Islamic but *jahili,* "ignorant" of the true religion in the same way as the society of pre-Islamic Arabia. The best known expression of his revolutionary position is contained in *Signposts,* a book written mainly in prison and published around the time of his release in 1964, but banned by the government not long after its publica-

tion. Shortly afterwards Qutb was again arrested, implicated in a new plot against Nasser, sentenced to death, and hanged on Aug. 29, 1966. His ideas and example inspired a number of members to leave the mainstream Brotherhood and form their own militant groups, such as **al-Takfir wa'l-Hijrah**. Meanwhile the more moderate leadership was later accommodated by Presidents Sadat and Mubarak and, although prevented from operating as a separate political organization, the Muslim Brothers participated in the April 1987 parliamentary elections by putting up candidates in alliance with the Liberals and Socialist Labour Party, and succeeded in gaining a number of seats. However, in an atmosphere of souring relations with the government, the Brothers boycotted the elections of November 1990.

Outside Egypt the Muslim Brotherhood has spread to other Arab countries, sometimes existing under other names, for instance in Algeria as Ahl al-Da'wa (People of the Call) and in Tunisia as al-Hizb al-Islami (the Islamic Party). In Jordan it achieved notable successes in the November 1989 parliamentary elections and Brotherhood candidates have been appointed to key ministries. In Algeria Brothers have been very active in 1991 in organizing Islamic opposition to the socialist régime and demanding an Islamic state. However, in Syria they have been suppressed and forced underground after violent struggles with the Baathist régime of Hafiz al-Asad from the mid-1970s to early 1980s. Since July 1980 membership in the Syrian Brotherhood has been illegal and punishable by death.

Muslim Institute. This London-based organization has been vocal in its support of the Islamic republic in Iran. Its director, Dr Kalim Siddiqui, attracted considerable public hostility for his outspoken support of Ayatollah Khomeini's *fatwa* according to which Salman Rushdie had merited the death penalty for the crime of apostasy as reflected in his novel *The Satanic Verses.*

Dr Siddiqui occasioned further controversy with his project for a **Muslim Parliament of Great Britain**.

Muslim Parliament of Great Britain. Established in the UK in 1991, this organization has made claims that it will become a truly representative expression of British Muslims. This seems unlikely, not least because its main protagonist, Dr Kalim Siddiqui, is also the Director of the **Muslim Institute**, and an ardent advocate of the current Iranian form of Islam. Initial concerns of the Muslim Parliament have included Muslim education in Britain, economic conditions of Muslims in Britain, and discrimination arising out of *The Satanic Verses* affair. It has also called for volunteers to fight (in defence of Muslims) in the former Yugoslavia.

Muslim World League. The Muslim World League (Rabitat al-'Alam al-Islami) was established in 1962 in Mecca, where it continues to be based. Founded partly to establish Saudi leadership against the leadership claims of President Nasser and his Arab nationalist cause, the League has come to assume many of the activities of the Pakistan-based **World Muslim Congress**, and currently reflects Saudi determination to appear as the chief spokesperson of normative (**Sunni**, even **Wahhabi**) Islam in order to counter Iran's (**Shi'ite**) claim to a comparable role.

The organization promotes the dissemination of the faith, and supports Muslims worldwide, including those in minority situations: its permanent Secretariat in Mecca includes Departments of Islamic Culture, of Publicity and Publications, of Muslim Minorities, and of Islamic Law and Jurisprudence. By its own admission, 99 per cent of its finances come from the Saudi government, and critics—not only the Iranians—regard it as a tool of the Saudi régime.

It has encouraged the formation of regional councils of Islamic organizations, for instance the Islamic Co-ordinating Council of North America, and the European Council of Mosques, and has sponsored a variety of Islamic associations, mosques (through its subsidiary, the Mecca-based Supreme World Council of Mosques) and conferences around the world. It employs approximately 1,000 missionaries worldwide (one third of these in Africa and another third in Indonesia), and trains *imams,* preachers and missionaries in its training centre in Mecca. It also sponsors the **World Assembly of Muslim Youth**, and publishes the informative English-language version of its monthly journal, *The Muslim World League Journal*. In 1974 it became a member of the non-governmental organizations of the UN. It has on occasion been referred to as the religious counterpart to the more political **Organization of the Islamic Conference**.

Musta'lis. The Musta'lis are the smaller of the two main surviving branches of **Isma'ili Shi'ism**. They are sometimes also known as the **Tayibis**. When the Fatimid Caliph al-Mustansir died in 1094, followers of his younger son al-Musta'li distinguished themselves from the **Nizaris**. The sect originally transferred its centre from Egypt to the Yemen, where it still exists under the name of **Sulaymanis**. In the early 17th century, a distinct line of leaders (*da'is*) emerged, whose followers are known as **Daudis** (or in India commonly **Bohoras**). Apart from their main centre in Gujarat, there are also numbers of Daudis in East Africa, Mauritius, Myanmar (Burma), and elsewhere. They probably number about 300,000.

N

Nadvat-ul-Mujahideen. The formal organization of the **Mujahids**, a movement of Islamic reform among the Mappila community of southern India. It was established in 1952 and has been active in promoting Muslim schools and publications as vehicles for its reformist ideas.

Nagas. The Nagas are the inhabitants of the hilly tracts of the north-eastern frontier of India, a people of Sino–Indian ethnicity. A large proportion of them were converted to Christianity from the late 19th century onwards, but about 1,000,000 of the Nagas still adhere to their traditional religious beliefs and practices, what is sometimes termed animistic religion.

"Naga" is a generic term (the name has nothing to do with snakes), and there are many different tribal groups among them such as the Angamis, the Semas, and the Konyaks. But they share many common religious beliefs and practices: indeed there is striking uniformity of belief among the tribes of the frontier. The concept of a high god, who has created the world and then withdrawn, is one such common feature. The Alhou of the Sema Nagas, the Gawang of the Konyaks, and the Terhopo of the Angamis are examples of a supreme being who is benevolently disposed towards human beings but remote and therefore not to be propitiated. Prayers and propitiation are directed rather to lesser deities, usually nature spirits inhabiting rocks, streams, hills and trees, some of them malevolent and the cause of sickness, death and misfortune. The Kukwobolitome of the Semas who causes stillbirth, the Teghas Kesa who destroys crops, and the Teghas Aghu Zuwu who inflicts people with delirium, are cases in point. Spirits of ancestors, the Kituri, can also cause trouble and have to be appeased. Fowls, and animals are sacrificed and the flesh shared among the worshippers. The Gennas are permanent annual celebrations of propitiation of the supernatural.

The Nagas believe in the immortality of the soul—or souls—as usually individuals are believed to have multiple souls. The Yimbu, or land of the dead, is a ghostly reproduction of the temporal world, and weapons and other equipment have to be buried along with the dead in order to properly equip them for the afterlife. The bodies are laid out in the open near their habitation, and when sufficiently decomposed the head is wrenched off and then cleaned and kept in the house or in a special place in the tribal village where it is fed during festive occcasions.

There is no hereditary or ordained priesthood. Usually people who are naturally endowed with psychic abilities take on the role of a *shaman* or seer. The Nagas believe in the ability of the soul to leave the body while sleeping. The *shamans* have the ability to enter the land of the dead in their dreams, and if they meet a person there who is still alive on earth they predict the imminent death of the individual. Most groups believe that animals also possess souls.

The Nagas used to practice headhunting till it was banned by law. The belief that powerful magical forces adhere to the skull and could be used to the benefit of the possessor seems to be the rationale underlying this practice as well as the practice of preserving ancestors' heads previously alluded to. The possession of heads, and with it the tattoo and rank of the unfortunate owner, used to bring prestige to the warrior and also the tribal village as a whole. Incidentally the Ibans of Sarawak also practised tattooing and headhunting, and they are believed by some anthropologists to be ethnically related to the Nagas.

As described above, the Nagas practise a variant of the **tribal religions of India.** They should not be confused with the **Nagas (Saivite).**

Nagas (Shaivite). Nagas are a semi-military ascetic order in Hinduism, venerating Shiva as their deity. The Nagas go naked or "sky-clad", covering their bodies with ashes, bearing tridents, and wearing their hair long and matted in imitation of their god. As part of the **Dashanami** monastic order, philosophically they adopt the monism of Shankara's **Advaita Vedanta.** Nagas live in monasteries or can be peripatetic ascetics. Every twelve years at the great Kumbha Mela festival, the Nagas are among the first to enter and bathe in the holy Ganges, indicating their high esteem in the hierarchy of Hindu monastic orders. The name *naga* probably comes from *nagna* or "naked", rather than from the name for the snake-deities of Indian mythology.

Nagô. One of the names used in the Maranhão region of Brazil for the **Afro–American spiritist** movement **Candomblé.**

Nagoshias (Nagushis). The Nagoshias are a tiny sub-sect of the **Daudis** within Indian Islam. The Daudis, in turn, form a branch of the **Musta'li** sect of **Isma'ili Shi'ism.** They are commonly (though slightly inaccurately) identified as **Bohoras.** The Nagoshias split from another sub-sect of the Daudis, the **'Alia Bohoras**, in 1789. Various reasons were involved, but the most notable was that the schismatics regarded meat-eating as a sin. Their name means, in fact, "not meat eaters", and they remain a vegetarian group today.

Nahda Movement/Party. These terms are used somewhat loosely to refer to one of two groups. One is the Mouvement de la **Nahda Islamique, or Islamic Renaissance Movement,** in Algeria; the other is the currently more influential **Hizb al-Nahda,** or Renascence Party, in Tunisia. The latter was known until 1988 as the Mouvement de la Tendance Islamique, or Islamic Tendency Movement.

Nahdatul Ulama. The Nahdatul Ulama (NU) — Union of Muslim Teachers — is perhaps the largest Muslim organization in Indonesia. It was founded in 1926 by traditionalist *ulama* disturbed by the rapidly growing appeal of the Islamic modernist organization, **Muhammadiyah,** founded 14 years earlier in 1912. Against the reformist challenge of the system of more modern education being established by the Muhammadiyah, the Nahdatul Ulama sought to safeguard the position of the traditional, largely rural, centres of learning known as *pesantren* or *pondoks.* These were in effect the power base of the *ulama*, or *kyai* (*kiyayi*) as they are known in Java, the religious leaders who taught in them and indeed often owned them.

The continued flourishing of the *pesantren*, with the families of the *ulama*, staff and students all living together on the premises, would be seen by the Nahdatul Ulama as a sign of its success, yet although it is today a larger organization than the Muhammadiyah, the latter's record in education and welfare work is stronger. Moreover, while committed originally to preserving a very traditionalist curriculum of Islamic education in the face of the **Salafiya-**inspired reforms advocated by the Muhammadiyah, over the years the NU-run *pesantren* too have adopted a broader outlook, and subjects such as science, technology, modern languages, economics and business studies are now widely accepted. In that sense it would be misleading today to present the difference between the NU and the Muhammadiyah in terms of a simple traditionalist-modernist dichotomy despite continuing major differences in theology.

In 1953 the NU became a political party, with a concentration of electoral support in East Java, and under Sukarno it held responsibility for the Ministry of Religious Affairs. In the 1970s it emerged as the dominant party in the federation of four Muslim political parties imposed by the Suharto régime and deliberately given a non-Muslim label, Partai Persatuan Pembangunan (PPP), Unity Development Party. The government's policy of undermining specifically Muslim parties culminated in the PPP's adoption, in 1984, under intense pressure, of the state Pancasila ideology as its sole ideological foundation. The Five Tenets include belief in one God, but deliberately refrain both from specifying this in Muslim terms and also from including a clause specifying that Muslims are bound by the *syaria* (Shari'a).

The intense pressures to which the NU was subject during the government's Pancasila campaign were a prime cause of the factionalism to which it succumbed in the early 1980s, and since 1984 it has withdrawn from politics with the aim of reverting to being the sort of socio–religious organization it was before 1953. One effect of this has been to weaken dramatically the power of *ulama* to deal with local grievances, because there are no longer NU politicians whose support they can enlist. Electoral support for the PPP has declined dramatically too.

Although the NU's abdication of political involvement derives from a declared aim of "returning to its 1926 roots", the current climate of Islamic resurgence is very different from that prevalent when the NU was founded. It remains to be seen how it will adapt to the changed circumstances. Now as then, though, the *pesantren* constitute its indispensable base.

Nakali Nirankaris. Literally, false **Nirankaris**. A Sikh-derived splinter group more regularly called the **Sant Nirankari Mandal.**

Namdharis. A **Sikh** reformer of the 19th century, Baba Balak Singh, 1799–1861, protested against moral laxity in the Panth, especially the use of drugs and alcohol, lavish weddings and the giving of dowries. He also condemned meat-eating though this was never proscribed by the Gurus. In 1872 the movements then leader, Baba Ram Singh (1816–1885) was exiled by Burma by the British for causing disturbances and 66 of his followers were executed. Namdharis also believe that Guru Gobind Singh did not die in 1708 or end the line of human guruship but appointed Balak Singh in his stead. The present Guru has his headquarters at Baini Sahib in the Punjab.

Khalsa Sikhs often lump Namdharis and **Nirankaris** together as heretical movements. In fact Namdharis differ significantly from the latter by their insistence on a reformed and restored *khalsa*, rather than a return to the pristine teachings of Nanak. Nevertheless they are more obviously wayward than the Nirnakaris because of their continuing belief in a living *guru*. Namdhari men are distinguished by their white homespun cotton clothing and turbans tied horizontally across the forehead. They are also known as **Kukas.**

Nanak Panth. The community of followers of Guru Nanak (1469–1539). A name applied to the early **Sikh** community, for whom Nanak is the first *guru* in a sequence of 10, and more latterly to those **Sahajdhari Sikhs** who disregard the discipline of the *khalsa* as established by the final *Guru*, Gobind Singh in 1699. The central practice of Panthis is the remembrance of the Divine Name (*nam simaran*) though Nanak himself may also be venerated. The **Nirankaris** are in essence part of the Panth.

Nanaksar Movement. A **Sikh** *sant* named Baba Nand Singh (1870–1943) used to meditate in this place in the Punjab which has now become the headquarters of a movement led by his successor, Bhai Mani Singh. It is characterized by personal devotion to the living teacher and to the memory of Nand Singh, vegetarianism, the observance of the full moon when an all-night service is held, and the encouragement of celibacy. Nanaksar *gurdwaras* usually have a room laid aside for the use of Bhai Bani Singh.

Nañiguismo. This is a Cuban **Afro–American spiritist** cult about which, due to its secretive nature, relatively little is known. It appears to involve secret societies which practise certain rituals derived ultimately from **African traditional religion** in Nigeria.

Naqshabandiya. This great **Sufi** order is probably the most widespread after the **Qadiriya**, frequently associated with reform and with resistance to attacks on Islam. Originating in Central Asia in the 12th–13th centuries, the first Naqshabandi masters traced their spiritual line of descent back to the early caliphs of Islam, Abu Bakr and 'Ali, and are said to have followed in the tradition of the Malamatis ("Blameworthy ones"), who sought to attract blame by disguising their true inner piety by outwardly impious behaviour. 'Abd al-Khaliq al-Ghujdawani (d. 1220) is credited with laying down the basic rules of the order and developing the practice of the silent recollection of God (*dhikr khafi*) as against the vocal *dhikr* of other orders. The name of the order derives from Baha al-din al-Naqshabandi (1318–89), himself a Tajik from a village near Bokhara, whose famous mausoleum became one of the major places of pilgrimage in Central Asia. Probably his best known saying, and one which epitomizes the Naqshabandi outlook, is that "the exterior is for this world, the interior for God".

Naqshabandis believe in seeking spiritual communication with the holy dead, especially past masters of the order, who may make contact in dreams and visions, sometimes in the vicinity of their tombs or shrines. Thus some Naqshabandi shaikhs

have claimed to be initiated by dead predecessors. Outwardly the Naqshabandis live fully in the world, at times associating with temporal rulers, at times active in opposing them, but always journeying inwardly with God and aspiring to replace base with virtuous qualities. They concentrate on God in their characteristic silent remembrance, seeking to form a mental image of the heart with God's name inscribed on it, and practising techniques of breath control as an aid to constant consciousness of God. They may also meet for gatherings with vocal remembrance, but in times of persecution this has not always been possible and is not essential.

The Naqshabandiya spread southwards into India in the 16th century, where it developed new directions under the inspiration of Ahmad Sirhindi (1563–1603), often known as the "renewer (*mujaddid*) of the second millenium". His branch of the order was therefore called the Mujaddidiya ("renewerist"). It was strongly **Sunni**, concerned with the strict application of Holy Law (Shari'a) and assertion of a purified Islam in the face of any attempts at accommodation with Hinduism. Probably the most celebrated among reforming Naqshabandi shaikhs in India was Shah Wali Allah of Delhi (1702–62), who pioneered the translation of the *Quran*, urged a fresh examination of the *Quran* and Traditions and the need to compare them with the views of all four Sunni legal schools in order to overhaul the system of Islamic law. He also wished to see a range of social and economic reforms, and his ideas have had a continuing influence among Muslims of the Indian sub-continent far beyond Naqshabandi circles.

The Mujaddidi branch of the Naqshabandiya was introduced into the Ottoman Empire in the 17th century, where it flourished in Turkey and Syria, enjoying special popularity among religious scholars. In Damascus it gained yet another new sub-order at the hands of the Kurdish Shaikh Khalid al-Shahrazuri (1776–1827), who, like Sirhindi, emphasized strict uncompromising Sunnism and adherence to the Holy Law, and was notably hostile to Christians and Jews. The Khalidi influence extended to Turkey and Iraq (where it became linked to Kurdish nationalism) and into South East Asia, where it remains active in rural communities in Sumatra and Java. In Turkey the Naqshabandiya was officially suppressed by Ataturk in 1925 along with other orders, following a rebellion by Kurdish Naqshabandis. Although still banned, it has resumed its activities in recent years and appears to have a large, politically conscious membership opposed to the Turkish secular state.

In its homeland in Central Asia the Naqshabandiya was in the forefront of resistance to 19th century Russian imperialism. Under the Soviet state it managed to survive in secret with very wide support. It seems to have been helped by its ability to infiltrate the ranks of the Communist Party and KGB in line with the traditional Naqshabandi policy of seeking to influence rulers. It was also well-designed not to attract attention by its practices of silent *dhikr* and inconspicuous small group meetings. It can be expected to flourish in the present atmosphere.

At the peripheries the Naqshabandiya was introduced into China in the 18th century, where it gave rise to the New Sect marked by its militancy and involvement in rebellions in the 19th century. In Western Europe Naqshabandis are reported as active in Germany, France and Britain, with groups meeting in a number of cities, including Birmingham and Oxford.

Nara. The first forms of Buddhism to arrive in Japan from continental Asia (in the 6th century) were scholastic and aristocratic schools, which later became known as the six Nara sects, after the capital city of the period in which they were incepted. Membership to the three surviving sects is now almost negligible, as popular Japanese Buddhism has cast off continental influences and adapted to a new environment. However, the Nara sects are worthy of mention here not only because they rep-

resent the epoch-making transmission of Buddhism from China and Korea to Japan, but they also contain, in embryonic form perhaps, ideas and tenets which continue to influence the development of Japanese Buddhism.

Naths. Naths or **Kanphatas** are an order of Hindu yogis, recognizable by their split ears (*kan-phata*) and large earrings given them at initiation. Naths either shave their heads or grow their hair long, wear ochre robes, apply ashes from their fires to themselves and carry a begging bowl and a staff. They have a number of monasteries throughout India, some of which belong to the sub-sects of the order. Naths are generally **Shaivas,** though in western India they tend to be **Vaishnavas** and in Nepal they can be Buddhists.

Theoretically only higher castes are initiated, though there are exceptions to this rule and sometimes women are admitted. At initiation the yogi takes a vow of celibacy and vows not to engage in paid employment thus ensuring poverty and reliance on the laity. The tradition's founders are said to have been the legendary figure Matsyendranath and his disciple Gorakhnath (c1200 CE) who wrote one of the tradition's major texts. Naths teach that liberation from the cycle of reincarnation is possible in life by developing a perfected or divine body. Such a body is created through the practice of *hatha yoga* and by awakening the dormant energy within the body called the "snake-power" or *Kundalini Shakti*. Another practice of the Naths is turning the tongue, after cutting the frenum, back into the throat in order to catch the drops of the nectar of immortality (*amrta*) dripping from the crown of the head.

Nation of Islam. This was the name originally given to the US movement which later became famous as the **Black Muslims.** This movement subsequently changed its name twice, in 1976 to World Community of Islam in the West, and in 1980 to American Muslim Mission.

These changes were accompanied by major doctrinal shifts which were not to everyone's taste within the movement. The original name has been retained by two or three different groups which sought to perpetuate the original Black Muslim ideology. Easily the largest of these is that led by Louis Farrakhan, with an estimated 5,000 to 10,000 members, but there is also a small splinter group led by the self-styled Caliph, Emmanuel Abdullah Muhammad, and another led by John Muhammad, brother of the founder Elijah Muhammad.

National Council of Hindu Temples. The major co-ordinating body of Hindu Temples in the UK.

National Council of Young Israel. *See* **Orthodox Judaism.**

National Religious Party. *See* **Mafdal.**

Native American Church. This is a loose umbrella organization drawing members from over 50 different tribes, and best understood as an expression of **Peyotism.**

Native American Religions. The native tribes of the North American continent have developed, over thousands of years, an enormous variety of religious beliefs and practices. Each tribe effectively has its own unique religious configuration, thus making it essential that we speak of religions and making it difficult to make generalizations. Although much has been lost and/or destroyed following European contact, much still survives, necessitating the use of the ethnographic present tense in describing Native American beliefs and practices.

Underlying all these religions are none-theless some common core concerns: the first has to do with a world view based around origin myths which speak of a time when humans and other beings were not differentiated as they are today. This forms the basis of the widespread native American concern with the essential cosmic harmony in the universe—a harmony in which humans, animals, trees and plants, natural phenomena and supernatural powers each play a role. It is often difficult to distinguish "natural" and "supernatural" in native American thought, since the natural world is imbued with the sacred. This is not to suggest that the whole universe is sacred, since native Americans distinguish certain places, objects and phenomena as sacred. Nonetheless, the natural world is of prime concern since sacred power manifests commonly through natural phenomena. Relationships to the sacred are of central concern, particularly to animal aspects of the sacred and in most of North America it is common for individuals to seek a "guardian spirit", often through a "vision quest".

The acquisition of a guardian spirit is widespread among native Americans, except in the south-west. One acquires a guardian spirit through vision or dream, or in some cases through inheritance or purchase. Guardian spirits are usually animal in form, though they can take virtually any form. Guardian spirits give power and help to their owners and the latter often carry amulets, medicine bundles or other outward representations of their spirit. Powerful spirits can give an individual the power to cure others and he or she usually becomes a *shaman* or medicine man (*see* **Shamanism**).

Most typical is the acquisition of a guardian spirit through "vision quest". One of the most distinguishing features of many native American tribes, the vision quest reflects the importance of a personal relationship to, and experience of, the sacred. Typically associated with a rite of passage as well as the acquisition of a guardian spirit, the practice involves the supplicant retiring, after a period of purification through fasting, praying and use of sweat lodge (see below), to an isolated place where he continues to fast and pray until granted a vision or dream where a spirit appears, which will then grant a song and bestow certain powers. The individual then assembles a medicine bundle comprised of objects associated with the spirit. If the vision so indicates, the individual may embark on a career as a *shaman*, or medicine man. Repetition of the experience is seen as a way of renewing power.

The sweat lodge is a widespread native American rite of purification involving the construction of a domed lodge made from saplings and covered with blankets or skins. A pit in the centre holds heated rocks on to which water is poured, making the dark interior hot. Individuals pray and smoke. The rite serves both as a means of renewing a close relationship with the sacred as well as purifying oneself in preparation for further rites, such as the vision quest. The sweat lodge has undergone a considerable revival, and is one of the central rites to be found in the movement called **Pan-Indianism**.

Native Americans traditionally perceive time in cyclical terms, not linear ones; some Indian languages lack terms of past and future, consequently everything is potentially in the present, including the time of myth, which is why myth and the world of the sacred are so potent and accessible. This cyclical view is represented symbolically in the widespread use of circles to denote the universe. Each tribe generally has established a close and intimate link to the territory they inhabit, and particular landforms and sites can have great religious significance.

A broad differentiation can be made between hunting tribes and agricultural ones in terms of religious orientation. Hunting tribes generally place strong emphasis on individualism and individual relationships to the sacred. There is much animal ceremonialism and crisis rituals mediated by a *shaman* or medicine man

who uses helping spirits to cure the sick, locate game and lead other rituals, including an annual ceremony of cosmic rejuvenation such as the Sun Dance.

One of the best-known ceremonies of the native Americans of the Plains, the Sun Dance is at heart an annual renewal ceremony, taking place during the summer and involving the construction of a lodge, having cosmological significance. At its centre is the Sun Dance pole, representative of the world pillar. Typically individuals made a pledge to perform a rite, involving purification and dancing facing the sun. Among the Lakota, there is the piercing of the supplicants' skin with skewers which are then fastened by rope to the pole. The supplicant dances and prays whilst attempting to tear himself free of his bonds, representing both sacrifice of flesh and freeing from ignorance. This activity is a means of achieving individual power, as well as cosmic renewal and reaffirming the well-being of the tribe as a whole. Suppressed at the end of the 19th century, this ceremony was practised clandestinely until the 1950s, and has undergone a significant revival since then.

Agricultural societies, on the other hand, in contrast to the hunting tribes, tend to have more anthropomorphic spirits, stress rain and fertility ceremonies, which occur regularly at the same time each year, and are usually under the direction of medicine societies, rather than individual specialists. Clearly the more settled peoples can develop more permanent shrines, temples and material artifacts than the more nomadic hunters. Some of the most elaborate ceremonialism was found on the north-west coast, where ample food supplies and large permanent settlements allowed the development of an enormously rich culture, with animal masks, totem poles (a form of family heraldic denoting spirits with which the family had a close relationship) and a sacred half of the year when individuals were initiated over a period of months into religious societies.

Much of this latter culture and many others were lost due to the destructive effects of European culture, in particular the deliberate suppression of native religious practices in the late 19th century. Resistance to White encroachment was mainly military, but there were some religious responses, notably the millenarian movement known as the Ghost Dance, which flourished at the end of the 19th Century under its founder, a Paiute Indian called Wovoka.

Most syncretic religious responses tended to be either short-lived or very localized, the most notable exception being the widespread Peyote Cult, or **Peyotism.** Many native Americans became Christians, whilst trying to maintain a distinctly Indian identity. In recent years on a tribal level there have been increased efforts to maintain and revitalize traditional practices, and to regain possession of, or access to, sacred sites lost under earlier unjust treaties. On a national level, certain religious practices, including "sweat lodge" have been utilised by younger Indians from different tribes in Pan-Indianism.

All tribes have been affected, in varying degrees, by the coming of the Europeans. Hunting tribes particularly have suffered enormously from loss of territory and game, as well as the universal effects of disease and cultural suppression, but traditional religious practices continue to flourish, particularly in the south-west.

Nazarenes. "Nazarene" means "from Nazareth", the town where Jesus (sometimes referred to as Jesus of Nazareth) grew up. It was an early name for Christians (Acts 24, 5) and later an early sect of Christianity.

The Church of the Nazarene is the largest of the **Holiness (Perfectionist)** churches. It was formed early in the 20th century through a number of mergers of Holiness churches, and came to Britain in 1906 through the work of George Sharpe in Scotland. Its headquarters is in Kansas, USA and is believed to have over 800,000 adherents. Church

government is democratic, and similar to the **Methodist** church. The Nazarenes administer colleges, hospitals and schools and are active in missionary work.

Neo-Buddhism. A term coined to denote the Buddhism of social protest established in India, more specifically in Maharashtra state, by Dr B. R. Ambedkar in the early 1950s. Neo-Buddhist ideals are represented today by the **Buddhist Society of India.**

Neo-Hasidism. (*See also* **Hasidism, Jewish New Agers.**) The name given to the diffuse and wide-scale interest in Hasidic literature and teachings among contemporary non-Hasidic Jews. Whereas Hasidim follow the *Rebbe* of their particular Hasidic dynasty, the neo-Hasid is not bound in this way. Also, Hasidim live completely within a social and religious framework centred on their Rebbe, while the neo-Hasid utilizes Hasidic materials as one of the sources and resources for his/her Jewish spiritual life. Neo-Hasidism is often associated with Martin Buber, whose translations and romantic renderings of Hasidic tales and interpretative writings on Hasidic themes were the main vehicle for the transmission of Hasidic teachings to the non-Hasidic world.

Neo-Paganism. This label is often used to refer to the modern revival of **Paganism**: the two terms are not infrequently used interchangeably.

Nestorians. The Nestorian Church represents an ancient form of Eastern Christianity separate both from the **Orthodox Church (Byzantine tradition)** and from the **Oriental Orthodox Churches,** though sometimes loosely grouped with the latter. Also known as the "Assyrian" or "East Syrian" Church, the Nestorian Church dates back to the fifth century, taking its name from bishop Nestorius, Patriarch of Constantinople, whose teachings were condemned by the Council of Ephesus (431). Nestorius taught that in Christ were two separate persons, the human and the divine, in opposition to the prevailing view that Christ was a single person with two natures. For Nestorius, Mary the mother of the human Jesus could not be venerated as "Mother of God" (Theotokos), as she was by those who accepted the decrees of the Council.

The original stronghold of Nestorianism was Mesopotamia (Iraq and Iran), and there were also Nestorian missions to India and the Far East. Nestorian missionaries probably established the original Malabar community of South India (*see* **Syro–Indian Churches**). The influence and population of Nestorianism in the Middle East and Asia were dramatically reduced during the Mongol invasions of the 14th century, and the surviving remnant was further reduced and dispersed during World War I.

The Nestorians worship in ancient Syriac, mainly using the Liturgy of Addai and Mari. The patriarch of the Church is known as the Catholicos of the East, which is (unusually in Christianity) a hereditary office, passing from uncle to nephew. Baghdad in Iraq was the main centre of the Nestorian Church for most of its history, but in recent decades the Catholicos has for political reasons lived outside Iraq, first (from 1940) in the United States, where there is a small Nestorian diasporate, and more recently (since 1976) in Tehran (Iran). A schismatic Nestorian Church also exists; its rival Catholicos was in 1972 officially recognized by Iraq as the true patriarch of the Nestorians. Today the Nestorians number roughly 100,000 worldwide.

Neturei Karta. (*See also* **Haredi, Orthodox Judaism, Zionism.**) The Neturei Karta (Aramaic, "Guardians of the City") are one of the groups that make up the **Haredi (Ultra-Orthodox)** community of Israel (Edah Haredi. NB. sometimes this term is used more narrowly to refer to the "hard" separatist communities). Neturei Karta is the most vocal of the **Ashkenazi,** anti-**Zionist** groups who do not recognize the legitimacy of the State of Israel, and maintain a campaign throughout the *diaspora* protesting at the "desecration" of Jewish life in the "unbeliever" state of Israel. Originally part of the communities that were represented by **Agudat Israel,** the Neturei broke away in the 1930s, rejecting what they saw as Agudat compromises with the secularists and breaches in the separatist Ultra-Orthodox life established in pre-state Palestine. They are still stridently anti-Agudat Israel.

Like other Haredi groups they live *Yeshivah*-centred lives, strictly observe the commandments, follow their rabbinic leaders and refuse to use Hebrew as their daily vernacular and speak Yiddish. In addition, they also refuse any activity that could be deemed as co-operation or recognition of the Zionists. Thus, they refuse to use Israeli currency; would prefer to live "in exile" under Palestinian Arab rule, and "celebrate" Israel's Independence Day as a day of mourning.

The ranks of the Neturei Karta are filled with the Reb Arelah (a Hungarian "sect" that follow the teachings of Rabbi Aaron (Reb Arelah) Roth, and broke away from the **Satmar Hasidim,** distinguished by their gold-braided frockcoats) and other extreme Ultra-Orthodox groups.

The Neturei Karta, although small in numbers, have been reasonably effective at limiting the activities of the "compromisers", such as Agudat Israel, by their constant programme of pressure and propaganda.

New Age. On the surface, the New Age looks as though it provides a bewildering and conflictual array of beliefs and activities. Virtually all forms of religious life are utilized, from eastern mysticism to "**pagan**" traditions of Europe and North America. New Agers work with crystals; serve as channels in order to receive messages from spiritual agencies; practice holistic healing; or tap into the energy provided by the earth Goddess. Some favour hallucinogenic drugs (ecstasy is currently in vogue); others go on enlightenment intensives, or practice meditation.

Beneath this apparent diversity, however, there lies a distinctive account of what it is to be human. Essentially, the New Age is all about self-religiosity. The self, itself, is held to be perfect, the source of truth, wisdom, energy, creativity and tranquility. Indeed, the Self is often called "God" or the "Goddess".

New Agers are able to engage in an apparently heterogeneous set of activities, drawn from many religious traditions, because they believe that these are all means to the same end: discovering the perfection that lies within. These paths—enlightenment seminars of the **est** variety, finding "attunement" with nature (for the Self-God is typically held to exist within the natural order as a whole as well as in the human body), or (even) hard and conventionally futile manual labour—are all held to serve to liberate the self from the contaminating effects of life in contemporary society. The New Age will dawn when people discover their true nature, casting off the destructive effects of having been socialized to perform in the unnatural constructs of mainstream life: the nuclear family; the capitalist enterprise; or the competitive educational system.

New Agers have a major problem: what should be done about the unenlightened mainstream of society? Some, following that earlier eruption of the New Age, namely the spiritual wing of the counter-culture of the later 1960s, have chosen to ignore this difficulty. They reject the mainstream as much as possible—in the UK, for example, living on the dole in squats, retreating to small-holdings in the Celtic fringe, or joining the bands of travellers who roam from free festival to free festival (at least during summer months)—of which Glastonbury

is perhaps the most well known. In contrast, others are hard at work aiming to "transform" mainstream institutions. They run management trainings for large companies, attempt to influence the political process (as with the Natural Law Party in Britain and the New Age wing of the environmentalist movement), or seek to find ways of interfusing New Age experiences with Christianity and the health profession.

Overall, the New Age is best regarded as a highly celebratory form of spiritual humanism. As such, it is rooted in deep-seated cultural trajectories: the Western Romantic tradition; the American evolution of New Thought-cum-**Positive Thinking**; the progressive introduction of Eastern spirituality to the West; and, more generally, the ever-increasing tendency for us to ascribe value to the self.

Conventionally dated from the 19th-century, when the East significantly impacted on religiosity in the West (cf. the founding of the **Theosophical** Society in New York in 1875), New Age retreats, programmes, "seminars" and disciplines have proliferated. They now number in the thousands. But this is not to say that there are commensurate numbers of fully-fledged New Agers. The Shirley MacLaines of this world, continually prepared to announce, and apparently to enact, their divinity, are few.

The New Age is best seen as comprising a diverse range of (oft-competing) means to the common end of self-sacralization, which is now firmly established as a significant "how to change your life" complex, pronounced by the spiritually informed experts of the field. There might not be many fully fledged New Agers, but there are plenty of people who tap into New Age cultural resources—the bookshops, the spiritual therapy centres, the New Age holiday facilities, the management training courses and the health provision outlets—when the occasion demands. A Gallup Poll (1989) reports that 12,000,000 are New Age inclined in the USA.

The future of the New Age seems assured. Here is a universalized spirituality grounded in a global scheme/vision. It claims authority from a wide range of traditions. Here is a development which chimes in with the celebratory indi-vidualism of so much of our time. Hence it is much more appealing than the "fallen man, listen to God out there" dynamic characteristic of traditional Christianity. And here is a development which appeals to all those who feel anxious about the effects of modernity: from the impact on the environment (Mother Earth) to humankind itself. The New Age might not be an organized and conspiratorial "movement" (as it has been described), but it is a movement in the sense of having a dynamic career.

Counting against this optimistic scenario of the future, the New Age is controversial. A number of key figures have disgraced themselves. Accusations of psychological coercion are not unknown. And leading New Agers have a habit (so it might seem) of going over the top with their promises: and so estranging those who might be looking in their direction to "unlock potential". Who can readily believe, with Shirley MacLaine, that they have "created" their parents?

The New Age exemplifies strands of "late" modernity—in particular, some argue, exaggerating the authority and value of the self—and in so doing it is almost certainly paving the way for its own "transformation", or day of reckoning, in the future. As some commentators suppose, the New Age is an Age too far. According to this account, its future appeal could well be undermined by the probability that faith in human-kindness will have to face the fact that there will be competition for ever-increasing scarcity of resources.

New Apostolic Church. The New Apostolic Church (NAC) has its roots in the **Catholic Apostolic** Church (CAC). The CAC had appointed 12 Apostles, in expectation of the imminent return of Christ, but by 1860, 5 of the 12 apostles had died already and the CAC accepted that the return of Christ was not as near as they had expected, so they did not appoint new apostles. The prophet H. Geyer of Berlin and the elder W. Schwarz of the congregation in Hamburg rebelled and were suspended from their offices in the CAC. So the congregation in Hamburg became the starting point for the NAC. On April 12, 1883 the Priest Carl Wilhelm L. Preuss was appointed into the office of apostle and the name was changed to "Allgemeine Christliche Apostolische Mission" (General Christian Apostolic Mission). In the same year the Elder Friedrich W. Schwarz became the Apostle for the Netherlands, where he founded the "Herstelt Apostolische Zending Kerk", (HAZK). In 1881 Fritz Krebs (1832–1905) was appointed as Apostle for North and East Germany. Against the wishes of the HAZK, he tried to reunite the now five Apostles of the movement under his leadership and authority as an arch-apostle (Stammapostel), an office which he had created for himself in 1895. After Krebs' death Hermann Niehaus (1848–1932) took over this office (1905–1930) and the ACAM was renamed in 1907 "Neua-postolische Gemeinde", (New Apostolic Congregation). Niehaus was responsible for the spread of the NAC throughout the world. Most significant for the NAC was the appointment of Johann Gottfried Bischoff (1871–1960) as his successor. Not only was the final name "New Apostolic Church" established in 1938 during his reign (1930–1960), but in 1951 he announced, during a service in Giessen (Germany), that the Lord had revealed to him that he would return during his lifetime. Bishoff's claim for unquestioned authority and his prophecy led to a number of congregations seceding from the NAC. On July 6, 1960 Bishoff died and his successor Walter Schmidt (b. 1891) simply stated that God had changed his mind. Schmidt resigned in 1974 and Ernst Streckeisen (1906–1978) took over the office as arch-apostle in 1975. He appointed a large number of new apostles so that their number reached 60. After his sudden death after only three years in office in 1978, H. U. Urwyler (b. 1925) was appointed as arch-apostle. The NAC is centrally organized from its Headquarter in Frankfurt/Main and in 1977 the NAC registered 407,000 members in West and East Germany, 38,000 in Switzerland, 5,000 in Austria and over 1,000,000 worldwide.

New Church. The name of the formal organization in **Swedenborgianism.**

New Sect Shinto. A name used to denote various modern groups within **Kyoha Shinto.**

New Testament Church of God. This is a West Indian **Pentecostal** church which is one of the black churches which have become well established in the UK with a national headquarters and regional organizations.

New Thought. This movement, originally of 19th century origin, is currently known as **Positive Thinking.**

Ngorpa. A branch of the **Sakyapa** tradition of **Tibetan Buddhism,** founded in 1429 by the great scholar Kunga Zangpo (1382–1456). Famous for their knowledge of the *tantras*, especially the "Path and Fruit" (*Lamdre*) system, the Ngorpa's headquarters at Ngor Ewam Choden became, after nearby Sakya itself, the second largest monastery following the Sakyapa teachings, and there were also many other Ngorpa monasteries throughout Tibet. Two major Ngorpa lamas are now based in the West, Kunga Rinpoche in California and Phende Rinpoche in France.

Nichirenshoshu. A form of Japanese *Mahayana* Buddhism derived from the teachings of Nichiren, although often classified as a new religion with its origins in the early 20th century.

Nichirenshoshu (the **True Nichiren School**) claims Nichiren (1222–1282), who has *bodhisattva* status in some circles, as its religious source, and Nichiko his disciple, as sectarian founder. This movement has become distinctly international, attracting the young, and remarkably, pop stars and entertainers. This is often accounted for by the "this-worldly" nature of **Nichiren Buddhism,** which in its modern milieu has become notable for advocating chanting the *daimoku* for mundane and material ends, based on Nichiren's teaching that the benefits of practice are attainable here and now. Nichirenshoshu, in accordance with the teaching of Nichiren, claims that Nichiren Buddhism should be established as the state religion and that Japan should be the platform from which the Lotus is introduced to the rest of the world.

The Daisekiji on Mt. Fuji is the head temple of this denomination. Membership is difficult to quantify because **Soka Gakkai** (the lay movement affiliated to Nichirenshoshu) numbers are often included in statistical reports, though 16,000,000 seems a reasonable estimate. Nichiren Buddhism appeals predominantly to the working class, partly because of its emphasis on a strong sense of membership, which appeals to the modern Japanese alienated by their overwhelmingly industrial environment.

Nichirenshoshu of the UK (NSUK). The British section of **Soka Gakkai International (SGI).**

Nichirenshu. A form of Japanese *Mahayana* Buddhism which originated in the Kamakura period.

Nichiren (1222–1282), a vociferous and prophetic nationalist, trained as a **Tendai** priest, and studied **Zen** and **Pure Land**

Buddhism on Mt. Hiei. Ultimately he left the mountain, though not in complete rejection of Tendai, in order to propagate the doctrine of absolute faith in the Lotus Sutra. To Nichiren, the most important part of this sutra is its second half, the *honmon*. This stand was later to become the source of dissension amongst disciples. Nichiren vehemently opposed all other Buddhist sects on the grounds that the fate of Japan rested on there being one true sect, and he utilized a method of conversion called *shakubuku* (break and subdue), a practice that deliberately provoked a decisive response, whether positive or negative. Nichiren was exiled twice, and his movement was persecuted. This he interpreted positively; this rejection by the misguided state confirmed his mission.

Nichirenshu advocates the chanting of the *daimoku, Namu Myohorengekyo* "Adoration to the Lotus Sutra", the five Chinese characters of which embody Absolute Truth in its essential form. Also venerated is the *daimandara* or horizon, a mandala depicting the *daimoku* surrounded by Sakyamuni, *bodhisattvas, kami* and **Tendai** masters. This is an abstract representation of the cosmos with Sakyamuni at its centre. The final element of Nichiren's thought, the *Kaidan,* represents the place of ordination also understood as a secret place within the believer's heart.

Nichirenshu itself claims nearly 2,000,000 devotees, although there are larger denominations e.g. **Nichinenshoshu, Reiyukai** and **Soka Gakkai,** which also claim Nichiren as founder. The head temple, the Kuonji, is on Mt. Minobu in Yamanashi Prefecture, at the site of Nichiren's tomb.

Nihangs. A warrior sub-group of **Khalsa Sikhs.**

Ni'matullahiya. One of the very small number of **Shi'ite Sufi** orders, the Ni'matullahiya traces its origins to Shah Ni'mat Allah Vali (1329–1431), a Syrian-born **Sunni** teacher of Iranian origin who spent the last part of his life in Mahan near Kerman, in southeast Iran. After Ni'mat Allah Vali's death, leadership of the order moved to India. In the 18th and 19th centuries, however, there was a significant Ni'matullahi revival in Iraq and Iran. In the twentieth century, many educated and middle-class Iranians belonged to the order. There are three main branches of the Ni'matullahiyya in modern Iran: Gunabadi, Dhu'l-Riyasatayn, and Saf: 'Ali Shahi. Estimates of membership range from 50,000 to 350,000. Recently, Ni'matullahi missions have been established in Europe and America under the tutelage of the leader of the Dhu'l-Riyasatayn branch, Dr Javad Nurbakhsh (Nur'Ali Shah).

Nimbarka Vairagins. An order of Hindu **Vaishnava** ascetics closely linked to the **Sanakasampradaya.**

Nippon Kirisuto Kyodan. The United Church of Christ in Japan has almost 200,000 members, and is the largest **Protestant** Church in the country. Founded by American **Presbyterian** and **Reformed** missionaries in 1858, it was forced by Government decree to unite with other Protestant bodies in 1941. After the war, it reaffirmed its distinctiveness and several churches withdrew. It has accepted its share of war guilt, and is increasingly concerned about the revival of nationalist currents, such as the Theocratic emperor system.

Nippon Sei Ko Kai. The **Anglican** Church in Japan came into existence in 1859 when missionaries arrived from the American Episcopal Church. It was recognized in law in 1887. In 1930 a province of the Anglican Church was formed. Its bishops and other church leaders are all Japanese and it is financially independent. Immense effort is being put into the building up of the Church tomorrow—"Asu no kyokai o kizuku Kai". It has 55,000 members.

Nipponzan Myohoji. Founded by Nichidatsu Fujii early this century, this sect, one of the overwhelming number that trace their lineage back to Nichiren, promotes radical pacifism. Although a small denomination in Japan (about 1,500 celibate ascetics) Nipponzan Myohoji is famous worldwide for its "peace pagodas" as well as drum beating and chanting the *daimoku* at peace demonstrations.

Nirankaris. Baba Dayal Das (1783–1855), a shopkeeper from Rawalpindi is the founder of this **Sikh**-derived movement. Though not a **Khalsa Sikh,** he grew up in an environment in which marriages were conducted by Hindu priests and images of Hindu gods were often found in *gurdwaras*. He taught a return to the pristine teachings of *guru* Nanak and in particular the discipline of meditating on the Divine Name (*nam simaran*). He also attempted to eliminate alien accretions from Sikh practice and to affirm the nature of God as formless (*nirankar*). The present character of ceremonies, especially marriage owes much to his efforts. A belief emerged amongst some of his followers that he was a successor to Guru Gobind Singh and since his death there has been a succession of *gurus* to whom authority is given, rather than to the Guru Granth Sahib. After the partition of India, the Nirankaris abandoned their base in Rawalpindi and are now found centred on Chandigarh. Khalsa Sikhs often, misleadingly, lump the Nirankaris together with the **Namdharis** as heretics. In fact the two groups are quite distinct. The Nirankaris are essentially part of the **Nanak Panth** in that they wish to return to the pristine simplicity at the root of the Sikh tradition. In the beginning members did not join the *khalsa*, though nowadays many adopt *khalsa* insignia. **Sahajdhari Sikhs** and Hindus are also attracted to Nirankari teachings.

Nishkam Sevak Jatha. An organization founded by the charismatic Kenyan **Sikh,** Sant Puran Singh, also known as Kerichowale Baba. He spent the final part of his life in Birmingham, England, where he died in 1983, his funeral attracting over 10,000 mourners. The movement continues to grow, particularly in the Leeds and Birmingham areas. The teachings emphasise the need for proper initiation into the *khalsa*, though reverence is also paid to the founder. Members are vegetarian, consume no alcohol and are dedicated to the reconversion of **Patit Sikhs.**

Nityananda Institute. Based in Masschusetts and headed by its American-born abbot, Swami Cetanananda, the institute propogates the **Trika** philosophy within **Kashmir Shaivism.**

Nizamiya. The Nizamiya is one of the two main branches of the **Chishtiya Sufi** order, popular in South Asia. It is sometimes referred to, indeed, as the Nizamiya-Chishtiya.

Nizaris. The Nizaris are the larger of the two chief branches of **Isma'ili Shi'ism.** They are also commonly known as the **Aga Khanis.** The sect emerged on the death of the Fatimid Caliph al-Mustansir in 1094, giving its allegiance to his displaced elder son Nizar. They established communities in Syria and in Iran, where their chief centre was at the fortress of Alamut. Known as "Assassins" (*Hashishiyyin* or *Hashshashin*), they represented a powerful political presence until the destruction of their strongholds by the Mongols in the 13th century. The Iranian line of Imams remained quietist until the mid-19th century, when the first Aga Khan (as their Imam now began to be called) rebelled and subsequently fled to India, where he and his successors allied themselves to the British.

A Nizari community had already existed

in India from the 14th century. They are generally known as **Khojas**, although the term strictly applies to individuals born into an Indian caste grouping, and some Indian Nizaris belong to quite different groupings. Under the leadership of the Aga Khans, the Isma'ili Khojas have become a wealthy and widely distributed community, with a major presence in East Africa.

Nuer and Dinka Religion. The Nuer and Dinka are closely related Nilotic peoples mainly living in the southern Sudan. Traditionally pastoralists, the economic and religious life of the Nuer and Dinka have been greatly affected by recent civil war and famine, as well as earlier mission influence and colonialism. Their religion is an example of **African traditional religions**.

Both the Nuer and Dinka live in patrilineal clans, with no centralized authorities. A supreme deity, *Kwoth*, ("spirit"/"breath") among the Nuer, and *Nhialic*, ("sky") among the Dinka, is distant but concerned with the world and its affairs. Myths of origin speak of separation from the sky, the dwelling place of the deity, who is petitioned with prayers, hymns and offerings, an activity which forms an integral part of an individual's everyday life. Lesser spirits, classified by the Nuer as spirits of the air and spirits of the below, and divided by the Dinka into sky spirits and those associated with clan groups or ancestors, are closer to human affairs, and may form relationships with particular groups or individuals. Sickness is often caused by spirit possession. Ritual specialists belonging to particular lineages, (Leopard-skin priests—Nuer; Masters of the Fishing Spear—Dinka) are capable of interceding on behalf of the people and of performing efficacious sacrifices. Prophetic leaders have also been active in the nineteenth and twentieth centuries, possibly as a response to colonial pressures and subsequent political turmoil, although they may have much older roots in Nuer and Dinka society.

Nurcus. The "Followers of Divine Light" — a movement also sometimes known as Nurcular Camaati (Jama'at al-Nur), Association of Light, or simply as the Nur movement — is a movement of renewal within Turkish Islam based on the ideas of the religious leader "Bediüzzaman" ("without equal in his times") Said Nursi (1876–1960).

Born in Nurs in the Eastern, Kurdish, part of Turkey, Said made somewhat rebellious progress through the education system established in that region by the **Naqshabandiya Sufi** order, but also studied some secular, modern Western science, and the theme of the compatibility of the *Quran* with modern science (he went so far as to claim that the *Quran* predicted the aeroplane, the railway, the radio, electricity) is prominent in his writings and amongst his followers, the Nurcular.

Although indebted to the Naqshabandiya (Turkish: Nakşibendiler) in various ways, he was also highly critical of the Naqshabandi establishment, and defiantly adopted as his patron the figure of the founder of their great rivals, the **Qadiriya**. A notable theme of his later thinking is that all the Sufi orders have a contribution to make to Islam, and one should not display exclusive allegiance to any single one. (The Nur movement has been described on occasion, incorrectly, as a Sufi order itself.)

Having been to some extent supportive of the Ottoman state's appeal to Islam as a means of mobilizing popular support, Said Nursi fell foul of the Turkish Republic established in 1923, being exiled to a village in Western Turkey for alleged involvement in the Kurdish revolt of 1925. Convinced of a divine calling as mucedded (*mujaddid*), he gained a sizeable and growing number of disciples and followers, to the alarm of the authorities who imprisoned him for a period as a potential threat to the state. Further jail terms were to follow in 1943 and 1948. Yet throughout this period of state-enforced secularization, his influence spread as he conveyed his message of revitalizing Islam through a renewal of faith in the heart of the ordinary believer. He ended up being wooed by Prime Minister Menderes in pursuit of increased electoral support, and today former Prime Minister Demirel writes frequently for the Nurcu periodical *Köprü*.

Said Nursi's main work, the *Risale-i Nur* (Discourses on Divine Light), is revered almost as a sacred book, and adherence to the Nur movement (and Nur philosophy — Nurculuk) involves group study of this text. The publication of his writings in Turkey has been permitted since the 1950s, and they are now being translated into several languages — including German, since the Nurcular have a significant following in what was formerly West Germany. There are also small Nurcu groups elsewhere in Western Europe, as also in North America.

Nurcus oppose the Kemalist notion of a secular state, but advocate peaceful persuasion rather than violence. Consistently with this, they have disparaged the Iranian revolution. Their apparent success in gaining some support amongst cadets in a Turkish military school — where normally Kemalist principles are presupposed — caused the authorities considerable concern. They also oppose the 'Turkish-Islamic Synthesis' of **Aydinlar Ocagi**, being emphatic that Islam is a universal religion and not a nationalist creed.

Both in Turkey and in Germany, one way in which they gain followers is through the support they offer students (and in Germany, workers) living away from home — often by providing friendly accommodation. (In this respect they resemble the **Süleymancis**.) In their basically non-political approach to Muslim renewal, they bear comparison with another missionary movement, of South Asian origin, the **Tablighi Jama'at**, rather than with organizations such as the **Muslim Brotherhood** or the **Jama'at-i Islami**. From within Islam, nevertheless, critics might claim with some justification that direct study of the *Quran* has been unduly neglected by the Nurcus in their enthusiasm for the *Risale-i Nur*.

Nusayris. A quasi-Muslim sect, also known as **'Alawis** ('Alawiyun), mainly found in Syria. The name is taken from Abu Shu'ayb Muhammad ibn Nusayr, a representative (*bab*) of the tenth **Shi'ite** Imam (d. 868), but the sect was first organized in Iraq by a certain Abu 'Abd Allah al-Khasibi (d. 968). By the 12th century, however, the Nusayris were firmly established in Syria. Nusayri doctrine, like that of other extremist Shi'ite sects, is a complex mixture of Islamic, gnostic, Christian, and local elements. The Imam 'Ali is raised to the status of the divinity, figuring in a Trinity alongside Muhammad and the early Shi'ite saint Salman. In contrast to Muslim belief, they regard women as lacking a soul. Conventional Islamic practices are discarded in favour of an allegorized interpretation and a range of distinct festivals and ceremonies. Their meeting places are closed to outsiders.

In recent years, the Nusayris have exercised disproportionate political power in Syria, through their control of the Baathist party and the army. They have sometimes sought greater religious legitimacy by claiming to be a community within **Twelver Shi'ism**. Several million Nusayris live in the region between Latakia in Syria and Antakya in Turkey.

Nyingmapas. "Followers of the Ancient Teachings". Tibet's oldest Buddhist tradition, named for its emphasis on the first Buddhist *tantras* to reach Tibet. After defeating his mainly Buddhist neighbours in China, Bengal, Nepal, Kashmir, Uddiyana, and Central Asia, Tibet's Emperor Trisongdetsen (756–797) nevertheless felt shamed by Tibet's simpler culture; so inducing, possibly as tribute, many famous Buddhist teachers to visit Tibet, he commanded a translation of the Buddhist canon, a process his successors continued for nearly a century. The Nyingmapa tradition is based upon these first translations; hence they follow the

Mahayanist philosophy of Bengal's monk-logicians, Santaraksita and Kamalasila, the formless Atiyoga meditation of Western India's Vimalamitra, and the tantric yogas of Padmasambhava, from Uddiyana (modern Pakistan). Padmasambhava's royal descent and unmatched spiritual powers earned him the role of imperial guru and the gift of an imperial wife, Yeshe Tsogyal, later his leading disciple. His prestige established, devotion to Padmasambhava as founding guru for the whole Tibetan nation remains central for Nyingmapas and other Tibetans alike.

Nyingmapas have three unique features; mystical revelations called **Termas**, a decentralised cellular structure and minimal political involvement. Nevertheless invading Mongols, Manchus, and their Tibetan puppets occasionally attacked Nyingmapas, apparently through fear of their occult powers.

Beloved by Tibetans for its beauty, tolerance, and freedom, as well as its profundity and power, the Nyingmapa tradition specializes in integrating Buddhism into real-life situations, accommodating married lamas as well as monks and hermits. Since China's destruction of Tibet, the Nyingmapa tradition has begun attracting many new converts worldwide. In particular, the work of the incarnate lama, Tarthang Tulku, who in 1969 established the Nyingmapa Centre in Berkeley, California, has done much to bring western attention to these teachings.

O

Obaku Zen. The smallest school of Japanese **Zen Buddhism** with approximately 460 temples and 340,000 followers at this time. Doctrinally not dissimilar to the much larger **Rinzai** school, the Obaku was brought to Japan by Chinese missionary monks in the mid 17th century as a response to religious stagnation during the early Tokugawa Shogunate. Shortly after establishing itself on Japanese territory, it published a staggering 6,956 volume canon of Buddhist writing which represented the doctrines of all Buddhist schools in operation at that time.

Obeah. A secretive Jamaican cult of African origin—the name probably derives from the Ashanti word *obayifo,* meaning "witch". The term is used more generally for conjuring and magic, in particular harmful magic. The spirits of deceased practitioners of obeah are used by devotees of **Convince** to assist them in their divination practices.

Occultism. Western Occultism ("occult" literally means "hidden") encompasses various methods of developing latent powers ("psychic"/"magical") through extensive training in order to discipline the will. An occultist's training takes many years and involves the balanced development of intellectual, emotional and physical potential. The highest ideal of the occultist is to "work for the sake of the work" (or for the sake of mankind), with no personal benefit. The history of occultism shows many who have fallen short of this.

Many occultists pursue their work within a mystery tradition. One or more central mysteries are understood by the novitiate to the best of his/her ability, and through ritual, meditation and long periods of study the meaning of the mystery is deepened.

Schools of occultism and mystery schools have an exoteric (outer) and esoteric (inner) teaching, and the school is structured to reflect this.

Common to most Western traditions of Knowledge is the study, in both theory and practice, of **Kabbalah** (also Cabala or Qabalah). It is best known as the ancient and inner teaching of Judaism, and is also central to the mystical teaching of the Abrahamic religions. Kabbalah is a living tradition in its own right, and is periodically reformulated to meet the needs of the time. One of its foremost exponents today is Z'ev Ben Shimon Halevi, author and teacher of groups in a number of countries. Kabbalah, in Hebrew, means to receive. Kabbalists use a key symbol of the tree of life, a structure which sets out the macro- and microcosmic order and, through awareness of these different subtler levels of reality, knowledge (not information) is received. It is variously practised as a key to mysticism, meditation and magic. Gareth Knight is one of the most widely known teachers of Kabbalah as a magical training system and his work on archetypal symbolism is highly regarded.

The most significant group in the late 19th century occult revival was The Golden Dawn, a magical order whose origins were a mixture of **Freemasonry, Rosicrucianism** and, indirectly, **Theosophy**. One of today's direct descendants is The Servants of the Light, a school of occult science whose director of studies, Dolores Ashcroft-Norwicki, was herself trained by Dion Fortune's Society of the Inner Light. The Servants of the Light offer a Kabbalistic training into the mysteries of the tree of life and the symbolism of the Grail.

Old Apostolic Church. This church was originally set up in Zimbabwe and has spread to neighbouring countries. Its founder disappeared for two years, reputedly to heaven where he received instructions about the new church. He returned bearing a written set of rules to be used in conjunction with the Old Testament laws. Zulu is a significant language for the church members.

Members of the Old Apostolic church are distinct for their white robes, headdresses scored with a red T-shape for the women, and the fact that their meetings are held in the open air. All members carry a carved staff which is deemed to have special powers, particularly with regard to staving off witchcraft attacks.

Alongside adherence to certain Old Testament practices, including dietary taboos and acceptance of polygamy, the church members also claim to have special gifts through God's Holy Spirit coming into them. Such gifts range from healing, usually involving a ritual with washing and inhalation, to being in direct communication with God via a magical telephone.

While in rural areas the Old Apostolic church attracts the poorest sector of the population, in urban areas it has a self-help business enterprise orientation based on its exclusive network of members.

Old Believers. The most significant sectarian group within Russian Christianity, the Old Believers, or Old Ritualists, were those millions of **Russian Orthodox** who refused to accept the ecclesiastical reforms initiated by Patriarch Nikon (1652-58) and continued under the auspices of Peter the Great. Despite excommunication (from 1657), prolonged periods of persecution, and a lack of bishops to ordain their priests, they survived alongside the reformed Orthodox Church, relying on the latter for a steady supply of disaffected priests. Their status was much enhanced when in 1846 a bishop joined their ranks, and in 1881 they were recognized as a legitimate Church body. Numbering perhaps as many as thirty million in 1917,

they survived the communist years and in the new era of religious freedom in Russia continue to thrive.

There was also a minority party of Old Believers who, despite their original conservatism, denied the necessity of a priesthood, and from there evolved into a number of more extreme sects, whose religious enthusiasm found expression in a variety of bizarre beliefs and practices. These sects have always remained marginal minorities.

Old Calendarists. When from the 18th century onwards the western Churches changed from the Julian to the more accurate Gregorian calendar, the **Orthodox** Churches (Byzantine and Oriental) continued to follow the Julian calendar, which runs 13 days behind the Gregorian. Beginning with the Ecumenical Patriarchate in 1924, most of the individual Orthodox Churches also came to adopt the Gregorian calendar, continuing exceptions being the Churches of Jerusalem, Sinai, Serbia and Russia, together with most of the monasteries on Mount Athos. The Oriental Orthodox Churches also continue to follow the Julian calendar, except in some diasporate communities. The term "Old Calendarist", however, particularly applies to those dissident groups within the calendrically reformed Churches, mostly associated with monastic communities, who claim that only a collective decision by the whole Church could have legitimated such a reform. For them, adherence to the "Old Style" calendar has also become something of a symbol of a refusal to adapt to modern customs and usages. The Old Calendarists are particularly strong in Greece, where excommunication by the Church and persecution by the State have given them a strongly sectarian image. The chief practical difference for those following the "Old Style" calendar is that the Church year is consistently out of step with the calendar used by other Churches and in secular life. For example, the Russians celebrate

Christmas on January 7th rather than on December 25th. It should be noted, however, that the Orthodox Churches continue to use the Julian calendar as a basis for the complex lunar-based computation of Easter.

Old Catholic Church. The Old Catholic Church numbers about 400,000 members worldwide and compromises those churches belonging to the Union of Utrecht. These churches accept the doctrines of the Church prior to 1054 (the year of the Great Schism which divided the Eastern and Western churches) and reject more modern doctrines such as the infallibility of the pope. Clergy may marry and services are in the vernacular. The doctrines were stated in the Declaration of Utrecht made in 1889 by the then five Old Catholic bishops of Holland, Germany and Switzerland.

The Church falls into two distinct groups, West European (German, Austrian, Swiss, Dutch) and, a larger group, East European (Polish, Yugoslavian, American Polish). The earliest of these was the Church of Utrecht (in Holland) founded in 1724 after Dutch Roman Catholics were accused of the heresy of Jansenism (a belief in the necessity and irresistibility of the grace of God). After the First Vatican Council in 1870 Roman Catholics in Germany, Austria and Switzerland rejected the doctrine of papal infallibility. To preserve the apostolic succession of bishops they aligned themselves with the Church of Utrecht which led to the 1889 Declaration.

The Polish National Catholic Church was founded in Pennsylvania, USA in 1897 by Polish Catholics, after conflicts with the Roman hierarchy over Church property and ecclesiastical control. The first bishop of this church was consecrated by Old Catholic bishops in Utrecht in 1907. It now has over 250,000 members in the USA and Poland. The Old Catholic Church in Yugoslavia is much smaller and began with the Croatian Old Catholic Church in the early 1920s. It has since united with other small ethnic Old Catholic churches in the region.

Since 1932 Old Catholic Churches have been in full communion with the Anglican Church.

Old Catholic Mariavite Church. The Mariavite movement began in Poland with Feliksa Kozlowska, an impoverished gentlewoman after she claimed to see visions in the 1890s. She believed that she was called to the Third Order of **Franciscans,** and later to create a new exemplary order of priests to replace the corrupt **Roman Catholic** clergy. She depended on the spiritual support of the Virgin Mary and especially Our Lady of Perpetual Succour, focus of a late medieval **Orthodox** cult. She found little support before 1900 when a Catholic priest, Jan Kowalski, turned to her for spiritual and sexual satisfaction. Kowalski provided leadership for the tiny sect and recruited a few young priests. But he also drew it to the attention of the Inquisition in Rome, which ruled that Kozlowska's visions were bogus. The sect would probably have been suppressed at that point had not the Russian Tsar who ruled over Poland issued a decree on religious toleration in 1905 which provided some legal cover.

The Mariavites found some support from those dissatisfied with the Catholic clergy. Whereas the latter behaved in an authoritarian and worldly manner and frequently dabbled in Polish nationalist politics, Mariavite priests followed Franciscan ascetic ideals, addressed popular spiritual needs, and shunned politics. By 1907 about 250,000 people supported the movement particularly in the rural areas of central Poland. Despite the opposition of the Catholic hierarchy, the Mariavites were protected by the Russian government because they were apolitical and diverted the energies of priests and people away from subversive activities. They also called for the fusion of Catholicism and Orthodoxy. In 1909 Kowalski was consecrated bishop by the **Old Catholic** Bishop of Utrecht, but when the Polish state was created after World War I, numbers declined and in 1924 the Old Catholics withdrew their recognition. During World War I the Church was the target for severe persecution.

Today the Church is reduced to 24,000 members in 41 parishes, who are urged to make an annual pilgrimage to Plock. It manages a home for the elderly, seven workshops, four bakeries and three mineral water factories. It joined the World Council of Churches in 1969.

Old Religion. Adherents of contemporary **Witchcraft** and **Paganism** tend to regard themselves as practising some variant of "the Old Religion", which in Britain means mostly pre-Christian Celtic religion, but also elements of Norse, Saxon and Greco–Roman religion.

Old Ritualists. This is an alternative label for the **Old Believers** within **Russian Orthodoxy**.

Olive Tree Church. Like the **Unification Church** of the Moonies, this is a new religious movement originating in South Korea, where it has developed extremely large property holdings, and major urban-industrial complexes. It was founded in 1955 by Pak T'ae-son, who is regarded as the immortal Olive Tree of Revelation 11.4, and an oracle of God who has magical powers of healing.

Omotokyo. A relatively new Japanese **Shinto**-oriented sect. Omotokyo was founded in 1892 by the widow Deguchi Nao after revelatory visions of the god Ushitora no Konjin. The sect is essentially messianic, calling for the establishment of the kingdom of heaven upon earth (a clear rejection of the Emperor's divinity),

through the realization that god and humanity are interdependent. Deguchi's son-in-law, Deguchi Onisaburo, famed for his healing and shamanistic powers, systematized the religion, and was seen by many as the predicted messiah. Omotokyo proclaims itself an international religion, and advocates world peace and social reform in accordance with its tenets. Membership has recently waned, and is reckoned at about 150,000.

Ontakekyo. A Japanese mountain worship group, based on Mt. Ontake and one of the traditional 13 constituent sects of **Kyoha Shinto.**

Open Brethren. In 1829 a group of Christians from various denominations met privately in a Dublin room to share in a Communion service. This was a remarkable event since in those days only the members of a denomination could participate in its Communion Service. The men and women in Dublin believed that the Bible showed that Christians were free to "break bread" together as Christ had told them to, regardless of particular church affiliation.

These early "ecumenical" meetings gradually attracted more people who were concerned that the communion service should be an act of unity between Christians, not divisive. One member of the group was Francis Newman, younger brother of John Henry Newman. Others included J. N. Darby (see **Exclusive Brethren**), A. N. Groves, Lord Congleton and Edward Cronin (a converted Roman Catholic).

Francis Newman's friend Benjamin Newton became convinced that this view of scripture was correct. Newton lived in Plymouth and a strong congregation preaching these doctrines was established there, leading to the present tendency to refer to "Plymouth Brethren" a name not used by the Brethren themselves. A similar situation arose in Bristol where a friend of A. N. Groves, George Müller, founded a chapel and later a famous orphanage. Gradually the movement spread across the country.

After the split with the **Exclusive Brethren** in 1849 the Open Brethren continued to expand both through missionary work and writing. Many Brethren were involved in innovative social work and included people with influence in national politics. Dr. Barnado is perhaps the most famous. Abroad, missionaries went to Europe, to Australia and New Zealand (where they are still strong today) to Persia, India, Africa and America. Churches today still have the Breaking of Bread as their central weekly service. Open Brethren (unlike Exclusive Brethren) observe believer's baptism, and continue to assert the importance of preaching and the Bible, and the need for total commitment to Christ. Worldwide membership is about 1,500,000.

Opus Dei. Opus Dei, a **Roman Catholic** religious order, was founded in 1928 as a right-wing student movement. Its founder was the Spanish priest Jose María Escriva de Balaguer (1902–1975), who was beatified by the Pope in 1992. Its aim is to sanctify everyday life, particularly professional work. Opus Dei is a personal prelature of the Roman Catholic Church. A personal prelature is the equivalent of a bishopric: just as all Catholics within a diocese fall under their Bishop's authority, so all members of this world-wide prelature answer to their Prelate, in matters relating to Opus Dei. The current Prelate is Bishop Alvaro del Portillo. Opus Dei has more than a thousand priests, and 75,000 lay members in more than 80 countries. It is the Roman Catholic church's fastest growing, wealthiest, and most controversial society. Criticism has arisen over allegations of secrecy about membership and involvement in the worlds of politics, high finance and academia.

Order of Buddhist Contemplatives (OBC). Founded by an Englishwoman, Reverend Master Jiyu-Kennett, who is one of the few women Buddhist leaders. She founded, and is Abbess and Spiritual Director of, Shasta Abbey in California in 1970, followed by Throssel Hole Priory in England, then other temples and meditation groups in America and Canada. The Order is within the **Soto Zen** ("Serene Reflection Mediation") tradition but with a strong emphasis on adapting Buddhism to the West—including the incorporation of some Christian ritual and terminology.

Men and women are given equal training and status, both being fully ordained into the Buddhist priesthood and called monks. The monastic order is celibate. Lay training is also catered for with a full programme of meditation courses and retreats. The Order emphasizes the need to establish and deepen practice in daily life. There is no charge for teaching or accommodation, though donations are requested. Visitors are welcome.

Organization of Islamic Action. The Organization of Islamic Action (Munazzamat al-'Amal al-Islami) is a **Shi'ite** oppositionalist group which emerged in Karbala in Iraq in the 1960s. Its foundation is associated with Ayatollah Hasan al-Shirazi who, however, was forced to leave Iraq in 1970. He lived first in Kuwait and then Beirut, where he was influential in establishing several Islamic institutions until he was assassinated by Baath agents in 1980.

The party still has some underground cells in Iraq, but is now based in Tehran, Damascus and London. Unlike other similar groups, its membership is quite international, and it has been active in the Gulf, especially in Kuwait and Bahrain. (Its leader until the late 1980s, was Muhammad Taqi al-Mudarrisi, who fled to Kuwait in 1968; his brother, Hadi al-Mudarrisi, founded the **Islamic Front for the Liberation of Bahrain.** Both were originally based in the Shi'ite religious centre of Karbala in Iraq, where they trained as clerics.) In the eighties it was involved in international terrorism, but this now appears to have ceased.

Organization of the Islamic Conference (OIC). The OIC (al-Mu'tamar al-Islami) was established in 1971 and is based in Saudi Arabia. It is an international organization whose declared aims include promoting Islamic solidarity among member states, of which there are currently 45. Its supreme body is the Conference of Heads of State which is scheduled to meet every three years: the sixth such summit meeting took place in Dakar, the capital of Senegal, at the end of 1991. There is also an annual conference of member countries' foreign ministers.

The OIC supports education in Muslim communities worldwide, and through its Islamic Solidarity Fund, established at the second summit conference in Lahore, Pakistan, in 1974, it has helped to establish Islamic universities in Niger, Uganda and Malaysia. Humanitarian assistance to Muslim communities affected by wars and natural disasters is also given. Politically the OIC opposes Israel and seeks to play a constructive role in troublespots involving Muslims, e.g. in Afghanistan, Chad, Lebanon, and the Iran-Iraq and Gulf wars.

Following the break-up of the USSR, Azerbaijan has joined the OIC, Kazakhstan sent a delegation to the 1991 summit, and all six predominantly Muslim republics are expected to join in due course. Albania was also represented at the Dakar summit, having been granted observer status.

The organization suffers, however, from tensions between its Arab and non-Arab members, and is weakened in many people's eyes by its identification with Saudi interests. Moreover, the hostility between many Muslim states (as in the Iran–Iraq and Gulf wars) has also very often been a major factor in preventing the OIC from moving beyond passing resolutions to developing a strong, united and effective

stance in world affairs. It remains to be seen whether current, tentative exploration of the basis for an Islamic Common Market will eventually yield positive results.

The OIC is seen as complementing the other major Saudi-based organization, the **Muslim World League.**

Oriental Orthodox Churches. The term "Oriental Orthodox" identifies an important but often neglected group of Churches of the Middle East which represent some of the oldest traditions of Christianity. They include the **Armenian** Church, the **Coptic** Church the **Ethiopian** Church and the **Syrian Jacobite** Church (*see also* **Syro–Indian Churches**). The **Nestorian Church,** sometimes loosely counted among them, strictly belongs in a group of its own.

The identity of these Churches is defined positively by their fidelity to the Council of Ephesus (431) and negatively by their repudiation of the decrees, or at least the authority, of the Council of Chalcedon (451). The latter affirmed that Christ united two natures, human and divine, within a single person; the opposing monophysite view, that Christ's humanity was a function of his single divine nature, was condemned as undermining the reality of the incarnation. But these non-Chalcedonian Churches are not necessarily accurately described as monophysite: their rejection of Chalcedon owed something to ecclesio–political factors and something to theological misunderstandings, and the extent to which their adherents still affirm the more extreme forms of monophysitism is open to question.

The Oriental Orthodox Churches, ethnically and geographically separate in the past, have in modern times established close ties with one another, as was demonstrated at a conference of their heads and representatives held in 1965 in Addis Ababa, where intentions were formulated to work for greater understanding between themselves and other Churches. Moreover, despite their undoubted monophysite emphasis, the Oriental Orthodox are very close to the Byzantine Orthodox in their general theology, style of worship and ecclesiastical customs. All this leaves open the possibility of future re-union between the Byzantine Orthodox and at least some of the Oriental Churches, and a number of constructive meetings between representatives from the two traditions have already taken place.

Orthodox Bahai Faith. The largest of several dissident groups which broke from the mainstream **Baha'i** organization following the death of Shoghi Effendi in 1957. This group has its headquarters in Roswell, New Mexico, and adheres to a belief in the continuation of the Bahai Guardianship through Charles Mason Remey and his successors.

Orthodox Church (Byzantine tradition). The Orthodox Church is a family, or federation, of independent and in most cases national Churches bound together by common traditions of worship and theology which were developed within the Greek-speaking, Byzantine culture of the eastern Mediterranean. Officially defining itself as the "Orthodox Catholic Church", and in the creed as the One, Holy, Apostolic and Catholic Church, the Orthodox Church, like the **Roman Catholic** Church, claims to be the true representative of the original undivided Church. It constitutes the second largest communion of Christians in the world, numbering something over 150,000,000 baptized members.

The simple title "Orthodox Church" is potentially misleading, just as the title "Catholic Church" is for the Roman Catholic Church, since the term "Orthodox", like the term "Catholic", is used by other Churches too. It is nevertheless preferable to the popular title "Eastern Orthodox Church" (or "Orthodox Eastern Church"), which risks confusion with the Churches describing themselves as the **Oriental Orthodox** Churches. More accurate would be a title such as "Byzantine Orthodox Church" or "Orthodox Church of the Byzantine tradition".

The early Church was based on five principal metropolitan centres: the patriarchates of Rome in the West, and of Constantinople, Alexandria, Antioch and Jerusalem in the East. In the fifth century, **Syrian, Armenian** and Egyptian sections of the hitherto undivided Church became separated from the mainstream Church, which now consisted of a Greek-dominated eastern half with its centre at Constaninople (Byzantium) and a Latin-dominated western half with its centre at Rome. Religious disputes and misunderstandings, exacerbated by cultural and political differences, eventually led to open schism (1054), and thence to the emergence of two separate institutions; the Byzantine Orthodox Church and the Roman Catholic Church. It is worth emphasizing, however, that despite their many differences (most crucially about ecclesiastical authority) these two Churches affirm fundamentally the same doctrines and recognize the validity of each other's sacraments. A symbolically significant event was the meeting in 1964 between Pope Paul VI and Patriarch Athenagoras I at which they withdrew the mutual excommunications of 1054.

For the Orthodox Church, authority is exercised collectively and not by any individual Church or single senior bishop, though the inevitable tendencies towards ecclesiastical centralism have been checked as much by historical circumstances as by any straightforward adherence to principle. This "de-centralized" view of ecclesiastical authority is expressed through the tradition of autocephalous Churches, so-called because each is completely independent of the jurisdiction of any other Church. Each autocephalous Church governs its affairs through a council, or synod, of bishops headed by a senior bishop, variously ranking as patriarch, catholicos, metropolitan or archbishop, whose seat is normally in the chief city of the country. Churches still dependent on a parent Church for the election of their senior bishops are *autonomous* but not (yet) autocephalous. Although no Church or bishop has overall authority, the Church of Constantinople, known as the "Ecumenical Patriarchate" and headed by the Ecumenical Patriarch, is traditionally accorded primacy of honour and certain rights of initiative on account of its historical role as the mother Church of Byzantium. Thus the Ecumenical Patriarchate may be called upon to mediate in disputes and to express the whole Church's official recognition of an individual Church's claim to autocephalous status.

Although the distinction between one Church and another is in theory territorial (like that between one diocese and another), in practice the complexities of history have produced national or ethnic Churches without coherent geographical boundaries. Thus within the same country, particularly in the West, may be found Orthodox Christians attending different national Churches who should logically be members of a single Church. The main dividing factor is language, since Orthodox worship is meant to be conducted in the local vernacular (which in practice is often a language now become archaic). This close identification of each individual Church with the language and culture of a particular national or ethnic group has proved a source both of strength and of weakness. On the one hand it has helped preserve national identity, especially during the long periods of foreign occupation suffered by most Orthodox countries. On the other hand the independence and inward-looking character of its member Churches have made it difficult for the Orthodox Church to express a collective view or common purpose. Orthodox believers from one group may not readily recognize those of other nationalities or cultures as their own co-religionists.

The various Churches can be conveniently described under five main headings; (1) the four ancient patriarchates; (2) the principal Greek-speaking Churches; (3) the Churches which are neither Greek nor Slavonic; (4) the principal Slavonic Churches; and (5) the newer Churches of Slavonic origin.

(1) The four ancient patriarchal Churches are surviving outposts of Orthodox Christianity in what for centuries have been predominantly Islamic countries. The Church of Constantinople (in Istanbul in Turkey) is all that is left of the once powerful and extensive Church that formed the spiritual and cultural centre of the Byzantine Empire. Its original heartland was Greek Asia Minor (conquered by the Turks in the 15th century) and what is now modern Greece (where the Church eventually became autocephalous). Today it has jurisdiction over a number of disparate groups: a dwindling community of Greek Orthodox Christians in Turkey; the Greek and Slavonic monastic communities of the semi-independent republic of Mount Athos; Greek Orthodox dioceses on Crete, Patmos and the Dodecanese islands; and emigrant communities in Western Europe, North America and Australia, including autonomous Slavonic communities wishing to be independent of the jurisdiction of Churches in communist countries. Turkey continues to impose restrictions on the Patriarchate: for example, the Patriarch himself must be a Turkish citizen. Worldwide the Church numbers around 5,000,000 members.

The Churches of Alexandria and Antioch are Byzantine versions of the original patriarchates which split off from the mainstream Church in the fifth century to become, respectively, the **Coptic Church** and the **Syrian Jacobite Church.** The Church of Alexandria (in Egypt, originally part of greater Greece) has jurisdiction over Orthodox Christians throughout Africa, but its members are mainly Greeks and Arabs living in Egypt,

Ethiopia, the Sudan, Kenya, Uganda and Tanzania (about 250,000 in all). Its ecclesiastical traditions and language of worship are Greek. The Church of Antioch preserves traditions of Syriac Christianity and worships in Arabic. It has jurisdiction over Arab Orthodox communities in Syria, Lebanon, Iraq and various emigrant communities in the United States (around 500,000 in all). The patriarch, since 1899 an Arab rather than a Greek, now resides in Damascus (Syria) rather than in Antioch (Turkey). The Church of Jerusalem (until 451 part of Antioch) is dominated by Greek senior clergy, while the vast majority of its members are Palestinian Arabs living in Israel and Jordan (about 75,000 in all). It is this Church which has custodianship of most of the Christian holy places in Israel and Jerusalem. It also has responsibility for the tiny autonomous Church of Sinai (St Catherine's monastery).

(2) Apart from the Churches of Constantinople Alexandria, Sinai and Jerusalem, the main Greek-speaking Churches are those of Cyprus and of Greece. These, despite their shared language and customs, are administratively quite separate. Each Church is governed by a "Holy Synod" of archbishops, one of whom has primacy but not patriarchal status. The Orthodox Church of Cyprus is one of the oldest independent Churches, established by the apostles Paul and Barnabus and autocephalous since 431. The primate is the archbishop of Constantia (Famagusta), resident in Nicosia. His traditional role as ethnarch, or national leader, of Cypriot Christians is a legacy of the Ottoman system of governing the Christians through their Church leaders. The Church of Cyprus has nearly 500,000 members. The Orthodox Church of Greece was originally part of the Church of Constantinople, but assumed autocephalous status in 1833, following the creation of modern Greece after four centuries of Turkish occupation. The archbishop of Athens is primate.

The Church of Greece is now the only Orthodox Church officially recognized as a State Church, though formal ties between Church and State, often a source of tension in the past, are gradually being loosened. Even so, national and religious identity still go hand in hand. The membership of the Church is four-fifths the population of Greece itself: namely 8,000,000.

(3) Up until the 20th century all but two of the autocephalous Churches were either Greek or Slavonic in culture. The exceptions were the patriarchal Churches of Georgia and Romania. The ancient kingdom of Georgia, in the Caucasus, was converted to Christianity in the fourth century. Headed by a Catholicos-Patriarch, and also known as the Catholicate of Georgia, it became independent of its parent Church, the Patriarchate of Antioch, in the eighth century. In the 19th century it was incorporated into the Church of Russia, and from 1917 until the collapse of communism remained under the control of Moscow. Always one of the smallest Churches, today it numbers roughly 1,000,000 members. The Church of Romania, by contrast, is the second largest Orthodox community in the world, numbering at least 15,000,000. Though much influenced by their Byzantine and Slav neighbours, and during Turkish rule dominated by Greek clergy, the Romanians have remained basically a Latin people. An autocephalous Romanian Church was established in 1864, but the present Church, a much larger entity brought into being with modern Romania, dates from around 1925.

(4) With the loss of its original heartland, first to the Arabs and then to the Ottoman Turks, the Church's centre of gravity gradually shifted from the Greek to the Slavonic world, though most of the new Churches themselves passed through a period of Turkish rule. The principal Slavonic Churches are the Patriarchal Churches of Serbia,

Bulgaria and Russia. Established by Greek missionary monks, these Churches followed the ecclesiastical traditions of Constantinople, but worshipped in their own language, the now somewhat archaic "Church Slavonic", for which the missionaries devised the Cyrillic alphabet, based on the Greek alphabet. Each of these Churches was eventually to gain independence from Constantinople, though in the Ottoman period, when the Turks used the Patriarchate to govern their Christian subjects, they were again controlled by Greek clergy.

Byzantine missionaries established Orthodoxy in Serbia and Bulgaria during the ninth century, and autocephalous Churches existed in the mediaeval period. A Serbian Orthodox Church was recognized in 1879, but the modern Church, uniting a number of originally separate dioceses, dates from 1922, following the creation of Yugoslavia after World War I. Serbian nationalism and Serbian Orthodoxy have always gone hand in hand. During World War II the Serbs suffered heavily from their Croatian compatriots, many of whom were Nazi supporters as well as Catholics. Bitter and violent conflict between Orthodox Serbs and Catholic Croats were resumed following the post-communist division of Yugoslavia into independent states. Today the Church numbers about 8,000,000. The modern Church of Bulgaria proclaimed its autocephalous status in 1870, against the wishes of the Ecumenical Patriarchate, which finally accepted its autocephalous status only in 1945 (later granting it patriarchal status). Today it numbers about 6,000,000 members.

Russia officially became Orthodox at the end of the 10th century, remaining dependent on Constantinople until 1448, when it claimed autocephalous status. The Patriarchate of Moscow, until the end of the 20th century the centre of the greater Russian Church, was officially established in 1589. While other Orthodox countries passed through a period of Ottoman rule, Russia alone remained a free Orthodox country. The Church grew into a powerful institution, extending its domain both as result of Russian expansionism and through its own missionary effort (in Japan and Alaska). The history of the **Russian Orthodox** is complex and contentious, especially in relation to the rival Roman Catholic Uniate Churches established among Orthodox populations in territories along Russia's shifting western frontiers (*see* **Eastern Rite Ukrainian Church**). The Patriarchal Church of Moscow and all Russia has for centuries been the largest single Orthodox Church, numbering just under 100,000,000 in 1917, though only around half that number by the end of the communist era. This number has now been reduced further by the independence of Churches formerly part of or dependent upon the Moscow Patriarchate.

Following the Russian revolution and the spread of communism, the Orthodox Churches in eastern Europe entered seven decades of oppression, deprivation and persecution. Church leaders in response evolved various strategies of co-existence and co-operation, not always compatible with their professed Christian principles, and even when compatible not always sympathetically understood by those living in the free world.

(5) The political upheavals of the 20th century resulted in the emergence, or re-emergence, of new independent Churches among the Slavs. The break-up of the old Russian Empire freed a number of autonomous Churches from the control of Moscow (though it resumed control of some of them during World War II). In 1923 the small Church of Finland, founded in the 12th century, placed itself under the jurisdiction of the Ecumenical Patriarchate. In 1924 the Ecumenical Patriarchate granted autocephalous status to the Church of Poland, a status recognized by

Moscow only after World War II. In 1951 Moscow itself recognized the independence of the small Church of Czechoslovakia, made up of a small minority of ex-Uniate Carpatho–Russians. The Church of Albania was granted autocephalous status in 1937; but, in a country populated mainly by Muslims and ruled by a repressive régime which in 1967 declared Albania the world's first officially atheist state, it had at one time virtually ceased to exist.

The "Orthodox Church in America", which traces its origins to Russian missions in Alaska in the 19th century and which was previously called the "Russian Orthodox Greek Catholic Church of America", gained independence from Moscow in 1970 and has had aspirations, never fully realized, to bring together the Orthodox of all national groups living in the United States. The Orthodox Church of Australia, an autonomous body based on the large Greek emigrant community, has corresponding aspirations.

With the disintegration of the communist bloc national Churches again began to proclaim in their newly independent homelands the independence from Moscow they had long proclaimed as disasporate groups: these include the Estonian, Latvian, Lithuanian, Belorussian and Ukrainian Orthodox Churches. Likewise, with the break-up of Yugoslavia, the Macedonian Orthodox Church reasserted a long-standing claim to autocephalous status persistently refused by the Serbian Orthodox Church.

The teachings of the Orthodox Church are defined by the decisions of the seven ecumenical councils (325–787), and given philosophical and mystical expression in the writings of the Church fathers. In theory further ecumenical councils might be convened, though it is difficult to imagine under what circumstances. The Orthodox Church does not accept the authority of any of the subsequent councils recognized as enumenical by the Roman Catholic Church. Nor have the basic teachings of the Orthodox Church been subject to the kind of doctrinal elaborations and scholastic definitions characteristic of Latin Christianity. Orthodox Christianity tends to emphasize prayer and worship rather than doctrine, in this respect resembling Judaism and Islam.

Orthodox worship and theology are strongly Trinitarian; God is never viewed as an abstract being above and beyond the three divine persons. Great devotion is paid to the saints and especially to Mary, who is venerated not in her own right but as Mother of God (Theotokos, "God-bearer"). As in Roman Catholicism, seven sacraments are recognized: baptism, chrismation, eucharist, confession, anointing of the sick, marriage and priesthood. Baptism is traditionally by full immersion, including for those baptized as adults. Chrismation (the equivalent of confirmation) follows immediately after baptism; baptized infants receive communion along with the rest of the congregation. Communicants receive by spoon a fragment of bread from a chalice of wine. Orthodoxy accepts the "real presence" of Christ in the sacrament, without attempting to define this doctrinally. There is a three-fold ministry of deacons, priests and bishops. Secular priests are always married, while the bishops are celibate, recruited from the monastic clergy. Some parishes are served by archimandrites (celibate monastic priests). Monasticism has always been a vital part of Orthodox tradition: the monasteries helped keep the faith alive in difficult times, combating heresy and political interference alike. There are no separate "orders" such as exist in western monasticism. The main occupation of Orthodox monks and nuns is prayer and worship, though monasteries also attract many lay visitors.

Perhaps the most distinctive features of Orthodox Christianity are to be found in its rich tradition of worship and religious art. The long and elaborate services, sung or chanted by choir or cantor, are celebrated in churches richly decorated with lamps and images, the congregation standing throughout. Musical instruments are never used. The high point of the Church year is Holy Week (Easter), culminating in the feast of the Resurrection, which in Orthodox countries retains the importance it had in the early Church. The veneration of icons (images of Christ and the saints) in churches and homes link all the main themes of Orthodox belief and practice: devotionally they provide a focus for prayer and worship, theologically they express the themes of divine incarnation and human salvation, institutionally their presence confirms the victory of the Orthodox Church over the heresy of iconoclasm (destruction of icons) in the eighth century, which marked the end of its basic doctrinal development. Orthodox Christianity is easily criticized for its doctrinal and ecclesiastical conservatism, rather unfairly given the extent to which the life and development of its various member Churches have been constrained by the rule of non-Christian or anti-Christian powers. Nowadays, however, the Orthodox Church commands considerable respect among other denominations, not only on account of the sufferings of its various communities under communism, but also because of its great ecumenical potential. For it offers a model of Christianity from an era prior to the divisions and upheavals which occurred in western Christendom. For their part, and largely through their diasporate communities in western Europe and North America, the various Orthodox Churches have become more sympathetic to non-Orthodox Christian traditions, as well as more aware of deficiencies and problems within their own tradition. Most of the Orthodox Churches are now members of the World Council of Churches, and many Orthodox Christians are involved in one way or another in the ecumenical movement.

Orthodox Judaism (Orthodoxy). (*See also* **Haredi.**) Orthodox Judaism holds that the written *Torah* (the first five books of the Bible) were revealed verbatim to Moses by God and that the rabbinic commentary on it, the oral *Torah,* is divine in origin and is just as binding as the written version. (Although teaching the same beliefs, Hasidic Judaism is considered in a separate article due to differences in its ethos.) Some refer to it as "Orthopraxy" because it emphasizes correct practice, yet the term is useful as it locates the reasons for observance and hesitancy to change Jewish practice in theology, not just respect for tradition.

Orthodoxy, as well as its sub-divisions, stems from the beginning of the Jews' ability to participate in Europe's modern nation-states. Just as European Christians attempted to "modernize" their religion, so too did some Jews, particularly German **Reform** Jews. These efforts were vigorously opposed by Hungarian rabbi Moses Sofer (1762–1839), known as the Hatam Sofer ("the perfect scribe"), whose dictum "Novelty is forbidden by the Torah" became the watchword of those who considered modernity an enemy of traditional Jewish culture. In his eyes, all of Jewish tradition, whether from the *Mishnah* and *Talmuds* or from later local *minhag* ("custom") was equally valid and immutable.

At the other end of the traditionalist spectrum was German rabbi Samson Raphael Hirsch (1808–1888), the leader of "neo-" or "modern" Orthodoxy. He argued that one could be fully modern and fully traditional, although favouring some minor liturgical changes. Yet this support for combining Judaism and modernity, encapsulated in his interpreting the rabbinic phrase, *Torah im derekh Eretz* ("Torah and an occupation" [Avot 2:2]), to justify participation in the modern state, did not stop him from becoming the leader of a German Jewish group which broke from the Reform-dominated "official" Jewish community recognized by the government.

While issues of modernity and emancipation produced Hungarian and German forms of Orthodoxy, traditional Judaism in Russia, Lithuania and Poland was divided by Hasidism, a pietistic movement emphasizing prayer over *Torah* study, and in its second generation, teaching that certain men, *tzaddikim* ("righteous ones"), could intervene with God on behalf of their community. Hasidism's critics, the Mitnagdim ("opponents"), led by Rabbi Elijah Shlomo Zalman, "the Gaon (Sage) of Vilna" (1720–1797), stressed the importance of diligent Torah study at its *yeshivot* ("seminaries"). Rabbi Israel Lipkin (Salanter (1810–1883)) began the *Musar* movement ("ethics") which stressed rigorous self-examination and fear of God. Later, the Hasidic–Mitnagdic rift ended as they joined in opposition to non-traditional forms of Judaism originating in the West. Today, these two groups comprise the **Haredim** ("those who fear (God)") or as they are sometimes referred to, the "ultra-Orthodox."

The Orthodox communities of Britain, America, and Israel, traditionalism's main centres after the *Holocaust,* have been influenced by all these trends as well as by local conditions. Regardless of personal observance, most British Jews affiliate with Orthodox synagogues, which are divided into several organizations, the largest being the **United Synagogue** founded in 1870. Jews' College (London) established in 1856, is the principal institution for the training of Orthodox rabbis and *cantors* for Britain and the Commonwealth. It also offers academic degree courses in Jewish Studies. Other groups include the **Federation of Synagogues,** founded in 1887 by Lord Swaythling, which is oriented towards Eastern European Orthodoxy and the **Union of Orthodox Hebrew Congregations,** founded in 1926 by Rabbi Victor Schonfeld, to unite Western Orthodoxy. The latter group included **Adat Israel,** which was established to perpetuate German-style Orthodoxy.

In America, the Orthodox are a minority of the Jewish population, behind the Conservative and Reform branches of Judaism. Major Orthodox organizations include **The Union of Orthodox Congregations of America** (founded 1898, and representing more than 700 congregations) and **The National Council of Young Israel** (1912), a synagogue group founded by Americanized Orthodox laity and under lay leadership until after World War II. American Orthodox rabbis are organized in two major groups, **The Union of Orthodox Rabbis of the United States and Canada** (1902), comprising of Eastern European rabbis and **The Rabbinical Council of America** (1923, reorganized in 1935), comprising more than 800 American-trained rabbis, and supporting the institutions for their training. Orthodox educational institutions include the **Torah Umesorah** ("Torah and tradition"), the National Society for Hebrew Day Schools, founded in 1944 with 498 schools in 1985 and Yeshivah University (1928, with component units dating to 1897). Recent American Orthodox leaders include rabbis Joseph Dov Soloveitchik (1903) and Moshe Feinstein (1895–1986) whose *halakhic* ("Jewish legal") decisions were respected universally by Orthodox Jews.

In Israel, the Orthodox are also a minority, but comprise a majority of religious Jews. Institutionally, only Orthodox rabbis may perform marriages, divorces, and conversions, **Zionism** itself was originally controversial among Orthodox Jews with some calling for a return to Zion and others arguing that not only must Jews wait for God's messiah to restore Jewish sovereignty but also that traditional Jews could not co-operate with the secular Zionists. Today there are four main groups of Orthodox Jews in Israel: an anti-Zionist minority, comprised of **Neturei Karta** ("Guardians of the City") and the **Edah Haredi** ("Haredi community"); a number of haredi communities, hasidic and mitnagdic, who have limited contact with the state; **Sephardi** traditionalists, represented politically by the **Shas** party; and **religious Zionism,** which sees religious value in Zionism and the State of Israel, despite its secular leadership. One group of religious Zionists, the **Gush Emunim** ("the bloc of the faithful"), following the teachings of Rabbi Abraham Isaac ha-Kohen Kook (1865–1935) as mediated by his son, Rabbi Tzvi Yehudah ha-Kohen Kook (1891–1982), were instrumental in the establishment of the settlement movement, believing that Israeli history, especially the 1967 Six-Day War, was part of God's redemption of the Jews. They are opposed by the Orthodox peace groups, Oz V'Shalom ("Strength and Peace") and Netivot Shalom ("Paths of Peace"). In

recent years, a number of religious Zionists have also tended towards greater rigour in observance.

Other important current trends in Orthodoxy are the **Baalei Teshuvah** ("masters of repentance") and the Hozrei be-Teshuvah ("returning in repentance") movement in which formally non-traditional Jews become Orthodox, generally, *haredi*. The movement, strongest among Israelis and travellers, rejects Western culture and has led to the creation of a unique Orthodox sub-culture.

P

Paganism. The word Pagan (from Latin *paganus*) means country dweller, and Paganism (or Neo-Paganism) uses ritual as a tool to end the alienation arising from a separation from nature. The terms "Paganism" and "Neo-Paganism" are often used interchangeably, and are sometimes also used as synonyms for **Witchcraft.**

Pagan beliefs date back to early man, and aspects of the legacy handed on include working in stone circles, celebration of season festivals, worship of the old gods and especially the Goddess in her manifestations as maiden, mother and crone. Similar kinds of **shamanic** nature religion that worships a goddess are sometimes linked with modern political movements— green witches with the ecological movements, etc.

Important seasonal festivals include the Winter Solstice (adopted and adapted by Christians in the form of Christmas), Beltane (the Spring Festival of the first of May associated with maypole and Morris dancing), and the Summer Solstice (with Glastonbury and Stonehenge as favoured venues in the United Kingdom for this celebration of midsummer).

Pajelança. One of the names used in the central regions of Brazil for the **Afro–American spiritist** movement **Candomblé**.

Palace of Sacred Peace. A small sub-group within the modern Taiwanese **Compassion Society.**

Palang Dharma Party (PDP). Founded in the early 1980s by Maj.-Gen. Chamlong Siimeuang, a prominent lay follower of **Santi Asok,** this Thai political party propounds a "path of righteousness" and is morally and politically conservative. It has had little electoral success.

Pan-Indianism. "Pan-Indianism" is a term used to describe beliefs held by many young native Americans who hold that, at heart, all **Native American religions** and cultures are the same and present an integrated set of beliefs and rituals common to all tribes. This is a recent idea, formed in response to white domination, and would not find favour with many representatives of traditional tribal religions. Nonetheless, Pan-Indianism is an important feature of contemporary native American religious life, underlying such rituals as **Peyotism** and the increasing use of the sweat lodge, vision quest and other rites, as well as being an important impetus in asserting native American rights, particularly in regard to sacred sites and land disputes.

Pangestu Pangestu — Paguyuban Ngesti Tunggal in full — is one of the larger **kebatinan** sects which have proliferated in Indonesia this century: its membership is estimated at around 100,000. It was founded in 1949, but its origins lie in an alleged revelation from God in February 1932 to R. Soenarto Mertowardojo, or Pakde Narto as he became generally known. The revelation was written down not long afterwards by Pakde Narto (b. 1899) and two friends, and published as a book entitled *Sasangka Jati* which later appeared in English under the title *True Light*. This functions as the basis for the group's teachings, lectures and discussions.

The content of the teachings includes elements related to several major religions, for example a trinitarian doctrine of God, what has been described as a Javanese spiritual version of Genesis, a Hindu doctrine of reincarnation, and a variant of Buddhism's Panca Sila or five basic values.

The movement attracts members among

the village population but is also very strong in the state bureaucracy and the army, and has appealed too to prominent intellectuals.

Parsis. Literally "the Persians". The **Zoroastrian** community in India, so-called because they migrated from Iran in the 10th century CE and settled in north-west India. They maintained little contact with the community they had left behind, although between the 15th and 17th centuries priests in Gujarat corresponded with those in Iran in an attempt to obtain authoritative rulings on religious matters. Parsi fortunes improved early in the 19th century with a movement from Gujarat into Bombay. This provided opportunities for business and professional activities, underpinned by education in Western-style schools. Increased contact with other religions, the criticism of Christian missionaries, and western scholarship caused internal divisions over theological and doctrinal problems. These mostly concerned the question of whether dualism, some form of monotheism on the Semitic model, or even monism lay at the heart of their tradition. In particular, the inability of Parsi priests to rebut these criticisms satisfactorily engendered a new self-consciousness among lay people and signalled a decline in priestly influence. This crystallized into a number of reform movements, variously influenced by outside agencies, including the **Theosophists.**

Within the context of the wider Indian society Parsis operate as a caste, which helps to sustain both their religious exclusiveness and their economic strength as a group. Apart from the fire temples, Parsi institutions are controlled by a *panchayat*, or community organization. Among the properties they own are the *dakhmas* or "towers of silence", where corpses are placed to be consumed by vultures and other carrion-eaters in conditions that are minimally polluting. The fire temples, which are the concern of the priests, fall into two categories, on the basis of their grade of ritual fire. Among the eight holiest in India is one at Udvada, north of Bombay, where the fire is said to have been burning continuously for a thousand years; consequently it is a special place of pilgrimage for Parsis. Of the "ordinary" fire temples (*agiari*), there are 40 in Bombay alone.

Since Independence Parsi fortunes have faded; there has been a quickening of the outside influences working on the community, and the population (approximately 100,000) has continued to decline. This has led to a further attempts to define what constitutes Parsi identity. Their economic, political and cultural influence continues, nevertheless, to exceed massively their numerical strength.

Parti Islam Se-Malaysia (PAS). This is the main political organization representing resurgent fundamentalist Islam in Malaysia. It was established in 1951, prior to Independence, to promote radical reformist Islam in the polity of the emergent nation, its founding members having left UMNO (the United Malay National Organization), the Muslim–Malay party which has dominated the multi-racial government coalitions since Independence in 1957, because of its refusal to endorse the establishment of Malaysia as an Islamic state. PAS and UMNO have been rivals ever since.

PAS has achieved intermittent power in three states of the Federation, but has only a small but vocal group of members of parliament, despite an increasing share of the national vote (43 per cent in 1986). PAS is committed to the establishment of an Islamic state based on the *Quran* and *Sunna*, and the promotion of Islamic economics.

In the 1980s it sought to broaden its appeal by attacking religious–ethnic chauvinism and advocating Islam as the solution to problems of social injustice for all, not just Muslims. UMNO-led government repression has increased, however: in the "Memali incident" of 1985 14 villagers died and many more were arrested in a police attack on a community of militant PAS supporters led by Ibrahim "Libya" — who was also killed. While that remains an extreme instance, tensions between PAS and UMNO supporters continue to grow: symbolic of this is the way in which they may now well meet separately in the mosques for prayer, or indeed build entirely separate mosques.

In the October 1990 election PAS gained control of the northern state of Kelantan, and now faces the challenge of living up to its supporters' hopes in practice.

Parvezis. Followers of the Pakistani Muslim thinker, Ghulam Ahmad Parvez (1903–1985), a notable developer of the position of the **Ahl-i Quran.** His followers are based in London and hold annual functions.

Pasdaran. The Pasdaran organization in Iran is the corps of the **Islamic Revolutionary Guards.**

Patit Sikhs. A lapsed **Sikh.** From the point of view of **Khalsa Sikhism** any initiated Sikh who cuts their hair or smokes is regarded as having a gross sin against the code of discipline (*rahit maryada*). As such they are lapsed (*patit*). Repentance can only come about through re-initiation.

Pax Christi. Pax Christi is a **Roman Catholic** peace organization. It was founded in 1946 by the French Bishop Theas. Its immediate aim was to bring about "reconciliation between the French and German peoples". As the Cold War escalated, it broadened its purpose to include healing the rift between Soviet Russia and the West. Thus, in 1985, Pax Christi published *Looking at the Russians: a Christian Perspective.* Against the widespread Western stereotype of the Soviet Union as being in some way inhospitable to religious believers, the Editor, Peggy Attlee points out that "the majority" of Christians imprisoned in Russia are "unregistered Baptists who will not accept the restrictions placed upon the exercise of their ministry" by the Soviet state. In the 1970s and 1980s the group was vocal in its opposition to nuclear weapons.

According to its current English spokeswoman, Pat Gaffney, Pax Christi continues to campaign against the "poverty and the arms trade", which it perceives as "the root cause of war". Armed with unassailable conviction and vivid poster displays, Pax Christi disseminates its beliefs in parishes and schools. The English section seeks to put an end to world religious conflict and, closer to home, to curtail the deployment of Trident missiles. Since the conclusion of hostilities between East and West, Pax Christi has turned its attention to the North/South axis.

At the May 1992 annual general meeting of Pax Christi International, the group noted with some disapprobation the 500th anniversary of Christopher Columbus' arrival in the United States, and expressed "its solidarity with the indigenous peoples in their struggle for political, economic, religious and cultural self-determination". Pax Christi publishes the journal *Justpeace.* It has 2,000 members, in 22 sections, worldwide.

Pentecostal Churches (Charismatic). Pentecostalism is not so much a doctrine as an experience. Members of pentecostal churches believe that all the gifts of the Holy Spirit mentioned in 1 Corinthians 12 are available to Christians today. In particular they will expect to receive and practice the gifts of speaking in tongues, healing and prophecy.

Although there are suggestions that in previous revivals (for instance that of the 18th century leading to the foundation of **Methodism**) these experiences occurred, the historical evidence is ambiguous. Pentecostalism is usually regarded as having begun in America at the turn of the 20th century, when meetings at the Azusa Street church in Los Angeles became the springboard for the movement. The flamboyant preaching of Aimee Semple MacPherson based at the Angelus Temple made the movement more widely known. In 1907 it reached Britain through the preaching of T. B. Barrett at All Saints Church in Sunderland.

There are many pentecostal denominations. The two main ones in Britain are the Assemblies of God and the Elim Pentecostal Church. The Assemblies of God are linked with the worldwide Assemblies of God Church, one of the largest international pentecostal denominations which has its roots in the Azusa Street revival. The Elim Pentecostal Church grew out of the ministry of George Jeffreys in Ireland in 1915. It has a more central organization, being governed by a conference and having its own ministerial training college.

A third strand of Pentecostalism is the House Church movement. This began as groups of Christians who had had a pentecostal experience meeting informally in each others houses for informal worship. Nowadays local groups meet in Community buildings, and structures of leadership and some formal national organization is being established. However the movement cannot yet be described as a denomination, and some former house group members have returned to the established churches.

Within the established churches, particularly the Anglican and Roman Catholic churches, the charismatic movement has become a significant influence on worship and liturgy. The distinctive style of pentecostal worship, worship songs with simple words and music (often sung with raised hands), times of silence giving any member of the congregation the opportunity to pray or give a prophecy, services of healing, all these are now an accepted part of mainstream church life in many places. The Pentecostalists (named after the Jewish feast of Pentecost when, according to Acts 2 the church first received the Holy Spirit) or Charismatics (from Charism—"Gift") are acknowledged to be the fastest growing movement in the church, with worldwide membership (excluding those within existing other denominations) estimated as over 25,000,000.

People's Buddhist Study Society. A Singapore based Buddhist organization founded to encourage and to finance the missionary visits of Thai **Theravada** monks to Singapore.

Perfectionists. Perfectionists are discussed in the entry on the **Holiness (Perfectionist) Movement**.

Perwalian Umat Buddha Indonesia (Walubi). An association of Indonesian Buddhist sects more widely known as the **All Indonesia Federation of Buddhist Organizations**.

Peyotism. A syncretic ritual of the Native Americans, peyotism, or the peyote cult is a ritual which spread across much of the Plains area at the end of the 19th century. Involving the use of the hallucinogenic cactus *Lophophora Williamsii*, it combines traditional elements with Christian ones, centred round the central ethics of the "Peyote Road", a life of responsibility to family and tribe, avoidance of alcohol and curing of illness. Ceremonies, usually lasting one night, involve drumming, singing and visions under the direction of a "Road Chief". It has attracted significant numbers of followers among many tribes, notably the Navajo.

Most adherents belong to the Native American Church, originally the Native American Church of Oklahoma, incorporated in Oklahoma in 1918 at the instigation of James Mooney, an anthropologist sent from Washington to investigate peyote use. In 1945 it became the Native American Church of the United

States. Peyotists from over 50 different tribes belong to this loose inter-tribal organization, which allows much individual tribal variation in ritual. In 1978 the *American Indian Religious Freedom Act* protected the sacramental use of peyote by members of the Church. In 1990 the Supreme Court challenged the law and the legality of peyote use is now decided on a state-by-state basis.

Peyotism is also a feature of some **Mesoamerican Traditional Religions,** notably in Mexico.

Philippine Independent Church. This church should probably be seen as a New Religious Movement (see opening essay). Its members are commonly referred to as the **Aglipayan.**

Phuntsok. A sub-group of the **Tibetan Buddhist Sakyapa** school named after a branch of the influential Khon family who have overall control of the movement.

PL Kyodan. A new religious movement in Japan, PL Kyodan (**Church of Perfect Liberty**) is a synthesis of **Tokumitsukyo** which included faith healing, patriotism, Buddhist and **Shinto** elements, and **Hito no Michi Kyodan.** The first movement died with its founder, the second was convicted of *lèse majeste* in 1937. However, a leader of the second, Miki Tokuchika, regrouped the faithful in 1946 under the new name PL Kyodan. The central teaching of **PL** is "life is art". Humanity is essentially divine, and this nature must be developed creatively. PL has a high public profile and is involved with social programmes. It claims over 2,000,000 adherents, with headquarters in Osaka.

Plymouth Brethren. This widely used label refers to the group known as the **Open Brethren.**

Pocomania. Meaning "little madness", Pocomania is an Afro–Protestant cult found in parts of Jamaica and similar in many ways to **Revival Zion.** Singing round a pole with a flag induces possession by ancestors or angel spirits. Full baptism by immersion is also a feature of the movement.

Polynesian Religions. Polynesia is the largest of the island groupings of the Pacific, ranging all the way from the north central Hawaiian Island group, to the south-east where the statues of Easter Island continue to exert their fascination. The area includes the Line Islands, the Marquesas, Society and Austral Islands of French Polynesia, the Cook Islands, Kiribati, Tuvalu, Tokelau, Samoa (Western and American), Niue and Tonga. Christianity strongly influenced religious beliefs in the area with the epoch of European colonization, and very nearly destroyed the primal religious nature of the area. However, in more recent times, traditional spiritualities have emerged as stronger factors in the religious life of the people of these islands. Moreover, churches throughout the region have become interested in indigenous theologies related to the island cultures, and this has meant a renewed interest in the primal religions. A large number of anthropologists and religious specialists and historians of Christianity have become interested in this part of the world.

Hawaii occupies a position of particular significance in Polynesian spirituality, as its name is also given to the legendary homeland where the spirits of Polynesian people go after death. It is also seen as the distant ancestral home of the gods and chiefs of Polynesia. But this Hawaii of legend and myth is probably not to be associated with the island people themselves, but is best interpreted as the mythological point of origin of Polynesia. The religious structure of Hawaiian society was the most advanced in the region. There were 10 colleges of priests each specializing in different aspects of spirituality—sorcery, necromancy, divination, medicine, surgery and sacred architecture.

A chief characteristic of Polynesian spirituality is its concept of life as a journey or a pilgrimage across vast watery spaces, and here one sees the strong influence of the geographical characteristics of the region on the development of the religious life of the people. Polynesian creation mythology is similar to that of many other indigenous cultures worldwide, with the concept of primal emptiness (*Kore*) and primal darkness out of which the gods have given birth to all creation. *Tane*, one of the major deities, plays the role of trickster and cultural hero who pulls up land out of the oceans for human beings to live on. But he was also a tragic figure, for he dies trying to win immortality from the Goddess of Death.

Polynesian religion has given rise to two particular concepts of major significance. *Mana* is the name given to the sacred power which is believed to infuse the whole of creation. Wherever *Mana* erupts is a place of danger and that is represented by the concept of *Tabu* or *Taboo*. When a place or a person is Taboo, they might not be approached or touched by anyone who has not gone through the correct preparations. Chiefs and the dead were Taboo as were all who came in contact with them. During pregnancy and menstruation women are regarded as Taboo. Wherever the spirits are said to abide is also Taboo. The medicine man or medicine specialist and the priest are Taboo because they deal with sacred matters. In fact it is the priest who plays the major role in the community—educating, healing, exorcizing and enabling the people to keep in contact with the living dead. The Tohunga undertake rituals at key moments in a person's life: birth, death, marriage, and there are various initiation points in the human journey. Sanctuaries were set aside for worship, and as the place where the divine and the human realms touched each other. Tribal traditions and religious knowledge were all held in high esteem,

and were believed to have been brought from Heaven by Tane in three baskets, and revealed to the people by the priests under strictly controlled circumstances in their houses of sacred learning. Beside the priests there were other specialists of the sacred who concentrated, for example, on divination. Others were specialists in black magic. A sorcerer was someone who was believed to have particularly strong power which could be used to cause disaster in the lives of individuals and communities unless harmony was established between people in the tribal group and between the tribal group and nature.

Positive Thinking. Better known as New Thought which as a movement formed itself in the middle of the 19th century. In the 1820s the magnetic healing of Franz Anton Mesmer, an Austrian, was introduced to America. Mesmer claimed the existence of a magnetic cosmic fluid which could be focused in one person and transferred to another. In the transfer a hypnotic trance and the healing of the physical body occurred. Through the writings of Charles Poyen, these ideas were handed on to Phineas Pankhurst Quimby. Pupils of his, Warren Felt Evans, a **Swedenborgian** minister, philosopher and author, and Mary Patterson, later known as Mary Baker Eddy, founder of **Christian Science,** continued and promulgated Quimby's work. Dissenting Christian Scientists also contributed through their independent teachings and writings to shape New Thought ideas. These can be summarized as follows: while they accept the Scriptures as divine revelations, they deny their literal meaning by Spiritual Interpretation, a method which allows the discovery of new connotations. Although the Bible stands as Truth, its meanings stand at variance to those held by orthodox religion, sometimes to the point of constituting a complete repudiation of the latter, such as the Calvinist doctrines of sin, predestination, and damnation. New

CONTEMPORARY RELIGIONS: A WORLD GUIDE

Thought emphasizes health, happiness and prosperity as legitimate religious concerns. Others proclaimed the principles of New Thought in a variety of ways: Ralph Waldo Trine, for example, by publishing books, Emma Curtis Hopkins by teaching, the Fillmores, Nona Brooks and Ernest Holmes by creating the bases for churches. Today the influence of New Thought extends well beyond the membership of its churches (**Christian Science**, Divine Science, Religious Science, Unity School of Christianity), with its literature reaching a wide audience and its ideas being promulgated by writers such as Norman Vincent Peale, Dale Carnegie and Maxwell Maltz.

Prajapita Brahma. The religious name taken by a Sindhi diamond merchant, Dada Lekh Raj (d. 1969), after he had a vision of Vishnu in 1937 in Hyderabad, Sindh, and subsequently of Shiva and of the nuclear holocaust (there is a definite apocalyptic strain in his ideas), as a result of which he felt divinely inspired to abandon his business interests in order to create a pure new world. He developed his concept of **Raja Yoga** (usurping a name applied to an older Yoga tradition) and founded a community which before long settled in Karachi and in 1950 moved again to Mt Abu, becoming the **Brahma Kumaris** Spiritual University, run entirely by women, since, according to Prajapita Brahma, a mark of the degeneracy of the world is that only women are pure enough to propagate his teachings.

Pratyabhijna. One of the philosophical schools of **Kashmir Shaivism**, it expounds a doctrine of strict monism.

Presbyterians (Reformed). The **Presbyterians** were, like the **Lutherans**, products of the European **Protestant** Reformation.

In 1533 John Calvin, a French legal and theological scholar was expelled from the University of Paris for his reformist views.

He found his way to Geneva, Switzerland, where he became the inspiration and leader of the reformed church over much of Europe.

Like Luther, Calvin believed that the Bible contains all that is needed for the Christian faith. Any doctrine or practice not supported by scripture should be rejected. But Calvin also had a deep sense of God's power and therefore believed that in all his dealings with people, God takes the initiative. This led to the doctrine of predestination, that God has chosen some people for salvation and others for damnation, and to believe in the irresistibility of grace (that God's grace cannot be rejected by an individual). These doctrines were rejected by other protestant groups, notably **Methodists** who believed Christ died for all, but that Christians could fall away from their faith.

Calvin was a gifted administrator and his belief in the sovereignty of God led to a belief that the state, though a body separate from the church, should conform as far as possible to the will of God. In Geneva under Calvin laws reflected the teaching of the Bible, and education, which enabled people to read the Bible for themselves, was encouraged and expanded.

The movement spread and took root particularly in Holland and Scotland. From there it was taken overseas by emmigrants to South Africa, India and Northern Ireland (which was being populated in the 17th and 18th centuries by Scottish immigrants). Today the Presbyterian Church of Scotland is the state church of Scotland and is the largest presbyterian church in the world. Styles of worship vary, but churches are usually led by a Presbyter, responsible for preaching, sacraments and spiritual guidance, elders responsible for administration and church discipline and deacons who care for the poor and needy.

Calvin's emphasis on the importance of Christian principles in the life of the state has led many Presbyterians to take an active role in political life. In the 16th century John Knox preached in Scotland against both Mary Queen of Scots and Queen Elizabeth I (the "monstrous regiment of women"). Today in Northern Ireland most Unionists have Presbyterian backgrounds (the Rev. Ian Paisley is a minister of an independent strict presbyterian denomination) and in South Africa the **Dutch Reformed** Church has both conservative branches (such as the NGK and GK to which the present and former prime ministers belong) and a liberal branch, which vigorously opposes apartheid (the NGS church) associated with Dr. Alan Boesak, a leading proponent of Liberation Theology (that the church must side with the oppressed, as God does).

In many countries (including England) Presbyterian and **Congregational** churches have joined to form a United Reformed Church. Most Presbyterian and Reformed churches belong to the **World Alliance of Reformed Churches.** Worldwide membership is estimated at around 40,000,000.

Primal Therapy. Seen by many as belonging to the **Human Potential Movement,** or indeed to what has been labelled the **"self religions",** Primal Therapy has attracted considerable numbers of Americans and Europeans who have sought to process deep-seated emotions by acquiring the skill of emitting a primal scream.

Progressive Judaism. *See* **Reform Judaism.**

Protestantism. Protestantism arose in the 16th century as a protest against certain doctrines of the **Roman Catholic Church.** In 1517 Martin Luther nailed a statement of "95 Theses" of belief to the door of Wittenberg Church in Germany, and four years later he was excommunicated for those beliefs by the Roman Catholic Church. Within 20 years, due in great part to the administrative gifts of John Calvin (see **Presbyterians**) the movement

had spread throughout Europe and later, through emigration and missionary work, to every country in the world.

Protestants treasure their direct personal relationship with God, and reject the need for church or priest as an intermediary. The Christian who has sinned is made acceptable to ("justified") a wholly good God by faith through grace alone, not through the sacraments of the church nor through his own good works.

The understanding of this came to Martin Luther through his study of the Bible, particularly the Epistle to the Romans. Protestants give high priority to the individual study of the Bible, and therefore to preaching: though the object of both is to witness the Word of God i.e. Jesus Christ ("the Word was made flesh" John 1, 14). It is his dying which reconciles humanity to God, despite the estrangement of sin. Personal response to God's love and forgiveness, and to freedom from guilt is the gratitude of good works and love for others.

For many years the conflict of ideas centred around the meaning of the Eucharist. Roman Catholics believed that the "substance" (an abstract mediaeval philosophical concept) of the bread and the wine was changed when they were consecrated so that by "transubstantiation" they become the body and blood of Christ. Protestants dismissed this as superstition and insisted that Christ was present with the worshippers as they enacted a memorial of the Last Supper. Many of these arguments and much of the debate about justification by faith have been explored and reconciled through the work of ARCIC—the **Anglican,** Roman Catholic International Commission.

A central doctrine of Protestantism is the "universal priesthood of all believers" (based on 1 Peter 2,9). Certain people may be set aside for ministry (and most Protestant churches have a structure of authority) but it is recognized that every Christian may be a priest to every other. This is in contrast to the concept of priests who have sole access to, and power to administer, the grace of God by virtue of their priesthood. This is now the main area of conflict between the Roman Catholic and Protestant churches (and between the Catholic and Protestant wings of the Anglican Church) and affects the debate on such matters as the ordination of women, administration of the Eucharist and the authority of the Pope.

The emphasis on a personal relationship with God through individual Bible study and revelation has led to many splits in the Protestant church as individual Christians strive to live and worship to the glory and purpose of God. During the past century this divisive trend has been to some extent reversed by the growth of the ecumenical movement which encourages denominations to work together and eventually to unite. The **Charismatic** movement has affected both Catholics and Protestants and may be a means of healing this 500-year-old schism.

Psychosynthesis. A method of spiritual awakening designed by Roberto Assagioli, an Italian psychiatrist. The goal is a euphoric state of joy and mental illumination and love in the realization that all life is one. There is an emphasis on the self as a centre of pure consciousness, and this has led to its being described as one of the **"self religions"** within the much larger complex of "new religious movements" (see the essay in Part I).

Pujeras. An alternative name for the **Murtipujakas**, a sub-sect of **Svetambara Jainas.**

Pure Land School. Also known as the Japanese Buddhist **Jodoshu.**

Pushtimarga. "The Way of Grace", a Hindu **Vaishnava** devotional movement also known as the **Vallabhasampradaya.**

'Pygmy' Religion. Various groups of indigenous hunter-gatherers inhabit the equatorial forests of the Central African Republic, Cameroon, Zaire and Rwanda. They are usually referred to by the slightly disparaging term "Pygmies" (which is used here for lack of a clearly understood alternative). Pygmy groups speak the languages of neighbouring Bantu peoples, who have increasingly invaded their traditional territories. Recent estimates put the Pygmies' numbers at around 150,000. There are also Pygmoid groups which have intermarried with Bantu villagers, although outside the forests the Pygmies quickly appear to lose their distinctive cultural and religious characteristics.

Most accounts of Pygmy religion refer to a creator-god who is distanced from the world, but whose progeny include the god of the forest, a benevolent force, and the first human ancestors. The dead become ghosts inhabiting the forest, and may be neutral or malevolent, according to whether they are accorded respect, and depending on how humans treat one another. Evil spirits, primarily associated with the forest edge and Bantu settlements, may also be attracted by human discord.

Ritual activity is concerned with obtaining the blessings of the god of the forest (or of the forest itself, seen as a sacred force), propitiation of the spirits, to ensure success in the hunt, or to restore social harmony, or in setting up a new camp, the focus of civilized activity. Ceremonies designed to reawaken the forest, after a death or some other disaster, may last for a month, and are accompanied by polyphonic singing in which both women and men participate. Among the Mbuti of Zaire initiation ceremonies socialize children into the adult world, and are marked by periods of seclusion and the acquisition of esoteric knowledge. Seen in relation to their Bantu neighbours, Pygmies exhibit a lack of concern over witchcraft and a positive, sacred, attitude towards their forest environment. Their religion is just one example of **African traditional religions.**

Q

Qadianis. *See* **Ahmadiya (Qadianis).**

Qadiriya. The Qadiriya is one of the oldest and most widely spread **Sufi** orders, represented in most Islamic countries from West Africa to South East Asia, although in many areas there are other more popular orders. The name is taken from the great saint 'Abd al-Qadir al-Jilani (1077–1166), the details of whose life pose many contradictions and who does not seem to have intended the founding of any Sufi Way. He is known principally as a **Hanbali** preacher who, after a period of legal training in Baghdad, led a wandering ascetic life in Iraq for about 25 years before returning to preach in the city. Many stories are told about his piety, unworldliness and miracles, but their historicity is open to question. After his death (his tomb is in Baghdad) he became generally regarded as a saintly miracle-worker with many popular shrines. His intercession was often sought, and many followers claimed to have seen him in visions and dreams. However, some Qadiris tried to play down the miraculous aspects of al-Jilani's role, notably the famous Hanbali Ibn Taimiya (d. 1328), who considered such visions to be the work of demons. He was himself to have an important influence on the thought of the anti-Sufi **Wahhabis** as well as on the **Salafiya,** the **Muslim Brotherhood,** and recent radical Islamists.

The Qadiriya has not developed any rigid system of teachings and practices, which vary from country to country and among different Qadiri groups. At their communal gatherings Qadiris normally recite verses in praise of the Prophet, and other sacred songs, sometimes to the accompaniment of musical instruments and with various bodily movements designed to induce ecstasy, typically the slow turning from right to left, while uttering pious formulae. A 40-day retreat is also practised by Qadiris, who reduce their consumption of food until they are fasting completely for the last three days. In some areas local pilgrimages are made to shrines of 'Abd al-Qadir al-Jilani, and festivals are celebrated in his honour, for example at Salé, Morocco, where the Jilali branch of Qadiris present sheep and oxen to his descendants during the third month of the Islamic lunar year.

In the early modern period the Qadiriya has at times been associated with reformist activities and also with *jihad* against lax and syncretist Muslims and against European colonialists. In Hausaland (northern Nigeria, Niger) Usuman dan Fodio (1754–1817) experienced a dream vision of 'Abd al-Qadir al-Jilani, who girded him with the Sword of Truth to use against the enemies of Islam. He then led a successful *jihad* to counter un-Islamic practices connected with **African traditional religion** and to enforce the Holy Law. In Algeria another Qadiri shaikh, 'Abd al-Qadir (1808–83), was a reformist Sufi anxious to establish the Law (Shari'a) and opposed to saint cults or **maraboutism.** He also fought a lengthy *jihad*, in this case against the French from 1832–47, but was finally vanquished and imprisoned in Paris until 1852, after which he was allowed to settle in Damascus. Other Qadiri jihadists fought against the Dutch in Indonesia in the late 19th and early 20th centuries. Like some **Naqshabandis, Sanusis** and **Tijanis,** they represent an activist strand of Sufism, but other Qadiris have continued in the older quietist pattern of the medieval Qadiriya.

Qalandars. The Qalandars are one of the better known "irregular" **Sufi** orders, of which numerous examples are to be found in the Indian subcontinent. To call them irregular is to refer to their being *bi-shar'*, or "outside the Islamic law", in contrast to mainstream orders like the **Chishtiya.** In this respect they resemble the **Malangs.** Their name is derived from the alleged founder of the order, a native of Spain called 'Ali Abu Yusuf Qalandar (known too as Bu 'Ali Qalandar, d. 1323) who settled in India. His tomb at Panipat near Delhi is venerated as a shrine. The Qalandars are mendicant beggars who have a reputation for calling down a curse on any household where their request for alms is refused.

Qimbanda. Practised by a small minority in Brazil, this is a movement of the type known generally as **Afro–American spiritist,** but differing from the much more widely practised **Umbanda** in that it involves the invocation of evil spirits rather than benevolent ones.

Qizilbash. Qizilbash (from Turkish—"red head") is a term applied in a broad sense to designate ethnically diverse heterodox Muslim communities whose origin can be traced back to the historical encounter between the **Sunni** Ottoman Empire and the **Shi'ite** Safawid dynasty during the 15th to 17th centuries. The name itself was given by the Ottomans to nomadic Turkic partisans of the Safawid dynasty who used to wear 12 red bands on their head-cover as a token that they worshipped the 12 imams.

The Qizilbash contributed a lot to the rise of the Safawids to power and after the establishment of the Safawid state in 1501 enjoyed the status of military aristocracy and high-ranking bureaucracy. Known to have been mighty warriors, they are the only troops in the Muslim world that could rival the Ottoman janissaries.

To the contrary, in the Ottoman Empire the Qizilbash were considered a religion of opposition and a threat to the established political order; therefore they were persecuted and scorned. The term Qizilbash itself had a pejorative meaning in the Turkish vernacular and their religious practices and beliefs were regarded as a counter-culture. The Qizilbash enjoyed the moral support and guidance of the **Bektashiya** which seems to have become a receptacle for all sorts of non-Sunni currents.

The faith of the Qizilbash is rather syncretic, comprising elements of Islam, **Zoroastrianism** and Christianity. It is marked by sometimes far-reaching disregard of Muslim ritual and worship. A central figure in their system of beliefs is Ali, the fourth caliph, who is not less revered than Muhammad himself. Therefore followers of the sect have also been called **Alevi,** Aliani, **Ali-ilahi.** The deification of Ali comes only next to pantheism—tiny particles of God, according to their doctrine, are to be found everywhere in nature and universe. They also have elaborated a cult for fire and stone. The Qizilbash do not honour the Quran as a holy book or mosques as sites of worship and drink alcoholic drinks during their ceremonies, which usually take place at night. They usually live in esoteric communities practising extreme endogamy and their doctrine is kept a secret from strangers. Vertical linkages within each community are very strong, but contacts between Qizilbash groups in different countries seem to have been scarce. Because of so little exchange it is hard to speak of a uniform Qizilbash doctrine.

Qizilbash women in general are much less secluded than their orthodox Muslim counterparts. They do not cover their faces, speak freely to male relatives and neighbours and participate in all ceremonies side by side with men. Since the honour of women in Islam is often regarded as derivative from seclusion, this has given grounds for allegations (eg in Turkey) of immoral practices and even promiscuity.

Qizilbash communities are to be found today in Turkey, Iran, Azerbaijan, Afghanistan, in Kurdish-inhabited lands, and Bulgaria. In Afghanistan they constitute an important and politically influential social group; in Azerbaijan the name Qizilbash has sentimental overtones derived from the past glory of the Safawid dynasty; while in modern Turkey they are still considered to be an inferior group with stigmatized identity.

Quakers. This is the long-standing popular name applied to members of the **Society of Friends**.

R

Rabbinic Assembly (of America). *See* **Conservative Judaism.**

Rabbinical Council of America. *See* **Orthodox Judaism.**

Rabita. Taken from the Arabic name of the **Muslim World League**, this is sometimes used in an English-speaking context as an abbreviation for that organization.

Rahmaniya. The Rahmaniya is a **Sufi** order founded by Muhammad bin 'Abd al-Rahman (1715–1793). It is a branch of the **Khalwatiya.** The founder was initiated into the Khalwatiya in Egypt, and brought its practices back with him to his native Algeria. There he firmly placed his own stamp on the order.

An affiliation to the Rahmaniya, reverence for the founder, pilgrimage to his tomb, or hearing the mystical phrases of the order—all these would guarantee immunity from hell-fire. Other, already established, Sufi orders reacted very sharply to the active proselytization of the Rahmaniya. However, the large following impressed the Turkish authorities of the Ottoman Empire, and protected the founder from action being taken against him by the other orders.

The initial succession to the founder went undisputed, but by the middle of the 19th century the order was divided into a series of local branches. The Rahmaniya instigated a number of small-scale insurrections against the French which were generally unsuccessful but had a wide following. The local branches of the order became more independent, some fostering good relations with the French colonial authorities. At the end of the last century more than 150,000 disciples were initiated into the order, and its sphere of influence reached from Algeria into Tunisia and the Sahara.

By the 1950s the order was considered to be the strongest in Algeria, numbering 230,000 followers, and today it is represented, not only in Algeria and Tunisia, but also elsewhere in the Arab world, for instance in Jordan and the West Bank.

Rajneeshism. The movement centred on Bhagwan Shree Rajneesh (born 1931), a former professor of philosophy who in 1974 founded a community in Poona: the Shree Rajneesh Ashram. With a permanent population of some 2,000 people, it attracted many thousands more visitors, but in 1981 Bhagwan suddenly disappeared, to reappear shortly afterwards in Oregon where a new base was established, known as Rajneeshpuram. An astonishingly wide variety of courses was available, making the identification of a common underlying philosophy virtually impossible. In broad terms, though, Rajneeshism has been identified as one of the **self religions.**

Followers were known as the Orange People because of the colour of the clothing they wore. They also took a new name, and wore a picture of Bhagwan on a necklace of wooden beads. In 1985, however, scandal occurred when Bhagwan's personal secretary, Ma Anand Sheela, was arrested and later imprisoned for various irregularities, and Bhagwan himself was expelled from the United States, leaving his followers in a state of confusion and upset.

Bhagwan was now known as Osho ("Friend") Rajneesh, and sought to re-establish himself in Poona. The distinctive orange colour for clothing disappeared, though during meditation followers were encouraged to wear white or maroon.

However, before the movement could regain anything of its former strength in 1990 Rajneesh died, rendering its future all the more uncertain.

Ramakrsna Society. The Rāmakrṣṇa Society, one of the most successful of modern Hindu religious movements, has its roots in the life of the Bengali saint Rāmakrṣṇa. Born Gadādhar Chattopādhyāya in Kamarpukar, Bengal on Feb. 18, 1836, Rāmakrṣṇa began at an early age to experience religious ecstasies. After migrating to Calcutta, he became a priest of the temple of Kālī at Dakṣineṣwar which had been constructed by Rani Rasmani, a wealthy *śudra* widow. Rāmakrṣṇa was particularly attached to the worship of Kālī, and his devotion to that goddess, coupled with his religious ecstasies, began to attract disciples. As a result of pressure from his family, he married his wife Śāradāmani in 1859 when she was only five years old, but the marriage appears to never have been consummated. In fact, Rāmakrṣṇa saw in his wife the embodiment of the goddess he worshipped, and in 1872, when she finally came to live at Dakṣineṣwar, he formally worshipped her as the goddess, giving her the name Śāradā Devī.

Among the many disciples that Rāmakrṣṇa attracted from the intellectual, Europeanized upper classes of Calcutta was Narendranāth Dutt, who is better known by his *sannyasin* name of Swāmi Vivekānanda. After Rāmakrṣṇa's death in August of 1886, his disciples decided on Christmas Eve of the same year to form a formal Order to perpetuate his ideals. Although Rāmakrṣṇa himself thought little about philosophy, holding to a vague Advaitanism, and concentrated heavily on meditative practice tinged with tantric elements, the newly constituted Rāmakrṣṇa Order sought to meld the traditional life of meditation and renunciation of the world with service to society and the practice of more orthodox yogic techniques. Thus was born what

one might characterize as the first Hindu missionary society, with Vivekānanda carrying the message of Rāmakrṣṇa throughout India and, ultimately, to the West in 1893 when he spoke to the World Parliament of Religions in Chicago. Subsequently, a number of centres, under the aegis of the newly-formed Vedānta Society, were established in the United States. After his return to India in 1897, Vivekānanda established the Rāmakrṣṇa Mission to ensure their continued success. This institution still functions to-day with its headquarters at Belur near Calcutta. It boasts over 100 centres in India itself and more than 50 others around the world. It also administers impressive medical and educational facilities throughout India, and has remained in the forefront of charitable institutions in that country. *See also* Guru, Vedānta and Yoga.

Ramanandis. A sect perhaps founded by legendary teacher of Kabir, Ramananda, sometime in the 15th century. Today they are probably the largest Hindu **Vaishnava** ascetic order (*sampradaya*), regularly vying with their **Shaiva** rivals, the **Dashanamis,** for the best site at the great pilgrimage grounds of India. There is a threefold membership of householders, non-renouncers and renouncers with the first group providing lay support for the other two categories. Non-renouncers dwell in monasteries and hermitages which are found in large numbers throughout western and central India, the Ganges basin and the Himalayan foothills as well as in Nepal. Renouncers, who hold pride of place in the order, are homeless but unlike other Indian *samnyasins*, who wander in solitude, the Ramanandi renouncers travel in small groups which constitute an itinerant monastery or *khalsa*. The wanderings of these groups are not aimless for they obey an annual cycle in which all the major Vaishnava pilgrimage centres are visited at the astrologically correct time. The Renouncer smears his body twice a day with ash from a sacred fire and, while he has no permanent place of residence, Ayodhya, in northern India, is traditionally considered to be the central focus of the order. Ayodhya, the birth place of the god Rama, is today the focus of militant Hindu activity, and in particular organized agitation to have a *mosque* demolished since it is held to occupy the actual site of Rama's birth (*Ramajanmabhumi*). Non-renouncer Ramanandis, together with members of other groups such as the **Bharatiya Janata Party** and the **Vishva Hindu Parishad,** are prominent in this enterprise.

Ramanna Nikaya. One of the three main divisions of **Theravada Buddhist** monks in Sri Lanka. It was established in 1865 when a new ordination lineage was received from the Mon *Sangha* which had its centre in the Ramanna country of lower Burma. It arose as the result of dislike for the élitism of the **Sivam Nikaya** of Kandy and of disillusion with the internal strifes of the **Amararupa** fraternity. While originating among low-country *bhikkhus* and not being too seriously affected by caste issues (due to the pioneering work of the Amararupas), there are at present two caste-defined sections of this fraternity: those belonging to the Goyigama caste and those of the lower Padu caste. It is "modernistic" or "radical" in its approach, being critical of traditional "Buddhist" notions concerning cosmology, deities, spirits, and the efficacy of ritual. It is by far the smallest of the Sinhala fraternities, with about 2,000 monks. However, despite its size, it has been an influential voice within the Buddhist community in Sri Lanka.

Ramdasis. A Hindu **Vaishnava** devotional movement based on the teachings of the Maharashtrian saint and poet, Ramdas (1608–1681). Ramdas' main word is the *Dasbodh*, in which he outlines the philosophy of **Advaita Vedanta.** He also stressed the supreme importance of the *guru* and devotion to Rama, hence his name which means "slave of Rama". In his lifetime he established a large number of monasteries (*math*) in the region of western India and is perhaps best known as the spiritual preceptor (*guru*) of Shivaji, the founder of the Maratha state. The Ramdasi movement went into decline after the fall of the Maratha kingdom in 1817, but since Indian independence the group has risen to prominence once again, partly on the back of the Maharashtrian nationalist cult of Shivaji. Ramdasis wear orange/brown clothing and may be celibate monks or laity. About 40 *maths* currently flourish and devotees concentrate their attentions on study of the *Dasbodh* and worship of Rama.

Rashtriya Swayamsevak Sangh (RSS). The Rashtriya Swayamsevak Sangh (RSS) grows out of a tradition of Hindu communalism that stretches back to the beginning of the 20th century. The Hindu Mahasabha, formed in 1906, was itself a direct offshoot of the Ārya Samāj, and under its most influential leader, Veer Savarkar, the idea of Hinduatva (militant Hinduism) and non-democracy developed. The RSS itself was founded by Dr. Keshav Hedgewar in 1925. The organization holds to the promotion of the Hindu religion, Hindu society and Hindu culture. It opposed the pluralistic stance of Gāndhi and Nehru, preferring instead to work for a governmental system that more accurately reflected the majority status of Hindus in India. Although it avoided involvement in the struggle for independence, the RSS came to public attention as a result of its activities in the Hindu-Muslim riots at Nagpur in September of 1927. It grew in influence during the communal disruptions that marked the last days of the British Raj, commanding some 10,000 cadres in 1945, but it was the assassination of Gāndhi in 1948 by a Hindu sympathetic to its aims that thrust it into the front ranks of Indian politics. Banned until July of 1949, it was subsequently allowed to resume functioning. It continued to forge bonds with non-Congress political parties and during the Emergency (1975–1977), it was again banned for a short period. The power base of the RSS is the urban middle class and particularly the petty bourgeoisie who have been most directly in economic competition with the Muslim minority. Increased sectarian tensions in recent years have resulted in a significant strengthening of the RSS's support base and an increase in its political influence. *See also* Bharatiya Janata Party and Modern Hindu Reform Movements.

Rastafarianism. The Rastafarian movement appeared in Jamaica during the 1930s. It was inspired by the Jamaican Marcus Garvey's Back to Africa movement, and his prophecy of a black messiah who would liberate black people. The accession of Ras ("Prince") Tafari to the imperial throne of Ethiopia in 1930 as the emperor Haile Selassie was seen by some as fulfilment both of Garvey's prophecy and of Psalm 68 with its alleged claim that the black race had been singled out by God for special attention.

Rastafarian beliefs are fluid and varied, but in general they regard themselves as one of the twelve tribes of ancient Israel, and some believed Haile Selassie to be the Messiah who would redeem them from white oppression—which they identify as due to the modern Babylon of Britain, the United States, and the Jamaican state (plus, for some, the church)—and return them to the homeland Africa. This last belief, in the return to the promised land, is today often interpreted symbolically rather than literally. Harmony with nature is important, and most Rastafarians are vegetarians (or, indeed, vegans).

In Dominica, Rastafarians are known as "Dreads", meaning simply the power that lies within every individual. Uncombed hair (dreadlocks) and beards are characteristic of male adherents, and hats and other garments may use typical Rastafarian colours: black for the race, red in memory of the blood of slaves, green for the promised land, and gold for a golden future. Strict moral standards are fostered, and members may renounce alcohol and tobacco, but there is widespread use of cannabis (ganja) which is considered to be sanctioned by the Bible.

Anti-white sentiment has been important but is not universal. Christianity has been rejected by many as the white man's religion, but some Rastafarians have been baptized into the **Ethiopian Orthodox** Church. The Bible is accepted as God's word—as interpreted by Rastafarians—and readings from it feature in their meetings, as does the singing of hymns, the words of which have been adapted to reflect Rastafarian beliefs. This is characteristic too of their other songs, which often combine social comment with praise of Ras Tafari (and ganja). Their influence on popular music through the development of reggae is well known.

It is estimated that Rastafarians in Jamaica number approximately 100,000. Numbers elsewhere in the Caribbean, in Britain, or in the United States are not known, but their cultural influence in terms of poetry, music or art is of still wider international significance.

Ratana. Nov. 8, 1918 at 2 p.m. Tahupotiki Wiremu Ratana was standing on the verandah of his home, looking out across farmland to the vast stretches of the sea, when a small cloud arose out of the water, then approached and swirled around him. To his astonishment a voice spoke in Maori: "Fear not, I am the Holy Ghost . . . . Ratana, I appoint you as the mouthpiece of God for the multitude of this land. Unite the Maori people, turning them to Jehovah of the thousands, for this is his compassion to all of you". His family thought him mad or drunk when he told them about this experience. Later, an angel appeared to him and repeated the message and commissioned him to preach the Gospel to the Maori people, and to heal their spirits and their bodies.

After Christmas 1918 he turned to ministry full-time, and soon his fame as a preacher and faith healer had spread. On Christmas Day 1920 an undenominational church was opened, built with Ratana's own funds. It was a great occasion with **Roman Catholic** and **Protestant** clergy taking part in the dedication, in the presence of more than 3,000 people. A religious revival spread throughout the Maori. By 1921 more than 19,000 had joined Ratana and his movement. Although the Catholic Church withdrew its support, the movement had strong backing from **Anglicans** and **Methodists.**

At Pentecost (May 31) 1925 the Ratana Church came into existence as a separate organization, and on July 21 that year it was recognized by the Government when the Registrar General of Births, Deaths and Marriages gazetted the names of 38 representatives authorized by the state to conduct marriages. The break with the Anglican Church followed two years later, but the Methodists left relationships open.

According to the Ratana Church Creed deposited at the time of its registration with the Registrar General, the Church had a firm Christian basis—belief in Jehovah, Father, Son and Holy Ghost; Jesus Christ as the human form of God's son; the Holy Ghost, the breath of Jehovah; the Holy Christian Church; humans as co-workers with God; the Holy Bible as the record of Jehovah's greatest revelation; the faithful agents who are God's workers and messengers, and finally Ratana as the mouthpiece of Jehovah.

As the movement grew in influence, a temple was opened on Jan. 25, 1928, the prophet's birthday. As the Labour Party emerged as a major force in New Zealand politics there were contacts with Ratana. Closer relationships were forged in 1928, and since 1936 the four political representatives of the Maori people who sit in Parliament have considered themselves part of the Labour Party and have served the country, when the Labour Party has been in government, with distinction.

Ratana died on Sept. 18, 1939, but his influence has continued in the Ratana Church, and has touched all of Maoridom as well as the political life of the nation. In recent years Ratana has shown a noticeable growth.

Ravidas Panthis. Ravidas (1414?–1526), also known as Rai Das was a *chamar* (cobbler), and mystic of deep spirituality. At the end of the nineteenth century, *chamars*, in the hope of improving their social status, converted to **Sikhism** in large numbers, but religious acceptance did not result in them achieving this aim. Socially they remained untouchable. Some, therefore, began to proclaim themselves to be neither Hindu nor Sikh but Ravidasi. The *Guru Granth Sahib*, which contains 41 of the hymns of Ravidas continues to be the focus of worship which is of a similar nature to Sikh worship and the word *gurdwara* is often used to describe the place of worship. Ravidasis tend to keep the *kesh*, i.e. uncut hair, and turban and are frequently mistaken for Sikhs. Currently, however, a *granth* using only the hymns of Ravidas is being prepared and the time may come when it replaces the *Guru Granth Sahib*, and *sabha*, association being used instead of *gurdwara*. The celebration of the birthday of Guru Ravidas in February/March is another development paving the way for this movement to becoming a distinct religion. Sikhs describe Ravidas as a *bhakta* or *bhaghat*, composer of devotional hymns, not as *guru*. Members of the Panth are mainly found in the Punjab.

Rebirthing. Seen by many as belonging to the **Human Potential Movement,** or to the **"self religions"**, Rebirthing involves immersion in hot water as a means of re-experiencing one's own birth, and at the same time processing related deep-seated emotions, often using concepts of Divine Mind/Energy. It became well known through the Theta movement founded by Leonard Orr in the late 1960s in the USA.

Reconstruction Crusade. This is the Iranian Muslim organization **Jihad-i Sazandigi** which has been influential in combining dedication to Islam and work on rural development projects.

Reconstructionist Judaism. Most recent of the Jewish "denominations", Reconstructionist Judaism is based on the teachings of Rabbi Mordechai Menahem Kaplan (1881–1983). Kaplan, an instructor in the **Jewish Theological Seminary** from 1909–1963, originally had no intention of forming a new movement, hoping instead that his understanding of Judaism as a religious civilization, as presented in his 1934 *Judaism as a Civilization,* would offer a new way to all branches of Judaism. He argued that Judaism is a culture whose primary aim is the perpetuation of the Jewish people. Thus, Judaism is to serve its people not vice-versa. He defined the "God-idea" in Judaism to be the power that makes for salvation which, in this era, must be this-worldly.

In 1935 he and others founded *The Reconstructionist,* a monthly journal, and later issued a new Passover *haggadah* (1941) and Sabbath Prayerbook (1945), changing prayers claiming Jewish exclusivity and challenging the belief that all Jews would return to the Land of Israel when the Messiah came, arguing that Israel must be restored but not all Jews must return to it. Despite his attempt to write liturgy for all Jews, his work was condemned by the Orthodox Union and he was "excommunicated".

In 1955, The Reconstructionist Foundation of Congregations was organized, requiring member congregations to belong either to the Reform or Conservative movements following Kaplan's opposition to creating a new movement. In 1968, however, the movement became a separate organization, The Federation of Reconstructionist Congregations (since 1982, The Federation of Reconstructionist Congregations and Havurot) with its own seminary, The Reconstructionist Rabbinic College,

open to both men and women and since 1975 having its own rabbinic organization, The Reconstructionist Rabbinical Association. Currently, Reconstructionist Judaism estimates a membership of 50,000 and over 60 congregations worldwide with 40,000 members in America, 8,000 in Canada, and 2,000 in Curacão, the Netherlands, and Israel.

Redemptorists. The Redemptorists are the Congregatio Sanctissimi Redemptoris, the **Roman Catholic** Congregation of the most holy Redeemer (CSsR). They were founded in 1732 by St. Alphonsus Ligouri. The original purpose of the order was to convert the rural inhabitants of the countryside around Naples, who had gone unattended by other priests. Because many priests at this time tended to backslide after taking their vows, St. Alphonsus instituted in addition to the vows of poverty, chastity and obedience a fourth vow of "perseverance unto death". There are currently 6,000 Redemptorists. They retain the main purpose of evangelization. This is achieved in different ways in different countries. In some of the very poor countries of the Third World, Redemptorists undertake to live amongst their most impoverished parishioners. In England, they maintain six parishes of their own, run parish missions elsewhere, administer retreat centres, and write the *Living Word,* the weekly religious commentary familiar to practising Catholics from the back of their parish newsletter.

Reform Judaism. Reform Judaism, also known as **Liberal** or **Progressive Judaism,** is the denomination most concerned with creating a modern Judaism. At times, quite radical in its jettisoning of older Jewish ideas and practices, the movement has, in the past generation, become more receptive to certain elements of tradition.

Reform rejects the traditional view that the written *Torah* (the five first books of the Hebrew Bible) were revealed verbatim by God and that the oral *Torah* (the Mishnah and the Palestinian and Babylonian *Talmuds*) is the sole basis for interpreting the written *Torah,* while stressing Judaism's universalistic and ethical qualities, and more recently participating in the American Civil Rights movement, and similar causes.

Reform Judaism began in Germany and its development is related to events and ideas both inside and outside the Jewish community. European society, especially German society after Kant, was swept by the ideas of the Enlightenment which demanded that religion be "reasonable" and modern (even a major opponent of Reform Judaism, Rabbi Samuel Raphael Hirsch (1808–1880) emphasized the concord between Judaism and modernity). This was also the age of European Jewry's emancipation, which came with the stipulation that Jews modify their religion in order to become "proper" citizens. Many Jews also saw "modernization" as an ideal though they were less enthusiastic about abandoning their Jewish identity. These Jews looked for a way to become full citizens while still being committed to what they saw as the rational and universal core of Judaism.

The first Reform institutions were Israel Jacobson's Seesen temple (1810), with Jacob Herz Beer's temple in his Berlin house (1815), and the more permanent temple in Hamburg (1818) following. At the time, the name "temple" was used by some traditional Jews but Jacobson saw his as a universalist replica of the ancient shrine and later Reformers considered theirs replacements for it. Worship in these temples included organ music, not only challenging prohibition using instruments during worship as a sign of mourning for the Temple in Jerusalem and its instruments, but using an instrument identified with Christianity. The liturgy was changed also, now including the vernacular and rejecting the hope that the Messiah would appear and lead the Jews back to the Land of Israel.

These changes were justified by the argument that Judaism had developed historically and thus, contemporary Jews could modify their religion and reject what were considered to be rabbinic additions. These views were put forward most strongly by Abraham Geiger (1810–1874), an early leader of German Reform and scholar of *Wissenschaft des Judentums* ("the scientific study of Judaism"). The movement drew traditionalist anathemization and was hindered by Prussia's government which feared making a potentially more appealing Judaism. The movement, however, spread throughout Germany, also having some impact in the rest of Europe.

In America, the absence of governmental control or interference with religion made it possible for Reform to grow rapidly. The first non-traditional synagogue was founded in Charleston, South Carolina (1825) but did not last long. German–Jewish immigrants in the mid- and later 19th century had had exposure to Reform and their children warmly embraced the Reform tradition. As in Germany, there were disputes between the more moderate and radical factions; the former being championed by men such as Isaac Meyer Wise (1819–1900), and the latter being led by David Einhorn (1809–1879). Wise hoped to find a way to both modernize and unify American Jewry but after some unity was achieved in Cincinnati, it soon became clear that Reform was to be a separate domination. By 1883, the institutions Wise founded, the **Union of American Hebrew Congregations** (1873) and the seminary, **Hebrew Union College** (1875, merged with the **Jewish Institute of Religion** in 1950) became exclusively Reform. The date marks the graduation of HUC's first students, an event celebrated by a banquet featuring shellfish, prohibited by traditional dietary laws.

Einhorn's son-in-law, Kaufman Kohler (1843–1926), re-established the supremacy of the radical wing by writing the "Pittsburgh Platform" which was considered at an 1885 Reform rabbinic conference and then adopted at the 1889 founding meeting of the Reform rabbinate, the **Central Conference of American Rabbis.** The platform, which defined Reform for 50 years, repudiated Jewish dietary laws, belief in Heaven and Hell, the messiah, and the return to Zion.

The ideas embedded in this document dominated American Reform Judaism until the 1930s when they were challenged by the rise of anti-Semitism in Europe and America as well as the long-term impact of waves of Russian immigrants (beginning in 1881) who were less assimilationist than German Reform Jews. Reform's change of attitude was shown in the 1937 Columbus (Ohio) Platform which implicitly supported Zionism while also affirming the importance of Jewish life in the diaspora, as well as universal social justice. Any doubts about Reform's stand on Zionism was eliminated in 1942 when it endorsed the *Biltmore Program* for the creation of a Jewish State.

Recent decades have seen Reform retrace its steps towards greater appreciation of tradition with the movement's 1976 "Reform Judaism—A Centenary Platform" (The "San Francisco Platform") listing of a number of ritual practices among Reform Jewish "obligations" being quite different from the Pittsburgh Platform's approach. The most recent series of prayerbooks *(Gates of Prayer* and *Gates of Repentance)* have much more Hebrew than their predecessors, *The New Union Prayerbooks.*

Yet Reform has also remained innovative, ordaining women rabbis since 1972. It also has changed its definition of Jewish identity to include as Jews those with Jewish fathers and non-Jewish mothers. This adoption of patrilineal descent in addition to matrilineal descent was opposed by Israel's Progressive Jews. Reform also officially tolerates its gay and lesbian rabbis though it urges them to consider the implications of "coming out of the closet" before doing so.

Despite the refusal of its Orthodox rabbinic establishment to recognize them as a *bona fide* Jewish movement, Reform has remained committed to Israel. In 1963, HUC-JIR established a campus in Jerusalem and requires its rabbinic, cantorial and Jewish education students to study there for a year. **The Association of Reform Zionists of America** (ARZA), made significant inroads at the last World Zionist Organization conference and was instrumental in having that body call for plurality in Israeli Judaism. Reform has established two *kibbutzim* in Israel, Yahel and Lotan.

Reform Judaism is the largest component of the **World Union for Progressive Judaism,** founded in 1926. In addition to North America's 846 Reform congregations and 297,435 families, Progressive Judaism counts among its ranks at least 30,000 Liberal and Reform Jews in Great Britain, 5,000 families (six congregations) in Argentina and Brazil, 8,000 members (11 congregations) of the Australian and New Zealand Union for Progressive Judaism, 800 Israeli families (15 congregations) and smaller groups elsewhere in Europe and South America.

Reformed Apostolic Community. With headquarters in Dresden, the Reformed Apostolic Community (Reformiert-Apostolischer Gemeindebund) is a schismatic group which broke away from the **New Apostolic Church.** It has several hundred members.

Reformed Catholic Churches. A number of churches owe their origin to schism from the **Roman Catholic** Church by a group of priests. Of these the largest is the Czechoslovak Hussite Church (membership mainly in Czechoslovakia but with branches in the USA). This was founded in 1920 after demands by a group of Roman Catholic priests for a liturgy in the Czech language, the abolition of the celibacy of the priesthood and lay participation in church government had been rejected by Rome. The church does not believe in the

Apostolic Succession (bishops are elected for seven years only) and rejects the doctrines of Original Sin and Purgatory.

Other such churches are the Italian Catholic Reformed Church (formed 1881 by a schism of 12 priests and six churches) and the Lusitanian Church in Portugal (formed 1871 by a schism of 11 priests).

Reformed Church. This **Protestant** organization is discussed in the entry on **Presbyterians (Reformed)**.

Reiyukai Kyodan. A Japanese new religious movement, the doctrine of Reiyukai Kyodan (**Society of Companions of the Spirits**) is rooted in **Nichiren Buddhism,** and rites include the recitation of an abridgement of the Lotus Sutra. This predominantly lay organization is based on the belief that salvation of one's ancestors will pre-empt one's own salvation. Interpreted on a national level, social discord and calamity in Japan are due to the ritual neglect of ancestral spirits.

Reiyukai was founded by Kubo Kakutaro (1892–1944) and his sister-in-law, Kotani Kimi, a charismatic and shamanic personality. The sect claims around 3,000,000 adherents, and is noted for its promotion of traditional values, especially relating to the family.

Religion of Heavenly Wisdom. A Japanese, **Shinto**-based, new religious movement more widely known as **Tenrikyo.**

Religion of the Heavenly Way. The English rendition of **Chondo-Gyo,** a Korean new religious movement.

Republican Brothers. The Republican Brothers (or al-Hizb al-Jumhari, Republican Party, as it was known until 1969) attracted attention during President Nimeiri's Islamization programme in the

Sudan in 1983–1985 in particular. More of a religious movement than a political organization, its inspiration lay in its leader, Mahmud Muhammad Taha. Revered for his spirituality and learning, Taha had developed a radical methodology for transforming and liberalising the traditional shari'a. His views were regarded with abhorrence by the mainstream Muslim leadership, to the extent that he could be reviled as a heretic. Whatever the merits or otherwise of his methodology, the fate of this 76 year-old non-violent reformist Muslim leader under Nimeiri evoked international criticism. He was widely regarded as a victim of internal politics when he was arrested, summarily tried, and then hanged in January 1985 for alleged sedition and apostasy. His followers continue to propagate his teachings.

Republican Party. Until about 1969 this was the name of the reformist Islamic movement in the Sudan currently referred to as the **Republican Brothers.**

Restorationism/New Churches. New Christian congregations began to appear in the early 1970s and, for a few years, grew alongside and in the shadow of the **Charismatic** renewal in the denominational churches. The emerging leaders of the **House Churches,** as the movement became known, increasingly recognized the Charismatic renewal as only a partial restoration of what they believed to be church patterns and principles laid down in the New Testament. As the Charismatic renewal ran out of its initial steam, disaffected adherents moved across to join other Christians from **Brethren, Baptist,** Independent Free Church and **Assemblies of God** backgrounds to form the House Church movement which, in addition to being more lively, more participative and more free (less structured) in its worship, put into practice the full restoration of the Ephesians gifts of apostle, prophet, evangelist, pastor and teacher. As the movement grew it became necessary for congregations to move their main worship services from members' homes into local halls (redundant church buildings, schools and cinemas etc.). In recognition of the restoring of Biblical principles of Kingdom (Church) life in the practising of both spiritual gifts and in the supposed Divine appointment of leaders, the term "Restorationism" was adopted by some to describe the developing movement.

In recent years the "movement" (it is not really organized as such) has grown less through proselytization and increasingly through aggressive church planting linked to blanket local evangelism. Scores of new congregations have emerged and there now are in excess of 1,000 churches in Britain which share similar **Pentecostalist** and **Fundamentalist** theology, who eschew denominationalism and clericalism and who are characterized by the full commitment and passion of their members. Individual membership is probably well over 120,000 adults, with some congregations numbering over 500 worshippers.

A large number of New Church congregations are entirely without formal external links, although on occasions they may support a large regional or national gathering for Charismatic Christian worship. Many others, however, are linked to a number of more or less informal "streams". New Frontiers (with 100 congregations) is led by Terry Virgo; Pioneer (almost 50 congregations) is led by Gerald Coates: both of these networks are in the South of England. Ichthus, also in the South (with almost 50 congregations), claims not to be Restorationist, but its worship and theology are similar to other New Churches: where it differs radically is in its practice of recognizing women as local leaders. The Jesus Fellowship Church in the Midlands (with over 50 "church households") emphasizes communal living and celibacy: this grouping has been particularly successful in recruiting from amongst working class people and young unchurched "street" people. Covenant Ministries, in the North of England with almost 60 congregations, is the

most structured and introspective of the New Church streams, although there are indications that this group, along with many other New Churches, is seeking to add social concern to its evangelistic outreach.

Most New Churches are located in the South of England with the largest numbers having been identified in Greater London, Essex, Hampshire, Kent, Surrey, West Sussex and Devon. They tend to be middle-class, although significant numbers of working-class people attend in some areas and some, at least, of the earlier pioneers came from non-professional backgrounds. Few New Church congregations have more than a very small minority of black or Asian members, even in areas where this might be expected. New Churches often can be recognized by their name: frequently they take the name of their catchment area and add such words as "Community Church", "Christian Fellowship", "New Life Church", "New Covenant Church" or "King's Church".

New Church streams are led by "Apostolic teams", small groups of men who are recognized (some would say self-appointed) as having an ability to plant new congregations and to advise and support local leaders. One man is usually recognized as the "Apostle" of the organization although the title is rarely used. Each local congregation is almost totally independent: sanctions can be applied by the Apostolic team but this is rarely necessary as, on the one hand, the links are so informal as to be able to be cut at any time and, on the other hand, local leaders appreciate and come to rely on the wider support, advice and care offered by such a system. Regular meetings between the elders within a stream (and increasingly across streams) ensure vibrancy and flexibility through the sharing of ideas and vision. Leaders usually have no formal theological or pastoral training (although a few streams are now establishing their own training programmes and colleges). They exercise a high profile, charismatic and paternalistic ministry. Leaders never operate alone: New Churches believe strongly in "team ministry" where members of local teams exercise their own particular spiritual gift but consult and operate together in complementary roles. Many leaders rely on secular employment for remuneration. New Churches, in the main, reserve all leadership of congregations for men, at the same time declaring that women have a crucial and important role to play in family life and in supporting and "releasing" their husbands in the exercise of headship.

Membership of New Churches is open to those who have had a "born again" experience in conversion, who have been baptized by total immersion and who have received or are seeking the "Baptism in the Holy Spirit". The majority are under 50 years of age, many worshipping together as young families. The percentage of men is greater than in most denominational churches, sometimes coming close to the societal percentage. New Churches are not without significant numbers of professional people (doctors, teachers, psychologists, lawyers, etc.).

The submission, or covering of members by each other is a central tenet of the movement: children and wives submit to the male head of the household, congregational members submit to house-group leaders and church elders, elders and pastors to apostles and apostles, at least in theory, to each other: all claim to submit to God. This benevolent theocracy appears to work for those involved.

Worship takes place at three levels. The "cell" meets mid-week, the "congregation" on Sundays and the "celebration" more occasionally on a weekend. Most New Churches follow this pattern of worship life. The cell functions as a caring, house-based fellowship of a dozen or so people who respond to each other in situations of spiritual, physical, social and financial need and who stimulate and support one another in the practising of individual spiritual gifts such as praying in tongues, healing, words of knowledge etc.

Sunday worship is fully participative:

members are free (often after an initial checking with the officiating elder) to contribute in tongues, prophecy, dancing, words of knowledge, prayer or in any other way that it is acknowledged that the Spirit is leading. Services may also include drama, poetry, solo or group singing, Bible readings and prayers in addition to a large proportion of communal singing. Songs are usually short and sung several times: most have been composed within the last 20 years by members within the movement. Services often give time for the ministry of healing, laying-on of hands or congregational corporate prayer. Limited time may be given for quiet contemplation but rarely are intercessory prayers offered for people or events outside of the immediate contacts of the congregation. A "typical" worship service will consist of 45 minutes worship followed by a 45 minute sermon. It will be patronized by around 100 adults dressed casually and behaving in an informal but intense manner. Worship provides the attender with a confirmation of salvation in an all-providing, ever-present, personal God who reigns over all the world and has power to defeat the Evil One: this is the basis for those who accuse the New Churches of triumphalism. Worship also promotes a sense of camaraderie and a sense of purpose in life.

The regional celebration is a "jamboree" style of meeting and is supported by several local congregations: services usually continue for three hours or more. These events give an opportunity for deeper Biblical teaching as well as demonstrations of such phenomena as healing or other "signs and wonders".

Congregations are "planted" by the process of splitting an existing flourishing congregation: some members may be expected ("asked to consider") to move their homes into the newly evangelized area in order to form the nucleus of the new group.

New Churches look for and expect the whole Church to be restored but, unlike most Fundamentalists before them, many leaders are prepared to spend time in fellowship with denominational leaders. New Church leaders tend to be less judgemental of non-Charismatics than, for example, leaders of the Charismatic renewal in the 1970s. Similarly, New Church leaders, whilst they speak much of "spiritual warfare" against "the powers and principalities of this world", do acknowledge what they see as good in their local communities. In this sense New Churches are neither isolationist nor introversionist.

Members are expected to contribute "tithes and offerings" to their local congregation (some leaders are known to expect a double-tithe) as loans taken out to erect extravagant new buildings become liable for repayment. Observers of New Churches often note that leaders demand a flexibility and commitment of their members which is not expected in denominational churches. Many of these churches now have been established for a generation: this fact has not dimmed their pioneering and trail-blazing spirit of adventure. The expression from within the movement that "constant change is here to stay" adequately summarises the New Churches phenomenon.

Revival Zion. An Afro–Protestant cult found still in parts of Jamaica, and similar in many ways to **Pocomania.** Weekly services involve drumming, prayers and Bible readings as in **Convince,** but here the spirit possession that occurs involves the spirits of prominent Old Testament figures (for instance Moses, Joshua, Jeremiah), apostles and evangelists from the New Testament, archangels (for example Michael), Satan, and the dead. Possession by the Holy Spirit also occurs. The ritual of baptism is a further feature of the movement.

Rifa'iya. The Rifa'iya is one of the oldest **Sufi** orders, founded in the marshes of southern Iraq by Ahmad b. 'Ali al-Rifa'i (1106–82). Rifa'i gatherings are accompanied by the beating of drums and dancing, and by the accomplishment of extraordinary feats while in a state of ecstasy. Characteristic Rifa'i practices are dancing in fires and eating the flames until they are extinguished, putting heated iron into one's mouth, and biting the heads off live snakes. In India the Rifa'is are often known as Gurzmar because of the practice of striking their bodies with a gurz, a sort of iron mace. All such acts are taken as exemplifying the ability of the spirit to overcome the base flesh. In modern times critics have sometimes accused Rifa'is of resorting to jugglery.

The Rifa'iya is well established in Iraq, Syria and Egypt, although in Syria it has been repressed since 1979 for allegedly harbouring anti-governmental members of the **Muslim Brotherhood.** Small communities of Rifa'is have been documented in Yugoslavia and East Africa, and they are active in parts of the Indian sub-continent (Gujarat, the Deccan, Malabar, the Laccadives and Sri Lanka).

Rimay. "The eclectic movement." A movement of spiritual and cultural renaissance originating in Eastern Tibet's Kham region in the 19th century, which changed the face of **Tibetan Buddhism.**

Rimay began as an enlightened response to the sectarianism that plagued 18th century Kham; skirmishing had occurred when the **Sakyapas** lost royal patronage to the **Nyingmapas** and many died when the **Gelugpas** attempted to annihilate an entire **Bon** community. Hence Rimay's basic premise is non-sectarianism; all religious traditions are seen as equally valid paths to salvation, suitable for different persons.

Rimay's founders were Sakyapa Khyentse Wangpo (1820–1892) and his equally brilliant **Kagyudpa** disciple Jamgon Kongtrul (1813–1899). Together with a host of like-minded and talented individuals from different schools, they began a process of eliminating sectarian barriers which culminated in a literary florescence unparalleled in Tibetan history. In the belief that all the multifarious Buddhist teachings are of value to somebody somewhere, innumerable forgotten texts were re-edited and printed. Alongside the literary rediscovery went a powerful renewal of spiritual enthusiasm that first swept the entire region, and eventually engulfed all non-Gelugpa Tibetan Buddhism. Today, all non-Gelugpa Tibetan Buddhists are Rimay, respecting and often practicing each other's teachings; hence Rimaypas can profess quite different philosophies, while still remaining close spiritual friends.

Ringatu. The founder of the Ringatu Church, Te Kooti, was educated at a mission school and read the Bible. During the Land Wars of the 1860s he was employed as an ammunition carrier by the Government, and five years later was arrested on a charge of spying. He was condemned without trial and exiled to the Chatman Islands off the coast of the South Island of New Zealand.

In 1867, following an illness, Te Kooti was spoken to by God in a series of religious experiences and assured the role of a prophet. In 1868 he escaped and returned to New Zealand where he was hunted by the Government for four years. Te Kooti had a number of religious experiences during this period. Out of these he came to identify himself with Moses, and saw it as his vocation to deliver the Maori people from the oppression of foreigners. He fully identified the Maori people with the children of Israel and the experience of the Hebrews in Egypt. He saw his escape from exile as a parallel to the escape of Moses and the people of Israel from Egypt.

Ringatu attracted a strong following from among the Maori people, and it was Te Kooti's rejection of Christianity that led him to base his church on Old Testament and Jewish ideas. The celebration of harvest festivals was begun, and the feast of the Passover was inaugurated, commemorating the deliverance of the

escape of the exile from the Chatham Islands. Services were held on the 12th day of every month, and Saturday worship was instituted. Ringatu is a Maori Christian Church today. Although it has a smaller following than **Ratana**, it still is widely respected throughout Maoridom.

Rinzai Zen. The roots of Zen reach back to early Buddhism. The purpose of Zen adepts is to reproduce here and now the Enlightenment experience of the Buddha through meditation and related practice. Zen attempts to reach the absolute as simply and directly as possible, rejecting the rituals and formalism characteristic of the aristocratic Buddhism which was its predecessor in Japan.

Zen arrived in Japan from China. The most significant early transmitter was Eisai (1141–1215), a **Tendai** monk, like all the Kamakura era reformers, who studied in China and brought back the Rinzai branch of Zen. It seems that to some extent he retained his esoteric Tendai allegiances, and the Kenninji temple in Kyoto over which he presided some time after his return provided for Tendai and **Shingon** rituals, as well as being one of the great centres for the propagation of Rinzai Zen.

Rinzai, essentially a monastic school, places emphasis on the precepts, and on meditation. It is also characterized by the use of the *koan*, a type of riddle designed to expose human reason as severely limited. These are set by Rinzai masters to encourage disciples out of their habitual modes of thinking. The master–disciple relationship is crucial. Only a master can declare a disciple enlightened, and the onus is on the aspiring disciple to seek out the right master.

Rinzai achieved a strong early footing through the patronage of the newly emerging *samurai* class, who were attracted by its simplicity and the aura of propriety and order of the neo-Confucian values which had accompanied Zen in its transmission from China.

The sects of Rinzai are mainly based in the Kyoto area, displaying institutional rather than doctrinal differences; the largest of which is **Rinzaishu Myoshinjiha.** All have a proportionally large lay following, in total around 3,000,000 adherents, who meet not only in temples, but also in factories, offices, schools and universities for sitting meditation (*zazen*) sessions and discussions with masters. The Rinzai monk D. T. Suzuki (1870–1966) was influential in bringing Zen teachings to the West where they were popularized in the 1950s by the Beat poets of America.

Rinzaishu Myoshinjiha. The largest **Rinzai Zen** sect in Japan. It currently has about 3,000 temples and 600,000 adherents.

Rismed. *See* **Rimay.**

Rissho Koseikai. A Japanese new religious movement founded in 1938 by former members of **Reiyukai Kyodan,** Niwano Nikkyo and housewife Naganuma Myoko, Rissho Koseikai (**Society for the Establishment of Righteousness and Harmony**) advocates a spiritual path in which specific individual and societal problems are examined in the light of a collection of Buddhist doctrines, predominantly **Nichiren**-influenced. Folk religious practices, such as divination and healing, have played a diminishing role since the war. The administrative set up is complex, and there is significant stress on strong member-leader relationships. Headquarters are in Tokyo, and the sect claims almost 5,000,000 members, making it the largest of those groups that have emerged from Reiyukai.

Risshu. One of the six **Nara** sects of Japanese Buddhism. Emphasizing strict adherence to monastic discipline (*vinaya*), it has about 30,000 members.

Ritsu emphasizes the Buddhist monastic precepts. For a long period it provided the only legal means of ordination. Together with the affiliated **Shingon Risshu School,** Ritsu claims around 500,000 adherents.

Ritsu. *See* **Risshu.**

Roman Catholic Church. More than 872,104,646 people call themselves Roman Catholic. This means that they were baptized by a Roman Catholic priest, who in turn has been ordained by a bishop. The Roman Catholic bishop is believed to be bound both in an historical chain which leads in unbroken succession to the first Apostles, and in a hierarchical chain which binds his own episcopal authority to that of the Pope. In the Roman Catholic Church, the Pope is both bishop of Rome and, as the successor of Peter, the guide of Christian doctrine and morals. The Church does not lightly depart from historical precedent. When this latter draws on the unanimous voice of the Church at ecumenical Councils, it is taken to be infallible Christian dogma. Roman Catholicism is thus hierarchical, traditional and sacramental. For Roman Catholics a sacramental act is one in which Christ is made effectively present. The Church recognizes the Eucharist as the sacrificial offering of the body and blood of Christ. There are seven sacraments. They are baptism, confirmation, eucharist, ordination, anointing of the sick, confession, and marriage. The sacramental prinicple is the mid-point of Catholic life. As Karl Barth, the greatest of Protestant theologians, noted, it is founded in Catholic belief in the analogy of being between God and creation: that is, in faith that God the Creator is authentically represented by created realities. Nonetheless, as the Fourth Lateran Council (the Church's 12th ecumenical Council, held in 1215), stated: "however great the likeness (between God and the world), the dissimilarity is always greater". The Catholic theologian of the analogy of being is Thomas Aquinas (1224-1274). St. Thomas, a rotund Dominican friar, is also renowned for his synthesis of nature and grace, his five proofs of the existence of God, his ethics, based in natural law, and for the hymns which he composed for the feast of Corpus Christi.

By the eighth century, the Popes had made a pact with the Frankish kings of the West. The latter supplied armed protection to Christian mission, whilst the former conferred a sacral charisma upon the Holy Roman Emperor. A transition has been made from Christian societies (c.100–300) to *Christendom* (312–1303), finally dissolved in the struggle between Pope and Emperor for the upper hand (the "higher sword"), and to the unstable fusion of modern nationalism and Catholicism (c.1450–1789) created in France, the Austro–Hungarian Empire and in Spain and her South American dominions. Catholicism was wedded to the public expression of her faith and morals. This is not a principle to which the modern westernised world is unduly attached. The Church cannot start afresh in the two continents in which it is now most prominent: South American and African Catholicism inherit the dilemmas and the riches of this history. Contemporary phenomena as diverse as the Charles Maurras's Action Française (condemned at Rome in 1907 and 1926) in the first half of this century, and the flourishing of Marxist theology in South America (if not condemned, discouraged) in the second, pay tribute to the persistent refusal of Catholics to acknowledge either an autonomous secular State or an autonomous market economy.

The 19th century saw the retreat of Christianity from the claim either to dominate public institutions or to explain external reality. In 1878, Pope Leo XIII responded to the Christian need for an objective and rational theology and to the secularization of European politics and social life with *Aeterni Patris*: this encyclical recalled Catholics to the thought of St. Thomas. In *Rerum Novarum* (1891) Leo castigated the evil consequences of an economic liberalism uninhibited by objective morality. The errors of the age were perceived as subjectivism, relativism and historicism. Each was condemned during the "Modernist Crisis" of 1905–1908, during which the Roman Curia invoked its full authority against a spectre partly projected by itself. The influential mid-twentieth century Catholic theologian, Bernard Lonergan noted that the catholicism of 1905–1960 is summed up in the fact that it named the worst of all heresies "modernism". For some, it was a time of the flowering of Catholic thought: in Germany and Poland, Max Scheler, Ida Görres, Edith Stein, Erich Przywara and Roman Ingarden invented an admixture of Thomism and phenomenology; in France, Jacques Maritain and Gilson devised neo-Thomistic philosophies, whilst their compatriots Charles Péguy, Bernanos, and Claudel created Catholic novels and poetry; the "New French Theology" of Henri de Lubac, Louis Bouyer, Yves Congar and Jean Danielou bloomed; as did the "English Catholic Spring" of the 1920s and 1930s, and whose spokesmen were Chesterton, Christopher Dawson, Belloc, Eric Gill, David Jones, Evelyn Waugh, Martin D'Arcy and Ronald Knox. For others it was a fallow time, a time of stifling conformism.

In the 1950s, the French "New Theologians" worked under the shadow of condemnation by the Roman Curia. They uncovered elements of the Church's spiritual inheritance more manifold than those revealed by the Thomist revival. Above all, they argued that the objectivity of the sacraments must be met by the faith of a believing subject. Their theology undergirds that of the Second Vatican Council (1962–1965), the Church's 21st Ecumenical Council, convened by Pope John XXIII). They were appalled by the disarray which ensued. After what seemed to some to have been a century's confinement in a medievalist straitjacket, Catholics embraced the new liberties which the Council enshrined: pluralism in theological method, the encouragement of ecumenical contacts, the freedom of Biblical scholars to practice historical criticism, the relaxation of the plethora of rules encircling religious life, the devolution of episcopal control ("collegiality"), and the translation of the old, beautiful Tridentine Mass from Latin into the vernacular of the "New Mass".

How much had changed? The encyclical *Humanae Vitae* was published by Pope Paul VI in 1968 to a roar of disapproval. It became a symbol of the chasm between Papal loyalists and *refuseniks* which rent the Church for the next 20 years, and of which there are few signs of repair. *Humanae Vitae* taught that artificial contraception is contrary to the natural law. There followed an exodus from seminaries, and the new phenomena of public dissent on the part of prominent theologians, and private dissent from a central moral teaching on the part of perhaps the majority of lay people and their local clergy. The novelty is that the dissent refers, not only to the pastoral application of Catholic ethics, but to their underlying principles. Sexual issues, such as contraception, abortion, homosexuality, and the celibacy of the clergy, have become the storm-centre of the Church. The question of the purpose of the sexual act is not a recondite one: it underlies the current medical ethical debates about abortion, in vitro fertilization and scientific experimentation upon human embryos. The present Pope is John Paul II. His 1991 commemoration of *Rerum Novarum, Centesimus Annus* describes campaigns to enjoin Third World countries artificially to regulate births as a form of "chemical warfare". It is highly improbable that his successors will depart from his stand. The resulting friction has led both to the diminution of belief in Papal authority, and to its centralization. If, as some believe, there is an implicit schism in the Catholic Church, it is probable that it may at some date become explicit. In 1988, Cardinal Archbishop Lefebvre led numerous Catholics who had refused to countenance the New Mass into a breakaway Church. Conservatives are unlikely to be those distressed by the Church's future leadership and direction.

The divisions are not only caused by acceptance or rejection of ecclesiastical authority. They have no less been brought about by the alienation of middle-class Catholics from the social structures and paradigms of rationality on which Catholic doctrine is based. The Pope's pronouncements appear to these men and women to be the strident assertion of impracticable ideals. Catholics will remain within their Church only if convincing restatement(s) and practice(s) of Catholic thought and social life are found. Thus, the most significant growth areas of contemporary Catholicism are the new religious communities. Reflecting the emphasis of Vatican II, they are largely composed of lay people. These base communities thrive in varying forms from Central Europe to Brazil. They include, amongst others, the biblically oriented "Neo-Catechumenal Way", the intellectually reflective, Italian-based "Communio e Liberazione", founded by Don Giovanni Giusseppe and attached to Henri de Lubac's theology, and the élitist and reactionary purism of "Opus Dei". The founder of Opus Dei, Msgr. José María Escriva, is about to be canonized, an expression, perhaps unfortunate, of Papal enthusiasm for the new communities. They are significant for the Church because her ethic is fitted to members of a community, not to isolated individuals, and because any new Catholic theology will be grounded in the experience of Christian society, as was St. Augustine's *City of God. Centesimus Annus* gives its support to "intermediary groups" and claims that the primary task of "a business firm is not ... to make a profit but [to be] ... a community of persons ... ".

Pope John Paul II appears as an authoritarian to many in the West, whilst demonstrating a open-mindedness unthinkable in his predecessors. Thus,

Mulieris Dignitatem (1988, *On the Dignity of Women*) is neither acceptable to Christian liberals nor the rehash of conservative dogmas which both his opponents and his supporters might prefer. The encyclical disavows the notion of the ordination of women to the priesthood. Having cited the Fourth Lateran Council's proviso about God's "greater dissimilarity", it recalls that in the Christian Bible " . . . God's love is presented . . . sometimes as the "feminine" love of a mother". *Mulieris Dignitatem* dwells upon the personal and personalizing relations between Christ and women. Responding to the unresolved debate as to whether the locus of the objectivity of "natural law" is biological, metaphysical, or social, it states that motherhood is *not* merely physical but " . . . a *human fact* . . . linked to the personal structure of the woman . . . ", thereby lifting the argument about natural law out of the realm of biology. This is of a piece with the author's "Personalist" philosophy, drawn from Thomism, from Gabriel Marcel's existentalism, and from the realist phenomenology of Max Scheler. These may be the intellectual roots of the future re-statement of Catholic philosophy.

Romanian Church. Eastern Rite Romanian Catholics use the Byzantine rite. Their Church came into being in 1698, when, under the less-than-casual influence of the Austro–Hungarian Empire, the **Orthodox** Church of Transylvania forged a union with Rome. Most current members of the Eastern Rite Church of Romania are Hungarians who, due to the demise of that Empire, found themselves domiciled in Transylvania. Theirs was a national church from 1919 until the Communist seizure of power after 1945. At the Synod of Cluj in 1948, the Church was compelled to be assimilated into **Russian Orthodoxy.** After this, Romanian officialdom knew Orthodox and Latin Rite Christians, but not the Church of the Eastern rite. Thousands of clerical and lay Romanian Eastern Rite Catholics received jail sentences; six were bishops, of whom the last to die in prison was Juliu Hossu, in 1970. In 1975, there were an estimated 900,000 secret Eastern Rite Romanians. They were enabled to practise their faith by the bravery of hundreds of underground priests. The overthrow of President Ceaucescu at Christmas 1989 has allowed the Eastern Rite Romanian Catholic Church to come above ground. It has met continuing Romanian dislike of Hungarian "separatists". Its good health as a Christian community will depend on its capacity to outgrow its enforced absorption in private devotion alone.

Romanian Uniate Catholic Church. *See* **Romanian Church** and **Uniate Churches**.

Rosicrucianism. Rosicrucians follow the teachings of Christian Rosenkreutz (1378–1484?) whose life, possibly mythic, was recounted in documents that aroused considerable interest when published in Germany in the early 17th century. Rosicrucianism integrates esoteric Christianity with a mastery of the laws of nature through alchemy and other magical practices. Many **occult** groups claim a Rosicrucian origin—notably today the Ancient and Mystical Order Rosae Crucis (AMORC). AMORC was founded by the prolific writer H. Spencer-Lewis in 1915, and is now an international organization offering tuition by correspondence course.

Russellites. This is a label sometimes used for **Jehovah's Witnesses**.

Russian (Orthodox) Church Abroad. The Russian Orthodox Church Abroad—or the Russian Church in Exile—is an emigré organization based in New York and currently led by Metropolitan Vitali. Up to 1976 they recognized only the underground **True Orthodox Church** within the Soviet Union, and not the official **Russian**

Orthodox hierarchy (the Moscow Patriarchate), but then they opened up relations with the Moscow Patriarchate, and in 1990, in a complete *volte-face*, they rejected the priesthood of numerous True Orthodox clergy. They have now begun to establish themselves inside Russia as the **Free Russian Orthodox Church**.

Ruthenian Church. This is the local church of the Subcaparthian Ukraine. It has been allied to Rome since the Union of Uzhorod in 1646. In 1944, it had 461,555 members, using the Byzantine Rite. It was ingested by the **Russian Orthodox Church** in 1949. By the mid-seventies, it had just 290,170 members. The break-up, first of state-imposed Communism, and by the close of 1991, of the Soviet Union itself, may enable it to recover the modicum of self-government required for its survival. (*See too* **Uniate Churches**.)

S

Sabaeans (Sabians). The Sabaeans are a scriptural group mentioned in the *Quran* and identified by some Muslims with the **Mandaeans**.

Sabbateans. *See* **Donmeh**.

Sabiriya. The Sabiriya is one of two main branches of the **Chishtiya Sufi** order, popular in South Asia. It is sometimes referred to, indeed, as the Sabiriya–Chishtiya.

Sadahnm Mithuru Samuluwa. *See* the **Saddhamma Friends Society (SFS)**.

Saddhamma Friends' Society (SFS). Also known as the **Sadahnm Mithuru Samuluwa**, the SFS was founded in Sri Lanka in 1962 by D. C. P. Ratnakara as a response to spirit messages urging him to do so. Some of their spirits or *devas* are claimed to have been former disciples of the Buddha. The SFS therefore represents a reformed version of **Theravada** Buddhism which aims to "follow the philosophy of the Buddhas while continuing the lay life and receiving all advice to eradicate suffering (*dukkha*)." Such advice often comes from *devas* and the organization is consequently fairly hostile to the *sangha*. Ratnakara continues as chief organizer and influences at work in the movement appear to include Theosophy, yoga, tantricism, mother goddess worship and the meditation traditions of Theravada forest monks.

Saddhammavamsa. A prominent **Theravada** Buddhist monastic grouping within the Sri Lankan **Amarapura Nikaya**.

Safi 'Ali Shahi. A branch of the Iranian **Ni'matullahi Sufi** order.

Sahaja Yoga. Sahaja Yoga is unusual among new religious movements originating in the East in being founded and run by a woman, Nirmala Devi (b. 1923), known as the Divine Mother. *Sahaja* means spontaneity, and she teaches spontaneous union with the divine within by awakening a powerful spiritual energy called *kundalini*. She has a large following in India, but only a few hundred British disciples, some of whom live in a communal ashram. Most continue with their normal lives, though all members are encouraged to make donations to the movement.

Sahajdhari Sikhs. A non-**Khalsa Sikh**. The term is popularly used in contrast to **Amritdhari** or **Keshdhari**. A Sikh who has not been initiated into the religious community established in 1699 by the 10th Sikh *Guru*, Gobind Singh. By disregarding the significance of the *khalsa* the Sahajdhari Sikh may be assenting to the view that Nanak and his early followers did not see themselves as members of a new group wishing to dissociate itself from the Hindu mainstream. By cutting his hair and shaving, the Sahajdhari is certainly indistinguishable from his Hindu neighbour. Loosely speaking, Sahajdharis are part of the **Nanak Panth**.

Sai Baba. *See* **Satya Sai Baba**.

Sakyapa. "Grey Earth School". One of the four major traditions of **Tibetan Buddhism**, named after the colour of the soil at the site in Central Tibet where its first monastery was built by Khon Konchog Gyalpo in

1073. Following an Indian *tantric* model still followed by Tibetans and Nepalese, leadership of the Sakya school is the hereditary property of a single family, the Khon. Hence the Khon hand down several **Nyingmapa** *tantras* bestowed on their ancestors directly by Padmasambhava in the eighth century. But the main body of Sakyapa doctrine comes from the newer *tantras* that Khon Konchog Gyalpo received from Drogmi, a Tibetan trained in Nepal and India. The Sakyapa are particularly renowned for their practice of the Hevajra Tantra and the related teachings of *Lamdre* ("Path and Fruit").

The Sakyapas are special devotees of Manjusri, Bodhisattva of Wisdom. Through the agency of Sakya Pandita (1181–1251) they exerted a major formative influence on Tibet's entire monastic higher education system. Skilful logicians, debaters and philosophers, the Sakyapas excel in preserving in their full diversity all the many different traditions Tibet received from India. It was a Sakyapa, Khyentse Wangpo (1811–1892), who initiated and intellectually underpinned the **Rimay** movement.

A Sakyapa hierarch Phagpa (1234–1280) was made ruler of Tibet by Khubilai Khan, and Sakyapa rule in Tibet continued for a century. Always retaining their headquarters at the holy site of Sakya, the Sakyapas developed thousands of monasteries throughout Tibet, and produced the two sub-schools of **Ngor** and **Tshar.** Following the Chinese invasion of Tibet, the Sakyapa tradition continues in exile. The **Phuntsok** branch of the Khon has established a monastery in Seattle, USA, and the reigning hierarch from the **Dolma** branch, His Holiness the Sakya Trizin, is currently developing a Sakya College in Dehra Dun, India.

Salafiya. The Salafiya may be compared with the **Islamic Modernists (South Asia).** It owes its inspiration to the late 19th century Islamic Modernists Jamal al-din al-Afghani (1839–97) and Muhammad 'Abduh (1845–

1905). Both had called for a return to follow the example of the *salaf*, the elders or ancestors, i.e. the members of the earliest community of believers in 7th century Medina, rejecting the blind imitation of later generations. In so doing, Muslims would be rediscovering the true Islam, a religion of reason not hostile to modern science and technology, but capable of meeting the needs of man in the modern world. At the hands of Muhammad Rashid Rida (1865–1935), 'Abduh's best known disciple, the Salafiya developed into a reform movement with a following from Morocco to Indonesia. Rida was interested in the creation of a just system of Islamic law and government suited to modern conditions. To achieve this, he stressed the importance of establishing as exactly as possible the actual practice of the *salaf*, and then relating it to current needs.

The Salafiya played an important role in Algeria and Morocco from the 1920s until independence, bolstering Muslims' awareness of their Arab and Islamic cultural identity in the face of French colonialism, and assuring them that Islam did not have to hold them back from social and economic progress. In Algeria the major figure associated with the movement was 'Abd al-Hamid b. Badis (1889–1940), who in 1931 founded the Association of Reformist Ulama to work for the reform of Algerian Islam in opposition to both **maraboutism** and French cultural influence. A major part of their programme involved the establishment of schools to teach Arabic and Islam alongside modern sciences, and the publication of journals to disseminate their ideas. In Morocco a parallel pattern marked the development of Salafi activities centred on the old capital of Fez.

The Salafiya continues to exist as a trend in reformist thought, but appears to have been largely overtaken by the new radicalism, to whose emergence it has made such a significant contribution.

Salvation Army. In the summer of 1865 a former Methodist minister preached to a crowd in a tent in a Quaker cemetry in the East End of London. His congregation was composed of the poor, the illiterate, the immoral, the dirty; the people who felt that society and certainly the Church had no place for them. William Booth spoke to them of the dangers of hell and the love of God and demanded that they turn away from their sins and be saved.

Many did come forward wanting to give their lives to God. Wealthy Christians who had taken an interest were so impressed that they supported William Booth financially and enabled him to start a "Christian Mission" in a former public house, with a reading room, hall and accommodation for eight missioners. At first William Booth encouraged the new Christians to join a church but soon found that they were not accepted.

In 1878 he gave the movement a new name "The Salvation Army". A book of *Orders and Regulations* soon appeared, the first brass band performed at an Army event and new Christian words were written to popular tunes of the day, in response to William Booth's often quoted words "Why should the devil have all the best tunes?" In 1880 the uniform was created including the famous bonnet for women which was specifically designed to protect the wearer from the rotten eggs, overipe tomatoes and even physical blows of the Army's opponents.

From the start women have had total equality in the Salvation Army. This was greatly due to the influence of William Booth's wife Catherine, who was a gifted preacher and practical administrator. As the movement spread rapidly worldwide her children became its first overseas leaders, with such success that today the Army is active in over 70 countries with more than 4,000,000 adherents.

The ordinary members are "soldiers" and sign Articles of War and belong to a corps. Officers are the equivalent of ministers in other churches and are in command of a corps. Ranks of officers are similar to those in the secular army, the highest rank being General, of whom

William Booth was the first. The Salvation Army concentrates on Christian action running hostels for the homeless, a missing persons bureau, rehabilitation centres for alcoholics, hospitals, schools, food kitchens etc.

The Salvation Army still seeks for the conversion of people to a life of commitment to God and the experience of His love for them. Members are encouraged to give publicly their personal testimony. They believe that the Bible is divinely inspired, and preaching is central in their services. The decision was made by William Booth early in the Army's history that the movement would not celebrate the Lord's Supper. Two reasons were given; the problem that was created for reformed alcoholics who could not safely receive even a sip of wine, and the uneasiness in Victorian times on the part of both men and women at the possibility of women officers giving communion to male soldiers. However the hallmark of the Salvation Army is its music—the brass bands on the street corner, tambourines and recently pop and rock bands.

Samaiya Panthis. An alternative name for the **Taranapanthis,** a sub-sect of **Digambara Jainism.**

Samaritans. The Samaritans, sometimes labelled a Jewish sect, are a group which has its origins in northern Biblical Israel but which separated from the rest of the people today known as Jews. The precise history of this separation is debated but it appears to have been completed by Jesus's time if not 300 years prior. Like the Jews, their holy text is the *Torah* but unlike them, their holy site is Mt. Gerizim, where they continue to offer a Paschal sacrifice. Their current population is around 400, centred in Holon, a Tel Aviv suburb, and Shechem (Nablus).

Samaya. One of the two major divisions with Hindu **Tantricism.**

Samkauw Hwee. Literally, "the three religions". An Indonesian new religious movement more widely known as **Tridharma**.

Samnak Paw Sawan. Literally "the Abode of Heavenly Fathers", this is an urban Thai movement which practises spirit exorcism. It was founded in the early 1970s by Professor Kloom Vajroban, a professor of zoology at Chulalongkorn University, Bangkok. Mediums have included a Vietnamese member of the **Cao Dai** sect.

Sanakasampradaya. One of the four contemporary Indian **Vaishnava** teaching and monastic traditions which has its origins in the writings of the orthodox Hindu thinker Nimbarka, a 14th century Telugu brahmin. Followers hold to a form of **Vedanta** philosophy described as "dualism and non-dualism" and believe that Brahman is really none other than Lord Krishna. The *sampradaya* contends that liberation may only come about through Krishna's grace and in this, as in many other matters, there is great theological similarity between the Sanakas and the **Sri Vaishnavas**. The movement underwent a reformation in the 15th century and is now important only in Bengal, as well as in the immediate vicinity of the cities of Mathura and Agra. A monastic order of ascetics (*samnyasins*) exists and is known as the **Nimbarka Vairagin**. Monks are distinguished by their white *dhoti,* necklace with a single bead, and U-shaped white, or black, forehead marking.

Sanatan Sikhs. This term is used less now than in the 19th century. It refers to a Sikh who is conservative in the sense of not over-emphasizing the disctinctions between Hinduism and Sikhism which came to be stressed in the latter part of the century. Such a person would argue that Sikhism has many identities, the **Khalsa** form being only one of them.

Sant Nirankari Mandal. Also known as the **Nakali Nirankaris** (false Nirankaris) to distinguish them from the more established **Asali Nirankaris**. A modern **Sikh**-derived movement which enjoys profound hostility from **Khalsa Sikhs**. It may be traced back to Babu Buta Singh, a prominent **Nirankari** who, in the 1930s, was requested by his peers to cut back on his drinking. His disciple, Baba Avtar Singh seems to have founded the movement a few years after his master's death in 1943. The canonical writings of the Mandal differ in a few minor respects from that of the Nirankaris. They rose to public prominence when Jarnail Singh Bhindranwale, an up-and-coming Khalsa militant, led a violent demonstration against a Mandal conference in Amritsar in 1978. Shortly after this, in 1980, the then leader of the movement, Baba Gurbachan Singh, was assassinated. Since that time the Mandal has kept a low profile.

Santería. This Spanish word meaning image-worship is the name given to the syncretic mix of **African traditional** and **Roman Catholic** religion in Cuba. It is also practised by Cuban immigrants and exiles in North America, and by some African Americans, in such cities as Miami, Los Angeles, New York, Chicago and Detroit. In Cuba itself, partly as a result of measures of control introduced by Castro, there is evidence of some decline.

In Santería, as in **Candomblé** in Brazil, most of the African elements—the names and functions of the gods, type of spirit possession and sacrifice—are derived from the Yoruba traditional religion. However, the Catholic counterparts of the Yoruba gods often differ in the two places, Shango the god of thunder and lightning being equated with St. Barbara in Cuba and with St. Jerome in Bahia in north-eastern Brazil.

Stones hidden under the altar are believed to contain the life and power of the gods. They have to be baptized and fed with herbs and the blood of animal sacrifices. In return, some of the participants in the ceremonies become possessed by some of their spirits.

Santi Asok. A this-worldly Thai Buddhist movement founded in 1975 by former TV producer and singer Phra Photirak (1935–). Having received ordination in both Thai **Theravada** monastic fraternities, Photirak came in for hostile criticism from the ecclesiastical authorities after claiming to have achieved the highest level of spiritual perfection (*ariya*). His relation with the *Sangha* is now ambiguous but he has built up a considerable lay and monastic following. Santi Asok teaches an individualistic programme of "dhammic action" of a moral reformist kind. Emphasis is placed on diligence, moderation and a simple lifestyle and the traditional practice of meditation is repudiated. Followers meet together in discussion groups and a strong value is placed on reason. In consequence superstitious practices, including many of the activities of the *Sangha,* are condemned. Lay and monastic members often live together in urban "Dhamma families" and the laity wear distinctive blue Thai peasant clothing. Males commonly sport military style haircuts. The **Palang Dhamma Party (PDP)** of Maj.-Gen. Chamlong Siimeuang, Photirak's most prominent lay follower, though electorally ineffective, supports Santi Asok's "path of righteousness". Santi Asok has its origins in downtown Bangkok, but now has established itself in four Thai provinces. Unlike its companion movement, the **Thammakaai Religious Foundation,** it accepts donations only from proven followers.

Sanusiya. The Sanusiya is a **Sufi** order associated with Libya in particular, and which takes its name from its Algerian founder, Muhammad b. 'Ali al-Sanusi (1787–1859), known as the Grand Sanusi. After a period spent in Mecca as a disciple of the reformist Moroccan Sufi Ahmad b. Idris

(1760–1838), along with his subsequent rival Muhammad 'Uthman al-Mirghani, who went on to found the **Khatmiya,** he set up his own Sufi centre (*zawiya*) there, but was forced to leave Mecca in 1840. He then settled in Cyrenaica (eastern Libya) before moving in 1856 to a new base at an oasis in the Libyan desert to the South, where he could avoid the interference of the Turkish authorities and build up the strength of his order among the nomadic tribes of the Sahara and beyond in Chad and further areas of West Africa. A network of Sanusi centres was established, each with its own mosque, school, accommodation for teachers and students and for passing caravans. Each had its own lands cultivated by the Ikhwan (brethren), a practice similar to that of the **Wahhabis** in early 20th century Arabia.

During the later 19th century the Sanusiya spread peacefully, but from 1902 came under attack by the French in its bases south of the Sahara. From 1911 the order was then engaged in resistance to the Italian occupation of Libya, surviving despite the destruction of its centres and, with British support, enthroning the head of the Sanusiya as King Idris I of Libya on achieving independence in 1951. It remained the only Sufi order to create a modern state with its leaders as hereditary monarchs until their overthrow in September 1969 by Colonel Muammar al-Qaddafi. One of the first acts of the new régime was to bring the order under government control and prevent the opening of new Sanusi centres. The Sanusiya was declared to be responsible for allowing corruption and drunkenness, for spreading a perverted mystical conception of Islam, and the monarchy itself was condemned as an un-Islamic institution. Sanusis have continued to provide one of the strands of religious opposition to the Qaddafi régime.

Sanusis are widely regarded as reformist neo-Sufis. Like the **Tijaniya** they are opposed to the noisy recollection of God (*dhikr*), emphasize the need to seek contact with the Prophet Muhammad and encourage their members to work rather than seeking charity. In a spirit of fostering reform they insist on the fresh examination of the Quran and Tradition, bypassing the early authorities of the four **Sunni** schools of jurisprudence, and making new interpretations of legal points through independent reasoning (*ijtihad*). However, unlike the Tijanis and the Arabian reform movement of the **Wahhabis**, they permit practices associated with the veneration of saints.

Sapta Darma. Sapta Darma (Sevenfold Teaching) is one of the larger **kebatinan** sects which have proliferated in Indonesia this century. Its founder has been known by several names — originally called Hardjosapuro, then Brahmono, then Rodjopandito, and finally Sri Gutama. He allegedly began to experience God directly in December 1952, a process which continued for several years and involved both automatic movements and receptivity to teachings.

The latter include a theory of energy points and pathways, and part of the aim of the movement is to enable members to awaken the life energy within them and to help it flow more freely.

Sri Gutama died in 1964, and leadership is currently exercised by Ibu Sri Pawenang. The estimated 100,000 members are found mainly in village communities, in Bali as well as in Java, although the leaders tend to be urban middle-class intellectuals.

Sar cult. An alternative rendering of the more commonly used designation, **Zar cult.**

Sarbat Khalsa. At one time it was practically possible for almost all **Khalsa Sikhs** to assemble to discuss and resolve matters of concern. Such gatherings evolved into ones where representatives of groups within the Khalsa met, but the term which means "all the Khalsa" continued to be used. Maharaja Ranjit Singh, (1780–1839) abolished such assemblies in 1809 but they have recently been revived though no formula has been devised in respect of representation. Who, if anyone, for example, should be the voice of Sikhs in Britain or other parts of the Sikh dispersion? In such circumstances decisions, known as *gurmatta*, do not always win the total approval of the Panth.

An improperly convened Sarbat Khalsa, on Jan. 26, 1986, held in the precincts of the Golden Temple, Amritsar, led to the demolition of the holy Akal Takht after its desecration by the Indian army during Operation Blue.

Sarvodaya Sramadana. A modern Buddhist movement aiming to present a purely Buddhist model of social development. It was established in 1958, following a spiritual transformation of a team of college-based missionaries working in a deprived community of Sri Lanka. Its founder, A. T. Ariyaratna, roots its ideology in the Buddhism of Anagarika Dharmapala, instigator of the **Maha Bodhi Society**. Its function is to promote village renewal through various collective–community projects. Work groups are based upon the concept of *sramadana* (selfless gift of labour) and draw on all members of the community irrespective of religious status. Praxis is seen as essential to the nature of Buddhism and consequently monks have been a target of recruitment and are encouraged to emerge from their monastic ghettos. Although Gandhi first used the term *sarvodaya* (welfare of all), Ariyaratna developed the concept into "the awakening of all", implying a moral awakening to self-sufficiency of villages in contrast to the Western non-Buddhist model of industrialization. The village awakening (*gramodaya*) has four stages: (i) community cognition; (ii) community organization; (iii) community action; and, (iv) balanced technological upgrading. The main emphasis is not upon an improved quality of life but on a full understanding, through praxis, of the nature of reality as defined by **Theravada** Buddhist tradition.

Although peasant-based, the ideological infrastructure originates with the Sinhala Buddhist urban upper-middle-class. On the governing body of Sarvodaya, all are educated, 24 per cent being professional educationalists (professors, lectures and teachers) with little personal experience of village life. To date, the Sarvodaya movement has been actively promoting its ideals in over 5,000 of the 25,000 villages of Sri Lanka and is the largest non-governmental organization in the country. This socially engaged Buddhism has also appealed to Western Buddhists, and is strongly advocated by the North-Amercian Buddhist scholar, Joanna Macy, who has used the movement in her own analysis of social involvement for Buddhists.

Satanism. Satanism encompasses a number of practices, the essence of which is the profaning of Christian worship. Included in these are the Black Mass, reciting the Lord's Prayer backwards and the desecration of Christian sacred objects, including the symbolic replacement of symbols of light with those of dark.

Satanic themes have provided the basis of a number of well known films, plays and novels. The imagery used is often distorted in its meanings by the media to such an extent that the practices of true Satanists are lost. The Satanist's philosophy is a hedonistic one of living life to the full through gratification of physical, emotional and mental desires. As very little authoritative material has been published it is impossible accurately to gauge the size of membership, but numbers are small in comparison to those for **Paganism** and **Witchcraft**, and commitment tends to be short-lived.

The Church of Satan, founded in America by Anton Le Vey in 1966, has functioned largely as a movement teaching self-assertion.

Satmar Hasidism.
Satmar is a Hungarian Hasidic movement, now based in Williamsburg (Brooklyn, New York), with followers in Israel and other Jewish centres. Although the Satmar, named after Satu-Mare (St. Mary), the place of its Transylvanian origins, is a comparatively recent development in Hasidism, it draws on older northern Hungarian Hasidic traditions. The current leader is Rabbi Joel Teitelbaum, whose father, Rabbi Moshe Teitelbaum (1888–1982) escaped from Hungary in 1944 and established his court in America. The centre in Brooklyn became a focal point for Hungarian Jews in the years immediately after the war and the Satmar made great efforts on behalf of refugees.

The Satmar are among the most rejectionist of all Jewish communities, in terms of their encounter with the modern world. They do not attribute value to any form of secular studies, see themselves at war with modernity and have attempted to re-create a complete and perfect replica of pre-Holocaust Jewish life—in America. Moshe Teitelbaum, in his work, *Vayoel Moshe,* advocated a staunch anti-**Zionism** and the Satmar continue to be among the most vociferous opponents of all types of Jewish nationalism. They regularly publish and disseminate anti-Zionist materials and hold public anti-Israel rallies. Teitelbaum's opposition, utilizing an argument found in the *Talmud,* reflects what once was a dominant Orthodox rabbinic viewpoint. He also gained notoriety in the Jewish world for his claim that the Holocaust was divine punishment for the "sin" of Zionism.

The Satmar have been involved in a series of disputes (theological and legal) with other Hasidic and non-Hasidic groups. They have created a community almost totally closed to other Jews and the modern world. In many ways the Satmar represent the continuity of the 19th century, **Ultra-Orthodox** (particularly Hungarian) life-style and theology once so much a feature of European Jewry.

Satpanthis. The Satpanthis, or "those who follow the true path", are a small sub-group

of the **Nizari Khojas** in India. The Nizaris
are a Muslim sect within **Isma'ili Shi'ism**,
and the Khojas are a caste, or caste-like,
group who were converted by a Nizari
missionary in the 14th or 15th century.
The Satpanthis split away from the Nizari
Khojas in the 16th century on the issue of
leadership. Related to this, they are also
known as Imam-Shahis.

Imam Shah too was a Nizari missionary,
active in Gujarat. After his death in the
early 16th century, he was declared by
his son to have been the spiritual leader
(*Imam*) of the Nizaris. The son, Nur (Nar)
Muhammad Shah, further claimed to have
inherited his father's mantle as *Imam*, thus
breaking definitively with the official Nizari
Imam based in Iran. He and his followers,
and their successors, are known as Imam-
Shahis, or alternatively as Satpanthis.

Satpanthis have their centre near Ahma-
dabad in Gujarat, and are to be found
mainly in Gujarat and Khandesh. They share
much of the religious literature of the Nizari
Khojas from whom they originally broke
away. This literature is known as the *Sat
Panth*, or True Path. It contains elements
of Hindu thought, and many Satpanthis have
now reverted to Hinduism.

Satya Sai Baba Satsang. Satya Sai Baba
claims to be the reincarnation of the 19th
century mystic Sai Baba, and also an *avatar*
of the Indian god Vishnu. His teaching is
traditionally Hindu. However, he is best
known as a "miracle worker" or magician
who regularly "materializes" sacred ash
and other objects (including gold watches)
at *darshans* in his Indian ashrams. He
claims 10,000,000 followers, mostly in
India, but also many Westerners, including
about 10,000 British. There are many
tales of his supernatural powers, such
as telepathy, precognition, and weather
control, but some of these have been
disproved.

Satya Samaj. A modern Indian **Jain**
sect, founded in the 1960s by Pandit

Darabarilala, who is also known as
Swami Satyabhakta. It has several hundred
adherents and is primarily concerned with
social, rather than religious matters. In
particular, it opposes the caste system
and welcomes muslims as full members.
Its main temple and headquarters are to
be found at Wardha, Madhya Pradesh.

Sauras. The name applied to Hindu
worshippers of the sun god, Surya, one
of the five traditional deities of **Smarta**
devotion. This style of devotion is thought
to be extremely ancient though it has
declined greatly since its peak in the
13th century CE. Numbers of devotees
today are small and the majority of Surya
temples are neglected. An exception to this
rule is the Temple of the Sun at Konarak,
in the eastern state of Orissa, which is well
preserved and acts as the prime focus of
the movement.

Scientology. A religio-therapeutic system
founded in 1950 by L. Ron Hubbard,
an American who once wrote science
fiction novels. Hubbard called his system
"Dianetics", but when it was attacked by
doctors and psychiatrists, he buttressed it
with a quasi-religious philosophy, based on
transmigration, and an ecclesial structure.
"The Church of Scientology", as it
became, is instrumental in orientation,
offering explanations for personal failure,
mental and physical ill health. These
ills and inadequacies are put down
to "engrams", the physiologically or
neurologically recorded experience of
trauma in early life, the womb, or a
past life. The aim of Scientology is to
provide a technique to erase fully the
"engrams", leaving the individual free
to act unimpeded by time, space, mass,
and energy, and capable of realizing
effectively the reserves of superhuman
powers. Achievement of this goal comes
to those who complete expensive courses.
For its core members, Scientology is often
experienced as totalitarian.

Sect Shinto. *See* **Kyoha Shinto.**

Seicho no Ie. Founded in 1930 in Kobe by Taniguchi Masaharu, a former member of **Omotokyo**; Seicho no Ie (**House of Growth**) claims the doctrinal integration of all Japan's major religions, including Christianity. Emphasis is on positive thinking. Suffering is an illusion which arises from ignorance that mankind is essentially perfect. Realization of this "truth of life" through certain practices, such as chanting and meditation, will restore humanity's filial relationship with the divine. Seicho no Ie is characterized by a mainly middle class, conservative membership, of well over 2,000,000, and by its championing of the Emperor, the military and patriotic causes.

Sekai Kyuseikyo. A Japanese new religious movement founded by **Omotokyo** member Okada Mokichi (1882–1955), Sekai Kyuseikyo (**World Messianity**) advocates healing through the laying on of hands using power derived from the deified founder, and advances the ideal of an earthly paradise through communion with divine beings. Membership is quoted at around 700,000.

Sekai Mahikari Bunmei Kyodan. The founder of this new religious movement, also known as the **World True-Light Civilization**, Okada Kotama, previously a member of **Sekai Kyuseikyo**, received a revelation from the creator god, Su, in 1959. It claimed Japan as the centre of the universe, and Okada as the mediator of divine rays of light from Su which would effect the purification of humankind, who had become polluted by restless spirits, often those of ancestors.

The central ritual, claimed by **Mahikari** as scientific, is a purification rite, *Mahikari-no-waza*, in which the performer, by virtue of his or her initiation (a three day "seminar") and the amulet worn by all members, exorcises his or her restless spirits facilitating among other beneficial effects, healing. On a larger scale *Mahikari-no-waza* is thought to prevent natural and political catastrophes (the products of spirit possession) and its widespread practice will result in the return of humankind to divine stature.

The sacred centre of Mahikari is in Shizuoka, although it also has headquarters in Tokyo, and some international membership, predominantly in the United States. Membership is approaching 100,000, and though small the sect has a high public profile.

On the death of Okada in 1974 a succession dispute resulted in a schismatic movement named **Sukyo Mahikari** and led by Okada Sachiko, the adopted daughter of the founder. Sekai Mahikari Bunmei Kyodan is presently led by Sekiguchi Sakae, a disciple of Okada. The doctrinal differences between the two groups are negligible.

Self Realization Fellowship (SRF). One of the first Hindu-oriented movements to establish itself in the West. Founded by Paramahansa Yogananda (1893–1953), who is held to be the fourth in a line of Indian *gurus*, the distinctive teaching of the SRF is *kriya yoga*. In 1920, Yogananda was sent by his teacher, Sri Yukteswar, to the International Congress of Religious Liberals in Boston. Shortly after arriving in America he established the mother centre of the SRF in Los Angeles. It remains the headquarters of the movement. The SRF is noteworthy in having pioneered correspondence courses for its membership based on the writings and oral teachings of the founder. A six-month minimum initial study period is required before initiation into *kriya yoga* can take place. Initiation by a minister of the SRF, followed by sustained practice is said to result in a merging of consciousness with the *guru*. Monks and nuns belonging to the **Self-Realization Order** reside at the Los Angeles centre and the movement has active branches throughout the world. The SRF is perhaps best known through its founder's highly popular and classic exposition of the spiritual life, *The Autobiography of a Yogi*.

Self-Realization Order. A name applied to the monastic grouping within the **Self-Realization Fellowship (SRF).**

Self Religions. As noted in the opening essay on New Religious Movements by P. Clarke, some of these movements may usefully be grouped together under the label of "self religions". What they have in common is a focus on the inner self as the source of true divinity. Psychological techniques may be used to uncover the "god" within. Instead of submitting to a transcendent God, who is in some sense "outside" or "beyond", people aim to "live *as* gods" themselves. Examples of such movements include **Scientology, est, Rajneeshism, Insight, Primal Therapy, Rebirthing, Psychosynthesis** and **Silva.** They are connected too to **New Age,** and its psychological wing, the **Human Potential Movement.**

Sephardi. (From biblical "Sepharad" (Obadiah 1:20) later interpreted as Spain). Refers to Spanish and Portuguese Jews and their descendants, sometimes used to describe all Mediterranean Jews, although most Jews from North Africa and the Near East (excepting Turkey) are not Sephardim, rather they are members of the Edot ha-Mizrah ("Eastern Communities").

Spanish Jewry was the largest and most important medieval Jewish community until 1391 but its influences came to an end when Jews were expelled from Spain in 1491 and Portugal (1497). From 1391–1491, many Jews converted to Catholicism but continued to practise Judaism secretly. These crypto-Jews, derogatorily referred to as *Marranos* ("swine"), were the target of the Spanish Inquisition (established in 1480). After 1492, the Sephardim and many *conversos* fled to Turkey, Italy,

Holland and the Land of Israel and later England and the Americas. By the end of the 17th century, Sephardi Jewry had lost much of its influence in the Jewish world. Many European Sephardi communities were destroyed during the Holocaust. Current Sephardi centres include Latin America, the USA and Israel.

Sephardi Judaism differs from **Ashkenazi** (Central and Eastern European) Judaism in cultural, liturgical, and linguistic ways (differing pronunciation of Hebrew, as well as Sephardi use of Judeo–Spanish and Ladino). While both hold the written and oral *Torahs* to be the basis of Jewish law, later Sephardi and Ashkenazi legal codes differ in many areas, such as Sephardi law permitting certain foods during Passover, which the Ashkenazim forbid. The Sephardi community has its own Chief Rabbi in Israel and systems of courts and education.

Sephardi Torah Guardians' Party. *See* **Shas.**

Servants of the Light. A contemporary school of **Occultism** offering a **Kabbalistic** training into the mysteries of the tree of life and the symbolism of the Grail.

Sevener Shi'ites (Seveners). The label Sevener Shi'ites (or simply Seveners) is sometimes given to the **Isma'ilis** as a convenient way of distinguishing them from both the **Twelver Shi'ites** and the **Zaydis** (Fivers) within Islam.

Shadhiliya. Dating back to the 13th century, the Sadhiliya is to this day one of the most thriving **Sufi** orders across North Africa from Morocco to Egypt, and is also active in Syria and Jordan. The founder, Abu'l-Hasan 'Ali al-Shadhili (1196–1258), is surrounded by pious legends, but his few surviving letters show him as a great spiritual master with humanitarian concerns.

He led a wandering ascetic life in North Africa, but met with hostility towards his teaching and moved to Egypt where he was more favourably received, both by the ordinary people and by religious scholars. He died in Upper Egypt on his return from a pilgrimage to Mecca in 1258, and his tomb became a venerated site.

Shadhilis, in common with the **Tijanis, Sanusis** and **Murids**, stress the importance of combining work with devotions, and the demands of the order do not conflict with the pursuit of a trade or profession. They discourage begging, and see no necessity for a life of poverty. Members may live in comfort or even luxury, provided that they cultivate inner humility and are not attached to worldly goods. They are frequently active in charitable works and concerned with the welfare of the poor. They are usually noted for their sobriety and strictness in following the example of the Prophet.

In Egypt one well established branch of the Shadhiliya is the Idrisiya, founded by Ahmad ibn Idris (1760–1837), a great reformer of Sufism. It has an estimated 10,000 members.

A much more recent branch of the order, the **Hamidiya Shadhiliya** in Egypt, was made the subject of a major study by the anthropologist Michael Gilsenan in his *Saint and Sufi in Modern Egypt*, resulting from a period of fieldwork in Cairo in 1964–6. This sub-order was founded by Shaikh Salama Hasan al-Radi (1867–1939), a civil servant regarded by his followers as a saint. He was credited with many miracles, such as confounding the religious scholars by posing them theological questions that they could not answer, and also saving members of the order from drowning or in traffic accidents. Gilsenan noticed the highly organized bureaucracy of the order with its hierarchy of officials and many regulations. In the 1960s he saw that members came mainly from the lower middle class and urban poor. However, on a return visit to Cairo in 1977 he found that there had been a split in the leadership, with one section being taken over by

a prosperous group of businessmen and professionals who had built a new mosque in the smart district of Zamalek. Despite this, the majority of lower class members remained attached to the original centre with the saint's shrine in the old port area of Bulaq, and the split marked serious social divisions in an order intended to be dedicated to the service of the poor.

In Jordan another recent sub-order of the Shadhiliya, known as Dar al-Qur'an, is currently active in Amman. Members regard themselves as a modern, reformed branch, are involved in welfare services for the poor and have had representatives elected to the Jordanian parliament.

Shafi'is. The Shafi'i rite or school of Islamic law (madhhab) traces its foundation to Muhammad al-Shafi'i (d. 820), a pupil of Malik b. Anas, the founder of the Medinan **Maliki** school. Al-Shafi'i is generally admired for his intellectual contribution to studying the principles of Islamic jurisprudence. He recognized four "roots" or sources of the Holy Law: the *Quran*, Prophetic Traditions, consensus of the religious scholars (*ijma*) and analogical reasoning (*qiyas*). He held that the Prophet was divinely inspired in all his acts and sayings, and that God had commanded men to obey the Prophet. Therefore, in common with the Malikis, he attached great importance to Traditions. There could be no disagreement with matters that were clearly decided by reference to the *Quran*, Traditions or consensus. However, in other cases he accepted the use of analogy subject to stricter rules than those employed by the **Hanafis**. For al-Shafi'i, it was not man's concern to work out laws for himself, but to discover God's laws by applying the methods of jurisprudence to the four sources of the Law. Unrestricted reasoning could not be allowed in order to deal with new situations, and the jurist should not question God's purposes if he found a law thus discovered to be inconvenient, or contrary to his wishes.

In Egypt, a cult of al-Shafi'i flourishes, centred on his tomb in Cairo, in a manner normally associated with **Sufi** shrines. By coincidence his name, Shafi'i, means "intercessor", and he is addressed as such in letters sent (or taken) to the shrine, a practice that has been going on for centuries. The letter-writers are normally concerned to seek help in having an injustice remedied. The mosque-tomb is a centre of international pilgrimage, visitors often rubbing the wooden screen surrounding the actual tomb in order to absorb the saint's *baraka* (sacred power). Once a year a colourful festival is celebrated in the mosque's immediate neighbourhood.

At present most Egyptians are Shafi'is, especially in Lower Egypt, and the Shafi'i school, which is **Sunni**, is to be found in South Arabia, the Gulf state of Bahrain, East Africa, along the western coast of India, and in Sri Lanka, South East Asia and some areas of Central Asia.

Shaivas. In Hinduism devotees of the god Shiva are known as Shaivas. The Shaiva religion possibly has its roots in the pre-Aryan Indus valley civilization (c.2000 BCE) where a seal was found depicting a horned, phallic figure reminiscent of Shiva as Lord of animals and ascetics. Most Shaivas revere the Shaiva *agamas* and *Tantras* as their scriptural authority, though other texts are held in esteem such as the Shaiva *Puranas* which depict the mythology of Shiva, rituals and other aspects of Shaiva religion. While accepting the reality of other Hindu deities, Shaivas maintain that Shiva is the supreme God, though what this precisely means varies from tradition to tradition within Shaivism. For example, **Kashmir Shaivas** are monists, maintaining that Shiva is the ultimate reality with which all particular souls are identical, while **Shaiva Siddhantins** are dualists maintaining that there is a plurality of souls eternally distinct from Shiva. Shaiva ascetics or renouncers adopt the insignia of their god: covering themselves in ashes, wearing

their hair long and matted and bearing a trident. Some Shaiva ascetics practise yoga in order to attain liberation, while others smoke hashish in order to commune with their deity. Notable orders of Shaiva ascetics are the **Naths** and **Aghoris**. The **Lingayats** or **Virashaivas** who worship Shiva in his phallic form as the *linga* are prominent in South India where temple priests, the *Adishaivas*, administer to their ritual needs. Chidambaram, the site of Shiva's dance, should be particularly noted as a centre of Shiva worship. Even if not dedicated to Shiva as their primary deity, most Hindu temples will have a shrine to Shiva, especially in his phallic form as the *linga*.

Shaiva Siddhantins. The tradition of **Shaiva Siddhanta** originated in Kashmir, where it was supplanted by Kashmir Shaivism, but now exists only in South India particularly in Tamil Nadu. It contains two strands, one derived from the Kashmiri tradition which used Sanskrit as its medium of expression, the other derived from Tamil devotionalism (*bhakti*) expressed in the poetry of the Nayanmars (4th–9th centuries CE). Among this collection of poetry is Tirumular's *Tiruvacakam* (fifth century CE), about the soul's absolute dependence upon Shiva, which is sung daily in Shaiva temples and in the home. The most important text upon which Shaiva Siddhanta theology is based is the *Civananapotam* by Meykantatevar (c1200). Here there are three eternal realities: Shiva the transcendent Lord who is also immanent in the world; the soul (or "beast") who is utterly dependent upon Shiva and caught in a cycle of transmigration; and the cosmos or that which binds. The soul, of which there are an infinite number, upon liberation becomes omniscient and omnipotent like Shiva. In the Kashmiri Shaiva Siddhanta liberation was achieved through ritual which eradicated the pollution clinging to the soul, while for the Tamil version, liberation is through surrender to Shiva and his grace. Shaiva Siddhanta is the tradition behind the popular worship of Shiva in Tamil Nadu and is the philosophy of the Adishaiva priests who administer the South Indian Shaiva temples.

Shakers. The Shakers of Saint Vincent are an Afro–Protestant cult similar in many ways to the **Spiritual Baptists,** or Shakers, of Trinidad, with the main differences being that the order of worship is based on that of the Methodists rather than the Baptists, and there is a hierarchy of offices. Proceedings may also be more informal.

Shaktas. Shaktas are Hindu devotees of the Goddess (*Devi*) in one of her forms as mother, ferocious destroyer or as a young virgin. Devi is also worshipped as the power (*shakti*) of Shiva manifested in his consorts such as Parvati and Sati and as the consorts of Vishnu such as Lakhsmi. At a popular level Devi is worshipped in regional forms throughout India and paid homage at many pilgrimage sites where, according to legend, parts of Sati's corpse fell, dismembered by Vishnu, as Shiva danced wildly with it. She is worshipped particularly in Bengal, Assam and Nepal, though Hindu temples throughout India will have a shrine to the Goddess as Durga, the slayer of the buffalo demon. Shaktas generally are concerned with the power manifestations of the absolute and are characterized by rituals involving actual or visualized sex, the worship of virgins as manifestations of the Goddess and by animal sacrifice.

A broad distinction can be made between those who follow orthodox or Puranic worship of Devi and unorthodox **tantric** worship. Tantric devotees can be further divided into the **Sri Vidya** and the **Kalikula** traditions.

The *Shakta Tantras* categorize devotees according to three hierarchical and progressive dispositions: the condition of the "beast", of the "hero" and of the "divine". This classification is directly related to the use of five ritual ingredients called the five "m"s, which are regarded as an anathema to the orthodox, namely meat (*mamsa*), fish (*matsya*), wine (*madya*), parched grain (*mudra*) and sexual intercourse (*maithuna*). The "beast" worships in the "right-hand" mode using the five "m"s purely symbolically, whereas the "hero" uses the five "m"s as actual ritual ingredients; the ritual probably being performed within a circle of devotees. The heroic mode of worship with its emphasis on the erotic and the terrifying is described more in the **Kalikula** tradition than in the gentler **Sri Vidya.** The "divine" is a state of awareness which transcends different modes of worship, in which the devotee is identified with the Goddess.

Shaktas also practise *Kundalini yoga*, the awakening of *shakti* within the body. The body is visualized in a subtle form as having a central channel from the crown of the head to the region of the anus. Six or seven centres of power (*cakras*) are located along its axis, at the anus, genital organs, navel, heart, throat, between the eye-brows, and at the crown of the head. Either side of this are two further channels from the nostrils, joining the central channel at its base. The "snake power" Kundalini residing in the anal *cakra,* once awakened by yogic breathing exercises, rises up this central channel, piercing the *cakras* as she moves to finally unite with Shiva at the crown of the head. The *sadhaka* is then filled with the bliss of divine union.

Shamanism. The word "shaman" originates among the Tungus tribe of Siberia where it refers to a religious specialist whose contact with the sacred rests on ecstatic abilities. In essence shamanism (the configuration of beliefs and practices surrounding the shaman) involves a tripartite cosmology—earth, heaven and underworld—linked by a central axis, the world tree or pole. By virtue of his or her special abilities, the shaman can, in trance, travel to the different parts of the cosmos in order to contact spirits. The aid of the spirits is solicited by the shaman to aid members of the tribe in his capacities as healer of the sick, diviner, hunting magician and psychopomp. The shaman can induce trance at will, commonly with the aid of a drum, and his initiation into the profession involves an experience of death and rebirth. By extension, the term is used to describe comparable figures in cultures in other parts of the world, eg. Northern Eurasia, North and South America, Australia, Japan, and Africa.

Shamanism may predominate in the society or be peripheral to it. Strictly speaking the terms shaman and shamanism should only be applied where the characteristics outlined above are present. Where certain elements are present, but not all, it may be more appropriate to speak of medicine men, sorcerers, mediums etc.

'Medicine man' is a general term used to describe a Native American sacred specialist who cures through the use of sacred power. Although the term is often used to describe all such specialists, strictly speaking a differentiation should be made between shamans, who use trance states to contact helping spirits to cure, and medicine men (or women) who will commonly use a combination of learned knowledge and helping spirits, or in some cases, learned knowledge solely. In certain areas, medicine men may form medicine societies. The term medicine refers to both physical artifacts—herbs, fetishes, etc.—and to sacred power and knowledge.

Also to be distinguished from shamanism is spirit-possession, such as occurs eg. in various Afro-Brazilian or Afro-Caribbean cults such as **Candomblé, Convince, Pocomania** and **Shango.** In spirit-possession the spirits invade the practitioners, whereas in shamanism the specialist (shaman) seeks to enlist the aid of the spirits.)

Shamanism is undoubtedly one of the oldest forms of religious practice and is mainly characteristic of hunting societies. As such it has declined along with traditional hunting cultures. Nonetheless it survives in many areas (indeed is being revitalized in some) and its influence can be detected in some form in most religions.

In addition, Shamanism has begun to exercise an appeal in modern western societies as part of the **New Age** movement, including the **Human Potential Movement.** The practice of urban shamanism is advocated, for example, as a means by which modern urban dwellers can rediscover the sanctity of Nature and tap into the energy of the universal life-force which underlies and interconnects all forms of animate and inanimate existence. Thus it is seen as a way in which people can expand their consciousness to embrace realities which transcend normal everyday experience, yet which should not be regarded as "supernatural" since they are part of Nature. From being the province of a limited number of specialists (shamans), shamanism is being changed, in this context, to become a spiritual technique open in principle to all.

Shango. Shango, the name of the Yoruba god of thunder and lightning, is also the name given to the syncretic mix of **African traditional** and **Roman Catholic** religion found in Trinidad and Grenada. In many respects it is similar to **Candomblé** in Brazil, one variant of which is also known as Shango (Portuguese: Xangô), to **Santería** in Cuba, and numerous other forms of African–Catholic syncretism found in the Caribbean and South America in particular.

African gods (not only Shango) are identified with Catholic saints, and a four-day ritual held annually is of central importance. Prayers, drumming, dancing and singing conduce to the possession of a number of the participants by the spirit of the god recognized in that particular cult centre. There follow animal sacrifices involving for example doves, pigeons, chickens, turtles, goats or sheep. Spirits of the dead are regarded with caution, as they can trouble people. Cult leaders may be revered as healers.

Shas (Sephardi Torah Guardians' Party). (See also **Orthodox Judaism, Zionism.**) Israeli non-**Zionist,** religious, **Sephardi** political party, created to contest the 1984 general election. Shas is the largest (along with **Mafdal**) religious party in Israel and highlights the strength of Sephardi religious support and the significance of the ethnic factor in Israeli politics. Shas was founded by former members of **Agudat Israel** and sponsored by Rabbi Eleazer Schach and the former Sephardi Chief Rabbi, Obadiah Yosef. It expressed Sephardi dissatisfaction at the way their interests were pursued by the **Ashkenazi** Agudat. A major issue was the amount of government funding being used for Ashkenazi projects, other concerns include the marginalization of Sephardi concerns as reflected in that Yiddish is the official language of the Council of Torah Sages. Separate Sephardi lists had operated at the municipal level since 1983. Shas, although sharing many positions with Agudat Israel, took a broader view of its potential constituency and is less hawkish over the future of the occupied territories. Shas joined the government of National Unity (1984–1988). Unexpectedly Shas doubled its support by taking 6 Knesset (Israeli parliament) seats in 1988—Agudat gained only 5. Shas retained its 6 seats in the 1992 elections and is part of the coalition government with control of the important Interior and Absorption ministries.

Although Shas has been beset with scandals and resignations it appears to have become a stable electoral party on the Israeli political scene representing the religious voice of the Sephardi community.

Shattariya. The Shattariya is a **Sufi** order found today in the Indian sub-continent. The founder was Shaikh Bayazid Taifur Bustami who lived in Iran in the ninth cen-

tury. Shah 'Abdallah al-Shattar (d. 1485), an Iranian, introduced the order into India in the 15th century and gave it its present name. The term *shattar* can be translated as "speed". In Sufi terminology this describes practices which, for example, produce the state of mystical self-annihilation (*fana*) in the shortest possible time.

The order became popular in northern India and Bengal, but did not establish itself throughout the sub-continent. It is said originally to have attracted mainly rich men and scholars. It had close links with the Mughal court, enjoying the patronage of Babar and Humayun, though less favoured by their successors.

The Shattaris have excelled in scholarship, and produced a large number of influential mystical works, with saints of the order using pantheistic expressions to illustrate their experiences. The Shattariya is noted too for its accommodating attitude to Hindu cults, and interest in magic and the occult. Perhaps the most formative leader of the order, Saiyid Muhammad Ghawth (d. 1562), wrote on the influence of Hindu ideas on Muslim mysticism; his book *Jawahir-i Khamsa* is still used as a major guide in mystical matters.

Shaykhis. A quasi-heterodox school (also known as Kashfiya) and part of **Twelver Shi'ism**, within which many of the traditions of the **Shi'ite** theosophy of the Safavid period (1502–1722) have been continued and developed. The school was created in the early 19th century on the basis of the personal reputation and writings of an important Shi'ite theologian, Shaykh Ahmad al-Ahsai (1753–1826), an Arab who spent most of his later years in Iran. In the process of defending his master's theories from orthodox criticism, his successor, Sayyid Kazim Rashti (1798–1844), inadvertently brought a separate school into existence.

On Rashti's death, the school was split between radical millenarians who created the **Babi** sect and conservatives led by a wealthy Iranian cleric, Hajj Mulla Muhammad Karim Khan Kirmani

(1809–70). Kirmani strove to play down the heterodox elements in al-Ahsai's thought and insisted on the essential orthodoxy of the school. Leadership remained until recently in the hands of his descendants, residing in the south-eastern Iranian town of Kirman. There were also important local centres in Tabriz and Kirmanshah. Since 1979, leadership of the school has been located in southern Iraq, but the majority of adherents still live in Iran.

Shi'ism. Shi'ism is a generic term covering a variety of sectarian movements in Islam, all of which have in common some principle of hereditary succession from Muhammad's cousin and son-in-law 'Ali ibn Abi Talib (d. 661). The largest groups are the **Twelvers** (Ithna 'Asharis, or Imamis), **Isma'ilis** (with numerous subdivisions), and **Zaydis.** There have also been numerous extremist groups (*ghulat*), among which the most important survivors today are the **Nusayris, Druzes,** and **Ahl-i Haqq.** There are a few Shi'ite **Sufi** orders, including the **Ni'matullahiya** and **Dhahabiya.** Modern Twelver Shi'ism has spawned a number of heterodox movements, some of which have passed outside Islam entirely (for example **Shaykhis, Babis,** and **Bahais**). It has also given birth to a number of religio–political movements, including the **Hizbollah** and the **Hojjatiya Society.**

Shin Buddhism. A name commonly applied to the Japanese True Pure Land School or **Jodoshinshu** after its founder Shinran Shonen (1173–1262).

Shingon Risshu. A sub-group of the Japanese Buddhist **Risshu.** It has approximately 90 temples and 400,000 adherents.

Shingonshu. The major form of **tantric** Buddhism in Japan, Kukai (774–835) was the founder of this school. Shingon is based on the premise that human understanding cannot approach absolute truth. The only reliable practice, are therefore symbolic rituals; in the case of Shingon, *mantra, mudra,* and *mandala.* Dainichi Nyorai (Skt. *Mahavairocana*), from which all Buddhas and bodhisattvas emerge, is the absolute and immanent Buddha-nature pervading all phenomenal reality. When this Buddha-nature is awakened through subtle changes in consciousness prompted by the complex matrix of Shingon ritual, "enlightenment in this body" (*sokushin jobutsu*) takes place.

Shingonshu has continued to prosper throughout the centuries. This must in part be due to the centrality of Kukai's personality. He was man of remarkable talent, famous for his contribution to the arts and literature, as well as for his complete systematization of Shingon thought. His ability to curry aristocratic favour through the performance of quasi-magical rites was clearly influential. Shingon has maintained a fairly passive stance toward other Japanese religions, which has doubtless aided its survival.

Central scriptures for the sect are the *Mahavairocana* and *Vajrasekhara sutras.* Shingon's centre almost since its inception has been Mt. Koya on the Kii peninsular, still one of the most popular destinations for pilgrims in Japan. Including its various sub-sects Shingon claims around 11,000,000 adherents.

Shinrikyo. A Japanese revivalist **Shinto** group and one of the traditional 13 constituent sects of **Kyoha Shinto.**

Shinshu Honganjiha. A major sub-grouping within the Japanese Buddhist **Jodoshinshu.** It has approximately 10,000 temples and 7,000,000 adherents.

Shinshu Otani. A major sub-grouping within the Japanese Buddhist **Jodoshinshu.** It has approximately 9,000 temples and 6,000,000 adherents.

Shinshukyo. A Japanese purification movement and one of the traditional 13 constituent sects of **Kyoha Shinto.**

Shinto. Shinto, Way of the *kami* (gods), is the indigenous religion of Japan, emerging with the mythic foundation of Japan and the world through sexual and spontaneous generation by *kami*, and developing into a complex structure of rituals and institutions which have served to underpin Japanese culture throughout the centuries.

Rather than being soteriological in character, Shinto is the outward signifier of the way the Japanese identify with their environment. *Kami* are not only mythological divinities, but include all aspects of nature, agricultural activities, and spirits of the dead. The early clans would venerate their own particular ancestor *kami,* and even now certain *kami* are believed to preside over particular localities, specific groups of people, and different aspects of human life. Often it is difficult to differentiate *kami*.

Early Shinto was never defined or systematized. In fact it was not until the arrival of Buddhism in the 6th century that the word Shinto was introduced to distinguish it from the newcomer. Whilst Shinto is institutionally organized now, it has never had a doctrine as such, no system of ethics and no theology. Ritual purification and the accurate execution of devotions to *kami* (who can be malevolent, but more commonly benign) in a total affirmation of the goodness of life and fertility, provide the contours of Shinto, and its here and now concerns. Shinto has a celebratory character. Most Japanese have Shinto weddings, children have special ceremonies, and shrine festivals often take to the streets. Portable shrines shouldered by young males, in which the local *kami* is believed to be temporarily enshrined, are paraded in an often ecstatic atmosphere. Shinto exists today in three main forms: Shrine or **Jinja Shinto**, Sect or **Kyoha Shinto**, and Folk or **Minzoku Shinto.**

Shinto Shuseiha. A Confucian-oriented Japanese movement which is also one of the traditional 13 constituent sects of **Kyoha Shinto.**

Shinto Taikyo. A Japanese revivalist **Shinto** group and one of the traditional 13 constituent sects of **Kyoha Shinto.**

Shinto Taiseikyo. A Confucian-oriented Japanese movement which is also one of the traditional 13 constituent sects of **Kyoha Shinto.**

Shiromani Gurdwara Parbandhak Committee (SGPC). This committee was set up in 1920 in anticipation of the *Sikh Gurdwaras Act* of 1925 to take responsibility for the *gurdwaras* in the Punjab which would pass into Sikh control. Its activities have been extended as diversely as publishing material on Sikhism and taking a political role in Punjabi affairs. Some Sikhs, but by no means all, would regard it's the voice of Sikhism. It has 175 members who are elected every five years.

The custodians (*jathedars*) of the five historic thrones (*takhts*) of Sikh temporal power at Amritsar, Anandpur, Bhatinda, Patna and Nanded are appointed by the SGPC.

Shotokushu. A modern form of Japanese Mahayana Buddhism. Prince Shotoku (574–622CE) is considered the father of Japanese Buddhism, and is venerated as a cultural figure of great worth. In 1950 the Shotokushu seceded from the **Hossoshu,** claiming the oldest Buddhist temple, commissioned by the Prince himself, the Horyuji, as its head. Membership is around 12,000.

Shouters. This is a designation used for the **Spiritual Baptists** of Trinidad, although according to some accounts it refers to a particular variant of this in which places of worship include both an altar with a crucifix and a central pole (poteau–mitau), the latter being derived from African Fon religion. The Shouters of Trinidad are also similar in many ways to the **Shakers** of Saint Vincent.

Sri Shankaradeva Sangha. A Hindu reform movement in Assam. The Vaishnava movement in Assam owes its origin to Shankaradeva (1449–1548), whom his followers believe to be an *avatara* of Vishnu. The Sri Shankaradeva Sangha was founded in 1933, and claims today to be Assam's largest religious organization. The reforms which it introduced involve the rejection of the role of the brahmin priest, especially in funeral rites, the prohibition of worshipping any deity other than Vishnu, the breaking down of caste rules within the Sangha, and the substitution of an initiation committee for the individual initiating guru. The key scripture of the Sangha is the *Bhagavata-purana*.

Shrine Shinto. *See* **Jinja Shinto.**

Shugendo. Literally, the way (*do*) of controlling (*shu*) sacred power (*gen*), Shugendo is a Japanese religious tradition probably deriving from the life and teachings of its mysterious founder En no Gyoja (634–701?), also known as Shokaku. Master En is said to have led an ascetic life on Mt. Katsuragi, Nara Prefecture, where he developed the capacity to fly through the air and command the powers of nature. The sect was first institutionalized in the 11th century and has always remained an essentially lay organization hostile to the priestly and monastic establishment. From the 13th century, Shugendo became influenced by the cosmological thought of the Buddhist **Shingonshu** though it is now often classified as a denomination within

Tendaishu. Strictly speaking, however, Shugendo is an amalgam of many traditions including the indigenous, **Shinto**-based, respect for nature, Buddhism and **Taoism.** In 1872 Shugendo was officially abolished by government decree, in an attempt to purify Shinto from extraneous elements, though since 1945 it has been rehabilitated. At present the sect has six main shrines, 180 temples and approximately 100,000 adherents. Initiated practitioners are expected to undergo a series of severe mountain retreats and for this reason are referred to as *yamabushi*—those who sleep in the mountains.

Shuha Shinto. *See* **Kyoha Shinto.**

Shwegyin Nikaya. The second largest monastic fraternity (*gaing*) within the **Burmese Theravada** Buddhist *Sangha*. Founded as a reform movement in the mid-19th century by the abbot of the village named Shwegyin, the order now has around 50,000 ordained monks and differs from the other three fraternities mainly in its highly puritanical interpretation of monastic discipline (*vinaya*). Monks may not smoke, drink after the noon meal, nor witness popular entertainments. Despite its size, in comparison with the **Thuddama Nikaya** which comprises about 90 per cent of the total monastic population of Burma, it has been historically influential, particularly in its support for the monarchy. Its political standpoint in present day Burma is difficult to assess.

Siddha Yoga. An organization claiming great antiquity though established in recent years to promote the **Kashmir Saivite** teachings of the late Swami Muktananda. The present leader of the movement is Guru Mai, Muktananda's American translator, who succeeded him on his death in 1982. The headquarters are at Ganeshpuri, 60 miles from Bombay and there are approximately 40 centres (*ashrams*) worldwide. Siddha Yoga has established itself quite successfully in South America and there are thriving centres in Mexico, Japan and New York. The movement uses satellite links for communication between members.

Sikh Dharma of the Western Hemisphere. In 1969 Sant Harbhajan Singh Puri, also known as Yogi Bhajan, began to teach *yoga* in Los Angeles. Some Americans became attracted by his Sikh faith and within a few months the first conversions had taken place. Such western Sikhs are **Amritdhari** and, besides keeping the five Ks, both men and women wear the turban. They can be distinguished from other Sikhs by their clothing which is Punjabi and white in colour. Yogi Bhajan also teaches *kundalini yoga* at a secular university and is co-president of the World Fellowship of Religions. The movement is also known as the **Happy, Healthy and Holy Organization (3HO).**

Sikhism (Sikh Panth). Sikhism originated based missionary organization working within the **Sikh** community itself. It focusses its activities primarily on children and conducts camps in *gurdwaras*, or on school premises, at which the young learn Punjabi, music, Sikh ceremonies, history and philosophy. The Society also publishes pamphlets on aspects of Sikhism for interested non-Sikhs.

Sikhism (Sikh Panth). Sikhism originated in the Punjab region of north-west India in the early years of the 16th century CE. It has been commonplace for writers, including Sikhs, to describe the religion as a fusion or synthesis of Hindu, and Muslim ideas. Such an interpretation neglected the inspirational contribution of the Sikh Gurus themselves and was seen by most Sikhs to deny the elements of revelation and grace which lie at the heart of the message of Guru Nanak and his successors. The view that Sikhism is a form of syncretism perhaps intended to form a bridge between Hinduism and Islam is one which is almost universally rejected today.

Guru Nanak, the initiator of the Sikh movement was born in 1469 CE in the village of Talwandi (now in Pakistan and called Nankana Sahib). He worked, probably as an accountant in the service of Daulat Khan Lodi in the town of Sultanpur until his call to begin his preaching mission in 1499. This is not regarded by Sikhs as a conversion experience but a commissioning. The Guru, Sikhs believe, was born already in a state of perfection, as the result of God's will not the consequence of his own *karma*. The purpose of his life was to bring the divine word to an age which had replaced direct knowledge and experience of God with Hindu ritualism and Islamic formalism.

Guru Nanak travelled widely between 1499 and about 1521 preaching the message of one God and one humanity in which differences of caste and class, gender, and colour as well as religion were irrelevant and contrary to the divine order. In these journeys he was often accompanied by a Muslim bard named Mardana. His message, and that of the other Gurus who continued his work, was contained in devotional songs (*shabads*). These provide the content of the Sikh scriptures.

Guru Nanak taught that God is one. Though he was happy to use Hindu and Muslim names when referring to the deity he also used the term *Akal Purukh*, the Being Beyond Time or the Timeless One and held the view that God was personal though neither male nor female. God as Creator, *Karta Purukh*, is an idea which features strongly in the Guru's teachings. God is ultimately ineffable but has become manifest as Word (*shabad*). God is often, therefore, described as the *Sat Guru*, the True Guru, who is the preceptor of all human kind.

The householder (*gristhi*) stage of life was the one which Guru Nanak commended and practised. In this way he not only included people of all castes and also outcastes or untouchables in his teaching, he also made work a virtue and laid the foundations for a movement based on three principles, *nam japna, kirt karna*, and *vand chakna*. These may be translated as personal spirituality, honest work, and care for one's fellow human beings. Nanak rejected and stressed the development of the inner presence of God through meditation. This, however, should not result in a selfish piety. Guru Nanak required his disciples to come together for congregational worship and mutual support. An institution known as *langar* which he began and other Gurus developed is one which requires all Sikhs, and others who share in their worship, to eat together. Its negative purpose is to denounce the practices of some socio–religious groups who will only take food with and from members of their own fellowship; positively it affirms belief in one universal community. So as to put as few obstacles as possible in the way of participants in Sikh worship or other activities such as weddings, the food provided in *langar* is always vegetarian. A small handful of *karah parshad*, made of wholemeal flour, sugar, and ghee, prepared in an iron pan (*karaha*), hence the name, is also given to those who attend most Sikh functions. It serves the same purpose as *langar*.

It is unlikely that Guru Nanak's intention was to create another religion but by the time of his death in 1539 the movement had assumed such a size and distinctiveness that he felt it necessary to appoint a successor. In all there were 10 Gurus, the line ending in 1708 when the last declared that in future Guruship would be invested in the scripture, now known as the *Guru Granth Sahib*, and the community, the **Guru Panth**, which adheres faithfully to the teachings contained in it. This decision actually focussed attention where it had always really been, upon the message not the messenger and upon all who lived by it. Anyone who visits a *gurdwara*, as a Sikh place of worship is called, will see the devotees gathered together listening to and singing the divine Word which is manifest in the scripture which they face. Anyone, man or woman, may read from the *Guru Granth Sahib* and conduct any Sikh ceremonies. The movement is totally lay, though a professional *granthi* (literally reader), may be sometimes be appointed to conduct services and ceremonies and provide teaching.

The importance of the scripture has already been mentioned. It contains the compositions of six of the Gurus, Hindu and Muslim teachers such as Namdev, Kabir, Ravidas and Ramanand, and bards who played at the court of the fifth preceptor, Guru Arjan. Sikhs point to this as additional evidence of the inclusive nature of Sikhism. It was compiled by Guru Arjan in 1604 and revised by the 10th Guru. Guru Gobind Singh, who also gave the Sikhs the physical form by which they are best known. In 1699 he introduced a new method of initiation, no longer carried out by the Guru but by five initiated Sikhs. Members of this new family, the **Khalsa** (the Pure), were required to take certain moral vows and to wear the five Ks, five distinguishing features which in Punjabi all begin with the initial K. They are: (i) *kesh*, uncut hair, including body hair; (ii) kirpan, sword; (iii) *kaccha*, trousers, often worn in a short form as an undergarment; (iv) *kara*, steel wristlet worn on the right forearm; and (v) *kangha* (comb,)—used to keep the hair tidy and in order. Bodily hygiene is something which Sikhs emphasize strongly, whilst at the same time rejecting any belief in physical purity and pollution. Guru Nanak taught: "If the mind is unclean, it cannot be purified by worshipping stones, visiting holy places, and wandering about like an ascetic. Only one who cherishes the True Lord (in the heart) acquires honour".

Sikhs are now to be found world wide, especially in English-speaking countries. Most of them, some 13,000,000, still live in the Punjab area of India and have links with that part of the world. Punjabi is the spoken language of the community and is used in worship. The Sikh population is about 16,000,000. Britain's Sikhs number some 350–400,000, the largest group outside India.

In India itself many Sikhs, dissatisfied with promises of greater autonomy within the state, have called for the establishment of a completely independent Sikh state which they refer to as Khalistan (the land of the pure), in which the *khalsa* will rule supreme. The increasing militancy employed by some Sikh groups in attainment of these aims is a cause for concern for Hindus, moderate and non-*khalsa* (ie. **Sahajadhari Sikhs**). Jarnail Singh Bhindranwale is perhaps the most prominent militant of recent years closely associated with the **All India Sikh Students' Federation (AISSF)** and the **Damdani Taksal** religious school Bhindranwale and many of his followers lost their lives when the Indian army stormed and descrated the Golden Temple. Amritsar in June 1984. Operation Blue Star, as it was named, and the massacre of over 2,700 Sikhs in Delhi in the wake of Mrs. Indira Gandhi's assassination, have caused a deep sense of injury to almost all Sikhs. Sikh militancy therefore continues and many outrages have been committed. Such tragedy must, nevertheless, be placed against a background of rising Hindu fundamentalism.

Silva Mind Control. One of the "new religious movements" (see the essay in Part I). It has attracted several hundred thousand people in recent decades with its claims to be able to enhance problem-solving capacities, memory and health through enhanced states of awareness. A scientific aspect is introduced when it claims to teach people how to function at lower brain frequencies. It is seen by some observers as belonging to a group of **"self religions"**.

Singapore Buddhism. The dominant ideology of Singapore's collection of Indians, Malays, Sri Lankans and Chinese has been described as economic post-**Confucianism,** where learning and virtue are essential for success. Within this overall system traditional religious practice represented by *Buddhism, Taoism, Christianity* and *Hinduism* find their place.

In Singapore, as in Malaysia and Indonesia, there are several **Theravada** monasteries which have been set up under the Thai government-sponsored Phra Dhamma-duta missionary programme. It was from one such temple in Singapore that General Thanom Kittikachorn, one of Thailand's most repressive dictators, returned home as a monk in 1976 and contributed to the collapse of democratic government.

There is currently a shortage of Thai monks in Singapore, and the **Peoples' Buddhism Study Society** and the **Bodhi Society** have recently started to finance visits by monks from Thailand.

Singh Sabha Movement. The name is given to many Sikh associations and means precisely that. The term dates back to 1873 when the first "sabha" was established in Amritsar to counter the work of Christian missionaries and later the Hindu **Arya Samaj.** Its policy was to educate the Panth in its beliefs by establishing schools and colleges and producing Sikh literature. The Khalsa Colleges which are to be found in many parts of northern India owe their existence to the Singh Sabha movement.

Sino–American Buddhist Association (SABA). This eclectic yet very traditional Buddhist group was established by Tripitaka Master Hsuan Hua in 1968. The aim of the association is to provide Westerners with access to Chinese Buddhist teachings as transmitted within a valid ordination tradition. For this reason one of Hsuan Hua's first acts after founding the SABA was to send five of his American disciples to Taiwan in 1969 so they could receive the threefold ordination of Chinese tradition: novice (*sramanera*), monk (*bhiksu*) and awakening being (*bodhisattva*). Hence the Sino–American Buddhist Association is now able to provide full ordination in America for those who aspire to the monastic life.

The community (*sangha*) itself has four divisions; monks, nuns, laymen and laywomen. The monks' lives are regulated by 250 rules, the nuns' by 348. There are also nine categories of SABA membership ranging from life membership as a founding patron (i.e. one who donates $100,000) to annual student membership for $25. Membership bestows the right to attend all events organized by SABA, a newsletter and reduced prices on publications, meditation retreats and *sutra* recitations. By western standards the meditation retreats are quite austere. Participants rise at 4.00am and retire at 10.00pm. In between these times they attend lectures and language study classes as well as meditation and recitation sessions.

The Sino–American Buddhist Association offers what is, perhaps, the most traditional and disciplined version of the Buddhist lifestyle in contemporary America. In the course of spreading its message it has taken on some substantial financial commitments (including $6,000,000 for the purchase of 237 acres plus buildings that form the basis for the City of Ten Thousand Buddhas near San Francisco) and it has plans for further expansion. Should all its projects come to fruition SABA could well become one of the most influential Buddhist groups in America today.

Siv Sena. Śiv Sena (the Army of Sivaji) is a Hindu communal party of Mahārāṣtra which belongs to that region's long history of militancy. Its immediate predecessor was the Sampoorn Mahārāṣtra Samiti which transcended traditional political party lines to crystallize resistance to the perceived incursion of South Indians into Mahārāstra. Śiv Sena, founded in 1967

by Bal Thakare, had a paramilitary cast which made it very useful to the Congress Party which wished to weaken the left-wing parties then on the ascendant in Bombay. Initially active only in Bombay proper, the party soon expanded into the suburbs and to Pune, the old capital of Mahārāṣtra. After initial successes, however, the party has declined in importance, being an essentially regional phenomenon.

Siyam Nikaya. The oldest and most influential fraternity of Buddhist **Theravada** monks in Sri Lanka. It was founded in 1753 when monks from Siam (now Thailand) were invited to Sri Lanka to re-establish an authentic ordination lineage after an earlier form of monasticism had fallen into disrepute. Centred on the ancient capital of Kandy, the Siyam Nikaya once enjoyed the patronage of Sinhalese royalty and still retains considerable affluence. The Temple of the Tooth, containing an important relic of the Buddha, is administered by the fraternity. Traditionally ordination has only been possible for the landowning (*Goyigama*) caste and the Nikaya remains highly conservative. It has two principal subdivisions based on the Malwatta and Asgiriya monasteries and a highly elaborate hierarchical structure. The current number of monks overall is about 12,000.

Siyane Vipassana Bhavana Samitiya. A modern Sri Lankan lay meditation society established in the mid 1950s to promote insight (*vipassana*) meditation according to the traditions of **Theravada** Buddhism. Rather like the **Lanka Vipassana Bhavana Samitiya,** though less dependent on Burmese monks for its introduction, the society has pioneered meditational practice in a number of non-traditional ways, for instance as a means of alleviating stress. The society is popular and now trains monks as well as members of the laity. It has centres throughout the island though its headquarters remains the Kanduboda centre, established by Ven. Kahatapitiya Sumathipala soon after the inception of the movement.

Slavonic Orthodox Church. See the entry on **Russian Orthodox Church.**

Smartas. Smartas are a community of brahmins in South India who adhere to orthodox Hindu practice, maintaining caste distinctions and passing through, at least in theory, a series of four prescribed life-stages. The Smartas are so called because they follow the *smrtis,* the "remembered", non-revelatory texts of Hinduism, particularly following the Puranas in their forms of worship, while at the same time adopting the non-dualist metaphysics of **Advaita Vedanta.** Smartas are characterized by worship of five deities: Vishnu, Shiva, Durga, Surya, and Ganesha. The **Shakta** cult of the goddess Tripurasundari has been absorbed by some members of the group and worship of the Goddess's symbol the *shri cakra* is found in their temples. Although the Smartas are householders, they also practise renunciation into one of the **Dashanami** orders of Shankara.

Society for Companions of the Spirits. A Japanese new religious movement also known as **Reiyukai Kyodan.**

Society for Social Reform. The Society for Social Reform (Jam'iyat al-Islah al-Ijtima'i) was, prior to the Iraqi invasion, a powerful **Sunni** Islamist organization whose headquarters were in Kuwait, but which had branches in other Gulf states. Its views were similar in many ways to those of the **Muslim Brotherhood**, to which, according to some reports, it was linked. It was also described as enjoying the patronage of the Saudi establishment. It published an important journal, *al-*

Mujtama, organized lectures and Quran study groups, and encouraged a more Islamic lifestyle. It was active both in the student union and in the national assembly. Its current status is unclear.

Society for the Establishment of Righteousness and Harmony. A Japanese new religious movement also known as **Rissho Koseikai.**

Society of Friends (Quakers). The Religious Society of Friends of Truth was the result of an 18 year-old, George Fox, leaving his home in Leicestershire in 1643 to discover religious truth. After travelling the country talking to many preachers and spiritual counsellors he came to believe that God is in everyone, and that each person should trust his "Inward Light".

George Fox went first to the north-west and then to London sharing these views, and groups of like-minded people were established. They rejected church customs, denying the need for clergy, liturgy or sacraments. Their services consisted of silence, waiting for God to move someone, man or woman, to speak. They refused to pay church tithes. They refused to take oaths, including the Oath of Allegiance to the King. They would not remove a hat to persons of higher rank, even to a court judge. These views brought members into conflict with the authorities; many were imprisoned, some died. While justifying his beliefs in court, George Fox told the judge "You should tremble at the Word of the Lord!", which led to the popular epithet for the Friends, "The Quakers".

By 1680 it is estimated that there were 60,000 Quakers in England and Wales. However by 1800 this had fallen to only 20,000. This was partly due to massive emigration to America, particularly to the Quaker colony in Pennsylvania ("Penn's Woods") established by William Penn. King Charles II owed a substantial debt to Penn's father and in lieu of this granted Penn extensive land rights in America.

Mainly because of their refusal to take the necessary oaths, Quakers were barred from the universities. Consequently they used their gifts in other ways such as banking and industry. Quaker colleges and schools often had a special emphasis on science. As a result Quakers became eminent in a number of fields. Joseph Lister and Francis Galton in medicine, the Barclay and Lloyd families in banking and the Rowntree, Cadbury and Fry families in chocolate making.

Quakers were also pioneers in social concern. They took responsibility for the welfare and education of the workers in their factories. Perhaps the most famous reformer is Elizabeth Fry (née Gurney) who in the early part of the 19th century campaigned for improvement in prison conditions. Her brother Joseph John Gurney was active with other Quakers in the anti-slavery campaign.

In the 19th century the Society of Friends was influenced by the evangelical revival and some groups became more formal in their worship, with hymns, sermon and even sacraments, all previously rejected. However in the 20th century the trend towards silence and simplicity has returned. Women still have equal rights in worship and may be "Recorded Ministers"—members who are set aside and may be supported in full-time ministry. Quakers continue to reject formal creeds and for this reason do not belong to the **World Council of Churches.** They now number about 500,000, mostly in the USA and the UK. Church government is through the monthly meeting of members of local churches, the County Quarterly meeting and the National Yearly meeting. Through the writing of members (for instance Gerald Priestland, former BBC journalist) they have a significant influence on modern thought.

Society of Militant Clergy. The Society of Militant Clergy (Jam'iyat-i Ruhaniyun-i Mobariz; also Jame'eh-ye Ruhaniyat-e Mobarez) is an Iranian organization whose roots go back before the revolution to 1976, when a nucleus formed around Ayatollah Beheshti. Since the 1979 revolution it has been pivotal in radicalizing the traditionally conservative **Shi'ite** clerical structure and organizing support for the ruling Islamic Republican Party. When the latter was dissolved in 1987, the Society's function as a political arm of the *ulama*, endorsing candidates for elections, increased. A channel of influence for many radicals, it opposed Iran's neutrality in the Gulf conflict of 1991, denouncing the United States. However, it failed to command popular support for its stance.

Soka Gakkai. The "**Value Creating Society**", Soka Gakkai was founded in its preliminary form on Nov. 18, 1930 in Tokyo by a teacher, Makiguchi Tsunesaburo. Its religious foundations are in **Nichiren Buddhism.** Since 1952 it has been a juridically independent lay organization, related to **Nichirenshoshu.** It was originally created as a forum for the educational theories of the founder, although it is to all intents and purposes a new religious movement based on Nichiren's belief that the benefits of spiritual practice can be reaped here and now.

In 1943 Makiguchi and his associates were imprisoned for violating the Peace Preservation Law (i.e. opposing State **Shinto**). After the war Soka Gakkai grew dynamically under the controversial leaders Toda Josei (1900–1958) and Ikeda Daisaku (b. 1928) and international membership is currently approaching 16,000,000.

Soka Gakkai International (SGI) is a world-wide organization with branches in about 115 countries, including Britain (**Nichirenshoshu of the UK — NSUK**). In Japan, Soka Gakkai has a high public profile, with its impressive rallies and meetings, and extensive range of social reform programs in keeping with Nichiren's utopian ideals for the country. It has launched a campaign for world peace, and in its international capacity endorses the ideals of the United Nations, in which it plays a consultative role. It has its own education system, including Soka University, and its emphasis on conversion accounts for its wide usage of the mass media, and the production of its own daily newspaper, *Seikyo Shimbun*. Until 1970 **Komeito** (the "Clean Government Party") was the political wing of Soka Gakkai.

Soka Gakkai, in accord with Nichiren-shoshu, holds that positive social reform will take place when each individual realises the all-permeating Buddha-nature. This process has been defined as the "human revolution" and it is towards this end that all Nichiren Buddhism applies itself.

Soka Gakkai International (SGI). The international arm of **Soka Gakkai** with branches in about 115 countries.

Son. Son is the Korean version of the Chinese Buddhist meditation (*Ch'an*) school. Being Korean, it differs from its counterparts elsewhere in that it presents a unique blend of teachings and practices from various Buddhist schools. The Son tradition was taken to Korea during the unified Silla period (668–935 CE) by a monk called Pomnang who combined two Chinese traditions of Ch'an with the teachings of *The Awakening of Faith in the Mahayana* (a Chinese text ascribed by tradition to the Indian Buddhist master Ashvaghosha).

During the eighth and ninth centuries CE nine schools of Son developed. Oldest was the **Huiyang-san**, founded by a disciple of Pomnang. The others were founded by various Korean masters after their return from studying on the Chinese mainland. Each had a headquarters on a mountain site and hence they came to be known as the Nine Mountains Schools. In the late 12th century the Son master Chinul (1158–1210) developed what is recognized as a distinctively Korean version of Son: the **Chogye Chong**. This was essentially a synthesis of Nine Mountains practices with Kongan (Jap: *Koan*)techniques for culti-

vating sudden enlightenment along with the teachings of various scholastic schools that had been introduced from China.

From 1424 until the Japanese annexation of Korea in 1910 the Chogye Chong was amalgamated with two Chinese-derived schools to form a unified Son school (**Son Chong**). Throughout this period the Son was one of just two schools of Korean Buddhism, the other being the Doctrine School (**Kyo Chong**). In 1935 these two were amalgamated with the Chogye Chong.

Under the Japanese, Buddhist monks were allowed to marry and by 1935 almost all of the senior incumbents in monasteries were married. This state of affairs was, however, anathema to traditionalists. After World War II a division emerged between the **T'aego Chong** (a faction representing married monks) and the Chogye Chong. In 1954 the South Korean government supported the Chogye Chong in its attempt to control the monasteries and now only celibate monks are allowed to become abbots. At the present time about half of the 45,000 or so Korean monks and nuns are married. They serve the needs of approximately 6,000,000 Korean Buddhists.

Today, the Son Buddhists of Korea are seeking to revitalize their distinctive synthesis of doctrines and practices whilst making their tradition relevant to the needs of people living in the modern world. They emphasize education and social involvement, run retreats for the laity, operate a number of newspapers and, at the Donnguk University, are sponsoring a systematic translation of Buddhist texts into Korean. Buddhism appears to be regenerating itself in modern Korea and at the heart of that regeneration lies the distinctive synthesis of thought and practice that is Son.

Son Chong. The unified **Son** school of Korean **Zen** Buddhism, renamed **Chogye Chong** in 1935.

Soto Zen. A Japanese form of Buddhism which places great stress on meditation.

Dogen (1200–1253) brought Soto to Japan from Sung China. He, like other Kamakura period innovators, spent some time at the **Tendai** centre on Mt. Hiei. He travelled to China with Myozen, a disciple of the **Rinzai** founder, Eisai. Many sources suggest that he met with Eisai himself before his trip.

Soto puts near exclusive emphasis on the practice of *zazen,* sitting meditation. This is based on the principle that practice and attainment are essentially one and that enlightenment is not a goal which can be approached or grasped. In Dogen's words, "All existents are the Buddha nature". All sentient beings are potentially enlightened. So simply sitting in meditation, or going about one's daily tasks in accordance with the precepts and with awareness, is to live out the realisation that *samsara* and *nirvana* are not separate but totally interrelated.

In his major work, the *Shobogenzo,* Dogen sought to express the nature of the intuitive transmission of Enlightenment outside words which tend to engage the intellectual mind only (hence his suspicion of the Rinzai practice of the *koan*). His concern was to precipitate the fundamental reorientation of perception towards Enlightenment, with as little distracting paraphernalia as possible.

Dogen, more than Eisai, wanted to purify Zen practice in Japan; to separate it from Tendai and the burgeoning **Pure Land** devotion of the time, and to remove Soto from Rinzai's shadow. Some time after his return from China, he left the capital for the remote Eiheiji in Echizen (now Fukui prefecture), which was to become Soto's centre for around 200 years.

Despite Dogen's puritanism, Soto embraced many aspects of folk religion throughout its history. This was partly because membership was drawn mostly from the agrarian classes, who were attracted by its simplicity.

Like all Buddhist schools in Japan, Soto has undergone periods of repression, particularly during the Tokugawa Shogunate (1603–1867), but has emerged to be one of the largest forms of Japanese Buddhism, with over 6,000,000 adherents, its own university, Komazawa, and ample training facilities for its monks. The restored Eiheiji and the Sojiji in Yokohama are joint head temples and the priesthood numbers around 15,000.

Both Rinzai and Soto Zen have achieved a solid footing in the West, initially through the efforts of such figures as Dr. Daisetz Suzuki, Christmas Humphreys and Alan Watts, during the 1950s and '60s and more recently Dr. Irmgard Schloegl (Ven. Myokyo-ni). Zen's minimalism appears to hold particular appeal for Westerners coping with the ever expanding complexities of modern life, and the number of practice centres continues to grow both in Europe and in the United States. The **Order of Buddhist Contemplatives** is a Western, Soto-devised monastic order.

South American Traditional Religions. The total indigenous population of South America is well over 15,000,000. The majority are highland peoples such as the Quechua and Aymara of the Andes, whose total exceeds 11,000,000, while about 1,000,000 forest dwellers live in the Amazon region. All these peoples retain in varying degrees their pre-Christian religious views, many of which have been the subject of detailed studies by anthropologists and specialists in comparative religion and mythology. As in central America the contemporary situation of these peoples is bound up with their political survival, and religious and political issues are closely linked all over (see **Mesoamerican Traditional Religions**).

In Brazil the Amazonian tribes are some of the least assimilated indigenous peoples on the entire planet, continuing to hold to their way of life, including traditional religious outlook, free from European encroachment. With the development of the Amazon basin, however, this heritage is under intense threat and has led to a concerted politicization of the Amazon indians in which religious leaders have shown a strong commitment to protect and sustain their natural habitat and environment.

In 1989 an extraordinary convention took place under the auspices of Indian tribal leaders at Altamira, joined by many environmentalists and political leaders; the conference opened with a religious peace ceremony staged by the Xavante tribe from the South Amazon. The government of Brazil has since promised to review its ambitious "Plan 2010" which called for the development of virtually all the Amazon's water resources and the flooding of an area of rain forest the size of the UK.

The federation of the indigenous nationalities of Ecuador has declared itself willing to use armed struggled if the jungle regions of that country are not converted to an autonomous territory for their peoples, and Ecuador declared officially a multinational country.

Bolivia has the highest proportion of pre-Columbian religious traditions surviving, with 66 per cent of its population belonging to one of several indigenous cultures, such as the Aymara and the Quechua tribes descended from the Inca civilization. Traditions of magic, witchcraft, divination and therapeutic sorcery continue to play an important part in the lives of the impoverished descendants of Incan civilization. Among the agricultural peoples practising small-scale subsistence farming in Columbia, Bolivia and Chile, the modern-day descendants of the Incas remain closely bound up with the obligations imposed on men and women by the cycles of nature. In Peru the Sendero Luminoso (Shining Path) guerrilla movement is mostly made up of Indians from the highland regions, and the dispossession of Indian lands is one of the great motivating factors behind the unrest throughout the

region. In Chile the Mapuche people of the highlands have fallen foul of both right- and left-wing attempts at assimilation, and continue to demand autonomy.

As in Central America, spirituality is closely linked to hallucinogenic and narcotic drugs, such as cocaine, the consumption of which remains an everyday reality to the native peoples. Such practices hark back to the Incan practices in which narcotics played an important part in divination through enabling the priesthood to contact the spiritual worlds.

One of the most intriguing survivals of South American paganism is that of the Tairona culture of northern Columbia's Atlantic coast along the Sierra Nevada. There the Kogi Indians have maintained, in almost complete isolation from contact with Western civilization, the spiritual and cultural traditions of their ancestors. The Kogi comprise a microcosm of pre-Columbian spirituality of great significance, in which the priests, the Mamas, devote themselves rigorously to the concentrated development of mental and spiritual energy (*aluna*), maintaining contact with the spiritual worlds on behalf of the community as a whole, performing the function of sacred guardianship.

Attitudes to sexuality among South American peoples generally were far more full-blooded and liberal than among their Spanish and Portuguese conquerors, as the large numbers of erotic objects, such as terracotta pots and figurines, testify. In South America as in Central America it is to be hoped that recent changes towards democratization in the world at large will advance the cause of Indian emancipation, both spiritual and political, and there are signs that this is indeed the case. The large UN conference on the Environment and Development in mid-1992 in Brazil marked a further watershed in the recognition of indigenous rights throughout the region. Native peoples have a vital role to play in the quest for patterns of sustainable development. The contemporary world has therefore, not surprisingly, seen a growing interest, reflected in publications and research, in the indigenous spirituality of South America.

Southern Baptists. The Southern Baptists are a denomination of the American branch of **Baptists.** The split between North and South in America (strictly, in the USA) came in 1845 when the board of the American Baptist Home Mission Society decreed that they could not appoint as a missionary anyone owning slaves. This led to a decision that it would be best if a separate and independent Southern Baptist Convention should be formed, consisting of 14 southern states who stated that slaveholders were no less eligible than others to serve as missionaries. During the American Civil War the Southern Baptist Convention publicly supported the Confederacy and afterwards voted to continue to function independently. Until World War II membership was confined to the southern states, but since then it has expanded across the USA.

Three factors distinguish the Southern Baptist Convention from other Baptist churches. Their theology is conservative and they speak out strongly on ethical issues. They have opposed gambling, pornography, homosexuality, violence on television, and abortion. They have also led campaigns against racial discrimination, anti-Semitism and religious persecution. The second feature is a deep concern for evangelism and missionary work: they have the largest number of missionaries of all the American denominations, and make full use of modern technology and communication techniques. Finally the stewardship of talents, and especially of money, is a central belief. This leads to high levels of giving by members of affiliated churches, ensuring the effectiveness of their work.

The evangelist Billy Graham comes from the Southern Baptist tradition and his methods and message reflect the above attitudes. Former president Jimmy Carter is also a Southern Baptist, and his election is a reminder of the fact that the Southern Baptists are now the largest American Protestant denomination.

Spanda. Literally "vibration". One of the three philosophical schools of **Kashmir Saivism** principally concerned with the exposition of relevations received by Vasugupta (9th–10th century) from the Hindu god Shiva.

Spiritual Baptists. This Afro–Protestant cult in Trinidad—also known as the Shouters—is similar to **Revival Zion** in Jamaica. Baptism by full immersion in a river or the sea occurs, but services do not feature the drumming which is prominent in Revival Zion and numerous other Afro–Caribbean religions (for instance **Kumina** and **Shango**). Moreover, the spirit possession that occurs involves, in most cases, the Holy Spirit only, and not the further range of spirits found in Revival Zion.

Spiritualists. Although spiritual mediums existed in Bible times (King Saul visited a medium at Endor to consult the dead prophet Samuel, I Sam 28) modern Spiritualists go back to 1848 following the experiences of the family of John D. Fox in New York State, USA. After hearing mysterious tappings in their house his teenage daughter Kate set up a code of communication with the spirit believed to be causing the phenomenon—a man who had been murdered in the house. As an adult Kate became a medium in the Spiritualist Church.

Interest in the spirit world spread quickly. Spiritualism was brought to England in 1853 by David Richmond, starting in Yorkshire but soon spreading south. At one time the movement claimed 10,000,000 believers, including such notables as the author of the Sherlock Holmes detective stories, Sir Arthur Conan Doyle and the eminent Scientist, Sir Oliver Lodge. A famous Victorian medium D. D. Hume demonstrated his powers in front of a gathering of eminent scientists and convinced many.

Spiritualists believe that God is Infinite Intelligence. They reject the deity of Christ but believe he was a medium. A medium is someone who is sensitive to vibrations from the "spirit world", where the disembodied spirits of the dead are believed to exist. He mediates with this spirit world at seances via a specific spirit called a "control". The means of communication vary, and may include a change of voice or automatic writing. Mediums can also specialize in clairvoyance (the knowledge of future or hidden events) or healing.

The largest group of adherents is in the USA where the International General Association of Spiritualists has a membership of over 100,000. However there have been a number of splits in the movement. In the United Kingdom the Greater World Christian Spirtualist League has about 30,000 members, although the beliefs of Spiritualists have never been accepted by mainstream Christianity. The Spirtualists National Union has a similar membership, but is open to non-Christians. Spiritualists were prominent in the Natural Law Party which put up candidates nationally (but unsuccessfully) in the 1992 General Election. Their most well-known medium is Doris Stokes, who has written several books. Worldwide membership is about 500,000.

Sri Lankan Dharmadhuta Society. Founded in 1952 as an offshoot of the **World Fellowship of Buddhists,** this organization is involved in **Theravada** missionary activity around the world.

Sri Lankan Theravada. Theravada Buddhism was almost certainly brought to Sri Lanka by Mahinda, the missionary son of the converted Indian emperor Asoka Maurya,

some time in the 3rd century BCE. Mahinda succeeded in converting the king of the time and ordained the first monks. His sister subsequently brought an ordination lineage for nuns. Sri Lanka has consequently been a Buddhist country for over 2,000 years, at least as far as the majority Sinhalese population is concerned. The Pali canon (*tripitaka*) was committed to writing on the island between 29–17 BCE. One of the most famous Buddhist writers, Buddhaghosa, moved to Sri Lanka from northern India in the 5th century to undertake the translation of Sinhala commentaries into Pali. While there he composed his classic treatise on the spiritual life the *Path of Purification* (*Visuddhimagga*). From the 10th century we find evidence for the rise of an ascetic forest monk tradition which survives down to the present day. Divisions such as these can be traced back to about the beginnings of the Christian era and we know of royal attempts to reform the *sangha* in the 12th century. The three monastic fraternities (*nikayas*) today (i.e. **Siyam, Amarapura** and **Maha-nikayas**), though only dating back to the 18th century, are heirs to some of these disputes. The influence of the *sangha* has ebbed and flowed across the centuries though periods of stagnation have generally picked up from a fresh impetus supplied by fellow Theravadins in Thailand or Burma. In the last hundred years, or so, Sri Lankan Theravada has undergone many changes. Millenial movements have been relatively common, and **Theosophy** has played a significant role in a number of developments. Similarly, lay meditation and therapy of the type offered by the **Siyane Vipassana Bhavana Samitiya** has grown in prominence. The appearance of this-worldly movements such as the developmentally-oriented **Sarvodaya Sramadana** has been another feature of Buddhist modernism in the country while sections of the Theravada *sangha* still regard themselves as the bulwark of national identity in a longstanding and bitter dispute with Tamil separatists in the north. Recently an ordination lineage for nuns has established itself again in the country after an absence of almost

1,000 years and, although not universally approved, the number of women coming forward for ordination is growing.

Sri Vaishnavas. One of the oldest Vaishnava *sampradayas*. Its name is derived from the fact that its members worship not only Vishnu, but also his consorts, chiefly Sri/Lakshmi, the goddess of prosperity. The first teacher of the *sampradaya* was the South Indian Nathamuni, who lived at about the end of the 10th century CE. He collected together the hymns of the Alvars, the poet-saints of Tamil Nadu who lived from the sixth century to the ninth century CE. They are thought to have derived their inspiration from Vishnu himself. The theology of the Sri Vaishnavas was given a philosophical basis by Ramanuja (c.1017–c.1137) and his philosophy is known as "qualified non-dualism" (**Visistadvaita**) because it posits Brahman alone (identified with Vishnu) as the supreme reality, yet gives to individual selves and the material world a sufficient degree of dependent reality to allow *bhakti* to take place. Ramanuja used the analogy of the soul's relation to the body to express the relationship of Brahman to the world and his idea of *bhakti* is akin to that of the *Bhagavad-gita*: continuous meditation upon Visnu as the supreme reality.

There are two sub-sects, the **Vatakalai** ("northern culture") and **Tenkalai** ("southern culture"), which are divided not only by their respective emphases upon Sanskrit or Tamil origins, but also by their theories regarding divine grace. Following their teacher Vedanta Deshika, the **Vatakalai** believe that human beings make some contribution to their salvation, whereas the **Tenkalai** teacher Pillai Lokacarya held that salvation depends entirely upon God. The Tenkalai call these two positions the "cat-hold" and the "monkey-hold" schools, for they say that the Vatakalai believe that the soul must cling to God as a baby monkey clings to its mother, whereas in their own view the soul is like a kitten which is picked up by its mother without making any effort of its own. The Sri Vaishnavas today are most numerous in Tamil Nadu, but are found in the other south Indian states also. They have 108 major temples, the most famous of which are those of Tirupati and Shrirangam.

Sri Vidya. A south Indian version of Hindu **Tantricism**. The movement worships the beautiful and gentle goddess Tripurasundari especially in the form of the geometrical design, the Sri Cakra or Sri Yantra which can be found in the major Shaiva temples of south India, and in the 15-syllable *mantra* (called the Sri Vidya). Tripurasunari is worshipped externally in the temple where offerings of flowers, incense and vegetarian food are made to her, and internally where the practitioner identifies himself in his private worship and meditation with the Sri Vidya, the Sri Cakra, his guru and the goddess. Liberation is becoming omniscient and omnipotent in realizing the identity of these forms. The metaphysical basis of this tradition is the **Pratyabhijna** monism of **Kashmir Saivism** though the tradition has been adopted by the **Smarta** brahmans of south India who follow the philosophical system of **Sankara**.

Srimad Rajchandra (Raychandbai Mehta). A **Jaina** layman (1867–1901) well-known for his asceticism, who refused to become a monk or align himself with any particular sect. On his own admission, **Mahatma Gandhi** was personally influenced by him. Rajchandra's followers now constitute a sub-sect, called the **Kavi Panth**, within Jainism, propagating his biography, as well as translating and publishing his writings. They have, to date, established 46 temples, including two outside India.

St Thomas Christians. *See* Syro–Indian Churches.

Sthanakavasis. Literally "dwellers in halls" also known as **Dhundiyas.** A 17th century development from an earlier "reforming" sub-sect of the **Svetambara Jainas.** They came to assert that there is no authority for image worship in the canonical texts and so have no temple ritual. They acknowledge only 31 canonical texts as authentic, as opposed to the 45 accepted by other Svetambaras.

Subud. Subud—Susila Buddhi Dharma (or Susila Budi Darma) in full—is the only one of the numerous **kebatinan** movements that have proliferated in Indonesia this century to have become truly international. Founded in 1947, its origins lie in a revelation which is claimed to have occurred to Muhammad Subuh Sumohadiwidjojo—later known as Bapak ("Father") Subuh—in 1932, although a sense of spiritual awakening had begun already in 1925, and had been followed by extensive contacts with a teacher of the **Naqshabandiya Sufi** order.

The movement's emphasis is on *latihan*, practice, rather than theoretical teachings, although an authoritative summary of the latter is contained in the book which originated with Bapak Subuh in the 1940s and whose title is also that of the movement, *Susila Budi Darma* ('Susila'—right living according to God's will, 'Budi'—an inner force inherent in human nature, and 'Darma'—submission to God).

Subud advocates its form of spiritual practice as supportive of, and complementary to, the spirituality of other religions, rather than claiming to be a religion itself. For this reason it in 1979 withdrew from the umbrella *kebatinan* organization in Indonesia (which at that time was named the Sekretariat Kerjasama **Kepercayaan**).

Since the mid-1950s, however, Subud has become well-known outside Indonesia, including in Europe and America. Bapak Subuh (1901–87) was invited to England from Indonesia in 1956 by **Gurdjieff's** chief English disciple John Bennett, and initially attracted many of Gurdjieff's and Ouspensky's students. His system, consisting mainly of *latihan,* performed twice a week, involves letting the "divine power" take over the body and mind. Effects can include movement, dance, prayer and catharsis, often leading to increased well-being, and sometimes profound spiritual changes. Membership is open to anyone over 17, and is said to be about 10,000 worldwide (1,000 in Britain). There is no fee, but a voluntary donation of three per cent of one's income is suggested. Its enterprises include various social welfare projects and businesses worldwide.

Sufism. Sufis are traditionally described as the mystics of Islam, but this is in important respects misleading: Sufism covers quite a variety of beliefs and practices.

In early Islam, Sufis were pious Muslims who reacted to what they saw as the corruption bred by worldly success by practising austerities, and they marked their more ascetic lifestyle by wearing garments of wool—*suf*—hence Sufi.

Their spiritual concerns led them to focus on the inner life; and ever more elaborate theories of the possible states of the soul, and how to achieve them, were developed. Methods varied, but included singing and chanting as well as types of meditation. Interpretation of the goal varied too. The famous (or notorious) al-Hallaj apparently claimed identity with God, and was crucified in 922 CE for blasphemy. That kind of monistic mysticism was henceforth to be avoided, and Sufism had to keep within the bounds of Islamic law and traditional belief. Due to a considerable extent to the work of al-Ghazali (d. 1111), it secured an accepted place within Islam on those conditions (although they were not always adhered to: a notable exception was the monism of the Spaniard Ibn al-'Arabi, 1165–1240, with his theory of the "unity of all existence", *wahdat al-wujud*). It is in respect of this core development that Sufis are properly known as Muslim mystics. They also emphasized the love of God rather than his justice.

The methods of prayer and meditation were handed down from master to pupils. This was often facilitated by groups of Sufis living together in communities. In this way the Sufi orders emerged. Particular traditions, e.g. of *sama*—music performed for spiritual purposes—and forms of *dhikr* (or *zikr*)—rhythmic repetition, aloud or silently, of the names of God in order to attain ecstasy—were passed down from a given spiritual leader to succeeding generations of disciples who venerated his memory and gave him their personal allegiance. Such a chain of spiritual allegiance is known as a *silsila*. The founder is referred to as a *shaikh*—a term also used, along with others (*murshid, pir*), for subsequent spiritual guides within the orders at any particular time. Followers may be known as *murids*, and Sufis in general are sometimes called dervishes, as reflected in a label such as Whirling Dervishes which highlights a distinctive feature of the ritual of individual orders, in this case the **Mawlawiya**.

The number of orders has proliferated enormously. The vast majority are **Sunni**, but a few, like the **Ni'matullahiya**, are **Shi'ite**. Some, like the **Naqshabandiya** and the **Qadiriya**, are international in scope; others are regional, like the **Chishtiya, Suhrawardiya** and **Shattariya** which have their focus in the Indian sub-continent, the **Darqawiya** and **Tijaniya** in Africa, or the **Shadhiliya** more particularly in North Africa and the Middle East; others are relatively local, like the **Hamadsha** in Morocco or the **Kubrawiya** in Turkmenistan, or else associated with certain countries in particular, like the **Muridiya** and Senegal, the **Khatmiya** and Sudan, or the **Sanusiya** and Libya.

The followers or disciples of a shaikh lived in, or visited and travelled between, Sufi centres which often received endowments from wealthy patrons and in some cases became elaborate complexes known as *zawiyas*. These might contain a mosque, college, library, refectory, and a lodging house for travellers, servants, and students. A more basic centre may be known as a *tekke, ribat* or *khanaqah*.

The tombs of the founders of orders in particular, but also of subsequent venerated *shaikhs*, were of major importance. They were likely to become the centre of a *zawiya* complex, and centres of pilgrimage. The anniversary of the death of the *shaikh*, the *'urs*, became the occasion of a great gathering of people, and a major festival. This is true still today, for example in the Mawlawiya, the **Bektashiya**, the Chishtiya, the **Badawiya**, and the **Madariya**. A host of other festivals and pilgrimages is associated with Sufism too: part of what some observers label "popular" or "folk" Islam as opposed to the "orthodox" Islam of Quran and *ulama*.

Here Sufism again became controversial. A very great number of tombs of holy men, usually referred to in English as saints, became the focus of shrine cults. Visitors implored the intercession of the saint on their behalf, or his miraculous intervention, whether for healing or some form of worldly success. Simply by touching his tomb the devotee would acquire some of his special sacred power, *baraka*. This is now a long way from mysticism. In North and West Africa the term **maraboutism** has been used in relation to this phenomenon, but it is an extremely widespread one, being common, say, in Pakistan and India, but also in the Muslim states of the former USSR. It incurred the intense hostility of the **Wahhabis**, and in Saudi Arabia the once common Sufi shrines have all been destroyed. In South Asia, attitudes to the saints remain a subject of often bitter controversy between the **Barelvis** and the **Deobandis**.

The vast majority of orders have remained "with the law" (*ba-shar'*), as stipulated centuries ago by al-Ghazali. A few, e.g. the **Malangs**, have developed "without the law" (*bi-shar'*), and their members may in truth be Muslim in name alone: one is here on the very fringe of Islam and Sufism alike.

The fortunes of the orders have fluctuated a good deal, but they (i.e. the *ba-shar* ones) have been enormously influential in a variety of ways, sometimes through the education or social services they have provided, sometimes politically, and very often in the spreading of the faith—even if not always in a form approved of by the *ulama*, or modern reformers (e.g. the **Salafiya**), or today's Islamists (e.g. the **Muslim Brotherhood** and the **Jama'at-i Islami**).

Suhrawardiya. The Suhrawardiya is a **Sufi** order found in Afghanistan and the Indian sub-continent. Its roots go back to Shaikh Abu Najib 'Abdul Qahir Suhrawardi (d. 1168) who taught for a time at the Madrasa Nizamiya in Baghdad before cutting himself off from society to live on the banks of the Tigris. His nephew, Abu Hafs 'Umar Suhrawardi (1145–1234), is regarded as the actual founder of the order, having a reputation as a great teacher of Sufism.

The Suhrawardiya was introduced into north India in the 13th century, and the main credit for its successful establishment there goes back to Shaikh Baha ud-din Zakariya, who died at Multan, in present-day Pakistan, in 1267. Multan remains the centre of the order to this day. The Suhrawardis have flourished particularly in the Punjab, Sind and Gujarat, and the tombs of their saints remain centres of pilgrimage.

The Suhrawardiya, in contrast to their great rivals the **Chishtiya,** maintained close connections with the rulers of the day. They stated that in this way they acted as mediators between the people and the court, and that they were able to reform the character of the rulers. Saints of the order were active in politics and accepted posts within the government. They also accepted cash and land offerings. At one stage during the 15th century the order

actually emerged as the ruling dynasty in the Punjab. In Gujarat, the Suhrawardiya helped legitimize the provincial rulers by closely working together with them. The demise of their patrons, however, meant also the decline of the order: their survival depended on the success of their political allies. Nevertheless, they remain firmly associated still today with the higher status social groupings of Ashraf.

There were several *ba-shar'* (with the shari'a) and *bi-shar'* (without the shari'a) offshoots of the Suhrawardiya. An important sub-division is the Jalaliya which developed in the 13th century. The *silsilas* (lines of discipleship) of the Jalali Suhrawardiya go back to Saiyid Jalal ud-din Mir Surkh-posh of Bukhara (d. 1291), whose tomb is to be found in Uch in the Punjab. The Jalali *silsilas* spread to other parts of North India and the Deccan. By the early 19th century many Jalalis had accepted **Shi'ite** practices, for instance, the cursing of the **Sunni** caliphs. Some of the Jalalis moved outside the Shari'a and favoured the use of drugs.

Sukyo Mahikari. A sub-sect of the Japanese religious movement **Sekai Mahikari Bunmei Kyodan,** established in 1974 by the daughter of the founder of the original group.

Sulaymanis. The Sulaymanis are a branch of the **Musta'li** sect of **Isma'ili Shi'ism** within Islam. Along with the other branch, the **Daudis,** they represent an essentially conservative form of Isma'ilism as developed originally in Egypt under the Fatimid dynasty.

At the end of the 11th century, a split occurred within Isma'ilism between the **Nizaris** and the Musta'lis. The latter transferred their centre from Egypt to the Yemen. The religious leadership was invested in a Da'i Mutlaq. By the early 17th century, the Indian Musta'li community (the **Bohoras**) having eclipsed the Yemeni community in importance, the Da'i transferred to Gujarat. However, there followed a further split, resulting in two lines of Da'is, one in India, the other in the Yemen, representing the Daudis and the Sulaymanis respectively, the two branches of the Musta'lis to emerge from the split.

The division revolved, indeed, around the leadership issue. In 1591 two rivals emerged, Daud ibn Qutb Shah and Sulayman ibn Hasan. Those who supported the former as Da'i became known as the Daudis, while those who supported the latter became known as the Sulaymanis. Most of the Yemeni community became Sulaymanis, and the Sulaymani Da'is resided in the Yemen from 1677 until 1936. At this time, however, with the incorporation (in 1934) of the traditional centre of Sulaymani authority into the kingdom of Saudi Arabia, with its strict **Wahhabi** ethos, the Sulaymani Da'i transferred his residence to India, where he had in any case traditionally had a representative in order to maintain contact with his followers among the Bohoras.

Both Da'is are now resident in India, where both are also called by the title Mulla-ji. Yet most Sulaymanis are probably still to be found in the Yemen, and in the Najran area of Saudi Arabia, their traditional centre, where however their religious activities are now restricted. The Indian community, with its centre in Baroda in western India, has remained small and scattered, though containing highly influential members (including the first Muslim President of the Indian National Congress).

Süleymancis. A Turkish Islamic renewal group founded by Süleyman Hilmi Tunahan (1888–1959), and similar in some ways to the **Nurcus.** A **Sufi** sheikh of the Nakşibendi order (**Naqshabandiya**), Süleyman opposed the Kemalist policy of establishing the Turkish state on a secular basis, and was arrested in 1933 for setting up Quranic schools as rivals to the state schools. Attempted state control of Islam in Turkey through a Directorate of Religious Affairs (Diyanet Isleri Baskanligi)

was a particular target of criticism, and remains so amongst his followers today. Inded Süleymancis, in expressing their disapproval of the secular state, refuse employment in government service. Nor will they become teachers in state schools, though they are active in running hostels for schoolchildren. In their quest for new members, their strategy resembles that of the Nurcus.

The Süleymancis, with a centre in Köln, are particularly influential among the Turkish community in Germany (being in this respect the envy of rival groups like the Nurcular and **Milli Görüs**), and this has led Diyanet to step up its opposition to the movement, which it currently denounces as heretical. The Suleymancis are also represented, in Islamic Cultural Centres, in most western European countries. In Turkey they have been the object of criticism, not only by Diyanet, but also by the **Alevis.**

Sumarah. *Sumarah*, which roughly means "total surrender to God", is one of the numerous **kebatinan** movements which have proliferated in Indonesia this century. Its founder, Sukinohartono (also known as Pak Kino, or simply Sukino), may have been connected early on with the founder of another kebatinan organization, **Subud.**

Sukino (1897–1971) claimed a series of revelatory experiences beginning in August 1935 and extending over two years. He was taken through nine spiritual planes, culminating in an experience of union with God, but also including visions of Muhammad and Christ. He felt himself to have been commissioned to guide others towards *sumarah*, complete and absolute surrender to God.

Sumarah's estimated 10,000 followers are found mainly among East and Central Javanese villagers, but also include some Chinese. The leadership is largely urban middle-class.

Summit Lighthouse. This was the original name of the movement currently known as the **Church Universal and Triumphant**.

Sunists. One of the two major sects within the modern Taiwanese **Unity Society.**

Sunnism. Sunnis are variously described as mainstream or orthodox Muslims. They form the overwhelming majority of all Muslims. The designation Sunni is based on the word *sunna* meaning the path set forth by Muhammad. This path is contained in the Quran, and in the authoritative collections of hadith—the reports of the sayings and actions of the Prophet. The shari'a, the religious law, is widely regarded as normative too. Sunnis recognize four schools of law, or four rites, as they are also known: the **Maliki, Hanafi, Shafi'i** and **Hanbali.**

Sunnis are defined negatively as not being **Shi'ites** (or **Ibadis**). However, they recognize Shi'ites as being Muslim, which they do not do with regard to members of the **Ahmadiya.**

Most of the numerous **sufi** orders that have developed within Islam are Sunni orders, but some Shi'ite ones also exist, so Sufism transcends the Sunni–Shi'ite distinction rather than forming a third category alongside the other two.

Within Sunnism a number of different movements and schools of thought are to be found. Of considerable significance are the **Wahhabis** of Saudi Arabia because of their trusteeship of the historic cities of Mecca and Medina. Among South Asian Muslims two major groups are the **Barelvis** and the **Deobandis**, but there are also the **Ahl-i Hadith** and the **Ahl-i Quran**, while the **Tablighi Jama'at** is of wider appeal internationally.

The resurgence of Islam in recent years undoubtedly owes much to the revolution in Iran, a Shi'ite country, but it has certainly seen a proliferation of religio–political organizations in the Sunni world too—as well as vigorous activity by older-established ones such as the **Muslim Brotherhood** and the **Jama'at-i Islami**. The label "fundamentalist" is often used in this connection, but is not terribly satisfactory. The attitude to scripture that it characterizes is supposed to be held by all Muslims, not just the so-called fundamentalist ones; alternatively put, it is not their attitude to scripture that distinguishes the Muslim fundamentalists. In many cases it is their attitude to the *shari'a*, but this is not uniform either. Amongst Muslims themselves they are increasingly referred to as Islamists, a usage adopted here. The meaning remains vague—like many of their programmes—but it serves to pick out those religio–political organizations which aspire to establish an Islamic state as a means of transforming Muslim society. And outside Iran, most Islamists are Sunnis.

Supreme Assembly for the Islamic Revolution in Iraq (SAIRI). The Supreme Assembly (or Council) for the Islamic Revolution in Iraq (al-Majlis al A'la li'l Thawra al-Islamiya fi'l-Iraq) was founded in 1982 in Tehran as an umbrella organization for the various **Shi'ite** opposition organizations in Iraq, but also functions as a parallel organization in its own right. Like the leadership of the associated **Da'wa Party**, its leaders tend to be drawn from students of Ayatollah Muhammad Baqir al-Sadr of Najaf. Its supreme leader, Ayatollah Muhammad Bakir al-Hakim, is the son of the late Grand Ayatollah Muhsin al-Hakim, one of the most distinguished religious leaders of Najaf. He is also regarded as Iran's preferred replacement for Saddam Hussein as Iraqi head of state.

Iranian financial support for the movement is considerable. It recruits among Iraqi exiles and prisoners of war in Iran, where it also enjoys some civilian support. It has its own unit in the Iranian army, the Iraqi Revolutionary Guard, and engages in political, cultural and social work in a manner similar to al-Da'wa, but on a larger scale. The extent of its support within Iraq is not known.

A related organization — perhaps an extension of it — was founded in 1980 by the leader's younger brother Abd al-Aziz al Hakim. This is called al-Mujahidun.

It concentrates on recruiting 'pure souls', members aged between 10 and 25, who proudly claim to be suicide squads.

In the Shi'ite uprising in Iraq after the Gulf War, SAIRI forces were active, and at one point Ayatollah al-Hakim appeared to be directing fighting in Basra. Subsequent developments are currently unclear.

Svetambara Jainas. "White-clad" **Jainas** — one of the two major sects of Jainism so-called because their ascetics wear white robes. The practice of nudity has always been regarded as optional for Svetambara monks who, unlike the **Digambaras**, consider that women are capable of the same spiritual and ascetic attainments as men. The fact that nuns are clothed presents no obstacle to liberation. Indeed, according to the Svetambara (but not the Digambara) account, the 19th *tirthankara*, Malli, was a woman. They have an extensive canonical literature, and a very large body of commentarial and philosophical texts in classical and vernacular languages.

The majority of Svetambaras have been, and remain, **Murtipujakas** or "image worshippers". That is to say, lay religious practice is characterized by temple worship: the making of offerings and other devotional practices in the presence of images of the *tirthankaras* and their attendant deities.

Outside the rainy season, monks and nuns separately lead itinerant lives in small groups under the overall direction of an *acarya* or teacher. They beg food and water from householders two or three times daily, taking the alms away in small pots.

After the Muslim invasions, various "reforming" sects arose within the Svetambara community. One line of reform led, in the 17th century, to the formation of the **Sthanakavasis** ("dwellers in halls"), who came to assert that the canonical texts do not sanction image worship. Consequently, they took (and take) no part in temple ritual. A further division within this group led to the formation, in the 18th century, of the **Terapanthis.** In 1948, under the leadership of the monk, Acarya Tulsi, Terapanthis began the **Anuvrat movement** with the purpose of spreading reformulated Jain values to all communities. Recently, an ex-Svetambara ascetic, Chitrabhanu, has acquired a following outside India, establishing a Jain meditation centre in the USA.

Today Svetambaras are especially influential in north-east India (Gujarat, Rajasthan and the Panjab). The ascetic community comprises approximately 4,400 nuns and 1,650 monks.

Swami Narayan Hindu Mission. The worldwide missionary arm of the **Swaminarayan** movement. It is particularly active in Britain and north America.

Swaminarayans. The Hindu followers of the ascetic Sahajanand (1781–1830) who came to be regarded as a manifestation of the Supreme God and thus given the name Swami Narayan. There are perhaps 5,000,000 members of this movement, mostly living in Gujarat, but there are members in other parts of India, especially in large urban centres, and in East Africa, the United Kingdom and the USA. The **Swaminarayan Hindu Mission** acts as an international umbrella organization.

Swami Narayan was born near Ayodhya in Uttar Pradesh, but spent most of his life in Gujarat. At the age of 20 he became the leader of an ascetic order which, in the next 30 years, he turned into a well-organized group made up of both ascetics and householder families. He was happy, in his lifetime, to be seen in a mythic framework as an *avatara* of the Supreme God. In other ways he is one of the earliest Hindu reformers of the modern age: he opposed female infanticide and the practice of *sati* (the self-immolation of a widow upon her husband's funeral pyre) and was in favour of the remarriage of younger widows.

The chief Swaminarayan temples are in Gujarat at Vadtal and Ahmedabad. The scriptures of the movement (along with some mainstream scriptures such as the *Vedas*, the *Vedanta-sutra,* the *Bhagavad-gita* and the *Bhagavata-purana*) consist of Swami Narayan's writings and sermons (for instance the *Shikshapatri,* his rules for his followers' conduct, and the *Lekh,* a document which sets out the two administrative divisions for his movement in Gujarat). Spiritual guidance is undertaken by ascetics, but the overall leadership and control of practical affairs is in the hands of a householder, a descendant of one of the two nephews whom Swami Narayan chose as his successors.

The Vaishnava character of the movement manifests itself in three ways. One is that Swami Narayan is often identified with Krishna. Another is that the pattern of daily worship of the Swaminarayan temples is closely modelled upon that of the **Vallabha-sampradaya.** Thirdly, Swami Narayan saw himself as firmly within the philosophical tradition of Ramanuja's **Visistadvaita,** even though he was prepared to modify this in some ways.

The lifestyle of the Swaminarayan movement is puritanical. Men and women are rigidly separated in worship, and ascetics must be particularly careful to avoid any contact whatsoever with women. There is an insistence upon charitable works, social concern and high moral standards.

Since Swami Narayan's time there have been some schisms among his followers. The most important schismatic group is the **Akshar Purushottam Sanstha,** whose members reverence one of Swami Narayan's first disciples, Gunatitanand, along with Swami Narayan himself. Gunatitanand is said to be the *akshar,* the abode in human form of the Supreme Person, and therefore an appropriate object of worship together with the Supreme Person.

Swedenborgianism. Emanuel Swedenborg (1688–1772), a Swedish scientist who developed a dominant interest in religion, became concerned to expound the hidden meaning of scripture and to communicate his own mystical/supernatural/visionary experiences. According to his philosophy, the spirits of the dead, located in two groups with characteristics roughly corresponding to heaven and hell respectively, jointly constitute Maximus Homo, a huge human being. He judged Christ to be the highest form of humanity, but his views are not in general in line with Christian belief. He established the New Church, which for a time became a flourishing worldwide movement. It still has a number of congregations in various parts of the world, and Swedenborgianism is seen as influencing the contemporary **New Age** movement (e.g. by Peter Clarke in the essay on New Religious Movements in Part I).

Synagogue Council of America. Founded in 1926 as an umbrella body representing the major rabbinical and/or synagogue organizations in America. The Council consists of the **Rabbinical Council of America** and **Union of Orthodox Jewish Congregations of America** (Orthodox); **Rabbinical Assembly** and **United Synagogue of America** (Conservative) and **Central Conference of American Rabbis** and **Hebrew Union College** (Reform). The Council's work has been, in the main, to fight prejudice, particularly anti-semitism and to develop inter-religious contacts. In recent years the Council has been under considerable pressure as the boundary lines between its constituent groups have hardened.

Syrian Jacobite Church (Oriental Orthodox). Also known as the "Syrian Orthodox Church", the Syrian Jacobite Church is one of three main traditions among the **Oriental Orthodox** Churches. It derives directly from the monophysite majority within the original Patriarchal Church of Antioch which in the fifth century rejected the authority of the Council of Chalcedon and split off from the mainstream Church. The term "Jacobite" comes from the monk,

Jacob Baradaeus, who in the sixth century renewed the monophysite tradition in Syria and rescued the Church from absorption into the Byzantine Church. Its adherents once included almost all the Christians native to Syria and western Mesopotamia (Iraq), but a large proportion of this population later converted to Islam. Now living in predominantly Muslim countries, the Syrian Jacobite minority suffers from restrictions and insecurities unlikely to diminish in the face of nationalistic and fundamentalist Islam.

Heading the Church is a Patriarch of Antioch who now lives in Homs (ancient Edessa) in Syria, though for several centuries the patriarch lived near Mardin in Turkey. The liturgy follows the West Syrian (Antiochene) Liturgy of St. James, which now combines Syriac with Arabic. Its members are to be found in Syria, Iraq and elsewhere in the Middle East, numbering around 200,000. The Church also claims jurisdiction over Jacobite Christians living in North and South America (50,000) and in Southern India (see **Syro–Indian Churches**).

In addition to the Syrian Jacobite Church there are a number of distinct Uniate (Roman Catholic rite) Churches with a history and presence in Syria, most notably the Chaldean Church, which follows the East Syrian rite (Syriac); the **Melkite** Church, which originated with those Christians in Syria, Palestine and Egypt who rejected monophysitism and which follows the Byzantine rite in Arabic; and the **Maronite** Church, which uses the West Syrian Liturgy and which is the only Uniate Church with no counterpart in the Byzantine or Oriental traditions.

Syro–Indian Churches. Since at least the fifth century, and possibly much earlier, there has been a community of Christians on the Malabar coast of South West India (Kerala State). This community, probably established by Syrian missionaries, traditionally trace their origin to the missionary activity of St. Thomas the Apostle. Also known as the Malabar Christians, or St. Thomas Christians, they have had a complex history and now exist in at least five distinct groups.

Originally the community seems to have followed the beliefs of the **Nestorians** and maintained ecclesiastical contacts with the hierarchy in Iraq. Following the Portuguese colonization of South India in the 16th century, they repudiated their Nestorianism and joined themselves to the **Roman Catholic** Church, but in the following century undue pressure to adopt Western customs and usages alienated the community, which in 1653 broke with Rome. In 1662 the majority were persuaded to renew their union with Rome, while the remainder, prevented from rejoining the Nestorians, joined themselves to the **Syrian Jacobite** Church. In 1874, within the Roman Catholic group, a small minority split off from the Catholics to re-establish links with the Nestorians; these are the Mellusians, so named after Bishop Mello, their original leader.

In the twentieth century continuing disputes among the Syrian Jacobites produced new groupings. Around 1910 a split developed between those accepting the jurisdiction of the patriarch of Antioch and those placing themselves under their own locally elected catholicos. Protestant and in particular Anglican influence produced a small minority of Reformed Jacobites, who have appropriated the title "Mar Thoma" (St. Thomas) Christians and who in recent years have been associated with the ecumenically inspired Church of South India. In 1930 a further group of Jacobites became reunited with Rome, this time retaining their Jacobite traditions: these are the Malankarese Uniates (Malankara being the old name for Malabar).

Thus there are now five distinct groups of Churches: (i) the original Malabar Catholics, numbering around 1,500,000, who use a Romanized version of the East Syrian Liturgy of Addai and Mari (originally used by the Nestorians); (ii) a Jacobite (Oriental Orthodox) community, who use the West Syrian (or Antiochene) Liturgy, and who number around 500,000; (iii) the second Catholic group, the Malankarese Uniates, who also use the Antiochene liturgy, but translated into the vernacular Malayalam language. They number about 125,000; (iv) the nominally Nestorian Mellusians, now numbering only a few thousand; and (v) various Protestant Churches.

T

T'aego Chong. A Japanese influenced school of Korean Buddhism which argues that monks should be allowed to marry. In 1954 the South Korean government decided against the T'aego Chong in their dispute with the traditionalist **Chogye Chong** and now only celibate monks are permitted to become abbots though ordinary monks are still allowed to marry.

Tablighi Jama'at. Tablighi Jama'at, or "Missionary Society", which is also known as the Tahrik-i Iman (Faith Movement) and the Dini Dawat (Religious Mission), is probably the most popular reform movement in the Islamic world today. With the **Jama'at-i Islami** it is one of the two great Islamic movements to emerge from South Asia in the 20th century. The founder was Maulana Muhammad Ilyas (1885–1944), who came out of the **Deobandi** tradition. Dissatisfied by the Deobandi focus on those who were literate, he aimed to take the message of Islamic reform to the masses. His followers were required to adopt the following practices: (i) inculcating missionary spirit; (ii) acquiring and transmitting Islamic knowledge; (iii) enjoining what is right and forbidding what is wrong; and (iv) working together in mutual love.

In executing their mission members of the Tabligh go on tour in groups. They wear a specific uniform (a beard, Muslim cap, a long Indian shirt and trousers cut off above the ankles), and preach both door by door and in the local mosques. Their methods bear comparison to those of the **Salvation Army** of the Christian tradition. The movement is notable for its total focus on the renewal of faith, for its prohibition on the involvement of politics in their mission, for its avoidance of all religious controversy, and for its following of Islamic law as set out in the medieval law books. Since the death of Muhammad Ilyas, the Tabligh has spread throughout Asia, Africa and North America. In Europe it has had most success in France, Belgium and Britain, where its main centre is in Dewsbury, Yorkshire.

Tahrik-i Iman. Tahrik-i Iman, or Faith Movement, is an alternative name for the Indian—and now international—Muslim reform movement, the **Tablighi Jama'at.**

Taizé. This **interdenominational** religious community began in September 1940 when a 25-year-old Swiss theology student, Roger Schutz, bought a house in the French village of Taizé. At first he lived there alone, helping refugees on their way to safety, but the German occupation made it necessary for him to return to Switzerland. In 1944 he came back with two like-minded friends and in 1949 a group of seven "brothers" committed themselves to a life of community in celibacy at a service in the Taizé village church, which they had received permission to use as a chapel.

The community was from its foundation non-denominational and includes brothers from all traditions including **Roman Catholic.** The daily routine is organized around three times of Common Prayer when the brothers join together for worship, often in white prayer robes. They have always worked to support themselves, initially in farming or their own profession (one of the first brothers was a doctor); nowadays in printing, pottery and enamels. Since the early 1960s young people have come to Taizé; as many as 5,000 may be staying at any one time, living mostly in tents. They are given food, washing facilities etc. but above all the opportunity (which is not optional) to join in a life of Bible study, prayer and a sharing of ideas. In 1962 the Church of Reconciliation was designed by Brother Denis, an architect, and built by German volunteers on the Taizé community site. Its rear wall can be taken out and a tent added so that up to 6,000 people can be accommodated at one service.

The brother have always rejected any tendency to become a separate denomination. Visitors are encouraged to remain in their own denominational tradition but to take back the Taizé ideas of love, trust and openness to God. As well as the writings of Brother Roger and others (for example Max Thurian and Brother Leonard) the music of Taizé (composed by Jacques Berthier) is known all over the world and evokes the peace and tranquility of the Taizé rule. Each song is short, two or four lines, usually based on a biblical text or from one of the great spiritual writers such as St. Teresa. It is chanted many times so that the mind becomes immersed in the meaning not the words. Musical texture is given by a cantor or a second choir singing a contrasting melody with complimentary words or by an instrumental *obbligato*. Many different languages are used, including Latin, reflecting the many nationalities who visit Taizé.

Taizé has been influential both in the church and, indirectly, in politics. Brother Roger was a friend of Pope John XXIII and Taizé brothers attended the Second Vatican Council. In 1986 Pope John Paul II visited Taizé. The brothers have also been active in the **World Council of Churches,** exploring ways, both practical and theological, of bringing denominations together. Each year five-day meetings are organized by the brothers in a European capital, which young people from all over the continent attend. With the easing of East–West tension it has been possible for meetings to be held in former Communist countries, with many hundreds of visitors from the West attending. In 1985 Brother Roger met the Secretary-General of the United Nations, J. Pérez de Cuéllar to encourage the United Nations to become a "catalyst of trust" between nations.

There are perhaps 100 Brothers, some living at Taizé, others in "fraternities" among the poor in Third World countries. However, because many thousands of people travel to Taizé each year, the influence of the community is profound in all branches of the church and throughout the world.

al-Takfir wa'l-Hijra. See page 79.

Takadaha. A significant sub-group of the Japanese Buddhist **Jodoshinshu.** It has about 600 temples and 250,000 adherents.

Tak Kaau. This is the Cantonese version of the Chinese new religious movement **De Jiao.**

Taklung Kagyudpa. Smallest of the four surviving **Kagyudpa** schools of **Tibetan Buddhism,** it was founded by Taklung Tangpa Tashi Pal (1142–1210), a student of Phagmodrupa (1101–1170), the leading disciple of Gampopa whose students founded so many branches of the Kagyudpa tradition. The Taklung Kagyudpas had their headquarters at Taklung Tang in Central Tibet, and were famous for their strong emphasis on monastic purity. They had another famous monastery at Riwoche, in East Tibet, where all the different Buddhist traditions were studied in different colleges. Leadership of the Taklung Kagyudpa passed within Taklung Tangpa's Ragasha family, usually from uncle to nephew, until the **Gelugpas** forcibly annexed Taklung in the 17th century, depriving it of its estates and disinheriting the Ragasha family, replacing them with a system of reincarnating abbots. The Taklungpas are beginning to re-establish themselves in exile in India, under the Shabdrung Rinpoche based in Sikkim, but are not yet very active in the West.

Taklungpas. *See* **Taklung Kagyudpa.**

Talaeh al-Fidaa. This Tunisian "comman-does of sacrifice" organization achieved some prominence in 1992 with the major trial of over 100 alleged members of the clandestine network running parallel to the other major trial of over 170 members of the banned **Hizb al-Nahda**. The Talaeh al-Fidaa is alleged to have been a separate Islamist organization that was later incorporated into al-Nahda as its military wing.

Tambor de Mina. One of the names used in the Maranhão region of Brazil for the **Afro–American spiritist** movement **Candomblé**.

Tantrics. Tantrism is a tradition within Hinduism which looks to the scriptural authority of the *Tantras* (composed 400–800 CE) as opposed to the Vedas of or-thodox Hinduism. Tantric ideas, images and practices pervade Hinduism, but one who accepts the authority of the Tantras seeks liberation and enjoyment through initiation by a Tantric *guru* into a school (*sampradaya*) and lineage. While many *Tantras* are **Shakta** in orientation there is not always a clear distinction between **Shaiva** and **Shakta** texts. There are also **Vaishnava** and **Jain** *Tantras* and a large body of Buddhist *Tantras*, translated into Tibetan, of the *Vajrayana* tradition.

Perhaps the most characteristic feature of tantric traditions is that a female force or power called Shakti is integral to their idea of deity. The absolute is often conceived and represented as Shiva in union with Shakti who, as it were, gives him life. Within the universe a polarity exists between Shiva and Shakti which is resolved or unified at liberation, though in Shakta traditions, Shakti is not subordinated to Shiva. She may take gentle or ferocious forms and these latter manifestations often demand blood sacrifice in contrast to the "pure" Hindu gods who accept only vegetarian offerings. Various centres of Goddess

worship in India are places of pilgrimage for tantrics.

Three broad categories of tantrics might therefore be identified. Firstly at a village, low-caste level there is popular worship of tantric deities, usually female, ministered to by low-caste priests. Such cults will be concerned with possession and exorcism. Secondly there is private worship of Tantric deities by high caste, usually Brahmin, householder Hindus who have been initiated into a tantric tradition. Such a tantric might be quite orthodox but accept, on top of his Vedic obligations, the ritual obligations of his tantric lineage. He thereby fits the formula quoted by a 13th century tantric author, Jayaratha, that in the outer social world one should behave as an orthodox Hindu, externally as a Shaiva, but privately or internally one is a **Kaula,** (a tantric). A third group is that of the tantric ascetics such as the **Aghoris,** who live outside of the householder's world, perhaps in cremation grounds, practising tantric yoga and imitating their terrifying Lord.

The Tantric householder will perform rituals and *yoga* designed to awaken the Shakti within the body called Kundalini. Such rituals might involve the purifica-tion of the body through its visualized destruction; the construction of a divine body by the use of magical formulae or *mantras,* the internal or mental worship of the deity; and finally external worship involving the offering of incense, flowers and food. This rite will be accompanied by the repetition of *mantras* and possibly by the use of five ritual ingredients (the five "m"s), namely wine (*madya*), meat (*mamsa*), fish (*matsya*), parched grain (*mudra*), perceived as an aphrodisiac, and caste-free sexual intercourse (*maithuna*). Alcohol, non-vegetarian food and sex outside of the constraints of marriage and caste, are taboos for orthodox brahmins. By a "right-hand" Tantric these ingredients are substituted by other acceptable ingredients, such as vegetables for meat, meditation for sex, while for a "left-hand" tantric they are taken literally. It is these ritual practices which have given tantrics a reputation of immorality among high caste Hindus. The extent to which a Tantric householder will take part in sexual rites varies. Many Nepalese tantrics, for example, do not perform these rites but simply read the appropriate passage in the Sanskrit ritual manual.

Liberation is not barred to women nor to low-castes in Tantrism and there have been female tantric *gurus*. However at a practical level, the role of women is generally subordinated to men and images of the divine as female, so central to Tantra, are nevertheless male images.

Tantrics can be found mainly in Nepal, Bengal and Assam and there are respectable tantric traditions in south India. For example, the **Sri Vidya,** stripped of its hard tantric elements has been adopted by the **Shankaracaryas.**

Taranapanthis. Also known as **Samaiya-panthis,** a sub-sect of the **Digambara Jainas,** who oppose outward religious practices and concentrate on their sacred texts.

Taro cult. A spiritist movement in Papua New Guinea. It arose in 1914 when a prophetic figure, Buninia, following a visionary experience of his dead father's spirit, developed rites aimed at increasing the taro crops. Spirit possession, communal meals and ecstatic musical gatherings for singing and dancing are prominent features.

Tayibis. The **Musta'lis,** the smaller of the two main surviving branches of **Isma'ili Shi'ism,** are sometimes referred to as the Tayibis (or Tayibiya). The name derives from that of a putative grandson of al-Musta'li called al-Tayib, who acquired significance following the assassination of his father al-Amir in 1130. Either he or one of his descendants functions as an *imam* figure in Musta'li belief.

Tendai Jimonshu. A prominent sect within the Japanese Buddhist **Tendaishu.** It currently has approximately 400,000 adherents.

Tendaishu. The Chinese *T'ien T'ai* tradition was introduced to Japan by Saicho (767–822 CE), not only marking an epochal change in Japanese Buddhism, but also laying the foundations for almost all future Buddhist developments. Highly prestigious, partly due to its proximity to the new capital (modern Kyoto), the Enryakuji complex on Mt. Hiei became its centre, and at its height housed 30,000 monks in 3,000 temples.

Tendai embraced a wide range of rituals and practices and scholarship in other schools, including **Zen** and **Pure land,** was undertaken on the mountain. Its eclecticism, however, was underpinned by a consciousness that the last phase of the *dharma,* in which the teachings of Sakyamuni Buddha would be inoperable due to the degenerate nature of humanity was imminent. This was held in tension with a belief that all sentient beings are capable of enlightenment. Tendai's great influence in the Heian period (794–1160 CE) provided the foundation for the development of *Mahayana* Buddhism in Japan. The Lotus Sutra is a central text for the school, although almost all the *Mahayana sutras* (brought from China by Saicho) are studied and venerated. Tendai is a monastic order, and practices are ascetic and meditative, directed towards the great pantheon of Buddhas and Bodhisattvas.

Tendai's support came from the aristocracy, so with their fall, the sect suffered greatly. Also violence and schisms, one in particular in the 9th century when Enchin founded the esoteric **Tendai Jimonshu,** have plagued Tendai's early history. Including all the splinter sects, there are now 5,000,000 Tendai believers, and ascetics still inhabit Mt. Hiei.

Tenkalai. Literally "southern culture". A sub-sect of the south Indian **Sri Vaishnava** school.

Tenrikyo. A Japanese new religious movement, also known as the **Religion of Heavenly Wisdom,** Tenrikyo is one of the 13 sects of **Kyoha Shinto** and places great emphasis on healing through faith. Founded by Nakayama Miki (1798–1887), a farmer's wife and miracle worker, the movement today has about 3,000,000 followers, 17,000 churches and 20,000 mission stations worldwide. Nakayama taught a monotheistic and highly mythological version of **Shinto** which stressed that sickness (*mijo*) is the result of acts (*hokori*) which contradict the divine will of God the Parent, who is also known as Tenri O no Mikoto—the Lord of Heavenly Reason. From the age of 41 she regularly underwent possession by *kami* and in this condition she wrote the two principal scriptures of the sect. She is also said to have identified the site of the original birthplace of man. Iburi Izo (1833–1907) took over the leadership of Tenrikyo on the death of Nakayama and it is he who laid down the present structure of the church.

The twin aims of Tenrikyo are to deliver from suffering and to prepare the path for the establishment of a "perfect divine kingdom". The movement concerns itself with the observance of domestic rather than state values, perhaps as a result of its early history of persecution, and stresses the virtues of loyalty, charity, obligation and gratitude. Shrine building is regarded as an important duty and great emphasis is placed on sacred dance, most notably in the central rite known as the "salvation dance service".

Terapanthis. A name with two applications: (i) a sub-sect of the **Digambara Jainas,** characterized by a restrained form of temple worship and the rejection of non-mendicants as leaders, and (ii) a sub-sect of the **Svetambara Jainas** which broke away from the **Sthanakavasis** in the 18th century. Their current leader, Acarya Tulsi began the **Anuvrat movement** in 1948 with the intention of making Jain values accessible to the whole of society.

Terma. "Spiritual Treasures". Tibetan Buddhism has highly complex and strictly institutionalized systems of ongoing scriptural revelation, closely modelled on those used to produce India's *Mahayana sutras*, though in this case intricately combined with specifically tantric systems for recovering spiritual treasures, or Terma, as described in early Sanskrit writings. **Nyingmapas** are Tibet's Terma specialists, revealing innumerable scriptures for themselves and many for the other traditions too; but all schools have produced some treasure revealers, called *Tertons*. Sacred objects of all kinds can also be discovered. Several Tertons are presently active, some even revealing new sacred texts during visits to the West. Famous Tertons include the Fifth Dalai Lama (1617–1682) and Jigme Lingpa (1729–1798).

Thai Theravada. Thailand's ability to avoid colonization during the last two centuries has been due primarily to two kings, Mongkut (1804–68) and Chulalongkorn (1868–1910). Both played a major part in reforming Buddhism to accommodate modernist influences to enable it to become a source of spiritual and ethical well-being.

Although Mongkut and Chulalongkorn inherited the respect and power ascribed by mainland South–East Asian Buddhist monarchs as successors of Asoka Maurya (the ideal Buddhist emperor of India), they rejected the accompanying cosmology according to which the king, as universal monarch, occupies the centremost position in a three-decker universe. Heaven and hell, gods and demons, were interpreted not so much as places and vehicles of reward and punishment, but as states of mind.

Mongkut's detailed familiarity with Buddhism during his period as a monk enabled him to question many Thai Buddhist practises which were incompatible with the Pali canon. He re-ordained according to the strict and somewhat puritanical Mon tradition and effectively founded a new branch of the Sangha, known as the **Dhammayutika Nikaya** ("the branch of those who adhere to the Dhamma"). The older group subsequently became known as **Mahanikaya** ("the great branch").

The **Dhammayut** part of the Sangha gained influence among the educated élite and was paralleled in Cambodia, where a separate patriarch was eventually appointed for each branch. In Thailand both groups remained under a single Sangharaja and were governed by a council made up of senior representatives of each branch, known as the Maha Thera Sama Kom. Dhammayut temples (or *wats*) exemplify some of Thai Buddhism's finest architecture, and include the Wat Bovorniwes in Bangkok, which houses Mahamakut Buddhist University and the **Phra Dhammaduta** missionary programme, that sends monks to other countries. Its nearby Mahanikaya equivalent, the Wat Mahathat, houses Mahachulalongkorn Buddhist University, which in recent years has pioneered development work among its up-country monks who ordain at an early age partly to secure a good education, ultimately migrating to Bangkok to obtain a degree.

King Chulalongkorn continued his father's reforms, centralizing the Sangha under government supervision, and setting up educational establishments such as the university which bears his name. Though the absolute monarchy was abolished in 1932, monarchs continued to play a major role in providing stability in times of crisis.

During recent decades lay Buddhists have organized themselves into a variety of groups. The **Buddhist Association of Thailand** came into being in 1934 with the aims of encouraging the study and practice of Buddhism and the consequent promotion of social welfare work and public service. In 1950 the **Young Buddhist Association of Thailand** was founded with

similar objectives among young people. By 1970 there were 73 provincial Buddhist associations affiliated to the Buddhist Association of Thailand, while their Young Buddhist counterparts numbered 44. By 1984 this had risen to 54.

The World Federation of Buddhists was set up in 1940 as an international organization to promote Buddhist causes and realise Buddhist goals. At its ninth general conference in 1969 it was decided that the permanent headquarters of the Federation should be located in Thailand.

The centralization of the Thai Sangha has not prevented it from encompassing a wide variety of viewpoints. Politically, Phra Kittiwudho's anti-communist stance represents one end of the spectrum, whereas leftist monks were obliged to take refuge during the repressive military *coups* of the mid-1970s. Sulak Sivaraksa, a leading lay intellectual and social critic, is representative of the latter.

From a much less political point of view Buddhadasa Bhikkhu (or Putatat, as he is known to most Thais) represents a progressive reformist approach which reinterprets traditional Buddhist doctrines in a practical and ethical manner which appeals especially to professional lay Buddhists and the younger scholar monks. According to Putatat rebirth refers not so much to existence beyond this life as to our moment-to-moment transformation as we progress via the Noble Eightfold Path and the Precepts from a condition of egocentredness towards selflessness. Ironically, though, most Thais continue to believe in a variety of spirits ranging from the *winyan* (essentially "soul") to different sorts of *phii*, which inhabit the small spirit houses to be seen in most streets.

Thammakaai Religious Foundation. A this-worldly Thai Buddhist movement founded in 1970 by Phra Thammachayo (1944–), an economics graduate and abbot of Wat Thammakai in the northern outskirts of Bangkok. His deputy, Phra Thattachiiwo is well-known for driving his Mercedes on the traditional Buddhist morning alms round. The movement indulges in an open display of wealth and uses the media in a sophisticated manner to obtain funds. It invests heavily in property, land, tourism and oil and was responsible for one of Thailand's more recent financial scandals, the "Chamoi chit fund", which collapsed in 1986. It is said that Wat Thammakai itself needs about $600,000 per month in order to maintain its overheads. Thammachayo himself receives some support from senior monks of the conservative **Mahanikay.** He teaches a form of lay asceticism adapted from the Thai forest monk tradition and places great emphasis on a meditational method in which a crystal ball is visualized at the base of the stomach. This is said to represent the *dhamma*-body of the Buddha. Monks within the order are, distinctively, ordained for life and are in general very well educated. General Aathik Kamlang-ek, the well-known ex-Commander-in-Chief of the Army, sacked for financial irregularities in 1986, is a prominent lay-follower.

Thammayutika Nikaya. Also known as the Thammayut or **Dhammayut,** this Theravada monastic fraternity controls 1,502 of the more than 28,000 monasteries in Thailand. Founded in the late 19th century as a reformed group within the *Sangha* by King Mongkut, a monk of 27 years standing, the Thammayut adheres to a strict interpretation of monastic discipline (*vinaya*). Despite its size, in comparison with its rival—the **Mahanikay**—the Thammayut exercises a disproportionate influence in Buddhist and national affairs. This is in part due to the way the order has been used by royal circles to increase the power of the monarchy. Senior members of the royal family still act as patrons and, despite the abolition of absolute monarchy in 1932, the order is still strongly establishment-oriented. With the rise in influence of the Mahanikay after 1932, the Thammayut has tended to align

itself with the authoritarian side of the Thai political spectrum and has maintained close links with the military. The Thammayut and Mahanikay have few differences over matters of Buddhist doctrine though the former supports the ancient and ascetic forest monk tradition more forcefully. Many monks of this tradition are popularly believed to possess supernatural powers of prophecy and healing. The Thammayut was found in Cambodia, where it was known as **Thomayat,** until its suppression by the Heng Samrin government in the 1970s.

Theosophical Society. The Theosophical Society was founded in America in 1875 by Helena Blavatsky (1831–91) and Henry S. Olcott (1832–1907), and later established its headquarters in Madras, India. Blavatsky claimed to have received the wisdom of the ages from Hidden Masters in Tibet, with whom she was in psychic communication. The teaching is a synthesis of Hindu and Buddhist mysticism with Western **occultism.** The society's motto is "There is no religion higher than truth", and it was the first movement to claim that all religions have the same goal. Although disparaged by some as a charlatan (for her claimed psychic powers), Blavatsky is generally acknowledged as the first Westerner to bring Indian religion and philosophy to the West in an accessible form, thus paving the way for later seekers. Theosophy also popularized the now widespread twin doctrines of *karma* and reincarnation.

Several schismatic offshoots occurred, including one in 1891 led by one of the original founders, William Q. Judge in Pasadena, California, and known today as the Theosophical Society International; and also the United Lodge of Theosophists, founded in the USA in 1909. Its best known offshoot, however, was **Anthroposophy;** and Blavatsky's successors, including Annie Besant, discovered and trained **Krishnamurti.**

The Theosophical Society is still going strong though with a predominantly elderly membership. Although it claims that esoteric wisdom is revealed only to the spiritual élite, many of its programmes are open to the public. Membership is open to anyone in sympathy with its objectives, although they need two members as sponsors.

Theravada Buddhism. The term Theravada is used for the distinct Buddhist movement which emerged from a less well-defined group known as the *Sthaviras* (i.e. elders) in India in the 3rd century before the Christian era. The term means "way of the elders". Theravada Buddhism is based on the Pali canon, known as the *Tipitaka*, and stresses the central role of the *arhat* (derived from *ari*, or enemy, and *ham* meaning to kill: i.e. the one who slays the warring passions), rather than the *bodhisattva*, which is taken up in **Mahayana** Buddhism.

Our knowledge of the history of Buddhism following the Buddha's death is based on the early scriptures (of which the Pali canon forms a significant part), the characteristics of the many sects which transmitted, and sometimes distorted, early versions of those scriptures, and information about the early Buddhist councils. Of these the first three were held at Rajagaha (very early), Vesali (100 years later), and Pataliputra (in 236 BCE, at the end of Asoka's reign).

The Indian emperor, Asoka Maurya, came to the throne probably in 268 BCE. He became a Buddhist following a bloody war in Kalinga; thereafter he set an example of virtuous kingship which became an important ideal for subsequent Hindu and Buddhist leaders (especially in mainland south-east Asia). Asoka's son, Mahinda, took Buddhism to Sri Lanka, where the Pali scriptures were written down and Theravada Buddhism began to take on a distinctive form.

As Buddhism declined in India, **Sri Lankan** (Sinhalese) **Theravada** Buddhists came to think of their island as especially blessed by the Buddha, and a legend grew up that he had actually visited there. They incorporated certain Hindu and Mahayana ideas into their tradition (e.g. the building of shrines to gods inside temples and the use of Buddha statues), but otherwise Theravada Buddhism remained largely unchanged for many centuries. Monarch and *sangha* co-operated together in a symbiotic relationship which was eventually imitated in Thailand, Cambodia, Burma and elsewhere.

Early Buddhism had emphasized meditation and careful adherence to the Pali scriptures. In time public festivals such as Vesak, the full moon in May, celebrating the Buddha's birth, enlightenment and decease, were incorporated into the tradition.

Monks and nuns made merit for the laity, and the Buddha statues became objects of personal piety. When Sinhalese Buddhism was transmitted to south-east Asia in the early centuries of the Christian era, these meritorious and pietistic elements were reinforced by existing animist and brahmanistic practices (e.g. the veneration of *nats* in Burma).

Theravada monasticism was regulated by the detailed Vinaya rules of the Pali canon. Since the *sangha* is based on a republican form of government established in the Buddha's time it is possible in theory, though difficult in practice, for the rules to be changed. In Thailand, where King Mongkut based his 19th century Sangha reforms on strict adherence to the Vinaya, conservative influences have remained strong, though in recent years monks have managed to take on new and progressive development roles within the framework of their monastic tradition. Orders of nuns have lapsed in many places, though there are moves in some Theravada countries (e.g. Thailand) to restore them.

Theravada Buddhism is to be found in almost all parts of the world. Its adherents tend either to be nationals from Buddhist countries or European and north Americans who are attracted by meditation and the Theravada Buddhist way of life.

Thomayat. A Cambodian **Theravada** Buddhist monastic fraternity closely aligned to the Thai **Thammayutika Nikaya** and monarchical in outlook. It suffered accordingly under the Khmer Rouge- and Vietnamese-backed governments, but with the return of Prince Sihanouk to Cambodia in 1991 its influence may recover to some extent.

Three HO. *See* **Sikh Dharma of the Western Hemisphere.**

Thuddama Nikaya. The largest monastic fraternity (*gaing*) within the **Burmese Theravada** Buddhist *Sangha* with approximately 250,000 ordained monks. Founded in the late 18th century by an ecclesiastical council called by King Bodawpaya, the order takes a fairly flexible view of monastic discipline in contrast to the more puritanical **Shwegyin Nikaya.**

Tibetan Buddhism. Buddhism initially arrived in Tibet, under royal patronage, in the 8th century. The first monastery, at Samye, was founded in 779. It seems that, at this early period, both Indian and Chinese forms of Buddhism were taught though, as the tradition developed, the former came to predominate. Tibetan Buddhism consequently shares many of the features of the Buddhism taught and practised in the great monastic universities of northern India at the end of the first millenium CE. In particular, **Tantric** and scholastic versions of the *Mahayana* are widely found. Older, unreformed schools like the **Nyingmapas** have tended to stress the former while the **Gelugpas** place great emphasis on scholarly activity. Despite these differences, the Tantric element is integral to all schools of Tibetan Buddhism.

After China's 1950s' invasion of Tibet, about 100,000 Tibetans, including the Dalai Lama and many other leading lamas, escaped Tibet's sealed borders into India, Nepal and Bhutan. While attempting to re-establish the shattered remnants of their tradition in precarious South Asian refugee camps, they witnessed in horror the determined attempts of China's Red Guards to systematically eradicate every trace of Buddhist culture within Tibet.

In India their focal point is the 14th Dalai Lama, Tenzin Gyatso (b. 1935), who set up his headquarters in the Himalayan foothills north-west of Delhi in 1960. There are, however, other Tibetan Buddhist groups in India, concentrated mainly in the Himalayan and sub-Himalayan parts of the north-east, especially in the border areas of Arunachal Pradesh. At Tawang, for instance, there is a large **Gelugpa** monastery. The effect of Buddhism on the local tribal peoples appears to have been minimal.

With Tibetan Buddhism thus on the verge of extinction, the lamas in exile began teaching interested Westerners in all earnestness, first in India, then abroad. Often stateless persons, refugee lamas even now sometimes face serious travel restrictions, but by 1967 the first Western Tibetan Buddhist centre, Samye Ling, had opened in Scotland. Twenty-five years later, there are hundreds of Tibetan Buddhist centres and monasteries throughout Europe, North America, and Australasia, as well as some in East and South-East Asia. Smaller groups exist in Latin America and Southern Africa. Non-Tibetans are successfully becoming monks, nuns, and Buddhist scholars, as well as practising the strictly enclosed three- and twelve-year retreats demanded of serious meditators. The translation of Tibetan texts has become a flood, both within and outside the universities, while many Tibetan lamas, especially younger ones, can now speak some English.

The first Western incarnate lama, the **Karma Kagyudpa** school's Sangye Nyenpa, was recognized in the 1970s, son of an

American poet and an English artist. Since then several others have been recognized, including a woman. Many of Tibetan Buddhism's leading lamas now regularly visit the West, some even living there permanently. This development is largely decentralized, each lama or tradition operating with total autonomy. Most of the Tibetan traditions have by now had some success in the West, but the Gelugpa and the Karma Kagyudpa schools have had the biggest initial impact.

Buddhism in present-day Tibet has, to a very limited extent, been revived since the early 1980s with the restoration of some important monasteries such as Drepung and Tashilhunpo under the auspices of the **Chinese Buddhist Association (CBA),** though monastic numbers remain very small.

Tien Te Sheng Hui. This is a new religious movement found among Chinese communities in East and South East Asia. It is known in English as the **Heavenly Virtue Church**.

Tijaniya. The Tijaniya is a **Sufi** order which was founded by Ahmad al-Tijani (1737–1815) in Algeria in the 1780s. After facing problems with the authorities, al-Tijani was forced to seek refuge with the sultan of Morocco, and remained in Fez from 1798 until his death. He claimed to have experienced a daylight vision of the Prophet Muhammad, who informed him that he was the "seal of the saints" and taught him the litanies of his new Tijani order. He then left previous Sufi orders to which he had been attached and instructed his followers to do likewise, committing themselves solely to the Tijaniya. Regarding his own position, al-Tijani held that he was the vice-regent of God in all affairs of the universe, and that the world was preserved in existence by his spirituality. He taught that, due to the Prophet's fa-

vour towards them, Tijanis did not have to forsake the world, but should work, preferably in trade or agriculture, and not make themselves a burden on the community by depending on charity. In common with other Sufi reformers of the 18th–19th centuries, he stressed the need to enforce the Holy Law (Shari'a) and also the central importance of seeking to draw near to the Prophet, whose presence might be felt within the Sufi gathering. He trained his followers to perform the *dhikr* (recollection of God) quietly, without the loud chanting characteristic of many orders. Like the **Wahhabis,** al-Tijani was opposed to cults of both living and dead saints, although in his own case he claimed to have been granted the power to intercede even for unbelievers, and his tomb became a place of visitation.

In West Africa the Tijaniya was propagated by al-Hajj 'Umar Tal (1794–1864), who preached and led a *jihad* to establish the order in Guinea, Senegal and Mali. Membership of the order was open to all, including women and slaves.

At present the Tijaniya is a widespread and well-established order in North and West Africa, and is also to be found in the Sudan. In Turkey, its adherents attracted attention in the 1950s by an active campaign against secularist state policies, resulting in the gaoling of leading activists and the apparent disappearance of the order. It is no longer found in the Balkans, but some members are still active in Indonesia.

Tikhonite Church. An alternative label for the underground **True Orthodox Church** in the former USSR. Patriarch Tikhon was the leader of the **Russian Orthodox Church** at the time of the Bolshevik revolution, and the underground church claim that it is they who are the true successors of the church at that time, not the Moscow Patriarchate which usurped the legitimate power of Patriarch Tikhon in 1927.

Tokumitsukyo. A Japanese new religious movement now subsumed within **PL Kyodan.**

Tonghak. Literally, "eastern learning", a Korean socio–political religious movement hostile to the influence of the European powers and in particular to **Sohak,** ie. western learning. The manifesto of the movement, the *Tonghak Scripture,* was written by Ch'oe Suum (1824–1864) who is regarded as the inspiration for the populist Tonghak revolution of 1894. Under Tonghak leadership the Korea of the early 20th century moved gradually into the modern era and writings of the movement predict that Korea will ultimately become the most powerful nation in the world. Tonghak thought undergirds the religious teachings of **Chondo-Gyo.**

Torah Umesorah. *See* **Orthodox Judaism.**

Transcendental Meditation (TM). Maharishi Mahesh Yogi (b. 1911) "the Giggling Guru", was the first of the post-war Indian *gurus* to capture the public imagination, when the Beatles and other showbusiness personalities learnt TM. He was also the first to offer young people an alternative to drugs for self-awareness. TM is a Hindu meditation technique, practised for 20 minutes twice a day, using a *mantra* to calm the mind. Mantras were originally believed to be individually allotted, though it is now known that there are only 16, allotted according to age. TM calls itself a science but not a religion (though critics see it as a Hindu revivalist movement). Empirical research has validated some of the claims for TM's physiological and psychological benefits, such as stress reduction, though not for the attainment of cosmic consciousness.

The Maharishi's Spiritual Regeneration Movement (later registered as a charity) originally had the aim of saving the world through meditation in three years. When this did not happen, the methods became more and more elaborate—and expensive—and the organization now comprises a worldwide, commercially successful chain of international centres and "universities" (300 in America, 60 in Britain). The movement claims that if one per cent of a city practises TM, the crime rate drops dramatically. This is called the Maharishi Effect. Recent media attention has focused on its courses in *siddhis* (psychic powers), especially levitation.

It is claimed that millions of Westerners have learned TM, though many have subsequently stopped practising. Current practising meditators worldwide are estimated at 4,000,000 (100,000 in Britain, with about 100 full-time teachers). The technique is taking off in a big way, being taught in schools, prisons, and even business corporations.

Tribal Religions of India. According to the 1981 census of India there are 414 different tribal groups in India (total population 51,628,638—about 7.8 per cent of the population of India). It is therefore manifestly impossible to describe in detail the characteristics of the religious beliefs and practices of all these tribes. But a study of these groups yields some general patterns, and it is with these common features that this article is concerned. The beliefs and practices of two particular groups, the **Nagas** and the **Colonaikans,** are described separately.

Theistic concepts: In common with most tribal people in other parts of the world, the tribes of India believe in, and worship, supernatural entities. Most of the Indian tribes are polytheistic, but have a conception of a supreme creator god, who is not much involved in the day to day affairs of the world—a kind of *Deus Otiosus*—who has created the world and then withdrawn from mundane concerns. The Alhou of the Sema Nagas, the Kittung of the Vanars, the Thakur

Jiu of the Santhals are all examples of this remote high God. The tribal people however are more concerned with lesser deities, most of them associated with some element of their natural surroundings such as trees, rivers and hills. Some of them are malevolent spirits, causing diseases, natural calamities and misfortune. Worship is directed to these lesser spirits rather than to the supreme creator God, and the concern of tribal people is to appease and propitiate them with rituals of various kinds, including sacrifices. In addition most tribes worship departed members of their tribe, clan and family, some of the most famous and long-standing ancestors having reached almost divine status. There are no temples, but most tribes have shrines which are built either inside the household or in the open. According to most anthropologists the motivation for worship seems to be fear of the spirits, both divine and ancestral, to turn away their wrath, and to keep them at arm's length, so to speak. Most groups have priest-like functionaries, such as the Bhumka of the Gonds, and the Ato Naeke of the Santhals, who lead the rituals and whose duty is also to identify which of these spirits is responsible for illness or other misfortune.

Eschatology: Tribal people of India have quite complex conceptions regarding the human personality. Most believe in the existence of an extra-corporeal element, and as a matter of fact in more than one soul for each individual. The Konyak Nagas for example believe that one soul, the *mio,* remains attached to the body for some time after death, while another soul, the *yaha,* goes to the world of the ancestors, and yet another soul, the *biba,* appears to the living as a ghost. The *jiu* and *roa* of the Uraons is another example of multiple souls. Life after death is very similar to worldly existence, except that it is a dimmer and less happy world. Most tribal people are buried, not cremated, and they take care to bury some of the essential equipment with the dead for their

eschatological life, such as their weapons. Almost invariably there is a second burial ceremony designed to properly rehabilitate the soul into the ancestral world. This may in some cases take place as late as six months after the first burial. Some tribes keep a part of the body, such as the skull, in the house, so that some element of the departed remains in the household, to be worshipped, and more commonly to be fed at the time of festivities. But generally the worship or feeding is designed to keep the ancestral spirit away from the family, and to ensure that it is not offended and bring sickness or some other calamity on its living members. Many tribes erect menhirs to the dead, and in exceptional cases to the living as well.

The soul's actions while living do not substantially affect its after life, in contrast to Christianity or Islam. However tribes do believe that the good and the sinful are distinguished in some way or other in the eschaton. The Sema Nagas, for instance, believe that good souls go east towards the rising sun, whereas the wicked go west to the setting sun. According to the Konyak, those who die abnormal deaths or have committed much wickedness in life follow a path to the ancestral world which is very difficult and troublesome, while the virtuous follow a less arduous path—the very opposite of Christian conceptions! But eventually both types land up in the same ancestral world. Life in the ancestral world is a shadowy version of the temporal world. The souls till, hunt and fight each other as they do here. The partners of the first marriage are man and wife in the hereafter also.

Morality and ethics: Tribal people in India are generally more honest, sincere and upright in their actions than their compatriots from more sophisticated societies, but often their norms of morality and ethics differ from the latter. The *gotuls* of the Nagas, for example, where adolescent boys and girls sleep together and gain some sexual experience before marriage, will be frowned upon by most non-tribal societies. Though many tribal groups have strict taboos regarding extra-marital sex and incest, sexual relations before marriage are not looked upon with severity, especially if the union does not result in children. Many tribes, the Mundas and the Sarna for example, believe that God led man and woman to the first marital act and blessed the union, and hence such union cannot be viewed as sinful action. Some anthropologists opine that among tribal people morality is dictated not so much by any intrinsic value that virtuous action might have but by the adverse consequences that immoral acts might bring, particularly from the gods and ancestral spirits. The Konyaks, for instance, believe that the supreme god Gawang has great concern for moral behaviour and acts as the guardian of the moral order.

Finally it should be mentioned that a process of Hinduization, or "Sanskritization" as Indian scholars term it, has affected the religious life of many Indian tribes. Hindu gods and goddesses and Hindu rituals are now being gradually incorporated into tribal religious praxis.

Tridharma. "Three teachings." A combination of the teachings of Buddha, Confucius and Lao Tzu which came into being in Jakarta in 1938. Its Chinese founder, Kwee Tekhoay, edited a magazine called *Moestika Dharma*, and initially called his new teaching **Samkauw Hwee,** (three religions). Adherents of Tridharma maintain that their religion is not syncretistic but a combination of three distinct sets of teaching, and tend to be non-political. It is difficult to estimate their number, but it is probably in the region of a few thousand.

Trika. Literally, "threefold". One of the three philosophical schools of **Kashmir Shaivism.** It venerates the three goddesses Para, Apara and Parapara and is primarily concerned with initiatory ritual and cosmology.

True Nichiren School. *See* **Nichirenshoshu.**

True Orthodox Church. The True Orthodox Church, also known as the Catacomb Church and the Tikhonite Church, claims to be the authentic successor of the **Russian Orthodox** Church as that existed prior to Communist rule, or more precisely up to 1927. At that time a declaration of loyalty to the Communist state by Metropolitan Sergi of Nizhni Novgorod marked the beginning of a new period of church-state relations, and the numerous priests and bishops who rejected this declaration were severely persecuted, generally being sent to the camps or shot. Survivors went underground, forming the True Orthodox Church, as it came to be known, separate from the Moscow Patriarchate.

Numbers of adherents are unknown due to the extreme secrecy maintained as a necessary condition of survival: even today members themselves lack an overall picture. Small groups were served by priests moving from one village to another in the guise of workmen, and distanced themselves from Soviet life as much as possible; indeed young men refused to join the Red Army even during World War II, not wanting to play any part in defending "the achievements of October", and many were shot in consequence.

From time to time members were identified and brought to trial. In 1976, Metropolitan Gennadi was betrayed to the authorities: he had organized a network of underground monasteries in the Caucasus, and also a seminary. Members are reputed to revere Tsar Nicholas II and his family, murdered by the Bolsheviks. They are to be found in all parts of the former USSR.

Until 1976 the True Church was the only one recognized by the emigré **Russian (Orthodox) Church Abroad**, but relations subsequently cooled, and today many members of the True Orthodox Church are joining the **Free Russian Orthodox Church**, which is the branch of the emigré church now active within the former Soviet republics. Thus the future of the True Orthodox Church remains uncertain.

True Orthodox Church of Greece. This is the group also known as the **Old Calendarists**.

True Orthodox Church of Romania. This underground organization of the Communist period has, since the downfall of the Ceausescu régime, emerged into the open and begun an extensive programme of church-building. Metropolitan Silvestru has appeared on Romanian television.

True Pure Land School. *See* **Jodoshinshu.**

Tsharpa. A branch of the **Sakyapa** tradition of Tibetan Buddhism, founded by Tsharchen Losal Gyamtso (1502–1560), a great scholar and meditator who studied under 63 masters from both the **Nyingmapa** and the newer schools. The Tsharpa are particularly famous for their "Thirteen Teachings of Gold" and their *Mahakala* practice, as well as the other Sakyapa doctrines. The current head of the Tsharpa tradition is Chogay Trichen Rinpoche, born in 1920. In exile from Tibet, he is now based at the holy place of Lumbini, Nepal, where the historical Buddha was born.

Twelver Shi'ites. Following the death of Muhammad in 632, the Islamic community was at first ruled by a succession of three caliphs, ending with the assassination of 'Uthman in 656. During this period, however, a small group of Muslims remained loyal to the Prophet's cousin and son-in-law, 'Ali ibn Abi Talib, and insisted on his right to leadership of the community, which they claimed had been directly granted him by Muhammad. 'Ali himself was acknowledged Caliph on 'Uthman's death, holding the office until his own assassination in 661.

Leadership of the burgeoning Islamic empire now passed to the Umayyad dynasty, with its capital in Damascus, but a now much-expanded body of 'Alid loyalists (styling themselves Shi'a bayt 'Ali—the Party of the House of 'Ali) continued to promote the claims of the descendants of 'Ali (mainly his offspring from the Prophet's daughter Fatima), beginning with his sons Hasan and Husayn.

It is with the martyrdom of Husayn in the year 680 at Karbala that **Shi'ism** may be said to emerge as a distinct religious movement. His death still figures as the central event of religious history for Shi'ites, for whom his sufferings (and, more broadly, those of his family and descendants) have connotations similar to those of the passion of Christ in Christianity.

After Husayn's death, his successors (*Imams*) adopted a politically quietist stance. Various strands of Shi'ism developed under different leaders, some from other branches of the Prophet's family, but in time an identifiable mainstream emerged, generally designated Imami (i.e. Imam-centred) Shi'ism. The chief divisions in this early period were those of the **Zaydiya** after the fourth *Imam*, and the **Isma'iliya** after the sixth.

The death of the eleventh *Imam*, Hasan al-'Askari, in 874 led to controversy over the succession, since it was not clear that Hasan had left a son. One group maintained that the true Imam was a boy of four or five named Muhammad, who had been placed in hiding. For a period of some seventy years this hidden Imam could be communicated with only through a succession of four vice-regents or gates; but on the death of the last of these in 941 there began an indefinite era of "greater occultation", which still continues, in which the twelfth *Imam* remains alive in a supernatural realm, from which he exercises spiritual sovereignty.

The Imamis now maintained that there could never be more than twelve *Imams* (hence their designation as Ithna 'Asharis or Twelvers) and that the last of these would in due course emerge from hiding as the Mahdi to inaugurate an age of peace and the universal triumph of Shi'ite Islam.

Since then, authority within Twelver Shi'ism has lain with the clergy, who claim the right to act as representatives of the unrevealed *Imam*. Clerical authority developed considerably in the eighteenth and nineteenth centuries, with the triumph of the Usuli school, which emphasized the role of the clergy as sources of legal innovation. This laid the foundations for the establishment of a religious state in Iran following the revolution of 1979 led by *Imam* Khomeini.

In general, the Twelver Shi'a have been deprived of political power, with the notable exceptions of the Buyid rulers in Iran and Iraq, and the Safavis (from 1502), Qajars (1794–1925), and Pahlavi (1925–1979) dynasties in Iran. Nevertheless, Shi'ism has spread widely in the Islamic world, and it is estimated that there are today some 73,000,000 Twelvers, with substantial communities in Iran (34,000,000), Pakistan (12,000,000), India (10,000,000), Iraq (7,500,000), the former Soviet republics (4,000,000), and elsewhere. The large Shi'ite community in Lebanon has acquired considerable political significance in the past decade.

Mainstream Shi'ism has never diverged markedly from **Sunnism** in its basic religious beliefs or legal norms. God, the Prophet, the *Quran*, and the religious law are viewed almost identically in both groups. The chief differences lie in the fields of ritual, the role of the *Imams*, and the authority given to the clerical establishment. The Shi'a also have a wholly distinct canon of religious traditions (Hadith), derived from the *Imams* rather than the Prophet.

Distinctive Shi'ite practices include the performance of pilgrimages to the shrines of the *Imams* and their relatives (particularly the sacred sites in Iraq: Najaf, Karbala, and Kazimayn); the permissibility of temporary marriage (mut'a) and the concealment of religious belief; and the celebration of the events of Husayn's mar-

tyrdom during the month of Muharram in the form of passion plays, threnodies, and processions in which significant numbers of participants engage in ritual flagellation.

From purely political figures, the *Imams* developed the characteristics of direct intermediaries with the divinity or even, in more extreme contexts, earthly representations of the Godhead, having come to be regarded as pure and sinless. It is in and through the Imams (particularly Husayn) that the believer finds salvation, and it is through their activity that the universe is both created and sustained. Extreme views of this kind have generally been rejected by the more orthodox, and restricted to sectarian movements such as the **Nusayris**, but several have passed into the mainstream. During the Safavid period (1502–1722), such ideas were greatly matured in a sophisticated form of philosophical speculation (known as "divine wisdom") which was developed by Twelver thinkers in Iran. This theosophical tradition was developed in the 19th century by the **Shaykhi** school and laid the basis for the radical millenarianism of the **Babis** and the subsequent move away from Islam of the **Bahais.**

Among the Twelver clergy, certain individuals are singled out as exceptional authorities, known as "Centres of Imitation" (*maraji'-i taqlid*), to whom all other believers are expected to defer in matters of religious judgement. At times, this degree of authority has been centred in single individuals, and at others spread among several (as at present). There is, nevertheless, a general tendency to concentrate authority in one figure, as occurred in the case of *Imam* Khomeini after the Islamic Revolution. The future of mainstream Shi'ism depends in some measure on how it chooses to tackle the problem of where and how widely to locate religious authority and how far to identify it with political power.

Tz'u Hui T'ang. *See* **Compassion Society.**

U

Udasis. An order of ascetics which traces back its origins to Baba Siri Chand. (1494–1512) the elder son of Guru Nanak. It is now part of mainstream Hinduism, and has no links with **Sikhism.** In its centres (*akharas*) children learn Sanskrit and their temples have images of the principal Hindu deities. It is thought that the Udasis may have been influenced in their formative years by the teachings of the **Naths.** Again it is said that members may have acted as Sikh *gurdwara* custodians through the 18th century.

UK Islamic Mission. A British organization arising out of the Pakistan-based **Jama'at-i Islami**. Founded in 1962, it has some 50 centres located in various parts of Britain. Islamic education for Muslim children is a major concern, and it provides speakers to schools and colleges. It co-operates with the **Islamic Foundation**.

Ukrainian Uniate Catholic Church. The "Uniate" Catholic Church of Ukraine was created by the Union of Brest in 1595–96. Whilst retaining allegiance to the **Roman Catholic Church,** it was to conserve **Orthodox** liturgical and pastoral traditions, celebrate its rites in Old Church Slavonic, and permit its clergy, excepting Bishops, to marry. In modern times, it was termed, first, the "Ukrainian Greek Catholic Church", and now the "Eastern Rite Ukrainian Church" or **"Ukrainian Uniate Catholic Church"**. Under the Austro–Hungarian empire, its preservation of local character enabled it to fuel Ukrainian patriotic sentiment. Ukrainian national self-determination was no less a threat to the Soviet Union. In order to neutralize it, Joseph Stalin compelled the Ukrainian Catholic Church to accept absorption into the **Russian Orthodox** Church. The Orthodox Patriarch of Moscow collaborated enthusiastically. At the Synod of Lvov, in 1946, the Ukrainian Church signed its own death warrant. During the 40 years of persecution which ensued, the 4,000,000–5,000,000 suppressed Ukrainian Catholic laity attended Orthodox services, if they participated at all. They retained a concealed loyalty to the Eastern Rite Church. In the mid-1980s, there were no active Eastern Rite clergy, all having been imprisoned or murdered. The tide may have been turned by the accession in the late 1970s of a Pope, the Polish John Paul II, who emphatically proclaimed the rights of religious believers under communism, and by the heroic example of men such as Iosp Terelya, who spent 20 years in Soviet labour camps and psychiatric hospitals. Christian resistance movements now became visible in the Ukraine. The most potent was the "Action Group for the Defence of the Rights of Believers and the Church", led by Terelya. The years 1988–1989 saw mass public demonstrations in support of the Ukrainian Catholic Church, with hundreds of thousands on the streets. There followed the registration of numerous formerly Orthodox parishes within Ukrainian Catholic jurisdiction. In 1989, because of *glasnost* in the Soviet Union, and just two days before President Gorbachev's historic meeting with John Paul II, the Ukrainian Catholic Church was legalized. A serious confrontation now looms between the remaining Orthodox hierarchy, and the Ukrainian Catholics, who wish to reclaim their church buildings. A synod was held in 1990 to resolve the issue; it broke down amid recriminations about the "violent seizure" of churches, on the one hand, and accusations of lies on the other. It will be long before any mutual trust is restored. The Eastern Rite and Orthodox churches have it in common that their combined resurgence of religion and nationalism have created fears of the revival of anti-Semitism. The Ukrainian Catholic Church will be one of the livelier Christian communities in the Europe of 2000.

Umbanda. This Brazilian religious movement, although often described as African (Afro-Brazilian), is in fact much less so than **Candomblé** both in terms of its content and membership. Found chiefly in the south of Brazil, Umbanda emerged in the 20th century as a syncretistic religion with little in the way of central unifying doctrine but incorporating Amerindian, **African traditional** and **Roman Catholic** beliefs and practices (including a priesthood), and also the spiritualism of Allan Kardec (well known in Brazil as **Kardecismo**). Salient elements include belief in reincarnation, with rebirth higher or lower in the socio-economic scale as appropriate punishment and reward for conduct in this life, and belief in harmful spirits who need to be placated.

Its membership is generally more affluent and more Euro-Brazilian than that of Candomblé, and unlike the latter it produces a range of publications which promote its cause. With over 20,000,000 adherents, it is a force to be reckoned with politically, being wooed at election time in particular, and has members up to government level. Again in contrast to Candomblé, some attempt has been made to establish a federation of congregational groups, so that it might become a truly national religion, although hitherto this is not a trend that has proved particularly successful.

At times Afro-Brazilian spiritist cults—which also include **Macumba**—have been persecuted, but today Umbanda enjoys legal recognition and is a still-growing force in Brazilian society.

Uniate Churches. In Eastern Europe and Asia there are a number of churches which are in communion with the **Roman Catholic** Church but which follow Orthodox rites, observe the Eastern calendar, and permit the marriage of clergy. They include the **Maronites, Syrians, Armenians, Chaldeans, Copts, Ethiopians,** and others. Some of these churches in the USSR had been handed over by the Government to the **Russian Orthodox** Church, and since 1990 have been the subject of dispute between the two faith-communities. In Uzhgorodin, Western Ukraine, the local authorities intervened when the Orthodox were unwilling to return the cathedral to the Uniates. It arranged for a Roman Catholic Church to be refurbished in return for the handing back in 1991 of the cathedral to the Uniates.

Unification Church. The Unification Church (UC) was founded by the Reverend Sun Myung Moon in 1954 in Korea as Tong Il movement. In the West it is popularly known as "the Moonies", while its official name is The Holy Spirit Association for the Unification of World Christianity (HSA UWC). There are many offshoots and branches, such as **CARP, ICUS, CAUSA,** etc.

In 1936 Moon received his mission in a vision, which is to establish God's Kingdom on earth. Over the following 20 years Moon is said to have communicated with God and other religious leaders, including Moses and Buddha, the result of which is *Divine Principle,* the movement's sacred text. The book offers a reinterpretation of the Bible, claiming that Jesus failed in his task of restoring the original state of man by establishing a "Perfect Family"; another messiah (believed to be Moon) must now accomplish this mission.

It was not before the early 1970s, when the founder himself arrived in the USA, that Unificationism began to take off. The movement pursued a strategy of active recruitment and high public profile: lecture tours, large rallies, mass weddings, international conferences, daily newspapers and businesses. Its strong anti-communist stance was represented in CAUSA, particularly active in Latin America. By the late 1970s the "Moonies" had become a household name, branded as a sinister "cult that breaks up families", coupled with allegations of brainwashing and "Heavenly Deception", that is street recruitment teams presenting themselves as conventional Christians. This image was exacerbated by the libel action which the Church brought unsuccessfully against the *Daily Mail* in the UK.

Despite active recruitment it is believed that the movement's full-time membership never exceeded 10–15,000 in the West. Estimates of actual membership in the UK today put it in the lower hundreds. With the "House Church" movement within the UC, members do not necessarily live communally or work full-time for the Church.

In recent months UC's activities have spread to Eastern Europe with conferences, youth services and English-teaching projects, the high point of which was a meeting of Moon with President Gorbachev in May 1990 during the UC organized World Media Conference.

Unified Buddhist Church. *See* **Unified Vietnamese Buddhist Church.**

Unified Buddhist Congregation. *See* **Unified Vietnamese Buddhist Church.**

Unified Vietnamese Buddhist Church. Also known as the **United Buddhist Association,** came into being as a result of the Vietnamese Buddhist Reunification Congress held in Saigon in December 1963. It united **Theravadins** and **Mahayanists** in a single organization presided over by a patriarch and governed by an assembly of elders consisting of 50 or so senior monks.

Although the majority of Vietnamese Buddhists are technically members of the Unified Vietnamese Buddhist Church, most speak of their religion in terms of *cung*

to tien ong ba ("the cult of ancestors") and especially the grandfather and grandmother. They follow the lunar calendar, and on the first and 15th of every month go to the temple and put incense sticks on altars in front of photographs of deceased relatives. They also eat vegetarian food on this occasion.

Union of American Hebrew Congregations (UHAC). *See* **Reform Judaism.**

Union of Muslim Organizations of UK and Eire. Founded in 1970, this was an attempt to create an umbrella organization for all the separate Muslim organizations in the UK and Eire. The attempt did not succeed, and critics might argue that it has become just one other separate organization. However, approximately 200 local organizations are affiliated to it. It holds an annual conference, and in 1978 it set up the National Muslim Education Council of UK to promote the cause of education for British Muslims in accordance with the principles of Islam.

Union of Orthodox Congregations of America. *See* **Orthodox Judaism.**

Union of Orthodox Hebrew Congregations. *See* **Orthodox Judaism.**

Union of Orthodox Rabbis of the United States and Canada. *See* **Orthodox Judaism.**

Union of Traditional Conservative Judaism. *See* **Conservative Judaism.**

Unitarians. Unitarians reject the doctrine of the Trinity: that there is one God but three persons, Father, Son and Holy Spirit. By corollary they reject the divinity of Jesus Christ (the Son). The doctrine of the

Trinity was first formalized at the Council of Nicea in AD 325, in response to the unitarian doctrines of Arius (Arianism). Since then unitarianism has been regarded as heresy.

Unitarianism was strong in Eastern Europe in the 16th and 17th centuries and was spread to England in 1652 by John Biddle of Gloucester, who was later banished to the Scilly Isles. The movement had a resurgence in the 18th century Age of Reason; the scientist Joseph Priestley was a Unitarian leader. It spread to the United States which still has the largest number of Unitarians. In the 19th century, under the influence of James Martineau the movement moved from an emphasis on the Bible to a basis of rationalism and scientific thought.

Unitarian churches today are independent and organized on a congregational basis. There is a tension between those who would regard themselves as Christians (although rejected by mainline Christianity) and those who reject most Christian dogma. Unitarians are often active in the community and have been prominent in civil rights movements. Worldwide membership is over 600,000.

United Buddhist Association. *See* **Unified Vietnamese Buddhist Church.**

United Churches. These are churches in which a number of existing (and continuing) denominations have joined together to form a single entity. The largest is the Evangelical Church in Germany which consists of **Lutheran** and **Presbyterian (Reformed)** churches.

One of the most famous united churches is the Church of South India, founded in 1947, which includes Anglicans, Methodists, Congregational and Reformed churches. Anglicans are also members of the Church of North India and the Church of Pakistan. However, the belief of Anglicans in the apostolic succession (that it is essential for priests to be ordained by a bishop coming from an unbroken line traceable to the apostles) has made their involvement limited in other areas.

The Uniting Church in Australia (Congregational, Presbyterian and Methodist) and the United Church of Canada (Congregational, some Presbyterian, Methodist and United Brethren) are examples of churches choosing to unite in former colonies. The origins and differences between the denominations are rooted in Europe; away from this situation, and in an environment which may be unsympathetic and even actively hostile to Christianity, Christians became more aware of how much they have in common, and wish to become visibly united.

Occasionally unity is enforced by the state. This happened in the middle of the 20th century in both China and Japan where Protestant denominations were compelled to merge. In Zaire in 1970 the Congo Protestant Council voted (by majority, not unanimously) to form a single church; when some denominations subsequently dissented the government forced them to remain in the united "Church of Christ of Zaire".

Although members of united churches still form the largest group in Protestant churches, in recent years there have been fewer schemes of union. In part this may be inevitable because all the uncontroversial and "natural" schemes have already taken place. However, there has also come about an awareness that it is better that unity should come "from below" and a desire that local churches should work together so that unity may be an existing experience translated into an administrative reality, rather than a system imposed "from above". The failure of some proposals on the final vote after years of preparatory work (for instance the Anglican–Methodist union proposals in the 1970s) has caused many to draw back from such attempts at organic union.

There are about 65,000,000 people in united churches worldwide, over one third of whom are in the Evangelical Church of Germany.

United Church of Christ. This **Protestant** church came into existence in the USA in 1957 as a result of the union of the **Congregational** Christian Churches and the Evangelical **Reformed** Church, both of which, though products of various mergers, had colonial roots. It thus brought together the English Puritan and Separatist tradition and the German pietist and evangelical traditions. This pluralist denomination has 1,700,000 members.

United Jewish Appeal. American organization founded in 1939 which seeks to co-ordinate the raising of funds by American Jews for Jews outside the USA. It is the largest vehicle for the collection and distribution of such funds. Its work includes aiding Jews to settle in Israel, America and other places. In recent years its focus has become more and more centred on Israel, reaching a peak of more than US$280,000,000 in 1967. Since then considerable although lesser sums have been contributed annually.

United Reformed Church. The United Reformed Church represents a fusion of the **Presbyterians (Reformed)** and the **Congregationalists**.

United Synagogue. *See* **Orthodox Judaism.**

United Synagogue of America. *See* **Conservative Judaism.**

United Torah Judaism (UTJ) or **United Torah Party.** (See also Orthodox Judaism; Zionism; Shas.) The UTJ, a non-Zionist Israeli political party, a coalition of **Agudat Israel** and **Degel Hatorah,** was formed to contest the 1992 Israeli general election and secured four seats in the Knesset (Israeli parliament). The spiritual mentor of this **Ultra-Orthodox (Ḥaredi), Ashkenazi** party, Rabbi Eliezar Schach

(1896–), is one of the leading figures in religious politics in Israel. The UTJ was an unsuccessful attempt to consolidate Ultra-Orthodox support, fragmented in the 1988 elections when Agudat Israel (largely, Ḥasidic, gaining four seats in 1988) and the then newly formed, Degel Hatorah (largely Lithuanian–Midnagdic, gained two seats in 1988) split the Ultra-Orthodox vote. UTJ stood on a platform supportive of peace on the political level and the support of Ḥaredi institutions on the communal front.

Unity Sect. Also known as **I kuan-Tao,** this Taiwanese ethical society incorporates Buddhist, **Confucian** and **Taoist** teachings. Its origins are obscure though it was probably founded as an independent entity in 1928 by Chang T'ien Jan in northern China. Sect members themselves claim an ancient ancestry for the movement and hold Confucius, Lao-Tzu and Bodhidharma to be early members of an unbroken apostolic line. The sect centres on the cult of the Venerable Mother from whose womb Buddhas of the past, present and future are said to emerge. Initiation within the sect causes a person's name to be erased from the rolls of purgatory and transferred to the records of the saved. Knowledge of the "three treasures" (*mantra*—the name of Amitabha Buddha, *mudra*—a bodily posture symbolically revealing the relation between humans and the Venerable Mother, and the Mysterious Gate—a point between the eyes) is also communicated during the initiation rite. The Unity sect encourages traditional religious exercises such as shadow boxing, meditation, chanting of scriptures and vegetarianism and places great emphasis on the education of its members. Texts held to be particularly worthy of study include the *Tao Te-Ching* and Sun Yat-Sen's *Three Principles of the People.* Because of allegations of Japanese collaboration during the war the Unity Sect only achieved legal status in 1983. Two main sub-sects exist. The first, the

Lui-ist, was founded by Chang's second wife, Madame Lui. The other, the **Sun-ist,** looks to the authority of Sun Su-chen, Chang's mistress. There is considerable rivalry between the two groups.

Universal Saiva Trust. Based in California, the trust provides a Western base for the dissemination of the **Kashmir Shaivite** teachings of Swami Lakshman Jee (d.1992).

V

Vaikhanasas. A Hindu **Vaishnava** community of South India. Although comprising only about 2,500 brahmin families in Tamil Nadu, Andhra Pradesh and Karnataka, the Vaikhanasas have an importance beyond their numbers because of their claim to an unbroken tradition of ritual performance which goes back to Vedic times. From references in ancient texts it seems likely that the community existed before the beginning of the Common Era, even though the oldest of their own texts date from no earlier than the fourth century CE. Most of their literature deals with temple ritual and with the construction and dedication of temples and images.

Vaishnava Sahajiyas. An esoteric Bengali cult, formed by a blending of Tantric and Vaishnava ideas and practices. The Sahajiyas regard their practices as the natural expression of human sexuality, which is a microcosm of the unity-in-duality which characterizes the universe as they see it. As such their ritual involves sexual intercourse between the practitioner and an unmarried woman, in order to re-enact at a physical level the pure love between Krishna and Radha and to transform worldly desire (*kama*) into spiritual love (*prema*). Semen is not emitted but "redirected" through a channel thought to traverse the centre of the body, to the thousand petalled lotus at the crown of the head where the bliss of Krishna and Radha is enjoyed. The Sahajiyas adopt and interpret the theology of the **Gaudiya Vaishnavas** and credit Chaitanya himself with the origin of the cult's doctrines.

Most of our knowledge of the Vaishnava Sahajiyas is derived from the cult's texts. Since it has always been esoteric, and since Sahajiya practices are now illegal, it is difficult to know how many adherents, if any, it may still have today.

Vallabhasampradaya. A branch of the Hindu *bhakti* tradition founded by Vallabhacarya (1479–1532) also called the **Pushtimarga** or Way of Grace. It flourishes chiefly in Bombay, Rajasthan and Gujarat, and its adherents belong mainly to the commercial castes. The most characteristic feature of its worship is *seva* (service), which consists of a dedicated attendance upon Krishna's image understood as the Lord's own true and living form. There are eight periods in each day when the Lord Krishna is believed to grant the sight of himself to his faithful and this means that the priests of the Pushtimarga spend most of their day in dressing the image and providing its meals. The key scripture of this *sampradaya* is the *Bhagavata-purana,* upon which Vallabhacarya wrote a commentary. In this and his other writings, Vallabhacarya expounded his philosophical doctrine of Suddhadvaita (pure non-dualism). According to this, the only true reality is the Lord Krishna, and liberation can be attained by his grace alone. He is to be worshipped in particular by recitation of the *mantra* "Sri Krishna is my refuge".

Renunciation plays little part in the movement for Vallabhacarya spent most of his life as a householder and believed that his Lord had commanded him to marry and have children. His followers today dedicate "mind, body and wealth" to Krishna. The leaders of the *sampradaya* are householders and have the title *maharaja*. Its places of worship are known by the name *haveli*, which means a private mansion, implying that the Lord Krishna lives there as an honoured guest of the *maharaja*.

Valmikis. *See* **Balmikis.**

Varkari Panth. *See* **Warkaris.**

Vatakalai. Literally "northern culture". A sub-sect of the south Indian **Sri Vaishnava** school.

Vedanta. "Vedānta" is the term used to describe one of the six classical schools of Indian philosophy, its name meaning literally "the end of the Vedas". The aphorisms which form the core of its teachings were first set down by the philosopher Bādarāyaṇa early in the Common Era, it was technically classified as *uttara* (later) Mimāṁsā to distinguish it from another major philosophical school, *pūrva* (earlier) Mimāṁsa. Based on the *Upaniṣads*, and, ultimately, on the *Vedas*, Vedānta holds that the individual is one with Ultimate Reality, and the object of the religious quest is realization. Thus knowledge alone dispels the ignorance which obscures one's real nature and brings dissatisfaction with life. Unlike another of the six schools, Nyāya, which believes that ignorance may be dispelled through logical analysis, Vedānta concludes that human intellect is incapable of comprehending the Infinite by its very nature. This being the case, one may only rely on the direct intuitive experiences of the great sages as recorded in the *Upaniṣads* as the basis for realization of Reality.

What the *Upaniṣads* communicate is, however, open to diverse interpretation. As a result, Vedānta has sub-divided into three major schools. The oldest of these, if one excludes the relatively amorphous pantheistic monism of Bādarāyaṇa, is Advaita, or non-dualism. This school found its greatest exponent in the eighth century CE philosopher Śaṅkara. Śaṅkara, building on Bādarāyaṇa, held that Ultimate Reality is integral and "unsplit." Consequently, all phenomena are illusory (*māyā*). This illusion can be dispelled by means of meditative insight (*jñāna*). So antithetical was this position to the religious sensibilities of the time that Śaṅkara was branded by many as a crypto-Buddhist. Śaṅkara's thought was later expanded by Padmapāda, Vachaspati Miśra, and others. Śaṅkara was also said to have set up the major monastic institutions of India and is held to be the spiritual progenitor of the still-influential Jagadgurus, the titular heads of these institutions. The tradition of Śaṅkara's school is maintained by this lineage of the Jagadgurus (world teachers) or Śaṅkarāchāriyas of the four major monastic centres that he supposedly founded. In recent times, one of the most respected of these was Śrī Candraśekharendra Sarasvatī of the Kāñcī Kāmakoṭi-pīṭha in South India. The position of Jagadguru is hereditary in certain families.

The second great school of Vedānta, Viśiṣṭadvaita, was founded by Rāmānuja in approximately 1100 CE. In this school, the human soul is seen to be a fragment of all-pervasive Ultimate Reality and unconscious of it. Nevertheless, this soul possesses identity in its own right and will retain individuality and self-awareness on re-uniting with Ultimate Reality, but it is in all senses subordinate to that Reality which pre-existed all things and was their Creator. Religious dis-ease, for the Viśiṣṭadvaitans, is not only a function of ignorance, but more importantly of disbelief or lack of faith. Thus *bhakti*, or devotion, not *jñāna*, is the essential factor in gaining liberation from suffering. Rāmānuja's influence is evident in the works of Madhva, Vallabha, Chaitaniya, and modern Hindu reform movements such as the Brāhmo Samāj. Finally, there is the Dvaita school of Madhva founded in around 1250 CE. Madhva believed in a clear, substantial difference between Ultimate Reality and the individual soul. The soul, he held, was an active and responsible, if imperfect, agent in its own right. Only through the gracious intercession of Ultimate Reality, which

Madhva identified with the god Viṣṇu, could the individual be saved from the endless rounds of rebirth.

The various schools of Vedānta are still active. Indeed, many of the ideas espoused by various reform movements in modern Hinduism draw heavily on their doctrines as the metaphysical foundations of their own programs. Vedānta also forms the philosophical basis for many forms of yoga and it is central to the teachings of most contemporary Hindu gurus.

Vietnamese Buddhism. Buddhism entered Vietnam towards the end of the second century AD when the country was under Chinese rule. Both **Theravada** and **Mahayana** Buddhism were taught and practised. **Confucianism** was the basis of the royal court, and **Taoism** probably formed the bridge between these elements and folk religion. This was achieved partly through **shamanistic** mediums (male and female) and partly via national and local deities.

Between the 15th and 19th centuries the frontier Vietnamese pushed the state of Champa out of what is now their south. Towards the end of the 19th century Vietnam became part of the French Union Indochinoise.

Under French rule **Roman Catholicism** was no longer prohibited. Monks engaged periodically in resistance to the French, and both monks and laymen were active in educational and reform programmes. There was renewed interest in **Pure Land Buddhism.** Associations for Buddhist studies were founded in Saigon (1931), Hué (1932) and Hanoi (1934).

Following French withdrawal from Vietnam and the partition of the country into north and south, Buddhist monks became increasingly involved in politics. In the south, on Visakha Puja Day (May 8), 1963, government troops of Saigon President Ngo Dinn Diem, a Catholic, tore down Buddhist flags; monks responded by leading political protests and hunger strikes. On June 11, 1963, Thich Quang Duc, a 73-year-old monk, performed self-immolation. He was followed by a number of monks, nuns and lay Buddhists. Among the demands of the Buddhists were the free practice and propagation of the Buddhist religion and equality under the law for Buddhists and Catholics. Madame Nhu, the President's sister-in-law, condemned the protesters as Communists. "If another monk barbecues himself, I will clap my hands" she said.

By the end of August 1963 the Buddhist headquarters had been overrun. But Buddhist opposition had paved the way for a successful coup against the Diem régime, which was overthrown on Nov. 1. By now the Buddhists were seen as a major political force in Vietnamese politics. The military therefore gave permission for them to hold the Vietnamese Buddhist Reunification Congress in 1963, which led to the establishment of the **Unified Vietnamese Buddhist Church.** This body united Theravadins and Mahayanists in a single ecclesiastical structure.

The **Buddhist Chaplain Corps,** responsible for the welfare of soldiers' families, came into being at about this time. In 1964, largely at the initiative of Thich Nhat Hanh, the new Church also set up the Institute of Higher Buddhist Studies within the Department of Education. This later became Van Hanh University in Saigon.

In 1966 the populations of north and south Vietnam were 18,000,000 and 16,000,000 respectively. Of these there were 1,500,000 Roman Catholics, of which three quarters lived in the south. The remaining 80 per cent of the population were Buddhists, of which two million of South Vietnam's 12,000,000 Buddhists were distinctively Theravadin. The remainder practised a mixture of Mahayana Buddhism, Taoism and Confucianism. South Vietnamese Buddhist temples of all kinds then numbered 4,856.

Struggles continued between the Unified Buddhist Church and the Saigon government, though by 1968 the moderate faction, led by Thich Nhat Hanh, was on the ascendancy. Many Buddhists increasingly adopted a politically neutral stance, wanting neither Marxism nor Western materialism. The Catholics were anti-Communist.

There were also in the south some new religions, such as the Buddhist-inspired **Hoa Hao,** the synchretistic **Cao Dai,** and the highly politicised **Binh Xuyen** (now defunct) whose leaders were monks and laymen who had been educated in the local schools.

Vinaya Vardhana Society. Literally, "The Association for the Protection of Buddhist Discipline", a Sri Lankan **Theravada** Buddhist movement dedicated to the improvement of morals amongst the laity. Founded in 1932 by G. V. S. Jayasundera the group is vehemently anti-clerical and excludes monks from membership. The society is hostile to all forms of superstition, including the veneration of Buddha images and encourages lay preaching of the *dharma*. Its heyday seems to have been in the 1950s. Violent opposition from the *Sangha* had an adverse effect on membership after this time though it still remains high in some, mainly urban, areas of the island. Members are expected to undergo quite severe temporary retreats and, unusually for Theravadins, there is considerable optimism about the possibility of the laity attaining *nirvana*.

Viniyoga. The modern tradition of Viniyoga, "the discipline of gradual progression", traces its origins back to the ninth century **Vaisnava** saint Sri Nathamuni. The present leader of the movement is T.V.K. Desikachar, who promotes the tradition from his Yoga Mandiram in Madras. It was Desikachar's father, Prof. T. Krishnamacharya, who first made the teaching available to Western students. Initiated into the Nathamuni tradition as a young man, Krishnamacharya learned many of the traditional yoga texts by heart, including Nathamuni's own *Yoga Rahasya*. Chapters 1–4 of this text are currently being published by the movement from dictation given by Krishnamacharya before his death in 1989.

A central teaching of the *Yoga Rahasya* is that yoga can be practised by all people, men and women, householders and renunciants. It also stresses that each person's practice of yoga should be tailored to their individual needs. For this reason much of the teaching is arranged on a one-to-one basis. Stress and pain are to be avoided. Ideally, each individual progresses physically, mentally and spiritually in small increments to produce a gradual and harmonious realization of their potential as a human being.

At the present time Viniyoga teachers can be found throughout Europe and the USA as well as in India. Each of these has received regular personal instruction from Desikachar himself and is involved in training others to teach within the tradition. Desikachar's British representative is Paul Harvey who runs the **Centre for Yoga Studies** in Bath and offers a four-year diploma course on Viniyoga for practising yoga teachers.

Virashaivas. *See* **Lingayats.**

Vizhitz Ḥasidism. (*See also* **Ḥasidism.**) Rabbi Menahem Mendel ben Ḥayyim Hager (1830–1884), who led the Jewish community of Vizhitz from 1854, founded this Ḥasidic movement. Famous as an amulet maker and miracle worker, he established Vizhitz as a centre of Ḥasidism. His grandson, Rabbi Israel (1860–1938) moved his Ḥasidism within the Austrian empire to Grosswardein (Hungary). A number of the Vizhitz dynasty moved to Israel (Bene Berak, Haifa, Jerusalem) where they have attempted to re-create pre-*Holocaust* **Jewish Orthodox** life in a new setting. The Vizhitz founded a number of *yeshivot* in Israel and there are communities centred around these.

Voodoo (Vodun). This is the name given to the syncretic mix of **African traditional** and **Roman Catholic** religion found in Haiti. In many respects it resembles **Candomblé, Santería, Shango** and those numerous expressions of African-Catholic systems of belief and practice found in the Caribbean and Central and South (and to some extent North) America. Loa (lwa) is one of the principal terms used to refer to the numerous African gods and Catholic saints (the two groups having been conflated) on which this religion is based. (Vodun, or Vudu, is the name of a god in African religion in Togo and Benin.) Spirit possession rituals, involving trances in which a loa spirit possesses certain individuals, are of central significance.

Although it has retained fewer African myths than Candomblé, in Vodun too special songs are sung and dances performed in honour of each individual deity. Animal sacrifices are performed to elicit favours from them. Respect for the dead is extremely important in this as in all other new world varieties of African-Catholic religion. The dead are second in importance to the loa, and must not be angered. Sacrifices to the family dead co-exist with Roman Catholic funeral rites on the occasion of a bereavement.

The particular importance of Vodun in Haiti is partly the result of the successful slave rebellion of 1791, as a result of which it enjoyed considerable freedom to flourish. More recently it was sanctioned by President Duvalier (Papa Doc, 1957–1971) as a means of gaining black majority support over the Roman Catholic mulatto élite. Yet despite receiving official recognition as a religion in the constitution of 1987, there is currently evidence of some decline.

W

Wahhabism. Wahhabism is a strict, puritanical form of **Sunni** Islam associated in particular with Saudi Arabia, a state which it contributed to creating, and whose society it continues to help mould.

The fundamentalist reform movement of the Wahhabis first arose in the mid-18th century in the isolated region of Najd in central Arabia. Wahhabis are so-called after Muhammad b. 'Abd al-Wahhab (1703–92), the movement's founder. Ibn 'Abd al-Wahhab came from a family of religious scholars, and spent many years studying under teachers of different legal schools and **Sufi** orders in Medina and Basra before returning to preach in his native Najd. In 1744 he formed an alliance with a local prince, Muhammad b. Su'ud, and together they launched a *jihad* to extend their community, to enforce the Holy Law (Shari'a) and suppress what they held to be corrupt beliefs and practices, notably all aspects of Sufism, popular cults of saints and sorcery. **Shi'ism** was also attacked and in 1802 the Wahhabis were raiding deep into Iraq, sacking the Shi'ite holy city of Karbala. By 1805 they had seized control of the Hijaz, capturing the holy cities of Mecca and Medina.

On the orders of the Ottoman sultan, the viceroy of Egypt, Muhammad 'Ali, organized an expedition into Arabia, putting an end to the Wahhabi Su'udi state in 1818. The second such state re-emerged within central Arabia, only to be ended again in 1891, when its Su'udi rulers were sent into exile by a rival tribal leader. It was 1902 before 'Abd al-'Aziz b. Su'ud was able to win back Riyad, and with the enthusiastic support of the Wahhabi **Ikhwan** (Brethren) to expand the territory under his control until he succeeded in founding the present Kingdom of Saudi Arabia in 1932.

Wahhabis stress that their faith is the "religion of unity" and that other Muslims have gone astray from the strict assertion of the absolute unity of God. Shi'ites and Sufis are held to be especially guilty. Therefore, only Wahhabis can be considered by them as true Muslims. All others are unbelievers against whom it is legitimate to fight a *jihad*.

However, King 'Abd al-'Aziz effectively ended the practice of continuing *jihad* in the late 1920s, when he suppressed the *Ikhwan* in order to halt their attacks on non-Wahhabi pilgrims to Mecca, their raids against Shi'ites and British in Iraq, and their demands for the forcible conversion of the Shi'ite population of eastern Saudi Arabia. With the ending of *jihad* there has also been an end to the strict Wahhabi prohibition against all mixing with non-Wahhabis, thus enabling the introduction of a foreign work force in Saudi Arabia, and the free movement of Saudis abroad. Nevertheless, the Gulf War of 1991 strained the tolerance of strict Wahhabis to the limit, as it involved the stationing of large numbers of "unbelieving" forces on their land.

Wahhabis condemn everything that they regard as innovation, for example all doctrines and practices with no sanction in the *Quran*, the Tradition of the Prophet Muhammad, or the consensus of the earliest Muslim community. Thus they disapprove of Hellenistic-influenced Islamic philosophy, Sufi theosophy, Shi'ite concepts of the Imam, and speculative theology. Among prohibited acts are the celebration of the Prophet's birthday, seeking the intercession of saints and making offerings at their tombs, dancing and playing music, wearing gold and jewellery, and smoking tobacco. Although there has been relaxation in practice in contemporary Saudi Arabia, this has met with disapproval in some quarters. This was manifested in November 1979 in the seizure of the Holy Mosque at Mecca by dissident Wahhabi **Ikhwan** under the leadership of Juhaiman al-'Utaibi.

The **Hanbali** school of Holy Law is followed by the Wahhabis, but they are also ready to accept the views of other schools where they consider them to be more soundly based on the *Quran* and Tradition, or where the Hanbali school does not offer relevant guidance. They believe in the need for creative interpretation in matters of law not covered by the sacred texts or consensus of the early community, introducing scope for reform in a manner which has had a wide influence outside Wahhabi circles.

Waldensians (also Waldenses or Vaudois). A twelfth century reform movement in France whose founder figure was Pierre Valdes, or Peter Waldo, a merchant of Lyons, France. About 1170 Valdes was converted in response to Matt. 19:21. Valdes tried to follow the example of Christ's life on earth and took to a life as a wandering preacher who lived in poverty, dependent on alms. From 1177 he was joined by men and women who followed his teachings of poverty and simplicity as the way to follow Christ. They organized themselves and became known as the "Poor men of Lyons". They translated the Bible into French and other vernacular languages, ordained priests, allowed women to preach, rejected purgatory, some sacraments, requiem masses and good works by the living for the death, celebrated Lord's Supper once a year, abolished holy days and opposed swearing and military service. Their message and unauthorized preaching alarmed the **Roman Catholic** church. At their request, during 1179 their beliefs were examined by Alexander III which was followed by excommunication in 1182–83 and in 1184 they were declared a heretical sect.

Centuries of severe persecutions followed. Despite this they developed into a genuinely popular movement. At Valdes's

death in 1217, the Waldensians had spread into Languedoc and northern Italy, Germany, Spain and later into central Europe. In 1532 contacts with Swiss **Protestants** resulted in a synod and the Waldensians became a part of the **Reformed** Churches known as "la Chiesa Evangelica Valdese". Persecution continued until 1848 when they were granted religious freedom.

Recently Waldensians and **Methodists** have merged to an united church without losing their identities. Today the movement has about 20,000 followers and is mainly found in the Waldensian valleys and in Sicily and Naples. Waldensian institutions are amongst others a theological faculty (Rome), a religious publishing house (Claudiana in Turin), a theological school (Torre Pellice), the well-known Waldensian centre in the Sicilian village of Riesi and the Agape centre. Its social consciousness undiminished, the Waldensian movement continues an active witness throughout society.

Walubi. *See* the **All Indonesian Federation of Buddhist Organizations.**

Warkaris or Varkari Panth. A Hindu devotional movement in Maharashtra, usually regarded as having been founded by Jnanesvar in the 13th century, but in fact so deeply rooted among the lower castes of Maharashtra that it is impossible to attribute its origin to any single source. The Supreme God of the Warkaris is Vitthal, also known as Vithoba, whom they worship in his chief shrine at Pandharpur in South Maharashtra. Indeed, the name of the *sampradaya* is derived from the word *vari* (pilgrimage), because this is such a central feature of their worship. The origins of Vitthal/Vithoba are uncertain, but the names used for him in Warkari hymns identify him with Krishna. The Warkari movement has produced several devotional poets, the best-known of whom are Namdev (1270–1350) and Tukaram (1608–1650). Although it has cultivated an oral style of expression rather than a written one, Jnanesvar's commentary in Marathi on the *Bhagavad-gita* has been handed down as an important text for the group. The Warkaris today are mostly householders. They avoid meat and alcohol, and belong mainly to low castes, as did many of their poet–saints and leaders. It is their pilgrimages, to Pandharpur and other shrines, which distinguish them most sharply from other groups. These are made on foot and in well-organized groups which carry representations of past saints and sing hymns as they go.

Watchtower Society. The movement once generally known as the Watchtower Society is today more generally known as the **Jehovah's Witnesses**.

Way International. Founded by Victor Paul Wierwille (1916–1986), formerly pastor of the "United Church of Christ". In 1942 he claimed to have received from God "the secret of a powerful and victorious life" and the "real" teaching of the "word" as given to Christ's apostles. This teaching, especially the fact that Christians should be financially prosperous and that the "right" believing will bring material rewards in abundance, is passed on by way of a study course, called the "Power for Abundant Living" (PFAL): 33 hours of recorded material which is studied in 3 weeks. The Bible is interpreted by the teachings of Wierwille, according to whom Jesus is the Son of God but not God the Son. Graduates of the PFAL course can move on to the intermediate and advanced courses. Then a member may become a "Word over the Word (WOW) Ambassador" so that he can recruit and set up groups. WOW ambassadors are expected to hold a part-time job and spend at least eight hours a week witnessing. A WOW ambassador may take a 3-year course at the "Way Corps College" in Emporia, Kansas, which trains future leaders. The course is said to be austere and students are financially sponsored by other members, the annual fee in 1979 being over US$4,000.

The Way's international headquarters are in New Knoxville, Ohio. Since 1982, L. Craig Martindale has been its president. The organization claims to have trained 40,000 adepts in 40 countries. The structure of the movement is that of a tree. The headquarters in Ohio is the trunk, states and counties are limbs, cities are branches (British branch headquarters are in Manchester), house fellowships with about six members are known as twigs, and followers as leaves.

The financial assets are said to be considerable. A large proportion of the income is provided by course fees, college tuition and the sale of books, records, T-shirts, etc. Since 1976 it has published *The Way*. The Way's image of a "Biblical Research Centre" has helped it to escape being branded as a "cult".

Wesleyan Church. The theological teaching contained in the 44 published sermons of John Wesley, the founder of **Methodism,** have often been used as a title to indicate an emphasis on evangelism and holiness. In Britain the small Wesleyan Reform Union, centred on Sheffield, perpetuates one of the 19th century Methodist splits. The Wesleyan Holiness Church, based on Birmingham is one of the black churches. The Free Wesleyan Church of Tonga has the allegiance of 35 per cent of the island's population, including the King, and particularly promotes education and evangelism.

Western Buddhist Order (WBO). The name applied to the most committed, quasi-monastic members of the **Friends of the Western Buddhist Order (FWBO).**

Whirling Dervishes. A popular name for a Turkish **Sufi** order, the **Mawlawiya**.

Wicca. This term is preferred by some to the alternative label, **Witchcraft.**

Winti. Winti—also known as Afkodré (Dutch afgoderij, "idolatry")—is the folk religion of the Creoles of Surinam, and continues to be important to many Surinamese currently resident in the Netherlands. Of African origin, it is a spirit-possession cult, dealing with everyday concerns such as illness or misfortune. A great variety of gods and spirits, and also the spirits of the dead, need to be placated and honoured, and their help sought. Their intervention in human lives is regular, and through their possession of mediums, both male and female, they can communicate with participants in the frequent rites that take place and which involve dancing, drumming and singing such as occurs too in Afro-Christian movements such as **Kumina** and **Shango.** For Surinamese Creoles, though, typically they juxtapose the practice of Christianity and Winti and have not effected a syncretic mixture of the two.

A form of religion akin to Winti, but more systematically African in character, is practised by the Maroons—or Bush Negroes—of Surinam, descendants of escaped slaves who have lived in relative isolation in the interior.

Witchcraft. Witchcraft (the craft of the wise) or Wicca (wise—its Anglo-Saxon meaning is to bend or shape, i.e. those who can shape the unseen to their will), is regarded by many as the **Old Religion.** It has its origins in pre-Christian and pre-Celtic sources, and was traditionally worked in covens under one of the six ancient houses. Traditional craft was family-based and the lineage passed from mother to daughter. The teachings are

traditionally passed on orally through its folklore and myth. A specific example of this occurs on All Hallows Eve when, as part of the celebration of Samhain (Oct. 31—adopted by the Christian faith as the Feast of All Souls), the lineage of an ancient house may be recounted.

Witches worship the Goddess under various names. She manifests as the Triple Goddess—maiden, mother and crone, and at other times as Goddess of earth, moon and sea. The Goddess represents the universal female. The Horned God, her counterpart, is also important—symbolizing creativity. In Christian times he was seen as the Devil because of his associations with fertility and nature worship.

Magic may be used for healing or for gaining some worldly success (e.g. a new job or a lover), but its use is governed by the Wiccan Rede: Except ye harm none, do what thou wilt.

Traditional craft is distinct from the approach of Gerald B. Gardner (1884–1960) and that developed subsequently by Maxine and Alex Sanders. Gardner, in the '50s, began publishing rituals, or "Gardnerian" Rites, regarded by traditional witches as fragments of the whole craft and much more sexually explicit. Gardnerian craft has gained popularity rapidly since then in the United Kingdom, and even more so through the **Neo-Pagan** movement in America.

In the minds of the uninformed, Witchcraft may be wrongly construed as being equivalent to **Satanism.**

Won. Won Buddhism was founded in 1916 by Pak Chung-bin (sometimes called Sao-Tae San) a Korean who, through the practice of rigorous asceticism, attained a Great Enlightenment in that year. Initially the movement consisted of just the founder and a few close disciples, but by 1924, when the group gave itself the title of **The Society for the Study of the Buddha Law**, its numbers had increased considerably. However, not until the end of Japanese occupation (1945) was it able to disseminate its teachings beyond its place of origin, the region of Iri in the south-western part of the country, and into Korea at large.

The term *won* means "round" and refers to the primary symbol of the movement: a black circle on a white background. This represents the Dharma-body (*Dharmakaya*) of the Buddha and hence the totality of existence. A primary concept of the Won tradition is adaptability. All its teachings are designed to make Buddhism accessible to ordinary people living in the modern world. Consequently, its centres are all located in the cities, its translations of Buddhist texts are in modern Korean, its rituals are simple and women play a prominent role in its activities.

Whilst essentially Buddhist, the Won tradition has drawn upon **Confucianism, Taoism, Chondo Gyo** and Christianity to achieve its aims. Unlike more traditional Buddhists, adherents of Won emphasize the importance of serving society, hence the movement has been active in the establishment of educational institutions from universities down to nursery schools. At the present time the Won movement can claim well over 500,000 members.

Word of Life (Livets Ord). An evangelical, charismatic ministry, based in Uppsala, Sweden. Formed in 1983 by Ulf Ekman, previously a student priest in the Swedish **Lutheran** Church. The ministry includes a congregation and Bible school, an extensive media business (selling videos, tapes and books), a television studio, and a primary and secondary school. Administrative leadership is primarily invested in a committee consisting of Ekman, members of his family, and the second pastor of the congregation. The congregation contains over 1,500 adult members, while the Bible school trains around 1,000 students a year. Probably the majority of adherents are under 40 years old.

Although it describes itself as a non-denominational church, the group is at the centre of a growing **"Faith Movement"** in Sweden. This involves perhaps 100 new congregations and 20,000 adherents. Ekman is also chairman of "The Faith Movement's Organization of Preachers in Scandinavia" (Trosrörelsens Predikant-organisation). Close links with North American Faith ministries are also maintained including Kenneth Hagin's Rhema Bible Church in Tulsa, Oklahoma, where Ekman studied in 1981–2. Since 1989 the Word of Life has focussed missionary work on Eastern Europe.

Faith teaching in the United States and Sweden is frequently called the "Gospel of Prosperity" (Framgångangsteologi). Financial prosperity and bodily health are held to be available to those who are "born-again" although it is stated that the "Last Days" may be approaching, believers are encouraged to achieve material success in order to appropriate worldly resources for Christian ends.

The "Word of Life" is a significant expression of the contemporary growth and global spread of evangelical Protestantism and the **"electronic church"**.

Its emergence is particularly interesting in a country as apparently secularized as Sweden, and has caused considerable controversy. The group has been accused by journalists, theologians and politicians of representing a politically right-wing ideology, opposed to the ideals of Social Democracy. It is frequently characterized by State and Free Church clergy as destructive of ecumenical relations, and eager to poach members from other congregations.

World Assembly of Muslim Youth. The World Assembly of Muslim Youth was established in 1972 by the Saudi-based **Muslim World League.** It organizes conferences, publishes books and pamphlets, and runs popular youth camps in countries as far apart as Morocco and Malaysia, as well as in Brazil, Britain and the US.

World Buddhist Sangha Council (WBSC). Formed in May 1966, its headquarters are at Colombo, Sri Lanka. It was designed to meet the growing need for an international organization of Buddhist monks (*bhikkhus*) which could deal with problems of the *Sangha* worldwide. The Sri Lankan Department of Cultural Affairs provided initial patronage and *bhikkhus* were sent abroad to establish Buddhist centres and propagate the *Dhamma*.

The WBSC has been instrumental in the resurgence of traditional **Theravada** Buddhism in South East Asia and, to date, many monks have been supported during their missionary work in the USA and Africa.

World Community of Islam in the West. This was the name used for a while, from 1976 to 1980, by the US organization known before that as the Nation of Islam, and subsequently (and currently) as the American Muslim Mission. Through all these changes, however, the label which stuck was the popular one of the **Black Muslims.**

World Conference on Religion and Peace. This international network of people of different faiths united by a concern for peace and justice was initiated with a conference in Kyoto in 1970. The immediate practical concern was to promote peace initiatives in the Vietnam war. Subsequent conferences were held in Leuven (1974), Princeton (1979), Nairobi (1984) and Melbourne (1989). The international headquarters of the organization, formerly in Geneva, is now in New York in order to facilitate its contributions to the UN (it is a Category II United Nations Non-Governmental Organization associated with the Economic and Social Council). It has established an international network of local groups, and is seeking to establish an interreligious aid programme for refugees. It supports programmes of peace education, and links its concern with promoting positive disarmament measures

with analyses of the international economic and political structures which perpetuate injustice and poverty. Conflicts which are rooted in religious allegiances, or which take on that guise, are its particular concern.

World Congress of Christian Fundamentalists. The keynote address of the 1990 World Congress of Christian Fundamentalists, held in London, was delivered by the veteran American **evangelical,** Dr. Bob Jones, chancellor of Bob Jones University. The definition of Fundamentalism put forward by a committee which included the Rev. Ian Paisley of Northern Ireland and printed in the Congress programme stated that "A fundamentalist is a born-again believer in the Lord Jesus Christ who maintains an unmovable allegiance to the inerrant, infallible, and verbally inspired Bible". Previous World Congresses had developed this definition and its implications. At Greenville, USA in 1986, it was resolved to reaffirm the unique and special place of the Authorized (King James) Version of 1611 and condemn all modern versions such as the New English Bible, Revised Standard Version, Good News Bible and the New International Version. At Singapore in 1980 apostasy and compromise which were to be found in dialogue with Roman Catholics, Jews and other religions, were rejected. The **Roman Catholic** Church was claimed to be revealed in Scripture as "the mother of harlots and abominations" (Revelation 17:5). Also condemned at Edinburgh in 1986 was the alleged growth of Satanism, the Unification Church of Sun Moon, and the charismatic movement "as being a satanic counterfeit of true revelational Christianity . . . emotional experience is exalted, true doctrine is minimized".

World Congress of Faiths. This organization exists to promote inter-faith activity and understanding of the kind that began in 1893 with the World Parliament of

Religions held in Chicago. The moving spirit behind its establishment was Sir Francis Younghusband, who was influenced in part by the 1933 gathering of a World Fellowship of Faiths in Chicago held in conscious imitation of the earlier World Parliament gathering.

Although no follow-up occurred in the United States, Younghusband was encouraged to organize a World Congress of Faiths in London in 1936, and this then inaugurated a permanent organization under the same name. Younghusband had developed a personal philosophy of his own, and this perspective, according to which there was an underlying unity of experience beneath the surface differences between religions, has been one major strand in the work of the Congress throughout its life. It has sought to promote a shared recognition of spiritual reality through shared understanding by members of different faiths, without, however, seeking to generate a new synthetic faith.

A more recent focus of interest has been the search for a global ethic, in which the relationship between human rights and religious traditions is explored. An interest in seeking common moral values contained in the different world religions became prominent from the 1960s onwards, inspired in the first instance by the then chairman, Baron Reginald Sorensen.

Inter-faith dialogue is today far more common than when the Congress began its work, but remains a central concern of Congress members. For others, the aim of inter-faith dialogue may be primarily, or indeed exclusively one of removing misunderstandings and promoting tolerance, but within the Congress there is the added dimension of the search for a shared truth.

With the development of multi-religious societies in Europe in particular, the Congress has taken an interest in the inclusion of a world religions perspective in religious education.

An annual conference is held, the journal *World Faiths* is published, and s substantial number of inter-faith services have been organized. The headquarters are in London.

World Council of Churches. Formally inaugurated at Amsterdam in 1948, the World Council of Churches began as an international fellowship of autonomous **Protestant** and **Eastern Orthodox** churches which "accept our Lord Jesus Christ as God and Saviour". It marked the fusion of two strands: Faith and Order, concerned with the common expression of the Christian faith, without compromising the doctrinal integrity of any particular denomination, and Life and Work which attempted a Christian response to social, political, and economic problems. The discussions at Amsterdam were inevitably coloured by the experience of World War II, the threat of Communism, and the neo-orthodox Theology of Karl Barth. Its headquarters was set up in Geneva and its first General Secretary was the Dutchman W. A. Visser 't Hooft.

The reality of world political and economic power was recognized in the decision to hold the second congress at Evanston, USA in 1954, but it was the third congress in New Delhi in 1961 which marked a watershed through the vastly increased representation from the Third World which included 11 African churches, many of which owed little to Western missions. Criticism of the doctrinal basis of the WCC that it was not sufficiently Trinitarian, was addressed at this congress by the addition of a reference to the scriptures and to "their common calling to the glory of the one God, Father, Son and Holy Spirit".

At New Delhi reconsideration was also given to the use of the word "churches" in the WCC's title and stress was increasingly placed on the notion that "churches" applies only to diverse manifestations of the one Holy, Catholic Church. It was the 1975 Congress at Nairobi which called for "visible unity in one faith and in one eucharistic fellowship". The acceptance of this goal was eased by creative thinking about "reconciled diversity" and "conciliar fellowship" which led up to the Lima text on Baptism, Eucharist, and Ministry.

In 1968 the Uppsala assembly accepted a trusteeship over creation, "guarding, developing and sharing its resources", and coming to the conclusion that "Christ takes the side of the poor and oppressed". A few weeks later, the **Roman Catholic** Episcopal Conference of Latin America, meeting at Medellín in Colombia, declared that the Church should take an option for the poor. This parallel thinking had been institutionalized in the creation of a joint Roman Catholic and WCC secretariat and committee on the issues of society, development and peace (SODEPAX).

The 1975 Assembly in Nairobi agreed to what in Britain became a highly controversial *Programme to Combat Racism*, and in the wake of the oil crisis, to a "just, participatory and sustainable society". This was carried further at Vancouver in 1983 when the fellowship was extended in response to pressure from women, youth, the physically disabled, and children for their voices to be heard. The 1991 Assembly in Australia seemed to some critics to move too far in accepting the religious experiences of social and cultural minorities like Australian Aboriginals and American Indians.

In 1993 a new General Secretary, Dr. Konrad Raiser, will take office at a time of restructuring, partly in response to diminishing financial resources. He brings to the post a strong awareness of the disquiet expressed by the **Orthodox** at recent developments.

World Council of Synagogues. *See* **Conservative Judaism.**

World Federation of Buddhists. *See* **World Fellowship of Buddhists.**

World Fellowship of Buddhists (WFB). First established in 1950 by G. P. Malalasekere and sponsored by the **All Ceylon Buddhist Congress,** this is a predominantly a non-denominational lay organization. Its aim is to carry on the spirit of the historical Buddhist councils as an expression of true religious ecumenism. At its first World Buddhist conference in Colombo, Sri Lanka (1951) lay and monastic representatives from 27 countries, covering nearly all Buddhist schools, were in attendance. Its headquarters has been in Bangkok since 1969 and there are 82 active regional centres throughout the world. The WFB is involved in social and humanitarian programmes, supports the establishment of Buddhist education and has been instrumental in developing Lumbini in southern Nepal, the birthplace of the Buddha, as a major pilgrimage site. It maintains a large number of **Dhammaduta** missionary centres around the globe. About 50 monks per year are supported in this work. The organization publishes a journal, the *WFB Review,* and a book series in Thai and English. The WFB flag, comprising the five colours of the Buddha's halo, is much used by Buddhists today. It was designed by Col. Olcott, a leading **Theosophist,** in the 1880s.

World Islamic Call Society. This Libyan-based would-be rival to the Saudi-based **Muslim World League** is still more commonly known by its original and simpler title, the **Islamic Call Society.** It promotes Qaddafi's atypical interpretation of Islam, and his view of modern Western societies as centres of Christian hostility to Islam in the manner of the medieval Crusaders.

World Jewish Congress. International association of Jewish representative bodies founded in 1936 in Geneva "to assure the survival and to foster the unity of the Jewish people". Presently there are representatives from more than 60 countries. The Congress has addressed issues of concern to Jews worldwide, such as War Crimes after the *Holocaust*; compensation from Germany after 1945; anti-semitism. Its research branch, the Institute of Jewish Affairs, is in London.

World Messianity. The English rendering of **Sekai Kyuseikyo,** a Japanese new religious movement.

World Methodist Council. Formed in 1951 in succession to the *ad hoc* conference held since 1881, the World Methodist Council under its chairman, Donald English, and secretary Joe Hale, has plans for a decade of indigenous evangelism by galvanizing the 26,000,000 **Methodists** in more than 90 countries.

World Muslim Congress. The World Muslim Congress (Mu'tamar al-'Alam al-Islami) is one of the main international Islamic organizations, along with the **Muslim World League** and the **Organization of the Islamic Conference.** Founded in 1926 during an international Muslim conference in Mecca, subsequent conferences were held in Jerusalem in 1931 and Karachi in 1949 and 1951. Its present structure was established at the last of these, and Karachi remains its main base.

Primarily a cultural organization to promote unity and co-operation among Muslims, it is seen by some observers as one of the ways in which Pakistan seeks to establish important Islamic credentials rivalling those of Saudi Arabia. Most of its activities have now been assumed, however, by the Saudi-based **Muslim World League.**

There are five regional offices internationally, in Senegal, Somalia, Lebanon, Malaysia and the Philippines.

World True Light Civilization. The English form of **Sekai Mahikari Bunmei Kyodan,** a Japanese new religious movement.

World Union for Progressive Judaism. (See also **Reform Judaism.**) Founded in London in 1926 in order to foster the cause of **Progressive Judaism (Reform and Liberal Judaism)**, the World Union moved its headquarters to Jerusalem in 1973 and includes the recognition of Jewish religious pluralism in Israel among its aims. It represents communities in more than 20 countries worldwide.

Worldwide Church of God. Also known as Armstrongism, after the founder Herbert W. Armstrong who founded the Church in Oregon in 1933 as the Radio Church of God. He had left his ministry at a **Seventh Day Adventist** Church in Missouri. Since 1947, the international headquarters have been in Pasadena, California. The propagation of The Worldwide Church of God (WCG) teachings is based on the media and established the WCG in American evangelism. With the acquisition of a property near St. Albans in 1959 the WCG started its activities in Britain. As in America, the media (pirate radio stations, magazines and newspapers) were used to make the Church known. Today, it boasts 800 congregations in 120 countries. In Britain 22 full-time ministers look after 3,000 baptized members. The UK headquarters are in Borehamwood, Hertfordshire.

However, with the death of Armstrong's wife Lorna (1967) schisms and power struggles occurred, exacerbated by allegations of moral and financial misconduct in the leadership. Armstrong himself was accused of dictatorial and totalitarian style of leadership. Several splinter groups broke away, among them one led by Armstrong's son, Garner Ted Armstrong, who set up his Church of God International in 1978, with its UK headquarters in Lincoln.

The organizational structure of the WCG is hierarchical, with offices only open to men. Armstrong was the head bearing the title "Apostle"; after his death in 1986, he was succeeded by Joseph

W. Tkach, called "Pastor-General". The second-in-command is called "Evangelist", followed by pastors, preaching elders, local elders, and deacons. Total membership of baptized members is claimed to be 94,000 worldwide. The WCG gives a literal interpretation of the Bible, lays great store by prophecy, teaches the Second Advent of Christ, celebrates Saturday as the day of rest, observes Jewish Holy Days (Passover, Atonement, Tabernacles, etc), claiming that Easter and Christmas are unbiblical. In its teachings of ethics and morality the Church appears conservative, emphasizing marriage and family life. Adherents eat kosher food. There is a stress on spiritual healing, with some members discouraging the use of modern medicine, although others see no contradiction between the two.

Funds are raised through tithing (members give 10 per cent of their net income) and appeals for "offerings". The movement's main publication is *Plain Truth,* a monthly magazine with a purported circulation of 2,000,000 copies in six languages. The Church publishes a number of booklets on specific topics addressing "the big questions of life", like The Ambassador College Bible Correspondence Course. The Ambassador College (founded in 1947) in Texas offers 4-year undergraduate courses in humanities, training ministers and personnel for the Church.

Y

'Yan Tatsine ('Yan Isala). The 'Yan Tatsine is a Nigerian Islamic sect which shot to prominence in December 1980 when large-scale rioting broke out in Kano. Followers of Alhaji Muhammadu Marwa, known as Maitatsine—Hausa for "he with powers of cursing"—fought pitched battles with police and army, resulting in several thousand dead, including Marwa himself (who had gradually built up a large following over the previous 20 years). The sect, which preaches a radical denunciation of materialism and privilege—and curses or damns (hence the name it acquired) all who are attached to modern materialist objects from bicycles and watches to economic wealth—recruits among refugees from Chad and Niger as well as among poor rural migrants to the cities and alienated wandering Quranic students (*gardawa*) and teachers (*mallams*). It has continued in existence despite the disaster of 1980, which was precipitated by the sect's attempt to take over the Friday mosque in Kano as a prelude to an insurrectionary attempt to establish control of Kano itself, and further outbreaks of violence occurred in 1982 (in Maiduguri and Kaduna), 1984 (in Yola), and 1985 (in Gombe).

There are certain similarities between the 'Yan Tatsine (meaning followers of Maitatsine, but sometimes also known simply as Maitatsine, or as 'Yan Izala) and the **Ikhwan** who occupied the mosque in Mecca in 1979.

Yasawiya. A **Sufi** order centred on the town of Turkistan in Kazakhstan. In former times it had some prominence in Central Asia, but is now rather limited in scope and influence. Two offshoots are the **Laachi** and the **Hairy Ishans**.

Yazidis. A small but widely-dispersed religious and tribal community mainly found in western Iran, Iraq, and Syria, Kurdish-speaking but distinct from the main body of Kurds. The origins of the cult are obscure, but it seems to involve a syncretistic mixture of early Iranian beliefs, Christian, Muslim (including **Sufi**), and related doctrines and practices. The Yazidis are often mistakenly referred to as "Devil-Worshippers" through a misunderstanding of their dualistic belief system in which the creation and continuation of the world are shared by God and Malik Taus, the peacock angel. Although some Muslim writers have regarded them as an Islamic sect, this does not appear to be historically or doctrinally accurate. The cult possesses a large priestly class and has distinct prayers, pilgrimages, festivals, and other rituals. There is a small body of sacred literature in Arabic, accessible only to the senior priesthood.

Current conditions in Iraq and Iran make it difficult to say with any precision what the fate of the Yazidis has been in recent years.

Yoga. Yoga is perhaps the best known of the six orthodox Hundu philosophical systems. Supposedly founded by the ancient sage Yājñavalka, the system was first codified in the *Yogasutra*, traditionally ascribed to Patanjali who redacted the work in approximately 200 CE. The term is derived from the root *yuj*, to "yoke" or "join." Yoga is often seen as the practical embodiment of the Samkhya school of philosophy, but it forms a part of most forms of Hindu meditative practice. Like Sāṁkhya, early Yoga downplays the importance of God, and references to God in Patanjali may well be later interpolations. This is not to say that later schools of thought which appropriated yoga's "technology" for their own purposes did not introduce theological elements, but rather the primary aim of yoga has always been to teach the means by which the individual human soul may gain release from the phenomenal world regardless of the existence or non-existence of a personal deity. This is accomplished through the "eight limbs of yoga". Those who practice these techniques believe that these "limbs" results in the individual's liberation from rebirth in the world. The first of these techniques is *yama*, external control and restraint of the senses. Next is *niyama*, internal control of the mind through meditation. This is followed by *āsana*, the well-known bodily postures of yoga, and *prāṇayāma*, control of the breath. These lead to *pratyāhāra*, control of the senses and *dhāraṇa*, meditation. As these deepen, the practitioner enters the states of *dhyāna*, contemplation, and finally *samādhi*, super-consciousness.

There are a number of different schools of yoga which have different emphases. *Karma-yoga* is primarily concerned with salvation through works or action in the world. *Bhakti-yoga* places its emphasis on devotion to the gods and salvation through faith. *Jñāna-yoga* focuses on the pursuit of wisdom. These three forms of yoga are mentioned, and their practice sanctified, in the *Bhagavad Gītā*. The esoteric *laya-yoga* deals with the acquisition of magical powers through the activation of the subtle centres of the body. *Haṭha-yoga* is concerned with physical culture, while *rāja-yoga* emphasizes spiritual aspects of the system. *Haṭha-yoga* is perhaps the system most recognizable to the Westerner. Rāja, or "royal" yoga lays far more stress on the psychological and spiritual elements of yoga than does *haṭha-yoga*. Theoretically, it consists of the eight "limbs" described above practiced on the spiritual plane, but in point of fact it is really a concentration on the final four "limbs". The culmination of this system is held to lie in the so-called *mahā-yoga*, the "great yoga" which is free of any and all external forms and techniques. This was held to

result in a mind free of hatred, greed, fear and lust. A mind which was, in a word, free of the ties that bound it to the phenomenal world. Here one might also note the various "yogic" practices, such as *kuṇḍalinī yoga*, practiced by the non-traditional schools of Hinduism. Yoga is one of the most prevalent forms of Hindu religious practice and forms a significant part of the teachings of most contemporary Hindu gurus.

Young Buddhists Association. Founded in Bangkok in 1950 with aims similar to those of the **Buddhist Association of Thailand,** though in this case targetted towards the young. There are approximately 45 provincial organizations throughout the kingdom which run lecture programmes, libraries and holiday work camps. The Association is strongly involved in propogating the *dhamma* through the medium of radio and television.

Young Christian Workers. This **Roman Catholic** organization is an extension into the English-speaking world of Jeunesse Ouvrière Chrétienne, whose members are often referred to as **Jocists.**

Young Men's Buddhist Association (YMBA). A Sri Lankan **Theravada** Buddhist lay movement which aims to "advance the moral, cultural, physical and social welfare of Buddhists" whether young or old. Founded in 1898 by an ex-Catholic and now based in Colombo its activities are island-wide. It sponsors Buddhist Sunday schools in most villages, though these have been the overall responsibility of the Department of Cultural Affairs since 1961. The YMBA publishes a journal. *The Buddhist.* The leadership committee is known as the **All Ceylon Buddhist Congress.**

Z

Zar Cult. The zar cult is to be found in the Nile area in Egypt and the Sudan, in Somalia (where the zar is known as the sar), and in Ethiopia (where it appears to have originated). It is a spiritist cult, or spirit possession cult, similar to others found across Sudanic Africa from Ethiopia to Senegal. The *zar* is a spirit believed to possess women, causing depression or frustration. The afflicted woman engages a *shaykha*, or female religious specialist (although on occasion it may be a male), before whom she dances, speaking in the voice of the *zar*, and acting out its character. There may also be blood sacrifice. The *shaykha* then diagnoses the root of the problem, and relieves the woman of her affliction by suggesting a way of appeasing the spirit.

Confined almost exclusively to women, the *zar* cult tends to be despised by the men (themselves often members of **Sufi** orders).

Zaydis. The smallest of the main branches of **Shi'ite** Islam. The sect originated in allegiance to Zayd ibn 'Ali (d. 740), a brother of the fifth mainstream *Imam*. Unlike the **Imami** leaders, Zayd advocated armed rebellion to establish Shi'ite rule, and was himself killed in an abortive uprising. Zaydi states were established in Tabaristan (864–928) and Yemen (from 893 to the present, with interruptions). In doctrinal and legal matters, the Zaydis come closest of all the Shi'a to **Sunni** orthodoxy. During this century, attempts to intensify a traditionalist religious rule in Yemen have been modified by wider political conditions in the country and its division in 1970. Zaydis form about 40 per cent of the population of the former Yemen Arab Republic, with their traditional centres in the northern and central highlands and the eastern desert.

Zen. An important form of Japanese Mahayana Buddhism. The word *zen* means meditation and is a translation of the Chinese term *ch'an*. The Ch'an tradition arrived rather late in Japan, though earlier forms of Buddhism, particularly **Tendai, Hosso** and **Kegon,** eased the way by making rigorous meditation practice more familiar to the Japanese people. Myoan Eisai (1141–1215) is generally regarded as the founder of Zen. Travelling to China in 1168 and studying under masters of the Lin-chi (Jap. **Rinzai)** tradition, Eisai gained enlightenment and established the first Zen temple at Hakada, on the southern island of Kyushu, in 1194. He later directed the influential Kenninji temple in Kyoto at which Zen practices were taught alongside those of the Tendai and Shingon schools. His disciples successfully purged Zen of doctrines associated with the older schools of Japanese Buddhism and a variety of Chinese Lin-chi (Rinzai) masters were encouraged to visit Japan to complete this work in the late Kamakura period.

Soto Zen was brought from China, during the Sung period, by Dogen Kigen (1200–1253). Since that time the Koshoji near Kyoto has been its major temple. Soto is characterized by the centrality of *zazen* (sitting meditation) in its practice, while Rinzai gives great prominence to meditation on the *koan* (public utterance). Both schools have continued to flourish down to modern times, though the former was riven by schism throughout the 13th century. After a period of stagnation, Soto began a renaissance in the 17th century. Its spread throughout Japan has led to it becoming the second biggest Buddhist school, the largest being **Nichirenshoshu.** Another Zen school, the **Obaku,** owes its existence to the missionary activities of Chinese monks during the Tokugawa Shogunate (1603–1867). Established first in Kyushu and soon after (1661) in Kyoto, the Rinzai-based Obaku has remained reasonably small.

In the Middle Ages literature, calligraphy, painting and garden creation flourished, particularly in connection with the Rinzai Five Mountain (*gozan*) movement centred on Kyoto and Kamakura. Similarly, the way of tea (*sado*) owes its existence to a variety of Rinzai masters based at the Daitokuji temple, Kyoto during the 16th century. Finally two Zen practitioners of the Edo period deserve mention. Takuan Soho (1573–1645) was Japan's greatest teacher of swordsmanship and is regarded as an important influence on the later chivalric tradition. Basho (1644–1694) is the most prominent exponent of the *haiku* poetic form. His naturalism is a recurring theme in later Zen-inspired culture. In the Meiji period (1868–1912) non-Shinto religion was briefly suppressed, though Rinzai, Soto and Obaku have continued to receive support since that time. In recent years a good deal of interest in Zen has developed in the West in response to the opening of Japan to the outside world. The writings of D. T. Suzuki and the beat poets of 1950s America have been influential in this regard. Similarly, the **Order of Buddhist Contemplatives** is one of the many quasi-independent Western-Buddhist based Zen movement to emerge in the last few decades.

Zionism. Zionism is the modern political movement which supports the Jews' re-establishing a national centre in their ancestral homeland. Contemporary Zionists disagree about the necessity of every Jew living in the State of Israel but all support its existence. Since the Romans' destruction of the Temple (70 CE) and subsequent exiling of the Jews, traditional Judaism hoped for a return to the Land of Israel. Zionism as a political movement, however, began at the end of the 19th century under the leadership of Theodor Herzl (1860–1904). Although a group of Russian Jews created the *Hibbat Zion* ("love of Zion") movement to create agricultural villages in the Land of Israel

following the 1881 Russian *pogroms*, it was Herzl who created a Jewish nationalist movement which united Jews from many lands and put their quest for a secure home on the international agenda.

Zionism was a response to both internal and external events in the lives of modern Jews. It began as a response to the failure of emancipation to provide full equality for all citizens, it becoming clear that Jews were expected to give up much of their identity in order to "fit in" but as the pogroms, Dreyfus Affair, and later *Holocaust* showed, even this was not enough. Internally, many Jews began to question both the passivity of many **Orthodox** Jewish leaders as well as others' assimilationist tendencies.

Against this backdrop, Herzl began his activities, organizing the first Zionist conference in Basle, Switzerland (1897). Herzl worked tirelessly on the project, seeking international support for a state for the Jews. Herzl held the movement together despite internal divisions over the place of traditional Judaism in Zionism and a British proposal to give the Jews Uganda—a plan which Herzl backed only as a temporary measure but which was rejected by the movement. Herzl's early death stunned the organization.

Nonetheless, Zionists kept immigrating. The 1904–1906 Second Aliyah ("ascendants", i.e. immigrants to the Land of Israel) from Russia included an influential group of secular socialists who sought to re-shape the Jews by making them into communal farmers. This structure eventually became the **Kibbutz** ("collective farm") movement which became the symbol of Zionism pioneerism. Kibbutzim were established by the prominent *ha-Shorner ha-Tza'ir* ("The Young Guard") movement as well as *ha-Kibbutz ha-Me'uhed* ("the united kibbutz") and *Kibbutz ha-Dati* ("the religious kibbutz"). The secular lifestyle of most kibbutzim outraged the majority of traditional Jews who insisted that only God could save the Jews. One of the few early religious Zionists, Rabbi Abraham Isaac ha-Kohen Kook (1865–1935), embraced the pioneers, arguing that their "insolence" was actually a harbinger of the Messianic era.

World War I radically affected the Middle East with the defeat of the Ottoman Empire. During the war, in 1917, the British issued the *Balfour declaration* which expressed support for "a national home in Palestine for the Jewish people". Although later British governments would attempt to limit Jewish rights, their support at this point was important for Zionism.

Four main trends developed among Jews in the *Yishuv* ("the dwelling," the Jews living in the Land of Israel). Of the Zionist "new" *Yishuv*, the largest were the Socialists, which dominated *Yishuv* and Israeli politics until 1977. Led by men such as Berl Katznelson (1887–1944) and David Ben-Gurion (1886–1973), much of the infrastructure of present-day Israel was created, such as the federation of labor unions, the Histadrut. In 1930, the various unions formed Mapai, which after merging with smaller parties became Ma'arach (Alignment or Labour).

Opposed to them were the Revisionists led by Ze'ev (Vladimir) Jabotinsky (1880–1940) who rejected socialism and a 1937 plan partitioning Mandatory Palestine into a Jewish and an Arab state. The movement evolved into the Herut party led by Menachem Begin, which, except for the years 1967–1970 (from the 1967 Middle East crisis to a dispute over the question of withdrawal from the territories), was in opposition to Labour-led coalitions until 1977 when Herut, at the centre of the larger Likud party defeated the Left. Since 1977, the Likud has either led or shared power in ruling coalitions.

The third trend, **Religious Zionism,** was represented by Mizrahi (an acronym for *Merkaz Ruhani*, "spiritual centre"), the forerunner to the **National Religious Party.** Founded in 1902 Mizrahi was the only traditionalist group to join the **World Zionist Organization.** While most religious Zionists did not consider Zionism to be concerned with the Jews' redemption, the influential Rabbi A. I. Kook, noted

above, did. His son, Rabbi Tzvi Yehudah ha-Kohen Kook (1891–1982), continued this line of thought, seeing the Six-Day War as confirmation that the redemptive process was unfolding. He and his students affected Israeli society by creating **Gush Emunim** ("bloc of the faithful"), which led the broader-based settlement movement in the occupied territories. Although the National Religious Party currently strongly supports the settlement movement, a minority of religious Israelis, clustered around the *Oz ve-Shalom* (strength and peace) and *Netivot Shalom* (paths of peace) movements, supports a more conciliatory approach.

The fourth group is comprised of non- or anti-Zionists. In 1919 they attached themselves to **Agudat Yisrael** (bloc of Israel), whose overall policy did not oppose Jewish nationalism but disagreed with Zionism's disregard for *diaspora* Judaism and its general secularity. The Jerusalemite chapter, however, was much more opposed to Zionism than overall movement. Yet as the Yishuv developed, Agudat Yisrael began having more contacts and inter-actions with Zionism, prompting an isolationist faction, the **Edah Ḥaredit** ("ḥaredit community"), to bolt the party. Today, Agudat Yisrael, despite philosophically opposing Zionism, takes part in the Israeli political system, and in recent years, participating in governmental coalitions in return for religious concessions. Recently, the party has splintered. In 1984, Sephardi members formed a new party, in response to perceived discrimination by Agudat Yisrael's **Ashkenazi** leadership. In 1988, Agudat Yisrael became further divided when Rabbi Eliezer Shach, supported the formation of the **Degel ha-Torah** ("banner of the Torah") party to combat what he saw as the undue influence of **Lubavitch** Ḥasidism in the party.

Zionist Churches. This is the label used primarily in a South African context to refer to African independent churches of the prophet-healing type. Whereas the so-called **Ethiopian** churches largely reproduced the dominant Western forms of Christianity, and were often based on group secessions from the European-run churches, the Zionist churches, which began to appear from the 1920s onwards, were typically founded by a charismatic leader, developed distinctive patterns of worship (e.g. with drumming and dancing) and emphasized gifts of prophecy and healing in the manner of the **Pentecostals.** In Nigeria the same kinds of churches are referred to as **Aladura** churches. They exercise a powerful appeal, and there are thought to be several hundreds of them. *See too* **African New Religious Movements.**

Zoe. Zoe ("Life") is the oldest and most influential of the several evangelical and reform movements that have been a notable feature of **Orthodox** Christianity in Greece since the beginning of the 20th century. Founded in 1907 by the archimandrite (monastic priest) and preacher Eusebius Matthopoulos (1849–1929), together with four other theologians, it entered the public arena in 1911 with the first publication of the periodical *Zoe,* from which the movement takes its name. Against a background of nominal Christianity and lax religious observance among a population served by a largely uneducated clergy, Zoe aimed to renew Orthodox Christian values among all sections of Greek society, particularly through preaching and Bible study; to encourage closer participation in the Church's sacramental life (especially through more frequent confession and communion); and to reform certain elements of Church worship and custom. Extremely well organized, the movement has pursued its aims in all sectors and age groups of the Greek population, through preaching, teaching, publishing, and social work.

Based in Athens, Zoe is registered as a private and voluntary corporation; it has no official Church ties or State support. At its centre is the Zoe Brotherhood, a body of theologically trained individuals organized along monastic lines and consisting mainly of unmarried laymen who undertake a life of poverty, obedience and chastity (though no strictly binding vows). Its members, who include a minority of priests, refuse all ecclesiastical preferments. They pursue their activities throughout Greece, initiating Bible study groups, organizing catechism classes, and working through various affiliated organizations, which include separate Christian Unions for Students, Teachers, Men of Science, and Young Workers. There is also a Women's Association, Eusebia. In addition to its widely circulated weekly *Zoe,* the movement publishes numerous popular and specialist books and periodicals, as well as translations of the New Testament in modern demotic Greek. It has shops in all the main towns and cities.

Relations between Zoe and the Greek Church have been mixed. On the one hand the members and work of Zoe have been regarded with suspicion and sometimes hostility, since the movement's very existence implies deficiencies in the theological and pastoral abilities of parish priest and bishop alike, while as an independent religious organization it is easily perceived as a rival, or as a Church within the Church (rather as **Opus Dei** has been regarded in **Roman Catholicism**). At the same time the more secular Greeks find it easy to despise Zoe for its moralistic and pietistic attitudes. On the other hand many among the clergy have welcomed and encouraged the work of Zoe, regarding its aims and achievements as one with their own. In 1930 the success of Zoe and other movements encouraged the official hierarchy to set up its own "home missionary" movement, the Apostoliki Diakonia ("Apostolic Service"), though this now co-operates with both Zoe and Sotir in the organization of catechism classes.

Despite its inherently conservative character, Zoe has undergone significant development. In 1960 changes within the movement led a conservative faction to defect and set up a rival organization, Sotir

("Salvation"), whose activities parallel those of Zoe though in a more puritanical and in some respects fanatical mode. In recent years Zoe theologians have become more aware of western theology, and to some extent influenced by it, and an interest in ecumenical issues is slowly developing. The main impact of Zoe has been in urban Greece, among the middle classes from whom the members of the Brotherhood themselves are drawn.

Zoroastrians. Followers of the ancient religion established by the Iranian "prophet" Zarathustra (known in the West as Zoroaster) who lived in Iran, c.1000 BCE. They sometimes refer to themselves as **Mazdayasnians,** "worshippers of Ahura Mazda", the "wise lord" and entirely good God (and so **Mazdaism**). Their early history is obscure, but from the sixth century BCE until the coming of Islam in the seventh century CE theirs was the most important, perhaps the official state religion in three successive Iranian empires. The precise nature of that religion fluctuated; the dominant tradition for perhaps four hundred years before Islam may have been **Zurvanism,** which proposed "Time" as a first principle and so compromised the absolute dualism of "orthodox" Zoroastrianism.

After the Arab invasions, Zoroastrians suffered persistent persecution and were marginalized numerically, economically and geographically. The faithful remnants of **Irani Zoroastrians** were forced to retreat to remote Iranian villages where they subsisted in poverty. As a result of these conditions, some Zoroastrians left Iran in the 10th century CE, eventually establishing a community in north-west India where they became known as **Parsis** ("Persians"). For those left in Iran, there was a brief improvement under the Pahlavi dynasty (1925–1979). Parsis now constitute the largest group of Zoroastrians (approximately 100,000 compared to: Iran, 30,000; Pakistan 4,000; Britain and North America 6,000).

The traditional teachings of Zoroastrianism are contained in its holy text, the *Avesta*, associated with Zarathustra himself. Of equal importance is the Pahlavi literature (about the ninth century CE). The central insight of the religion is that the world and human beings are the field in which the cosmic struggle between good and evil takes place. On the one side of this radical ethical dualism is the good God, Ahura Mazda, on the other the evil Angra Mainyu. Both at the cosmic and at the individual levels, the good or evil nature of things is the result of free moral choice. Human beings are at the centre of this struggle, and it is their duty to care for the creation of God (that is the spiritual and the material world) and to fight evil in all its forms. In the long term, the favourable outcome of this struggle is not in doubt. Zoroastrians also believe in heaven, hell, resurrection of the dead, and a final judgement, ideas that may have had a substantial influence on the Semitic religions.

Fire, representing God, plays the central role in Zoroastrian worship or sacrifice (*yasna*). It is tended by hereditary priests; physical and moral purity is essential to the ritual. Originally focussed on the ever-burning hearth fire, such worship has constituted a temple cult since the fourth century BCE. Boys and girls are initiated into the Zoroastrian community before puberty, when they are invested with a sacred shirt (*sudre*) and cord (*kusti*). Since it is considered to be the work of evil, death also involves substantial purificatory rituals.

Traditionally, Zoroastrians do not accept converts and favour marriage between blood relations (usually cousins). Similarly, they do not proselytize. Today a steady decline in their numerical strength has made them increasingly self-conscious about the essential nature of their community and religion and their need to preserve it.

PART III: COUNTRY-BY-COUNTRY SUMMARY

Afghanistan

Afghanistan has a population of approximately 20,700,000 composed of 20 indigenous language groups, including Pushtun, for which "Afghan" is a synonym. Some 99 per cent of the population are Muslims, with about 90 per cent being **Sunnis** of the **Hanafi** school of religious law, and about 9 per cent **Shi'ites**. Most of the latter are **Twelver** Shi'ites—comprising two ethnic groups in particular, the **Qizilbash** (also a religious group) and the Hazaras—along with some **Isma'ilis** (mostly **Aga Khanis**). Amongst the Sunni majority, certain **Sufi** orders have put down deep roots, above all the **Naqshabandiya** and the **Qadiriya**, both traditionally with strong links to the ruling élite in Kabul, but in the case of the former in particular mobilized into opposition to government by the arrest of their leaders in the wake of the 1978 *coup*.

In addition to the Muslim population there are some 100,000 Hindu and **Sikh** Indians, a few thousand tribal religionists, and a similar number of Christians, roughly equally divided between **Roman Catholics** and **Anglicans**, as well as a small number of Central Asian Jews ("Bukharan").

The country has traditionally been an Islamic monarchy, and this was recognized in the 1964 constitution which declared Islam to be the official state religion. However, the king was deposed in 1973, and since then the Islamic organizations have been the leading forces in opposing Communist rule, both before and after the Soviet invasion. Although these mujahidin have at times been described collectively as "fundamentalists", it is important to distinguish between the traditionalist (or "moderate") groups led by the *ulama* and the Sufi *pirs*, who are inclined to advocate the re-establishment of the monarchy, and the revolutionary groups, who wish to establish an Islamic state based upon Quranic law.

The three main conservative organizations are: (i) Mahaz-i Melli-i Islami (National Islamic Front) consisting of the personal following of the Sufi leader Pir Sayid Ahmed Gailani; (ii) Harakat-i Inqilab-i Islami (Movement for Islamic Revolution) led by an expert on Islamic law, Nabi Muhammadi, but tarnished by corruption; and (iii) Jebha-i Nejat-i Melli Afghanistan (Afghan National Liberation Front) led by Imam Sibghatullah Mujjaddidi who advocates the restoration of the monarchy.

The three main radical groups are the Ittihad-i Islami, which enjoys the backing of Saudi Arabia and is noted for its band of Arab volunteers, and the two rival factions of the Hizb-i Islami (Islamic Party), led by Maulavi Muhammad Yunus Khalis and Gulbuddin Hikmatyar respectively.

A seventh organization, Jam'iat-i Islami (Islamic Association)—not to be confused with the **Jama'iat-i Islami** in Pakistan—may be categorized as falling between the other two main groupings. It is led by Professor Ustad Burnahuddin Rabbani, but noted in particular for its outstanding field commander, Ahmed Shah Massoud, who emerged as a key figure in the new mujahidin-controlled Afghanistan.

Finally mention should be made of a Shi'ite organization, Hizb-i Wahadat, which is a coalition of nine smaller groups and backed by Iran.

Rivalry and hostility, both between differing Sunni organizations and also between Sunni and Shi'ite groups, and further complicated by ethnic rivalries, have been a continued problem for the mujahidin, reducing their effectiveness against the Communist régime. Following the Soviet military withdrawal in February 1989, as a result of the Geneva Accord of April 1988, they established an interim Islamic government in neighbouring Pakistan (which had functioned as a key base for all groups), but this remained internally divided. When, in April 1992, President Najibullah's régime collapsed, the mujahidin finally came to power, led in the first instance by Massoud's Jam'iat Islami. A coalition government was set up, yet rivalry and hostilities between conservatives and radicals, and between Sunnis and Shi'ites, continued. Gulbuddin Hikmatyar in particular seemed to rule out any compromise—his faction of the Hizb-i Islami has the support of the influential Pakistani Islamist organization, Jama'at-i Islami.

Albania

Albania has a population of approximately 3,300,000. Three-quarters of the population were Muslim at the time the Communist republic was formed in 1946, making Albania the only European country with a Muslim majority. Subsequently an attitude of initial religious tolerance soon changed to repression, and in 1967 organized religion was forced to end. Vast numbers of mosques and churches were closed, and Muslims and Christians forced to apostatize. The prevailing State atheism nevertheless remained superficial in some quarters; private religious belief remained. About 20 per cent of the population still profess to be Muslim, of whom 80 per cent are **Sunnis** of the **Hanafi** school of law, while the other 20 per cent are **Shi'ites**. Some Muslims still observe Ramadan. There is also about 5 per cent of the population which retains some allegiance to Christian belief; a small majority of these are Albanian **Orthodox**, and the others are **Roman Catholic**. The Christians were forced to operate underground, and many priests were imprisoned or executed for continuing to practise their vocation. With the recent changes of government in Albania, and the liberation from Communist ideological restrictions, religious organizations have begun to practise openly again, and it is anticipated that among the Muslim organizations will be found the formerly influential **Bektashiya Sufi** order.

Algeria

Algeria has a population of 26,700,000 of whom 99 per cent are Muslim, overwhelmingly **Sunnis** of the **Maliki** or **Hanafi** school of law, although there is also a tiny minority of **Ibadis** concentrated in five ancient walled cities in the Mzab valley of southern Algeria. The **Salifiya**-inspired Association of Reformed Ulama, founded in 1931 by Sheikh 'Abd al-Hamid b. Badis, campaigned effectively against what it considered to be the superstitions of **maraboutism**, and against the **Sufi** orders. The latter, however, although less influential today than formerly, nevertheless remain important—perhaps especially the **Rahmaniya**, but also the **Qadiriya, Shadhiliya, 'Alawiya, Darqawiya**, and **Tijaniya**, with some adherents of the **Hamalliya**.

The Association of Reformed Ulama co-operated with the FLN (Front de Libération Nationale) in the war of independence against the French from 1956 onwards, but subsequently became subordinated to it, as the state sought to control religion for its own purposes through the Ministry of Religious Affairs (Wizarat al-Shu'un al-Diniya). Islamic institutions and publications became subject to state scrutiny, and *ulama* became state appointees. It is in part as a reaction to these developments that the recent rise of Islamic fundamentalism must be seen.

This contemporary movement has its precursors. In the 1960s, Al-Qiyam ("the values") mobilized support for a less decadently Western, more explicitly Islamic form of society, until it was banned in 1970. In the 1970s, similar demands continued to be pressed, culminating in the emergence of a successor movement to Al-Qiyam, with some continuity of leadership, known as **Ahl al-Da'wa** ("People of the Call"). Meanwhile the government sought to counter this tendency by reasserting its own Islamic credentials, e.g. by outlawing gambling, and establishing Friday as the official day of rest.

Nevertheless, after the death of President Boumedienne in 1978, the Islamist movement developed rapidly. Outbreaks of violence in the early 1980s led the government to clamp down, yet despite deaths in clashes with the army, and the arrest and trial of militants, the movement went from strength to strength, feeding on wider social and economic discontent which found dramatic expression in traumatic riots, particularly in Algiers, in 1988.

Measures of political liberalization introduced in the wake of the riots led to the founding, in 1989, with state approval, of the first Algerian Islamic political party, the Islamic Salvation Front, or **FIS (Front Islamique du Salut)**. It promptly won 55% of the vote in the June 1989 regional election. Two other parties followed in 1990: **Hamas** (al-Haraka li-Mujtama' Islami—the Movement for an Islamic Society), and the **Islamic Renascence Movement** (Mouvement de la Nahda Islamique—MNI). A number of smaller groups (e.g. the League of the Islamic Call—Rabitat al-Da'wa al-Islamiya) also exist, but firm details about them are not currently available.

There was very widespread public support for Saddam Hussein's Iraq in the Gulf War of 1991. The triumph of the FIS in the first round of the general election later that year, when they won 49% of the vote, led to army intervention and the cancelling of the second round of elections which had been expected to bring the FIS to power. With the party's leaders under arrest, more militant members—including CIA-trained veterans of the war in Afghanistan, for which they had volunteered to fight alongside the mujahidin—have resorted to acts of violence. In June 1992 President Boudiaf was assassinated, but it is not yet known who was behind the plot. The future remains uncertain: however, the prison sentences (of between four and 12 years) which the party leaders received in July 1992 were less severe than expected.

Andorra

Andorra has a population of about 55,000, of whom at least two-thirds are foreign nationals. It owes allegiance to joint French and Spanish sovereignty. Over 99 per cent are Christian, and these are almost entirely **Roman Catholic**. The Spanish-speaking schools are supported by the Church. There is also a tiny Jewish community of about 100 people.

Angola

Angola is a former Portuguese colony with a population of about 9,900,000. Around 90 per cent of these profess to be Christian, although some of these may maintain indigenous patterns of belief and practice. Some 70 per cent of the population are **Roman Catholic**, and these are concentrated mainly in the west where the Portuguese colonialists had been. The 20 per cent **Protestant** contingent are mainly evangelical, including **Methodists, Baptists** and **Plymouth Brethren**. These are concentrated in particular ethnic groups to whom missions have been directed. Some of the Protestants have been active in supporting the UNITA rebel movement, with South African backing, against the former Cuban and Soviet-backed Communist regime. There are hardly any indigenous churches. The remainder of the population adhere to **African traditional religions**. Their rites express devotion to ancestral spirits; they fear the evil activity of witches and look to the beneficent function of medicine men to protect them.

Antigua and Barbuda

These Caribbean Islands are a former British colony with a population of about 80,000. Ethnically, 94 per cent of the inhabitants are African. Around 96 per cent of the population are Christian, with about 44 per cent **Anglicans**, 41 per cent other **Protestants**, and 10 per cent **Roman Catholics**. There is a tiny minority of 2 per cent **Rastafarians**.

Argentina

Argentina has a population of 34,000,000 of whom 98 per cent are ethnically European, and 2 per cent mestizo. Some 92 per cent of the population are **Roman Catholic**, although the Church has never enjoyed sufficiently cordial relations with the state to become a state religion. It is the major influence upon social values, but has suffered from a lack of priests throughout the past 200 years. Few Argentinians follow a calling to the priesthood, and many of the priests come from elsewhere. In many rural areas it is only possible to receive the sacrament occasionally from a travelling priest. A militant minority of Catholic clergy have been involved in movements for social reform, although the majority of the hierarchy supports the establishment.

Although the **Protestants** are in a minority of 3 per cent, Argentina is a base for a number of Protestant missionary societies. Protestants can be divided into two kinds: immigrant communities who have their own churches, and foreign missionary groups. No sizeable indigenous Protestant groups have arisen, and the evangelistic methods of the missionary groups are not accepted socially by the Catholic majority.

The Jewish community in Argentina comprises 2 per cent of the population, and is the fifth largest in the world. It exercises a significant role in business and politics. Around 78 per cent of the Jews are **Ashkenazi**, and 22 per cent **Sephardi**.

Australia

Australia has a population of about 17,000,000 which is predominantly Australian-born and of Anglo-Celtic origin. There is no state religion, but the country remains predominantly Christian. In the census of 1986 the population professed a denomination as follows: 26.1 per cent **Roman Catholic**; 23.9 per cent **Anglican**; 7.6 per cent Uniting Church; 3.6 per cent **Presbyterian**; 2.7 per cent **Orthodox**; 1.3 per cent **Baptist**; and 1.3 per cent **Lutheran**. The Catholics are mainly of Irish descent, although they have been supplemented more recently by immigrants from Italy, Malta, Yugoslavia and Poland. The Catholics tend to feel their minority status which gives them a cohesive identity, but also produces a tendency towards dogmatic conservatism. The Uniting Church is a combination of **Congregational, Methodist** and **Presbyterian** churches which was formed in 1977 after lengthy negotiation. There is a continuing Presbyterian Church which refused to enter this union. The Orthodox Church is mainly Greek.

Most of the Aborigines, who number 100,000–200,000, now profess to be Christian but the traditional **Australian Aboriginal religion** still continues in the large rural areas. Land is one of the key features of their spirituality, with a veneration of sacred sites. While all the major religious leaders of the Churches support federal Aboriginal land rights legislation, in practice the Aboriginal attitude to land is often actively opposed.

Finally, there are also significant minorities of Jews, Muslims and Buddhists.

Austria

Austria has a population of approximately 8,000,000, of whom 98 per cent are German-speaking, with a minority of 0.7 per cent Croatian, and 0.3 per cent Slovene. Around 84 per cent of the population are **Roman Catholic**, and there have been close links between the Church and State. Only 15 per cent of Catholics are regular in church-going, and major doctrines such as the Resurrection are only accepted by about one third of Catholics. The number of priests and nuns is declining, so lay people are taking more responsibility in teaching religion, as parish assistants, in synodal councils and in parish councils. Instructions are still sent to every baptized member of the Church to pay church taxes, as a result of which many people officially leave the Church when starting work.

About 6 per cent of the population are **Protestant**, and the main body of these is the Evangelical Church, which is a loose union of Helvetian **Reformed** and Augsburg **Lutheran**. Smaller groups include the **Methodists**, who are officially recognized, and **Adventists, Baptists, Brethren, Friends, Mennonites**, and **Pentecostals**. There are over 50,000 **Orthodox** Christians.

About 1 per cent of the population are Muslims, and these are mostly **Sunnis**—immigrant workers from Yugoslavia and Turkey. There are some 7,000 Jews, who are mostly drawn from **Liberal Judaism**, although about 20 per cent of them, mainly elderly, are drawn from **Orthodox Judaism**, and form a community based around Vienna. The Vienna synagogue administers three Talmud-Torah schools. There is also a small Buddhist group with a publishing house.

Bahamas

The Bahaman population is estimated at some 257,000, and is distributed over 700 islands and 2,000 cays. Eighty-five per cent of the population are black, and the 15 per cent white population are almost entirely of English, American or Canadian descent. Ninety-five per cent of the population are Christian, of whom 29 per cent are **Baptist**, 25 per cent **Roman Catholic**, 20 per cent **Anglican**, 7 per cent **Methodist** and 7 per cent **Pentecostal**. In addition there are small numbers of **Adventists, Lutherans**, Greek **Orthodox, Brethren**, and the **Salvation Army** and a number of black indigenous churches. A small group practise **Obeah**, which is a syncretism of Christianity with **African traditional religions**, and there are some **Rastafarians** from Jamaica. A small Jewish community is also present.

Bahrain

Bahrain's population of about 523,000 is 95 per cent Muslim. The minority of 2.9 per cent Christians are all expatriates, mainly from India, Britain, and the USA, but also including Arab Christians from Jordan, Palestine and Syria. In addition there are Hindus comprising 1.1 per cent who are expatriate Indians.

Amongst the Muslims, about a third are **Sunnis**, a minority who are nevertheless politically, and to a lesser extent economically, dominant. The ruling Khalifah clan adhere to the **Maliki** school of religious law, while Sunni members of the commercial élite tend to belong to the **Shafi'i** school. There are also small but significant groups who belong to the **Hanbali** school.

The other two thirds of the Muslim community are **Twelver Shi'ites**, many of Iranian origin. While some have succeeded in entering the commercial élite, most have not, and economic discontents have been reinforced, especially since the Iranian revolution, by social alienation derived from Sunni political dominance.

Iran's long-standing claims to the island were doubtless a factor leading to the establishment, in Tehran in 1979, of the **Islamic Front for the Liberation of Bahrain** (Jabhat al-Islamiya lil-Tahrir al-Bahrain) under the leadership of an Iranian cleric exiled from Bahrain for claiming to be Ayatollah Khomeini's representative there, al-Mudarrisi. In collaboration with underground cells of the Iraq-based **Hizb al-Da'wa**, this organization engaged in acts of sabotage, and in 1981 mounted a *coup* attempt. In response, the authorities handed out lengthy prison sentences but refrained from the death penalty. Perhaps partly as a result of this relative leniency, combined with a generally more accommodating attitude towards the Shi'a community, the IFLB has failed to engage widespread popular support. Nor, meanwhile, has there been much sign of the emergence of Sunni fundamentalism—a reflection, possibly, of the evident success of the Sunni community in Bahrain's entrepreneurial environment.

Bangladesh

The population of Bangladesh is now estimated to be over 110,000,000, making it one of the most densely populated countries in the world. Formerly part of the Muslim state of Pakistan (as East Pakistan), after its bloody separation in civil war it was originally constituted as a secular state on its foundation as a separate polity in 1972. However, amendments to the constitution in 1975 and 1988 resulted in Islam being reinstated as the state religion—83 per cent of the population are Muslim, and it is, after Indonesia, the second largest Muslim country in the world.

Believers are 95 per cent **Sunni** and adherents of the **Hanafi** school of law, although there is a sizeable **Shi'ite Isma'ili** minority in urban areas. A group of about 4,000,000 Urdu-speaking Muslims from Bihar in India form a despised ethnic minority. There are also about 60,000 members of the **Ahmadiya (Qadianis)**. Internationally Bangladesh is committed to an active role in the **Organization of the Islamic Conference**.

Sufi orders are prevalent to a greater extent than in most Muslim countries today, with strong representation of the **Qadiriya, Naqshabandiya** and **Chishtiya** in particular. Sufi influence on perhaps two thirds of the Muslims overall is opposed by Islamic purists, e.g. members of the **Jama'at-i Islami**, who regard the widespread interest in Sufism as a corruption by the Hindu environment.

A large minority of about 15,000,000 are Hindus, although due to a number of factors, including emigration during and as a result of the 1971–72 civil war, and a low birth-rate, the numbers of these are declining. In addition, over 500,000, mainly among the tribes, adhere to **Theravada** Buddhism, often with a strong admixture of animism. Animism itself still has about 100,000 adherents among the Garo, Santal and Chittagong Hill tribes. Christians form a minority of 500,000, with half of these being **Roman Catholic**, and the others belonging mainly to **Protestant** sects. There are a few small local assemblies of **Bahais**, with some new converts among the Hill Tract tribes.

Barbados

The population of Barbados, which numbers approximately 260,000, is almost entirely Christian, and half of these practise regularly. Membership of the **Anglican** Church, which was disestablished in 1977, extends to 50 per cent of the population, with 7 per cent **Pentecostals**, 6 per cent **Roman Catholics**, 6 per cent **Methodists**, 5 per cent **Seventh Day Adventists**, 4 per cent **Wesleyan Holiness** and **Moravians** being included among the other significant denominations. There are also over a thousand **Bahais**, who have spread very rapidly in recent times, and very small numbers of Muslims, Hindus, Jews and **Rosicrucians**.

Belgium

Belgium, with a population counted in 1983 at just under 10,000,000, is 90 per cent **Roman Catholic**, and over a half of these are still practising. Catholicism has a very significant influence upon Belgian society, with Catholic trade unions, worker movements, hospitals, schools and universities. There is a much stronger concentration of church attendance among the Flemish speakers in the northern half of the country than among the French speakers in the south. The Church itself experiences a split across the linguistic divide. The Church has relatively recently begun to ordain worker priests, who remain in their occupation during and after theological training. There were 85,000 **Protestants** in 1975, with 20,000 of these being foreigners from Africa, the United Kingdom, Germany and Scandinavia. The largest denomination is the Protestant Church of Belgium, which is a combination of the Protestants who had remained since the Reformation with the **Methodists**. The next largest are the **Reformed** Church of Belgium, and the **Pentecostal Assemblies of God**. The **Jehovah's Witnesses** are equal in size to the largest Protestant church. There are also over 50,000 **Orthodox** Christians, of whom most are Greek migrant workers, and others are Russians, mainly descended from refugees from the 1917 revolution.

There are about 200,000 Muslims, mostly immigrant labourers, nearly two thirds of whom are Moroccans and Algerians, and one third Turks, but also including Tunisians, Libyans and Egyptians. The **Muslim Brotherhood** has a few supporters, the **Sulaimancis** and the **Alawiya** many more, and the **Tabligh Jama'at** most of all. The Centre Islamique et Culturel de Belgique was at first designated the sole official organisation for Muslims, but this proved controversial because of its links to the Saudi-based **Muslim World League**. In an attempt to create a body more representative of the Muslim communities in Belgium, the Conseil Supérieur des Musulmans de Belgique was established.

In addition to Christians and Muslims, there are about 40,000 Jews, half of whom are still practising in 12 officially recognized Jewish communities whose members are largely **Ashkenazi** from Eastern Europe.

Belize

Formerly British Honduras, this country with a wide racial mix has a population of about 197,000. While over 60 per cent of these are nominally **Roman Catholic**, many of these syncretize folk-Catholicism with tribal animistic religions of a **Mesoamerican Traditional** or Black Caribbean origin. The numbers of Catholics have been growing recently due to an influx of refugees from neighbouring countries. Twelve per cent of the population are **Anglican**, and there is also a sizeable **Mennonite** community, as well as **Methodists** and the rapidly growing **Pentecostals** and **Adventists**.

Benin

Benin is a Marxist state with a population of over 4,900,000 over 60 per cent of whom still follow a variety of **African traditional religions**, which share the common properties of a mystical view of the universe, and a desire to communicate with and divine the will of deities. **Voodoo** is found among the Fon tribe. Some of these religions have survived slavery and now flourish in the Caribbean and Brazil. The 20 per cent who are Christian are largely **Roman Catholic**, although some **Methodists** and **Pentecostal Assemblies of God** are also found. Some 15 per cent are Muslims, located predominantly in the urban populations, and amongst them the **Qadiriya** and **Tijaniya Sufi** orders are well represented.

Bhutan

Buddhism is the state religion of this Himalayan kingdom with an estimated population of 1,700,000. Three-quarters of the population are Mahayanists who follow a form of **Tibetan Buddhism**, which is syncretized with a pre-Buddhist **shamanism, Taoism,** and animism. There are over 6,000 monks, some of whom hold a variety of governmental positions: conversely, the government supports major Buddhist temples and shrines. There is indeed rough parity between political and religious institutions, with the leader of the monastic hierarchy enjoying approximately equal status to the king.

The 25 per cent of the population who are Hindu are mainly Nepali settlers influenced by Buddhism.

Bolivia

Bolivia has a population of about 7,600,000, but as the poorest country in Latin America, it also has a fast rate of population growth. Ninety-five per cent of the population are **Roman Catholic**, but many of these practise a folk-Catholicism which retains elements from 16th century Spanish Catholicism, and **South American traditional religions**. The Church depends heavily upon foreign clergy, among whom Liberation Theology is strong in its drive towards social and economic change. The largest **Protestant** denomination is the **Seventh-Day Adventist** Church. There are some 20,000 **Bahais**, who are growing extremely rapidly in a massive missionary expansion. About 100,000 still follow the traditional South American Indian religions, venerating, in particular, deities of good luck, Mother Earth, and the multitude of spirits that people the phenomena of nature.

Botswana

Botswana has a population of about 1,350,000, among whom **African traditional religions**, for example **Khoisan religion** predominate. About 60 per cent still follow the old way, which is especially strong among the Bushmen tribe. The Tswana tribe have a rich mythology, and are notable for venerating God as mother. Christianity is the official religion, however, and the main **Protestant** denomination is the United **Congregational** Church, resulting from the efforts of the London Missionary Society. The **Roman Catholics** are growing rapidly, and number nearly as many as the Congregationalists. There are also a growing number of indigenous churches.

Brazil

Brazil has a population of 153,000,000. Eighty-nine per cent of the population are **Roman Catholics**, whose religion tends to take the local form of having a largely individualistic character, with devotion to saints and the aim of seeking personal protection. A progressive minority movement among the bishops and theologians has facilitated the emergence of liberation theology, the spread of ecclesiastical base communities, and the development of a "popular" church depending substantially upon lay leadership. The Vatican authorities have tried to curb the autonomy of the Brazilian Church, which constitutes the largest concentration of Catholics in the world. The Vatican has recently appointed a number of conservative bishops, who are committed to older pastoral and evangelistic strategies rather than to the "preferential option for the poor". The largest **Protestant** denominations are **Pentecostals**. About 2 per cent of the population profess to be spiritists, although it is estimated that at least 33,000,000 take part in their various rites. These are mainly **Umbanda**, which is an Afro–Brazilian syncretism and a form of white magic, but **Candomblé** and **Kardecism** are also important. The many Catholics who take part in spiritist rites see no contradiction between this and Catholicism. **Qimbanda**, a form of black magic invoking malevolent spirits, is also practised by a small minority, as is **Macumba**. There are over 1,000,000 Japanese immigrants, most of whom are Roman Catholic and are double the size of the Catholic community in Japan. Half a million of the Japanese are Buddhists. There are also about 200,000 Jews, mainly from Germany and central Europe. There are a few remaining who practise **South American traditional religions**, but the numbers of these are decreasing rapidly due to acts of genocide and the destruction of their territory.

Brunei

Brunei is a tiny, oil-rich Islamic sultanate with a population of some 256,000. The 65 per cent of the population who are racially Malay are entirely **Sunni** Muslims, of the **Shafiʻi** school of religious law. Some 13 per cent of the population are Chinese

Mahayana Buddhists, but there are also a few **Theravadins** from Sri Lanka. Christians constitute approimately 8 per cent of the population, and these are mainly **Roman Catholic** and **Anglican**. There is also some **Confucianism** and **Taoism** amongst the Chinese, and traditional animism among the aboriginal people.

Islam is actively promoted by the state, although in recent years the activities of independent Islamist groups have attracted suspicion, and these groups have been banned, as have the **Jehovah's Witnesses, Bene Brith**, and the **Maharishi Movement**.

Bulgaria

The population of Bulgaria is approximately 9,000,000. Prior to the establishment of a Communist state at the end of World War II, 85 per cent of the population belonged to the Bulgarian **Orthodox Church**, and a further 15 per cent were **Sunni** Muslims. The minorities of 70,000 **Roman Catholics**, and 20,000 **Protestants** were actively persecuted by the Communist régime, but succeeded in maintaining a precarious existence. The Orthodox Church was tolerated by the régime, after initially having its property confiscated, because it tended to conform to the state's requirements. After the restoration of the Patriarchate in 1953 it added a certain prestige to the official authorities, and facilitated some contacts in the international arena. A sociological survey in 1962 estimated that adherence to Orthodoxy had declined to 27 per cent of the population. However, the churches are now establishing themselves again in democratic Bulgaria, and according to the most recent opinion poll (March 1992) at least nominal adherence to Christianity was claimed by 90%, and to Islam by 10% of those asked. Among Christians the proportions were 87.5% Orthodox, 1% Roman Catholic, and 0.5% Protestant.

In the case of Islam, many mosques were closed during the Communist period, and though each village or community was allowed to retain one, Quranic teaching in them was forbidden by the state, as was public celebration of religious festivals. More recently, in the 1980s, the policy of forcing Muslims to adopt Bulgarian names caused much bitterness—and a major exodus of some 350,000 Bulgarian Turks to Turkey. The policy has now been relaxed. The heterodox Muslim sect known as the **Qizilbash** has also survived the years of Communist rule. Continued membership of some **Sufi** orders such as the **Rifa'iya** has also been reported.

Burkina Faso

This former French colony, known until 1984 as Upper Volta, has a population of some 9,400,000, of whom 65 per cent still adhere to **African traditional** religious beliefs. Thirty per cent are **Sunni** Muslims who adhere to the **Maliki** school of religious law. They are growing in number due to many conversions of tribal religionists, especially on their migration to cities, or in mass conversions of whole communities and villages due to healing practices. Conversions also take place among youths working abroad. Ten per cent are Christian, mainly **Roman Catholic**, and the largest **Protestant** denomination is the **Pentecostal Assemblies of God**.

Burundi

Burundi's population of 5,600,000 is approximately 60 per cent **Roman Catholic**, and the numbers of Catholics are said to be increasing by over two per cent each year. Five per cent are Protestant, mainly **Pentecostals** and **Anglicans**, and one per cent is **Sunni** Muslim. The remainder still adhere to **African traditional religions**, among which the Kiranga cult is influential, in which the former human, Kiranga, periodically possesses his highest initiate and serves as an intermediary between God and man.

Ethnically the country is divided between 84 per cent Hutu and 15 per cent Tutsi, with the latter politically dominant despite their small numbers. The same imbalance is to be found, however, in the country's Roman Catholic church, with the most eminent positions being given to the Tutsi. When Hutu resentment at Tutsi domination bubbled over into bloody, and ultimately unsuccessful, revolt in 1972, Roman Catholic priests, teachers and catechists were among the victims.

The Hutu were subsequently persecuted under President Bagaza (in power from 1976 to 1987), and Catholic church leaders were expelled or imprisoned, and weekday masses were proscribed. President Buyoya, who took power in 1987, has appointed Hutu members of his government, released religious leaders from prison, and introduced measures for human rights and freedom of expression. However, in August 1988 ethnic violence erupted again, in which 20,000 Hutus were killed by the Tutsi-dominated army, and 60,000 fled to neighbouring Rwanda. Meanwhile the church has continued to seek to play a reconciling role.

Cambodia

Cambodia, formerly Kampuchea, has a population of about 8,400,000. Before the Khmer Rouge took over in 1975, 95 per cent of the population were **Theravada** Buddhists, with nearly 3,000 monasteries (including the renowned Angkor Wat), and 70,000 monks. Since the displacement of Pol Pot's Khmer Rouge by the Vietnamese in 1979, there has been some revival of religious life at the popular level, but Buddhism is no longer a state religion and there are fewer monks (whose interests are nevertheless represented in the Patriotic Kampuchean Buddhist Association). There are minorities of **Sunni** Muslims, who adhere to the **Shafi'i** school of Islamic law, and tribal religionists, but the **Roman Catholics** were virtually wiped out in the violence leading up to the seizure of power by the Khmer Rouge in which 3,000,000–4,000,000 Cambodians perished.

Cameroon

The population of Cameroon, estimated to be about 13,000,000, is quite evenly distributed among **African traditional religions** (including **Bangwa religion**), Islam and Christianity. Nearly 40 per cent still adhere to the traditional religions, which often accord a special role to the traditional village blacksmith. The blacksmith plays a significant role in birth, death, illness, pottery making and iron smelting. Over 30 per cent are **Sunni** Muslim, among whom the **Qadiriya** is the principal **Sufi** brotherhood. Estimates of the numbers of Christians differ, with perhaps slightly over 20 per cent of the population being **Roman Catholic**, and nearly 20 per cent being **Protestant**; the main Protestant denominations are **Evangelical** and **Presbyterian**.

Canada

The population of Canada, currently estimated at around 26,800,000, is composed racially of 45 per cent of British origin, 29 per cent of French, 23 per cent other European, and 1.5 per cent indigenous Indian and Eskimo. There are over 300,000 Jews, including 170 congregations which belong to **Orthodox Judaism**, 25 to **Conservative Judaism** and 5 to **Reform Judaism**. The country is predominantly Christian, although relations with the state have never been particularly cordial, and all religious communities in Canada are outspoken on matters of social responsibility, particularly the avoidable levels of poverty and homelessness. Forty-nine per cent of the population still profess to be **Roman Catholic**, but there has been a recent decline in levels of religious practice, although quite high numbers still attend Church at least once a year. A de-confessionalization of institutions began in the 1960s, with schools, colleges and clinics being transferred to the state. There is a typical shortage of priests. Grass-roots communities have sprung up unofficially around parishes, and marginal groups, possibly influenced by **Mormons** and **Jehovah's Witnesses**, are influential among younger elements of the population.

The largest **Protestant** denomination is the United Church, which combines the **Methodists, Congregationalists**, and about half of the **Presbyterians**, and contains about 18 per cent of the population. The **Anglican** Church has 12 per cent of the population, and includes 80 per cent of the Eskimos. There are also 500,000 Presbyterians, a similar number of **Pentecostals**, a large number of **Baptists**, and about 200,000 Greek **Orthodox**.

There are about 150,000 Muslims, mainly immigrants from Pakistan, India, Guyana, and Uganda (Asians) including 20,000 **Aga Khanis** who maintain their own distinctive religious networks; 40,000 Hindus, mainly immigrants from India and Ugandan Asians; and 40,000 **Bahais**, having a total of some 800 centres. **Sikhs** are similarly well represented within the Asian business community. **Shamanism** continues to influence the Eskimo tribes, although most of these now profess to be Christian rather than adherents of traditional **Inuit religion**.

Cape Verde

This island group off West Africa, having a population of 386,000, is 95 per cent **Roman Catholic**. No tribal religions are practised, but the country has recently seen a marked de-Christianization. There are about 10,000 **Protestants**, who are Nazarenes and **Seventh Day Adventists**. The overwhelmingly Catholic nature of the culture was an important factor inhibiting union with neighbouring Guinea-Bissau, also a former Portuguese colony, but overwhelmingly **African traditional** or Muslim in religious character.

Central African Republic

The population of this country is estimated at a little over 3,000,000. Statistics on religious adherence are unreliable, and estimates vary from 20–60 per cent of the population as following **African traditional religions**. The numbers of Christians rose after independence, and are thought to be approximately 40 per cent, roughly equally divided among **Protestants** and **Roman Catholics**. The largest Protestant denominations are **Baptist** and **Brethren**. Some 5–10 per cent of the population are **Sunni** Muslims who adhere to the **Maliki** school of religious law.

Chad

Chad, with a population of 5,800,000, is mainly **Sunni** Muslim in the north of the country, believers following the **Shafi'i** or **Maliki** schools of religious law, and comprising 45 per cent of the population. The **Hamalliya Sufi** order is followed by about half of the Muslim population. The **Tijaniya** order claims a further 20 per cent of Muslims. Estimates differ on the numbers of Christians, ranging from six to 33 per cent of the population. The lower figure refers to full members and regular attenders of the churches, but due to missionary expansion, there are many others who have some contact with the churches and profess a Christian faith. The remainder follow **African traditional religions**.

Since 1965, there has been a continuing civil war across the north–south divide, exacerbated by Islamic ideas of jihad in the north, and bitter memories of Muslim slave trading and persecution amongst the non-Muslims in the south (where both Christians and followers of traditional African religions are grouped). Qaddafi's Libya has supported—some would say virtually annexed—the north (with which it shares a common border), while the former colonial power, France, has supported the south. The Tripoli-based **Islamic Call Society** has channelled funds for aid as Libya has adopted a benevolent public role. The growing influence of radical Islam in Chad has been further reinforced from Sudan as well as Libya, with Hassan Twabi, leader of Sudan's National Islamic Front, playing a significant role.

Chile

Chile, with a population of 13,400,000, is 93 per cent Christian, and 83 per cent **Roman Catholic**. The Catholic Church is progressive, and has found renewal through liturgical reform, pastoral reorganization, involvement of nuns in pastoral work rather than schools and clinics, diocesan synods, and concern with social issues. The Church was active in opposing human rights abuses by the Pinochet government, and was one of the first churches to organize a Christians for Socialism movement. It suffers, however, from the usual shortage of priests. Attendance is highest among women, and in the towns and middle classes. The folk-Catholicism in the rural areas expresses a devotion to the saints as if they were personal deities, and there is little contact with the institutionalized church.

About eight per cent of the population belong to an indigenous **Pentecostal** movement, which broke off from the **Methodists** near the beginning of this century, and has enjoyed a phenomenal rate of growth. One of the world's largest **evangelical** congregations is the Jotabeche Pentecostal Church in Santiago, with 80,000 regular members, mainly among the working classes. There are also about 10,000 Jews, although numbers have decreased due to emigration, 10,000 **Bahais**, and an estimated 100,000 people still practise some form of **South American traditional religion**.

China

China has a population of some 1,200 million, of whom 95 per cent belong to the Han race, and 80 per cent of the population are still rural dwellers. Most notable in recent history for its impact on religion was the Cultural Revolution, when in September 1966 the Red Guards launched fierce attacks upon all temples, mosques, churches, and against religious art, literature, believers and specialists, whether shamans, imams, monks or clergy. Religious freedom, however, was guaranteed in the constitution of 1982.

Many people are still deeply affected by **Chinese folk religions**, which include mixtures of ancestor worship, **Confucian** ethics, devotion to local deities and deified heroes, divination, magic, sorcery and **Taoism**. About 10 per cent of folk-religionists profess to be Taoists, although this is closely inter-woven with all folk-religion. Similarly, the Confucian ethical system can be measured by its influence, but its followers cannot be enumerated. The Communist régime has attempted to destroy all copies of the works of Confucius, since it objects to these as being feudalistic.

There are perhaps 50,000,000 practising Mahayana Buddhists along with many other supporters. These now suffer from a lack of temples, although the government has encouraged a Buddhist presence in Peking to show to visiting diplomats from neighbouring Buddhist countries in an effort to establish better relations. Muslims number in the region of 10,000,000–15,000,000 in ethnic minorities from Central Asia (Uyghurs, Kazakhs, Kirgiz, Tajiks, Uzbeks, Tatars), but also including Chinese Muslims (or Hui). They are mainly **Sunni**, although the Tajik race are **Shi'ite**. Mosques were re-opened in the large cities during the 1970s. The Muslims did not suffer such extreme repression during the Cultural Revolution as other religious groups, possibly because they threatened armed resistance to attacks on their mosques, and possibly because they were largely confined to ethnic minorities and were unlikely to influence the rest of the population. The recent upsurge of Islamic sentiment among related ethnic groups across the border in the former USSR has its counterpart in Xinjang (or the Sinkiang Uyghur Autonomous Region) where mosques are again flourishing and Islamic literature is in evidence.

In 1949, when Chairman Mao Ze Dong came to power, the **Roman Catholics** had 3,000,000 baptized members, the **Protestants** about 1,400,000 in 220 denominations, while in indigenous churches there were 440,000 as well as 300,000 **Russian Orthodox**. Foreign missionaries were soon arrested or expelled and the Three-Self movement attempted to rid the churches of imperialism, feudalism and bourgeois thinking. Following the Cultural Revolution, the number of Catholic priests was reduced to about 500. Only two churches were allowed to operate during the 1970s in Peking, and these were mainly attended by foreign diplomats and students. There has been a massive underground Protestant expansion, however, and there are now reports of at least 50,000,000 believing Christians in the Protestant churches alone.

Tibet, now annexed to China, was almost entirely Mahayana Buddhist, of the **Vajrayana** variety. The Dalai Lama, the pre-eminent political and religious leader, fled the country in 1959. He leads a government in exile in northern India. The persecution of Buddhism has been harsher here than in the rest of China: all the monasteries were destroyed or closed, and the number of monks fell from 100,000 to about 300. The few remaining monks took part in recent civil unrest in 1988 and 1989, and met with violence from the authorities. More recently young nuns have become a potent symbol of defiance. The Dalai Lama has proposed a new political status for the country, but has given up intentions of returning to political leadership there. Approximately one per cent of Tibetans are **Bonpos** and follow the ancient teachings of the Tibetan saint Shenrab.

Colombia

Colombia has a population of approximately 31,800,000, composed of mixtures of people of Spanish, Indian and Negro origin. The **Roman Catholic** church has traditionally exercised predominant influence, claiming the allegiance of 95 per cent of the population. It is mainly conservative, and tends to support the ruling élite, despite the radical counter-example set by Camilo Torres when, as a priest, he joined the guerrilla movement in 1968. There are also over 400,000 Protestants, who are mainly **Pentecostal**, and 300,000 Amerindian tribes who follow local customs and some variant of **South American traditional religion**. There are 70,000 Muslims, who are mainly **Sunni** immigrants from the Middle East (especially Palestine), 40,000 **Bahais**, and 14,000 Jews from Greece, Turkey, Germany, and other European countries.

Comoros

The Comoros is a country composed of three volcanic islands between Mozambique and Madagascar with a population of about 430,000. The population is almost entirely **Sunni** Muslim, of the **Shafi'i** school of religious law. A former French colony, it has been an Islamic Republic since 1978, with the shari'a (Islamic law) being enforced by a supreme court. There are some 780 mosques.

Congo

Congo, with a population of about 2,000,000, is largely a Christian country with over 50 per cent of the population being baptized members of the **Roman Catholic** Church. Up to a quarter of the population are **Protestant**, with the **Evangelicals** being the largest denomination. Three per cent are Muslim, and most of these are expatriate traders from North and West Africa. The remaining 20 per cent follow local forms of **African traditional religions** among which fetishism is widely practised and is indeed increasing. About 20 per cent of the population, however, have been involved in the **Mouvement Croix-Koma**, which is a campaign against magic that arose within the Catholic Church. This involves seven-day ceremonies in which people bring and leave their fetishes for public display.

Costa Rica

Costa Rica, with a population of close to 3,000,000, is predominantly **Roman Catholic**, with some 90 per cent of the population belonging to the Church. The Catholic Church here was once at the vanguard of Catholic social action, but is now becoming more conservative, and has used its influence to defuse potential civil unrest due to a deepening economic and social crisis. The Central American Mission and the **Presbyterians** are the historic **Protestant** churches, but these, like the Catholics, are now losing members to the growing **Pentecostal** churches.

Côte d'Ivoire

Côte d'Ivoire has a population approaching 13,300,000, and 45 per cent of its population adhere to **African traditional religions**. They have a fear of witchcraft, and there are secret societies of those who attempt to eradicate witchcraft by the use of rites involving transformation into animals. Some 30 per cent of the population are Christian, and there are more **Roman Catholics** than **Protestants**, although among the latter the **Harris movement** has been influential and Harrist churches enjoy official recognition. A high percentage of Roman Catholics are involved in government and business due to the prevalence of Catholic education in colonial times, and Catholics are to be found predominantly in the south. Twenty-four per cent of the population are **Sunni** Muslims, of the **Maliki** rite, and the numbers of these are growing due to the conversion of tribalists, Christians, and workers who travel abroad to Muslim countries. President Houphouët-Boigny has urged people to convert from animism to one of the major religions; he also recently constructed a massive basilica of the size of St Peter's in Rome, and gave it to the Pope as a gift.

Cuba

Cuba has some 10,900,000 inhabitants, and although 40 per cent profess to be **Roman Catholic**, only one per cent attend weekly mass. Many priests have been expelled in conflicts between the Church and state. The current shortage means that the life of faith is restricted entirely to the sacramental level. Nevertheless, there has been a tripling of numbers of baptisms in recent years, and the Church has been able to engage in dialogue with the government in order to effect the release of political prisoners. There about 150,000 **Protestants**, who are mostly **Pentecostal** and are undergoing a revival. Minor groups, such as the **Jehovah's Witnesses** and **Seventh-Day Adventists** have restricted rights to worship and association. Ten per cent of the population are influenced by **Afro-American spiritist** rites, which are on the increase, and fall into three main kinds: **Santería**, which is a mixture of Yoruba tribal religion from Africa with cults of Catholic saints; **Nañiguismo**, which is an occult practice of secret societies derived from Nigeria; and Bantu religions, which often evolve into magical cults. The president, Fidel Castro, is urging a return to the "spiritual" side of socialism, and these increases reflect his policy. Greater numbers of foreign workers have been allowed in recently.

Cyprus

Cyprus is now effectively split, after the Turkish invasion of 1974, between the Turkish, Muslim, north and Greek, Christian, south. Some 17 per cent of the population are Turkish Muslims, mostly **Sunnis** of the **Hanafi** school of Islamic law, although there are also a few **Shi'ites**. The majority, some 80 per cent, are Greek members of the Church of Cyprus, which has been autocephalous within the **Greek Orthodox** tradition since the fifth century, and distinct from the Orthodox Church of Greece. Traditionally, the Archbishop has also been Ethnarch, the political as well as the spiritual leader, due to the policy of the former Ottoman Empire. Most of the Orthodox priests have little theological training, but are adept at practising the ritual and conserving national culture. There are some 7,000 **Anglicans** who are expatriates, and 9,000 **Roman Catholics**.

Czechoslovakia

The population of Czechoslovakia is estimated to be 15,700,000, of whom 65 per cent are Czech and 30 per cent Slovak in origin. Eighty per cent of the population are affiliated to Christian churches, and 65 per cent to the **Roman Catholic** Church. Roman religious congregations were suppressed during Communist rule, and their activities were closely watched and constrained: brothers were only allowed pastoral work, and sisters, social welfare work. Two seminaries were tolerated, although the staff of these were appointed by the government.

The Greek Catholic, or **Uniate**, Church, affiliated to the Roman Church but following the Byzantine rite, was forced by the government to join the **Orthodox Church** in 1950, but largely returned to the Roman Church in a referendum in 1969. It was repressed because it was believed to be a hot-bed of Ukrainian separatism. Four per cent of the population now belong to the Czechoslovak Hussite Church, which was formed when 20 per cent of Catholics left the Roman Church in 1920 over issues such as having a vernacular liturgy, married priests, and participation of laity in running the church. It remains a **Reformed Catholic** rather than a **Protestant** church, and retains many Catholic features.

Seven per cent of the population are Protestant, and the largest denomination is the Slovak **Evangelical** Church, which is a brand of **Lutheranism** mainly found among conservative peasants. Also of significance is the Evangelical Church of Czech Brethren, which dates back to the Hussite and Brethren reformations of the 14th Century. It has some 670 congregations. One and a half per cent of the population are Orthodox.

Recent years have seen large religious gatherings: hundreds of thousands attended the celebration of the 1,100th anniversary of the death of St Methodius, who brought Christianity to the Moravians. In 1988 and 1989 mass gatherings of mainly young people demanding religious freedom, led by Cardinal Tomasek, and supported by the Charter 77 human rights movement, led towards the people's uprising of Autumn 1989.

Denmark

Denmark has a population of just over 5,000,000, and 93 per cent profess to belong to the State Church, the Danish Folk Church, which is **Evangelical Lutheran**. Only five per cent of the population attend weekly, however, and 40 per cent at Christmas. Bishops are appointed by the King, although they are nominated by priests. Women are ordained to the pastoral ministry. There are some 30,000 **Roman Catholics**, mainly urban and Danish by race, although Catholicism came to Denmark through immigrants in the last century. There are about 15,000 Muslims, and these are largely **Sunni** immigrant workers of Turkish, Pakistani, and North African origin. There is also a community of 7,000 Jews.

Faroe Islands

With their small population of 42,000, the Faroe Islands have been, since 1948, a self-governing overseas area of Denmark. Nearly all the islanders display allegiance to the Evangelical **Lutheran** Church, also known as the Danish National Church. Church attendance is higher than in Denmark. The **Roman Catholic** Church has been represented since 1931, having previously been suppressed in the wake of the Reformation, but has barely 50 members (a similar number to the **Bahais**). They fall under the jurisdiction of the Catholic diocese of Copenhagen. The Christian **Brethren**, established since 1865, have a significant following in the north, and there are small numbers of **Adventists** and **Salvation Army** members.

Greenland

With a population of some 64,000, Greenland has been, since 1953, a self-governing overseas area of Denmark. In the far north, a tiny minority of a few hundred Eskimos continue to practise **Inuit religion**, but otherwise Christianity prevails. Virtually all Greenlanders adhere to the **Lutheran** Church of Greenland, established in 1721 and itself part of the Evangelical Lutheran Church of Denmark. Church attendance is considerably higher than in Denmark, although secularization is now occurring on a significant scale. The **Roman Catholic** Church has been represented since 1960, but with fewer than 100 members. **Pentecostals, Adventists** and others have sought to establish themselves, but with little success.

Djibouti

The approximately 600,000 population of Djibouti is divided into two roughly equal ethnic groups, the Somali Issa and the Ethiopian Afar. This ethnic divide is bridged partly by their shared desire to remain independent of neighbouring Somalia and Ethiopia respectively, and partly by virtue of the fact that 94 per cent of the population are **Sunni** Muslims of the **Hanafi** or **Shafi'i** schools of Islamic law. **Sufi** brotherhoods are also represented, principally the **Qadiriya**, Salihiya, and **Rifa'iya**. The remainder of the population are mainly **Roman Catholic**, most of whom are metropolitan French on temporary contracts.

Dominica

The island of Dominica in the Caribbean has a population of around 84,000 which is almost entirely Christian. Ninety per cent of the population are **Roman Catholic**, but there are also 6,000 **Protestants** who are mainly **Methodists**, although the **Pentecostals** are becoming increasingly influential.

Dominican Republic

Over 90 per cent of the Dominican Republic's population of over 7,000,000 profess to be **Roman Catholic**, but church attendance is falling. Half the population are strongly influenced by spiritism and **Voodoo**, and 60,000 profess to follow such religions. The **Liborismo** cult, a syncretistic form of religion founded in 1900, is also influential. There are relatively few **Protestants**, who are mainly **Baptists, Evangelicals**, and **Seventh Day Adventists**. There are also some 5,000 **Bahais**, and 2,000 Chinese Buddhists.

Ecuador

Ecuador has a population of some 11,000,000, and over 90 per cent of these are **Roman Catholic**. The bishops have supported the "preferential option for the poor", and the base community movement is developing. The Bishop of Riobamba has been responsible for numerous social movements, and in particular has taken a stand in defending Indian rights. The majority of a generally ageing clergy remain rather conservative, however, and the hierarchy has been slow to criticise right-wing government abuses of power. Moreover, in 1988 a very conservative **Opus Dei** sympathizer was appointed Archbishop of Guayaquil, to the dismay of radical church activists.

In urban religions, attendance at mass is low, whereas in the mountain regions, the Catholic ritual is taken more seriously, though sometimes syncretized and practised in paganized forms. There is some Amerindian syncretistic folk-religion, while 50,000 tribes-people continue to practise their own examples of **South American traditional religions**. **religions**.

Egypt

The population of Eygpt is estimated to be 55,500,000. According to official census figures in 1984, 94 per cent were Muslim, but the Christian churches claimed to have as many as 12 per cent of the population as affiliated members. Amongst the Muslim population, the **Hanafi** school of law predominates in Lower Egypt, while the **Shafi'i** and the **Maliki** schools are adhered to in Upper Egypt. Large numbers of **Sufi** orders exist (over one third of the male population are estimated to be members), and gain official recognition by registering with the Supreme Council of Sufi Orders (al-Majlis al-A'la li'l-Turuq al-Sufiya). The most prominent are the **Qadiriya, Rifa'iya, Shadhiliya** and **Badawiya**. Sufi shrine cults abound, eg that of al-Badawi, founder of the **Badawiya**, in Tanta. A comparable, non-Sufi, cult is associated with the tomb of al-Shafi'i in Cairo.

Egypt is a major world centre for contemporary **Sunni** Islam. The ancient university of al-Azhar, founded in 973 CE, has great influence amongst Muslims worldwide, although it too has come to be subject to considerable government control. The Supreme Council of Azhar exercises, informally, great and perhaps supreme authority in the Sunni community internationally. Amongst al-Azhar's facilities is a large complex, the City of Islamic Research (Madinat al-Buhuth al-Islamiya) for training some 5,000 foreign students for mission work, and an Academy of Islamic Research (Majma' al-Buhuth al-Islamiya). The latter is administered jointly with the separate Council for Islamic Studies, established in 1961 with the aim of purifying Islam of political and sectarian fanaticism. Yet another influential organization is the Supreme Council for Islamic Affairs (al-Majlis al-A'la li'l-Shu'un al-Islamiya), established in 1960 to promote Islamic culture both nationally and internationally by dissemination of literature and building mosques.

In addition to this official Islam, and the Islam of Sufi orders, there is a third form of Islam, that of the various Islamist movements. Foremost among these is the **Muslim Brotherhood**, repressed as a violent subversive organization by President Nasser, but which today must be designated a moderate reformist movement in comparison with more radical groups: having participated (unofficially) in elections in the 1980s, it had some representation in the People's Assembly, although it subsequently boycotted the 1990 elections.

The policy of toleration towards the Muslim Brotherhood was initiated by President Sadat from 1970 onwards with the aim of channelling the growing Muslim resurgence (a reaction in part to the trauma of defeat in the 1967 Arab–Israeli war) into an organization that had renounced violence, and by the same token away from more extreme organizations which had begun to appear. The latter, however, persevered with their various campaigns, the **Islamic Liberation Organization** targetting the Cairo Military Technical College in 1974, **al-Takfir wa'l-Hijra** murdering a former government minister in 1977, and the **Jihad Organization** assassinating President Sadat himself in 1981. Al-Jihad and subsequent splinter groups have remained active throughout the 1980s, and continue to pose a threat to President Mubarak.

Meanwhile, outraged by Sadat's historic visit to Jerusalem in 1977, and his signing of the Camp David agreements the following year, militant Islamic Groups (**al-Jama'at al-Islamiya**) have flourished, especially among university students and youth groups in general. Clashes with the police have occurred, and some of the Islamic Groups are thought to be linked to organizations like al-Jihad which are engaged in violence.

Clashes with Christian Copts have also occurred most recently involving violence on the part of the Islamic Groups (or Leagues). Among the Christians, the **Coptic Church** dates back to the 1st century CE, and claims to have over 6,000,000 members (4,000,000 more than appeared in the official census). It has a strong monastic trait: all bishops are former monks, and there has been an increase in monastic vocations and literature concerning spirituality in recent years. Coptic saints, buried in a monastery or church, are often venerated in the way Sufi saints are by Muslims—indeed Copts and Muslims sometimes venerate each other's saints. The veneration involves pilgrimage to the shrine, and the celebration of festivals.

There are also **Greek Orthodox, Armenian** and **Syrian Jacobite** churches, and some 80,000 **Roman Catholics**, who are liturgically diverse and divided among seven different rites. There are also up to 200,000 Protestants: the largest Protestant community in the Middle East is to be found in the Coptic **Evangelical** Church, which is Presbyterian. In the Nile region of Upper Egypt the ancient ZAR cult is still to be found.

El Salvador

The population of El Salvador is estimated at 5,400,000, and around 80 per cent profess to be **Roman Catholic. Mesoamerican traditional religions** are adhered to in some areas. Among new religious groups, the **Bahais** are growing rapidly, and the **Pentecostal Assemblies of God** have seen a rise in urban areas in recent years. The Roman Catholics can be divided according to the following typology: bourgeois Catholics, the four per cent who form the upper classes; popular Catholics, with little education, who are about 30 per cent of the population; and the 60 per cent Mayanized Catholics, who mix Catholicism with **Mayan Indian** religious beliefs and customs.

A minority of clergy worked for political change with peasants in the 1970s, attacking "instutionalized violence", and American priests and nuns have joined others in sustaining and applying the vision of the "preferential option for the poor" through the 1980s into the 1990s. Many have been murdered by right-wing death squads, who regard them as subversives allied to Communist-inspired guerrilla movements. The Church documents human rights abuses, and Archbishop Rivera, who succeeded the more radical Archbishop Romero, murdered during mass in his own cathedral, attempts to mediate between guerrillas and government. The **Protestants** largely turn their back upon the conflict, except for the **Lutheran** and Emmanuel **Baptist** churches, both of which continue to suffer because of their commitment to social justice.

Equatorial Guinea

The population of Equatorial Guinea is estimated at nearly 400,000 having dropped to just 275,000 in the mid-1980s following large scale emigration and tens of thousands of murders in the previous decade: it has been estimated that during the reign of terror of President Macías over a quarter of the population fled the country. The population is 80 per cent **Roman Catholic**, but under Macías many priests were imprisoned or expelled, meetings forbidden, and churches closed. A more tolerant régime was instituted in August 1979, by President Obiang, who re-opened the churches. There are 5 per cent **Protestants**, most of whom are **Evangelical**. The remainder follow **African traditional religions**, including the Bwiti cult.

Ethiopia

Ethiopia is a densely populated country with an estimated population figure approaching 53,000,000. Forty to forty-five per cent of the population are **Sunni** Muslim, of the **Shafi'i** school of law, and the Muslims are strongest in Eritrea. There are some 10,000 local Quranic schools, and 100 advanced Quranic schools. The country receives a large number of missionaries from the Al-Azhar University in Cairo. The **Sufi** shrine of Sheikh Hussein, near Ginir east of Goba, has up to 100,000 pilgrims at festivals twice a year. Thirty-five to forty per cent of the population belong to the **Ethiopian Church**, a non-Chalcedonian Church dating back to the early centuries of Christianity and linked with the Egyptian **Coptic** Church. It is most prevalent among the Amhara and Tigray tribes, and supports one and a half thousand schools. Just four per cent of the population are **Protestant**, and the largest body is the Word of Life **Evangelical** Church which has 500,000 members, nearly 500 schools and supports six hospitals. There are smaller **Roman Catholic** and **Lutheran** churches. About 12 per cent of the population still adhere to **African traditional** beliefs and practices, and the **zar cult**, which appears to have originated in Ethiopia, is also to be found. There are also 28,000 **Falasha**, who are blacks who follow an archaic form of Judaism dating back to Jewish immigrants in the 1st to 7th centuries. Many of these emigrated to Israel in 1985. The conflict which lasted for many years between the former Marxist-Leninist government and the various rebel groups from Eritrea and Tigray has largely avoided religious issues, with leaders from several groups coming from the Christian part of the population.

Fiji

The population of Fiji, approaching 750,000, is largely urban, with 44 per cent belonging to native Melanesian tribes, and 51 per cent descended from Tamil workers whom the British brought from South India as indentured labourers to work on the sugar cane plantations. The native Fijians are almost entirely Christian, with 85 per cent of them being **Methodists**, and 12 per cent **Roman Catholics**. Traditional religions have apparently died out, with most Fijians professing Christianity, but witchcraft is still widespread and even the witch-doctors profess to be Christian. The Indian Fijians are 70 per cent Hindu, 25 per cent Muslim, with some Methodist Christians and 3,000 **Sikhs**. The military government, which came to power in a 1987 *coup*, espouses a fundamentalist Christianity.

Finland

The population of Finland, currently stable at just under 5,000,000, is 89 per cent **Lutheran**. The **Evangelical** Lutheran Church is the state church, and although only four per cent of the population attend weekly, over 40 per cent attend over twice a year, and others listen to religious radio and TV programmes. The Archbishop is the chairman of the Church Assembly, the Enlarged Bishops' Meeting, and the Administrative Board who run the Church. In recent years there have been a number of revivalist movements within the Church, and over 250,000 are involved in these. The Lutheran Church performs many civil religious functions. The Lutheran Synod takes its own initiatives and advises the government on social issues and remedies. 60,000 belong to the **Orthodox** Church of Finland, and although these were originally farmers from Russia in the East of the country, the church has now spread throughout the country. The numbers in all **Protestant** denominations are decreasing, but the 5,000 **Roman Catholics**, and the **Jehovah's Witnesses** and **Mormons** are increasing in numbers.

France

The population of France is now approaching 57,000,000, with a further 1,250,000 in overseas departments. The country is 77 per cent **Roman Catholic**, although the Church has never fully defined its role in relation to the state since the revolution in 1789. Many French profess no religion at all, or cease to attend Church after their first communion, but over 20 per cent still attend mass on a weekly basis. The French form of Catholicism is characterized by an orientation towards the working classes, and has ordained a number of worker-priests. The lay organization, **Catholic Action**, has been influential upon pastoral life and ecclesiastical appointments, and some eight per cent of regularly practising Catholics belong to it. Religious brothers occupy important roles in teaching, as well as in liturgical and theological renewal, and religious sisters are mainly involved in social or medical work, and teaching. A tiny number of Catholics are supporters of Cardinal Lefèvre, who was excommunicated several years ago for refusing to accept the changes to the Catholic Church which flowed from Vatican II.

In addition, there are 1,000,000 **Protestants**, among whom the **Reformed** Church of France is the largest grouping. There are also **Lutherans** of the Augsburg Confession in Alsace and Lorraine, and an **Evangelical** Lutheran Church. The **Pentecostal Assemblies of God** is the fifth largest denomination. There are some 400,000 **Orthodox**, who belong to the **Greek, Armenian** and **Russian** Churches respectively, and a large **Jehovah's Witness** Kingdom Hall.

An estimated 2,800,000 are Muslim, and these comprise the second largest religious grouping, and the largest Muslim population in Western Europe. They are mainly migrant workers, many of whom are naturalized, from Algeria (800,000), Morocco (450,000), Tunisia (250,000), Turkey (120,000), and Senegal, Mali, and Mauritania (jointly 100,000). There are also about 400,000 French Muslims of Algerian origin, and about 100,000 illegal immigrants. In addition, there are an estimated 30,000 French converts to Islam. Almost all of them are orthodox **Sunni**, with very little fundamentalism as yet—indeed the politically active among second generation Muslims are arguably becoming increasingly secularized. The Muslim Institute of Paris runs the mosques in other cities through representatives. Conflicts have arisen in some cities over the building of new mosques, and Le Pen's right-wing National Front party has sought to exploit anti-Muslim sentiment.

There are about 600,000 Jews, which is the largest community in Europe. These have increased due to immigration from many different areas; 100,000 came from Egypt. The **Sephardis** outnumber the **Ashkenazis**. The main communities are in Paris, Marseilles, Nice, Lyons, and Strasbourg. France has about 30,000 Buddhists, who are mainly Mahayana, and are Vietnamese, Laotian, Cambodian, and Chinese, along with 12,000 French. There are **Zen** and **Tibetan Buddhist** monasteries. There are also about 30,000 belonging to new religious movements; in particular, there are **Cao Daists** among the Vietnamese, and there is a **Soka Gakkai** mission which is derived from **Nichiren shoshu** Buddhism in Japan.

French Overseas Departments/Territories

French Guiana. French Guiana has a population of just under 100,000 that is 75 per cent **Roman Catholic**. Many of the Catholics are immigrant technicians from France, and a number of these work at the space station at Kourou. There is a residue of adherence to local tribal customs, particularly among the Oyampi, Cussuraris, and Emerillou. The **Anglican** Church is also represented, as are a few **Protestant** sects.

French Polynesia. This territory has a population of some 130,000 of which 95 per cent is Christian, made up of 47 per cent **Protestants** (the **Evangelical** Church of Polynesia is the main church), 40 per cent **Roman Catholics** and 8 per cent **Mormons, Seventh Day Adventists**, and independent, indigenous churches. The remaining 5 per cent of the population includes primal religious believers, Buddhists, a few adherents of **Chinese folk religion**, as well as non-religious Europeans.

Guadeloupe. While the 400,000 people of Guadeloupe profess to be 95 per cent **Roman Catholic**, magical practices continue and atheism is growing among the intellectuals. There are also some **Moravians** and **Seventh Day Adventists**.

Martinique. Martinique's population of approximately 400,000 is 95 per cent Mulatto, 2 per cent French, 2 per cent East Indians (Tamils), and 1 per cent Creole, Chinese, Syrian and Vietnamese. An overwhelming (95 per cent) majority are **Roman Catholic**, and in 1973 a Martinique national was made archbishop for the first time. Two per cent are **Protestant**, mainly Independent **Baptists, Reformed** (among metropolitan French) and **Seventh Day Adventists**. One and a half per cent drawn from the Tamils, adhere to the **Maldevidan cult**, of which there are scores of temples in the northern part of the island. There are small numbers of **Bahais** and Muslims (**Sunnis** among the Syrian Arabs).

Mayotte. With a population of some 50,000 Mayotte, an island in the Comoros group, has been a French overseas department since 1976. Ethnically it is 97 per cent Comorian (Swahili), and religiously it is 99 per cent Muslim of the **Sunni-Shafi'i** rite. The remainder are **Roman Catholics** with a few **Protestants.**

New Caledonia. This is a French administered territory and is one of the larger populated island groups with around 200,000 inhabitants. **Roman Catholic** missionaries arrived in 1843 and, today, this church claims more than 70 per cent of the population. **Protestants**, who are mainly indigenous people (Kanak), claim around 18 per cent with Muslims accounting for 4 per cent. Non-religious, mainly European people, number around 4 per cent. Tongan missionaries brought Protestant Christianity to the islands in 1834. **Seventh Day Adventists, Assemblies of God, Jehovah's Witnesses** and **Mormons** are also represented.

Réunion. The population of approximately 600,000 is over 90 per cent Creole with minorities of Chinese, Swahili, Indians, Pakistanis and Malagasy. It is 97 per cent Christian—overwhelmingly **Roman Catholic** with a few **Seventh Day Adventists** and members of **Assemblies of God** and the **Reformed Church**. Two and a half per cent are Muslim.

Wallis and Futuna. The population of these islands, administered by France, is around 9,000 and has been almost entirely **Roman Catholic** since the arrival of missionaries in 1836.

Gabon

Gabon's population of 1,200,000 is 60 per cent Christian following successful missions this century which have produced nearly all of these as converts. Most are now **Roman Catholic**. The main **Protestant** denomination is **Evangelical**. 60,000 belong to the *Religion d'Eboga*, a syncretism of the Fang ancestral cult with Christianity which employs the drug eboga in its rituals. Gabon is also the home of the **Bwiti Cult**. There are some 10,000 Muslims, and a mere 4 per cent still adhere to **African traditional religions**.

Gambia

The Gambia is a strip of land along an estuary that is entirely surrounded by Senegal, with a population of over 900,000. Eighty-five per cent are **Sunni** Muslim, of the **Maliki** school of law, and the Tariqiya and **Muridiya Sufi** orders are active. Eleven per cent still adhere to **African traditional religions**, and maintain close contact with ancestral spirits. There are special rites following funerals, when it is believed that the departed spirit may continue to hover over the houses of relatives. Three per cent of the population are Christian, mainly **Roman Catholic**.

Germany

Germany has a combined population of around 78,600,000, with 61,100,000 in the West in 1987, and the East having 16,700,000 in 1980. A number of demographic shifts have taken place in recent decades, with 15,000,000 refugees from Eastern Europe moving to the West prior to 1970, 4,000,000 immigrant workers arriving from mainly Muslim countries, and, just prior to the re-unification, a number of re-patriations of ethnic Germans from Eastern Europe.

Statistics on religious affiliation date from prior to re-unification. Germany is mainly Christian, with a greater degree of secularization in the East, where 55 per cent were **Protestant** and seven per cent **Roman Catholic**. The Communist régime allowed effective freedom of worship, and seminarians were exempt from military service, with faculties of Protestant theology being represented in universities. The Church did serve as a forum for dissident activities, however, such as the peace movement, ecology and human rights' groups. Only the **Jehovah's Witnesses** were illegal, and had a zealous underground following. The Roman Catholics in the East suffered a decrease due to the massive flight of people to the West; they were also dependent upon the West for financial support, but their leaders were unable to attain visas to visit the West for conferences. About 20 per cent of their members attend regularly.

Nearly forty-three per cent of the population in West Germany were Roman Catholic in 1987, giving them a slight numerical edge over the Protestants. They have been the dominant influence upon the Christian Democratic Party. A decrease in candidates for the priesthood has been matched by an increase in the number of lay theologians, and lay organizations openly oppose the traditional values of the hierarchy. In January 1989, 163 theologians from Germany, Austria, Switzerland and the Netherlands made public the "Cologne Declaration", a statement of disquiet about the way in which the Vatican was filling episcopal sees with little regard for the wishes of local churches, and was withholding the permission to teach from qualified theologians.

The Protestants in the East mainly belonged to the eight territorial churches, which are all members of the Federation of **Evangelical** Churches, and either **Lutheran** or United Lutheran-**Reformed** in tradition. These have neither a unified leadership nor liturgy, and became independent from the all-German counterparts in 1968, although since reunification a process of reorganization has begun to get underway. A decline in numbers of pastors led to a decline in practice, and some five per cent of professed adherents attend regularly. Also present in the East are **Baptists**, with **Pentecostal** groups associated, and **Methodists**, with **Plymouth Brethren** groups associated. There are also **Seventh Day Adventists**, the Conference of Reformed Congregations, Old Lutherans and **Moravian Brethren**. In the West, Protestants mainly belong to the 17 territorial people's churches which are members of the Evangelical Church in Germany. These comprised over forty-one per cent of the West's population in 1987, and are mainly Lutheran or Lutheran-Reformed in tradition. A 10 per cent church income tax is deducted automatically by the government for all registered church members—a tax now extended to the citizens of the former GDR—and this has resulted in some decline in membership in recent years. Twenty-seven per cent of the population attend monthly, and 10 per cent of the pastors were women in 1986. Protestant theology is strongly represented in the German universities. Major organizations include the Diaconal Work of the Evangelical Church in Germany, which has 130,000 members of staff engaged in medical and social services, and the Joint Committee for Church Development Service which handles many aspects of overseas aid. Other Protestant churches in the West include independent Lutheran and Reformed churches, **Mennonites, Moravians**, Methodists, and Baptists. There are over 680,000 Catholics who are non-Roman, and the third largest church in Germany as a whole is the **New Apostolic** Church, which is a sacramentalist and hierarchical body with extraordinary vitality and over 1,000,000 members worldwide. Other Catholics include the **Reformed Apostolic** Community and the **Old Catholic** Church. There are also some 650,000 **Orthodox** Christians, who are mainly **Greek** and **Russian** Orthodox respectively.

In the former West Germany, there are some 1,700,000 Muslims drawn from over 40 countries. The overwhelming majority, however, are guest workers from Turkey (1,500,000) and Yugoslavia (120,000). About 90 per cent are **Sunnis**, of whom 95 per cent adhere to the **Hanafi** school of religious law. The estimated 10,000 Iranians in Germany are **Twelver Shi'ites**, while among the Turks there are significant numbers of **Alevis**. The Federation of Islamic Associations and Communities in Berlin (or Islamic Federation) had strong links to the former National Salvation Party in Turkey, while the Islamic Cultural Centres (having a central office in Cologne, and being represented in most Western European countries), the largest Muslim organization, represents the **Suleymanci** movement. The Turkish government Directorate of Religious Affairs is also represented in the Turkish-Islamic Union for Religion (Diyanat Islerli Türk Islam Birligi).

Jews today number fewer than 30,000, mainly in small communities which continue to dwindle.

Ghana

Ghana's population of nearly 15,000,000 is evenly divided with 29 per cent Protestant, 16 per cent indigenous Christian, 14 per cent **Roman Catholic**, and 12 per cent Muslim, with the remainder adhering to **African traditional religions**. The number of traditional religionists is shrinking due to conversions to Christianity and Islam. They have a belief in Mother Earth, a pantheon of divinities, and make food offerings and libations to ancestral spirits. The **Protestants** are mainly **Methodist, Presbyterian** and **Evangelical**, with a few **Anglicans**, and together these sponsor some 2,000 primary and 10 secondary schools, and 15 teacher training colleges. The Roman Catholics have grown in numbers, largely during this century, but their growth has been outstripped by that of the spiritual indigenous churches, including **Harris** churches, who have over 400 denominations. In 1989, **Mormons** and **Jehovah's Witnesses** were both banned by the government for allegedly subversive activities. The Muslims are mainly found among the northern tribes, and while half of them are **Sunnis** of the **Maliki** rite, half belong to the **Ahmadiya** movement which is not recognized by other Muslims.

Greece

Greece has a population of about 10,000,000, of whom 97 per cent are members of the **Orthodox Church**. While Greece is a secular state, the Orthodox Church of Greece is recognized as the national religion of the Greek people in the constitution, making it the sole surviving officially Orthodox Christian country. There is a government Ministry of Education and Religious Affairs. The Orthodox Church of Greece has small dioceses, which allow bishops to maintain close relationships with the people, but the clergy are not usually well educated. The Universities of Athens and Salonika have replaced the monastery at Mount Athos as the centres of theological study, and this has consequently become more academic under German influence. The Monastic Republic of Mount Athos, the Church of the Dodecanese, the Patriarchal Exarchate of Patmos and the Church of Crete have developed independently of the state church, and are directly dependent upon the Orthodox patriarch of Constantinople, whom the state church also recognizes as its spiritual leader. Confusingly, all of these may on occasion be described as **Greek Orthodox Churches**.

There are also other small Orthodox communities: the Ancient Church of the East; the **Armenian** Apostolic Church; the Bulgarian Orthodox Church; the **Russian Orthodox** Church; and the Authentic **Old Calendar** Church. Church influence remains considerable: not until 1982 was civil marriage available in Greece as a legal alternative to church marriage.

The second largest Christian body is the **Jehovah's Witnesses**, with over 60,000 members in 400 congregations. There are also some 50,000 **Roman Catholics**, following Latin, Byzantine and Armenian rites, and a few **Evangelicals** and **Pentecostals**. Just over one per cent of the population are Turkish **Sunni** Muslims, and these have 300 mosques and several Quranic schools. There are under 4,000 Jews.

Grenada

Grenada has a small population of over 100,000, 99 per cent of whom profess to be Christian. 65 per cent are **Roman Catholic**, 20 per cent **Anglican**, and 12 per cent are divided between **Methodist** and **Seventh Day Adventist**. **Afro–American spiritism** is widespread in the form of **Shango**, a Yoruba syncretism. The last decade has seen an increase in the number of Conservative **Evangelical** missionaries, from societies such as "Youth With A Mission". A group of **Mormon** missionaries, on the other hand, were expelled in 1987 under allegations of racism.

Guatemala

Guatemala's population is estimated at 9,500,000 of whom 40 per cent are of pure Maya Indian descent, and the remainder mestizo and westernized Indian. While 99 per cent profess Christianity, and up to 94 per cent are baptized **Roman Catholics**, a quarter of the population practise a blend of aspects of Catholicism and **Mesoamerican traditional religions (Mayan)**. There is tension between the Indians and the largely foreign Church hierarchy. There is a resurgent traditionalist movement with large **Opus Dei** involvement, as well as a vibrant **charismatic movement** also present within the Roman Catholic Church. **Protestantism**, however, is growing steadily at the expense of the Catholics, with up to 35 per cent of the population now belonging to over 300 sects. These conversions have taken place in the past two decades, and so vigorous is the trend that by the mid 1990s Guatemala is expected to become the first Latin American country with a Protestant majority. Many of the new sects are fiercely anti-Communist in outlook, and the **Pentecostal** President of the early 1980s, Ríos Montt, incurred scathing criticism from human rights activists for sanctioning brutal counter-insurgency tactics. More recently, such excesses have abated, and the Catholic bishops have been active in (sometimes controversial) attempts at social arbitration, symbolized perhaps by one of their number being chairman of the National Reconciliation Committee established in 1988. There is also a small community of 1,000 Jews.

Guinea

Guinea has a population of just under 7,000,000, of whom 75 per cent are **Sunni** Muslim of the **Maliki** rite, 24 per cent follow **African traditional religions**, and 1 per cent are **Roman Catholic**. Most of the Muslims belong to the **Tijaniya** brotherhood, but their numbers include a few **Ahmadis**. Their numbers are officially increasing due to conversions from traditionalism, but it is probable that many professed Muslims are in practice traditionalist. Islam is associated with distant memories of the slave trade. The Kissi, Loma and Gbande tribes in the forests of the south-east are highly resistant to both Islam and Christianity. Guinea is the only black African Muslim state (although the more religiously heterogeneous Nigeria has recently joined the **Organization of the Islamic Conference**). In 1988 a National Islamic League was created to replace the Ministry of Religious Affairs.

Guinea-Bissau

The population of Guinea-Bissau has increased rapidly to nearly 1,000,000, making statistics for religious adherence unreliable depending upon which sectors of the population have the highest growth rate. It is estimated that about 60 per cent follow **African traditional religions**, and these are strongest among the western tribes. There are about

35 per cent Muslims, of the **Sunni Maliki** tradition, predominating in the south and east, and their numbers are growing rapidly due to conversions from tribalism. The Christians, mainly **Roman Catholic**, number about 5 per cent of the population, and are also increasing. Christianity is strongest among the Balanta.

Guyana

Fifty-one per cent of the population of Guyana, estimated at 833,000, are descended from East Indians brought in as indentured labourers by the British in the nineteenth century, making it an anomaly in the religious distribution of Latin America. Fifty-seven per cent are Christian, and these are roughly equally divided among the three main groups of **Roman Catholics, Anglicans**, who are mainly of **Anglo-Catholic** churchmanship and maintain close links with the Roman Catholics, and other **Protestant** denominations, including **Pentecostal Assemblies of God** and **Southern Baptists**. Among the Akawaio Indians the movement known as **Halleluja Religion** is to be found. Thirty-three per cent of the population are Hindu, and their active organizations include the American Aryan League on the reformed side, and the traditionalist Hindu Orthodox Guyana Sanathan Dharma Maha Sabha. Nine per cent of the population are **Sunni** Muslims, and there are a few **Ahmadiyas**. It was in Guyana that 900 members of the People's Temple cult committed suicide in 1978 in the so-called "Jonestown massacre". New religious movements have received a certain amount of government support in order to provide a counter-weight to the politically critical mainstream religious bodies.

Haiti

The population is estimated to be just under 6,000,000, and 95 per cent are pure Negro. While 80 per cent profess **Roman Catholicism**, 90 per cent of these practise **Voodoo**. Voodoo priests and priestesses have great authority among their followers, and their word is taken as law in some regions. They take part in ritual dances and drinking ceremonies, and black and white magic is practised. Voodoo was officially recognized as a religion by the 1987 constitution.

The **Roman Catholic** church, largely silent throughout the notorious excesses of the rule of "Papa Doc" Duvalier (1957–71), has become increasingly vocal in support of social justice, encouraged by the visit of Pope John Paul II in 1983. The Catholic radio station, Radio Soleil, was a principal channel for political criticism in the 1980s. Deep tensions exist, however, between radical supporters of Ti L'Eglise (Little Church) and of Père Aristide, expelled from his religious order for political agitation, and the more cautious hierarchy. The leftwing Père Aristide won a landslide 68 per cent of the vote in Haiti's first free elections in December 1990, but in September 1991 an army *coup* brought the short-lived democracy to an abrupt end, and Fr. Aristide fled to French Guiana, from where he hoped to return to power with American and French support. The coup was condemned internationally (leading to international sanctions)—but notably not by the

Vatican, the only state to have recognized the army rulers months later. In Haiti the *coup* was followed by brutal repression, probably worse than under the Duvalier dictatorship.

Twenty per cent of the population are now **Protestant**, with the **Methodists** as the longest established, while the denominations of **Baptists, Seventh Day Adventists**, and **Pentecostals** have enjoyed a rapid growth. There are some 12,000 **Bahais**, who have also grown rapidly.

Honduras

Honduras is one of the poorest countries in the Western hemisphere, and has a population of about 4,500,000 which is growing fast. Ninety-six per cent of its population are baptized **Roman Catholics**, but about five per cent of these practise a Christo-pagan religion, and their numbers are growing. The Church has not taken a political role until recently, when its activity in areas of society, laity and evangelization has been increased. This has taken the form of the creation of a lay apostolate, and integrating nuns into all aspects of pastoral work, but the concern for social development has brought it into conflict with the state. The state has encouraged **Protestant** missions from the United States which are indifferent to social activity on behalf of the poor, and a 1987 report numbers Protestants at 12 per cent of the total population. These are almost entirely fundamentalists or **Pentecostals**, with few historic denominations remaining.

Hungary

The population of Hungary is estimated at 10,500,000, of whom some 67 per cent are **Roman Catholic**, 20 per cent are **Reformed** Calvinists, and 5 per cent are **Lutheran**. There are also 0.5 per cent **Orthodox**, mainly Serbian and Rumanian, and also **Baptists** and **Pentecostals**. The Catholic Church is strongest in West Transdanubia, and elsewhere among ethnic minorities, intellectuals, and in rural areas. After initial opposition to the Communist régime, it resigned itself to co-operation, and won concessions and liberties towards the end of the 1980s before the régime collapsed completely. Fourteen per cent of the population attend mass weekly, and 20 per cent at Easter. The **Protestants** found it easier to adapt to Communism. There are nearly 100,000 Jews, 80 per cent of whom live in Budapest, and there they have 32 synagogues and a rabbinical seminary, with a library of 60,000 volumes. There are over 30 rabbis in the country, and 130 synagogues in all.

Iceland

Iceland's population has risen slightly to 253,000, and 91 per cent belong to the National Church of Iceland, which is also called the **Evangelical Lutheran** Church. It has over 100 clergy, and a seminary. About 12 per cent of Lutheran members attend weekly, and the state imposes a church tax, which non-members may choose to donate to the University of Iceland instead. The second largest religious organization is the **Roman Catholic** church. Also present are the **Salvation Army, Seventh Day Adventists, Plymouth Brethren**, and Swedish **Pentecostals**. Norse pagan religion has recently been re-introduced by a tiny minority.

India

The population of India is currently estimated at 844,000,000, 83 per cent of whom are Hindu. Of these, a further 83 per cent belong to the four major castes *(varnas)*, and 17 per cent to the scheduled castes or "Untouchables". Hinduism is divided into hundreds of sects, loosely divided into **Saivas**, who worship Siva and are predominant in South India, **Vaisnavas**, who worship Vishnu, and **Saktas**, who worship the goddess Sakti. There are some 9,000,000 priests, and 15,000,000 *sadhus*, or ascetic mendicants. Over 10,000,000 pilgrims attend the 12-yearly festival of Kumbh Mela at which they bathe in the holy river Ganges. On the fringes of Hinduism, 0.5 per cent of Hindus belong to intellectual movements concentrating upon **Vedantic** philosophy, for instance the **Arya Samaj**, and the **Ramakrishna Mission**. There are also new Hindu sects, such as the **Divine Light Mission**, following the Guru Maharaji, with 5,000,000 followers; the **Ananda Marga**, a politico–religious sect with 2,500,000 followers; and smaller groups such as the followers of Sri Aurobindo and **Sri Chinmoy**. The Hindu sects and reform movements have been active in proselytism, whereas most Hindus do not proselytize.

Some 10 per cent of India's population are Muslim, and this rises to 78 per cent in Kashmir, a state presently in turmoil. Most varieties of Islam are found, but the overwhelming majority of Muslims are **Sunni**, mostly of the **Hanafi** or (in the south) **Shafi'i** schools of religious law. However, a substantial 35 per cent minority are **Shi'ites**, who mostly live in Uttar Pradesh. Sunnis may be **Barelvis**, strongly influenced by the **Sufism** of brotherhoods like the **Chishtiya**, or stricter **Deobandis, Ahl-i Hadith**, or **Ahl-i Quran**. Again, different options are provided by the **Tabligh Jama'at**, the **Jama'at-i Islami of India**, or the tradition of the **Islamic Modernists (South Asia)**. The **All-India Muslim League** and **All-India Muslim Majlis-e-Mushawarat** are attempts to provide a national focus for Muslim interests, but their fortunes have fluctuated considerably, as have to a lesser extent those of the **Jam'iat ul-Ulama-i Hind**. Shi'ites include Ithna 'Asharis or **Twelvers, Isma'ili Khojas** (or **Aga Khanis**), and **Bohoras**. There are also over 100,000 **Ahmadis**.

An estimated 2.6 per cent of the population are Christian, with some 11,000,000 **Roman Catholics**, and 10,000,000 Protestants. The Church has seen some Indianization, with *ashrams* or communities being formed. Most Protestants belong to the **Church of South India**, or the Church of North India, but many **Baptists** and **Lutherans** remain separate. **Pentecostalists** are not as successful here as they are elsewhere. There are also over 1,000,000 in the Orthodox Syrian Church of the East, dating back to the

421

early centuries of the Christian era (see **Syro-Indian Churches**), and over 1,000,000 in indigenous Hindu–Christian movements.

There are 13,000,000 **Sikhs**, and Sikhism has its centre in Amritsar where the Golden Temple is to be found. Against a background of perceived Hindu triumphalism, Sikh separatist movements have become numerous in recent years. Prominent amongst more radical Sikh groups are the banned **Damdani Taksal** and the **All India Sikh Student Federation** (AISSF). Sikhs are in a majority in the Punjab.

India has 40,000,000 tribespeople, and although 10,000,000 of these are officially recorded as following **tribal religions of India**, the numbers may be larger, in spite of the fact that many are becoming Hinduized. Tribal religions are practised among the hill tribes of Assam, the **Nagas**, the Kandyans of Bengal, the Toda of Nilgiris, and many others.

India was the original home of Buddhism, and a significant number of Buddhists survive in unbroken lineage from ancient times. The northern state of Ladakh also possesses a flourishing Buddhist culture, of Tibetan descent, dating back to the 12th century. Since 1956, the Buddhist following of about 5,000,000 has spread among the Untouchables. Some of these have been re-converted to Hinduism by the Arya Samaj. There are also some 80,000 **Tibetan Buddhists** living in exile with their leader, the Dalai Lama.

India has 3,500,000 **Jains**, who are rarely found elsewhere in the world, and their numbers are decreasing. They emphasize asceticism, and have beautiful temples. There are also over 1,000,000 **Bahais**, and these have enjoyed a rapid expansion in recent years. **Parsiism**, which originated in Persian Zoroastrianism and has been in India for many centuries, has now declined to fewer than 100,000 adherents, not least because of prohibitions against inter-religious marriages.

Powerful new religious movements have swept through India in the 1980s, attracting millions of adherents, although statistics are not yet available. These include the **Swaminarayan** movement in Gujarat, the **Radhasoami Satsang** in Uttar Pradesh and Punjab, the **Satya Sai Baba Satsang** in South India, and the **Brahmakumaris** in Rajasthan.

Indonesia

With an estimated 190,000,000 people, Indonesia has—following the collapse of the USSR—the world's fourth largest population. It is approximately 87 per cent Muslim (predominantly **Sunni-Shafi'i**), and has the largest Muslim population in the world, although it is estimated (very approximately) that only some 43 per cent of these practise orthodox Islam, while the remainder practise a syncretistic blend of Muslim, Hindu, Buddhist and animistic elements. The former are known as *santri*, and the latter as *abangan*, a distinction parallel to that between **Agama Islam Santri** and **Agama Jawa** (or **Agama Islam Jawa**), as the two variants of Islam are known in Java, the main island. Many *santri* belong to **Sufi** orders, with purely local orders existing alongside major international ones like the **Naqshabandiya** and **Qadiriya**, but Sufi influence is obvious also in aspects of *abangan* practice such as repeated chanting of the basic Muslim tenet "there is no god but God". Otherwise the two main *santri* organizations are the **Muhammadiyah** and the **Nahdatul Ulama**, representing a modernist and a more traditionalist orientation respectively. The very different **Gerakan Pembaharuan** remains relatively insignificant. Many *abangan* belong to new religious movements known as **kebatinan** sects, of which **Subud** is the best known internationally. Since 1960, State Islamic Institutes (Institut

Agama Islam Negeri) have provided higher education in Islamic law and theology, and since 1975 the Muslim community has been represented by a Council of Ulama (Majlis Ulama).

Christians form approximately nine per cent of the population: there are about 4,000,000 **Roman Catholics**—some in Java but mostly elsewhere in the islands; and 8,000,000 **Protestants**, who are heavily involved in education, with 17 universities or institutes of higher education. There has also been a rapid rise in **Pentecostalism**.

Hinduism and Buddhism both antedate Islam and Christianity in Indonesia, but are today minority faiths, albeit experiencing something of a revival. Hinduism remains predominant in Bali, but is now spreading in Java too, and the total number of adherents is estimated at over 3,000,000. This process of growth in Hinduism is partly a result of the horror of the massacres which followed the military *coup* of 1965, for in their wake *santri*, often with military support, continued to attack *abangan*, and the latter found some protection being afforded by a new Hindu identity. In addition, since 1987 there has been a move to rebuild the court of Majapahit, last and greatest of the Hindu–Javanese kingdoms, as a symbol of an alleged pre-Muslim Indonesian national identity. Buddhism (Mahayana) is especially prevalent among the ethnic Chinese minority, but monasteries and temples are being built more generally, and huge celebrations take place at the great site of Borobudur. Although the modern revival of the sangha from the 1950s onwards was undertaken by **Theravada** monks from Sri Lanka and elsewhere, from the late 1960s onwards Indonesian Buddhism has reverted to its (Chinese) Mahayana roots.

Confucianism as a religion is also officially recognised by the state, being practised in a somewhat adapted form within the Chinese community.

Ancient tribal religions, officially designated as animism by the state, are practised by a very small per cent of the population in isolated regions and islands, although considerable elements from comparable religions appear as part of the syncretic Agama Java.

There is also a small number of adherents of the minority **Ahmadiya (Lahori)** group.

The *abangan/santri* divide has its political counterpart, reflected in the controversy over whether the official state ideology known as Pancasila should include, along with belief in one God, "the duty for all Muslims to follow the syaria" (shari'a). Santri leaders supported the clause, and *abangan* leaders opposed it, during constitutional debates prior to independence in 1945, and the controversy has continued ever since. With government members tending to be drawn from the priyayi—sometimes wrongly identified as a distinct religious grouping but in fact approximating to an *abangan* social élite—omission of the clause has been increasingly insisted upon: since 1985 there has been a legal requirement for all organizations to adopt the Pancasila in its non-Islamic form as their sole ideology. The acquiescence in this of the sole Muslim political party, the PPP (Partai Persatuan Pembangunan, or Unity Development Party, a federation of four previous Muslim parties imposed by the military government in 1973), underlines the current weakness of the *santri* quest for an Islamic state.

Yet the Pancasila campaign of the 1980s coincided with (and was in part intended to help control) a rise in radical Muslim activism, with a variety of groups, often purely local and firmly mosque-based, operating outside the traditional mainstream organizations like the PPP, Nahdatul Ulama, and Muhammadiyah. Occasional outbreaks of violence—incidents of bombings, arson, a plane hijacking, the Tanjung Priok riots of 1984—have reinforced natural government suspicion of Muslim "extremists", many of whom, including highly respected charismatic itinerant preachers known as muballigh, and editors of mosque-based periodicals, now languish in jail.

Nevertheless, networks of "sitting-room meetings" taking place in people's homes (so-called Usroh groups) proliferate despite an attempted clampdown by the state which regards them as a threat to state security. However, by their very nature their true extent remains unknown. What remains indisputable, though, is the wide dissemination of Islamic literature, often propagating the views of organizations abroad like the **Muslim Brotherhood** and the **Jama'at-i Islami**, and the unprecedented numbers of young people attending the mosques and taking part in other religious gatherings both in the cities and in the countryside.

In addition to its clampdown on Muslim "extremists", the government has sought to gain the support of moderate (and, it doubtless hopes, majority) Muslim opinion through such measures as its support for the organization of the Hajj, for the creation of Islamic banks, and for the establishment in 1990 of a national Islamic organization, ICMI (Indonesian Muslim Intellectual Association). Indonesia is also a member of the **Organization of the Islamic Conference**.

Iran

Iran has a population of nearly 58,000,000, and it is 99 per cent Muslim, with an estimated 85–90 per cent of the population being **Twelver Shi'ites** (Ithna 'Asharis), adherents of the **Ja'fari** school of jurisprudence. These include a number of **Shaykhis**. A small number of Shi'ite **Sufi** orders exist, including the **Ni'matullahiya** and the **Dhahabiya**. There are also several thousand **Isma'ili** Shi'ites, concentrated mainly in the North, who owe allegiance to the Aga Khan (hence **Aga Khanis**), and five per cent of the population are **Sunni** Muslims, mainly among the Kurdish minority or near the border with Afghanistan. Iran stands out as the only largely Shi'ite country in the world (although neighbouring Iraq has a 55 per cent majority who are Shi'ite, and there are also significant numbers of Shi'ites in Lebanon).

Small minorities of Jews, **Zoroastrians** and Christians are officially recognized and allowed to practise their religion, but not allowed to hold political office in this Islamic state. The Christians are mainly **Orthodox** members of the **Armenian Church**, and there are over 100,000 of these, and also of **Azalis**. There is a tiny community of **Mandaeans**, or Sabaeans, originating from the second century. Finally, there were, at the time of the revolution in 1979, over 300,000 **Bahais**. The Bahais, however, although constituting the largest religious minority, are denied recognition and have been persecuted, both as heretics and as alleged agents of **Zionism**: summary arrest and detention, torture and deaths in custody, as well as public executions have been their fate, although the level of persecution seems now to have declined from a peak in the mid-1980s.

Ayatollah Khomeini's authority remained supreme until his death in 1989. He was regarded as the divinely guided representative of the Hidden Imam of the Twelvers, often being referred to as "*Imam*" himself. His *fatwa*, issued a few months before his death, against author Salman Rushdie proved controversial even among his supporters. It was repudiated by his heir designate, Ayatollah Montazeri, a strong critic of human rights' abuses in Iran (he subsequently resigned as Khomeini's designated successor), and the **Organization of the Islamic Conference** refused to endorse it. Many ordinary Muslims, on the other hand, greeted it with enthusiasm, as did certain Muslim leaders.

As defined in the Iranian Constitution, Khomeini's position was that of Leader of the Islamic Republic. On his death, the Assembly of Experts, the body whose task it is to choose the Leader, selected as his successor the then President, Ayatollah Khamenei. (The Assembly of Experts consists of 83 elected members of the *ulama*.) Ayatollah Rafsanjani, at that time Speaker of the Majlis (Parliament), became President. By the autumn of

1990, these more pragmatic leaders had been able to exclude the radical faction within the leadership from positions of power. Under their influence, the release of Western hostages in the Lebanon was able to proceed the following year. Their position was further strengthened by the results of the election of April 1992.

The Islamic nature of the state and its policies is safeguarded, not only by having a Leader as spiritual leader (*wali faqih*) and an Assembly of Experts, but also through a 12-member Council of Guardians composed of *ulama*, jurists whose task it is to check that legislation conforms to Islamic principles, and that candidates to high elected office are equipped to govern in true Islamic fashion (in 1990 they vetoed the candidacy of several hard-line radical *ulama*—including "hanging judge" Khalkhali—in elections to the Assembly of Experts). All these institutions are an attempt to put into practice Khomeini's contested theory of Wilayat-i Faqih, or Rule of the Jurisconsult (which is rejected by many Twelver leaders).

From 1980 to 1988 Iran was locked in bloody conflict with Iraq. When Iraq invaded Kuwait in 1990, Iran condemned the move, whilst also condemning the subsequent presence of infidel American troops on Muslim territory in Saudi Arabia. Attempts by radical fundamentalists to press the latter issue as the greater of the two evils (and as justifying Iranian support for Saddam Hussein against America) failed, and Iran declared its neutrality. Clearly it encouraged the post-war Shi'ite uprising in southern Iraq through its support for the **Supreme Assembly for the Islamic Revolution in Iraq (SAIRI)**, but again refrained from active military intervention.

With the Tudeh, or People's Party (in effect the Communist Party), having been proscribed in 1983, and ex-Prime Minister Bazargan's Iran Freedom Movement (Nehzat-Azadi) allowed only limited freedom, the only organization remaining as a functioning political party, the Islamic Republican Party (IRP), has now also been disbanded. Established in 1979, shortly after the revolution, as a vehicle for the country's Islamization, and as the political arm of the *ulama*, it had at first been dominant in the Majlis, but became riven with factionalism. At the joint request of Rafsanjani and Khamenei, Khomeini ordered its dissolution in 1987. Concomitantly, the percentage of Majlis seats held by clerics fell from 70 per cent in 1980 to 27 per cent in 1988.

Several other Islamic organizations exist, some with mass participation. The **Society of Militant Clergy** (Jam'iyat-i Ruhaniyun-i Mobariz) at first grew in importance after the dissolution of the IRP, continuing to endorse candidates for elections. However, their hardline opposition incurred the hostility of President Rafsanjani (and Ayatollah Khamenei), and they were virtually eliminated from representation in parliament in the April 1992 general election. The **Islamic Revolutionary Guards** (Pasdaran-i Inqilab-i Islami) were formed on Khomeini's orders soon after the revolution in 1979 as an armed power base from which support for Iran's Islamic revolution could spread "throughout the world". The **Reconstruction Crusade** (Jihad-i Sazandigi), on the other hand, has a non-military character, being involved in such projects as building roads and schools. The present state of another group, the **Fada'iyan-e Islam**, remains uncertain, while the **Hojjatiya** remains rather secret. At the local level, the Komitehs, or Revolutionary Committees, are in charge of security and, under the rationing system, of food distribution in their neighbourhood.

Iran has been a strong supporter of **Hizbollah** in Lebanon, and has sought to extend its influence in the region of the Gulf through support for organizations such as Hizb al-Da'wa (**Da'wa Party**).

Riots in several towns and cities in April–May 1992 were the first serious signs of unrest since the revolution. Revolutionary Guards were withdrawn after being attacked, and replaced by units of bassijis, semicivilian members of the volunteer militia **Bassij-i Mostazafin**.

Iraq

Iraq has a population of approximately 20,000,000. There is some ethnic diversity: there are no recent reliable statistics but an estimated 79 per cent are Arab, 16 per cent Kurd, three per cent Persian and two per cent Turkish. Approximately 55 per cent of the population are **Twelver Shi'ites**, like their Iranian neighbours, and Iraq contains the most important shrines of the Twelvers, that of Imam Husain at Karbala, and that of Imam 'Ali at Najaf. Other important shrines are located in Kadhimain and Samarra. Ayatollah Khomeini lived in Najaf in exile from Iran from 1964 to 1978, and Najaf was the centre of a growing network of influential Islamic activists during the 1970s under the leadership of Ayatollah Muhammad Baqir al-Sadr, executed by the Saddam Hussein régime in 1980 for organizing opposition to the ruling Baath Party. Najaf activists have continued to be influential in oppositional organizations like Hizb al-Da'wa al-Islamiya (Islamic Call Party, or **Da'wa Party**), and not only in Iraq—Muhammad Husain Fadlallah, the Lebanese Shi'ite leader, was also an early collaborator of al-Sadr in Najaf.

Although less populous than the Shi'ites, the Sunni Arabs (**Sunnis** form some 40 per cent of the population, but nearly half of these are Kurds) have traditionally been disproportionately influential in government and the bureaucracy since the days of the (Sunni) Ottoman Empire. This remains true under current Baath rule. The war against Iran, begun in 1980, was motivated partly by a perceived need to prevent the export of the Iranian Revolution to Iraq via its large Shi'ite population, and Khomeini's known links with key militant leaders within the Iraqi Shi'ite community.

Christians form a tiny minority of some three per cent, mostly Catholics belonging to the **Chaldean** Church which is affiliated to Rome, though some of its priests are, or have been, married. The Ancient Assyrian Church, which is **Nestorian**, has 30,000 adherents, and there are smaller **Orthodox** communities. In addition there are 100,000 **Yazidis**, and a small number of **Mandaeans** or Sabaeans, only found elsewhere in south-west Iran. **Bahais** have been persecuted or repressed. Since the Iranian revolution of 1979, southern Iraq has been home to the leadership of the **Shaykhis**, while the well established **Sufi** order, the **Rifa'iya**, was originally founded in the south too.

There are, in addition to al-Da'wa, a number of oppositional Islamist organizations, all Shi'ite, which hitherto, however, have failed to command a mass following even within the Shi'ite community, although it remains to be seen whether the situation has changed following the régime's brutal repression of the Shi'ite uprising which was precipitated by the Gulf War. Among the more important of these organizations are the **Organization of Islamic Action** (Munazzamat al-'Amal al-Islami) and SAIRI, the **Supreme Assembly for the Islamic Revolution in Iraq** (al-Majlis al-A'la li'l-Thawra al-Islamiya fi'l-Iraq), with its associated al-Mujahidun. The Group of Combatant *Ulama* (Jama'at al-Ulama al-Mujahidin) may still be active, and there are various lesser organizations about which little is at present known—al-Afwaj al-Islamiya (the Islamic Batallions), Harakat Tahrir al-Mustad'afin (the Movement of the Liberation of the Oppressed), and Jund al-Imam (the *Imam's* Soldiers).

Iraq's invasion of Kuwait was denounced as un-Islamic by the Shi'ite groups, and they were baffled when many Muslims abroad supported Saddam in the subsequent confrontation. They were active in the subsequent uprising, but their precise role in it is unclear—as is the extent to which they have survived it.

In March 1991 the Shi'ite leader, Grand Ayatollah Abu'l-Qasim Khoi, was taken forcibly from the south to Baghdad. In a much publicized television interview with Saddam Hussein he denounced the uprising in the south, which he had been rumoured to be supporting.

Subsequently he was held under house arrest in Najaf until his death, at 93, in August 1992. Critics draw attention to the contrast with Ayatollah Baqir al-Sadr a decade earlier. The Shi'ite community apparently remains divided.

Ireland

Ireland, with a population of 3,500,000, is 95 per cent **Roman Catholic**. Catholic religious practice is extremely high, with over 80 per cent weekly attendance in some areas. The Church is strongly identified with Irish nationalism, and has a pervasive influence upon social life: controversies continue in relation to the laws against contraception and abortion in particular, and periodic scandals highlight the issue of clergy celibacy. The country has played a missionary role since the Middle Ages, and still sends a large number of priests and religious personnel abroad. The **charismatic movement** has grown in recent decades, and about 20 per cent of nuns and clergy are involved in this. Almost three per cent of the population are **Anglicans**, and the Church of Ireland once used to be the state religion in the time of British domination, although it never had more than 10 per cent of the population as members. About 0.4 per cent of the population are **Presbyterians**, and there are smaller minorities of **Lutherans, Baptists, Bahais**, and Jews. The **Protestants** are falling in numbers.

Israel

Israel has a growing population, the latest (1992) census figures give the total as 5,090,000 of whom 82 per cent are Jewish; 13.8 per cent are Muslim; 2.5 per cent are Christians; and 1.7 per cent are **Druze**. Since 1989 more than 418,000 new immigrants have arrived in Israel, largely from the Commonwealth of Independent States (87.6 per cent). There is officially no established religion, except for the Law of Return granting citizenship to Jews, all religions are equal in law.

Judaism, however, as the religious background of the majority of Israelis, plays a particular role in the public life of the "Jewish state" (the traditional Jewish calendar, the Jewish sabbath and religious holy days). Approximately 20 per cent of the Jewish population are strictly observant, with a further 40 per cent defined as traditionalists, subscribing in some degree to Jewish religious values and practices. The influence of the religious sector has been enhanced by the political system of proportional representation, with the religious parties often forming part of the ruling coalitions, and by the *status quo* agreement. This agreement entails the modern state of Israel maintaining a form of the Ottoman millet system inherited from the British mandate (1918–1948). This is a system of religious organization and corporate pluralism, whereby each recognized religious community is administered and funded under the auspices of the Ministry of Religion. Each community has the guaranteed right to its own rest days and holy days and a degree of autonomy in its jurisdiction over matters of personal status and family law. Religious functionaries are funded by the Ministry and operate parallel court systems (eg. Shari'a, Christian (canon law) Druze, and rabbinic).

Only the **Orthodox** form of Judaism is recognized: **Reform** and **Conservative** Judaism have no official status. The division of the Jewish population into **Ashkenazim** (Jews who derive from North, Central, Western and Eastern Europe) and **Sephardim** (from the Balkan states, North Africa and the Middle East) is reflected in the parallel offices of Ashkenazi Chief Rabbi and Sephardi Chief Rabbi. In addition there are rabbinical courts, with *dayyanim* (judges having the same status as district court judges), religious councils (responsible for local religious provision), religious committees responsible for *kashrut* (Jewish dietary laws), *yeshivot* (seminaries), synagogues (over 6,000), *mikvaot* (ritual bathhouses), burials, and inheritance. The rabbis have authority over the entire Jewish population in these areas, so that for example, there is no provision for civil marriage or divorce. This monopoly has been referred to as religious coercion by some factions and there have been calls for reforms. The recent influx of Russian Jewish immigrants will serve to lessen the power of the religious sectors.

There are both religious and secular state-funded Jewish school systems and some 35 per cent of parents elect to send their children to religious schools.

The Arab minority is made up of both Muslim (**Sunni** and **Shi'ite**) and Christian communities. In recent years there has been an upsurge in Muslim "fundamentalism", particularly in connection with the **Hamas** movement. The small Druze community still maintains its traditions and keeps its doctrines secret. There are also smaller communities of **Karaites** and **Samaritans** who reject the rabbinic tradition. Also, the world headquarters of the **Bahai** movement is in Haifa.

Christians are represented by a number of **Roman Catholic** churches (Armenian, **Chaldean**, Latin, **Maronite**, **Melkite** and Syrian) and **Orthodox** communities (**Greek, Armenian, Coptic** and **Russian**). In addition a number of other churches (for example the Evangelican Episcopalian Church in 1970) have been officially recognized in recent years.

Jerusalem is a sacred site for three world religions, with the Wailing Wall dating back to Second Temple Judaism, two mosques from the 7th and 8th centuries making it the third most important Muslim site after Mecca and Medina, and various Christian holy places looked after by the various churches.

Italy

Italy has a population of over 57,000,000, and until recently nearly all citizens were baptized as **Roman Catholics**. Now some 85 per cent profess to be Roman Catholic, and most of the rest claim to have no religious faith. Attendance at mass is low, however, with only six per cent receiving Communion regularly, and only 50 per cent of children being given catechetical instruction. Most participants in the Church are elderly, children, or women, and particularly those in the middle income bracket. The Vatican exerts its influence through its proximity and tight control over the Episcopal Conference. Rome has the highest proportion of attendance at mass, and here there are 17 pontifical universities, institutes and faculties of theology; 89 ecclesiastical institutes of education for secular and religious seminarians; and 10 pontifical academies. The Vatican city-state is situated in Rome.

In contrast to the presence of the Roman hierarchy and theology, some folk religion continues in the south of Italy with a belief in destiny which may be influenced by magical practices. There are about 200,000 **Protestants**, mainly **Pentecostals** belonging to the **Assemblies of God**, but also a small community of about 20,000 **Waldensians** who date back to the 12th century. There are also about 40,000 Muslims, mainly refugees from the Balkan states, as well as foreign students and diplomats. There are 21 Jewish communities, one of which dates back to the pre-Christian community in Rome. An agreement to repeal discriminatory laws dating from the fascist period was reached in 1987.

In the late 1980s, a politically active evangelical Roman Catholic group, **Communione e Liberazione**, continued to extend its influence within the Christian Democratic party, while in 1989 a major public controversy erupted over the traditional silence of the Church on the issue of the power and activities of the Mafia in the south.

Jamaica

The population of Jamaica of 2,400,000 is predominantly Christian, with an estimate of 70 per cent being **Protestant**, and 7 per cent **Roman Catholic**. The main denominations are **Anglican, Presbyterian, Baptist, Seventh Day Adventist**, and **Methodist**, with a recent rapid growth of the **Pentecostals** which makes them the most numerous. The largest Pentecostal church is the New Testament Church of God. The **charismatic movement** has affected both Roman Catholic and mainstream Protestant churches (represented by the Jamaican Council of Churches). In 1989 the Catholic hierarchy urged an end to capital punishment. Since 1988 the **Mormons** have also enjoyed official recognition as a church.

Jamaica is the stronghold of **Rastafarianism**, and this has over 100,000 followers, although its influence extends further. Rastafarianism is currently passing through a transition and becoming more widely acceptable. Spiritist cults are also widespread, including **Pocomania, Obeah, Convince, Kumina, Revival Zion** and the Black Israelites. These spirit-possession cults make use of strong alcohol and marijuana.

Japan

Japan has a population of 124,000,000, and it is estimated that 107,000,000 profess **Shinto** and 92,000,000 profess Buddhism. These figures illustrate the difficulty in quantifying religious practice in Japan, for many families will attend different temples for different rites, whereas on the private level the culture is predominantly materialistic. Nevertheless, there remains a high level of interest in religion in Japan, and it has the world's largest number, and fastest rate of increase, of new religious movements.

Shinto is the ancestral cult which reveres Japan's traditional gods (*kami*), and is composed of many sects. It became a national cult and the state religion for the first half of this century, and has been associated in Western minds with the belief in the Emperor's "divinity". The Emperor's nature as *kami*, however, merely indicates some vague numinous quality to do with descent or function which sets him apart from others, and is not related to Western ideas of God.

Shinto is not as widely practised as Buddhism, which has predominated since its entry from China in the seventh and eighth centuries. Buddhism is generally of the Mahayana variety, but may be divided into a number of widely differing sects. **Tendaishu** was once the dominant sect, but now has about 5,000,000 adherents and over 4,000 temples. Another ancient ascetic sect is **Shingonshu**, a **Tantric** religion, which has about 12,000,000 followers and 12,000 temples. Its centre is the small city Koya-San, which has a university of Buddhism. **Zen**, which has developed from Chinese Ch'an Buddhism, is divided into the three main schools of **Rinzai, Soto**, and **Obaku**, and together these have about 10,000,000 followers and 20,000 temples. Zen has had a significant impact upon Japanese culture, arts, gardens, and tea ceremonies, and is now popular largely due to its emphasis upon meditation. **Jodoshu**, with a reformed wing **Jodoshinshu**, is a version of **Pure Land** Buddhism which hopes for salvation from the Buddha Amida. It has a wide popular appeal, with perhaps 21,000,000 adherents and 30,000 temples, and has a university, Bukkyo Daigaku. The **Nichirenshu** sect, which dates back to the 13th century, is concerned with austerity and social justice, is also popular with the poorer classes, and has about 13,000,000 adherents and 6,000 temples.

Christian missionaries have been at work in the past two centuries, and there are about 2,000,000 Christians, including 500,000 **Roman Catholics**, 200,000 in the United Church of Christ in Japan, and 200,000 **Anglicans**. There are also a multitude of **evangelical** churches arising mainly from American missions, and a large number of indigenous Japanese churches.

A huge variety of new religious movements have been formed, some of which are break-away groups from Buddhism and Shinto, others of which are radically different. Approximately 16,000,000 participate in these. A variety of elements are found, including the promise of salvation, miracles and magic, belief in a divine spirit, **shamanism**, syncretism and authoritarianism. Among the most numerous are the following: **Soka Gakkai**, or **Nichirenshoshu** has 8,000,000 or more active members, and stems from Nichiren Buddhism. It is strong among the poor, and unites religion and politics in an ambitious and intolerant form. **Tenrikyo**, or the Religion of Divine Wisdom, derives from Shinto, and has about 2,000,000 adherents. **Reiyukai**, or the Association of Friends of the Spirit, has 4,000,000 followers, and follows a lay Buddhist tradition which has worldly concerns, an ancestral cult and patriarchal morals. **Rissho-Koseikai**, or the Society for the Establishment of Righteousness, is based upon Buddhism and aims at the personal perfection of individuals. There are also many marginal new religious movements, which often practise magic and occultism, and aim at psychotherapy rather than salvation.

Jordan

Jordan has a population of 4,000,000 with a further 1,100,000 in the West Bank currently occupied by Israel. It is 93 per cent Muslim, mostly **Sunnis** of the **Shafi'i** school of law, but with a small number of **Shi'ites** mainly among the Chechens. There are also about 3,000 **'Alawis**, and a few **Bahais** and **Druzes**. The nomadic Bedouins give priority to their pre-Islamic tribal law, but are also Muslim.

About six per cent of the population are Christian, of whom about 40,000 are **Orthodox**, mainly **Greek Orthodox** but also **Russian Orthodox** and members of the **Armenian, Syrian, Ethiopian** and **Coptic** Churches respectively. There are a similar number of **Roman Catholics** and **Melkites**, and a small number of **Anglicans** and **Evangelicals**.

While Jordan is not an Islamic state, King Hussein traces his descent back to the Prophet Muhammad (an important symbol of legitimacy), and a large mosque building programme together with numerous religious radio and television broadcasts indicate the importance which Islam has for the state. Islamist groups are represented by the **Muslim Brotherhood** in particular, but also the **Islamic Liberation Party**. However, a watchful monarchy has so far ensured that they do not develop into a threat to internal stability.

In the case of the Brotherhood, they have in many ways been successfully incorporated into the state. Not only do they enjoy official recognition, but they also hold seats in Parliament, and despite a period out of favour with the King in the mid 1980s they have influence at government level: they gained representation in the new Cabinet of January 1991 for the first time, controlling four ministries (Education, Religious Affairs, Health, and Social Development) until a new Cabinet was formed in June 1991. Thus their role in society is very different from that of the Muslim Brotherhood in neighbouring Syria.

The Islamic Liberation Party, on the other hand, remains illegal and has a limited number of supporters.

Iraq's invasion of Kuwait in August 1990 was at first criticized by the Muslim Brotherhood, but once US troops were stationed on sacred soil in Saudi Arabia, the Brotherhood became vociferously anti-American and finally supported Iraq, as did the majority of Jordanians.

Kenya

Kenya has a population of 27,700,000 of whom 28 per cent are **Roman Catholic**, 38 per cent **Protestant**, six per cent Muslim, and most of the remainder follow **African traditional religions**, including **Kikuyu religion**. These latter are characterized by a belief in magic power, medicine men, diviners, taboos and witchcraft. An ancestral cult is less prevalent than a belief in a single God. The Muslims are mainly **Sunni Shafi'i**, and 50,000 of them are Asian. There are about 20,000 **Shi'ites**, and also among the Asian community one finds many Hindus, and a few **Jainas** and **Sikhs**.

Christianity has arisen largely this century with numerous converts. Of the Protestant denominations, the **Anglican** Church is the largest, supporting many schools and Bible colleges, followed by the African Inland Church which arose from the African Inland Mission and has 2,500 congregations. Also present are **Presbyterians, Methodists, Pentecostals** and the **Salvation Army**. There are many indigenous churches (including **Maria Legio**), and the number of new churches registering, whether indigenous or missionary-sponsored, has led to restrictions on the numbers which are allowed to form. The **Jehovah's Witnesses** are banned.

Kenya is moving increasingly towards a one-party state, and the National Christian Council of Kenya (NCCK), which represents the Protestant Churches, together with the Roman Catholic Church, are the only effective opposition voices and are coming into increasing conflict with the state. In order to avoid involvement in this conflict, some Churches have taken the step of withdrawing from the NCCK, including the **Baptist** Convention of Kenya, the African Inland Church, the African Gospel Church, and the Full Gospel Churches.

Kiribati

Kiribati, formerly the Gilbert Islands, gained independence in 1979. It has a population of 70,300 scattered over 33 small atolls (including Christmas Island) in the South Pacific. It is predominantly Micronesian, with some Polynesians. Traditional religions have entirely ceased, and the population is now 48 per cent **Roman Catholic** and 45 per cent **Congregationalist**, with a few **Seventh Day Adventists** and **Bahais**. The churches play an important role in education and other aspects of life.

North Korea

North Korea has a population of 23,400,000, a people and culture very different from the neighbouring Chinese, and a Communist régime which officially discourages free religious associations. No accurate statistics of religious belief and practice are available, and no religious bodies functioned until recently when **Roman Catholic** and **Protestant** churches were built in 1988. The indigenous religion of **shamanism**, however, is still influential, in which the *shaman*, usually a woman, enters an ecstatic trance possessed by a spirit in order to cure diseases, secure blessings, and escort deceased souls to the nether world. The new religious movement, **Chondogyo**, has possibly 3,000,000 followers after a rapid growth in the first part of this century. It is a syncretic combination of shamanist, **Confucianist, Taoist** and Roman Catholic elements, with a great appeal for the poor. A further 500,000 may practise Mahayana Buddhism. Buddhists, Chondogyo, and Christian leaders have all recently spoken out in favour of national re-unification with the South.

Republic of Korea

South Korea has a population of 43,000,000, and in 1986 the Ministry of Culture and Information released accurate figures on religious distribution.

Buddhists have a membership of 15,000,000, with 21,000 clergy and 6,000 places of worship. Many of these belong to the **T'aego-chong** sect, which combines **Zen** meditation and **Pure Land** pietism, and shows considerable Japanese influence, though the largest Buddhist school at the moment is the more puritanical **Chogye-chong** which only achieved government endorsement in 1954 after many years in the wilderness. There are also some much smaller Buddhist sects, including **Won** Buddhism, which is a new syncretic movement drawing on features of Confucianism, **Taoism, Tonghak**—an indigenous tradition—and Christianity.

Confucianism has 10,000,000 adherents, 17,000 clergy and 230 places of worship, and had been the dominant religion for several centuries while repressing Buddhism. **Protestantism** has seen massive growth in recent decades, with numbers rising to 9,700,000, mainly in **Presbyterian** and **Methodist** churches, though **Pentecostals** are also growing. There are 43,000 pastors and 28,000 churches. The **charismatic movement** is strong, and the Korean churches have sent out one of the largest numbers of missionaries abroad. The **Roman Catholics** number 2,000,000, and have 6,000 priests and 2,000 churches. Leading Christians have clashed with the State, and have spoken out in favour of re-unification with the North. There have been a number of schisms from the churches to form indigenous churches, and some of these have incorporated elements from the indigenous **shamanism**. The influence of shamanism is still significant, and not measured in the Ministry's statistics.

Korea also has several new religious movements, the strongest of which is **Chondo-gyo**, which syncretizes shamanism, Confucianism, Taoism, and Roman Catholic elements, and has nearly 1,000,000 followers, 4,700 clergy and 270 places of worship. Another notable movement is the **Unification Church** of the Rev. Sun Myung Moon, who is believed by his followers to be the final Messiah. The **Olive Tree Church** is another new messianic movement.

Kuwait

Statistics on Kuwait are available only for the time prior to the Iraqi invasion of 1990: the exodus of refugees and the number of executions and other deaths will have altered them. They nevertheless provide the background against which the post-war situation will need to be judged—according to some estimates Kuwait's resident population has halved since the war, including the expulsion of thousands of Palestinians, Jordanians and Sudanese after liberation.

Prior to the war, the population was 1,900,000, of whom 40 per cent were indigenous Kuwaiti Arabs and the remainder expatriates, mostly also Arab, with large numbers of Palestinians in particular, but in addition a considerable Western community, and some 10 per cent South Asians. The ruling Al Sabah family, in power for over two centuries, has experimented with limited parliamentary democracy, most recently from 1981 to 1986.

Approximately 85 per cent of the population were Muslim, mostly **Sunnis** who—the indigenous Kuwaitis, at least—followed the **Maliki** school of law, but with a large 25 per cent minority of **Twelver Shiʻites**, many of them relatively recent immigrants from Iraq, but some of Iranian extraction. While some Shiʻites were members of the commercial élite, most were relatively underprivileged. Among the expatriates there were about 50,000 **Roman Catholics**, a number of **Anglicans**, and also of Hindus.

The ideas of the Egyptian **Muslim Brotherhood**, and of more extreme Islamist groups like **al-Takfir waʻl-Hijra**, have circulated in Sunni circles with the influx of expatriates, and there was an increase in fundamentalist Sunni Islam during the 1980s, without any pronounced militancy. The main organization embodying this trend was the **Society for Social Reform** (Jamʻiyat al-Islah al-Ijtimaʻi), which attracted support among professionals and some members of the ruling family and controlled the student union from 1979 onwards. It worked through representation in the national assembly to promote reforms in education and social practice that would encourage a more Islamic life-style, and published an important journal, *al-Mujtamaʼ*. Its aims were further pursued through lectures and numerous Quran study groups, and it had branches in other Gulf states.

In the wake of the Iranian revolution of 1979, Ayatollah Khomeini attempted to attract support among Kuwait's Shiʻites, and for a short time there were outbreaks of violence, coinciding partly with Saudi suppression of the Shiʻites in its eastern territories, but there was no sustained popular upsurge, although Kuwait's support for Iraq in the Iran–Iraq war led to attacks on some targets in Kuwait by underground groups, e.g. Iraq's Shiʻite organization Hizb al-Daʻwa, or the **Daʻwa Party**. The main organizational focus of Kuwait's Shiʻites was the Dar al-Tawhid, which tended to attract mainly intellectual support, and to be somewhat pro-Iranian.

In the wake of the Gulf War of January–February 1991, there is a feeling that, despite promises of increased democracy, the ruling Emir is out of touch with the realities of the situation. The traditional view that women should not have the vote has come under increasing criticism from the female population, many of whom braved tanks during the Iraqi occupation, and were active in the resistance.

Laos

Laos has a population of just over 4,000,000, of whom 85 per cent are **Theravada** Buddhists, and most of the others animist, with small Chinese and Vietnamese minorities practising forms of Mahayana Buddhism, and **Confucianism**. Thirty-five per cent of the people belong to hill tribes, and many of these still have a belief in spirits and practice ancestor veneration. As a result, Theravada Buddhism here is permeated by the cult of *phi*, the popular belief in deities, demons, spirits and souls, and is thus described separately (**Lao Theravada**). The two monastic orders, **Mahanikay** and **Thammayut**, were traditionally well supported, and the centre of each village is the *wat*, of which there are presently about 2,800. In the late 1970s the *sangha* was restructured, under the supervision of the Pathet Lao, and many monks fled to Thailand as a result. Sangha affairs are now the responsibility of the **Lao United Buddhists Association** (LUBA), which combines the dual function of propagating Buddhist and party teachings, which are seen to be mutually compatible. In 1985 it was calculated that Laos had some 7,000 monks and 9,500 novices, 20 per cent of whom live in the Vientiane area. Despite many restrictions, it could be said that Theravada Buddhism in Laos is recovering from its nadir in the early 1970s.

Lebanon

The population of the Lebanon is estimated at over 3,000,000, of whom 57 per cent are Muslim and 43 per cent Christian, a reversal of the proportions that prevailed according to the 1932 census which was the basis on which the (unwritten) "National Covenant" of 1943 allocated institutional power between religious groups. This reversal undermined the leading political role of the **Maronites**, leading to the outbreak of civil war in 1975.

Much of the population lives in peasant communities in the mountain ranges, and these people are either Maronites or **Druzes**. In the coastal areas and cities, **Sunni** Muslims (known as Mourabitun) and members of the **Orthodox Church** predominate. Other Orthodox groups include the **Armenian Church**, the **Nestorian Church**, and the **Syrian Jacobite Church**. Catholic groups other than the Maronites include the **Chaldean** and **Roman Catholic** Churches (with the Greek, Armenian and Syrian rites being used as well as the Latin rite). There are also small **Protestant** communities.

Immigration, particularly of Palestinians, has led to diversity of religious groupings. Estimates suggest that the Muslims are 45 per cent Sunni, 40 per cent **Shi'ite**, and 15 per cent Druzes. Most Shi'ites are **Twelvers**, and linked to the Twelver Shi'ite state in Iran: there are currently some 2,000 **Islamic Revolutionary Guards** from Iran in Lebanon in support of the main radical Muslim organization, **Hizbollah**. Among Sunnis are to be found members of **Sufi** orders such as the **Khalwatiya**.

Each Lebanese citizen must be a member of a religious group since these administer family law.

The civil war, which continued, with varying degrees of intensity, from 1975 to 1991, was started by both religious and ethnic tensions, and resulted in the cantonization of the country into confessional enclaves in which the militias often needed to take on nearly all aspects of government. Now, however, the Syrian-backed National Army of Lebanon—together with the occupying Syrian Army—has firm control of the country down to the six-mile-wide buffer zone in the South controlled by the Israelis and their proxies the (largely Christian) South Lebanon Army (formerly known as the Haddad Militia).

(Between 1988 and 1990, the Maronite Christian army commander General Michel Aoun attempted to defeat both the occupying Syrian Army and the militias—including the Christian militia, the Lebanese Forces, the armed wing of the Phalangist Party (established in 1936 as a right-wing Maronite grouping) and responsible for the 1982 massacres of possibly more than 700 people in the Sabra and Chatila Palestinian refugee camps—but the attempt was unsuccessful.)

The Taif Accord of 1989 established the framework within which the militias were to disarm. The only militia which has so far refused to disarm in accordance with this framework is Hizbollah, which continues to wage guerilla war against the Israeli troops and the South Lebanon Army in the southern buffer or "security" zone. In February 1992 the Israelis responded by assassinating the Hizbollah leader, Sheikh Abbas Mousawi, bombing the car in which he and his family were travelling.

Hizbollah has attracted international attention due to its prominent role in the Western hostage affair. Its stance here parallels that of **Islamic Jihad** and **Islamic Amal**. Its chief rival, **Amal**, however, has opposed hostage-taking.

Members of the disarmed militias are being encouraged to join the National Army of Lebanon, which is becoming more truly "national" as a result, incorporating increasing numbers of Muslims alongside Christians. Constitutional amendments endorsed in September 1990 mean that membership of the National Assembly will be equally divided between Christians and Muslims. It remains to be seen whether effective government will now be possible on these new bases.

Lesotho

Lesotho has a population of 1,800,000, of whom 90 per cent are Christian, and the remainder follow **African traditional religions**. Forty-five per cent of the population are **Roman Catholic**, and four-fifths of these are regular church-goers. The emphasis is placed by the hierarchy upon building schools, churches, rectories and convents, and this has displeased some Catholics who would like to see more work in deepening people's personal faith. The Pope visited in 1988. Twenty-four per cent of the population belong to the Lesotho **Evangelical** Church and 12 per cent are **Anglican** of a high-church tradition. There are also **Methodists, Dutch Reformed**, and **Pentecostals**.

Liberia

Liberia has a population of 2,700,000 and was formed when freed slaves were returned from America. Their descendants are mainly Christian, and these have dominated the indigenous tribes ever since. Christianity is mainly **Protestant** or indigenous, and while perhaps 30 per cent may profess to be Christian, only about 10 per cent practise and the rest still follow **African traditional religions**. The **Roman Catholic** Archbishop and a number of priests have been critical of government repression, and suffered harassment by the state in consequence. Seventy per cent of the population follow African traditional religions, including such elements as the veneration of ancestors, divination, a belief in witchcraft and the beneficial power of medicine men. There are secret societies with elaborate initiation ceremonies. Twenty per cent of the population are Muslim, of the **Sunni Maliki** tradition, and the numbers of these are growing among the tribes. The **Qadiriya** and **Tijaniya Sufi** orders are active.

Libya

Libya has a mixed Arab and Berber population of approximately 4,700,000. Ninety-seven per cent are **Sunni** Muslims, the majority of whom adhere to the **Maliki** rite, and a minority to the **Hanafi**. The **Sanusiya Sufi** order has been associated with Libya in particular—indeed it remains so, although its power (and perhaps its authority) have been drastically curtailed by the Qaddafi régime.

Colonel Qaddafi's own revolutionary ideals, constituting the Third Universal Theory (instead of either Capitalism or Communism) and expounded in his *Green Book*, have increasingly been presented as a contemporary interpretation of the social message of the *Quran*, and a form of Islamic socialism. As implemented in Libya so far, this has involved, for example, the abolition of the private ownership of land, the transference of the ownership of rented accommodation to its occupants, the taking over of factories by workers, and a system of direct democracy (with people's councils and congresses, the working of which, however, remains under dictatorial state scrutiny). In consequence, the country is now appropriately (it is claimed) to be known as The Socialist People's Libyan Arab Jamahiriya (rule by the masses).

The Islamic credentials of Qaddafi's creed are rejected as idiosyncratic by the majority of Muslims outside Libya, however, since he rejects the authority traditionally attributed to the Shari'a (religious law) and the hadith (traditions of the Prophet). The *Quran* remains as the indispensable foundation, but its interpretation, traditionally the prerogative of the *ulama*, is now declared the right of every individual. Within Libya too this view antagonized the religious establishment, but opposition—expressed, for example, in mosque sermons—has been repressed. Raids by government security forces on mosques during the time of prayer have taken place, and religious leaders arrested: some indeed have simply disappeared.

Illustrative of Qadaffi's modern individual interpretation of the *Quran* are the existence, contrary to traditional Islamic law, of a women's military academy and of a ban on polygamy. These co-exist with the more tradition-oriented prohibitions on gambling, night clubs and alcohol. The government also established the **Islamic Call Society** (Jam'iyat al-Da'wa al-Islamiya) for the propagation of Islam internationally.

Prior to Qadaffi's 1969 *coup* against the ruling monarch (King Idris was also the head of the Sanusi order), the **Muslim Brotherhood** had a small but influential following in Libya. Their power too, like that of the Sanusiya and the *ulama*, has now been curtailed, as has that of the stricter **Islamic Liberation Party** (Hizb al-Tahrir al-Islami) which nevertheless remains perhaps the major Islamist organization in Libya. Smaller fundamentalist opposition groups continue to have some influence amongst students and the lower ranks of the armed forces, but they face ruthless repression: in 1987 six members of two groups, Jihad al-Islami (in full, Munazzamat al-Jihad al-Islami, or Islamic Struggle Organization) and Hizbullah (Party of God) were hanged and their execution televised in a special programme. Other public hangings have also taken place.

Meanwhile the **Shi'ite** community of the Lebanon (in particular) blame Qadaffi for another "disappearance", that of their leader Imam Musa Sadr while visiting Libya in 1978.

Liechtenstein

Liechtenstein, with a population of nearly 29,000, is a traditional **Roman Catholic** state and in a sense a relic of the Holy Roman Empire. It is 87 per cent Roman Catholic, and 8.6 per cent **Protestant** in the form of the **Evangelical** Church. There are tiny **Lutheran** and **Seventh Day Adventist** communities. Women were allowed to vote for the first time in 1986.

Luxembourg

Luxembourg has a population of 379,000, of whom 95 per cent are **Roman Catholic**. There is a high rate of attendance at Mass, and Catholicism is taught in schools. The three per cent who are **Protestant** are mainly immigrants from other European countries, and are **Lutheran** or **Reformed**. There are about 700 Jews.

Madagascar

Madagascar is a former French colony with a population of 12,500,000. The population is 97 per cent indigenous Malagasy, which is an ethnic mixture from both Africa and South East Asia. About half of the population adhere to **Malagasy traditional religion**. They have a strong belief in the interdependence of individuals, and of the dependence of living upon the dead. They take part in complicated burial and ancestral rites, have many taboos, but fear and abhor all sorcery. Another 45 per cent of the population are Christian, with half of these **Roman Catholic**, and half **Protestants**. There are several indigenous Protestant churches with Malagasy pastors. There are also about 100,000 Muslims, mainly **Sunnis**, and at least 75 mosques.

Malawi

Malawi has a population of 9,200,000 of whom 45 per cent are **Protestant**, with the main denominations being **Presbyterian, Baptist, Evangelical, Anglican**, and **Lutheran**, and 30 per cent are **Roman Catholic**. Up to 1926 all Western education was mission education, and one effect has been that the Christian majority in Malawi has benefitted from a higher level of education than the large Muslim minority. Styles of worship in many of the major churches, including the Roman Catholic and the Anglican, have been influenced by the **charismatic movement**.

The human rights record of Dr. Hastings Banda's increasingly autocratic rule has evoked criticism from members of the Roman Catholic hierarchy, leading to confrontation between church and state, and the expulsion of some clergy, a state of affairs which persists into 1992.

Muslims constitute between 10 per cent and 20 per cent of the population, and are **Sunnis** of the **Shafi'i** school of religious law. Islam was first introduced in the 19th century by Swahili Arabs from the East African coast who established trading networks in slaves and ivory. In the early part of the 20th century Muslim teachers were active in deepening people's faith, a process reinforced by the spread of the **Shadhiliya**, and then the **Qadiriya, Sufi** orders. Traditional custom nevertheless often continues to prevail over the Shari'a.

Some Asian Muslims, who follow the **Hanafi** rite, are also present as traders, although since 1978 they have been required to reside in the main urban areas.

An active national body, the Muslim Association in Malawi, promotes the well-being of the Muslim community, and there is an increasingly active Muslim Students Association.

The **Bahai** faith has spread here too, but the government has banned the **Jehovah's Witnesses** (or **Kitawala**).

African traditional religions, involving the making of periodic offerings to the ancestral spirits, continue to be influential, as do the **Chisumphi** and **M'Bona cults**: the person of M'Bona is regarded as a black Jesus.

Malaysia

Malaysia has a population of 18,600,000, of whom approximately 15,000,000 live in Peninsula Malaysia, and 3,600,000 in East Malaysia (Sabah and Sarawak). In Peninsula Malaysia 54 per cent of the population are Malay, 35 per cent Chinese, 10 per cent Indian and one per cent Thai and other races including the tribal orang asli.

Nearly all Malays are Muslim, along with (North) Indians, and around 20 per cent of the tribal peoples (making Islam the dominant religion). The Muslims are mainly **Sunni-Shafiʻi**, but **Shiʻite** elements are evident, and Malays are attracted to the mystical aspects of **Sufism**—the spread of Sufism having been a major factor in the Islamization of the Malay peninsula from the 14th century onwards, when it allowed the integration of elements of existing Malay culture and belief (originally Hindu and Buddhist) into the practice of Islam. These syncretic elements, which include elements of Indian and Malay magic and their control by local *shamans* (*bomoh*), and local laws and customs (*adat*), continue to influence Islamic practice today.

The Chinese mainly practise **Chinese folk religion**, with ancestor-veneration rituals, and elements drawn from Buddhism, **Confucianism**, and **Taoism**. Mahayana Buddhism is also important among the Chinese, as too, in Kelantan, is **Theravada**, and forms of **Tantrism** are also present through encountering Malay Hinduism which has been present since the first century CE. About 70,000 Chinese follow a new religion, Tien Te Sheng Hui, or the Heavenly Virtue Church, which was founded in China and stresses ethics, virtue and wisdom in a synthesis of elements of Confucianism, Taoism, Buddhism, Islam and Christianity. (*See too* **De Jiao**.)

About six per cent of the population are Christian, though in the East Malaysian states of Sabah and Sarawak this rises to 40 per cent. There are about 400,000 **Roman Catholics**, 150,000 **Methodists**, 80,000 **Anglicans**, and around 200,000 other Christians, including fast growing **Pentecostal** and independent neo-charismatic churches. The **charismatic movement** is increasingly influential in mainstream Christian and independent churches alike, and acts as a strong counterpoint to resurgent Islam.

The Indians are predominantly Hindu, mostly **Saivas**, though with some **Vaishnavas** among immigrant groups with roots in northern India. There are also small, well-knit communities of **Sikhs** in most urban centres, and as noted above, some Indians are Christian.

In the northern state of Kelantan there is a small but well established extension of **Thai Theravada**. The Buddhist temples are often supported financially by the local Chinese community, but run by ethnic Thais (Siamese). Interestingly the chief monk and the district ecclesiastical heads are officially appointed by the Sultan, a Muslim, whom the Sangha recognize as their patron and protector.

Tribal religions are strong among the indigenous peoples of Sarawak and Sabah, and these share beliefs in good and evil spirits who must be placated, omens, taboos, divination, magic, and the practice of seasonal rites. The life-style of the tribal people is under threat from deforestation, and they are also the object of proselytization efforts by government-backed *dakwah* (Muslim missionary or renewal) groups, and by **evangelical** Christian groups.

The question of the role of Islam in society has become increasingly controversial, involving tensions both between Muslims and non-Muslims, and also between different groups of Muslims.

The latter have, to some extent, deep historical roots. In the 18th century Malayan Islam came under the more orthodox influence of the **Wahhabi** reform movement, and in the 19th century ideas of the Islamic Modernist **Salafiya** gained ground, giving rise to tensions with earlier Sufi and syncretistic tendencies. These tensions persist in Malay Islam still today.

Islam was declared the official religion of the new independent nation of Malaysia in 1957, and in each of the states of the Federation ruled by its sultan (the sultans take it in turn to serve five years as king of Malaysia), the sultan is also the head of the Islamic religion. A system of Shari'a courts is in place, and its workings have been gradually strengthened since independence.

A Malay-Muslim party, UMNO (United Malay National Organisation), has been the leading force in the multi-racial coalitions that have governed the country since independence. Conscious of the precarious multi-ethnic nature of Malaysian society, however, in which, moreover, differences of ethnicity tend to be symbolized by differences of religion, UMNO, accommodating the desires of the multi-racial coalition it leads, has been less ardent in pursuing specifically Muslim interests than its traditional rival for the Muslim vote, **Parti Islam Se-Malaysia (PAS)**. Nevertheless, the government established the Islamic Welfare and Missionary Association (PERKIM) which has engaged in proselytizing campaigns among the Chinese, Indians and tribal peoples.

The economic and cultural influence of the Chinese (rather than the less favourably placed Indians), particularly in the urban centres, is seen as a threat to the Islamic *umma* by the predominantly rural Malays. Ethnic tensions exploded in urban riots in 1969 and these events in turn fuelled a radical Islamic resurgence which spread rapidly from urban to rural areas in the 1970s and 1980s. Urban Muslims appropriated the term *dakwah* to describe the teachings and practices of the resurgence, and distanced themselves by dress, religious practice and teaching from the rural ulama, and the state religious apparatus controlled by the sultans. Important *dakwah* organizations include **Angkatan Belia Islam Malaysiam (ABIM)**, which like PAS has been actively involved in politics, **Darul Arqam**, and Jama'at Tabligh. The last of these, founded in India (where it is known as **Tablighi Jama'at**) in the 1920s, began growing in Malaysia in the 1950s, and strengthened by the resurgence of the 1970s, spread in both rural and urban areas. Tabligh is an exclusively male organization and this limits its influence, particularly among dakwah students. Its apolitical stance may also be construed as unduly beneficial to the government.

There have been, at times, clashes between the state and Muslim activists involving violence: in 1980 a rural police station was attacked (leading to the death of eight of the attackers), while in the "Memali incident" of 1985, a bloody clash between 400 villagers and 200 police left four policemen and 14 villagers dead including Ibrahim "Libya", a former PAS official, whom the police were seeking to arrest. In 1978 there was also a spate of attacks on Hindu temples.

The ability of UMNO to represent Islam has been challenged by a shifting of electoral allegiance of *dakwah*-influenced Muslims to PAS (which increased its share of the West Malaysian vote to 43 per cent in the 1986 general election). In an attempt to counter this, the UMNO-led government has found it necessary to champion significant Islamizing measures through its control of the legislature and secular state bureaucracy. Islamic banking practices are promoted by the Islamic Bank; a large new Islamic University, established in Kuala Lumpur in the 1980s with support from the **Organization of the Islamic Conference**, promotes official Islamic teachings through a range of degree courses from business studies to tropical agriculture; strict Arab-inspired Islamic dress codes are spreading in government buildings and schools; and government leaders have even begun publicly to air the possibility of making Malaysia a Muslim state guided by *syari'ah* (Shari'a) law. Whether this policy of selective and gradual Islamization will succeed in weakening the appeal of the more fundamentalist groups—or have the contrary, and unintended, effect of strengthening them—remains to be seen. UMNO can afford neither to disregard growing Muslim claims, or it will lose its own Muslim supporters, nor to be too supportive of them, or it may strengthen the appeal of PAS which in the October 1990 election gained control of Kelantan (where subsequently gambling and the sale of alcohol to Muslims have been banned; Chinese female hairdressers may no longer cut Muslim men's hair; and the chief minister has stated his intention to introduce Quranic punishments).

Meanwhile, the number of Muslims taking the *Hajj* continues to rise, as does the number of young people taking part in Friday prayers in the mosque, and the number of women adopting more conservative dress. Moreover, given that Islamic revivalism in Malaysia is closely linked to ethnic identity, it has had serious effects on the plural nature of the society. The social interaction of Muslims and non-Muslims becomes more problematic as *dakwah* influence lays increasing emphasis on food and other social taboos, and religious freedoms are increasingly restricted: in 1984 the Malay language Bible was banned, as was all non-Muslim religious teaching in schools, even Christian government-aided ones; restrictions on the building of churches were introduced; while in 1987 the discovery of two alleged Christian plots against the government led to a number of arrests of Christian evangelicals and social activists. Fears are growing among the 45 per cent non-Muslim population of the possibility of the imposition of an Islamic state with the *syari'ah* applicable to Muslim and non-Muslim alike. A delicate balancing act is required, of UMNO in particular, if ethnic–religious divisions are not to be deepened, and tensions exacerbated even further.

Maldives

The Maldives comprise 1,200 coral islands in the Indian Ocean south-west of Sri Lanka, of which 200 are inhabited. The population of 220,000 is of Sinhalese, Dravidian, Arab and black African origin. **Sunni Shafi'i** Islam is the state religion, and 99.9 per cent of the population are Muslims. Shari'a law is enforced, but according to a liberal tradition. Women have many formal civil rites.

Mali

Mali has a population of 8,300,000 of whom 90 per cent (though some estimates suggest 70 per cent) follow the **Sunni Maliki** form of Islam which has been present in the country since the 11th century. The **Hamalliya** form of **Sufism** split from the **Tijaniya** here, and remains strong, as does **maraboutism** (the President and many of his ministers employ important *marabouts* to confirm their powers). The **Qadiriya** is also present. On the other hand, adherence to the brotherhoods is often purely nominal. Timbuktu is a famous holy place of African Islam.

Mali is a one-party state with a military and socialist ruler, President Traoré. No Islamic opposition to his rule has surfaced yet, but reform Islam is growing, both in a relatively tolerant form, and in a more radical exclusivist form, inspired by pilgrimage to Mecca and related opportunities to study in Saudi Arabia or elsewhere in the Middle East, and encouraged by the more favourable political climate in Mali following the military overthrow in 1968 of the previous Marxist-Leninist régime. In 1981 the government-controlled Association Malien pour l'Unité et le Progrès de l'Islam (AMUPI) was established, partly with the aim of controlling the spread of **Wahhabist** reformism (of which Bamako is one of the principal centres in West Africa), and preventing the outbreak of the sort of religious riots that had occurred in northern Nigeria, notably in the 'Yan Tatsine movement. About nine per cent of the population follow **African traditional religions**, and notable among these are the Dogons, whose myths of creation determine conceptions of the individual, family and society. About one per cent of the population are Christian, and half of these are **Roman Catholic**, with the other half being **Protestant**.

Malta

Malta has a population of 350,000, of whom 98 per cent are **Roman Catholic** and two per cent are **Anglican**. Church attendance is very high, and the Church organizes social and cultural movements, credit unions and an emigration service. The Church is dominant in education, and owns 16 per cent of all property in Malta. Malta is also notable for the number of missionaries it sends overseas, and for its continued ban on divorce in any form. Trading links with Libya have been accompanied by some cultural influences, and there are requests to establish mosques in Malta for use by visiting Libyan technicians.

Mauritania

Mauritania's population of 2,100,000 is 99 per cent **Sunni** Muslim, following the **Maliki** school of jurisprudence. The **Qadiriya Sufi** brotherhood is widespread, but there are also some members of the **Tijaniya** and a few of the **Shadhiliya**, while it was here that the **Harralliya** originated early this century. An Islamic State was declared in 1980 through the alliance of the native Hausa régime with the **Muslim Brotherhood**, and Shari'a law was introduced, as well as slavery being abolished. Chinguetti is the seventh Holy Place in Islam.

Mauritius

Mauritius, formerly a British Crown Colony, is an island in the Indian Ocean with a population of about 1,000,000 people. The British introduced indentured Indian labour to work on the sugar plantations, and their descendants today form some 68 per cent of the population. Three quarters of these are Hindus, over 300,000 of whom are traditional **Vaisnavas** and **Saivas**, and over 100,000 being part of the **Arya Samaj** reform movement. Thirty-five per cent of the population are Christian, and 17 per cent are Muslims, with 90 per cent of these being **Sunnis** who speak Urdu as their main language; the remaining 10 per cent belong to the **Ahmadiya**, a heterodox sect formed in what is present-day Pakistan near the beginning of this century which is highly successful at proselytizing with some **Isma'ili Daudis**. There are also about 10,000 **Bahais**, 6,000 Buddhists, and a few **Confucianists** who belong to the old Chinese population which is dying out.

Mexico

Mexico has a population of about 87,500,000 which is 96 per cent **Roman Catholic**. Nearly all the clergy and religious orders are nationals, and the catechism is often taught by Sisters and youths. The attitudes of Mexican Catholics differ between regions and social classes, but one of the uniting features is the veneration of the Virgin of Guadalupe. This has a vast iconography, and has been fused with Aztec worship of the earth goddess Cuauhtli. Cults of patron saints are prominent, and pilgrimages to venerate those with miraculous qualities are common. **Catholic Action** promotes Church-oriented social welfare programmes. Mexico also faces a growing amount of religious indifference and secularization. The Constitution forbids any interference of any religious leader in state affairs, or even the right to speak on political issues or vote. The Church has been traditionally conservative, and conflict with the State has not arisen until the past two decades in which more liberal and democratic elements have begun to oppose the authoritarian régime and its electoral frauds. The state assisted the Church with the construction of a monumental basilica in honour of Our Lady of Guadalupe.

Mesoamerican traditional religions are also to be found. The Huichol and Tepehuan tribes still practise their traditional Indian religions, and Aztec and **Mayan** beliefs are still very influential among all monolingual Indian groups who combine them with a form of folk-Catholicism. About 3 per cent of the population are **Protestant**, or marginal Protestant, and the **Mormons** have had spectacular success among Indians with 40,000 baptisms in 1976 alone. The **Jehovah's Witnesses** have also been successful, but the main Protestant groups are **Presbyterian, Baptist** and **Pentecostal**. There are also 50,000 Jews, and about 40,000 immigrants who practise Islam and Buddhism.

Monaco

Monaco, a small town on the Mediterranean coast of France, is an independent state of 28,000 who are 95 per cent **Roman Catholic**. It is a single diocese, directly subject to the Vatican. There are also **Anglican** and **Reformed** churches, and a Jewish synagogue.

Mongolia

The People's Republic of Mongolia, with a population of about 2,000,000 was formerly predominantly **Tibetan Buddhist**, of the **Gelugpa** school, until the Communist takeover in the 1920s. Subsequently Buddhism was completely suppressed, and effectively ceased to function, although there is now a Buddhist temple at Ulan Bator, with 130 monks. This seems to exist mainly for propaganda purposes in diplomatic relations, though the Buryats still retain their allegiance to the Gelugpa tradition. Traditional **shamanism**, however, may still be influential among as many as 30 per cent of the population, although it has no public temples or organizations. There are also about 80,000 Muslims in Mongolia.

Morocco

Morocco has a population of 25,700,000, of whom 98.7 per cent are Muslim, **Sunnis** of the **Maliki** school of law. 1.1 per cent of the population are Christian, almost entirely foreign **Roman Catholics**, and there are a very small number of Jews.

Sufi orders—notably the **Qadiriya, Shadhiliya, Darqawiya** and **Tijaniya**, with some adherents of the **Hamalliya, Haddawiya** and **Hamadsha**—have seen their considerable appeal weakened since the confiscation of their large estates by King Muhammad V in the years following independence in 1956. The move was justified in terms of their alleged collaboration with colonialism.

This undermining of institutional Sufism (largely rural) by the state attracted little criticism from the *ulama* (largely urban), in good measure because of the influence on the latter of the **Salafiya** movement and its strong attack on **maraboutism**. In other respects, however, the *ulama* were critical of the monarchy, and retained considerable independence until the early 1960s.

Since the accession of King Hassan II in 1961, though, the monarchy has gradually succeeded in establishing religious supremacy over Sufi orders and *ulama* alike. A member of a dynasty whose power and influence in Morocco can be traced back as far as the 17th century, the King further claims descent from the Prophet Muhammad himself, and supreme religious authority as the Commander of the Faithful or Defender of the Faith. The failure of two *coup* attempts in 1971 and 1972 were explained in numerous speeches as due to his possession of *baraka*, the sacred power traditionally attributed to Sufi saints.

Members of numerous militant Islamic groups in Morocco regard the King as a corrupt client of the West, a perception that is perhaps quite widespread despite the power of the religious mystique of the monarchy—reinforced where necessary by more mundane power: in the 1980s, trials of Islamic radicals ended in sentences ranging from imprisonment to death. The accused belonged mostly to the Society of Islamic Youth (Jam'iyat al-Shabiba al-Islamiya, also Jeunesse Islamique), founded in 1972, but riven by factionalism—five major sub-groups have been identified. Further trials in 1989–90 involved members of al-Adl wa'l-Ihsan (Justice and Charity), a movement refused registration as a political party in 1982 and dissolved by government decree in 1990. Its leader, 'Abd as-Salam Yassin, has emerged as Morocco's principal Islamist theorist—in the early 1980s he edited the influential but now illegal review *Al-Jama'a*.

The King has also sought to counter any potential Islamist threat by establishing a network of loyal *ulama* councils, with close supervision of the mosques. Nevertheless, some mosques remain centres of recruitment to radical groups, and sermons of some of the militant Islamic preachers, both from within and from outside Morocco, circulate in cassette tape form.

The aims of the Islamist groups range from the implementation of the Shari'a (Islamic law), to a social revolution that will end social injustice, to an end to foreign power domination. The methods envisaged—an ongoing source of controversy and factionalism—range from violent revolution to personal moral reform. Two groups which endorse the latter are the Bishishiya Sufi order and the **Jama'at Tabligh**.

Mozambique

Mozambique has a population of 16,100,00, of whom 50 per cent still follow **African traditional religions**, and 35 per cent are Christian, mainly **Roman Catholic**, with a further 10 per cent being Muslim. Islam has been present here for up to 10 centuries. The Catholic Church is largely a copy of the Portuguese, although it has seen increasing Africanization since the revolution of 1975 which brought the Marxist Frelimo to power, when all whites left: at that time the government confiscated many church buildings, but in 1988 they were returned, as part of a process of gradually diminishing hostility to religion on the part of the state. The Pope visited the country in September 1988.

The largest **Protestant** groups are the **Assemblies of God, Methodists**, and **Anglicans**. The churches have suffered under the civil war which has raged since 1975 between Frelimo forces and those of the South African backed Renamo, losing both members and buildings. The number of Anglican congregations has fallen by a third, and the **Baptists** have lost the active participation of two-fifths of their members. Few of the churches, however, have condemned the atrocities committed by the guerrilla movement, and some of the US-linked fundamentalist churches are suspected of assisting Renamo because of its professed anti-Communism.

Myanmar

The population of Myanmar (formerly Burma) is estimated at nearly 43,000,000, and 85 per cent follow **Theravada** Buddhism. There is a monastery in most villages, and nearly all male Burmese spend some time in their life in a monastery. Some elements of traditional primal religions have been incorporated into Theravada Buddhism. After independence from British colonial rule, the Prime Minister, U Nu, adopted a policy of Buddhist socialism which placed an enormous emphasis on Buddhist education and practice. This alienated the military who took over in 1962 and disestablished Buddhism as the state religion. The Sangha, the organization of Buddhist monks, has been the dominant force in opposing military rule, and the government has tried to regain their support by building a new pagoda. Monks have been prominent in popular uprisings against the government in recent times: the government allowed elections in May 1990 but refused to respect the outcome—a clear victory for the main opposition party, the National League for Democracy—and continued to keep its leader, Daw Aung San Suu Kyi (subsequently awarded the Nobel Peace Prize in 1991) under house arrest. Six per cent of the population are Christian, mainly **Baptists** (concentrated among the Karen, Chin and Katchin tribes) and **Roman Catholics**, and three per cent are Muslims, largely a compact minority (known as Rohingyas) concentrated in the north-west, and forced by recent army persecution to seek refuge in large numbers across the border in Bangladesh, where they are a source of recruits for guerrilla groups such as the Rohingya Solidarity Organization and the Arakan Rohingya Islamic Front. There are some Mahayana Buddhists, **Taoists**, and **Confucians** among the Chinese community, and some tribal religions among the hill inhabitants.

Namibia

Namibia has a population of about 1,400,000 although estimates vary considerably because of the number of refugees who have returned since the end of the civil war in 1989. Nearly 90 per cent are Christian: 50 per cent belong to the United **Evangelical** Church, which is a union of two **Lutheran** churches, with a further 10 per cent in the **Dutch Reformed** Church, and five per cent **Anglican. Roman Catholics** comprise 20 per cent of the population, and although they are almost all black, the priests are mostly white. About 10 per cent still follow **African traditional religions**, including **Khoisan religion**.

During the years of South African occupation, both **Protestant** and Catholic churches firmly supported the UN independence plan, and clergy and lay-people alike were among those killed and imprisoned. Three Anglican bishops were expelled in succession, the Lutheran Press at Oniipa was blown up twice, while an Anglican nursing and theological college (St Mary's, Odibo) was closed and largely destroyed by South African forces.

In independent Namibia, the churches' networks constitute a potentially vital part of the developmental infrastructure. The Committee for Repatriation, Resettlement and Reconstruction, part of the Council of Churches in Namibia (of which the Roman Catholic Church is a full member), has worked closely with the UN High Commission for Refugees, UNICEF, and other agencies.

Nauru

Nauru is a rich and small South Pacific island with a population of 9,000. The population is 82 per cent Christian, with 30 per cent belonging to the **Congregationlist** Church, 20 per cent **Roman Catholic**, two per cent **Anglican**, and a further 30 per cent professing to be **Protestant** but having no church. Eight per cent of the population are Chinese labourers from Hong Kong, and these follow **Chinese folk religion** and Buddhism.

Nepal

The Kingdom of Nepal is the only Hindu state in the world, and 90 per cent of the 19,000,000 population are Hindu. Nepalese Hinduism is distinctive since it incorporates elements of Himalayan **shamanism** and **Tantricism**. King Birendra is believed by the faithful to be a reincarnation of Vishnu. The worship of the mother goddess Kumari is widespread, and she is incarnated in the form of a young child. When the child attains the age of her first menstruation, another is chosen as the incarnate body of Kumari. In 1988 the King hosted the World Hindu Conference, attended by over 2,000 delegates from South and South East Asia.

Five per cent of the population follow Buddhism in its Mahayana and Tantric forms, and Gautama the Buddha was born at Lumbini, in the south of the country, around 600 BCE. Three per cent of the population are **Sunni** Muslim. There is a tiny indigenous church, and a number of foreign **Protestant** missions are involved in education and medicine, but evangelism is illegal.

Netherlands

The Netherlands has a population of 15,000,000 and over 70 per cent of these profess Christianity. Calvinism was once the national religion, but the numbers have declined so that only about 31 per cent of the population are **Protestant**. The principal denomination is the **Dutch Reformed** Church, which contains both orthodox and liberal Calvinists, but there have been a number of neo-Calvinist schisms which have led to small denominations being formed. The **Roman Catholic** Church is now the largest body, claiming the allegiance of about 40 per cent of the population. Levels of practice are high compared to other churches, and to Catholicism in neighbouring countries, but have also been declining. Many children of Catholic parents are no longer baptized. The Catholics have had a tendency to introversion, having their own press and media services, as well as trade unions and a political party. More recently, liberal ideas and theology have become more prominent, and the Pastoral Council has supported the abolition of celibacy as a requirement for the priesthood. There are small non-Roman Catholics, belonging to the **Old Catholic** Church and the **Catholic Apostolic** Church, as well as a few immigrant **Orthodox** communities.

Although the Netherlands has fewer immigrants than its immediate neighbours, (five per cent of the population, compared to 7.6 per cent in the former West Germany, 7.8 per cent in France, and 8.9 per cent in Belgium), there are three groups of considerable significance, namely the Surinamese, the Turks and the Moroccans. Among the 200,000 Surinamese, roughly half are Hindus, descendants of contract labourers from British India, but **Winti** also has adherents. The well over 100,000 Turks and Moroccans are **Sunni** Muslims. There are about 30,000 Jews in 46 communities, half of whom live in Amsterdam. There are also about 4,000 Buddhists, mainly Chinese.

Netherlands Dependencies

Aruba. Aruba, which separated from the Antilles in 1986, has a population of about 70,000, 80 per cent of whom are **Roman Catholic**. There are also **Dutch Reformed, Methodists, Evangelicals, Jehovah's Witnesses** and **Seventh Day Adventists** present.

Netherlands Antilles. The Netherlands Antilles islands, formerly the Leeward and Windward Islands, have a population of about 207,000, who are mainly **Roman Catholic** with 80 per cent having links with the Church. There is also a **Dutch Reformed** Church, and much smaller communities of **Anglicans, Methodists**, and **Moravians**. Foreign religious groups engaged in missionary activity have often offended the local population.

New Zealand

New Zealand has a population of 3,320,000. **Anglicans** account for just over 21 per cent of the population, **Presbyterians** for 16 per cent and **Roman Catholics** for just under 15 per cent. The last, in the latest census of 1991, have shown a very slight increase in numbers, arresting a recent decline, whereas Anglicans and Presbyterians continue to decline in percentage terms. The **Methodist** Church has just over four per cent of the population and is in sharp decline, as is the much smaller **Salvation Army. Baptists**, on the other hand, are on the increase during the last census period, and now account for 2.1 per cent of the population. The decline in religious affiliation has been noticeable in New Zealand since the 1960s.

The largest increase is in the proportion of the population who say they have no religion or who object to stating their preference: this has now topped 20 per cent. The **charismatic movement**, which has spread through all the churches during the 1970s and 1980s, is a major influence. As well as this, **Protestantism** tends to be **evangelical** and conservative in character. The increase in church attendances is noticeable among the smaller Christian groups of the **Pentecostal** charismatic strand.

The Maori form 10 per cent of the population and are highly represented in the Anglican, Catholic and Methodist churches where structural changes have taken place over recent years to give Maori more power and influence in decision-making and leadership. The indigenous **Ratana Church**, though small in actual numbers, has shown a 10 per cent increase during the last census period—an indication of the pressure on the Maori in a changing New Zealand society. All Maori religious groups relate well to each other, and are searching for a Maori way of expressing spirituality. All the major churches have taken recent steps to change their names to incorporate the Maori word for New Zealand—Aotearoa. (*See too* **Maori Religion** and **Maori Religious Movements**.)

Presbyterians, Methodists and Anglicans have also taken decisive steps to admit women to clerical orders, and to key leadership positions. The Conference of Churches of Aotearoa/New Zealand, formed out of the National Council of Churches, includes a wide range of Protestant as well as Catholic participation. There is a growing Pacific Island population which is well represented in all the churches, in some cases outstripping the Maori. The Church of Jesus Christ of Latter Day Saints (**Mormons**) has been active in New Zealand since the 1850s, and has increased its membership over recent years particularly amongst Maoris and Pacific Islanders.

A feature of religious life in New Zealand in recent times has been a growing pluralism with fragmentation among major groups. There are also growing minorities representative of other religions (Islam, Buddhism and various Hindu and Chinese religious groups) as Asian immigration is on the increase, but the numbers involved are still very small.

New Zealand Associated Territories

Cook Islands. The dominant Cook Island Christian Church (**Congregational**) claims 80 per cent of the almost entirely Christian population of around 25,000. This church began in 1820 and has a strong cultural and indigenous heritage. Thirteen per cent of the people are **Roman Catholic**, and 6 per cent of the islanders are **Seventh Day Adventists**. There is a small indigenous church also.

Niue. Niue, also a New Zealand territory, was evangelised as early as 1830. The **Congregational** Church is the largest group claiming three-quarters of the population of around 6,000. Just over 16 per cent are **Roman Catholic**, 9 per cent are **Mormon** and there is a small **Jehovah's Witness** presence.

Tokelau. The small island community of Tokelau, with a population of 2,000, is an overseas territory of New Zealand where most of the people now live. Sixty-five per cent are **Protestant (Congregational)**, 25 per cent are **Roman Catholic** and 10 per cent are **Bahai**.

Nicaragua

Nicaragua's population of 4,000,000 is about 84 per cent **Roman Catholic**, and 15 per cent **Protestant**, with the remaining 0.7 per cent including traditionalists, **Bahais**, members of spiritist cults, Buddhists and adherents of **Chinese folk religions**. The largest Protestant Church is the **Moravian**, which is prominent among Miskito Indians and blacks. The next largest is the **Assemblies of God**, but there are also **Baptists, Seventh Day Adventists** and others.

The Catholic Church has been split between members of the hierarchy, such as Cardinal Obando y Bravo, the only Latin American cardinal, who identified himself as actively supporting the Contra rebels, and the base communities and grass-roots groups who supported the Sandinista government which came to power in 1979. During his visit to Nicaragua in 1983, Pope John Paul II summoned Christians at the grassroots to obey their bishops and refrain from attempting to live apart from the true church. In 1985, three priest ministers in the Sandinista government were suspended from their priestly duties. In contrast to this rift between the Sandinistas and the Catholic hierarchy, the Protestant churches tended on the whole to support the Sandinista government and its programme of reforms.

Following the Sandinistas' defeat in the elections of February 1990, relations between bishops and state have eased, and the influence of the base communities is now declining.

Niger

Niger has a population of just under 8,000,000 of whom about 90 per cent are Muslim, **Sunnis** of the **Maliki** rite. The **Sufi** brotherhoods are widespread and active, including especially the **Tijaniya**, Senoussi, and **Hamalliya**. About 10 per cent of the population follow **African traditional religions**, and the Kurfei and Mauri tribes are particularly resistant to the proselytizing efforts of Islam and Christianity. There are few Christians, with the largest group being 15,000 **Roman Catholics** who are mainly expatriates.

Nigeria

Nigeria is by far the most populated of the black African nations, with a population of 88,500,000 recorded in the 1992 census. The religious distribution is estimated to be about 40,000,000 Muslims, 28,000,000 Christians, and 20,000,000 adherents of **African traditional religions**.

The northern and poorer peoples tend to be Muslim, and these include the main tribes of Hausa, Fulani, Kanuri, and Nupe, among others, as well as some Yoruba. The **Qadiriya** and **Tijaniya Sufi** brotherhoods are widespread, although their influence is strongly criticized by Muslim reformers and fundamentalists. The **Hamalliya** has also spread successfully since World War II. There are also 500,000 **Ahmadiyas**.

The southern people, mainly Yoruba and Ibo, have benefitted significantly from the colonial Christian system of education, and are disproportionately represented among the *intelligentsia*. The main churches are the **Roman Catholic** and **Anglican** ones, with about 10–12,000,000 adherents each, but there are about 10,000,000 in indigenous charismatic churches among which the **Aladura** are prominent. There are small **Methodist, Baptist** and **Presbyterian** churches.

African traditional religion is very influential in the thought and behaviour of most Nigerians, but is being weakened by technology which replaces the traditional powers with much stronger ones: for the Yoruba, the god of iron was run over by a lorry, and the god of smallpox was killed by a vaccination. Elements of traditional religion remain influential across the Atlantic too, as a result of the slave trade, in **Afro-American spiritist** religions such as **Santería** and **Candomblé**.

There has been widespread conflict between the under-privileged Muslim north and the educated Christian south. The Muslims regard Christianity as Western, and lacking in depth of commitment since it is more distant from political and social issues. The Christians see Islam as a malign political force holding Nigeria back from further progress and development. Some violence has occurred, and the nation appears to be increasingly divided.

A messianic Muslim movement, 'Yan Tatsine, precipitated widespread riots in Kano and elsewhere in the 1980s before being suppressed by the army. The Kafanchan riots of 1987, by contrast, appear to have been precipitated by the furious Muslim reaction to the activities of assertive Christian fundamentalists. The Shari'a debate of 1977–79, over the issue of whether to establish a federal Shari'a court system, proved deeply divisive, and this unresolved issue will certainly not go away. Also contentious was the government's 1986 decision to join the **Organization of the Islamic Conference**.

Radical or fundamentalist Muslims are represented by the Jamaatu Nasril Islam (Society for the Victory of Islam), the Muslim Students Society, the Young Muslim Association of Nigeria, and a rather looser organization, Bida Yan Izala (those who reject innovation). More moderate Muslim reformers are to be found in the Muslim Association of Nigeria, while the government-established Supreme Council of Islamic Affairs is intended as a channel for "wise" counsel to the Muslim community from the country's rulers.

Norway

Norway's population of 4,200,000 is almost entirely Christian, with 94 per cent belonging to the **Evangelical Lutheran** State Church. This has been the state church since the time of the Reformation, but did not experience the evangelical fervour common in other countries until the 19th century. The Church has a high-church tradition remaining from its pre-Reformation times, but also strong pietistic and low-church movements. There are about 1,300 churches and 1,000 clergy, and the Church is run by the state with little inner autonomy. Attendance stands at about 3 per cent of the population, but levels of belief and membership are remarkably high. The Norwegian Church has a tradition of private religion, with about 50 per cent of members listening to religious broadcasts rather than attending, and 50 per cent praying daily. Ninety-five per cent of children are baptized, and 80 per cent of these are later confirmed. The remaining six per cent of the population are largely **Baptist, Pentecostal, Methodist**, or **Roman Catholic**, but there is a very small immigrant Muslim population, mostly **Sunnis**, but also including a small community of **Alevis**.

Oman

Oman has a population of approximately 1,600,000 which is almost entirely Muslim. Over half the population, and perhaps as many as three quarters, are **Ibadi** Muslims, including the autocratic ruler, Sultan Qabus bin Sa'id, latest in a dynasty that has been in power since the mid-1700s. From that time on, the Ibadi leader, the *imam*, has been divested of his traditional political leadership functions, retaining only his role as religious leader. Numerous sultan–*imam* conflicts culminated in the 1957–59 revolt by tribal supporters of Imam Ghalib (backed by the Saudis and the Arab League) against the harsh rule of Sultan Sa'id bin Timur. The revolt was put down by British forces, and Imam Ghalib now lives in Saudi Arabia.

In addition to the Ibadi majority, there is a small **Shi'ite** community, and a larger **Sunni-Shafi'i** minority concentrated in the poorer Dhofar region bordering the Yemen. Here elements of pre-Islamic religion are also to be found, including blood sacrifices of animals, and exorcism of evil spirits.

Here too serious revolt broke out, lasting from 1965 to the mid-1970s, and again British troops were involved in its suppression. In 1970 Said was replaced by his son, the present Sultan Qabus, who has introduced Islamic law in Oman, and constructed a new network of government-supported mosques in an attempt to promote a more integrated Islamic culture. Development projects have also been encouraged, in a notable reversal of the previous sultan's policy.

In some desert areas may be found **Wahhabi** nomads who adhere to the **Hanbali** school of law. Small numbers of Indian migrant workers are Hindus.

Oman stands alone in the Muslim world as the only predominantly Ibadi country. The sultan is the target of strong criticism by Islamists outside the country, but no Islamist opposition has been allowed to develop within Oman itself. Meanwhile, however, support for Imam Ghalib has not disappeared among some of the mountain tribes.

Pakistan

Pakistan has a population of 115,000,000, 97 per cent of whom are Muslim. Seventy-four per cent are **Sunnis** of the **Hanafi** school of religious law (with a minority adherence to the **Hanbali** school). Some two thirds of these are under the influence of **Sufism** via two orders, the **Qadiriya** and **Naqshabandiya**, in particular. Nearly 20 per cent of the population are **Shi'ites**, mainly **Twelvers** (in Lahore and Karachi in particular), but with some **Isma'ilis**, many of whom are descended from the Isma'ili population of Hyderabad which had absorbed Hindu customs and practices: their festivals have been banned by the Sunni majority, and tension between Sunnis and Shi'ites continues. The latter have their own political party, the **Movement for the Enforcement of Ja'fari Law** (Tahrik-i Nifaz-i Fiqh-i Ja'fariya), established in 1980 as part of the protest by Twelvers in particular opposed to the blanket imposition of Sunni Hanafi law by the regime of General Zia ul-Haq. Some 2.7 per cent of the population belong to the **Ahmadiya (Qadiyanis)** who in 1974 were declared to be non-Muslims by the Pakistan parliament (and also, in the same year, by the **Muslim World League**).

Christians constitute approximately 1.4 per cent of the population, and these are mainly among the Punjabis. **Roman Catholics** number about half of these, while the leading **Protestant** churches are the **Presbyterians** and the Church of Pakistan, a union of **Anglicans, Methodists** and **Lutherans**.

A little over one per cent of the population remain Hindu, being located mainly in Sind, but emigration to India has continued since the state's foundation in 1947. There are also very small minorities of **Parsis**, Buddhists, tribal religionists and **Bahais**.

Pakistan forms, together with Saudi Arabia, the heartland of a strict interpretation of Islam. About 30 per cent of the Muslim population are estimated to practise all the necessary Islamic duties. There is considerable rivalry between traditionalists and modernists, and fundamentalism is widespread. Pakistan is the base for the **World Muslim Congress**, a cultural organization to promote unity and co-operation among Muslims, and the World Federation of Islamic Missions. At grassroots level the **Tablighi Jama'at** is active as a non-political revivalist organization, while several different *ulama*-led organizations are active: the **Jam'iat ul-Ulama-i Pakistan** represents the **Barelvi** movement within Pakistani Islam, with its emphasis on Sufism and the veneration of saints and religious shrine cults, and is particularly strong in the small towns and countryside of the Punjab; the **Jam'iat ul-Ulama-i Islam**, by contrast, represents the rival **Deobandi** movement and controls a majority of the mosques and *madrasas*—it is particularly powerful in Baluchistan and the North West Frontier; and the **Jam'iat ul-Ulama-i Ahl-i Hadith**, representing a

Wahhabi-style puritan Islam which enjoys close links with the Saudis, but has only a limited following concentrated in business communities in Karachi and some cities of the Punjab.

From 1977 onwards under General Zia ul-Haq, a policy of Islamization (Nifaz-i Nizam-i Islam) was enforced, with considerable influence being exercised by Maulana Maududi's fundamentalist **Jama'at-i Islami**. After a short hiatus under Benazir Bhutto, the policy has been continued, and the Jama'at-i Islami remains a powerful force. This policy has involved, for example, the introduction of Islamic taxes (based, however, on Hanafi law, thus antagonizing the Shi'ites who adhere to **Ja'fari** law, leading to protests and eventual uneasy compromise but also in some cases violent clashes and fatalities); an Islamic banking system in which interest has been replaced by elements of profit-sharing; a ban on alcohol; and the introduction of Quranic punishments for certain offences such as theft and adultery, culminating in the ordinance of 1988 declaring the traditional religious law, the Shari'a, the supreme law of the country.

On the other hand, the Jama'at-i Islami's vehement opposition to the widely influential Sufi *pirs* and shrine cults has not been reflected in government policy. Pakistan, unlike Saudi Arabia, has not sought to suppress Sufism; rather the government has sought to use it to enhance its own authority by building hospitals and schools on to numerous shrines, and ensuring government representation at the annual festivals at major shrines.

A clandestine organization, al-Zulfiqar (the Sword), has been held responsible for a number of assassinations of prominent government figures in the 1980s. Taking its name from the first name of the former Prime Minister, Z. A. Bhutto, hanged in April 1979, it was established in 1981 by his elder son, Murtaza Bhutto. The extent of its appeal is unknown.

Many Pakistanis work in the Gulf, and thousands of these expatriates were forced to leave Kuwait—and all their assets and life-savings—following the Iraqi invasion of 1990. Pakistani condemnation of the invasion was widespread, and the government sent 5,000 troops for the defence of Saudi Arabia. With the build-up of the massive US presence in Arabia, however, and the devastating bombing onslaught on Iraq, the mood changed and despite government opposition, popular support for Saddam Hussein was mobilized by the Jama'at-i Islami in particular, and its student wing, the Jam'iat-i Tulaba, joined by the Jam'iat ul-Ulama-i Pakistan, the Jam'iat ul-Ulama-i Islam, and finally the Shi'ite Movement for the Enforcement of Ja'fari Law too. Tablighi Jama'at members, by contrast, remained largely apolitical, turning instead to prayers for peace. In the aftermath of the war, the pro-Iraq stance of so many has become a matter of debate and controversy.

Pakistan has also functioned as a base for numerous mujahidin organizations fighting in Afghanistan, with the Jama'at-i Islami supporting Gulbadin Hekmatyar's **Hizb-i Islami** in particular. In 1992, however—prior to the establishment of mujahidin rule in Afghanistan—the government insisted on the closure of these bases: volunteers from over 30 countries had received guerrilla training in them, and when these subsequently returned to their own countries, their governments (for example in Algeria) came to regard them as a threat and lodged protests in Islamabad accordingly. Meanwhile in April 1991, the Pakistani government introduced a relatively moderate Shari'a Bill to promote further Islamization (of education, the media, the economy and so on), a move seen by some observers as designed to pre-empt the much more radical Shari'a Bill proposed by a new coalition of religious groups, the United Shari'a Front.

Panama

Panama has a population of 2,500,000, 85 per cent of whom are **Roman Catholic**. Many of the clergy and religious are engaged in education. The Church hierarchy has called for a "preferential option for the poor", and the Church constituted a leading voice in opposition to General Noriega prior to his arrest in the American invasion of December 1989: it sought in fact to walk a fine line, both criticizing General Noriega's violations of civil liberties on the one hand, and the US sanctions and aggression on the other hand.

Some six per cent of the population are **Protestant**, mainly **Evangelical**, and five per cent are Muslim Indians and Arabs. One per cent is **Bahai**, and there are tiny minorities of tribalists, Hindus, Buddhists, Jews and members of new religious movements.

Papua New Guinea

Papua New Guinea has a population of 3,800,000, and 64 per cent are **Protestant**, while 33 per cent are **Roman Catholic**. The Catholic Church was particularly active in promoting the movement for independence from Australian trusteeship which gained its goal in 1975.

Nevertheless, indigenous pantheistic beliefs and traditional rituals are an integral part of the Melanesian culture, and 2.5 per cent follow **Melanesian traditional religions**, and the **Cargo Cults**—messianic movements which have arisen in modern times under the impact of Western culture. The **Taro cult** is the most predominant, and this involves ecstatic singing, dancing, and communal meals to enhance the fertility of the Taro crop.

The main Protestant churches are the **Lutheran** Church, and the United Church of Papua New Guinea and the Solomon islands, but there are also **Seventh Day Adventists, Anglicans**, and **Pentecostals**. A large number of Protestant refugees from the Indonesian half of Papua New Guinea, known as Irian Jaya, are also present. In addition, there are about 20,000 **Bahais**.

Paraguay

Paraguay's population of 3,000,000 is 95 per cent *mestizo*, of Spanish and Guarani Indian descent. Ninety-seven per cent are nominally **Roman Catholic**, but **Protestants** are represented by **Mennonites**, the **Evangelical** Church of Rio de la Plata, **Baptists** and **Anglicans**. There is also 0.8 per cent engaged in **South American traditional religions**.

The Catholic Church has supported the non-violent *ligas agrarias* movement in opposition to unequal land distribution, and was a major critic of the cruel dictatorial régime of Gen. Alfredo Stroessner, ended by a military *coup* in 1989. In 1988, Pope John Paul II visited, and called for agrarian reform as well as denouncing human rights' abuses. The new régime of President Rodríguez has introduced some reforms, but remains dependent upon vested military, economic, and bureaucratic interests, and the Churches may currently be expected to retain their role as critics of social injustice.

Peru

Peru has a population of 22,900,000, 95 per cent of whom are nominally **Roman Catholic**. However, one third of these practise some blend of Roman Catholic beliefs and rituals with **South American traditional religions**. One per cent are nominally tribal, although their influence extends much further, and the largest of these, the Aymara Indian religion, concerns ways of controlling the various guardian, nature and evil spirits. The **Assemblies of God** and the **Seventh Day Adventists** are the largest Protestant denominations, and the latter are strong among the Aymara Indians. The Catholic hierarchy has been among the most radical, with one of the pioneers of liberation theology being the Peruvian priest, Gustavo Gutiérrez. The statement "Justice in the World" by the Peruvian episcopate says that evangelism cannot exist without fighting against domination. During his visit of 1988, however, Pope John Paul II expressed his reservations concerning liberation theology, and has since moved to appoint more conservatives to the episcopate. Radicals urge the inappropriateness of this response, given the acute social problems which fuel the cause of the Maoist Sendero Luminoso (Shining Path) guerrilla movement, and given Amnesty International's concern at the death and disappearance of 6,000–10,000 people during the last decade.

Philippines

The Philippines have a population of 63,000,000, and 85 per cent of these are nominally **Roman Catholic**. Catholicism is often permeated by traditional beliefs on the one hand, giving it the quality of a folk-religion, while on the other hand the hierarchy imitates Western Catholicism and is theologically conservative, lacking in a distinct Asian identity. Many rural areas are visited by priests only once a year, or not at all. The **Jesuits** have been the principal progressive leaders, with liberation theology developing in the 1980s. Base Christian communities have been introduced, and the Church gradually became critical of the corrupt Marcos régime (ejected from power in 1986), although only a small number of bishops had a consistent record of denunciation of human rights' abuses. Much more critical was the Association of Major Religious Superiors of the Philippines, representing priests from 48 orders and also 125 orders of religious women. Its Task Force for Detainees, established during the martial law period of the Marcos years, did impressive work in relation to human rights' violations. Some church people went as far as joining Christians for National Liberation, a member of the National Democratic Front, which works with the peasantry against the government, using violence where it thinks necessary.

Nine per cent of the population are **Protestant**, mainly in indigenous denominations arising out of protests against the Catholic hierarchy. The largest of these is the Philippine Independent Church (**Aglipayan**), with 3,500,000 members, which has an episcopal structure. Also influential is the Church of Christ (**Iglesia ni Cristo**), with 1,500,000 followers who are organized into a militant, nationalist and authoritarian structure, and whose clergy have been known to carry weapons. This has 3,000 congregations and has become a major political force. Other Protestant denominations include **Seventh Day Adventists, Methodists, Baptists, Assemblies of God**, and **Evangelicals**.

Five per cent of the population are Muslim, **Sunnis** of the **Shafi'i** rite, and these are mainly in Mindanao and Sulu, whose communities date back to immigrations of Malays in 1380 CE, nearly 200 years before the arrival of the Spaniards, who dubbed them *"Moros"* ("Moors"). There has been a longstanding conflict between the Christians and the Muslim minorities, accentuated in the 1950s by government confiscation of Muslim traditional lands in order to re-settle Christians from the provinces of Luzon, and indiscriminate military repression. From the 1950s onwards, young Muslims increasingly studied in Egypt, and a general renewal of Islam occurred, with increased mosque attendance, and a flourishing of Islamic schools. In 1972 the **Moro National Liberation Front** initiated armed struggle against the government, in the wake of several massacres by armed Christian bands, the creation of 100,000 refugees, a shift in political power away from the Muslims in the 1971 election, and a declaration of Martial Law by President Marcos in 1972. It received the support of the **Organization of the Islamic Conference**. Following the *Tripoli Agreement* of 1976, two formally autonomous regions were created in the Muslim south, but no real autonomy was allowed, although certain Muslim demands were gradually conceded, for instance in 1985 the appointment of judges to implement the Shari'a in matters of personal and family law. Under President Aquino a cease-fire has taken place, followed by protracted negotiations in respect of "real" autonomy: Mindanao was granted partial rule in October 1990.

There are also small numbers of Buddhists, **Bahais** and **Chinese folk-religionists**. Traditional religions may be found among 500,000 people in the mountain tribes.

Poland

Poland's population of 38,000,000 is 95 per cent **Roman Catholic**. Half a million belong to the Polish Autocephalous **Orthodox Church**, which dates back to the 10th Century, and split from the **Russian Orthodox** in 1918. Also present are **Uniate, Old Catholic** Mariavite, **Methodist, Baptist, Evangelical** and **Seventh Day Adventist** churches, along with 12,000 Jews and 2,500 Muslims. The Catholic Church, rather than the state, has traditionally served as a political and social focal point. Polish Catholicism sees a special link between God and the Polish people, and is characterized by a rigid faith, high levels of devotion and large numbers of vocations to the priesthood. Karol Wojtyla, of Polish origin, has been Pope John Paul II since 1978, and his visit in 1979 was instrumental in the inception of Solidarity. During the 1980s the Church took a lead over the aspirations of the Polish people, but instead of simply supporting the opposition forces to the Communist government, it operated a mediating role and urged against violence, while also speaking out on human rights and civil liberties. The Church has been successful in preventing unnecessary bloodshed in the passage of power to the democratically elected Solidarity movement, and maintained its spiritual role and importance in the life of the Polish people. A renewal movement known as 'Oasis' or 'Light and Life' attracts large numbers of young Polish Catholics.

Portugal

Portugal has a population of 10,700,000, 97 per cent of whom are **Roman Catholic**. The Church has an anti-clerical tradition, and the south of the country is short of priests, very low in church attendance, and effectively de-Christianized. In contrast, the Church is powerful in the centre and north, with very high numbers of priests and levels of weekly practice. The masses, in rural areas, follow a religion influenced largely by superstition and fatalism, and this has been encouraged by the conservative hierarchy to prevent social or political unrest.

One per cent is **Protestant**, and these have been restricted in their public and missionary activities. There are 15,000 Muslims, mainly from Pakistan, Mozambique, and Guinea-Bissau. There are also about 1,300 Jews.

Portuguese Dependent Territory

Macao. Macao is a toehold on the Chinese mainland which has existed as a Portuguese-run enclave since 1537, and has a population of 430,000. Only 15 per cent are **Roman Catholic**, however, and the majority of the population either follow **Chinese folk religions** (55 per cent), or Chinese Buddhism (15 per cent). One per cent is **Protestant**, mostly **Baptists**.

Qatar

One of the small Gulf States, Qatar has a population of about 500,000. Of these, 95 per cent are Muslims, mostly **Sunnis** who adhere, like their rulers, the senior sheikhs of the Thani clan, to the **Hanbali** school of law. Like the neighbouring Saudis, they are also **Wahhabi**. The *ulama* exercise considerable influence in education and in law, advising the ruling autocracy on the consonance of government decrees with the *Quran* and *Sunna* (Prophetic tradition).

Possibly 16 per cent of the population are **Shi'ites**, including a small number of relatively recent immigrants from southern Iran who have succeeded in entering the commercial élite. Some three per cent are Christians, mainly **Roman Catholics**, **Anglicans, Presbyterians** and **Lutherans** who belong to the expatriate community of Europeans, Indians, and Palestinian and Lebanese Arabs.

Despite the presence of a number of expatriate members of the Egyptian **Muslim** Brotherhood, there is little sign of Islamist fervour among the Sunnis; and although the Shi'ites are receptive to Iranian propaganda, there is little evidence of Islamist militancy.

Romania

Romania has a population of 23,000,000, and the national church is the Romanian **Orthodox**, which has the allegiance of 80 per cent of the population. This has very high levels of participation and devotion, and massive attendance at Easter. There are up to three times as many candidates produced by the seminaries as there are pastoral vacancies. The priests, in consequence, are extremely well educated, with most having degrees and some having doctorates. There are about 12,000 churches and 8,000 priests, over 100 monastic foundations and 2,000 monks and nuns. The Orthodox hierarchy accepted the dominance of the Ceaucescu régime, and opposed moves by younger priests and **Protestants** towards a pro-democracy movement. A revivalist group within the church, the **Lord's Army**, on the other hand, suffered severe persecution.

Six per cent of the population are **Roman Catholic**, and these are mainly Hungarians who live in Transylvania, but also include Germans (many of whom, however, have now returned to Germany), and Moldovians. The Roman Catholic Church has been introverted and concerned mainly with spirituality. The **Romanian Uniate Catholic Church** was forcibly suppressed by the Communist government and forced underground, where it continued to function and had up to 900,000 followers.

Four per cent of the population are Protestant, mainly **Reformed, Lutheran** and **Baptist**, but the **Unitarian Church** has a long tradition and 50,000 members, and the **Pentecostals** are growing rapidly. There are also perhaps 30,000 Jews and 40,000 **Sunni** Muslims, who are mainly ethnic Turks and adhere to the **Hanafi** school of Islamic law.

Russia and Successor States to the Soviet Union

The countries of the former USSR, with a population of 289,000,000 contain 104 nationalities which are widely distributed among the various states. The ethnic groups which number above 10,000,000 are Russians (137,000,000), Ukrainians (42,000,000), and Uzbeks (12,500,000). Russians are present in all the states, and rarely comprise less than 10 per cent of the population of any state.

The largest church is the **Russian Orthodox**, with an estimated 35–40,000,000 members dispersed among 76 dioceses with more than 6,500 churches (a number that is growing rapidly). The Russian Orthodox Church formed a controversial partnership with the Communist authorities in order to survive, and was compromised as a result, but it experienced something of a revival in the 1970s and 1980s with millions of baptisms taking place. Many churches have re-opened in the past four years.

Many Orthodox, however, were unhappy with the accommodation to the former Soviet régime, and formed schismatic, underground churches known as the **True Orthodox** (or Catacomb, or "Tikhonite") Church. The numbers of these are still unknown, but could be very significant — and the same may be said of the **Old Believers**, a sectarian group which has survived. A much more recent arrival on the scene is the Free Russian Orthodox Church which is an offshoot of the New York-based emigré body, the **Russian (Orthodox) Church Abroad**: it is now seeking to reclaim parishes in Russia and the Ukraine.

During the failed August 1991 *coup* against Gorbachev, a number of senior hierarchs welcomed the *coup*, although subsequently the Church denounced it. Following the failure of the *coup*, the opening of the KGB secret archives in Moscow revealed that the Russian Orthodox Church had been infiltrated to an even greater extent than had been suspected. Indeed three Metropolitans stand accused of having been KGB agents and one, Metropolitan Filaret of Kiev — who had been one of those who had publically welcomed the *coup* in a sermon — has been defrocked. However, he enjoys continued support in the Ukraine, and has so far been able to remain in office as part of the struggle that has developed between the Russian and the Ukrainian hierarchies.

The Ukrainian Orthodox Church, linked traditionally to the Russian Orthodox Church, and with a further 15,000,000 members, is now proclaiming and asserting its independence, a move fiercely opposed by the Moscow Patriarchate. A further major group in the Ukraine is the Ukrainian Autocephalous Orthodox Church, which was banned by the Communists in 1929 but survived. It competes today for support in western Ukraine with the other churches (including now the Greek-Catholic Church — *see below*), and its newly appointed nonagenarian Metropolitan arrived from the USA in October 1990.

On a smaller scale, and with a non-Chalcedonian theological inheritance, are the **Armenian Church**, which has a nationalist character, and the Georgian Orthodox Church. These **Oriental Orthodox Churches** have 1,000,000 and 500,000 adherents respectively.

The next largest Christian church after the Orthodox churches is the **Roman Catholic**, with 5,000,000 members, who are principally in Lithuania, Byelorussia and the Ukraine. The Catholic Church was without a hierarchy for most of the Communist era. In addition to the Roman Catholics, there are over 4,000,000 **Uniate** Catholics in western Ukraine who had broken away from the Orthodox. This **Ukrainian Uniate Catholic Church** (also known as the Greek-Catholic Church) was illegal until December 1989, and suffered severe persecution under Soviet rule, but continued to function underground. Since 1989, over 3,500 churches in western Ukraine have been handed over to the Greek Catholics, who now number from 4–5,000,000. In now seeking to expand eastwards, the Catholics are in conflict with the Russian (and Ukrainian, and Ukrainian Autocephalous) Orthodox — leading both to street fights and hunger strikes, and greatly heightened sensitivities about a proposed visit by John Paul II.

Among Protestants, there are 1,000,000 **Lutherans**, who are mostly in the Baltic states of Estonia, Latvia and Lithuania, 500,000 (or fewer) **Baptists**, who were heavily repressed by the Communist régime, and are mainly found in the Ukraine, the Baltic states, and the Far East. There are also a number of smaller groups, including **Reformed, Methodists, Mennonites, Seventh Day Adventists** and **Pentecostals**, most of which have functioned underground during the Communist era, and their numbers are unknown.

The second major religion is Islam, with an estimated 45,500,000 adherents in 1979, a number which has now risen to in excess of 60,000,000. Muslims are descended from the remnants of former Turkish and Iranian empires, and are in a majority in six states, as well as 10 eponymous 'Autonomous Republics' in Russia.

The Azeris, of whom there are 5,500,000 in the former USSR, along with one or two smaller related races, are 70 per cent **Twelver Shi'ites**, following the **Ja'fari** school of jurisprudence. They are closely related to Iranian Shi'ites, even speaking the same language, and they owe theoretical allegiance to the Iranian Ayatollahs. They have their own spiritual hierarchy, however, the Muslim Spiritual Board of Transcaucasia, which was supported by the Communists. Most Azeris live in Azerbaijan, which has a population of 6,800,000, 78 per cent of which is Azeri, but they have had a long history of rebellion against Russian domination, and large numbers have been deported to Central Asia. Azerbaijan is immensely rich in oil, and supplied much of the wealth of the former USSR.

Most Muslims, however, are **Sunnis** of the **Hanafi** school, although there are some adherents of the **Shafi'i** school in Daghestan and Armenia. Small groups of **Isma'ilis**

— **Aga Khanis** — are to be found in Tajikistan, and there are tiny heterodox groups of **Yazidis** and **Ahl-i Haqq**.

Uzbekistan (82 per cent), Kazakhstan (52 per cent), Turkmenistan (86 per cent), Tajikistan (88 per cent), and Kirghizstan (73 per cent) all have Muslim majorities, and a combined population of 57,000,000. Since the end of Communist rule, Islam has emerged in these Central Asian republics as a powerful force after years of official control, often as a cultural component of the fierce nationalisms now surfacing. In Tajikistan in particular there is a strong fundamentalist movement, and the **Islamic Renaissance Party**, active but banned in the other republics, has here been allowed to register legally: its leaders have close links with the **Muslim Brotherhood** in Egypt and the **Jama'at-i Islami** in Pakistan. While there were officially only 17 mosques in Tajikistan in 1989, today there are approximately 3,000. Mosques and madrasas (Muslim schools or colleges) continue to open in all the Central Asian republics, supported by public donations and in some cases by funds from abroad, in particular from the **Muslim World League. Wahhabi** influence, both directly from Saudi Arabia and in circles established from 1912 onwards which managed to remain active, is on the increase.

The "official Islam" of the Communist period was organized via four Spiritual Directorates (or Religious Boards). These have now begun to use their administrative structures to promote religious life more vigorously, including the preparation of translations of the meaning of the Quran into the local languages. The leader of official Islam, the Grand Mufti of Tashkent (capital of Uzbekistan), still retains control of the mosques.

In addition to "official Islam", and the emergence of radical fundamentalist political Islam (which is strongest in the Ferghana Valley, which cuts through Kirghizstan and Uzbekistan as well as Tajikistan), the third type of Islam is the **Sufism** (or "ishanism" as it was referred to in Soviet literature) that has remained very much alive throughout the period of Soviet rule. ("Ishan" is an alternative title for the Sufi leaders, or shaykhs.) The **Naqshabandiya** is particularly strong: its founder's tomb in Bukhara, Uzbekistan, is a centre of pilgrimage, as are countless other tomb shrines in Central Asia (as indeed they were under Soviet rule). The **Qadiriya** survives too, especially in the Ferghana Valley and the North Caucasus — in the latter it has split into several branches: the Kunta Haji branch, the Bammat Giray branch, the Batal Haji branch, and the Chim Mirza branch (also called the "drummers" — Barabanshchiki). A further, puritanical, branch of the last of these, the Vis (Uways) Haji, is particularly active: members were known in Soviet literature as "white caps" — *Beloshaposhniki*. Yet another order is the **Yasawiya**, active in the Ferghana Valley and southern Kazakhstan: two radical branches of this are the Laachi and the **Hairy Ishans**. The **Kubrawiya** barely survives, it seems. In addition there are large numbers of wandering "irregular" adepts, some of whom, the *divana* ("possessed ones") are comparable to the Indian **Malangs**.

At the moment there are approximately 1,900,000 Jews left in the former USSR, from both European and Central Asian communities, and 5,000 **Karaites**. These have suffered a history of severe repression, and anti-Zionism which became confused with anti-Semitism under Communist rule. Many have now left for Israel, and a large number continue to emigrate each year. *Glasnost* has brought freedom of religious expression for the Jews, but also a rise in anti-Semitism from the surrounding peoples, and the emergence of the anti-semitic *Pamyat* ("Memory") movement.

In the East, Mahayana Buddhism continues with about 500,000 (or possibly 1,000,000) adherents, especially among the Buryat, Tuvan and Kalmyk peoples. This has declined under Communism, and there are few monks. A further 400,000 still follow forms of **shamanism**, and these are mainly the peoples of Siberia. There are small groups of **Bahais** and **Hare Krishnas**.

Rwanda

Rwanda has a dense population of 7,300,000, 90 per cent of whom belong to the Hutu tribe. The Hutu drove the minority Tutsi from power in 1959, creating large numbers of refugees (an estimated 1,000,000 worldwide), many in neighbouring Uganda to the north. In October 1990, an invasion of several thousand refugees, mostly Tutsis, organized in the Rwandan Patriotic Front, was launched from Uganda. The invaders were defeated by government troops, assisted by contingents of French, Belgians, and Zaireans. There is a related Tutsi–Hutu conflict in neighbouring Burundi to the south.

Christian missions have had considerable success over this century, so that 65 per cent of the population are **Roman Catholic**, and about nine per cent **Protestant**. Christians are involved in educational and social work, and there is a high level of religious practice in all denominations. The Protestants are mainly **Seventh Day Adventists, Anglicans, Presbyterians** and **Baptists**. Some religious sects, including the **Jehovah's Witnesses**, are illegal, and 300 members of these were tried in October 1986.

Perhaps nine per cent of the population are **Sunni** Muslim, while the remaining 17 per cent are adherents of **African traditional religions**.

St Kitts and Nevis

St Kitts and Navis have a combined population of 52,000, which is 95 per cent of black African descent. At the last census, 36.2 per cent were **Anglican**, 32.3 per cent **Methodist**, 10.7 per cent **Roman Catholic**, and 7.9 per cent other **Protestant**, especially **Wesleyan**. The influence of fundamentalism and neo-pentecostal sects, under North American trained leaders, has been growing in the past decade.

St Lucia

St Lucia has a population of 157,000, which is 90 per cent **Roman Catholic** (due to early French influence), three per cent **Anglican**, and seven per cent **Seventh Day Adventist** and **Evangelical**. The **charismatic movement** has been widespread among the Catholics, and **Pentecostal** sects are successful. The Catholic Church recently prevented the partnership of a local television station with an American religious broadcasting network. **Rastafarianism** has spread among the unemployed, bringing them into communities where they work in crafts.

St Vincent and the Grenadines

These islands have a population of 122,000, which is 82 per cent black African, and 14 per cent mixed. In the 1981 census, 42 per cent were **Anglican**, 21 per cent **Methodist** and 12 per cent **Roman Catholic**. There is a small following of **Afro-American spiritists** (eg **Shakers**), and even fewer **Bahais**. A small number of (traditionally non-political) **Rastafarians** have been accused of occasional acts of violence, as well as of being involved in a rising on Union Island (in the Grenadines) in December 1979.

San Marino

San Marino is a city-state within Italy, having a population of 24,000. It is almost entirely **Roman Catholic**, but strong Communist support includes many atheists. Among marginal groups are included **Jehovah's Witnesses, Seventh Day Adventists**, and **Bahais**.

São Tomé and Príncipe

These islands in the Gulf of Guinea, until 1975 under Portuguese rule, are populated by 127,000 people of mixed races. Eighty per cent are **Roman Catholic**, and the Church is administered by the Archdiocese of Luanda in Angola. **African traditional religions** have nearly disappeared, but indigenous beliefs still underlie the prevailing Christian practice. **Seventh Day Adventists** and indigenous **Evangelicals** have considerable followings.

Saudi Arabia

Saudi Arabia, with a population of 16,000,000, is 90 per cent Arab and 10 per cent Afro-Asian. Islam is the only legal religion, and adherents are almost entirely **Sunnis**, although there are some five per cent **Twelver Shi'ites** in the Eastern areas along the Gulf (in Ahsa), a small number of **Zaydis**, and perhaps five per cent **Ibadis** among the Bedouin who follow their own strict form of Islam and largely ignore the state. Amongst the Sunnis, the **Hanbali** rite is followed by the ruling family, and in Nejd and the Eastern Province—approximately 55 per cent of the population—whereas in Hijaz and Asir the **Shafi'i** rite predominates. There are also **Hanafi** and **Maliki** minorities. Foreign workers are permitted in practice to hold private religious, for example Christian, services, although strictly speaking these are illegal.

Saudi Arabia is the centre of the Muslim world as the location of the two principal cities of Islam, Mecca and Medina, where Islam was founded by the Prophet Muhammad. The mosque in Mecca holds 300,000 people, and each year some 1,500,000 people from around the world participate in the annual Hajj, the pilgrimage which is one of the five pillars of Islam: a special government department has responsibility for the complex logistics involved in ensuring the smooth running of this mammoth event. Saudi Arabia is also the centre of the **Muslim World League** and of the **Organization of the Islamic Conference**. In Mecca and Medina there are Islamic universities, and elsewhere colleges which teach all aspects of Islamic law.

The King is both state and religious leader, and enjoys considerable international prestige among other Muslim states as the guardian of Mecca and Medina: he currently uses the title Servant of the Two Sanctuaries in preference to King, sensitive perhaps to the questionable status of the monarchy as a legitimate form of government in the eyes of Islamic fundamentalists. There is no secular constitution or law, except those laws necessary for the operation of commercial companies; nor are there any political parties or trade unions. All aspects of life are governed by religious law, and an Organization for the Enforcement of Good and Prevention of Evil established in 1929 remains active today, while the moral police (*mutawwi*) patrol the streets to uphold strict observance of the Shari'a-based law.

Saudi Arabia is unique in the Muslim world in upholding the puritanical form of Sunnism known as **Wahhabism** (or al-Muwahhidun, as the movement is referred to within Arabia). It is in consequence of this that all **Sufi** shrines, formerly numerous in the country, have been destroyed and all Sufi organizations suppressed (although recently some Sufi meetings in private premises have been tolerated). Critics, however, accuse the régime of hypocrisy because of alleged discrepancies between Wahhabi precept and Saudi practice, and opposition surfaced dramatically in November 1979 with the seizure of the mosque in Mecca by Juhaiman al-'Utaibi and some 2,000 of his followers in the movement of the **Ikhwan** (which in its latest phase has thus become Mahdist). The mosque was recaptured after a three-week-long siege involving heavy casualties.

At the same time, but independently, disturbances occurred amongst the Shi'ites in the eastern provinces. Inspired by the (Shi'ite) Iranian revolution, they took to the streets to celebrate 'Ashura, the annual commemoration of the martyrdom of Imam Husayn, in defiance of the Wahhabi-inspired legal prohibition on practising their distinctive Twelver rituals in public. Riots ensued. The Saudi authorities, alarmed no doubt by the coincidence of Sunni and Shi'ite discontent, and conscious of the significance of the Shi'ites beyond their numbers (they constitute 35 per cent of Aramco's employees in the crucially important oil industry), have subsequently directed more resources to Shi'ite areas, and tensions appear to have eased, although an underground Shi'ite movement with close links to Iran, the Organization of the Islamic Revolution in the Arab Peninsula (Munazzamat al-Thawra al-Islamiya fi'l-Jazira al-'Arabiya), continues to propagate the idea of an Iranian-style revolt against the Saudi régime. Iranian pilgrims have also demonstrated in support of this during the Hajj, leading to unrest and some loss of life.

A relatively radical Saudi branch of the **Muslim Brotherhood**, known as the Jama'at al-Da'wa (Society of Propagation of Faith), operates publicly and quite extensively. Saudi Arabia has given very significant financial support and encouragement to radical reformist groups throughout the Muslim world, and notably to the Muslim Brotherhood in Egypt and the **Jama'at-i Islami** in Pakistan and Bangladesh. Several such groups emerged, at least at grass-roots level, as strongly pro-Iraq in the Gulf War of 1991 following Saddam Hussein's invasion of Kuwait, and were critical of Saudi Arabia for inviting infidel Western troops on to the sacred soil of the homeland of Islam. Their leaders, however, conscious of the need for continued Saudi financial support, were far more cautious, a tension evident, for example, in the case of **FIS** in Algeria and **Hizb al-Nahda** in Tunisia.

Senegal

Senegal has a population of 7,500,000 and 91 per cent are **Sunni** Muslims of the **Maliki** rite (although Islam is not officially a state religion). Over 50 per cent of the Muslim population belong to the **Tijaniya Sufi** brotherhood (one of its major black African headquarters is in Kaolack), 25 per cent belong to the **Muridiya** (whose chiefs control at least 50 per cent of the economically important peanut production), and 16 per cent belong to the **Qadiriya**. Although the country is a pluralist democracy, in practice it is the leaders of the Sufi brotherhoods who are able to hold the highest political offices through their economic power and the support of their fellow members. The Sufi orders have something of a reputation for promoting conservatism and sectarianism, a trend resisted by the Union Culturelle Musulmane, founded in 1953, and which attracts young people and intellectuals. The West African regional office of the **World Muslim Congress** is situated in Kaolack too.

Six per cent are Christian, and mostly **Roman Catholic**, and three per cent adhere to **African traditional religions**. There are a few **Protestant** missions.

Seychelles

The 92 islands of the Seychelles have a population of 68,500 which is largely Creole, and gained independence in 1976. Eighty per cent are **Roman Catholic**, 19 per cent **Anglican**, and the remainder are **Jehovah's Witnesses** or **Seventh Day Adventists**. The priests are mainly indigenous, and there is one congregation of nuns. Smaller islands are visited twice a year by priests.

Sierra Leone

Sierra Leone has a population of 4,300,000 over half of whom follow **African traditional religions**. These are generally characterized by beliefs in charms, medicine men, divination and witchcraft, and often have secret societies which are increasing in importance. Ancestors serve as intermediaries between the living and God. Twenty-five to 40 per cent, mainly in the north and west, are **Sunni** Muslims of the **Maliki** school of Islamic law, while six per cent are **Protestant**, mainly **Methodist**, and two per cent **Roman Catholic**. The Christians are largely descended from freed slaves, have better education, and all the heads of government so far have been Christian.

Singapore

Singapore has a population of 2,700,000, 75 per cent of whom are Chinese, 15 per cent Malay, and six per cent Indian. Approximately 50 per cent follow **Chinese folk religion** or are **Taoist**, and a further seven per cent follow Chinese Mahayana Buddhism. A small minority of Buddhists, both Chinese and Sinhalese, are **Theravadin**. In the 1980s the government began promoting **Confucianism** as furnishing the necessary moral basis for society—a move criticized by Chinese academics, and rejected, in the main, by the Indian and Malay communities. Mention should also be made of the Chinese new religious movement **De Jiao**.

Seventeen per cent of the population are **Sunni** Muslim, a community composed of Malays, Indians and Pakistanis, and regulated by a Muslim Religious Council (Majlis Ugama Islam). This Muslim minority has a significance disproportionate to its size because of Singapore's location between its two large Islamic neighbours, Indonesia and Malaysia. About one per cent of the population is **Sikh**.

Christianity grew from 10.3 per cent to 18.7 per cent of the total population during the 1980s, and includes a wide ethnic diversity. Formerly, **Roman Catholics, Methodists, Anglicans** and **Presbyterians** were the most numerous, but the recent growth has largely taken place among **Protestant evangelical** sects. This massive change has led the government to accuse Christians of subversive activity: a number of Catholic activists involved in social work have been detained for two to three years without trial, accused of Marxist subversion, and in 1987 the government closed the offices of the Christian Conference of Asia, a regional ecumenical organization involved in the field of human rights.

Solomon Islands

Melanesian religion is still influential in these islands where the population is around 250,000. **Protestants** claim 38 per cent of the population, and **Roman Catholics** 34 per cent. The Church of Melanesia (**Anglican**) is the strongest Protestant denomination, followed by the United Church with its strong **Congregational** base. **Baptists**, independent **Evangelicals, Seventh Day Adventists** and **Jehovah's Witnesses** are also present. There is an indigenous church known as **Etoism** after its founder, Silas Eto, which has a following of around 3 per cent.

Somalia

Somalia has a population of 8,000,000, 85 per cent of whom are ethnically Somali, and 15 per cent Bantu. Almost all the population is **Sunni** Muslim, with the **Shafi'i** rite practised in the South, and the **Hanafi** in the North, but the **zar cult** is also found. Somalia is an Islamic state, but has until recently attempted a form of Islamic socialism similar to Algeria. However, since the overthrow of President Barre in January 1991, various factions of the successful rebels have been engaged in relentless internecine warfare, reducing the country to destitution and famine, and it remains to be seen what form of state and society will eventually emerge. At least until the events following the overthrow of the Barre régime, the Islamic Assembly in Mogadishu served as the regional office for East Africa of the **World Muslim Congress**.

There are a few **Shi'ites** and Hindus among the small Asian population. Missionary work by Christians was prohibited by the Barre régime, and there was some tension with the foreign community of 2,000 **Roman Catholics**: the Italian Bishop of Mogadishu was shot outside the cathedral in July 1989.

South Africa

South Africa has a population of 38,000,000, 8,000,000 of whom are resident in the nominally independent homelands. There are 4,600,000 whites, 2,800,000 coloured, 800,000 Asians, and the rest are black Africans. Sixty per cent of the blacks, and almost all of the whites and coloured are Christian, while the remaining blacks follow **African traditional religions** (eg **Khoisan religion**), as well as more recent spirit possession cults. Sixty per cent of Asians are Hindu, and 20 per cent are Muslim (mostly **Sunnis**). There are some 120,000 Jews.

Some 2,400,000 people belong to the **Dutch Reformed Church** (Nederduitse Gereformeerde Kerk), which is largely white, and the denomination of most members of government. It has, in the past, produced theological justifications of apartheid, but since 1986 members of other races, in principle, have been allowed to be members. Previously, non-white members of the Dutch Reformed Church had to belong to the three sister churches established through mission: for coloureds, the Nederduitse Gereformeerde Sendingkerk; for Indians, the **Reformed Church** in Africa; and for blacks, the Nederduitse Gereformeerde Kerk in Afrika. All four groups are represented biannually in a meeting of their federal council. There are also two more conservative, white breakaway groups from the Dutch Reformed Church: the Nederduitsch Hervormde Kerk (established 1858), and the Gereformeerde Kerk (the "Doppers", established 1859) to which President de Klerk belongs.

The traditional English-speaking denominations are predominantly black, and have consistently opposed apartheid, their members often suffering at the hands of the State as a result. There are 2,300,000 **Roman Catholics**, 2,000,000 **Anglicans**, and 800,000 **Evangelical Lutherans**.

Liberation theology is strong, and is associated with such church leaders as Allan Boesak, Desmond Tutu, Albert Nolan and Frank Chikane. It is also widely practised in university theology departments, and includes a social and contextual analysis to describe the struggle for salvation from public sin. Its best-known expression is the *Kairos Document*. Some premises of leading church organizations were destroyed by right-wing organizations in 1988. By contrast, there are also many right-wing Christian groups, which are fundamentalist and support the government. It remains to be seen whether they will flourish or wither in the emerging post-apartheid world of the new South Africa.

The remaining 12,000,000 black Christians belong to African separatist churches, and

South Africa has the greatest proliferation of separate churches in the world. The largest of these include the **Zionist Churches**, which is **Pentecostal** and syncretistic in retaining elements of traditional African religions, and the **Ethiopian Churches** which are nationalist in outlook.

Muslims, Hindus and Jews have all been active in opposing apartheid: Muslims constitute only a little over one per cent of the population, being roughly equally divided among Asians (of Indian, Pakistani, and Bangladeshi extraction) and Cape coloureds (Afrikaans-speaking ethnic Malays), with only a very small number of black Africans.

Spain

Spain has a population of 40,000,000, 99 per cent of whom are nominally **Roman Catholic**. The Church has been traditionally conservative in outlook, and was closely linked to Franco's nationalist régime, which contained a number of members of **Opus Dei**. A second Church, within the first, has started to emerge since the 1950s which is based more on personal faith than cultural context, and has finally become more prominent. It has introduced such innovations as local communities who meet for the Eucharist and agree on socio–political prophetic tasks; new communities, re-shaping the old parish concept; and synods including priests and lay people. This trend has coincided more recently with gradual withdrawal of state support for Catholicism (in contrast to the "national Catholicism" of the Franco period), although Church property still remains exempt from taxation. While there has been a fall in vocations to the priesthood, Spain still has the largest number of contemplative sisters of any nation.

Also present are **Anglicans, Baptists, Evangelicals, Plymouth Brethren, Greek Orthodox, Mormons** and **Jehovah's Witnesses**. There are up to 300,000 immigrant Muslims, and 13,000 Jews.

Sri Lanka

Sri Lanka has a population of 17,000,000, which is 74 per cent Sinhalese, 18 per cent Tamil, and 7 per cent Moor. Religious affiliation usually follows the ethnic divide. Sixty-nine per cent of the population, the Sinhalese, are **Theravada** Buddhists, and Buddhism has been present here since the 3rd century BCE. There are about 6,000 monasteries, 17,000 monks, and 14,000 novices distributed between the three monastic fraternities (*nikayas*). Theravada missionaries are trained and sent elsewhere, and social action and development is stressed particularly by the **Sramadana Sarvodaya** movement. The government propagated Buddhist nationalism in the 50s, but since then has maintained a secular stance which has made it the target of criticism and terrorist attacks by both Buddhist nationalists and Tamils. Monks often sympathize with the Sinhalese People's Liberation Front, which is opposed to the government. Fifteen per cent of the population, the Tamils, are **Saivite** Hindus, and in the face of repression have fought a separatist war which despite being suppressed by the Indian army is still under way. Many atrocities have been committed by both sides. Seven per cent are **Sunni** Muslim, and these are Moors and Malays. A further eight per cent of the population are Christian, drawn from both Sinhalese and Tamil populations. These are 90 per cent **Roman Catholic**, five per cent **Anglican**, and two per cent **Methodist**.

Sudan

Sudan is the largest country in Africa in terms of geographical spread. It has a population of some 26,000,000 with extraordinary ethnic and linguistic diversity. However, Arabic is the language of the majority, and correspondingly about 73 per cent of the population are at least formally Muslim, although they often retain pre-Islamic beliefs (for example in the spirits of the Nile, or the wearing of magic charms), and the **zar cult** is still to be found in the Nile area. They are located in the northern two-thirds of the country. In the remaining southern third are to be found mostly Christians (about eight per cent of the country's population), and adherents of **African traditional religions**, including **Nuer and Dinka** religion. Amongst the Christians, the **Roman Catholic** community has experienced phenomenal growth this century and now numbers over 1,000,000. There are half as many **Anglicans** (a product of the activities of the Church Missionary Society), and relatively few members of the **Coptic** and **Ethiopian Orthodox** churches.

Muslims are mostly **Sunni** and follow the **Maliki** school of law (or alternatively the **Shafi'i**), although the influence of the **Hanafi** system introduced under earlier Anglo–Egyptian rule still remains. There are also significant numbers of **Isma'ilis**. **Sufi** orders remain very strong: they include the politically influential **Khatmiya**, their historic opponents the Sammaniya (from among whose members had appeared the Mahdi in the 1880s), the **Sanusiya, Qadiriya, Shadhiliya** and **Tijaniya**. Indeed the central role of Sufism in the spread of Islam in the Sudan has meant that, in marked contrast to neighbouring Egypt, for example, there has never been a strong *ulama* class. The **Ahmadiya** movement is prohibited as heretical.

The Mahdist movement, the **Mahdiya** (whose members are known as the **Ansar**), despite periods of weakness, has survived as a very significant religious force. Its political extension, the Umma Party (Hizb al-Umma), has been one of the main forces in Sudanese politics since independence in 1956. So has its historic rival, the Khatmiya Sufi order (working through various political parties). In addition, since its foundation in 1954, the country's **Muslim Brotherhood** (Ikhwan al-Muslimin) has emerged as a powerful new religio–political force.

In 1983 President Nimeiri declared Sudan an Islamic Republic, having veered completely away from the secular socialist policies and alliance with the Sudanese Communists that marked his original stance on seizing power in the military *coup* of 1969. While a renewal of personal faith may have been a factor, he was perhaps also seeking to retain the initiative in the climate of heightened religious fervour following the Iranian revolution of 1979 and the assassination of President Sadat of Egypt by extremist Islamists in 1981. However, the civil war between the Muslim north and the non-Muslim south which lasted from 1956 to 1972 now broke out again as Nimeiri imposed Islamic law, often medieval in character, on the whole country, including the non-Islamic south.

While some Sufi groups supported the introduction of Shari'a laws, the Khatmiya leadership voiced only guarded support, eventually opposing them in their existing form.

Sadiq al-Mahdi, leader of the Umma Party (and of the progressive wing of the Ansar), and a great grandson of "the" Mahdi, emerged as an outspoken critic. While himself a supporter of Shari'a, he had worked for a modern interpretation based on the *Qur'an* and *Sunna*. He now found himself imprisoned. Less fortunate was the 76-year-old non-violent reformist Muslim leader Mahmud Muhammad Taha, leader of the **Republican Brothers**: he was hanged for alleged sedition and apostasy.

The Muslim Brotherhood, on the other hand, continued their controversial policy of pragmatic co-operation with Nimeiri, and sought to broaden their support base beyond their traditional campus strongholds by tapping the considerable popular support, at least initially, for the Islamization measures. So successful were they in this, however, that in 1985 Nimeiri cracked down on them, imprisoning their leader Hassan Turabi and many others. At the same time, their readiness to participate in Nimeiri's government and support his policies further deepened their alienation from their longer-established Egyptian counterparts.

Elections in 1986, following Nimeiri's deposition in 1985, led to a shifting sequence of coalitions involving the familiar religious forces of the Khatmiya, the Ansar-supported Umma Party, and the Muslim Brotherhood, but agreement on the future of the Shari'a measures proved impossible. They were finally frozen, a decision which provoked a series of protests by the National Islamic Front (Jabhat al-Mithaq), the party of the Muslim Brotherhood. This brief period of turbulent democracy ended in 1989 with yet another military *coup*. Political parties were dissolved, and the Muslim Brotherhood went underground. The latter, however, along with the Ansar, and the Khatmiya and other Sufi orders, retain their significance. Nor has the last been heard of Sudan's experiment with Islamization, even if there is no repetition of the wave of floggings and amputations of the hand that occurred in 1983–1984 following Nimeiri's peremptory imposition of Shari'a and its application by special "decisive justice courts": a new penal code based on the Shari'a was introduced in 1990, though not in the Christian south. By 1992, Hassan Turabi had emerged as the unofficial leader of Sudan behind General Omar Bashir, and the National Islamic Front's (i.e. the Muslim Brotherhood's) campaign to spread the Islamic revival retained its momentum. Links with Libya and Iran, and missions to Chad, formed part of this process.

Suriname

Suriname's population of 400,000 has a wide ethnic diversity, with Hindustani, Creole, Javanese, Bush Black, Amerindian, Chinese, and European races being represented. Some 27.4 per cent are Hindu, 19.6 per cent Muslim (mainly **Sunnis** of the **Shafi'i** rite), 22.8 per cent **Roman Catholic**, and 25.2 per cent **Protestant**—mainly **Moravian**, but also including **Dutch Reformed, Lutheran, Jehovah's Witnesses** and **Seventh Day Adventists**. Just 0.2 per cent of the population is Jewish, and the remaining five per cent follow indigenous religions, which are primarily **shamanist**, and found among the Bush Blacks (Maroons) and jungle Amerindians. **Winti** is the folk religion of the Creoles, being a form of **Afro-American spiritism**. A related but more African version is found among the Maroons.

In 1988, the Committee of Christian Churches, an ecumenical group, were accepted in a mediating role between the government and the anti-government guerrillas, the Suriname Liberation Army.

Swaziland

Swaziland's population of 827,000 is about 70 per cent Christian, while the remainder follow **African traditional religions**. Ten per cent are **Roman Catholic**, six per cent **Methodist**, three per cent **Anglican**, seven per cent **Zionist**, while the rest are divided among smaller traditional **Protestant** and indigenous denominations, many of which come from South Africa.

Sweden

Sweden has a population of 8,500,000, which contains minorities from Yugoslavia, Poland, Turkey, Iran, Germany, and Chile. There are about 16,000 Jews. Eighty-eight per cent belong to the State Church, which is **Evangelical Lutheran**. The Swedish church is a national state church, rooted in tradition and rural society. It sends a number of missionaries overseas. The supreme legislative body is the General Assembly, composed of clergy and laity (most of whom, however, are elected as members of political parties, and no seats are automatically reserved for bishops or the clergy). There are close links with the **Anglican Church**.

The church is broad in composition, and contains such diverse elements as orthodox Lutherans, liberals, pietists, liturgists, and those who prefer spontaneous styles of worship. Weekly attendance stands at about three per cent of the population. Ten per cent of the population are in the Free Churches, and the largest of these are the Mission Covenant Church, the **Baptists, Methodists**, and **Pentecostals**. All of these maintain a pietist tradition. A further 1.5 per cent of the population is **Roman Catholic**, composed of immigrants and their descendants, and there are also about 50,000 Muslims among the immigrant population, as well as a number of adherents of the **Orthodox** churches.

Switzerland

The population of Switzerland stands at 6,750,000 with 1,000,000 of these being foreigners. The linguistic composition of the Swiss stands at 74 per cent German, 20 per cent French, and four per cent Italian. Switzerland was the home of the reformers Zwingli and Calvin, and 48 per cent of the population are **Protestant**. The Free Church of Geneva, and the **Evangelical Methodist** Church are the largest denominations, but each church tends to be autonomous and local. Religious practice is declining, but "religiosity" increasing. The **Roman Catholics** have recently risen, through immigration, to 49 per cent of the population. The Synod is influential on religious life. The Catholic Church contains a religious diversity, with the Canton Schwyz objecting to the appointment by the Pope, in 1988, of a conservative bishop over them. In addition, there is the movement of traditionalist Catholics led by Archbishop Lefebvre, excommunicated from Rome in 1988, who is in opposition to the reforms of *Vatican II*, and has established his headquarters in Écône near Geneva. Just 0.3 per cent of the population is Jewish, and the same proportion Muslim—mainly Turkish labourers. There are small **Bahai**, Hindu, and Buddhist groups, and several important Buddhist centres.

Syria

Syria has a population of 12,500,000 of whom 70 per cent are Muslims, **Sunnis** of the **Hanafi** school of law, 12 per cent **'Alawis** (i.e. **Nusayris**), three per cent **Druzes**, one per cent **Isma'ilis** and 14 per cent Christians. The Christians are **Roman Catholics** and also members of the **Greek Orthodox** and **Syrian** and **Armenian** Churches. There is also a small number of **Yazidis**, and in the Israeli-occupied Golan Heights are some 10,000 Jewish settlers.

Syria is the only Muslim country whose ruling élite—including President Assad—is drawn from the 'Alawis, a community whose claim to be legitimate Muslims is challenged by the Sunni majority. In order to buttress their claim, the 'Alawis have made some moves to achieve recognition, not as Sunnis, but as **Twelver Shi'ites**. Any 'Alawi claim to Twelver identity remains, however, undoubtedly tenuous, and almost certainly opposed by the majority of Twelvers (perhaps too by the majority of 'Alawis who prefer to retain their separate identity). It needs to be seen rather in the political context of Syria's links with Lebanon and Iran: Syria is in opposition to most neighbouring Muslim states apart from Iran, which is of course a Twelver Shi'ite state; and Syria also supports a number of Lebanese Shi'ite organizations, notably **Amal** (and to some extent **Hizbollah**, though external support for the latter comes primarily from Iran). The ruling Ba'ath Party held originally to a secular nationalist ideology, but President Assad's régime is concerned to emphasize its Islamic credentials, and the attempt to secure recognition of 'Alawis as Shi'ites is a way of developing this profile: it remains to be seen with what degree of eventual success, if any.

The **Muslim Brotherhood** has been a major force in the country—indeed Syria became for a time the main centre for the movement following the government clampdown on it in Egypt in the mid- and late 1950s. As a predominantly Sunni organization it has combined socio–economic criticism of the Ba'ath Party with religious criticism of the 'Alawi party leaders. From the mid-1970s onwards—faced for the first time with an 'Alawi head of state—its members were increasingly involved in acts of violence against the régime, culminating in an uprising in the city of Hamah in February 1982 which, however, ended in brutal state repression: thousands of people were killed, and large parts of the city destroyed. The extent to which the Brotherhood has survived this traumatic defeat is far from clear. Not only is it now forced to operate clandestinely, but membership of the organization carries with it the death penalty.

A number of **Sufi** orders are well established in Syria, including the **Khalwatiya** and the **Rifd'iya**. Since 1979, however, the latter has been repressed for allegedly harbouring members of the Muslim Brotherhood.

Syria opposed Iraq's occupation of Kuwait in 1990, and sent troops to Saudi Arabia. The Iraqi oppositional group, Hizb al Da'wa (the **Da'wa Party**), is also permitted to organize openly in Syria.

Taiwan

Taiwan is an island of 20,500,000 people off the Chinese mainland whose military government, opposed to Chinese communism, encourages religion. Many religious leaders fled here from China. Most of the population follow **Chinese folk religions**, but there are 2,000,000 **Taoists**, with 23,340 priests, and 3,600,000 Mahayana Buddhists with 5,860 priests. Many follow both Taoism and Buddhism at the same time, as well as folk-religion, and so it is difficult to give accurate figures of religious adherence. There are also 500,000 **Protestants** (mainly **Presbyterian**), and 300,000 **Roman Catholics**, as well as small numbers of **Sunni** Muslims: the Chinese Muslim Association (founded on the mainland in 1937) is active in promoting friendship and cultural exchange with Muslim countries, while the Chinese Muslim Youth League promotes conversion to Islam as well as the study of Islamic culture.

Tanzania

Tanzania has a population of 26,500,000 which is 99 per cent indigenous Bantu. About 40 per cent are Christian, 30 per cent Muslim, and 20 per cent adhere to **African traditional religions**. Traditional religions are often characterized by the belief that natural phenomena are manifestations of God, involve the veneration of ancestors, and include spirit-possession cults. The Muslims are mainly **Sunni Shafi'i**, unlike most of black Africa which is mainly Sunni **Maliki**, but there are also **Isma'ili Shi'ites** (mainly **Bohoras**) and **Ibadis** present, the latter being mostly descendants of 19th century workers and traders from Oman, and concentrated on the island of Zanzibar (which is over 95 per cent Muslim). The Christians, expressed as proportions of the total population, are 25 per cent **Roman Catholic**, six per cent **Lutheran**, four per cent **Anglican**, and five per cent other **Protestant** including large **Moravian** and **Mennonite** communities. There are also 60,000 **Bahais**, and 20,000 Hindus. Former President Nyerere was a devout Catholic, but was replaced by President Mwinyi, a Muslim from Zanzibar. Recent years have seen the growth of some Islamic militancy. The National Muslim Council of Tanzania (Bakwata) is the major co-ordinating agency for Muslims, enjoying government recognition.

Thailand

The population of Thailand, currently estimated at over 57,000,000, is mainly composed of Buddhists (92 per cent), Muslims (four per cent), **Chinese folk religionists** (1.5 per cent) and Christians (one per cent). Although **Theravada** Buddhism plays a minimal overt role in national politics, it is the religion of the state according to the constitution of 1968. The king, H.M. Bhumipol Adulyadej, must accordingly profess and defend the Buddhist dharma and its community of monks (*sangha*). At present there are some 200,000 monks located in 24,000 monasteries throughout the kingdom. At any one time a significant number of lay Buddhists (80,000) will be temporary monastic residents. The *sangha* is formed by two fraternities (*nikayas*), the **Mahanikaya** and **Dhammayutika-nikaya**, which disagree over some matters of monastic organization, though relations between the two are cordial. Most senior monks tend towards conservatism in political matters, but some discord has materialized in recent times with Bhikkhu Buddhadasa as an influential focus of the more radical position. In recognition of the long-standing nature of Thai Buddhist culture, Bangkok is the headquarters of the **World Fellowship of Buddhists**.

The southern part of the country contains a significant minority of **Sunni** Muslims of the **Shafi'i** rite: although they constitute only 4 per cent of the country's total population, they form 85 per cent of the 1,000,000 inhabitants of the southern peninsula. Being primarily Malay in origin, elements in the Muslim population feel alienated from the ideology of the Thai state and for decades have sought either independence or closer relations with neighbouring Malaysia. At the moment the tension appears to be at a low level. This is in part due to attempts by the central government to provide increased levels of services. A certain amount of devolution of government power has also occurred in the south. As a complement to this the central Department of Religious Affairs pursues a policy of genuine religious toleration.

Nevertheless, in recent years a number of new religious movements, such as **Santi Asok** and **Hooppha Sawan** have developed. Their traditional and anti-Communist outlook has found much support amongst leading members of the Thai military. The popular uprising and overthrow of the government of General Kraprayoon in May 1992 may signal the end of their influence in Thai national life.

Togo

Togo has a population of 3,700,000 up to 70 per cent of whom adhere to **African traditional religions**, 20 per cent of whom are Christian, predominantly **Roman Catholic**, and 10 per cent **Sunni Maliki** Muslim. **Protestants** are mainly **Evangelical** or **Pentecostal**. The Ewe tribe is strongly Christian, and the Kotokoli tribe Muslim. Since 1974, "foreign religions" have been actively discouraged by the government of President Eyadema (in power since 1967), and this has resulted in a substantial return from Catholicism to traditional religions. The Muslim Union of Togo (Union Musulmane du Togo), founded in 1973, struggles against unorthodox **Sufi** brotherhoods and **maraboutism**.

Tonga

Tonga is composed of 172 islands, 36 of which contain the population of 97,000. Tonga is 99 per cent Christian, mainly **Methodist**, and Sunday is declared by the Constitution to be a day of rest when everyone goes to church. There are over 40,000 Free **Wesleyans** (the King is head of the Free Wesleyan Church, again under the terms of the Constitution), 10,000 Free Church (also Methodist), 15,000 **Roman Catholics**, and over 15,000 **Mormons** who have been growing rapidly at the expense of the Methodists. Many missionaries have been sent overseas by Tongan Methodists. Church leaders have been active and successful in opposing the use of the islands by the US as a location in which to dump hazardous wastes.

Trinidad and Tobago

Trinidad and Tobago's population of 1,300,000 has a wide racial mix with 43 per cent Black, 40 per cent East Indian, 14 per cent mixed, one per cent White, and one per cent Chinese. Sixty per cent of the population are Christian, with 36 per cent **Roman Catholic**, 15 per cent **Anglican**, and nine per cent other **Protestant**, including **Presbyterians, Methodists, Pentecostals**, and **Seventh Day Adventists**. Twenty-three per cent are Hindu, six per cent are Muslim, and there are a few **Afro–American spiritists** (for example adherents of **Shango**, and **Shouters** or **Spiritual Baptists**), **Rastafarians** and **Chinese folk religionists**. The society is tolerant, and in general there is little tension between the different ethnic and religious groups. In July 1990, however, there was an attempted *coup* in the capital, Port of Spain, by a **Black Muslim** group, Jamaat al-Muslimeen, founded in 1984. The Prime Minister was taken hostage, but the rebels were eventually persuaded to surrender by the offer of a pardon (and when brought to trial, they were released—with their legal costs and $12m compensation—because the view was upheld that the pardon was legally valid).

Tunisia

Tunisia has a population of 8,400,000, of whom 98 per cent are Muslims, **Sunnis** of the **Maliki** school of law (though a minority adhere to the **Hanafi** rite). There are small pockets of **Ibadis**, and the offshore island of Djerba has 50,000 Ibadis whose life remains almost untouched by modern civilization. There are also some 20,000 **Roman Catholics**, nearly all French expatriates, and approximately 9,000 Jews.

After independence from the French in 1956, Islam was officially declared to be the state religion in the 1959 constitution. However, Shari‘a courts were abolished, and a liberal Islamic modernist interpretation of the *Quran* was used to justify bringing the legal status of women very much into line with that of Western countries (e.g. prohibiting polygamy, allowed in traditional Islamic law, and revising the rules for divorce). Moreover, the mosques and the Islamic education system became dependent on the state (although the attempt by President Bourguiba in 1960 to cancel the fast of Ramadan, on the grounds that it was interrupting the holy war against underdevelopment, foundered because of the concerted opposition of the *ulama*).

The modernist Islam used by the state to legitimize its policies failed, however, to exercise popular appeal—partly, no doubt, because of the social and economic problems to which they led, and which precipitated serious disturbances in 1978, 1980, and 1984 in particular. Meanwhile, in the Grand Mosque of Zaytouna (the country's oldest mosque and traditionally a centre of Islamic learning until incorporated into the new University of Tunis) and elsewhere, groups began to meet in the 1970s to discuss and propagate very different interpretations of Islam similar to, and doubtless in part inspired by, that of the **Muslim Brotherhood**. It was this steadily growing movement of Islamic renewal in the 1970s that formed the seedbed for the emergence in the 1980s of organizations like the **Islamic Liberation Party**, the **Islamic Progressive Movement** (Mouvement du Progrès Islamiste), the Islamic Shura Party, and above all the Islamic Tendency Movement (Mouvement de la Tendance Islamique—MTI), now known as **Hizb al-Nahda**.

In 1981 and 1987, arrests and harsh sentences—including some death sentences—were the state's reaction to outbreaks of violence imputed to members of the MTI in particular. Following the 1987 *coup* which removed the ageing and mentally unstable Bourguiba, however, a more conciliatory line was adopted. In the 1989 parliamentary elections, Islamist candidates won 15 per cent of the national vote, but perhaps as many as 30 per cent in some of the urban centres. There is said to be some sympathy for the fundamentalists in the military, and they remain a movement of considerable significance in the early 1990s, although in the wake of public disturbances during the Gulf War of January–February 1991, al-Nahda officially suspended its activities in response to the arrest of many of its leaders and hundreds of followers, as the state cracked down on its opponents.

Turkey

Turkey has a population of 58,000,000, and the common assumption—reiterated by President Turgut Özal in 1991—is that a sizeable Kurdish minority constitute some 20 per cent (concentrated mainly, but by no means exclusively, in the south-east). Other estimates of the number of Kurds, however, are very much smaller, and the issue is a sensitive one. Over 98 per cent of Turkish citizens are Muslims, mainly **Sunni Hanafi**, although in the south-east the **Shafi'i** rite predominates. There is a significant **Alevi** minority, notably among the Kurdish population. Sectarian tensions between this minority—sometimes said to be **Shi'ite**, but not altogether correctly—and the Sunni majority persist. A massacre of Alevis (in Kahramanmarash) in 1978 led to a declaration of martial law, the killings being partly political, having been organized, it seems, by the right-wing Nationalist Action Party (banned in 1980 but now replaced by the Nationalist Labour Party).

The label "Alevi" (follower of Imam 'Ali) may also be used, confusingly, to refer to two other, quite different, minorities who are indeed—as the label implies—Shi'ite: namely, a community of Azerbaijani **Twelvers** in the east who originally fled the Bolshevik revolution, and **Nusayris** in the south-east near Syria. A minority **Qizilbash** community also exists, its relationship to the Alevis remaining rather unclear.

Apart from the Muslims there are approximately 130,000 **Orthodox** Christians, mostly following the Ecumenical Patriarch of Constantinople who has a unique position, although no direct authority, in all Eastern Orthodox Churches. There are also **Greek**, Bulgarian, Serbian and **Russian Orthodox** Churches present, and among the non-Chalcedonians, **Armenian** and **Syrian Jacobite**. There are also 130,000 **Roman Catholics** of various rites, 50,000 Jews, and **shamanism** is still present in a small minority of about 15,000.

Despite its pronounced Muslim profile, Turkey has officially been a secular state since 1937, when the Constitution was amended accordingly. This is a legacy of the Kemalism which prevailed during the inter-war period in particular. Mustafa Kemal, popularly known as Atatürk, founder of the modern Turkish state, attacked institutionalized Islam (for example, abolishing the Caliphate in 1924, and banning the **Sufi** orders in 1925), and placed it firmly under state control, seeking to remove Islam from politics and limit it to a purely private, individual sphere. This ideology has continued to be upheld by the army in particular, and amongst the reasons for the introduction of military rule in 1980 was what the army saw as the increasingly inflammatory and socially disruptive activities of the religious National Salvation Party (NSP).

This concern was heightened at the time by recent memories of the Iranian revolution, but the Khomeini line has not in fact commanded much support in Turkey, although a man known as "the Local Khomeini" (Cemalettin Kaplan, a former *mufti* of Adana—and former member of the **Milli Görüs** organization) seeks to emulate the Iranian leader's success by having sound and video cassettes of his fundamentalist sermons smuggled into Turkey in large numbers from Germany, where he now lives.

The very existence of a religious party—the NSP was re-established in 1983 as the Welfare Party—is an indication that, while the state has in many ways continued a Kemalist policy of secularization, its former rigours have softened. Some toleration is now shown to the Sufi orders, which had continued to exist unofficially despite being illegal, and annual festivals at the tombs of saints may now be celebrated, sometimes by large numbers of people (for instance at the tomb of the founder of the **Bektashiya** in Hacibektaş in central Anatolia, or that of Rumi, founder of the **Mawlawiya**—the Whirling Dervishes—in Kenya). Gatherings of the **Halveti-Cerrahis**, by contrast, are quite small. Faculties of divinity have been re-established in the universities, new mosques built, and *imam–hatip* schools for training prayer leaders and preachers flourish.

To members of groups like the **Nurcus** and **Süleymancis**, however, little of any of this is necessarily a sign of the Islamic reassertion they themselves seek. Rather, it represents either an element of post-war liberalism, or more recently the implementation by the state of the "Turkish-Islamic Synthesis" developed by **Aydinlar Ocagi**. It is true that the Welfare Party polled 17 per cent of the vote in the 1991 general election, and secularists express concern at indications of religious renewal (symbolized by a campaign by female students to be allowed to wear headscarves), but hitherto, at least, opinion polls reflect minimal support for the idea of establishing Turkey as an Islamic state. Admittedly, responsibility for a small number of terrorist killings in Turkey in 1990 was claimed by a shadowy group calling itself **Islami Hareket** (Islamic Movement), but there is no sign at present that such groups command significant support. Meanwhile groups akin to the Nurcus and Süleymancis, for example the **Isikcilar** and **Fethullahcilar**, continue to appear, but at the moment at least remain relatively small.

Tuvalu

Tuvalu (formerly Ellice Islands) has a population of 9,000, many of whom live and work overseas. Ninety-six per cent are Christian, mainly belonging to the **Protestant** Tuvalu Church. There is still some prejudice against the 100 or so **Roman Catholics**, a tiny community whose size is explained by the fact that until 1964 Catholics were prevented by law from working in the islands: not unnaturally, local prejudice remains. There are also tiny **Seventh Day Adventist, Bahai** and Muslim communities.

Uganda

Uganda's population of 18,300,000 are approximately 45 per cent **Roman Catholics**, 25 per cent **Anglicans**, eight per cent other **Protestant** including **Pentecostals** and **Seventh Day Adventists**, 16 per cent followers of **African traditional religions**, and 6 per cent **Sunni** Muslims, mostly adhering to the **Shafi'i** rite, although some in the north-west are Sudanese **Malikis**. The Ganda tribe, the largest Ugandan tribe, have a developed pantheon of divinities. There were also nearly 500,000 **Bahais** until these were banned by President Amin in 1977. The Anglicans are still growing rapidly, and the churches are active in reporting recent human rights' abuses by President Museveni. There is some religious rivalry between the more numerous Christians, and the Muslims who were dominant during Amin's régime—a period when the Anglican church in particular suffered terribly (former President Obote's party being predominantly Anglican). In 1987 Museveni's forces encountered resistance from the Holy Spirit Movement/Battalion led by 27-year-old Alice Lakwena, which relied on witchcraft in order to prevail, but who were defeated.

United Arab Emirates

Abu Dhabi and Dubai are the two largest of the seven sheikhdoms in this federation founded in 1971. The population of 2,000,000 are Muslims apart from a number of Christians and a sprinkling of Hindus among the expatriate population. The Muslims are 80 per cent **Sunni**, and 20 per cent **Shi'ite**. The *Quran* is the only constitution, and the **Maliki** school of law prevails except among the large community of Pakistani workers where the **Hanafi** school prevails. Islamist ideas associated with the **Jama'at-i Islami** are to be found among the latter, but not to the extent that there is a significant political threat to the rulers from that source, any more than from the small numbers of indigenous people, whether students or tribal elements, among whom there has been some evidence of Islamic renewal, although there is some internal pressure for greater political participation and a more equitable sharing of wealth.

The Shi'ites are mostly **Twelver Shi'ites** of Iranian extraction, although in Sharjah Shi'ites from South Asia predominate. Most are concentrated in Dubai, where some are members of the commercial élite. Pro-Iranian sympathies are quite common, and the federal authorities keep a watchful eye open for any signs of serious discontent, and also cultivate good relations with Iran, but Shi'ite radicalism has in truth been little evident.

United Kingdom

The United Kingdom has a population of 57,500,000, which is 81.5 per cent English, 9.6 per cent Scottish, 2.4 per cent Irish, 1.9 per cent Welsh, and about 2 per cent West Indian, Asian and African. The state religion of the United Kingdom as a whole is the Church of England (or **Anglican Church**), of which the monarch is the titular head, whereas the state religion of Scotland is the **Presbyterian** Church of Scotland; the Church in Wales and Church of Ireland, both Anglican, are disestablished.

The Church of England has 42 dioceses, each with a cathedral, and a bishop appointed by the Crown, and two archbishops. The Archbishop of Canterbury, at present the Most Rev. Dr George Carey, is the leader, and head of the worldwide Anglican Communion. The supreme spiritual and legislative authority is the General Synod which is composed of bishops, clergy and laity. Only men are ordained, although there has been much debate about the ordination of women over the past decade. About 29 per cent of children are baptized, and there are 1,200,000 attenders each Sunday, although numbers increase significantly at Easter and Christmas, and there are perhaps 2,200,000 active members. The Church contains a wide variety of theological and liturgical positions, including **Anglo-Catholics**, conservative **evangelicals**, supporters of the **charismatic movement**, and liberals, and this can produce a strain upon its unity. The Church of Scotland has 800,000 adult communicant members, 1,400 ministers of both sexes, and is governed by the Kirk session and the General Assembly.

The **Roman Catholic** Church, which was persecuted and without a hierarchy until 1850, has perhaps the highest number of active members, with 2,600,000, but considerably fewer people profess to be Catholic than Anglican. The Catholics are led by Cardinal Basil Hume, and have four archbishops and 14 bishops. It remains a matter of controversy to what extent the communal conflict in Northern Ireland is in fact a religious one, despite the relevance of the sectarian divide between the 28 per cent Catholic minority, and the Protestant majority (mostly Presbyterian, 23 per cent, and Church of Ireland, 19 per cent).

The Free Churches are generally in decline. The **Methodists** are the strongest, particularly in the north, with 450,000 adult members, but perhaps 1,200,000 active adherents. **Baptists** are particularly strong in Wales, and as a whole have nearly 3,000 churches and 300,000 members. The **United Reformed Church** has 1,000 ministers and 128,000 members. The **Salvation Army** have 929 churches, and 135 social service centres involving 1,575 officers, including hostels for the sick, homeless, elderly, abused children and teenagers on probation. The **Quakers** have 462 meeting houses, and 18,000 adult members, although most who attend their meetings are not full members. There are also **Greek**, Serbian and **Russian Orthodox** churches.

Recent decades in the United Kingdom have seen a considerable amount of secularization, with falling attendances particularly in the Free Churches. In contrast to this, charismatic and evangelical renewal, as well as fundamentalism, has seen a significant rise, both inside and outside the main churches, and a number of **House Churches**, perhaps 1,300 of them with 170,000 members, have enjoyed a rapid growth. The **Assemblies of God, Elim Pentecostals**, and **Seventh Day Adventists** are also growing, often as Black Churches among the Afro–Caribbean population. This popular Christianity is largely divorced from the study of theology, which largely takes place in university faculties and theological colleges and has a different range of intellectual problems.

The largest minority religion in the United Kingdom is Islam, and there are 1,500,000 Muslims, almost all **Sunni**, who are Pakistanis, Bangladeshis, Indians (especially Gujaratis), and Arabs. These are mainly in London, Liverpool, Manchester, Bradford and Glasgow, although there are communities in virtually all industrial towns. There are 385 mosques, and a number of other prayer centres. Muslims in Britain include, for example, **Barelvis, Deobandis, Ahl-i Hadith, Ahl-i Quran**, and the **Tablighi Jama‘at** among the South Asian communities, and the **Jama‘at-i Islami** is represented by the Islamic Foundation of Leicester. There are also some 10,000 **Isma‘ilis**, especially among Kenyan and Ugandan Asians, including **Bohoras, Khojas**, and **Aga Khanis**. Iranian **Twelver Shi‘ites** are represented by the **Muslim Institute**, whose director, Dr Kalim Siddiqi, has attracted notoriety by publicly advocating the implementation of the Ayatollah Khomeini's death sentence (*fatwa*) of 1989 against Salman Rushdie (the Rushdie Affair of 1988–89 having in turn attracted notoriety, notably through the public burning of the book by Bradford Muslims). Dr Siddiqi has also been influential in organizing an **Islamic Parliament** to represent Muslim groups in Britain—an aim not yet achieved, despite various attempts, including that represented by the **Union of Muslim Organizations of UK and Eire**. The Regent's Park mosque in London (or Central Mosque and Islamic Cultural Centre, London) has support from Saudi Arabia, and responsibility for its administration rests with ambassadors from a range of Muslim countries. It functions in some ways as an unofficial leader of the Sunni community.

The **Ahmadiya** movement has a major centre in Woking.

Concern for the proper religious education of British Muslim children has led to the formation of organizations to promote this cause. They include the Muslim Educational Trust, and Professor S. A. Ashraf's Islamic Academy in Cambridge.

A number of **Sufi** organizations are also represented: the **Naqshabandiya** is particularly strong among the Barelvis, but in addition, for example, the Shi'ite **Ni'matullahiya** has a presence, as do the **Darqawiya** and **Chishtiya**.

There are 500,000 **Sikhs**, and 300,000 Hindus from India, and these are mainly in Leicester, North London, Birmingham and Bradford. There are 330,000 Jews, the second largest group in Europe, with 300 synagogues. Buddhism has been growing, mainly among the indigenous population, and there are 134 Buddhist groups, 55 centres, and 13 monasteries which represent all major schools of Buddhism. Marginal groups include **Mormons, Jehovah's Witnesses, Christadelphians** and **Spiritualists**, each of which is quite influential, as well as **Christian Scientists** and **Unitarians**, and **Rastafarianism** has a following among the Afro–Caribbean population.

A feature of recent decades has been new religious movements such as the **Bahais**, the **Unification Church**, the **Hare Krishna** movement, the **Church of Scientology**, **Transcendental Meditation**, and the followers of Bhagwan Shree Rajneesh (**Rajneeshism**). Most of these have lost influence, but growing are **New Age** movements such as the **Human Potential Movement, est** and Exegesis, as well as softer, more therapy-orientated movements which do not constitute religions but often involve a set of beliefs.

United Kingdom Dependencies

Anguilla. Anguilla is a Caribbean island with a population estimated at 6,850 which is almost entirely Christian. About 49 per cent are **Anglican**, 43 per cent **Methodist**, and there are also **Seventh Day Adventist, Pentecostal**, Church of God, **Plymouth Brethren** and **Roman Catholic** churches.

Bermuda. Bermuda's population of 59,000 is 61 per cent black and 31 per cent white. It is 45 per cent **Anglican**, 15 per cent **Roman Catholic**, and also has sizeable **Methodist** and **Pentecostal** churches. The main opposition Progressive Labour Party draws heavily on the black churches for its support.

Falkland Islands. The Falkland Islands' population was 1,919 in 1986, plus a British military garrison of 2,000. It is 50 per cent **Anglican**, 25 per cent **United** Free Church, and 10 per cent **Roman Catholic**. Since the 1982 war, the churches have taken the lead in seeking to renew contact with people in Argentina.

Gibraltar. Gibraltar's population of 32,000 is mainly British with minorities of Genoese, Maltese, Portuguese, Spanish and Moroccans. It is 77 per cent **Roman Catholic**, nine per cent Muslim, eight per cent **Anglican**, and 1.5 per cent Jewish. There are also **Methodist, Presbyterian, Jehovah's Witness**, and **Seventh Day Adventist** groups.

Hong Kong. Hong Kong's population of just under 6,000,000 is 98 per cent ethnic Chinese. There is a lively religious culture, and most Chinese follow Buddhism, **Confucianism** and **Taoism**, and often elements of these will be found in the same temple. There are 400 Tao temples, and 500 Mahayana Buddhist temples with 180 monasteries. Hong Kong has important Buddhist and Taoist monasteries and seminaries. **Chinese folk religion** is also practised. There are 500,000 Chinese Christians, who are mainly **Roman Catholic**, but there are also many **Protestant** denominations, the largest of which are **Anglican, Baptist**, and Church of Christ in China. There are also small Muslim, Hindu, **Sikh**, and Jewish communities. Tien Te Sheng Hui, or the Heavenly Virtue Church, which (like **De Jiao**) is a syncretism of five major religions which it claims to complete, has 100,000 followers. **Soka Gakkai**, the Japanese new religion, also has a small following.

Montserrat. The Caribbean island of Montserrat has a population of 13,000 which is almost entirely Christian, and composed of **Anglicans, Methodists, Roman Catholics** and **Pentecostals**, as well as a few others.

St Helena. St Helena in the Atlantic Ocean, with a population of 5,600, is 90 per cent **Anglican**, having 12 churches, but there are also small communities of **Baptists, Roman Catholics, Salvation Army, Seventh Day Adventists** and **Jehovah's Witnesses**.

Turks and Caicos Islands. These islands near the Bahamas have a population of almost 11,700 which is 99 per cent Christian. The largest group is the Jamaican **Baptists**, but there are also **Anglicans, Methodists**, and small groups of other denominations.

United States of America

The population of the USA was estimated to be 256,000,000 in 1991, and in the 1980 census the racial division was 83.1 per cent white, including 19,300,000 Hispanic, and 11.7 per cent black, with the largest minorities being over 1,000,000 native Red Indians, 800,000 Chinese, 700,000 Japanese, and 700,000 Philippino. Sixty per cent of the population are members of a religious body, although religious cultural influence extends further, and most religions as well as new religious movements are represented, but the country is predominantly Christian.

Since questions of religion are not asked in censuses, it is not easy to enumerate the size of all the minor religious bodies. The **Roman Catholic** Church is the largest body, with 52,700,000 members, and these are mainly white and Hispanic. The Church is affected by both secularization and spiritual renewal, and up to 8,000,000 are involved in the **charismatic movement**. Most of the other churches are strongly **evangelical**, with fundamentalism and the charismatic or pentecostal movement being dominant forces. The **Baptists** have 25,800,000 members, of which 14,600,000 belong to the **Southern Baptist** Convention, and 5,500,000 belong to the National Baptist Convention. There are 12,800,000 **Methodists**, most of whom are in the moderate United Methodist

Church, but there are also many splinter groups in the **Holiness** movement which emphasizes the Wesleyan doctrine of sanctification. There are 8,500,000 **Lutherans**, 3,400,000 **Presbyterians**, 3,100,000 white **Pentecostals**, 2,500,000 **Episcopalians**, and 500,000 non-Roman Catholics. The **Orthodox** Churches, of which there are over 20, have 4,300,000 members, and the largest of these is the **Greek Orthodox**. There are a further 20,000,000 or so in a large number of small Black Churches, most of which are of Pentecostal, Baptist or Methodist origin. There are also indigenous churches begun by American Indians, Hispanics, and from the Third World.

The principal marginal Christian groups are **Mormons**, who have 3,900,000 followers and a huge centre in Salt Lake City; **Jehovah's Witnesses**, with 2,000,000 followers, **Christian Scientists, Unitarians**, and **Spiritualists**. The USA generates a huge number of small religious groups, many of which are closely related to the major religions, but some of which form cults or New Religious Movements (see introductory essay) that combine or abstract elements from a number of different places: examples include the **Gurdjieff** Foundation, **Subud, Krishnamurti Foundation, Transcendental Meditation** and the **Unification Church**. There are an increasing number of **New Age** movements, with an emphasis on psychotherapy, holistic philosophies, and healing. Magic, **paganism** and **Satanism** can also be found in newly formed sects.

The second largest religion is Judaism, which has a far-reaching influence upon American society through the success of Jews, 80 per cent of whom become college graduates. There are 5,900,000 Jews, which is the largest concentration in the world and greater than the population of Israel, constituting nearly half of world Jewry. More than 1,000,000 are **Conservative Jews** in the **United Synagogue of America**, 1,200,000 are **Reform Jews** in the **Union of American Hebrew Congregations**, and approximately 1,000,000 are **Orthodox Jews** many of whom are affiliated to the **Union of Orthodox Jewish Congregations of America**. Each branch has its own rabbinical seminaries and its national rabbinic body: for the Orthodox, the **Rabbinic Council of America**; for the Conservative Jews, the **Rabbinical Assembly**; and for the Reform Jews, the **Central Conference of American Rabbis**. All of these organizations are members of the **Synagogue Council of America**, founded in 1926 as an umbrella organization. Jewish organizations which are not members include the **Union of Orthodox Rabbis** and **Agudat Israel**.

There are approximately 3,000 Jewish schools, with nearly 500,000 children. Almost 3,000 out of the 4,000 synagogues are Orthodox, although these are not necessarily affiliated to national bodies. Education, social welfare, and community relations are undertaken by specialized agencies separate from the synagogues. **Hasidism**, the mystical branch of Judaism, is growing in popularity, particularly among the young. There are also some black Jewish movements of various kinds, in which Blacks prefer to identify with Jews rather than the dominant Christians, and some of which claim Jesus to have been black.

The majority of American Jews are **Zionists**, in the sense that they support the Jewish State of Israel and accord its existence a religious value. In recent years this support has resulted in difficulties for some American Jewry in the light of current US foreign policy.

There are 2,000,000 Muslims, who are perhaps 76 per cent Arab, 17 per cent Far Eastern, and seven per cent European. Iraqi immigrants are mainly **Shi'ite**, but most of the Muslims are **Sunni**. There are **Black Muslim** groups, often influenced by nationalism, and **Ahmadis** are often black. Since 1970, the Shi'a Association of North America has been active in promoting the traditional standards of belief and practice, though other important centres also exist, notably in Detroit (Lebanese–American) and Atlanta (Pakistani–American). The Islamic Center in Washington DC, opened in 1957 as a centre for diplomatic personnel, is a symbolic focal point for the Sunnis, although the most inclusive organization is the Council of Islamic Organizations of America, founded in 1977 under the auspices of the **Muslim World League**: two major affiliates are the Federation of Islamic Organizations in the United States and Canada, founded in 1952 (but in 1954 under its present name), and the Islamic Society of North America (which emerged in the early 1980s from the Muslim Students' Association, established in 1963). **Sufi** orders are also present: the **Sabiriya–Chishtiya** in the Chishti Order of America, and the **Nizamiya**–Chishtiya in the Sufi Order; the **Ni'matullahiya** in the Khaniqahi–Nimatullahi Order (headed by Dr Javad Nurbaksh); and the **Mawlawiya** in the Mevlana Foundation.

There are 250,000 Buddhists, and these are often influenced by the Japanese. They have several major academic centres for the study of Buddhist philosophy. There are also 110,000 **Bahais**, and 9,500 **Sikhs**.

The 800,000 native American Indians, in 150 tribes, are 90 per cent Christian. Some 20 per cent, however, adhere to **native American religions** and **Pan-Indianism** is also a movement of some significance.

US Dependent Territories

Micronesia. This federation of four island groups in the North Pacific Ocean was recognized by the United Nations in September 1991. It is composed almost entirely of indigenous races who are mainly **Roman Catholic** and **Protestant**, and has a population of 112,000 distributed over 607 islands.

Puerto Rico. Puerto Rico has a population of 3,300,000 which is 98 per cent Christian. Ninety-two per cent are **Roman Catholic**, and with largely foreign clergy from the USA and Spain, the Church is torn between the Hispanic and North American traditions of dominance or subservience, respectively, in relation to the state. Liberal and separatist clerics have been forced out of parishes. The **charismatic movement** has been strong.

Six per cent of the population belong to **Protestant** or indigenous denominations, the largest of which is the **Pentecostal** Church of God with 67,000 members. **Baptists, Methodists** and **Adventists** also have significant numbers, and Protestants have penetrated all levels of social, economic and political life. There are 15,000 **Jehovah's Witnesses**, 2,000 Jews, and a few **Bahais** and Hindus. **Afro-American spiritism** is found among some of those who have little or no links with the Roman Catholic Church, and this generally uses herbs to cure illness, mediums to contact the dead and divine the solutions to problems, and amulets to ward off evil.

American Samoa. In American Samoa the **Congregational** Church is losing ground, whilst **Roman Catholics**, **Assemblies of God** and **Pentecostal** churches are gaining.

Uruguay

Uruguay has a population of 3,100,000, 88 per cent of whom are of European descent. Sixty-six per cent are nominally **Roman Catholic**, but Uruguay has a strong anti-religious tradition which makes it the most secular state in Latin America, and only four per cent of these Catholics attend weekly. The Church hierarchy is polarized between progressive and conservative members. The Pope visited the country in 1988. The next largest denomination is the **New Apostolic Church**, a non-Roman Catholic group of German immigrants. Also present are the **Greek Orthodox** and **Russian Orthodox** Churches, and several **Pentecostal** sects. **Protestants** make up about two per cent of the population, and a further two per cent are Jewish. **Umbanda** spiritists, who practise an Afro–Brazilian form of syncretism introduced from Brazil in the early 1970s, and **Bahais**, are growing in influence. Thirty per cent of the population have no religious affiliation.

Vanuatu

Vanuatu has a population of 154,000 which is 94 per cent Melanesian, and five per cent follow **Melanesian religion**, popularly known in New Hebrides as Custom. Ninety-four per cent are Christian, and many of the leading figures in government are former clergy. Forty per cent of the population are **Presbyterian**, 18 per cent **Roman Catholic**, 13 per cent **Anglican**, six per cent **Seventh Day Adventist**, and five per cent are involved in the nationalist **John Frum cargo cult** which has developed out of Christianity, and is politically influential.

Vatican City

The Vatican is an independent city-state within the city of Rome ruled by the Pope, the last remnant of his once considerable temporal power in Italy. It is the administrative, judicial and religious centre of the **Roman Catholic** Church. There is no indigenous population, and the 755 citizens registered in 1989 comprise the Church hierarchy: they also retain their citizenship elsewhere. St Peter's basilica is the largest Catholic church in the world, and the scene of most official public engagements. The Pope is advised by a College of Cardinals, a Synod of Bishops, and appoints nuncios, pro-nuncios and delegates as diplomatic agents to other nations. The Roman Curia is the administrative and judicial body. A large proportion of the Cardinals and hierarchy are Italian, although these have no longer been in the majority for the past 20 years.

Venezuela

Venezuela has a population of 20,300,000, which is 67 per cent mestizo, 21 per cent white, 10 per cent black, and two per cent Amerindian. Ninety-six per cent are nominally **Roman Catholic**, but most of these are so through habit and few of them have any real conviction. The Church is predominantly conservative. 200,000 follow **South American traditional religions**, and these are mainly the Chibcha, Arawak and Carib tribes. Some 120,000 follow the **Maria Lionza** cult, which associated the goddess of water and vegetation with the Virgin Mary, as well as various historical people. There are over 35,000 **Bahais**, who have been growing rapidly, and 12,000 Jews. Also present are various **Protestant** and indigenous sects.

Vietnam

Vietnam has a population of 67,000,000 and the statistics of religious affiliation are difficult to estimate. Perhaps 55 per cent are Buddhist, mainly following the Chinese Mahayana variety. Popular sects include Japanese **Zen** Buddhism, and **Pure Land** Buddhism (Amidism). Cambodians, or those under Cambodian influence, follow **Theravada**. Many Buddhists, however, follow a folk-religion combining folklore, animism, ancestor cults, **Confucianism** and **Taoism** with Buddhism. There have been attempts to unify Mahayana and Theravada earlier this century in a **United Buddhist Church**, but this has had no profound impact upon religious practice. Eleven per cent follow new religious movements, and the largest of these is **Cao Dai**, a millenarian sect syncretizing all major world religions, with over 3,000,000 followers. Also significant—and like Cao Dai also mainly found in the Mekong delta—is **Hoa Hao** with 2,000,000 followers. There are also several other smaller sects.

There are about 2,000,000 **Roman Catholics**, mainly in the south where they fled during the civil war, and there have been strong tensions between them and the Buddhists. The Catholics tend to live in ghettos, espouse a traditionalist theology, and are threatened with persecution because they appear to follow a foreign religion. There are perhaps 200,000 **evangelicals**, who also live in groups in the south.

A tiny minority of **Sunni** Muslims is to be found especially among the Cham minority group along the banks of the Mekong. They are organized by the Cham and Vietnam Muslim Association based in Saigon.

Communist restrictions on religious organization and practice have been relaxed in the past few years.

Western Sahara

The Western Sahara is a strip of desert on the coast of Africa populated by 180,000 largely nomadic Arabs and Berbers (although a quarter of the population are now employed in the phosphate mines of Bu Cra‘a). These are all **Sunni** Muslims, of the **Maliki** school of jurisprudence. The Polisario Front have maintained independence against the attempts of Morocco and formerly Mauritania to divide the country.

Western Samoa

The **Congregational** Christian Church dates its beginning to 1830 and claims just over 50 per cent of the population which numbers around 200,000. The **Methodist** Church accounts for nearly 18 per cent and the **Roman Catholic** Church just over 20 per cent. The **Mormons** are the fastest growing group who now claim more than 12 per cent of the total population, and the **Bahais** also have an increasing following.

Yemen

Yemen was re-united in 1990, and now has a combined population of 12,500,000.

The former North Yemen has a population of 10,000,000 which is 100 per cent Muslim. 40 per cent are **Sunni** adherents of the **Shafi'i** school of Islamic jurisprudence, and these tend to have the dominant role in government which has recently brought about the re-unification with South Yemen, which is also predominantly Sunni. During the 1980s an Islamic Front, closely related to the **Muslim Brotherhood**, has gained increasing influence, and the Brotherhood's ideas are propagated by large numbers of Egyptian teachers employed in the country. The majority of the population, however, are **Shi'ites**, with 55 per cent following the distinctive **Zaydi** branch of Shi'a Islam, which has tended to be reactionary. The other five per cent are **Isma'ili** Shi'ites. There are a very small number of Yemeni Jews.

The former South Yemen has a much larger territory than the North, but only 2,500,000 in population. These are 99.5 per cent Sunni Shafi'i, with a few thousand Isma'ilis (including **Sulaymanis**), and very small communities of Christians, Hindus and Jews. It is the traditional base of the **'Alawiya (Hadrami) Sufi** order. The socialist government attempted to suppress religious beliefs until 1980, but after a period of liberalization, a civil war, and further socialist militancy, a re-united and democratic government has now been adopted. Shari'a law is merely one source for the law of the new Yemeni state.

Yugoslavia

Yugoslavia—or the former Yugoslavia—has a population of 23,900,000 and in the 1981 Census the ethnic proportions were as follows: 36.3 per cent Serb, 19.7 per cent Croat, 8.9 per cent Bosnian Muslim, 7.8 per cent Slovene, 7.7 per cent Albanian, 5.9 per cent Macedonian, 5.4 per cent unspecified Yugoslavian, 2.5 per cent Montenegrin, and 1.9 per cent Hungarian. Religious divisions follow ethnic lines, although there is some variation. Ten per cent (though other estimates suggest as many as 19 per cent) of the population are Muslim, following the **Sunni Hanafi** tradition, and these are mainly Bosnians and Albanians, but also include some Macedonians, Montenegrins, Serbs and Turks. The Muslim Supreme Assembly is in Sarajevo, and the head of its executive, the *reis-ul-ulama*, is the supreme Muslim religious leader. There are over 2,000 mosques, and over 1,500 *imams* including, since 1981, the first female imams. Traditional **Sufi** orders are currently represented by the **Rifa'iya, Khalwatiya,** and **Bektashiya.** In 1974 a new order was introduced, the Community of the Islamic Alia Dervish Monastic Order, and by the late 1980s this had over 50,000 followers organized in 70 monasteries in the south, but was not recognized by the Muslim leadership.

Fifty per cent of the population are **Orthodox**, and most of these belong to the Serbian Orthodox Church, which has 150 monasteries and convents, and over 3,000 churches. Separated from this, through the interference of the Communist state, is the Macedonian Orthodox Church, and unsuccessful attempts were even made to establish a Montenegrin Orthodox Church. Also present are small Romanian, **Russian**, Albanian and Bulgarian Orthodox Churches.

Thirty per cent of the population are **Roman Catholic**, and these are largely Croat and Slovene. Levels of practice are dropping in all the churches, but remain higher among Catholics than among Orthodox. A **charismatic movement** is active in the Roman Catholic church. The town of Medjugorje has been the site of recent apparitions of the Virgin Mary, and this, prior to the current hostilities, led to its becoming a pilgrimage centre for mainly young people from all over Europe.

There are also some **Protestants**, and these are mainly **Lutheran**, with some **Reformed**, and small numbers of **Baptists, Methodists** and **Pentecostals.**

Zaire

Zaire, with a population of 36,600,000, is predominantly Christian, but has only four officially recognized and legal churches. Nearly 50 per cent of the population belong to the **Roman Catholic** Church. The Church was a critic of the excesses of colonialism, and this has helped it to retain its influence during independence. The **charismatic movement** is widespread, and has brought a deepening of the spiritual life. The Church of Christ in Zaire unites the 20 per cent of the population who are **Protestant**, but since this contains communities from a wide variety of traditional churches and newer sects, it is one of the most religiously diverse churches in the world. Another 10 per cent of the population belong to the Church of Jesus Christ on Earth through the Prophet Simon Kimbangu (or **Kimbanguist Church**), which was founded in 1921, and is now the largest indigenous church in Africa with 3,500,000 adherents. It is largely Protestant-influenced and is a prophetic movement. There are also other indigenous churches, not all of which have joined the United Church of Christ and so remain illegal. The **Greek Orthodox** Church is the other legal body, with a mere 8,000 adherents. **Jehovah's Witnesses** (or **Kitawala**) were banned in 1987 for refusing to salute the flag.

There are 400,000 **Sunni** Muslims, who mainly adhere to the **Shafi'i** rite, and many of whom are influenced by **African traditional religions**. Their number also includes Arabs, Pakistanis, Indians and West Africans: among the last of these, mainly Senegalese traders, the **Qadiriya** and **Tijaniya** Sufi orders are strong. There is also a small number of **Shi'ites**, mainly **Aga Khanis** of Indian extraction.

There are nearly 1,000,000 tribalists, whose religion contains the usual elements of magic, ancestor veneration, and witchcraft. Several movements for tribal renewal have swept through the country this century: recent renewal sects include Muungism, Tonsi, and Dieudonné.

Zambia

Zambia has a population of 8,200,000 which is 70 per cent Christian. Twenty-six per cent are **Roman Catholic**, 14 per cent **Protestant**, eight per cent indigenous, three per cent **New Apostolic** (the German non-Roman but Catholic tradition), and two per cent **Anglican**. Eighteen per cent are **Jehovah's Witnesses** (or **Kitawala**), and this marginal group retains the sympathy of many others, for up to 25 per cent of the total population come under its influence at some point in their lives, although many return later to the main Christian churches. The mainstream churches have recently spoken out against corruption in the government and civil service.

One per cent of the population is Muslim (**Sunnis** of the **Shafi'i** rite), **Bahai**, or Hindu. At least 20 per cent retain their **African traditional religions** with emphases upon magic and witchcraft, and spirit-possession healing cults.

Zimbabwe

Zimbabwe has a population of 9,600,000, which is 71 per cent Shona and 16 per cent Ndebele. The influence of **African traditional religions** is so widespread as to prevent accurate statistical division, but perhaps a quarter of the population is solely Christian, half mix Christianity with animism, and a quarter are without Christian influence. Christianity is mainly **Protestant**, and is divided into a number of small denominations, both of missionary origin and indigenous, none of which have a dominant influence. The African Apostolic Church of Johane Maranke, founded in 1932, has over 250,000 followers. There has been a recent rise in fundamentalist sects. Fifteen per cent of the population come under **Roman Catholic** influence, and the Pope visited the country in 1988. The socialist government of Dr Robert Mugabe encourages free religious expression, but has been concerned by the rise in the number of anti-socialist fundamentalist groups. There is a tiny (one per cent) minority of Muslims, **Sunnis** of the **Shafi'i** rite.

Glossary

Abangan the term for a less strict, perhaps only nominal, Muslim in Indonesia.

Abhidhamma See **Abhidharma**

Abhidharma The latest collection of writings to make up the **Theravada Buddhist** three baskets (*tripitaka*) of sacred writings. Believed to derive from the teachings of the Buddha, these texts are rather technical and essentially contain lists and descriptions of the fundamental constituents of reality as understood by early Buddhism. The Abhidhamma corpus also contains material which sheds light on early Buddhist philosophical disputes.

Agamas A body of sacred writings revered by Hindu **Shaivas**. They are believed to have been revealed by Shiva himself and are therefore placed on a par with the Vedas.

Ahimsa Non-injury. One of the fundamental doctrines and practices of heterodox Indian religions. It is stressed in Buddhist literature but is perhaps most closely associated with the teachings of **Jainism** where *ahimsa* is observed with regard to all creatures.

Akal Purukh Eternal or timeless being, i.e. God. A name applied to the divinity by Sikhism.

'Alim The singular form of **ulama** (see below).

Amida A shortened form of the name **Amitabha**, mostly used in the context of Japanese Buddhism.

Amitabha The name of a celestial Buddha said to reside in the western region of space, hence his abode is termed the Pure Land of the West. Faith in the salvific capacity of Amitabha is characteristic of the Japanese **Jodoshu** and **Jodoshinshu**, the two major contemporary forms of **Pure Land Buddhism.**

Anabaptists A name applied loosely and widely in the 16th century Reformation to small groups of Protestants who had in common a rejection of infant baptism. Several strands can be picked out. Thomas Muntzer (1489–1525) believed the true gospel was a call to revolution. The Confession of Schleitheim, 1527, accepted by Anabaptists in Switzerland, Holland, and the Rhineland rejected force. In Moravia Jacob Hutter rejected private property. Anabaptist ideas reached England in 1534 and influenced Brownists and Separatists.

Animism the belief that items of the natural environment such as rivers and trees are inhabited by spirits.

Apostasy renouncing one's faith. The term (and the act) may have connotations of betrayal or even treason. It is for this reason that in traditional Islamic law apostasy is a crime which merits the death penalty. This verdict must, however, be based on due process of law, and satisfy the various legal requirements. Ayatollah Khomeini's fatwa against author Salman Rushdie appears to have been in contravention of these rules.

Aramaic Semitic language close to *Hebrew*. It is found in the later Biblical books and is the language of the *Talmud* and *Zohar*.

Arhat The goal of **Theravada** Buddhist practice. The arhat, through the cultivation of ethical behaviour, meditation and insight, is said to reach a state in which all desires are uprooted (*nibbana/nirvana*). As a consequence he or she will not be born again.

Arminianism The Dutch theologian, Jacobus Arminius (1560–1609) came to reject the deterministic logic of Calvinism and held that Christ died for all instead of only the elect. These ideas were accepted by English high churchmen including John Wesley. They form the basis of much liberal theology.

Aryans A highly influential ancient people with a much disputed homeland, perhaps in a region to the north of the Black Sea. One branch of the Aryans migrated to northern India sometime in the second millenium BCE and subsequently developed the religion of the Vedas. They can be seen as a fundamental element in the formation of the Hindu tradition.

Ashram A hermitage populated by temporary or permanently resident Hindu ascetics.

Ashrama A stage in the life of an orthodox Hindu. There are traditionally supposed to be four of these stages, i.e. studentship, householder, forest dweller and renouncer (*samnyasin*).

'Ashura An annual festival within **Twelver Shi'ism** in commemoration of the martyrdom of Hussein at Karbala in 680 CE. Passion plays are performed and processions take place in which participants beat and cut themselves in identification with the martyred son of Ali.

Atman The self. The essential part of a person according to the Hindu Upanishads. Realisation that *atman* is identical with *brahman* is said to lead to release from the endless cycle of birth and death. This monist doctrine is characteristic of many contemporary Hindu teachings, particularly those that trace their ancestry back to Shankara.

Autocephalous Churches *Autocephalous* ('self-heading') applies to nationally or ethnically based churches comprising the **Orthodox Church (Byzantine tradition)** which are completely self-governing—nearly all of them. They elect their own senior bishops. The historical expansion of the Orthodox Church consists of newly created Churches developing complete independence from their mother Church (usually the Church of Constantinople).

Avatara Descent. A characteristic teaching of **Vaishnava** Hinduism which holds that the god Vishnu has descended to earth on a number of occasions, in a variety of forms, to save it from unrighteousness and ultimate disaster. Krishna is perhaps the most celebrated *avatara*. Some **Shaivite Hindus** also adopt this doctrine with respect to their god.

Ayatollah 'Sign of God'—an honorific label for leading members of the ulama in **Twelver Shi'ism**.

Baal Teshuvah (Hebrew, one who returns; a newly-observant Jew) traditionally this referred to one who had repented, a penitent, now used as a designation for the Jew from a non-observant background who returns to the ways of a full Jewish religious life. This movement began in the US but is now centred in Israel, where since 1967 many thousands of Jews have consciously adopted an **Ultra–Orthodox** lifestyle. There are a growing number of new *Yeshivot* (eg Or Hahaim and Aish Hatorah in Jerusalem) to cater for these "returners". (Plural is Baalei Teshuvah).

Balfour declaration The November 1917 declaration by the British government of sympathy for the Zionist aim to establish a Jewish homeland in Palestine. This was the first statement of support by a major power and represented a significant development in the history of Zionism.

Bar Mitzvah (Hebrew, son of the commandments) at age 13 males are called to read from the *Torah* and become responsible for individual observance of the commandments. In this century an analogous ceremony has developed for girls during their 12th year.

Base Christian Communities (communidades eclesias de base) or CEBs. With over 200,000 CEBs said to be in existence in Latin America, they are best viewed as Catholic lay groups which campaign to improve the standard of living and raise consciousness about the practical implications of Liberation Theology.

Baraka A sacred power believed by many Muslims to inhere in shaikhs and other holy individuals. Associated principally with **Sufism** or **maraboutism**.

Ba-shar' 'with the law (shari'a)'. A designation for **Sufi** orders whose members observe orthodox practices of prayer, fasting etc.

B.C.E. (Before the Common Era) Jews frequently refer to BC (Before Christ) in this fashion.

Bhagavad Gita The Song of the Lord. The most widely known Hindu scripture which consists of a discussion between Krishna and Arjuna—a warrior. In the course of the text, the fate of the person after death, the importance of caste duty (*dharma*), and the necessity of devotion (*bhakti*) to the supreme being of the universe (i.e. Krishna) are discussed. The Bhagavad Gita is in fact part of the very much larger epic poem, the Mahabharata. Over the centuries the Gita has been subjected to a wide variety of interpretation.

Bhakti devotion. An important phenomenon in many traditions originating on the Indian sub-continent. Bhakti may be directed to a god (e.g. Shiva or Krishna) or to a *guru*. Bhakti derived movements are many and diverse and the theology of devotion is extensively discussed in sacred writings. Sikhism owes its origin to the strongly devotional currents present in northern India from the 12th century onwards.

Bhikkhu One who receives alms. The name applied to an ordained Buddhist monk, most frequently employed in the **Theravadin** context.

Bi-shar' 'Without the law (shari'a)': A designation for **Sufi** groups whose members do not observe orthodox practices of prayer, fasting etc. Members may indeed be only nominally Muslim, and better known for fortune telling or the making and selling of charms and amulets. They may also regard the use of alcohol and drugs to be lawful.

Bodhisattva A term employed by Mahayana Buddhists to describe a being who, over countless lives, has persevered in working altruistically to bring about the salvation of all beings. The bodhisattva, thoughout his or her career, must perfect a variety of virtues, the chief of which is said to be wisdom (*prajna*). Mahayanists are inclined to contrast this selfless activity favourably against the supposedly selfish **Theravadin** ideal of arhatship.

Brahma A Hindu god, traditionally said to comprise a trinity with Vishnu (the preserver) and Shiva (the destroyer). Hindu texts assign to Brahma the role of creator though it seems that he was never worshipped so extensively as the other two. Today few devotees remain, although a number of temples dedicated to Brahma continue to operate in south India.

Brahman The sole reality according to the monist teachings of the Hindu Upanishads. This doctrine is particularly stressed by those forms of Hinduism following the interpretation (*vedanta*) put forward by Shankara who held that conventional reality is essentially an illusion or dream (*maya*).

Brahmanas A collection of early Hindu ritual texts which explicate the role of the priesthood in the Vedic sacrifice. Also the term employed for the priesthood itself, more commonly rendered brahmins.

Buddha nature That essential aspect of a person or being held to be identical with the absolute body of the Buddha. A characteristic doctrine commonly found in various kinds of east Asian Buddhism.

Chakra A term employed in **Tantric** Hinduism to denote a number, usually seven, of spiritual centres arranged along the human spinal column. These may be activated by an assortment of practices.

Calvinists are those who share the doctrinal emphases of John Calvin (1509–64) which include the absolute sovereignty of God, the fall of man, justification by faith alone to those predestined for election, and to damnation to those who are preselected for condemnation. Calvinists have a high view of deity and a low view of humanity.

Cantor (Hebrew, Ḥazzan) originally a synagogue official now used for the prayer and liturgy leader in the synagogue.

C.E. (Common Era) Jews frequently refer to the Christian Era (CE) in this fashion.

Circumcision (male) The foreskin (or part thereof) of the penis is removed from the Jewish male child on the eighth day after birth as a sign of the covenant between God and the Jewish people. This practice, traditionally held to have begun with Abraham, is still almost universally observed by all Jews.

Daimoku The mantra "*namu myohorengekyo*" (lit. 'Adoration to the Lotus Sutra') said to symbolise the essence of absolute truth by the Japanese nationalist and religious teacher Nichiren Shonen (1222–1282). The chanting of the diamoku and its calligraphic representation are central to the Nichiren-derived schools of Japanese Buddhism.

Dakwah, da'wa A term referring to Muslim missionary and/or renewal movements or organizations.

Dede An elder among the **Alevis**.

Dervish Literally 'poor man', but a term applied to members of **Sufi** orders.

Deva A term employed by most Indian derived traditions for a spiritual being. Devas range in status from relatively lowly vegetation spirits to the great divinities of classical Hinduism.

Devi A name employed in Hinduism for any female personification of the divine. The precise characteristics, sphere of influence, iconography and epithet of Devi is highly dependent on regional factors. Goddesses falling into this category include Kali, Durga, Amba and Shakti.

Dhamma A term most commonly employed in **Theravada Buddhism**. Generally speaking **dhamma** refers to the moral and cosmic order of things. More specifically it is used to denote the teachings (conceived as law) of a Buddha. In the writings of the Abhidhamma, the term is used in a technical sense for the fundamental building blocks of reality.

Dharma A very common term in Indian derived religious systems. It has a multitude of meanings and is consequently difficult to define. In Hinduism it has three principal meanings: (a) the moral and physical order of the universe, (b) the duty of a person which is essentially defined by his/her caste (*varna*) and stage of life (*ashrama*), (c) the legal system as defined in ancient writings.

Dharmashastras Ancient Hindu law books believed to have been written by great sages of the past. The basic texts of the Hindu legal system which cover a wide variety of matters and in particular the duties of caste.

Dhikr Literally 'remembrance', i.e. of God. A **Sufi** ritual or liturgy which often took the form of rhythmic chanting of the names of God, perhaps using a bead rosary, or of dancing.

Diaspora Jews living in the "dispersion", i.e. outside the Land of Israel.

Dukkha Suffering. A key concept in almost all forms of Buddhism. The Buddha taught that all unenlightened human activity, because it is founded on a false understanding of the self, generates suffering. This doctrine is known as the First Noble Truth. Enlightenment (*nibbana*) is held to result from a complete uprooting of the desires which lead to *dukkha* and as such is the only true happiness.

Durga A Hindu goddess much worshipped in the north of India.

Ecumenical Derived from the Greek *oikoumene* meaning 'the whole inhabited earth', it was first used in the early Church when Ecumenical Councils were called from all parts of the world. It is now used to describe a movement begun with the Edinburgh Conference of 1910 which aims at the visible union of all Christians.

Evangelical Strictly means 'good news', and evangelism is spreading the good news of salvation. In Europe this tends to mean Protestants, while in England the Evangelical Revival of the eighteenth century was a widely based movement which was promoted by John Wesley, George Whitefield, Charles Simeon, Dan Taylor and others. In recent years there has been a world-wide polarization between Evangelicals, who see themselves as outward looking and Ecumenicals who are often perceived as inward looking. A conservative Evangelicalism has emerged which is cautious and sometimes hostile to Biblical criticism.

Exile (Hebrew, galut) The condition of Jews living outside the Land of Israel. Traditionally understood as a result of the Divine Will.

Fakir See **dervish**.

Faqih An Islamic expert in religious law; a jurisconsult.

Fatwa An official pronouncement, decision, judgment or ruling in Islamic law or theology by a recognised authority. The power of a fatwa is likely to depend on the status of the authoritative figure or body which issues it, and on whether contradictory fatwas are issued by rival authorities. The process is relatively informal in Islam compared, for example, with doctrinal and canon law judgements within the **Roman Catholic** church because of the much tighter authority structure within the latter.

Fetish An object believed to have preternatural or magical power.

Free churches Religious groups which are not established as state churches and are free to change their doctrines, forms of worship and polity.

Fundamentalist Used originally in a Christian context with reference to a person who believes in the verbal inerrancy of the Bible (or, allegedly, in its literal meaning—'allegedly' because literal interpretations are rarely adhered to consistently). Currently frequently applied to a variety of modern Muslim movements, but a misnomer since all Muslims believe in the verbal inerrancy of the Quran, not just the so called fundamentalists. Besides, the Muslim fundamentalists have a very different agenda from fundamentalists within Christianity, and in the entries here they are referred to as Islamists. A comparable misuse of the term is increasingly common in relation to other religious traditions too, e.g. Sikh or Hindu fundamentalists, where it also refers to some form of what is seen as divisive political activism in the name of religion with a readiness to resort to violence.

Ganesha The elephant headed god of the Hindu. Worship (*puja*) of Ganesha is held to destroy the obstacles that stand in the way of prosperity and good fortune.

Gentile A non-Jew, one not born of a Jewish mother or converted to Judaism.

Geshe The major monastic degree in the **Gelugpa** school of **Tibetan Buddhism**. During a training of many years the *geshe* will have mastered the content and exposition of a wide range of Mahayanist literature.

Get A bill of divorce.

Ghehenna The place of after-life punishment.

Ghetto Section of town or city enclosed by wall and gate(s) where Jews were forced to live and remain. The first ghetto was established in Venice in 1516. Ghettos were often overcrowded and conditions poor. The ghetto system was revived by the Nazis during the *Holocaust*. The expression "out of the ghetto" has become a sort of shorthand for Jews in modern times as leaving the ghettos of Europe marked the first sustained encounter that Jews had with the modern world and the end of their medieval isolation. Some Jews now look rather nostalgically back at ghetto life as poor and limited but fostering certain identity and a rich spiritual life.

Granthi Reader. The person responsible for reading the Sikh holy book, the *Guru Granth Sahib*, in the proper intoned manner during public worship in the *gurdwara*. A granthi is not a priest and he, or she, need have no theological training.

Gurdwara The door of the guru. A Sikh temple in which the *Guru Granth Sahib* is housed as the central object of veneration.

Guru An authoritative spiritual personage within the Indian religious tradition. Gurus may be human or divine, in some cases they may even be a book. Reverence is generally shown to such a figure for they embody the holy in some mysterious and perhaps terrifying way.

Guru Granth Sahib The sacred scripture of the Sikhs. Compiled by the fourth successor of Nanak, Arjan, in 1603–4, the book is regarded as *guru* by the majority of Sikhs.

Hadith In Islam, a report of sayings and actions of the Prophet Muhammad (or his close companions). Authoritative collections of hadith are second in importance for Muslims only to the Quran. They are also known as Traditions.

Hakim The term for a judge in an Islamic religious court in Indonesia.

Halakhah The system of Jewish law, including ritual, civil and criminal law. As a literary genre, usually distinguished from Aggadah (non-legal materials, especially narrative).

Harijans Children of god. A term employed by Gandhi and his followers to positively denote members of India's untouchable castes.

Haskalah (Hebrew, enlightenment)—movement by Jews for spreading modern European culture among Jews from the mid-18th century.

Hathayoga A practice with its origins in ancient Hinduism. Literally, a spiritual discipline (*yoga*) with violent or forced (*hatha*) characteristics. Exercises in which the body is placed in a variety of complex physical postures (*asana*).

Hebrew The language of the (Hebrew) Bible and of the Israelites. Part of the Semitic group of languages. Traditionally referred to as Lashon Hakodesh (Hebrew, the holy language) and reserved for religious usage.

Holocaust The systematic persecution and annihilation of six million European Jews by the Nazis (1933–45).

Ijtihad The use of independent reasoning and judgement in relation to matters of Islamic law and theology. In a famous phrase, the gates of ijtihad were said to have been shut when, centuries ago, a comprehensive system of law and theology had emerged. This inaugurated a tradition of entrenched conservatism which modern Muslim reformers have argued vigorously against. In **Shi'ism**, however, ijtihad continued to be regarded as legitimate provided it was exercised by a mujtahid.

Imam A prayer leader in a mosque, and generally its official custodian. In **Shi'ism** it is the supreme spiritual authority.

Islamist A term used in place of alternatives like 'fundamentalist'. The meaning is rather imprecise, but unlike Muslim conservatives (typically, the ulama) the Islamists seek to renew the Muslim world by returning to the Quran (and usually also the hadith) and rethinking their contemporary relevance rather than simply relying on inherited, often medieval, tradition. In this respect they are radical. Unlike liberal reforming Muslims, however, they advocate the harsh Quranic punishments of amputation of the hand for theft, and flogging or execution for certain sexual misdemeanours. They seek to establish Islamic states in which these, and some version of the shari'a, are enforced. They also advocate 'Islamic' economic policies and systems of government, but the details of these are quite varied, and, in the eyes of critics, vague. Islamists are highly critical of Western culture and society. Much of their appeal lies in the potent mix of anti-Western radicalism that they offer—combined with the apparent failure of the obvious alternatives.

Islamiyyun A self-designation used, perhaps increasingly, by people labelled in the West as 'Muslim fundamentalists'—but who are also, and less misleadingly, referred to as Islamists.

Jama'at khana The name of the religious centre and meeting place of the **Aga Khanis**.

Jati Kinship group. The major term used to denote caste in Hinduism. *Jatis* tend to be defined by specific occupations which are held to confer a particular level of ritual purity or pollution upon members. As such *jatis* are customarily arranged in a ritual hierarchy which is often different from one region of India to another. Caste members generally dine and marry within their own group.

Jatha A group of Sikh musicians who sing hymns of the *gurus (kirtan)*. The term can also refer to a meditational subgroup which follows the teachings of a *sant*.

Jihad 'Struggle' (in the path of Allah). A term in Islam for holy war, though strictly it has much wider connotations, including spiritual struggle within believers against temptation and sin.

Jina Victor. The name assigned to the omniscient teachers of Jainism.

John Paul II Born in 1920 as Karol Wojtyla, he became in 1978 the first Polish Pope. His opposition to Communism was rewarded in 1989–90 with the collapse of the system. Suspicious of some aspects of Vatican II, opposed to Liberation Theology and many goals of the women's movement, he has ensured the appointment of many like-minded bishops.

Kabbalah The esoteric teachings of Judaism, especially as found since the 12th century C.E.

Kali A particularly bloodthirsty Hindu goddess greatly revered in Bengal.

Kami The divinities of Shintoism. The *kami* are a disparate collection of beings including agricultural and nature spirits, ancestors and mythological heroes.

Karah Parshad Food served from an iron bowl (*karah*), traditionally made of equal parts of ghee, sugar and flour, as a sacramental gift (*parshad*) at the conclusion of a Sikh act of worship in the *gurdwara*.

Karma A doctrine found in all Indian derived religious traditions. Literally *karma* means action but more specifically *karmas* are actions carried out by a person unaware of his/her true nature. Such a person is held to act out of desire. In consequence his/her store of past actions will, at death, impell him/her into another existence. On the other hand, those who act in a true spirit of detachment from desire find release (*moksha*) from the endless cycle of birth and death. Some Indian religions, most notably Jainism, conceive *karma* as a dark substance that adheres to the surface of the soul, weighing it down and preventing it from finding its true abode in the bright, highest reaches of the cosmos.

Karta Purukh God as creator. One of the epithets of the divine in Sikhism.

Kemalism the particular tradition of secularism in politics established in modern Turkey by Kemal Ataturk (1881–1938). He sought to keep religion out of politics, and the army is a watchful guardian of this tradition.

Khalsa the pure ones. A religious **community** of Sikhs established by the tenth and final earthly *Guru*, Gobind Singh, in 1699. Upon initiation, male *khalsa* members adopt the name Singh (lion) while females take the name Kaur (princess).

Khanaqah A term used in Iran and the Indian subcontinent for a Sufi centre of worship.

Kharijite (also Khawarij) The first sect or breakaway movement within Islam, committed to a strict view about membership of the umma—a bad Muslim was not really a Muslim at all. The only surviving representatives of this movement in the contemporary world are the **Ibadis**.

Khwaja A Persian word meaning Lord. Used as an honorific for **Sufi** saints in India. Hence too the name **Khoja**.

Kiai (kiyayi) the name of village-based religious teachers in Indonesian Islam.

Koan An enigmatic saying or riddle given by a Zen Buddhist master to his disciple as a meditation device. The solution of the *koan* is held to have been accomplished only after the intellect has fully exhausted itself in the search. *Koan* meditation is characteristic of **Rinzai Zen**.

Kolel An advanced institute of Jewish learning, usually specifically for older married students. Also used as a designation of a community in Israel of people originally from a particular region.

Kosher (fit or proper) Can be used for any

ritual object but normally refers to the Jewish dietary laws.

Krishna One of the major Gods of Hinduism. Krishna is worshipped in a variety of forms and is believed by his devotees to have lived on earth in and around Vrndavan, a town near Mathura in northern India. Vrndavan is consequently an important pilgrimage site and many temples and monasteries are to be found in and around the town. Krishna is the principal character in the *Bhagavad Gita*.

Kundalini A female deity of Tantric Hinduism. Her devotees believe that she resides at the base of the human spine. Worship of the goddess through the use of *mantra*, visualisation, etc. is said to wake the goddess from her slumbers. She may then be encouraged to rise up the spinal column, activating spiritual centres (*chakras*) en route. This practice is known as *kundalini yoga*.

Ladino Vernacular language of Sephardi Jews.

Lama An authoritative spiritual teacher in the Tibetan Buddhist tradition. Many lamas, including the Dalai Lama, are held to be incarnations of earlier influential teachers.

Langar A communal kitchen characteristic of Sikhism. The *langar* is attached to the *gurdwara* and food is served to all, regardless of caste, creed or sex, at the end of worship. The food itself is also referred to as *langar*.

Liberation Theology A theological position developed by Latin American Roman Catholic activists such as Leonardo Boff and Paulo Freire which asserts that Christians should follow Christ in giving a 'preferential option towards the poor'.

Linga A phallic post or column which serves as an image of the god Shiva in many Hindu temples.

Madhhab In Islam, a school of religious law. Sometimes translated as 'rite' because ritual practices are affected by which madhhab one belongs to.

Madrasa(h) An institution of Islamic learning.

Mahabharata The longest of the two great Hindu epic poems, the other being the *Ramayana*. Mythically held to have been dictated by the sage Vyasa to Ganesha, the poem tells the story of the five sons of king Pandu who lose their kingdom in a game of dice to the evil Kauravas. Forced to wander in the wilderness for many years they prepare themselves for the great battle with their enemies which forms the core of this enormously lengthy story. The *Bhagavad Gita* was originally one small excerpt within the *Mahabharata*.

Mahathera A senior and authoritative monk within the **Theravada Buddhist** tradition.

Mahayana The Great Vehicle. Form of Buddhism which still manages to flourish, to a greater or lesser extent, in Japan, Taiwan, Korea, Tibet, Vietnam, China and adjacent states. Originating around the beginning of the Christian era in the north-western and southern extremities of the Indian subcontinent, the *Mahayana* de-emphasized the monastic rigour of the early Buddhist schools and propagated a variety of doctrines not much to the fore until that time. Prominent amongst these was the idea of the *bodhisattva* and the philosophical notion of emptiness (*sunyata*). Many *Mahayana sutras* exist which put these doctrines into the mouth of the Buddha. Adherents of the Great Vehicle maintain that these had been proclaimed during the Buddha's sojourn on earth, though they were subsequently hidden until such time as beings appeared with the spiritual capacity to understand them. With time the *Mahayana* proliferated into wide variety of forms. Some, such as the **Pure Land** schools, stressed a kind of devotionalism while others moved in a more scholastic direction. From approximately the fourth century C.E. *tantric* elements came to influence *Mahayana* doctrine and practice.

Mahdi A Muslim messiah figure. Although he does not feature in the Quran, the idea is firmly rooted in the hadith. He is expected to inaugurate the Last Days at the culmination of history by restoring a golden age of faith and justice. A famous claimant was the Sudanese mahdi whose **Ansar** movement is still influential. More recently the claim was made for al-Qahtani, a participant in the seizure of the mosque in Mecca in 1979 by the **Ikhwan**.

Maimonides Rabbi Moses ben Maimon (1135–1204), usually known by the acronym RaMBaM, philosopher and codifier of Rabbinic literature, was the author of the authoritative *Halakhic* code, *Mishneh Torah*; the classic text of medieval Jewish philosophy, *The Guide for the Perplexed* and the 13 principles of the Jewish faith.

Mandala A diagram, usually formed of interlocking squares and circles, used as a meditational device in many Indian derived traditions. Associated with the *tantric* current in Hinduism, Buddhism and **Jainism**, these diagrams may be entirely geometric or strongly iconic. Generally the devotee receives his/her *mandala* on initiation by a *guru* and sustained meditation on the device is held to reveal something important about both the deep structure of the world and of the human psyche.

Mantra A word or formula derived from Hindu scripture, particularly the Vedas. *Om* is the most well known of these, though there are many others. Tantric forms of Hinduism, Buddhism and **Jainism** also have recourse to these formulae. Usually received from a guru upon initiation the *mantra* is employed in meditation and ritual to help the initiate come into greater harmony with a particular manifestation of the divine. Some modern forms of Hinduism use *mantras* in congregational worship, a good example being the *mahamantra*, 'Hare Krishna Hare Krishna Hare Rama Hare Rama', much in evidence in the public worship of **ISKCON**.

Marja'al-taqlid 'source of imitation'. In principle this is the supreme mujtahid in **Twelver Shi'ism**, but in practice the term is used less strictly. In 1975, for example, there were seven of whom Ayatollah Khomeini was one. Their supreme authority emerges by informal consensus among their fellow ulama. Their 'centre of imitation' is an ayatollah whose judgement in religious matters is regarded as authoritative. There may be more than one, and Twelvers align themselves with one or other of these authorities.

Martin Buber (1878–1965) Jewish philosopher, Zionist thinker, Biblical scholar and translator and interpreter of Ḥasidism. He freely rendered Ḥasidic materials into German and was the major vehicle for the transmission of knowledge of Ḥasidism to the non-Ḥasidic world. These renderings (eg *The Legend of the Baal Shem Tov; For the Sake of Heaven; Tales of Rabbi Naḥman*) have not been without criticism particularly in terms of the influence of romanticism on his understanding of the Ḥasidic movement. Also his concentration on the narrative literature at the expense of the homiletic and commentarial works led some to consider his interpretations (including, *Ḥasidism and Modern Man* and *The Origin and Meaning of Ḥasidism*) as one-sided and distorted. As a thinker he is best known for his philosophy of 'dialogue' (*I and Thou*). He

left Germany and moved to Israel in 1938. Buber's influence has been as great, if not greater, in the non-Jewish world, and in the Jewish world as a major source for *Neo-Ḥasidism*.

Masgiah (Hebrew, supervisor) Supervisor of *Musar* in Lithuanian-type *Yeshivah*.

Masjid mosque.

Maskilim (Hebrew, enlighteners) Adherents of *Haskalah*.

Messiah (Hebrew, annointed one) The long awaited eschatogical King who will rule over Israel at the end of days and establish a time of peace. Jewish history has bourne witness to a series of false messiahs.

Maulana (mawlana) An honorific title in the Indian subcontinent meaning 'our master'.

Maulud The celebration of the birthday of the Prophet Muhammad in Islam. It is frowned upon by some Muslim critics as veering too close for comfort towards idolatry.

Maya Dream or illusion. According to some systems of Hindu thought, most notably **Advaita Vedanta**, the world is devoid of any real substance. From the ultimate perspective the sole reality is Brahman.

Metempsychosis Transmigration of the soul.

Mikveh Ritual bath house.

Millenarian A term applied to a belief in an imminent new age on earth to be inaugurated by divine intervention and in which the ideals of the movement or individual in question will be realised.

Minyan (number) A prayer quorum of ten adult males for communal prayers and the reading of the *Torah* in the synagogue. The age of majority is 13 years, following *Bar Mitzvah*.

Mishnah Hebrew text, edited c. 200 C.E. A codification of legal and religious materials, arranged in six "orders".

Mitnaggdim (Hebrew, opponents) The opponents of Ḥasidism (c. 1760–1850). Initially led by Rabbi Elijah ben Solomon of Vilna, who objected to both Ḥasidic theology and behaviour and instituted a ban of excommunication (Ḥerem) on all Ḥasidic leaders in 1772. Now refers to *Yeshivah* based communities that are part of the **Ultra-Orthodox** Jewish world.

Moksa Release or freedom. Many Indian derived religions teach spiritual techniques which are held to lead to perfection. Such perfection is said to consist of release from the endless cycle of birth and death (*samsara*).

Monism Literally 'one-ism', the belief that only one being exists. All apparently discrete entities are in reality parts or aspects of one whole. This whole may in principle be either material or spiritual, but in religious contexts the latter is far more likely. Spiritual monism differs from monotheism: for the latter maintains a dualism between God and world.

Monotheism Belief in only one God, often (as in Judaism, Christianity and Islam) conceived to be the creator of the cosmos—and in contrast to monism, the contrast between creator and creation is upheld.

Mount Meru The central, enormously high, mountain of our world system, according to various Indian derived traditions. The continents, usually four, are said to be arranged geometrically around Meru. Concentric circles of mountains and oceans may also be involved in an immensely complex cosmological scheme.

Mucedded The Turkish form of mujaddid.

Mudra A symbolic gesture, usually made with the hands, used in **Tantric** worship (*puja*). The *mudra* is often held to embody the essence of a deity. Thus, by practicing *mudra* the devotee becomes more closely identified with an aspect of the divine.

Muezzin The person who calls the faithful to prayer from the mosque in Islam.

Mufti A jurisconsult in Islamic law, qualified to offer authoritative interpretation of the shari'a.

Mujaddid 'Renewer'. Muslims believe that God sends a renewer at the beginning of each century, a charismatic leader who will actively renew Islam. Figures regarded in this light in the past have included al-Shafi'i, originator of the **Shafi'i** madhhab, and the great Muslim theologian al-Ghazali (dllll). The belief is based on a popular hadith.

Mujtahid A leading religious scholar among **Twelver Shi'ites** with the authority to exercise ijtihad.

Mullah The term commonly used in Iran for a member of the ulama, usually of lower rank.

Murid A follower of a murshid, or pir. Used in Soviet sources as a general term for a Sufi.

Murshid A spiritual guide within Sufism.

Nat Spirits and minor deities associated with popular Buddhist worship in Burma. *Nats* are particularly associated with specific localities, trees and other natural phenomena such as the wind and rain.

Nembutsu A *mantra* crucial to the practice of the various schools of Japanese **Pure Land Buddhism**. The *nembutsu "Namu Amida Butsu"* ("I take refuge in Amida Buddha") crystallizes the centrality of faith in this particular tradition of **Mahayana** Buddhism.

Oral Torah Traditionally, Judaism holds that the authoritative interpretation of the *Written Torah* was also revealed to Moses on Mount Sinai. The Oral Torah is rabbinic interpretation, in the main, the *Talmud* and its commentaries.

Pancasila The name for the constitutionally important five principles of national life in Indonesia, first enunciated by Sukarno (later President) in 1945. They are: belief in God (keTuhanan), humanitarianism (kemanusiaan), national unity (persatuan), democracy (kerakyataan), and social justice (keadilan sosial). Controversy has focussed on the first of these, involving the issue of which religions other than Islam and Christianity qualify for guaranteed protection by the state, and the members of the various **kebatinan** groups have perhaps felt most vulnerable in this regard.

Pali canon The Buddha's teaching as preserved by the **Theravada** school of Buddhism. Written down in the ancient Pali language in the first century B.C.E., some three hundred years after the Buddha's death, though preserved in oral form before this date, this extensive body of writing is arranged into three large collections individually entitled *vinaya* (monastic discipline), *sutta* (discourses) and *abhidhamma* (philosophical material). A term regularly applied to this corpus is *Tipitaka* (or *Tripitaka*), i.e. the Three Baskets.

Pandit A scholarly man or teacher.

Panth Path or way. An Indian system of belief or practice. Usually applied to religious communities arising out of the Sant tradition, e.g. the **Kabir Panth**.

Pantheism Belief that everything that exists is divine, and often implying in particular an identification of God and nature. Pantheism may be construed as a form of monism (see above) but does not have to be.

Pengadilan agama An alternative name for a hakim in Indonesian Islam.

Penghulu The name for the organiser of mosque affairs in Indonesian Islam.

Pentateuch The Five Books of Moses, the first five books of the (Hebrew) Bible.

Peot Side-curls, worn by **Ultra-Orthodox** Jews.

Pesantren A religious boarding school in Indonesian Islam.

Phii Rather like *nats*, the *phii* are regularly propitiated in the folk Buddhism and other folk traditions of Laos.

Pietism A reform movement amongst seventeenth century German Lutherans which saw faith as primarily a matter of personal experience which warms the heart rather than enlightens the mind. Pietism is suspicious of religious activism. Through the Moravians, it influenced John Wesley who wanted both a warmed heart and practical Christianity.

Pir A term in widespread use in the Indian subcontinent for a spiritual guide within **Sufism**, or for a holy man in general. It may have pejorative connotations when used to refer to hereditary custodians of Sufi shrines who, while commanding considerable obedience from the local populace, are in no sense spiritual adepts.

Pogrom (Russian) Outbreak of violent anti-semitism, often orchestrated by political or ecclesiastical authorities. The series of pogroms in the Russian empire beginning in 1871 were a major factor in the mass emigration of Jews to the U.S.A., western Europe and the land of Israel, and in the growth of the **Zionist** movement.

Pongyis The name given to an ordained **Theravada Buddhist** monk in Burma. The Burmese equivalent of the *bhikkhu*.

Primal religion A term for non-literate tribal religion, but unacceptable to many because of the possible connotation of 'primitive'. (Hence the use of 'traditional' by and large in the entries here.)

Proselyte Convert to Judaism.

Puja The name applied, in a majority of Indian derived traditions, to the worship of a deity. *Puja* may take place in the temple or at home. It may be accompanied by a great deal of external ritual. Alternatively it can be conducted through the medium of contemplative visualization and the like. Despite the wide range of practices falling under this general heading unifying themes can be found. Thus the majority of *pujas* involve the invocation of the deity, its entertainment, the making of offerings, etc.

Puranas A category of Hindu sacred texts.

Though not as revered as the Vedic writings, the Puranas nevertheless provide the basis of much current Hindu practice and belief. Many lengthy texts fall into this category and a good proportion of them are sectarian in the sense that they describe a specific deity, be it Vishnu, Shiva or some other god. Puranic writings are rich in mythological and cosmological material.

Pure Land A *Mahayana* Buddhist concept. From the inception of the *Mahayana* a belief emerged that supremely perfected beings, often called *bodhisattvas*, exist on other worlds. In contrast to our own impure world, these *bodhisattvas* are said to inhabit pure lands. A Buddhism of faith in the salvific power of these beings came into being in the early years of the Christian era. Perhaps the most well known quasi-diety in the Mahayanist pantheon is Amitabha. Belief in Amitabha is thought to lead the devotee to a future rebirth in his pure land, Sukhavati.

Qadi A judge in an Islamic religious court.

Rabbi Traditionally an expert in legal decisions. Now more generally the professional spiritual leader and religious functionary of a synagogue.

Rama The hero of the *Ramayana* and a popular Hindu god. Rama is regarded by **Vaishnava** Hindus as an important *avatara* of Vishnu.

Ramayana One of the two great Hindu epic poems, the other being the *Mahabharata*. Ascribed to the poet and sage, Valmiki, the *Ramayana* tells the story of Rama, Prince of Ayodhya, and his faithful wife Sita. Cheated of his heritage by demons who cleverly trick his father, the king, Rama and his retinue must, out of filial duty, withdraw to the forest. There many adventures befall them, the most significant of which is the abduction of Sita by the wicked demon king, Ravana. Only after an arduous campaign, in which Rama is ably assisted by Hanuman and his army of monkeys, is Ravana defeated. The story is still enormously popular in India and its yearly retelling provides the background to one of the more important annual festivals of northern India.

Rebbe Ḥasidic "master" or *tzaddik*. Charismatic leader of his followers (Ḥasidim), their spiritual guide and behavioural model. Except for a few notable exceptions, the leadership of Ḥasidic groups is dynastic with the new Rebbe being the son or son-in-law of the last. These dynasties trace their origins back to the beginnings of Ḥasidism.

Responsa (singular, responsum) The legal opinion of a qualified rabbinic authority, written in response to a question on specific issues of Jewish law. Responsa collections are often published.

Sabbath The seventh day of rest. Jews traditionally refrain from all forms of work on the Sabbath (Saturday).

Sacred Thread A thread of twisted cotton conferred on Hindu boys of the first three varnas on entering the first stage in life (*ashrama*), i.e. studentship. The thread, worn draped over the right shoulder and under the left arm, is a symbol that the boy has been born a second time and may now gain access to Vedic learning.

Samnyasin A Hindu ascetic who has renounced the world and its institutions so that he, less commonly she, may more effectively find release (*moksha*) from the cycle of birth and death (*samsara*). Renunciation is traditionally regarded to be the fourth and final stage (*ashrama*) of an orthodox life.

Sampradaya A Hindu religious order or sect.

Samsara The world, conceived as an endless cycle of birth and death. An Indian derived notion which is prominent in Hindu, **Jain** and Buddhist thought. Generally *samsara* is held to be an unsatisfactory state of affairs and many of these systems teach a spiritual technique claimed to be effective in gaining release (*moksha*) from its negative influences.

Sangha The community of Buddhists. Strictly speaking this is a fourfold community made up of laywomen, laymen, nuns and monks (*bhikkhus*). However the term *sangha* is generally applied to the monastic half of the equation.

Sangharaja A term employed by some Theravada Buddhists. Literally meaning "king of the *sangha*" this is a title conferred on a high monastic dignitary in some of the countries of southeast Asian.

Sant saint. A name applied to pious and renowned spiritual teachers, both Hindu, **Sikh** and Muslim, who lived in northern India from the 15th century until modern times. Kabir and Nanak are good examples of the *sant* tradition. *Sants* normally stress a form of devotionalism which places little emphasis

on external ritual, preferring instead the cultivation of an interior peace.

Santri The term for a strict or 'orthodox' Muslim in Indonesia, as opposed to the more nominal abangan.

Sat Guru The true guru. One of the epithets of the divine in Sikhism.

Sayyid A person claiming descent from the Prophet Muhammad himself.

Shaikh A Sufi master.

Shari'a The Islamic religious law. It is not a law code in the modern western sense: much of it is concerned with religious ritual. Its additional focus is on personal law, dealing with marriage and divorce, but also rules of property and inheritance. It is a characteristic of Islamists that they advocate the establishment of a state which implements the shari'a. They also object to modern Western law coexisting with it. However, since it is not comprehensive, it has always been supplemented by some kind of additional law, whether that of the ruler or of the state.

Shiva One of the great gods of Hinduism. Shiva is perhaps more widely worshipped than any other deity except Vishnu. His devotees are customarily referred to as **Shaivas** or Shaivites. Shiva is a paradoxical deity, being associated with enormous feats of asceticism on the one hand, and blatant sensuality on the other. He is the lord of *yoga* and of beasts and is said to reside high in the Himalaya with his consort, Parvati. Shiva's treatment of his devotees is unpredicatable and he is sometimes named the destroyer. The dance is his domain and he is regularly presented iconographically as the Lord of the Dance (*nataraja*). The *linga* is his other great symbol.

Silsila A line of discipleship in a **Sufi** order.

Six-Day War War in June 1967 when Israel reacted to Arab threats and decisively defeated her enemies. In many ways a turning point for world Jewry. In Israel the victory gave an impetus to messianic movements and advocates of a "greater Israel" (made up of Israel and some or all of the territories captured in 1967). In the *diaspora*, Jewish identification with Israel was strengthened.

Spiritism A form of religion in which at least some of the believers experience what they take to be being possessed by spirits, either of gods, demons or ancestors. Hence **Afro-American spiritism**.

Spiritism Cults involving some kind of spirit possession, as in **Afro-American spiritism**.

Sunna The 'path' or 'way' laid out by the Prophet Muhammad; in particular the example he set as recorded in the hadith, and regarded by Muslims as normative. Hence the term **Sunnism**.

Surya The Hindu god of the sun. An ancient deity not much worshipped today.

Sutra See **Sutta**.

Sutta A sacred text. In **Theravada Buddhism** the term denotes a discourse of the Buddha. These *suttas* are collected together and form on of the three baskets (*tipitaka*) of the Pali canon.

Svastika The Hindu symbol of auspiciousness. It is associated with the god Ganesha.

Synagogue (Greek, place of meeting, congregation) Jewish place of worship.

Talmud (teaching) There are two Talmuds (Talmudim). The Jerusalem or Palestinian Talmud (Yerushalami) comprising the *Mishnah* together with the commentary (gemara) of the Jerusalem schools, redacted c. 5th century C.E. The Babylonian Talmud (Bavli) comprising the *Mishnah* together with the commentary (gemara) of the Babylonian schools, redacted c. 7th century C.E. The latter is the larger and more influential work (that usually designated by the term "Talmud"). The study of the Talmud is the core of the *Yeshivah* curriculum.

Tantras Indian derived sacred texts. Tantras are found in Hinduism, Buddhism and **Jainism**. They are rich in symbolic language and are generally concerned with the explication of ritual acts.

Tariqa A Sufi order.

Tekke The name used in a Turkish context for a **Sufi** centre.

Temple The First Temple, built by King Solomon in order to sacrifice to God, was destroyed in 586 B.C.E. The Second Temple was destroyed by the Romans in 70 C.E. Orthodox Jews pray daily for its rebuilding. The term, "temple" is also used by some Reform Jews, particularly in the USA, to designate their synagogues. This practice, dating from the Hamburg Temple in 1818, marked a rejection of the hope for the restoration of the Temple in Jerusalem as the focal point of Jewish life.

Tirthankara A builder of the ford. The name used to designate the omniscient teachers, or victors (*jina*) of the Jains. According to Jain sources, there have been 24 *tirthankaras*. Mahavira, the last of the series, is customarily considered the founder of the tradition.

Tohunga A religious specialist in traditional **Maori religion**.

Torah (teaching, instruction, guidance) Normally refers to the *Written* and *Oral* Torot (plural). In its widest sense, Torah is used to mean the Jewish tradition. The study of Torah is a religious duty. Torah is also used as a shortened version of Sefer Torah (Hebrew, Torah Scroll) to refer to the actual scroll read in the synagogue three times weekly.

Tulku An incarnate *lama* of the **Tibetan Buddhist** tradition. Most schools of Tibetan Buddhism accept the existence of such individuals who are held to return to earth in a new body, after death, to maintain the continuity of a teaching lineage. Such *lamas* are regarded with especial reverence.

Tzaddik (plural, Tzaddikim) see *Rebbe*.

Ulama The 'clerics' of Islam: lawyer-theologians with a special education and training. They may be teachers in a madrasah, imams in a mosque, or qadis and muftis in the shari'a legal system.

Upanishads Hindu sacred texts. There are many writings which fall into this category, some of which are ancient (dating back to about the seventh century B.C.E.), while others were written in comparatively modern times. The *Upanishads* are disparate in terms of doctrine, though most are concerned with the notions of *atman* and *brahman*. Since the Upanishads form the concluding part of the overall Vedic corpus they are also known as *vedanta*, i.e. the end of the Veda.

Upasampada Initiation. A term used in **Theravada Buddhism** to describe the ceremony through which a candidate must go in order to become a fully ordained monk (*bhikkhu*).

'Urs The annual festival at the shrine of a **Sufi** saint in commemoration of his death.

Vajra A thunderbolt. The weapon of the ancient Hindu god Indra. In Tantric or Vajrayana Buddhism the *vajra* is a recurring symbol which represents the adamantine nature of the enlightened mind.

Vajrayana A form of *Mahayana* Buddhism. The term is generally employed to denote the kind of Tantric Buddhism that arose in northern India from about 600 C.E. This was probably the most influential strand of Buddhism to establish itself in Tibet and today almost all Tibetan groups regard themselves as part of the *Vajrayana*.

Varna The major word for caste in classical Hindu sacred writings. Unlike the term *jati*, varna refers to the fourfold division of ancient Indian society into priests (*brahmanas*), warriors (*kshatriyas*), farmers (*vaishyas*) and servants (*shudras*). The first three of these groupings are regarded as Aryan, or twice-born (*dvija*), castes and may, in consequence, be invested with the sacred thread. The relationship between *varna* and *jati* is complex, with the latter having a stronger contemporary relevance.

Vatican II A council of Roman Catholic bishops summoned by Pope John XXIII in 1962 to complete the work begun in 1870 by Vatican I and renew the life of the church. Amongst the changes it introduced was the use of the vernacular instead of Latin in worship, a less authoritarian attitude, and a new willingness to accept other Christians and engage in dialogue with them.

Vedas Ancient Hindu sacred writings. Believed to have been composed thousands of years ago by inspired sages (*rishis*), the Vedas are regarded as the revelatory basis of the orthodox Hindu tradition. As such, all later writings must, at least in principle, be in accord with the Vedas. Essentially a collection of hymns employed by a complex priesthood in the performance of sacrificial acts around a sacred fire, the Vedas are arranged in four collections (*samhita*) of which the Rig Veda is first in importance. The hymns are generally addressed to a deity of the Aryan pantheon of whom the most prominent are Agni—the god of fire, Soma — the divine essence of a plant, and Indra—the chief or the gods and archetypical warrior.

Vihara A Buddhist monastery. A term mainly used by the **Theravada**. The name of the Indian state of Bihar is a corruption of *vihara*. It is so called because of the enormous number of monasteries on its soil in ancient times.

Vinaya Buddhist monastic discipline. Also the name given to the first part, or basket, of the Pali canon of the **Theravada** in which the Buddha lays down the 227 rules for monks to follow after his death.

Vishnu One of the great gods of Hinduism. An ancient deity, Vishnu is mentioned in the Rig Veda. In later sacred writings the notion emerged that Vishnu has descended (*avatara*) to earth from time to time to rectify unrighteousness. Classical texts assign him a place in a trinity with Brahma and Shiva. In this capacity he is known as the preserver, for he maintains the moral and physical order of the universe. His devotees are known as **Vaishnavas** and many Vaishnava sects flourish today in India. Iconographically Vishnu is represented lying on a serpent, or accompanied by his consort Lakshmi. The mace and discus are among the symbols he holds in his four hands.

Vrndavan A town in northern India close to Mathura. This is the vicinity in which Krishna is held to have lived his earthly life, according to his devotees. As a result Vrndavan is a major pilgrimage site and many orders of ascetics have monasteries in the area.

Wahdat al-wujud A doctrine of the unity of all being taught by the controversial Spanish Muslim thinker Ibn al-'Arabi. Controversy centred on the apparent incompatibility of this doctrine of monism (see above) with the monotheism (see above) that is the basis of Islam. The teaching nevertheless continued to be influential in some **Sufi** circles.

Wat The Thai word for *vihara*. A **Theravada Buddhist** monastery.

Wilayat-i faqih The 'rule of the jurist'. This is the distinctive theory elaborated by Ayatollah Khomeini according to which supreme political authority in the state rests in the hands of the ulama. It diverges sharply from the view traditionally held in **Twelver Shi'ism**, and does not command universal acceptance within the community.

Written Torah The Written Torah usually refers to the Five Books of Moses, the first five books of the Hebrew Bible or *Pentateuch*. The Torah, in this sense, was given to Moses on Mount Sinai.

Yeshivah Institute of Jewish higher education with its origins in 2nd century C.E. Babylonia. The Yeshivah flourished in Eastern Europe until the 20th century. Currently there are Yeshivot (plural) throughout the Jewish world, especially in Israel where there are more than 70,000 students in some 700 Yeshivot. The curriculum is mainly made up of the systematic study of the *Talmud* and law codes. Although the Yeshivah does train *Rabbis* it is primarily for the Jewish education of all and not simply a seminary. The director is known as the Rosh Yeshivah. (Plural, Yeshivot).

Yiddish Jewish language, the sole vernacular language of the Ashkenazi Jews of Eastern Europe. Yiddish is a Judeo-German dialect made up of mainly medieval German together with *Hebrew* and Slavic elements. Referred to as Mama Loshen (mother language), still the daily language of the *Yeshivah* and **Ultra-Orthodox** communities. A secular literature developed in the 19th and 20th century. The *Holocaust* destroyed most Yiddish-speaking communities. In recent years there has been something of a Yiddish revival, particularly in the USA.

Yoga A difficult word to define. Arising out of the Indian religious thought universe, it refers to general spiritual discipline. More specifically it is applied to clearly defined practices and teachings within the Hindu tradition. Thus *bhaktiyoga*, devotion to the supreme being of the universe, is the essence of Krishna's teaching in the Bhagavad Gita, while *hathayoga*, a physically based series of exercises, is well known in the West. *Yoga* is also one of the six orthodox systems of philosophy in classical Hinduism.

Yogin A practitioner of *yoga*. Generally a term only employed for someone well advanced on the path.

Zawiya A Sufi centre, which at its most complex could include a tomb-shrine, a mosque, madrasah, library, hospital, lodging and caravanserai, and refectory.

Zazen sitting meditation. The distinctive meditational practice of **Soto Zen** Buddhism which is based on the principle that practice and attainment are one. As such, meditation is not seen as a means to an end but rather as a simple way of carrying out one's daily activities with awareness.

Zikr Another version of the word dhikr (see above).

Index of Personal Names

INDEX OF PERSONAL NAMES

INDEX OF PERSONAL NAMES

INDEX OF PERSONAL NAMES

INDEX OF PERSONAL NAMES